Principles of
Project Finance

Principles of
Project Finance

E.R. Yescombe

Second edition
© YCL Consulting Ltd. 2014
www.yescombe.com

AMSTERDAM • BOSTON • HEIDELBERG • LONDON
NEW YORK • OXFORD • PARIS • SAN DIEGO
SAN FRANCISCO • SINGAPORE • SYDNEY • TOKYO
Academic Press is an imprint of Elsevier

Academic Press is an imprint of Elsevier
The Boulevard, Langford Lane, Kidlington, Oxford, OX5 1GB
225 Wyman Street, Waltham, MA 02451, USA

Second edition 2014

British Library Cataloguing in Publication Data
A catalogue record for this book is available from the British Library

Library of Congress Cataloging-in-Publication Data
A catalog record for this book is available from the Library of Congress

ISBN: 978-0-123-91058-5

For information on all Academic Press publications
visit our website at **store.elsevier.com**

Working together
to grow libraries in
developing countries

www.elsevier.com • www.bookaid.org

Contents

List of Tables

List of Figures

INTRODUCTION

Project finance is a method of raising long-term debt financing for major projects through 'financial engineering,' based on lending against the cash flow generated by the project alone; it depends on a detailed evaluation of a project's construction, operating and revenue risks, and their allocation between investors, lenders, and other parties through contractual and other arrangements. In 2012, at least $375 billion of investments in projects around the world were financed or refinanced using project-finance techniques.

'Project finance' is not the same thing as 'financing projects,' because projects may be financed in many different ways. Traditionally, large scale public-sector projects in developed countries were financed by public-sector debt; private-sector projects were financed by large companies raising corporate loans. In developing countries, projects were financed by the government borrowing from the international banking market, development-finance institutions such as the World Bank, or through export credits. These approaches have changed, however, as privatization, deregulation, and the introduction of private finance through public-private partnerships have changed the approach to financing investment in major infrastructure projects, transferring a significant share of the financing burden to the private sector.

1

Principles of Project Finance. DOI: http://dx.doi.org/10.1016/B978-0-12-391058-5.00001-1

Unlike other methods of financing projects, project finance is a seamless web that affects all aspects of a project's development and contractual arrangements, and thus the finance cannot be dealt with in isolation. If a project uses project finance, not only the finance director and the lenders but also all those involved in the project (*e.g.* project developers, engineers, contractors, equipment suppliers, fuel suppliers, product offtakers, and—where project finance is used for public infrastructure—the public sector) need to have a basic understanding of how project finance works, and how their part of the project is linked to and affected by the project-finance structure. The nexus of contracts which make up a project cannot only be considered from a commercial perspective: a financial perspective is essential if much time and money is not to be wasted in creating projects which appear to work but cannot.

This book is therefore intended to provide a guide to the principles of project finance and to the practical issues that can cause the most difficulty in commercial and financial negotiations, based on the author's own experience both as a banker and as an independent advisor in project finance. The book can serve as a structured introduction for those who are new to the subject, and as an *aide mémoire* for those developing and negotiating project-finance transactions. No prior knowledge of the financial markets or financial terms is assumed or required.

'The devil is in the detail' is a favorite saying among project financiers, and a lot of detailed explanation is required for a book on project finance to be a practical guide rather than a generalized study or a vague summary of the subject. But with a systematic approach and an understanding of the principles that lie behind this detail, finding a way through the thickets becomes a less formidable task.

The subject of project finance is presented in this book in much the same way that a particular project is presented to the financing market (*cf.* §5.2.8), *i.e.*:

- *A general background on the project finance market and the rôles of the main participants:*
  - Chapter 2 explains how project finance developed, its key characteristics and how these differ from other types of finance, and why project finance is used.
  - Chapter 3 explains how investors develop projects, as well as the process for procuring public-sector projects using project finance.
  - Chapter 4 provides information on the markets for raising private-sector project finance debt.
  - Chapter 5 sets out the procedures for raising finance from private-sector lenders.
- *A review of the commercial contracts that can form a framework for raising project finance:*
  - Chapter 6 reviews the different characteristics of the main types of Project Agreements, which play a central rôle in many project-finance structures.

- Chapter 7 looks at terms and conditions which are common to most Project Agreements.
- Chapter 8 deals with the Sub-Contracts, which form a key part of a typical project-finance structure—including those for construction, operation and maintenance of the project, provision of fuel, raw materials and other input supplies, and insurance.
- *An explanation of project-finance risk analysis:*
  - Chapter 9 explains how lenders analyze and mitigate the commercial risks inherent in a project.
  - Chapter 10 similarly examines the effect of macroeconomic risks (inflation, and interest rate and exchange—rate movements) on project financing and how these risks are mitigated.
  - Chapter 11 analyzes regulatory and political risks and how these may affect a project.
- *A description of a project's financial structuring and documentation:*
  - Chapter 12 explains how the basic financial structure for a project is created.
  - Chapter 13 summarizes the inputs used for a financial model of a project and how the model's results are used by investors and lenders.
  - Chapter 14 sets out what lenders usually require when negotiating a project-finance loan.
- *Types of external support for projects:*
  - Chapter 15 explains how the public sector may provide financial support as part of the financing structure.
  - Chapter 16 reviews the rôles of development-finance institutions and export-credit agencies.

Finally Chapter 17 reviews recent market developments, new financing models and the future prospects for project finance.

Technical terms used in this book that are mainly peculiar to project finance are capitalized, and briefly explained in the Glossary, with cross-references to the sections in the main text where fuller explanations can be found; other specialized financial terms are also explained and cross-referenced in the Glossary, as are the various abbreviations.

Spreadsheets with the detailed calculations on which various tables in this book are based can be downloaded from www.yescombe.com.

References to books and articles are intended to provide some further reading for those interested in a particular topic, rather than as authorities for statements in this book, so they do not purport to provide a full bibliography. The main focus in these references is on those which can—at the time of writing—be freely downloaded from the internet (marked with an *). Again links to these and other similar resources are maintained at www.yescombe.com.

Chapter 2

WHAT IS PROJECT FINANCE?

§2.1 INTRODUCTION

This chapter reviews the basic features of project finance (§2.2), the factors behind its development (§2.3) and the 'building blocks' of a project-finance structure (§2.4), with examples (§2.5).

The benefits of using project finance are then considered from the point of view of the various project participants (§2.6).

§2.2 DEFINITION AND BASIC CHARACTERISTICS

Project-finance structures differ between various industry sectors and from deal to deal, since each project has its own unique characteristics. But there are common principles underlying the project-finance approach.

The Export-Import Bank of the United States (*cf.* §16.4.4) defines project finance as:

> "…*the financing of projects that are dependent on project cash flows for repayment, as defined by the contractual relationships within each project. By their very nature, these types of projects rely on a large number of*

5

Principles of Project Finance. DOI: http://dx.doi.org/10.1016/B978-0-12-391058-5.00002-3

*integrated contractual arrangements for successful completion and opera-
tion. The contractual relationships must be balanced with risks distributed
to those parties best able to undertake them, and should reflect a fair allocation of risk and reward. All project contracts must fit together seamlessly to
allocate risks in a manner which ensures the financial viability and success
of the project."*[1]

The rating agency Standard & Poor's (*cf.* §5.3.1) defines it as:

*"…non-recourse financing of a single asset or portfolio of assets where the
lenders can look only to those specific assets to generate the flow needed
to service its fixed obligations, chief of which are interest payments and
repayments of principal. Lenders' security and collateral is usually solely
the project's contracts and physical assets. Lenders typically do not have
recourse to the project's owner, and often, through the project's legal structure, project lenders are shielded from a project owner's financial troubles.*

*Project-finance transactions typically are comprised of a group of agree-
ments and contracts between lenders, project sponsors, and other interested
parties who combine to create a form of business organization that will issue
a finite amount of debt on inception, and will operate in a focused line of
business over a finite period."*[2]

An 'official' definition of project finance was provided by the Basel Committee
on Banking Supervision in the context of the 'Basel II' rules (*cf.* §17.3):

*"Project finance is a method of funding in which the lender looks primarily
to the revenues generated by a single project, both as the source of repayment and as security for the exposure. This type of financing is usually for
large, complex and expensive installations that might include, for example,
power plants, chemical processing plants, mines, transportation infrastructure, environment, and telecommunications infrastructure. Project finance
may take the form of financing of the construction of a new capital installation, or refinancing of an existing installation, with or without improvements. In such transactions, the lender is usually paid solely or almost
exclusively out of the money generated by the contracts for the facility's
output, such as the electricity sold by a power plant. The borrower is usually an SPE (Special Purpose Entity) that is not permitted to perform any
function other than developing, owning, and operating the installation. The*

---

[1] www.exim.gov – Home > Products > Loan Guarantee > Project & Structured Finance > Our
Approach to Project Finance*.
[2] *Updated Project Finance Summary Debt Rating Criteria* (Standard & Poor's, New York, 2007)*.

consequence is that repayment depends primarily on the project's cash flow and on the collateral value of the project's assets."[3]

The Organization for Economic Cooperation and Development (OECD) provides another 'official' definition of project finance in the context of the Export-Credit Consensus (*cf.* §16.2.3):

"a) *The financing of a particular economic unit in which a lender is satisfied to consider the cash flows and earnings of that economic unit as the source of funds from which a loan will be repaid and to the assets of the economic unit as collateral for the loan.*

b) *Financing of export transactions with an independent (legally and economically) project company, e.g. special purpose company, in respect of investment projects generating their own revenues.*

c) *Appropriate risk-sharing among the partners of the project, e.g. private or creditworthy public shareholders, exporters, creditors, offtakers, including adequate equity.*

d) *Project cash flow sufficient during the entire repayment period to cover operating costs and debt service for outside funds.*

e) *Priority deduction from project revenues of operating costs and debt service.*

f) *A non-sovereign buyer/borrower with no sovereign repayment guarantee (not including performance guarantees, e.g. offtake arrangements).*

g) *Asset-based securities for proceeds/assets of the project, e.g. assignments, pledges, proceed accounts;*

h) *Limited or no recourse to the sponsors of the private sector shareholders/ sponsors of the project after completion.*"[4]

So the principles of project finance can be summarized as:

- The project usually relates to major infrastructure with a long construction period and long operating life.
  - So the financing must also be for a long term (typically 15–25 years).
- Lenders rely on the future cash flow projected to be generated by the project to pay their interest and fees, and repay their debt.
  - Therefore the project must be 'ring-fenced' (*i.e.* legally and economically self-contained).

---

[3] Basel Committee on Banking Supervision, *International Convergence of Capital Measurement and Capital Standards—A Revised Framework* (Bank for International Settlements, Basel, 2005), p. 49*.

[4] Organization for Economic Co-operation and Development, *Arrangement on Officially Supported Export Credits* v. TAD/PG(2013)1 (OECD, Paris, 2013), Annex X: 'Terms and Conditions Applicable To Project Finance Transactions', Appendix 1: 'Eligibility Criteria for Project Finance Transactions", I.: Basic Criteria*.

- So the project is usually carried out through a special-purpose legal entity (usually a limited company) whose only business is the project (the 'Project Company').
- There is a high ratio of debt to equity ('leverage' or 'gearing')—roughly speaking, project finance debt may cover 70–90% of the capital cost of a project.
  - The effect of this high leverage is to reduce the blended cost of debt and equity, and hence the overall financing cost of the project.
- The Project Company's physical assets are likely to be worth much less than the debt if they are sold off after a default on the financing—and in projects involving public infrastructure they cannot be sold anyway.
  - So the main security for lenders is the Project Company's contracts, licenses, or other rights, which are the source of its cash flow.
  - Therefore lenders carry out a detailed analysis of the project's risks, and how these are allocated between the various parties through these contracts.
- The project has a finite life, based on such factors as the length of the contracts or licenses, or reserves of natural resources.
  - So the project-finance debt must be fully repaid by the end of the project's life.
- There are no guarantees from the investors in the Project Company for the project-finance debt.
  - So this is 'non-recourse' finance.[5]

Hence project finance differs from corporate finance, where loans:

- are primarily lent against a company's balance sheet and financial projections extrapolated from its past cash flow and profit record;
- has access to the whole cash flow from the spread of the borrower's business as security, instead of the limited cash flow from a specific project—thus even if an individual project fails, corporate lenders can still reasonably expect to be repaid;
- assume that the company will remain in business for an indefinite period and so can keep renewing (rolling over) its loans, which therefore do not need to be lent on a long-term basis; and
- may also be secured on the company's physical assets—its offices, factories, *etc.*, so that if the debt is not repaid these assets can be sold off to help recover the debt.

---

[5] Or there may be limited investor guarantees, in which case this is 'limited-recourse' finance—(*cf.* §9.13).

§2.3 DEVELOPMENT OF PROJECT FINANCE

Project finance has long been used in the natural-resources sector, lending against the cash flow which will be produced by extracting resources: *e.g.* in the 1880s the French bank Crédit Lyonnais provided finance in this way for the development of the Baku oil fields in Russia.[6] Lending techniques were developed further in the Texas oil fields in the 1930s. Such natural resources-based project finance was given a considerable boost from the 1970s by oil price increases—in particular it played a key rôle in the early development of the North Sea oil fields, as well as gas and other natural resources projects in Australia and various developing countries. The commodities boom of the 2000s saw another revival of such financing.

Similarly, project finance for public infrastructure projects is not a new concept: *e.g.* the English road system was renewed in the 18th and early 19th centuries using private-sector funding based on toll revenues; the railway, water, sewage, gas, electricity, and telephone industries were developed around the world in the 19th and early 20th centuries with private-sector investment debt raised through bond issues.[7] During the first half of the 20th century the state took over such activities in many countries, but this process began to reverse in the 1980s. Similarly, in developing countries, expropriations of foreign investments in the 1950s and 1960s caused foreign private-sector investment in key sectors such as infrastructure and natural resources to fade away, but this process also began to reverse in the 1980s.

The worldwide process of deregulation and privatization of utilities, and the use of private finance for public infrastructure in cases where privatization is not possible or desirable, have been key factors in the growth of project finance over since the 1980s. Project finance, as an appropriate method of long-term financing for capital-intensive projects where the investment financed has a relatively predictable cash flow, has played an important part in providing the funding required for this change, and its modern development and structuring really results from this. This has taken place both in the developed world as well as developing countries. It has also been promoted by the internationalization of investment in major infrastructure projects: leading project developers now run worldwide portfolios and are able to apply the lessons learned from one country to projects in another, as are their banks and financial advisors. Governments and the public sector generally also benefit from these exchanges of experience.

---

[6] Daniel Yergin, *The Prize* (Simon & Schuster, New York, 1991), p. 60.
[7] *Cf.* Barry Eichengreen, *Financing Infrastructure in Developing Countries: Lessons from the Railway Age* (World Bank Policy Research Working Paper 1379, Washington DC, 1994)*; Charles D. Jacobson & Joel A. Tarr. *Ownership and Financing of Infrastructure: Historical Perspectives.* (Policy Research Working Paper 1466, World Bank, Washington DC, 1995.)*

This modern development can be seen in successive 'waves':

- Project finance for natural resources projects was developed from the 1970s as discussed above.
- Project finance for independent power producers ('IPPs') in the electricity sector was first developed after the Private Utility Regulatory Policies Act ('PURPA') in the United States in 1978, which encouraged the development of cogeneration plants by allowing them to sell power based on long-term contracts priced at the marginal cost of the regulated utilities. The project-finance techniques developed for this purpose began to be used for power projects in developing countries such as Philippines and Chile in the 1980s, reached Europe with electricity privatization in the United Kingdom in the early 1990s, and then spread rapidly elsewhere in the world. In recent years project finance has also been widely used in the renewable power sector (*e.g.* wind- and solar-power generation).
- Project finance for other economic infrastructure (especially transportation) began in the mid-1980s with the first great modern privately-financed infrastructure project—the Channel Tunnel between Britain and France (signed in 1987), followed by two other major toll-bridge projects in Britain, along with privately-financed toll-road concession programs such as Australia's from the late 1980s and Chile's from the early 1990s.
- Project finance for social infrastructure (schools, hospitals, prisons, public housing, other public buildings such as government offices or police stations, *etc.*) was first developed through Britain's Private Finance Initiative ('PFI') from the early 1990s; PFI has been widely imitated elsewhere in the world.
- Project finance for the explosive worldwide growth in mobile telephone networks developed in the mid-late 1990s, but is no longer as significant.

Other changes in financing techniques, developed in the early 1970s, which helped the evolution of project finance included:

- *Long-term commercial-bank lending* to corporate customers—previously commercial banks only lent on a short-term basis, to match their deposits (*cf.* §10.3);
- The use of *export credits* for financing major projects (*cf.* §16.2);
- *Shipping finance*, where banks make loans to pay for construction of large vessels, on the security of long-term charters—*i.e.* construction lending against a contractual cash flow, with the borrower being a separate special-purpose company owning the ship, in a way very similar to later project-finance structures;

- *Real-estate finance*, again involving loans for construction secured against long-term cash-flow (rental) projections;
- *Tax-based financial leasing*, which accustomed banks to complex cash-flows (*cf.* §4.5.2).

The final vital element in the development of project finance was the creation (in the mid-1980s) of user-friendly *spreadsheet software*, without which project finance would be practically impossible.

Table 2.1 provides an analysis by industry sectors of the project-finance loan commitments provided by private-sector lenders in recent years. The effect of the global financial crisis after 2008 can be clearly seen, but as can also be seen the market recovered relatively strongly from 2010. (For a fuller analysis on a geographical basis, *cf.* §4.2.1.) Power generation has consistently been the most important market sector, although the figures in Table 2.1 do not show the sharp drop from $65 billion of lending in the power sector in 2001 to $25 billion in 2002, a product of the Enron débâcle and its knock-on effects elsewhere in the power industry. Infrastructure, especially transportation, has shown a remarkable growth during the 2000s, as has natural resources. Conversely, the decline in telecommunications from the boom years can be clearly seen.

These statistics do not include:

- direct lending (or lending through project-finance debt funds) by non-bank private-sector lenders (*cf.* §4.4; §17.4);
- public-sector finance for projects (*cf.* Chapter 15);
- finance from export-credit guarantors, insurers or banks, generally known as export-credit agencies ('ECAs'), and bilateral or multilateral development-finance institutions ('DFIs'), for which *cf.* Chapter 16.

Roughly speaking, if these other sources are added onto the figures in Table 2.1, the total project-finance debt raised in 2012 would exceed $300 billion. Assuming that debt averages 80% of total project costs, on the basis of this estimate some $375 billion of new investments worldwide were financed or refinanced (*cf.* §14.16.1—these figures include refinancings) using project finance in 2012.

It should be noted, however, that because it is debatable whether certain structured-finance loans should be classified as project finance or not (*cf.* §5.2.2), and the borderline between project finance and financing projects is not always clear (*cf.* Chapter 1), market statistics compiled by different sources can vary considerably.[8]

---

[8] For example, the Dealogic database recorded $358 billion of project finance investments (*i.e.* debt plus equity) in 2011 and $406 billion in 2012. The classification of reported loans into different market sectors is also rather unclear in both the *Project Finance International* and Dealogic figures.

Table 2.1 Private-Sector Project-Finance Commitments, 2000–2012.

($ millions)	2000	2007	2008	2009	2010	2011	2012
Power	56,512	76,518	90,236	57,642	78,177	85,947	73,416
Natural resources – of which:	16,518	56,432	67,859	38,005	50,589	59,756	75,485
Mining	629	4,607	11,486	4,071	10,858	11,158	4,745
Oil & gas	12,552	34,311	42,960	31,137	28,425	43,983	66,139
Petrochemicals	3,337	17,519	13,413	2,797	11,306	4,615	4,601
Infrastructure – of which:	16,755	67,620	65,212	40,233	64,998	56,676	65,610
Transportation		44,027	54,789	25,451	52,315	43,607	40,467
Other Infrastructure		16,423	6,940	8,890	9,838	11,348	21,060
Waste & recycling		2,989	550	1,194	1,267	724	842
Water and sewerage		4,181	2,933	4,699	1,578	997	3,241
Industry	3,538	17,473	11,979	3,454	6,306	12,155	6,833
Leisure and property	1,638	22,759	20,836		14,424	15,439	
Telecommunications	36,735	5,556	6,260	8,118	13,383	5,314	1,529
Agriculture		452	61		86	479	
Total	**131,696**	**246,809**	**262,442**	**147,452**	**227,964**	**235,766**	**222,873**

Source: Adapted from data published in the journal *Project Finance International*, issues 185 (January 26, 2000), 353 (January 9, 2008), 400 (January 9, 2009), 424 (January 10, 2010), 448 (January 13, 2011), 472 (January 12, 2012), 496 (January 16, 2013). Figures relate to commercial bank loans and bonds (*cf.* Chapter 4).

§2.4 ELEMENTS OF A PROJECT-FINANCE STRUCTURE

To look in more detail at the structure of a project financing, this usually has two elements:

- equity, provided by investors in the project; and
- project finance-based debt, provided by one or more groups of lenders.

The project-finance debt has first call on the project's net operating cash flow; the investors' return is thus more dependent on the success of the project. So as the investors are taking a higher risk, they expect a higher return on their investment, and the reverse is true for lenders.

A nexus of contracts signed by the Project Company provide support for the finance. A 'Project Agreement' is often at the centre of this contractual structure. This may take two main forms:

either an 'Offtake Contract', under which the product produced by the project will be sold on a long-term pricing formula to an 'Offtaker';[9]

or a contract with a central government department, regional or state government, county or municipality, or another public agency ('Contracting Authority' will be used to cover all of these),[10] which gives the Project Company the right to construct the project and earn revenues from it.

Alternatively, the Project Company may sell its production in commodity markets (which may apply, for example, to power or natural-resources projects) or have a license to operate under the terms of general legislation for the industry sector (*e.g.* a privatized port or airport, or a mobile-phone network), in both cases without an Offtake Contract or Project Agreement, as discussed further below.

The Project Company usually enters into 'Sub-Contracts', which provide support for the project finance, particularly by transferring risks from the Project Company to other parties, and which also form part of the lenders' security package.

The Project Agreement and Sub-Contracts are known collectively as the 'Project Contracts'. Project Agreements are discussed in detail in Chapters 6 and 7, and Sub-Contracts in Chapter 8.

---

[9] An Offtake Contract may be signed either with a private-sector counterpart or a Contracting Authority.

[10] Other terms for a Contracting Authority include 'Public Entity', 'Public Party', 'Government Procuring Entity', 'Institution', 'Public Authority', 'Authority' or 'grantor'. In the same context the Project Company may be referred to as the 'Private Party'.

§2.5 EXAMPLES OF PROJECT-FINANCE STRUCTURES

In this section some simplified examples of these structures in particular sectors—namely process-plant projects (§2.5.1) and infrastructure projects, including public-private partnerships (§2.5.2)—will amplify the basic structuring principles discussed above.

§2.5.1 PROCESS-PLANT PROJECTS

These are projects where there is an input at one end of the project, which goes through a process within the project, and emerges as an output, *e.g.*:

- *thermal power generation*: input—coal or gas; process—burning/conversion to steam; output—electricity (and sometimes heat);
- *water treatment*: input—untreated water; process—treatment of the water; output—potable water;
- *waste incineration*; input—household or commercial waste; process—incineration; output—electricity (and sometimes heat) and ash residue;
- *LNG (liquid natural gas) terminal*; input—liquid natural gas, brought in by sea in an LNG carrier; process—re-gasification; output—gas to pipeline.

Typical basic elements of this type of project, using a gas-fired power station as an example, are set out in Figure 2.1.

In this case the Project Agreement is in the form of a type of Offtake Contract, namely a Power Purchase Agreement ('PPA'), under which an electricity-distribution company purchases the project's output, *i.e.* electricity, based on a pre-agreed 'Tariff'[11] (*cf.* §6.2). This Offtaker may be either a public- or private-sector entity, depending on whether the electricity industry is privatized in the country concerned. The key Sub-Contracts are:

- an *Engineering Procurement and Construction Contract* ('EPC Contract')[12] for design and construction of the power plant;
- an *Input-Supply Contract*, in this case a Gas-Supply Agreement under which the gas to fuel the plant is supplied;
- an *Operation and Maintenance Contract* ('O&M Contract') with an experienced power-plant operator.

---

[11] The Tariff payable under a PPA or other process-plant projects, Service-Fee payments by a Contracting Authority for a PFI-Model Contract, and User Charges for a Concession (see below), will be referred to collectively hereafter as 'Contract Payments', and the formulæ in the Project Agreement based on which the Contract Payments are calculated, as the 'Payment Mechanism'.

[12] Also known as a design, procurement, and construction ('DPC') contract.

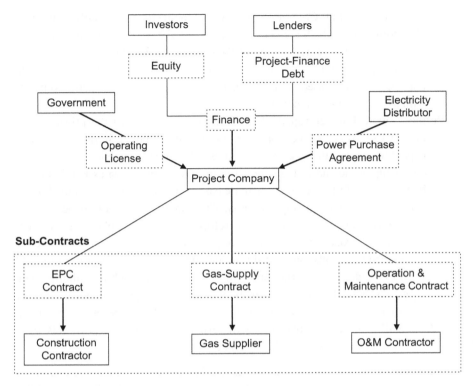

Figure 2.1 Process-plant Project.

§2.5.2 Infrastructure Projects

There are three main categories here:[13]

Privatized and Private-Sector Infrastructure. Economic infrastructure such as ports and airports may be privatized. In such cases the infrastructure company may raise debt on a corporate-finance basis,[14] with lenders relying on cash flow from the business as a whole, and security over the company's assets, or a particular self-contained new investment may be financed on a project-finance basis (*e.g.* a new terminal at an existing privatized port or airport). Typically in the latter cases there will be no Project Agreement but there may

---

[13] Of course power and other process-plant projects are also infrastructure (and may or may not be public-sector projects), but given their particular structure these are dealt with separately in this book.

[14] Corporate finance is sometimes referred to as 'equity finance', because no project-specific debt is being raised. However the term is confusing (because it could relate to the equity portion of a project financing).

be one or more Sub-Contracts with users of the facilities, *e.g.* airlines or shipping companies, which are very similar to Offtake Agreements since the contract counterparties agree to pay for their use of the facilities' services.

Similarly, a purely private infrastructure project such as a sports stadium may be financed based on the cash flow from medium/long-term contracts with users of corporate boxes.

Public–Private Partnerships.[15] These are projects in which the private-sector Project Company finances, operates and maintains public infrastructure, and is paid for its use; the asset concerned usually reverts to public-sector control/ownership at the end of the contract term. These are known as Public-Private Partnerships ('PPPs' or '3Ps'), and are based on a contract between the Project Company and a Contracting Authority. There are two main PPP models:

- 'Concessions': construction or refurbishment of public infrastructure such as a road, bridge, tunnel, airport, port, railway, *etc.*, with revenue derived from tolls, fares or similar payments by users ('User Charges');[16]
- 'PFI Model':[17] construction or refurbishment of a public building (such as a school, hospital, prison, public housing or government office), or other public infrastructure (such as a road, railway line, water-treatment facility or sewage plant),[18] with revenue derived from payments by a Contracting Authority ('Service Fee').[19]

---

[15] For further resources on PPPs *cf.* E.R. Yescombe, *Public–Private Partnerships: Principles of Policy and Finance* (Butterworth-Heinemann, Oxford, 2007); *Public–Private Partnership Handbook* (Asian Development Bank, Manila, 2008)*; European PPP Resource Centre, *The Guide to Guidance: How to Prepare, Procure and Deliver PPP Projects* (EIB, Luxemburg, 2011)*; *Public–Private Partnerships Reference Guide* (World Bank/PPIAF, Washington DC, 2012)*.

[16] The relatively-recent PPP type of Concession should be distinguished from the old form of concession (such as those for the Suez and Panama Canals), which was more akin to privatization, as it typically had a much longer term (*e.g.* 100 years or more), did not contain the detailed contractual controls and other terms which are found in modern Concessions (*cf.* Chapter 6 and Chapter 7), and granted rights now not given, such as extraterritoriality (exemption from local laws). The older concessions were often a kind of economic colonialism, rather than an agreement between two equal parties. PPP Concessions are also quite different to concessions in the natural-resources sector.

[17] The term refers to the British government's Private Finance Initiative program which began in 1992, the first major use of this structure, which has been widely adopted elsewhere in the world. PFI was renamed PF2 (which is not an abbreviation!) in 2012.

[18] Note that the actual services provided to the public may remain in the public sector under this model—*e.g.* a school may be provided by a PPP contract, but the teaching in the school is still a public-sector activity.

[19] This is often referred to as an 'Availability-based' model, because in the majority of cases the Project Company is paid for making the project available to the Contracting Authority, not for its usage as such However it is not correct to use the term Availability-based Contract to refer to all PFI-Model contracts, as there are exceptions where the PFI Model does not use this structure, for example 'Shadow Toll' roads (*cf.* §6.4.6), where the Project Company is paid by the Contracting Authority based on the number of vehicles using the road—*i.e.* effectively the Contracting Authority is paying tolls instead of the users doing so. But this term will be used elsewhere in this book where it is relevant.

It should be noted that the term PPP is often used very broadly, and PPPs do not necessarily involve project finance (*cf.* §6.6).

To a certain extent Concessions relate to economic infrastructure, and the PFI Model to social infrastructure, but this is not a precise dividing line. Any project which can be structured as a Concession can alternatively be structured as a PFI-Model PPP (although the reverse is not the case): the difference is simply the source of payments.

Process-plant projects like those discussed in §2.5.1, where the Offtaker is a Contracting Authority, are also often included under the PPP heading, but given their rather different structure, and the fact Offtake Contracts with private-sector Offtakers are also not uncommon and work on much the same basis, such projects are treated separately in this book. Conversely, it is also possible for contracts similar to those used for PPPs to be signed with a private-sector counterpart, but this is uncommon.

Privatized infrastructure and PPPs are collectively known as private participation in infrastructure ('PPI').

Revenue Bonds. This structure (only found in the U.S. market) makes it possible for a project owned and managed by the public sector to use private finance on a project-finance basis (*cf.* §4.3.1).

Figure 2.2 sets out the typical basic structure for a toll-road Concession. The Project Agreement here is a 'Concession Agreement', which provides for User Charges (tolls) to be paid by road users to the Project Company. The key Sub-Contracts are:

- a *Design & Build Contract* ('D&B Contract') to design and build the road;[20]
- an *Operating Contract* to operate the tolling system;
- a *Maintenance Contract* for the continued maintenance of the road.

Figure 2.3 sets out a typical basic structure for the PFI Model as used in a social infrastructure project such as a school or hospital. The term Project Agreement is usually used for the contract with the Contracting Authority, under which Service-Fee payments are made to the Project Company. The key Sub-Contracts in this case could include:

- a *Design & Build Contract* ('D&B Contract'), to design and build the building;

---

[20] The difference between an EPC Contract and a D&B Contract relates to the supply of equipment. In an EPC Contract the lead contractor is usually the supplier of equipment (*e.g.* power-generation turbines) which forms the greatest part of the project's costs, and it further sub-contracts civil works (*e.g.* the preparation of the project site and construction of any buildings). In a D&B Contract the civil works (*e.g.* construction of a road) form the main part of the contract's costs, and equipment supply (*e.g.* lighting for the road) is procured through sub-sub-contractors. The term 'Construction Contract' will be used hereafter to refer to either an EPC Contract or a D&B Contract.

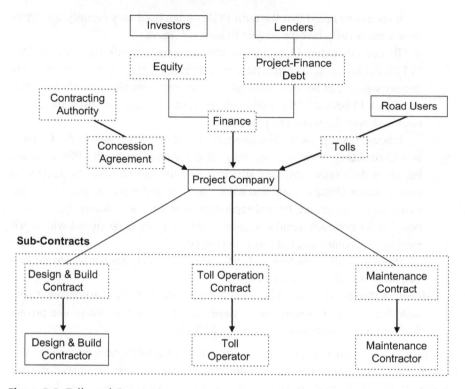

Figure 2.2 Toll-road Concession.

- a *Maintenance Contract*,[21] for maintenance of the building's physical structure and key equipment;
- one or more '*Building-Services Contracts*', for the provision of services such as cleaning, catering and security.[22] (Or this may be dealt with as part of one contract covering both maintenance and services.)

§2.5.3 OTHER STRUCTURES

There are many variations on the structures set out above, and all of the 'building blocks' shown in Figures 2.1–2.3 are not found in every project financing, for example:

- Various types of project do not operate under a Project Agreement, *e.g.* those that sell a product or service to private-sector buyers in a commodity-based

---

[21] Also known as a Facilities Maintenance ('FM') Contract, and as a 'Hard' FM Contract in contrast to a 'Soft' FM Contract (see next note).

[22] Building Services may be procured as part of the Project Agreement package, or under separate shorter-term contracts. A Building-Services Contract may also be referred to as a 'Soft' FM Contract.

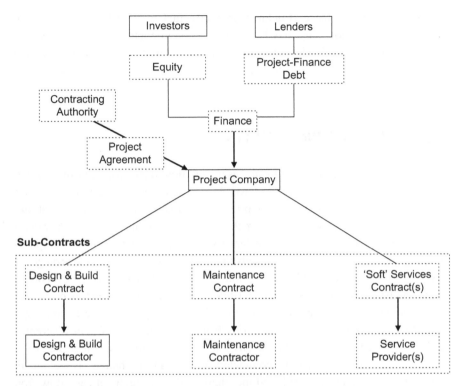

Figure 2.3 PFI Model.

or open competitive market, such as oil, gas, mining or telecommunications projects, or 'merchant' power plants (*cf.* §9.6.2), although they usually have some form of license to allow them to do this in lieu of a Project Agreement.

- Privatized infrastructure such as ports and airports are based either on a license to operate rather than a Project Agreement (but if the project is a PPP a Project Agreement would normally be used).

- The Project Company itself may operate the project rather than sub-contracting the operation and maintenance, perhaps with an agreement for technical assistance from one its shareholders.

- If the product of the project is a commodity for which there is a wide market (*e.g.* oil), there is not necessarily a need for an Offtake Contract (and as can be seen in Figure 2.2 a Concession does not have an Offtake Contract).

- Projects that do not use fuel or a similar raw material—*e.g.* hydro-, wind- or solar-power generation—do not require an Input-Supply Contract.

- A project for a mobile-phone network (and similar projects where a network of any kind is being constructed) is usually built in stages rather than under a single Construction Contract, and has no Offtake Contract.

Of course none of these structures or contractual relationships are unique to project finance: any company may have investors, sign contracts, get licenses from the government, and so on; however, the relative importance of these matters, and the way in which they are linked together, is a distinguishing feature of project finance.

§2.6 WHY USE PROJECT FINANCE?

A project may be financed by a company as an addition to its existing business rather than on a stand-alone project-finance basis. In this case, the company uses its available cash and credit lines to pay for the project, and if necessary raise new credit lines and new equity capital to do so (*i.e.* it makes use of 'corporate finance'). Provided it can be supported by the company's balance sheet and earnings record, a corporate loan to finance a project is normally relatively simple, quick, and cheap to arrange.

A Project Company, unlike a corporate borrower, has no business record to serve as the basis for a lending decision (unless a project-finance loan is being refinanced). Nonetheless, lenders have to be confident that they will be repaid, especially taking account of the additional risk from the high level of debt inherent in a project-finance transaction. This means that they need to have a high degree of confidence that the project can be completed on time and on budget, is technically capable of operating as designed, and that there will be enough net cash flow from the project's operation to cover their debt service adequately. Project economics also need to be robust enough to cover any temporary problems that may arise.

The lenders therefore need to evaluate the terms of the project's contracts insofar as these provide a basis for its construction costs and operating cash flow, and quantify the risks inherent in the project with particular care. They need to ensure that project risks are allocated to appropriate parties other than the Project Company, or, where this is not possible, mitigated in other ways. This process is known as 'due diligence.' The due-diligence process may often cause slow and frustrating progress for a project developer, as lenders inevitably tend to get involved—directly or indirectly—in the negotiation of the Project Contracts, but it is an unavoidable aspect of raising project-finance debt. (The issues covered during due diligence are discussed in Chapters 9 to 13.)

Lenders also need to continue to monitor and control the activities of the Project Company to ensure that the basis on which they assessed these risks is not undermined. This may also leave the investor with much less independent management of the project than would be the case with a corporate financing. (The controls imposed by lenders are discussed in Chapter 14.)

Besides being slow, complex, and leading to some loss of control of the project, project finance is also an expensive method of financing. The lenders' margin over cost of funds may be 2-3 times that of corporate finance; the lenders' due diligence and control processes, and the advisors employed for this purpose (*cf.* §5.5), also add significantly to costs.

It should also be emphasized that project finance cannot be used to finance a project that would not otherwise be financeable.

§2.6.1 WHY INVESTORS USE PROJECT FINANCE

Why, despite these factors, do investors make use of project finance?[23] There are a variety of reasons:

High Leverage. One major reason for using project finance is that investments in ventures such as power generation or road building have to be long term but do not offer an inherently high return: high leverage improves the return for an investor.

Table 2.2 sets out a (very simplified) example of the benefit of leverage on an investor's return. Both the low-leverage and high-leverage columns relate to the same investment of 1,000, which produces revenue of 100. If it is financed with 30% debt, as in the low-leverage column (a typical level of debt for a good corporate credit), the return on equity is 11%. On the other hand, if it is financed with 80% (project finance-style) leverage, the return on the (reduced level) of equity is 22%, despite an increase in the cost of the debt (reflecting the higher risk for lenders).

Table 2.2 Benefit of Leverage on Investors' Return

		Low Leverage	High Leverage
Project cost		1,000	1,000
a) Debt		300	800
b) Equity		700	200
c) Revenue from project		100	100
d) Interest rate on debt (*p.a.*)		5%	7%
e) Interest payable	[(a) × (d)]	15	56
f) Profit	[(c)–(e)]	85	44
Return on equity	[(f) ÷ (b)]	12%	22%

---

[23] *Cf.* Benjamin C. Esty, *The Economic Motivations for Using Project Finance* (Harvard Business School, Boston MA, 2003)*.

Project finance thus takes advantage of the fact that debt is cheaper than equity, so the higher the debt level (leverage) the better the equity return.

This example is highly simplified, and, as will be seen later, leverage is dictated largely by the lenders' requirements for a cash-flow cushion, which in turn may actually dictate the equity return on the project (*cf.* §12.8). Also Table 2.2 ignores the timing of the revenue (*cf.* §10.2).

In corporate-finance theory, an investor in a company with high leverage would expect a higher return than one in a company with low leverage, on the ground that high leverage equals high risk, and conversely the lenders would be happy with a lower return where there is lower leverage, so the overall cost of finance to a company should always be the same whatever its debt:equity ratio.[24] However, this correlation is not that close in project-finance investment, since its high leverage does not imply high risk—higher leverage can only be achieved in project finance where the level of risk in the project is limited, *e.g.* by passing risks down to Sub-Contractors.

Lower Cost. If the Project Company is selling a commodity such as electricity or LNG into a market, the lower the financing costs the more competitive its pricing can be, and hence the higher leverage may be beneficial if the weighted cost of an investor's capital (*i.e.* equity and debt on its own balance sheet) is higher (*cf.* Table 2.3).

Table 2.3 Effect of Leverage on Offtaker's/Contracting Authority's Cost

		Low Leverage	High Leverage
Project cost		1,000	1,000
a) Debt		300	800
b) Equity		700	200
c) Return on equity	[(b) × 15%]	105	30
d) Interest rate on debt (*p.a.*)		5%	7%
e) Interest payable	[(a) × (d)]	15	56
Revenue required	[(c) + (e)]	120	86

---

[24] This principle (known as the Miller–Modigliani theorem after its original authors) is that the value of a company is not affected by how it is financed; it follows from this that a company's weighted cost of capital should always be the same, whatever its financing structure (debt:equity ratio). However there are acknowledged exceptions which distort this approach, one of the key ones being that debt interest is generally tax-deductible whereas equity dividends are not (see comments on tax benefits below, and *cf.* §12.2.2), which is another reason for using a project-finance structure. It must also be assumed that there is perfect efficiency in the financial markets for both debt and equity, which may not be the case, especially in developing countries.

Borrowing Capacity. Project finance increases the level of debt that can be borrowed against a project; moreover non-recourse finance raised by the Project Company is not normally counted against corporate credit lines (therefore in this sense it may be off-balance sheet). It may thus increase an investor's overall borrowing capacity, and hence the ability to undertake several major projects simultaneously.

Risk Limitation. An investor in a project raising funds through project finance does not normally guarantee the repayment of the debt[25]—the risk is therefore limited to the amount of the equity investment (*cf.* §12.2). If the project goes well, the investor will get a good return on the investment, but if it goes badly the investor can simply walk away and hence limit the loss to the amount of the equity investment. In effect, in return for a relatively small fee (its equity share), an investor has established an 'option price' at which it may retain the investment if successful or walk away if its failure could otherwise have a high impact on its other business.

Risk Spreading/Joint Ventures. A project may be too large for one investor to undertake, so others may be brought in to share the risk in a joint-venture Project Company. This both enables the risk to be spread between investors and limits the amount of each investor's risk because of the non-recourse nature of the Project Company's debt financing.

As project development can involve major expenditure, with a significant risk of having to write it all off if the project does not go ahead (*cf.* §3.3), a project developer may also bring in a partner in the development phase of the project to share this risk.

This approach can also be used to bring in 'limited partners' to the project, *e.g.* by giving a share in the equity of a Project Company to an Offtaker who is thus induced to sign a long-term Offtake Contract, without being required to make a substantial cash investment.

Developer Leverage. Projects are often put together by a developer with an idea but little money, who then has to find investors. A project-finance structure, which requires less equity, makes it easier for the weaker developer to maintain an equal partnership, because if the absolute level of the equity in the project is low, the required investment from the weaker partner is also low.

Unequal Partnerships. Thanks to high leverage, the relatively small amount of equity required for a major project where project finance is used enables parties with different financial strengths to work together. It would be quite normal for example, for the investors to consist of a financial investor (say an infrastructure fund), a construction company, and a maintenance company, whose

---

[25] But *cf.* §9.13 for limited-recourse guarantees which may be provided by investors.

balance-sheet strengths would probably be very different, but with each bringing particular skills to this partnership. Creating a joint venture thus enables project risks to be reduced by combining expertise. In such cases the relevant Project Contracts (*e.g.* the Construction, O&M/Maintenance, or Services Contracts) are usually allocated to the partner with the relevant expertise (but *cf.* §3.2).

Long-Term Finance. Project-finance loans typically have a longer term than corporate finance. Long-term financing is necessary if the assets financed normally have a high capital cost that cannot be recovered over a short term without pushing up the cost that must be charged for the project's end product. So loans for power projects may run for nearly 20 years, and for infrastructure projects even longer. (Natural resources projects usually have a shorter term because the reserves extracted deplete more quickly, and telecommunication projects also have a shorter term because the technology involved has a relatively short life.)

Enhanced Credit. A company's credit rating is less likely to be downgraded if its risks on project investments are limited through a project-finance structure.

Also, if the Offtaker has a better credit standing than the investor (which is possible in a PPP Contract with a Contracting Authority), this may enable debt to be raised for the project on better terms than the investor would be able to obtain from a corporate loan.

Reduces Need for Outside Investors. Another important factor encouraging a high level of debt in Project Companies is the more equity that is required, the more complex the project becomes to manage (especially during the bidding and development phases), if the result of having to raise more equity is that more investors have to be brought in. Moreover if more investors have to be brought in, this means that the original developers may lose control of the project.

Tax Benefits. A further factor that may make high leverage more attractive is that interest is tax deductible in many countries, whereas dividends to shareholders are not, which makes debt even cheaper than equity, and hence encourages high leverage. Thus, in the example in Table 2.2, if the tax rate is 30%, the after-tax profit in the low leverage case is 60 (85 × 70%), or an after-tax return on equity of 8.5%, whereas in the high-leverage case it is 31 (44 × 70%), or an after-tax return on equity of 15.4%.

In major projects, however, there may be a high level of tax deductions anyway during the early stages of the project because the capital cost is depreciated against tax (*cf.* §13.7.1), so the ability to make a further deduction of interest against tax at the same time may not be significant. Moreover, if the shareholders invest most of their funds as subordinated debt rather than equity, interest on this is also usually tax-deductible (*cf.* §12.2.2).

Off-Balance-Sheet Financing. If the investor has to raise the debt and then inject it into the project, this will clearly appear on the investor's balance sheet. A project-finance structure may allow the investor to keep the debt off its consolidated balance sheet, but usually only if the investor is a minority shareholder in the project—which may be achieved if the project is owned through a joint venture. Keeping debt off the balance sheet is sometimes seen as beneficial to a company's position in the financial markets, but a company's shareholders and lenders should normally take account of risks involved in any off-balance-sheet activities, which are generally revealed in notes to the published accounts even if they are not included in the balance-sheet figures; so although joint ventures often raise project finance for other reasons (as discussed above), project finance is not usually undertaken purely to keep debt off the investors' balance sheets.

However investment in a project through an unconsolidated affiliated company may be useful during the construction phase of a project, when it is a 'dead weight' on the rest of a company's business, because it requires a high capital investment in the balance sheet which is producing no revenue.

§2.6.2 THE BENEFITS OF PROJECT FINANCE TO THIRD PARTIES

Equally, there are benefits for an Offtaker/Contracting Authority:

Lower Product or Service Cost. In order to pay the lowest price for the project's product or service, the Offtaker/Contracting Authority will want the project to raise as high a level of debt as possible, and so a project-finance structure is beneficial. This can be illustrated by doing the calculation in Table 2.2 in reverse: suppose the investor in the project requires a return of at least 15%, then, as Table 2.3 shows, revenue of 120 is required to produce this return using low-leverage finance, but only 86 using high-leverage project finance, and hence the cost of the project reduces accordingly.

So if the Offtaker/Contracting Authority wishes to achieve the lowest long-term cost for the project and is able to influence how the project is financed, the use of project finance should be encouraged, *e.g.* by agreeing to sign a Project Agreement that fits project-finance requirements.

Additional Investment in Public Infrastructure. Project finance can provide funding for additional investment in PPP-based infrastructure that the public sector might otherwise not be able to undertake because of economic or funding constraints on the public-sector investment budget.

Of course, if the Contracting Authority pays for the project through a long-term Project Agreement, it could be said that a project financed in this way is merely off-balance-sheet financing, and should therefore be included in the public-sector budget anyway. But if there are constraints on the public-sector investment budget, such public-sector accounting issues may be of limited relevance.

Capital at Risk. A project-finance structure transfers risks *e.g.* project-cost overruns or long-term maintenance costs, from the Offtaker/Contracting Authority to the Project Company (*cf.* Chapter 9). It also usually provides for payments only when specific performance objectives are met, hence also transferring the performance risks to the Project Company.

This risk transfer is made more effective in a project-finance structure because both the investors and the lenders have substantial 'capital at risk'. In non-project financed projects, the main contractors, *e.g.* for construction or maintenance, have limited liability which relates to the profits they are taking out of the transaction: *e.g.* a maintenance contractor's maximum liability may be two years' fees (§8.3.4). So if maintenance costs turn out to be much higher than projected, it is quite likely that most of these excess costs cannot be recovered from the maintenance contractor. In a project-financed project such overruns still fall first on the relevant Sub-Contractor, but then when the Sub-Contractor's liability is exhausted, they have to be dealt with first by the investors, and then the lenders. Only if these excess costs are so great that neither the investors nor the lenders would find it worthwhile to put in extra financing to protect their investment, would they both walk away (so incurring substantial losses on their investments and loans respectively): this is a quite unlikely scenario in most projects.

Lower Project Cost. As discussed above, private finance is now widely used for infrastructure projects that would previously have been built and operated by the public sector. Apart from relieving public-sector budget pressures, such PPP projects may also have merit because the private sector can often build and run such investments more cost-effectively than the public sector.

This lower cost is a function of:

- the general tendency of the public sector to 'over-engineer' or 'gold-plate' projects;
- greater private-sector expertise in control and management of project construction and operation (based on the private sector being better able to offer incentives to good managers);
- risk transfer, as discussed above, *e.g.* the private sector taking the primary risk of construction- and operation-cost overruns, for which public-sector projects are notorious;
- 'whole life' management of long-term maintenance of the project, rather than *ad hoc* arrangements for maintenance dependent on the availability of further public-sector funding.

However, whether such cost benefits offset higher private-sector financing costs is difficult to calculate because of the many assumptions which have to be made.

And of course this lower cost is not a function of project finance, but rather of the private-sector involvement.

Third-Party Due Diligence. The Offtaker/Contracting Authority may benefit from the independent due diligence and control of the project exercised by the lenders, who will want to ensure that all obligations under the Project Agreement are clearly fulfilled and that other Project Contracts adequately deal with risk issues.

Transparency. As a project financing is self-contained (*i.e.* it deals only with the assets and liabilities, costs, and revenues of the particular project), the true costs of the product or service can more easily be measured and monitored. Also, if the investor is in a regulated business (*e.g.* power distribution), the unregulated business can be shown to be financed separately and on an arm's-length basis via a project-finance structure.

Additional Inward Investment. For a developing country, project finance opens up new opportunities for infrastructure investment, as it can be used to create inward investment that would not otherwise occur. Furthermore, successful project finance for a major project, such as a power station, can act as a showcase to promote further investment in the wider economy.

Financial-Market Development. Also project finance may help to develop the domestic financing market in a developing country, as typically domestic banks in such countries only lend on a short-term basis. The involvement of DFIs and other parties from outside the country (*cf.* Chapter 16) may help develop the local financial market in parallel.

Technology Transfer. For developing countries, project finance provides a way of producing market-based investment in infrastructure for which the local economy may have neither the resources nor the skills.

PROJECT DEVELOPMENT AND MANAGEMENT

§3.1 INTRODUCTION

The life of a project can be divided into three phases:

- *Development.* The period during which the project is conceived, the Project Contracts are negotiated, signed, and come into effect, and the equity and project-finance debt are put in place and available for drawing—the end of this process is known as 'Financial Close'.[1] This phase is more complex than it might appear at first sight, and can easily run on for several years.
- *Construction.* The period during which the project finance is drawn down and the project is built—the end of this process will be referred to hereafter as 'Project Completion'.
- *Operation.* The period during which the project operates commercially and produces cash flow to pay the lenders' debt service and the investors' equity return.

The Sponsors (§3.2) play the primary rôle during the development phase of the project, managing this process (§3.3) with the support of external advisors (§3.4). Where more than one Sponsor is involved, a joint-venture structure has to be agreed

---

[1] Also known as the 'Effective Date', *i.e.* the date on which all the Project Contracts come into effect.   **29**

Principles of Project Finance. DOI: http://dx.doi.org/10.1016/B978-0-12-391058-5.00003-5

to (§3.5). The Project Company is usually set up towards the end of the development phase and manages the project from Financial Close (§3.6). The project may also be developed initially by parties other than the Sponsors through a bidding (public procurement) process for a PPP project, organized by a Contracting Authority (§3.7).

§3.2 SPONSORS AND OTHER INVESTORS

In order to obtain project-finance debt, the investors have to offer priority payment to the lenders, thus accepting that they will only receive their equity return after lenders have been paid their debt service. Therefore, investors assume the highest financial risk, but at the same time they receive the largest share in the project's profit (pro rata to the money they have at risk) if it goes according to plan.

The active investors in a project are usually referred to as the 'Sponsors',[2] meaning that their rôle is one of promotion, development, and management of the project. Even though the project-finance debt is normally non-recourse (*i.e.* the lenders have no guarantees from the Sponsors), their involvement is important. One of the first things a lender considers when deciding whether to participate in a project financing is whether the Sponsors of the project are appropriate parties.

Lenders wish to have Sponsors with:

- experience in the industry concerned and, hence, the ability to provide any technical or operating support required by the project;
- arm's-length Sub-Contract arrangements with the Project Company (if a Sponsor is also a Sub-Contractor);
- a reasonable amount of equity invested in the project, which gives the Sponsors an incentive to provide support to protect their investment if it gets into difficulty;[3]
- a reasonable return on their equity investment: if the return is too low there may be little incentive for the Sponsors to continue their involvement with the Project Company, and also limited cash-flow cover for the lenders (*cf.* §12.3);
- the financial ability (although not the obligation) to support the project if it runs into difficulty.

---

[2] The terms 'promoters' or 'developers' are also used. Confusingly, in PPP projects the Contracting Authority is sometimes called the sponsor.

[3] In this context, if a Sponsor is paid a large development fee (*cf.* §12.2.5), this may reduce its net equity to such an extent that it could be said that it no longer has a 'real' equity interest in the project. Lenders will therefore look with some skepticism on developers who just put projects together and effectively walk away from equity risk with development fees.

Typical Sponsors in projects using project finance include:

- Construction Contractors, who use the investment in a project as a way of developing 'captive' contracting business;
- equipment suppliers, again using their investment to develop 'captive' business;
- operators or maintenance contractors, here also using the investment to develop their business;
- Fuel or other Input Suppliers, who use the project as a way of selling their products (*e.g.* a company supplying natural gas to a power project);
- Offtakers of the project's products (*e.g.* electricity) who do not wish (or are not able) to fund the construction of the project directly, or who are constrained from doing so by government policy, but who have the resources to invest in part of the equity (or are offered equity in return for signing an Offtake Contract);
- companies that wish to improve their return on equity, or spread their risks among a wider portfolio in the relevant industry than could be financed on balance sheet with corporate debt (*cf.* §2.6.1).

It is evident that a Sponsor may have potential conflicts of interest between its position as a Sponsor and as a party with other contractual relationships with the Project Company. If the project is to pass the lenders' due diligence, these contractual relationships need to be conducted on an arm's-length basis. A Project Company that signs a Construction Contract with a contractor shareholder that is widely out of line with the market (either in its pricing or its detailed terms) is unlikely to find financing (*cf.* §9.5.4).

It is not just the lenders who are concerned about the Sponsors. Other parties contracting with the Project Company may be taking a higher than normal risk of payment, in the absence of corporate guarantees. For example, the Construction Contractor knows that if the lenders turn off the tap to the Project Company, amounts outstanding under the Construction Contract are not likely to be paid (*cf.* §9.5.11). The presence of the Sponsors, with whom the Construction Contractor may have other relationships and have completed Construction Contracts on other projects, is clearly relevant, as is the extent of their financial commitment to the project. Similarly, an Offtaker/Contracting Authority will want to ensure that the project will be properly developed, financed, and operated (*cf.* §9.14).

In summary, a project that looks viable but does not have credible Sponsors—even though the project finance is non-recourse—will probably not get financed. (The Sponsors' financial credibility will also be of importance if they have to fill up any gaps in the project risks by providing limited-recourse guarantees, as discussed in §9.13.)

§3.2.1 PASSIVE AND SECONDARY INVESTORS

Sponsors may bring in other, more 'passive', investors such as:

- investment funds specializing in project-finance equity, especially in the infrastructure sector (but such funds may themselves also act as Sponsors);
- institutional investors, such as life-insurance companies[4] and pension funds,[5] that are prepared to make direct equity investments in projects, rather than *via* investment funds;
- shareholders in quoted equity issued by the Project Company on a stock exchange;
- Contracting Authorities (*cf.* §3.2.2);
- local partners, where the Sponsor is a foreign investor;
- DFIs, such as International Finance Corporation (*cf.* §16.5.2), who may invest directly, or *via* investment funds;
- sovereign wealth funds, which have started to invest in this sector, again directly or *via* investment funds.

The passive investors may prefer to come in at Financial Close, rather than join the original Sponsors, in cases where the Sponsor group is bidding for the project in a public procurement, because they do not want to take the bid-cost risk, or the development-cost risk where the project is being procured by a Contracting Authority (*cf.* §3.3; §3.7; §12.2.5).

The investors who invest at Financial Close are known collectively as 'primary investors', as opposed to 'secondary investors'— *i.e.* those who come in at a later stage of the project by buying shares from the primary investors (*cf.* §14.17).

Lenders normally require the original Sponsors of the project to retain their shareholdings at least until the construction of the project is complete and it has been operating for a reasonable period of time; otherwise the perceived benefits of the particular Sponsors being involved in the project would be lost (*cf.* §6.3.2; §7.11; §9.13). Since Sponsors such as contractors and equipment suppliers may not have an obvious long-term interest in the project, lenders will be more comfortable in such cases if these Sponsors are in partnership with other Sponsors who do have a long-term interest and can ensure that contracts with the equipment supplier or contractor are set up and run on an arm's-length basis.

---

[4] Some life-insurance companies also manage infrastructure investment funds themselves.

[5] Typically very large public-sector pension funds such as those in the U.S. (*e.g.* California Teachers) and Canada (*e.g.* Canada Pension Plan, Ontario Teachers) some European countries (*e.g.* Britain, Denmark, France, Netherlands, Sweden) and elsewhere in the world (Australia, Brazil, Chile). Smaller funds usually invest through 3rd-party run investment funds. *Cf.* Raffaele Della Croce, *Trends in Large Pension Fund Investment in Infrastructure* (Working Papers on Finance, Insurance and Private Pensions No. 29, OECD, Paris, 2012)*.

§3.2.2 PUBLIC-SECTOR SHAREHOLDERS

A Contracting Authority (or another public-sector entity) may be a shareholder in a project in which it has an interest, *i.e.* a PPP Contract or an Offtake Contract where the Offtaker is a public-sector party. The motivations for such a shareholding may be:

- to reduce the cost of the project by offsetting equity revenues against the Contract Payments (but if this is the motive, the public-sector analysis must take account of the relatively uncertainty of receiving revenues compared to the relative certainly of having to pay the Contract Payments—*i.e.* the former should be discounted for risk);
- to share in any 'windfall' gains by the private-sector investors from equity sales (*cf.* §14.17.1).
- to ensure that the public sector is kept fully aware of developments in the project.

The difficulty with this is that there may be a conflict of interest if the project gets into difficulty—if the Contracting Authority enforces its rights under the PPP Contract it may lose its equity investment. However such shareholdings are the norm in some markets, *e.g.* process-plant projects in the Arabian Gulf. The British Treasury also announced a requirement for a public-sector shareholding in future PPP projects in 2012 as part of various changes to the PFI Model (*cf.* §2.5.2; §17.5.5). The shares will not be held by the Contracting Authority, but by a separate unit in the Treasury, to reduce the conflict problem.[6]

§3.3 PROJECT DEVELOPMENT

Like any other activity in project management, using project finance requires a systematic and well-organized approach to carrying out a complex series of interrelated tasks. The additional factor in project finance is that the Sponsors must be ready for outside parties—the lenders and their advisors—to review and perhaps get closely involved in what the Sponsors have been and are doing, a process that will take extra work and time. Finance can thus become a major critical-path item.

As with any new investment, the Sponsors normally undertake a feasibility study when initially considering the investment. If project finance is being used, then structural requirements resulting from this study (*e.g.* the terms of the Project Contracts) also need to be considered at this early stage since these may affect the commercial approach to and hence the feasibility of the project.

---

[6] Similarly a Contracting Authority has a conflict of interest if it provides or guarantees the Project Company's debt, as discussed in Chapter 15.

The Sponsors need to set up a development team with a mixture of disciplines, depending on the nature of the project, *e.g.*:

- design, engineering and construction;
- operation and maintenance;
- legal;
- accounting and tax;
- financial structuring;
- financial modeling.

It is important that this team is well-coordinated: one of the most common errors during project development is for the Sponsors to agree on a Project Contract that is commercially sound, but not acceptable from a project-finance point of view: for example, the fuel may be cheap, but the supply contract does not cover the loan period; or the Construction Contract may be at a low price, but the financial penalties on the Construction Contractor for failure to build on time or to specification are not adequate for lenders (*cf.* §8.2.8). Insofar as the Sponsors do not have the necessary in-house expertise to perform all these tasks, external advisors (*cf.* §3.4) also have to be used.

As the development process on all projects runs into months, and on many projects into years, Sponsors should not underestimate the scale of costs involved. High costs are unavoidable, with the Sponsors' own development staff working for long periods of time on one project, perhaps traveling extensively or setting up a local office. The costs of external advisors have to be added to this. Development costs can reach 5–10% of the total project costs, and there is always a risk that the project will not move forward and all these costs will have to be written off.[7] Cost-control systems are therefore essential. (There are some economies of scale—but large projects also tend to be more complex in structure, so the development costs may remain at a relatively high proportion.)

If the Sponsors are bidding in a public procurement, rather than developing the project themselves (*cf.* §3.7), it is inevitable that at best they will only win a proportion of the bids they make, and hence development/bidding costs on the bids that have been lost have to be recovered from bids that are won (*cf.* §12.2.1).

§3.4 THE RÔLE OF ADVISORS

Various external advisors are usually used by the Sponsors during the project development and financing process. They can play a valuable rôle, especially if the

---

[7] *Cf.* Gerti Dudkin & Timo Välilä, "Transaction Costs In Public-Private Partnerships: A First Look At The Evidence", *Economic and Financial Report* (EIB, Luxemburg, 2005)*, in the context of public procurement of PPPs (*cf.* §3.7).

Sponsor has not undertaken many such projects in the past, since they will probably have had greater experience in a variety of projects than the sponsors' in-house staff; if a sponsor is not developing a continuous pipeline of projects, employing people with the necessary expertise just to work on one project may be difficult. Using advisors with a good record of working in successful projects also gives the project credibility with lenders.

The Sponsors may also make use of other project counterparts in an advisory capacity—*e.g.* even if the O&M Contractor is not a Sponsor, it may offer advice on the design of the project based on the practical experience of operating similar projects.

The lenders use a parallel set of advisors to those employed by the Sponsors (other than a Financial Advisor) as part of their due-diligence process (*cf.* §5.5).

§3.4.1 FINANCIAL ADVISOR

Unless the sponsors are experienced in project development, problems are highly likely to be caused by negotiation of Project Contract arrangements that are later found to be unacceptable to the banking market. Therefore Sponsors without in-house project finance expertise need financial advice to make sure they are on the right track as they develop the project.

Financial advisory services may be provided by banks, accounting firms, or advisory boutiques. There are three ways in which a financial advisor may be involved:

- advice to Sponsors who are developing their own project;
- advice to a Contracting Authority undertaking a public procurement (*cf.* §3.7.1);
- advice to potential Sponsors bidding in a public procurement.

Table 3.1 is a league table of the 'top 20' financial advisors in the project-finance market in 2012, based on the size of the project at Financial Close. Banks often act as a lead arranger and financial advisor combined (*cf.* §5.2.3)—hence the occurrence of similar names to the largest lenders listed in Table 4.1 in Chapter 4. As can be seen from this Table, the other major types of financial advisors are accounting firms, investment banks, and advisory boutiques.

The financial advisor in project finance has a more wide-ranging rôle than would be the case in general corporate finance. The structure of the whole project must meet project-finance requirements, so the financial advisor must anticipate all the issues that might arise during the lenders' due-diligence process, ensuring that they are addressed in the Project Contracts or elsewhere.

The terms of the financial advisor's engagement are set out in an advisory agreement, usually signed with the Sponsors. (The Sponsors may transfer the

Table 3.1 Top 20 financial advisors—signed projects, 2012.

Advisor	Type	Country	Amount (US$ million)
Crédit Agricole	Bank	France	41,270
Mizuho	Bank	Japan	40,000
Royal Bank of Scotland	Bank	Britain	16,625
Macquarie	Bank	Australia	13,392
HSBC	Bank	Britain	12,053
KPMG	Accountants	Britain	9,830
Rothschild	Investment bank	Britain	9,570
Société Générale	Bank	France	9,470
Ernst & Young	Accountants	Britain	9,915
PwC	Accountants	Britain	8,439
Sumitomo Mitsui Banking Corp	Bank	Japan	8,065
BNP Paribas	Bank	France	4,696
ING	Bank	Netherlands	4,000
State Bank of India	Bank	India	3,342
Citigroup	Bank	U.S.A.	3,109
Natixis	Bank	France	2,468
Green Giraffe Energy Bankers	Advisory boutique	France	1,745
Bank of Tokyo-Mitsubishi UFJ	Bank	Japan	1,600
Unicredit	Bank	Italy	1,238

Source: *Project Finance International*, issue 496 (January 16, 2013).

advisory agreement to the Project Company in the latter stages of the project development process.) The financial advisor's scope of work under an advisory agreement typically includes:

- advising on the optimum financial structure for the project;
- preparing a financial model for the project;
- assisting in the preparation of a financial plan;
- advising on sources of debt and likely financing terms;
- advising on the financing implications of Project Contracts and assisting in their negotiation;
- preparing an information memorandum to present the project to the financial markets;
- advising on evaluating proposals for financing;

- advising on selection of commercial-bank lenders or placement of bonds;
- assisting in negotiation of financing documentation.

Financial advisors are usually paid by a combination of fixed or time-based retainer fees, and a success fee on conclusion of the financing. Major out-of-pocket costs, such as travel, are also paid by the Sponsors. These costs are charged on to the Project Company in due course as part of the development costs (cf. §13.5.1).

The financial advisor obviously needs to have a good record of achieving successful closure on projects of the same type, and (if possible) in the same country as the project concerned. Sponsors also need to ensure that the individual actually doing the work has this experience, rather than just relying on the general reputation and record of the financial advisor.

These financial advisory services are usually essential to the successful development of the project, but they are necessarily expensive (costing around 1% of the debt amount on an average-sized project; however a large part of this may be success-based). Costs may be reduced by using smaller advisory boutiques or individual consultants, but less experienced developers may feel uneasy about not using a 'big name' advisor. There is also always some risk that the financial advisor—however well qualified—thinks a project is financeable but the lending market does not agree.

§3.4.2 LEGAL ADVISOR

Legal advisors have to deal not only with the Project Contracts, but also with how these interact with project-finance requirements, as well as being familiar with project-finance documentation. This work tends to be concentrated in a small pool of major American and British law firms who have built up the necessary mixture of expertise. However, for projects outside the United States and Britain it is also necessary to employ local legal advisors with the expertise in doing business in the country concerned, so it may be necessary to coordinate two sets of lawyers.

Because so much of project finance is about the structuring of contracts, legal advisors play a key rôle. But their time needs to be used effectively, especially if they are paid for the time they spend working rather than by a fixed fee.[8] For example, the lawyer should not be unnecessarily involved in making decisions about the commercial structure of the project, and should not begin drafting contracts until the outline of the commercial deal is decided. On the other hand, lawyers' experience of commercial solutions in previous transactions can be very helpful to the Sponsors in their negotiations.

---

[8] 'Fixed' fees from both financial and legal advisors are seldom 100% fixed: the fixed fee will commonly be subject to a cap on the work, e.g. if Financial Close is not reached by an agreed backstop date, further fees would be payable for work thereafter. As project-development timetables are commonly optimistic, especially at the beginning of the process, such time overruns are common.

§3.4.3 Other Advisors

Various other advisors are usually retained. On the whole their costs are much lower than those of the legal and financial advisors.

Engineering. For the rôle of the Owner's Engineer, *cf.* §8.2.4.

Environmental. In most countries an environmental impact assessment (EIA) is needed before any major project can proceed, for which the Sponsors will probably have to engage specialized advisors. Environmental issues are of considerable importance to many lenders, who do not want to be associated with projects causing environmental harm, even if they as lenders have no legal liability for this (*cf.* §9.10).

Market Risk. Market-risk advisors are needed for aspects of the project not covered by contracts (*e.g.* fuel supply, product offtake, or traffic risks) if the Sponsors do not have their own expertise in the market concerned. The expertise of these advisors, and the degree of their involvement in the project, may be significant factors for the lenders' due-diligence process.

Accountants. Accountants are often retained to advise on the accounting and tax aspects of the project, both for the Project Company itself and for the Sponsors. (If an accountant is the financial advisor, then this rôle would be included under that heading.)

Financial Modeler. If the Sponsors have enough confidence in their own ability to raise finance, they may not retain a financial advisor, but may still retain a financial modeler. This is usually an accounting firm or a modeling boutique.

Insurance. For the rôle of the insurance broker, *cf.* §8.6.

§3.5 JOINT-VENTURE ISSUES

The equity investment in the Project Company may be split between several Sponsors (*cf.* §2.6.1), often referred to as a 'consortium', although this does not have any strict legal meaning.

Developing a project through a joint venture adds a further layer of complexity to the process: one partner may have a good understanding of project finance while the other does not; cultural differences become more acute under the heat of a project-finance scrutiny; or negotiations with the lenders may be undertaken before all intra-partnership issues have been clearly resolved. Indeed, it is not unusual for the development of a project to be held up, not because the lenders raise problems, but because the Sponsors have not agreed on key issues among themselves.

Good communication between Sponsors is therefore especially important when using project finance. They need to form a real joint team and ensure that the divisions of rôles and responsibilities are clearly defined. For example, one Sponsor may be primarily responsible for finance, another for the Construction Contract. If one of the Sponsors is going to sign a Sub-Contract with the Project Company, another Sponsor should control the negotiation of this contract from the Project Company side of the table to avoid the obvious conflict of interest.

Sponsors developing a project together usually sign a Development Agreement, which covers matters such as:

- the scope and structure of the project;
- an exclusivity commitment;
- management rôles and responsibilities;
- a program for feasibility studies, appointment of advisors, negotiations with the Construction Contractor and other parties to the Project Contracts, and approaches to lenders;
- rules for decision making;
- arrangements for funding of development costs—*i.e.* the costs of the Sponsors' staff and external advisors during the project-development phase (which can only be recovered if the project actually goes ahead)—and for crediting these costs against each Sponsor's allocation of equity, taking account of both the amount of the costs and the timing of when they were incurred (*cf.* §12.2.5);
- provisions for 'reserved rôles' (*e.g.* if one of the Sponsors is to be appointed as the Construction Contractor without being subject to third-party competition); this is a difficult provision unless the scope and pricing basis can be agreed at the same time;
- any completion, cost-overrun or other guarantees being given by one or more Sponsors (*cf.* §9.13);
- arrangements for withdrawal from the project and sale of a Sponsor's interest;
- provisions for dispute resolution.

Major decisions on the project have to be taken unanimously, because if the project develops in a direction not acceptable to one partner, that partner will not wish to keep funding it. Lesser issues—such as appointment of an advisor—may be taken on a majority-vote basis. If a Sponsor wishes to withdraw, the other Sponsors usually have a first option to purchase its share.

The Development Agreement is usually superseded by a Shareholder Agreement when the Project Company has been set up and takes over responsibility for the project (*cf.* §3.6.2).

§3.6 THE PROJECT COMPANY

§3.6.1 STRUCTURE

The Project Company lies at the center of all the contractual and financial relationships in project finance.[9] These relationships have to be contained inside a project finance 'box', which means that the Project Company cannot carry out any other business which is not part of the project (since project finance depends on the lenders' ability to evaluate the project on a stand-alone basis). Thus in most cases a new company is incorporated specifically to carry out the project. The corporate form of borrower is generally preferred by lenders for security and control reasons (*cf.* §14.7.2).

The Project Company is usually incorporated in the country in which the project is taking place, although it may occasionally be beneficial to incorporate it outside the country concerned.

The Sponsors may use an intermediary holding company in a favorable third-country tax jurisdiction, *e.g.* to avoid capital-gains tax if they sell their equity in the Project Company at a profit (by just selling the holding company instead), or to ensure that withholding tax is not deducted from dividends (*cf.* §13.7.6). A holding company structure may also be necessary as part of the lenders' security package (*cf.* §14.7.2).

In some projects a form other than that of a limited company is used. The commonest alternative is a limited partnership, so the Sponsors' liability remains limited in the same way as if they were shareholders in a limited company, but the income of the project is taxed directly at the level of the Sponsors, or tax depreciation on its capital costs can be deducted directly against Sponsors' other income, rather than in the Project Company.

In oil- and gas-field developments, the Sponsors may use an unincorporated joint venture as a vehicle to raise funding. The Sponsors sign an operating agreement, which usually provides for one of them to be the operator, dealing with day-to-day management, subject to an operating committee. The operator enters into the Project Contracts (*e.g.* for construction of a rig) and makes cash calls on the other Sponsors on an agreed basis. If a Sponsor defaults, the others may undertake to pay, and the interest of a defaulter who does not remedy the situation is forfeited. The liability of the operator to third parties needs to be made clear in the Project Contracts: is the operator directly liable and relying on being reimbursed by cash calls, or acting as an agent for the other Sponsors, incurring liability on their

---

[9] It is also referred to as a 'Special Purpose Vehicle' (SPV), 'Special Purpose Entity' (SPE), or—in the case of PPPs—the 'Contractor', or 'Private Party'.

behalf? In this structure the Sponsors usually participate through individual SPVs, and may raise funding individually through these companies to cover their share of the project costs, rather than raising finance collectively for the project. This structure is beneficial for Sponsors with a good credit rating who wish to raise funds on a corporate basis, while other financially weaker partners use project finance for their share. (However, the lenders' security position may be less than ideal in such cases.)

§3.6.2 SHAREHOLDER AGREEMENT

If there is more than one Sponsor, once the Project Company has been set up and is responsible for managing the implementation of the project, the Development Agreement previously signed by the Sponsors (*cf.* §3.5) is normally superseded by a Shareholder Agreement (although it is possible to have one agreement for both phases of the project). The Shareholder Agreement covers issues such as:

- percentage share ownership;
- procedure for equity subscriptions;
- voting of shares at the annual general meeting;
- board representation and voting;
- appointment and authority of management;
- conflicts of interest (*e.g.* if the Construction Contractor is a Sponsor, it may not be allowed to participate in board discussion or voting on issues relating to the Construction Contract);
- budgeting;
- distribution of profits;
- sale of shares by Sponsors, usually with a first refusal (preemption) right being given to the other Sponsors, or there may be 'tag along' rights, *i.e.* if one Sponsor agree to sell its share to a third party, the other(s) will have the option to sell to this party at the same price;
- reserved matters, *i.e.* decisions which require the approval of all shareholders;
- provisions for dispute resolution.

Some of these provisions may be included in the Project Company's corporate articles rather than a separate Shareholder Agreement. The Sponsors may also sign a separate Equity Subscription Agreement with the Project Company to pay in their agreed levels of equity as and when required during construction of the project (*cf.* §12.2.3); if so, this agreement is assigned to the lenders as part of their security (*cf.* §14.7.1).

50:50 joint ventures are not uncommon in the project-finance field, and they give rise to obvious problems in decision making. Even in cases with more

Sponsors, it may still not be possible to get a consensus where a minority partner can block a vote on major issues. Arbitration or other legal procedures are seldom a very practical way forward in this context. Clearly, if there is a deadlock one partner will have to buy out the other, for which a suitable process has to be established. One approach is to require both parties to bid for the other party's shares, with the highest bidder buying out the other Sponsor.

§3.6.3 MANAGEMENT AND OPERATIONS

The Project Company should have no assets or liabilities except those directly related to the project, which is why a new company should be formed rather than reusing an existing one that may have accrued liabilities. The Project Company also agrees with the lenders not to take on any extraneous assets or liabilities in future (*cf.* §14.10.2).

The Project Company is often formed at a late stage in the project-development process (unless project Permits have to be issued earlier, or it has to sign Project Contracts), because it normally has no function to perform until the project finance is in place. Sponsors may even sign some of the Project Contacts to begin with (*e.g.* a Construction Contract) and transfer them in due course to the Project Company (*cf.* §8.2.2).

Similarly, the Project Company may not have a formal organization and management structure until a late stage, as the Sponsors' staff will be doing the project-development work. There is, however, only a limited overlap between the skills needed at this development stage and those needed once the Project Company is set up and the project itself is under way, and so a new team may take over management of the project after Financial Close. Arrangements must be made to ensure a smooth transition between the two phases of the project, *e.g.* bringing the post-Financial Close team into the negotiations at an appropriate point so they can understand what is required. It is also useful for the development team to write an 'operating manual' for the project-finance aspect of the project to provide a guide to the documentation and summarize the lenders' requirements.[10]

Just as the transition from development to Financial Close needs to be well-managed, so the further transition from the construction phase to the operation phase may also involve a new team at the Project Company, and similar transition management is required.

There are two main models of how a Project Company can be organized to run the project after Financial Close. One is to run the project with its own staff, and the other is to outsource part or all of its operations to Sponsor shareholders or other third parties (and pay fees for this). The organization can also be a mixture

---

[10] *Cf.* §7.4 for a similar exercise by an Offtaker/Contracting Authority.

of these two approaches, with some functions carried out 'in house' and some outsourced. The decision on whether functions should be kept in house or outsourced is mainly a question of cost-effectiveness. If the project's Sponsors are undertaking a series of similar projects, a more centralized management of several Project Companies may be a more economical approach.

So during the construction phase the Project Company's personnel may be a combination of its own staff, the staff of the Construction Contractor, and outside advisors such as an Owner's Engineer (*cf.* §8.2.4). Once the project is complete, operation and maintenance may be carried out by Project Company itself or by a third-party operator under a O&M, or Maintenance Contract (*cf.* §8.3).

If one of the Sponsors is to take on any management rôles (other than O&M Maintenance Contractor, which is dealt with separately as discussed in §8.3), a Management Contract will be needed (and will ultimately be reviewed and approved by the lenders), setting out the scope and costs of such services. These may include matters such as accounting and tax, or personnel management.

Sponsors are generally well organized in ensuring that all the engineering and construction management expertise is in place at Financial Close, but sometimes they neglect the finance side of the Project Company's organization. The new Project Company needs to have systems in place with personnel who have an immediate grasp of the complex requirements of the finance documentation, not just in relation to drawing and spending the money provided under these arrangements, but also to deal with matters such as the lenders' reporting requirements (*cf.* §14.5).

If the Project Company intends to use its own staff to operate the project (*i.e.* with no external O&M Contractor), lenders naturally wish to be satisfied that the personnel involved have the requisite experience. Although operating personnel do not have to begin work until the construction process is complete, key personnel have to be in place at the beginning of construction, firstly to use their expertise to ensure that the design of the project is appropriate from an operating point of view, and secondly because the lenders wish to be satisfied that the key personnel are there before they start advancing funds. The Project Company will also have to set up clear guidelines on the structure and authority of its management, and the extent to which decisions have to be referred to the board: this would normally form part of the Shareholder Agreement (*cf.* §3.6.2).

A Support Services Agreement[11] with one or more of the Sponsors with relevant operating experience to provide the Project Company with back-up technical support, spare parts, *etc.*, may also provide some reassurance to lenders, even though one might expect that, whether or not there is such an agreement, the Sponsors will provide technical and operating support to protect their investment anyway.

---

[11] Also known as a Technical Support Agreement.

Because a Support Services Agreement should not cost anything unless support is actually required, there is no reason for the Project Company not to sign one if the lenders feel it to be necessary. Sponsors have to take care, however, that a Support Services Agreement is not used by the lenders as a 'backdoor' method of making them liable for the project's performance, *e.g.* by inserting widely-drawn clauses making the Sponsors liable for negligence.

§3.7 PUBLIC PROCUREMENT

The description of the project-development process above assumes that it is entirely under the control of the Sponsors, but this is often not the case. Projects involving provisions of products or services to the public sector under a PPP Contract are initially developed by a Contracting Authority, which then calls for proposals to finance and construct the project and provide the product or service. (A private-sector Offtaker—*e.g.* a privatized electricity distributor that requires a power plant to be built to supply its needs—may also choose to go through the same process.) Of course much of what is said above about the Sponsors' own project-development process still applies if they are making a bid for a Contracting Authority-developed contract.

Procurement of PPPs is inevitably a complex process. In a standard public procurement the project is designed by the Contracting Authority and then contractors are asked to build it. The scope of a PPP procurement is much wider:

- Design and construction are normally integrated.
- The procurement also has to deal with long-term operation of the project.
- The Contracting Authority also needs to understand project-finance requirements and hence the bankability of bids.

As with Sponsors, it is important for the Contracting Authority to use an efficient and project-management process to handle the procurement (§3.7.1), as well as appropriate advisors (§3.7.2). Formal approvals are usually required at each stage of the project-development process (§3.7.3).

There are various different types of procurement system (§3.7.4). In general, the bidding process itself is normally carried out in several stages:

- pre-qualification (§3.7.5);
- a request for proposals to the pre-qualified bidders (§3.7.6);
- negotiation (§3.7.7);
- bid evaluation (§3.7.8).

Various issues may arise during the bid process (§3.7.9). In some cases the Project Company's own Sub-Contracts may have to go through a similar process

(§3.7.10). A Contracting Authority may also have to deal with unsolicited bids (§3.7.11). The prospective lenders supporting the bidder also play an important part in this process (§3.7.12).

Once Project Completion has been reached, the Contracting Authority also needs an effective contract monitoring system (§3.7.13).

§3.7.1 PROJECT MANAGEMENT

Best-practice project management for the Contracting Authority in a PPP procurement process is to create a project board which is separate from the project team.

Project Board. The project board consists of the heads of the relevant functions within the Contracting Authority and other relevant parties in the public sector. Its rôle is one of general oversight of the procurement and approval in all major policy areas, usually subject to final approval at the ministerial/political level. However the project board cannot be involved in detailed negotiation, and this should be left to the project team, within agreed policy guidelines. The project board is usually chaired by a senior official of the Contracting Authority, often known as the 'accounting officer', who is primarily responsible for ensuring that the project progresses in a appropriate way.

Project Team. The project team itself should be led by a project director/manager, for whom this should be a full-time job, not one combined with other responsibilities within the Contracting Authority. The project director should report to the project board at regular intervals. Other project-team members would be drawn from relevant specialties within the Contracting Authority, both technical and financial, thus possibly cutting across normal reporting lines. Some of these team members may be able to combine their work with routine responsibilities, but others, *e.g.* the key technical people, will not.

Sourcing people within the Contracting Authority to undertake this work may not be easy. Public officials may have no previous experience of working on a PPP, and indeed may never work on another PPP again. So a PPP procurement does not fit easily into their normal career path, and they may feel disinclined to get involved since the risks of something going wrong are greater than the career benefits if it succeeds. Also once public officials have secured the experience of working on a major PPP they become attractive to the private sector, whose salaries cannot be matched by the public sector, and so that experience is easily lost again, leaving the public sector at a constant disadvantage against the private sector. Even if this does not happen, officials with PPP experience may be deployed back to their original departments and not brought back the next time a PPP comes up in another department—*i.e.* the public sector's experience base in PPPs is easily eroded.

This problem can be partly overcome if there is a central PPP unit in the country concerned to provide support (and in some cases to control) for PPP procurements. Many countries have formed such units, usually, but not always, as a department or agency of the Ministry of Finance.[12] Such units can provide expertise at both the project board and project team level, and also ensure consistency of approach to PPP Contracting within government as a whole (but still have to cope with 'leakages' of staff to the private sector).

§3.7.2 ADVISORS

The Contracting Authority also makes use of external advisors, who perform similar rôles to those of the Sponsors' advisors discussed in §3.4, and form part of the project team. It is important to ensure that weak project management by the Contracting Authority does not result in the procurement being run by the advisors.[13]

The costs of advisors are usually substantial (especially legal and financial advisors), and the Contracting Authority may not have any budget available to cover these costs. There are various solutions to this:

- *Costs paid by winning bidder*: The winning bidder pays the Contracting Authority's advisors' costs, and adds these to the overall project cost, so that the advisors' costs are covered by Contract Payments. The problem with this is that if the Contracting Authority decides not to proceed with the transaction, it will have to pay these costs itself, which in the worst case may encourage the Project Board to press forward with a project which they know should really be dropped.
- *Costs paid by Ministry of Finance*: The Ministry of Finance provides finance for the advisors, which it recovers on signature of the Project Agreement.[14] This is quite a common approach, but it still puts on pressure to sign the deal even though it may not be the best choice.

---

[12] Cf. *Public-Private Partnership Units: Lessons for their Design and Use in Infrastructure* (World Bank/PPIAF, Washington DC, 2007)*, *Dedicated Public-Private Partnership Units: A Survey of Institutional and Governance Structures* (OECD, Paris, 2010)*; Emilia Istrate & Robert Puentes, *Moving Forward on Public Private Partnerships: U.S. and International Experience with PPP Units* (Brookings Institution, Washington DC, 2011)*.

[13] Cf. *Toolkit: A guide for hiring and managing advisors for private participation in infrastructure* (World Bank/PPIAF, Washington DC, 1999)*.

[14] Some countries have special funds which act in a similar way. For example the India Infrastructure Project Development Fund (IIPDF), set up by the government in 2008, will finance up to 75% of project development costs if the Contracting Authority funds the remainder; again this funding is recovered from the winning bidder.

- *Project Preparation Facility*: There are a number of sources for non-refundable grants for project development in developing countries.[15]

§3.7.3 PROJECT DEVELOPMENT

Best-practice public procurement for PPPs usually involves formal reviews and approvals (*e.g.* from the Ministry of Finance's PPP unit) at various stages of the project-development and procurement processes, which provide a basis for moving forward to the next stage. Typical stages for review are:

Initial Business Case.[16] Looks at the project from a high level to confirm that it fits into government strategy, considers the various options for achieving the project, and whether it is inherently suitable for procurement as a PPP. Typically fairly short and simple. If the Initial Business Case is approved, the Contracting Authority normally engages external advisors at this point.

Outline Business Case.[17] Considers in detail the need for the project, based on a cost/benefit analysis (which would apply to any major public-sector investment). Based on this, the scope and estimated costs of a PPP Contract are estimated in detail, and a financial model based on these estimates (known as a 'Shadow Bid Model') is prepared. The Shadow Bid Model will take account of the estimated capital (construction) costs and lifetime operating costs of the project, and the likely structure and costs of private-sector project finance (*cf.* Chapter 12 and Chapter 13), thus estimating the total costs of the project to the Contracting Authority over its life. This model will therefore enable the Contracting Authority to decide whether the project is 'affordable', either within its own budget in the case of a PFI Model or process-plant project, or for users in the case of a Concession.

These PPP cost estimates may be compared with the estimated costs of a public-sector procurement of the same project, the latter being known as a public-sector comparator ('PSC'). Clearly private finance is inherently more expensive than public finance, so it might be expected that this comparison would rule out a PPP. However the cost of public finance does not take into account the risks inherent in the project (which are absorbed by taxpayers

---

[15] *Cf.* Infrastructure Consortium for Africa (ICA), *Infrastructure Project Preparation Facilities: User Guide–Africa* (ICA/PPIAF, Tunis, 2006)*; James Leigland & Andrew Roberts, *The African project preparation gap* (Gridlines Note No. 18, PPIAF, Washington DC, 2007)*; Cambridge Economic Policy Associates, *Assessment of Project Preparation Facilities for Africa (Report for ICA)* (African Development Bank, Tunis, 2012)*.

[16] This analysis may also be described as a 'pre-feasibility study', or 'strategic business case'

[17] This is the same thing as a feasibility study.

generally),[18] whereas private finance does, so that risk adjustments have to be made in the PSC comparison. In addition the tendency for a greater degree of 'optimism bias' (*i.e.* the tendency to overestimate usage of a project and underestimate its costs) in conventional public-sector procurements needs to be taken into account. Quantification of risk and optimism bias to make such adjustments is difficult to do with real accuracy, and it is easy to impugn the detailed numbers in the PSC.[19] The PSC therefore has to be considered as a rough indicative comparison with a PPP rather than a real measurement of comparative cost. Moreover a PSC is not that relevant if the government budget does not have funds for the project, because of limits on spending imposed either within government or by the need to borrow to fund the project.[20]

Readiness for Market. The commonest error made by the public sector during the procurement phase of a PPP project is lack of adequate preparation before approaching the market—known as the 'project preparation gap'.[21] This may not be the fault of the project team: political pressure may lead to a requirement to be seen to be 'doing something', and behind the scenes preparation work is not conspicuous enough to meet such political imperatives. In fact, throughout a procurement there are likely to be conflicts between a political timetable and a realistic and prudent approach.

As part of the preparation process, the project needs to be structured to ensure that it can in fact attract private finance: *i.e.* the risk transfer to the private sector has to be 'bankable' (*cf.* §9.3). This may involve preliminary market testing[22]—sometimes inviting prospective bidders to provide an expression of interest ('EoI')—to check that there is a market appetite for this investment and its financing, and also that potential contractors with relevant expertise are interested in joining bids for the project. A formal presentation on the project to all interested parties may be organized. Informal discussions may be held with prospective bidders, who can also be asked to comment on the proposed PPP Contract. The Contracting Authority can then

---

[18] *Cf.* Michael Klein, "Risk, Taxpayers, and the Role of Government in Project Finance", *Policy Research Working Paper No. 1688* (World Bank, Washington DC, 1996)*.

[19] Risk transfer can also be eroded by 'deal creep' (*cf.* §3.7.7).

[20] For a detailed discussion of the issues here *cf.* E R Yescombe, *Public-Private Partnerships: Principles of Policy and Finance* (Butterworth-Heinemann, Oxford, 2007), Chapters 2 and 5; James Leigland and Chris Shugart, *Is the public sector comparator right for developing countries?* (Gridlines Note No. 4, PPIAF, Washington DC, 2006)*; Federal Highway Administration, *Value for Money: State of the Practice* (US Department of Transport, Washington DC, 2011)*.

[21] For a more detailed review of this process, *cf.* Edward Farquharson, Clemencia Torres de Mästle & E.R. Yescombe with Javier Encinas, *How to Engage with the Private Sector in Public-Private Partnerships in Emerging Markets* (World Bank/PPIAF, Washington DC, 2011)*.

[22] Sometimes called 'soft' market testing.

make adjustments based on the feedback received, and prepare the Request for Proposals (§3.7.6).

Project preparation also involves 'stakeholder involvement'—good communication between the Contracting Authority and the users of the project as well as citizens generally to ensure that the case for a PPP is fully understood. Also, it is important—especially where User Charges are concerned—that the public consider that they are getting value for money, *e.g.* because the PPP is providing an attractive new service, or a significant upgrade on an inadequate existing one. The public's 'willingness to pay' is a major risk factor in projects such as toll roads (*cf.* §9.6.3).

PPPs can easily become mired in political controversy (*cf.* §11.2): inappropriate comparisons are often made between the cost of public procurement and a PPP which ignore risk transfer, or between initial construction costs in the public sector and the lifetime costs of a PPP. Opponents may also claim that the private sector should not make profits from the provision of a public service—but the private sector is already involved in many different ways in the provision of public services. Again good communication from an early stage is essential to ensure public understanding and support.

The project's 'readiness for market' is thus an important further review/decision point.

Final Business Case.[23] This will be prepared when the procurement process has narrowed down to one bidder (often referred to as the 'Preferred Bidder'), and takes account of the changes that have taken place in the project structure, risk transfer and costs since the Outline Business Case, with the aim of confirming that the original basis on which the PPP project was approved still applies.

§3.7.4 Procurement Systems

A competitive bidding process for public procurements is a legal requirement in most countries where public funding is being provided (*e.g.* for a PFI-Model contract), or services are being provided to the public (*e.g.* under a Concession), and it is generally also required if finance or guarantees are provided by multilateral DFIs, such as the World Bank.[24] The main framework for public-procurement procedures is provided by the Agreement on Government Procurement ('GPA'), administered

---

[23] Also called a 'bid report' or 'bid evaluation'.

[24] *Cf.* South Africa National Treasury, *Public-Private Partnership Manual* (Pretoria, 2004)* for a useful manual including covering the procurement process.

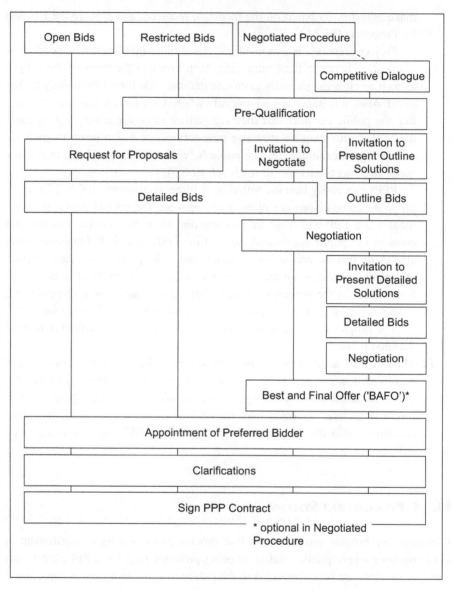

Figure 3.1 PPP Procurement Systems Under GPA.

by the World Trade Organization, to which most developed countries are parties. This was first signed in 1979, and last amended in 1994. These procedures can also be considered best practice for countries which are not signatories to the GPA. There are several procurement procedures within GPA rules, as summarized in Figure 3.1.

Open Bids. This procedure allows anyone to bid, *i.e.* there is no pre-qualification stage (*cf.* §3.7.5; given the complexity of a PPP, pre-qualification of bidders is generally preferable, so as not to waste time on bidders who are obviously unsuitable.

Restricted Bids. Under this procedure, following pre-qualification, the requirements of the bid may be discussed with bidders, and then the 'Request for Proposals' (RfP) is issued (*cf.* §3.7.6). Further clarifications may be made thereafter, but once bids are received, that should be the end of the process: the decision is made on the basis of the bids, and there should be no further negotiation with bidders other than any minor clarifications, who are expected to sign the PPP Contract on the basis set out in their bids.

This approach provides a relatively quick and hence potentially lower-cost procedure for bidders. It is also considered preferable in countries where there is concern about post-bid discussion being open to suggestions of corruption. But it can only be used if there is a general market consensus about the project requirements and the terms of the PPP Contract, so that detailed negotiation is not considered necessary—bidders just sign up to the Contracting Authority's draft of the Project Agreement and related documents.

Negotiated Procedure. This is intended for complex contracts where the Contracting Authority's requirements cannot be fully specified at the initial stage, and bidders may provide different solutions for the service concerned, so requiring further discussion after bids are received. The procedure is therefore as follows:

- Pre-qualification (§3.7.5).
- The pre-qualified bidders receive an 'Invitation to Negotiate' (ITN), which is basically the same as a Request for Proposals (*cf.* §3.7.6).
- Bids are submitted and negotiations on the responses take place with all bidders, and a Preferred Bidder is chosen.[25]
- After selection of the Preferred Bidder, only 'clarification' of this bid is allowed. In practice, however, it is generally very difficult to draw the line between clarification and significant changes to the bid terms.

Experience of this system in Britain was that the time period between selection of the Preferred Bidder and Financial Close was often very lengthy—two years or more in some cases—and it is obvious that dealing with minor clarification issues does not need this length of time. In fact 'deal creep' (*cf.* §3.7.7) was endemic.

---

[25] Or the bidders may be required to submit their 'best and final offer' (BAFO) after these negotiations, based on which the Preferred Bidder is selected.

Competitive Dialogue. This is a variation of the Negotiated Procedure introduced in the European Union in 2006 to deal with its inadequacies. A typical procedure (as used in Britain) is as follows:

- Pre-qualification (§3.7.5).
- Following this the Contracting Authority issues an 'Invitation to Present Outline Solutions' (ISOS) to pre-qualified bidders. Bidders are not expected to produce a full proposal: typically only a conceptual design, outline pricing and basic risk-transfer positions are required from them at this stage.
- Based on a review of the ISOS responses the bidders are reduced to two, based on their ability and willingness to meet the requirements of the project.
- Then the Contracting Authority issues an 'Invitation to Present Detailed Solutions' (ISDS), which is basically the same thing as a Request for Proposals (*cf.* §3.7.6).
- The Contracting Authority enters into detailed discussions with the bidders on any issues that they may raise on the project scope and requirements, and on the terms of the PPP Contract.
- Finally the bidders are required to present a BAFO taking these negotiations into account, under which they to present their final terms and pricing.[26]
- There is still provision for clarifications of bids after they are presented, but these should be minimal, and the PPP Contract should be signed without much delay.

This system makes bidding considerably more expensive for both sides: the Contracting Authority has to run at least two full negotiations, while at least one of the bidders will have wasted a lot of money on its bid (*e.g.* design/engineering costs, legal fees, *etc.*), but there is little doubt that it can produce a better deal for the Contracting Authority because competitive tension between bidders is maintained throughout (*cf.* §3.7.7).

§3.7.5 PRE-QUALIFICATION

The first stage in the formal pre-qualification process is to advertise the project in official publications and the financial and trade press. Interested bidding groups are provided with the 'request for qualifications' (RfQ), which is a summary of the project and its requirements. Prospective bidders are then invited to set out their qualifications to undertake the project,[27] demonstrating:

---

[26] This may be referred to as a 'Call for Final Tenders' (CFT).

[27] This is known as the 'PQQ' (pre-qualification questionnaire).

- technical capacity to carry out the project;
- experience of the personnel to be involved;
- experience and performance with similar projects;
- financial capacity to carry out the project;

and also to provide letters of support from prospective lenders.

This may be followed up with a 'bidders conference' where the Contracting Authority explains the project to interested parties, and answers initial questions about the project or the procurement procedure.

Bidders that do not meet minimum criteria at this stage are then excluded, and the other bidders invited to bid.

Pre-qualification may go a stage further by drawing up an initial short list of bidders (preferably no more than about four), if the relevant procurement rules allow this. (World Bank procurement rules, for example, do not.) This procedure is desirable because if there are too many bidders for the project the chances of winning the bid may be too small to make it worth the prospective bidders' while, given the considerable time and cost involved in preparing and submitting a bid. Of course fewer bidders also make managing the whole process easier.

§3.7.6 REQUEST FOR PROPOSALS

A formal request for proposals ('RFP')[28] is then sent out to the pre-qualified or short-listed bidders. This is accompanied with an information package that sets out, *e.g.*:

- executive summary;
- general legislative background;
- project background and *raison d'être*;
- availability, service, and other output requirements (*cf.* §5.6);
- risk matrix showing risk allocation (*cf.* §9.2);
- data on the market, traffic flows, and so on (especially for Concession projects);
- proposed pricing formula;
- draft PPP Contract;
- contact details for clarifications or requesting further information;
- procurement timetable.
- instructions on bid submission:
  - common financial assumptions—if bidders do not use the same basic assumptions it may prove difficult to compare the bids properly, *e.g.*:

---

[28] Also known as an 'invitation to tender' ('ITT'), and as an 'invitation to negotiate' ('ITN') in the case of the Negotiated Procedure.

- market interest rates;
- exchange rates;
- inflation indexation of the Contract Payments (*cf.* §10.4.1).
- response format for financial proposal—which should set out the detailed information to be provided on:
  - costs of construction and operation;
  - financial structure (including evidence of support from prospective lenders);
  - calculation of Contract Payments (which should be mapped onto the Contracting Authority's own financial-model template to ensure that comparisons can easily be made between bids);
- required bid validity period;
- bid evaluation criteria (*cf.* §3.7.8);
- Contracting Authority's right to cancel the bid process.

It is important that the RfP does not over specify what is required. In particular, the output—a product or service—should be ideally specified, not the input, or how the output is delivered (*cf.* §6.4.2). Thus if bids are requested for a power station, the RfP should specify the capacity in megawatts, but not the model of turbine that should be used to generate the power. In some projects, however, especially if the project assets have a longer useful life and are taken over at the end of the contract period under a PPP structure (*cf.* §7.10.7), there will also inevitably be a degree of input specification.

The response to the RfP is likely to be required to cover aspects such as:

- technology;
- design and engineering;
- construction program;
- details of works or services to be provided;
- management structures for both the construction and operation phases;
- quality and safety assurance procedures;
- commercial viability (*e.g.* traffic or demand projections);
- operation and maintenance policy;
- insurance coverage;
- financing strategy and structure;
- qualifications to RfP contract or other requirements;
- proposals for the Contract Payments.

Bidders should be required to include a financial model in their proposal, which will *inter alia* demonstrate how they have arrived at their bid proposal. There may be concerns about confidentiality here, but the model is needed by the Contracting Authority, partly to enable proper evaluation of the financial feasibility of the bid, and partly because it may also make it difficult to deal with later changes in circumstances (*cf.* §7.6.5), or payments on early termination (*cf.* §7.10.1).

Apart from responding to specific requirements in the RfP, bidders' proposals need to demonstrate:

- an understanding of the requirements of the project;
- how the bidder will achieve these requirements;
- any advantages the bidder's approach may have over the competition.

Fairness and transparency in the bidding process are essential; if bidders do not understand or trust the process, or do not believe there is a genuine competition in which they have a good prospect of winning, it is evident that the best results will not be achieved. Thus, a full and detailed record should be kept of the bid comparisons and why a particular bidder was chosen.

§3.7.7 NEGOTIATION

The extent to which negotiation takes place after the bid submissions depends on which procurement system is being used, as indicated in §3.7.4. Assuming there are negotiations, the Contracting Authority should make the same information available to all bidders. This can be achieved in several ways:

- by holding meetings and site visits which all bidders attend, which helps to flush out any major issues that bidders may have with the project;
- written answers to questions or issues raised by one bidder can also be copied to all of them, without indicating who asked the original question; however information which is confidential to one bid should obviously not be disclosed to other bidders.

Whichever procurement system is used, the key aim for the Contracting Authority should be to maintain competitive tension. As soon as there is only one bidder, the Contracting Authority is in a very poor position. Political pressure to get the project under way may seriously affect the ability of the Contracting Authority to resist the Preferred Bidder making changes to the PPP Contract, even after a detailed bid. This danger of 'deal creep' becomes much greater if the requirements for the project are not initially specified in enough detail, or are changed after the Preferred Bidder has been appointed, which is especially likely in a large and complex project. Much of the benefit for the public sector of using private-sector finance may be eroded in this way. Ideally, one or more other bidders should be required to keep their bids on the table in case the Preferred Bidder tries to take advantage of this position, but this is likely to be difficult as the losing bidder will not want to waste time and money keeping its bid team 'on ice'. This issue should not arise if the Competitive Dialogue procedure (*cf.* §3.7.4) is used.

§3.7.8 BID EVALUATION

The Contracting Authority obviously needs to be able to compare the bids with each other. This means that bids must be submitted using common assumptions where this is appropriate (*e.g.* as to the cost of fuel, raw materials, interest rates, inflation, *etc.*), and presented using the financial model template referred to in §3.7.6. The pre-qualification process should have already eliminated bidders for whom there are questions about financial capacity (as Sponsors), technology, or ability to undertake the project, so further fundamental qualitative comparisons of this nature should be limited in scope. However, the financial model and the overall financing plan for the project (*i.e.* the terms on which project finance debt is to be raised) does need to be examined (*cf.* §9.14).

There are two main approaches for comparing the bids:

Price Comparison. If the bids can be submitted on virtually identical bases, then the final decision may be a question of simply comparing the bid prices. If the price bases of different bids fluctuate over time (*i.e.* payments under a long-term PPP Contract), it is necessary to discount the amounts payable in future to a net present value ('NPV'—*cf.* §10.2.1) to compare like with like.

Scoring. However if the bids are not identical apart from price a more sophisticated system is needed: such a system is often based on scoring different aspects of the bid—giving points for price, speed of Project Completion, reliability, quantity or quality of whatever is being provided, the technology or technical proposal, risk assumption by the bidder (*i.e.* transfer of risk away from the Contracting Authority), and any other characteristics that are important to the project. Further adjustments may be made for bids that are considered overambitious in their projections of performance and financing plans, as well as for the cost of exceptions to the proposed terms of the PPP Contract. The aim is thus to identify the bid that is both realistic and the most economically advantageous to the project. Usually a minimum 'pass' score is needed in each aspect of the bid which is which is being measured.

A half-way house between price comparison and scoring is to split the bids into technical and financial bids. The technical bids are evaluated first on a scoring system, and bids which secure, say, 75% of the possible marks in the scoring are only then compared as to price, with the highest price winning.

Some procurements may not be based on the price to be charged for the product or service but the level of subsidy to be provided by the public sector (*cf.* §15.19). This approach is relevant if the bid relates to a Concession in which the User Charges cannot produce sufficient revenue to cover the financing required for the project.

§3.7.9 DEALING WITH BIDS

Various issues may arise at this during the bid process:

Nonconforming Bids. It is beneficial not to be too prescriptive about the bid requirements, since bidders may be able to come up with innovative solutions for the project which, although not previously considered, may actually be more beneficial. A standard procedure is that bidders must make at least one bid that conforms to the requirements of the RfP, but they may also offer alternative bids that do not conform. The Contracting Authority then has the option to choose a nonconforming bid if it offers a better solution.

Modifications. Discussions with bidders may lead to modifications in the bid requirements: in such cases the bid schedule may have to be delayed to give bidders enough time to deal with these modifications.

Bid Consortium Changes. After a particular bidding consortium has been pre-qualified, one of its members may not wish to proceed, and the consortium may wish to introduce a new member, perhaps a bidder in a consortium that previously did not pre-qualify. Other bidders may object to this, but it may be preferable not to exclude changes of this kind completely and to leave some discretion on the matter (*e.g.* if the new member can demonstrate it is as well-qualified as the one it is succeeding). An alternative approach is to allow changes in the consortium only after the winning bid has been selected; however, no bidder should be allowed to participate in more than one consortium at the same time, as this could lead to leakages of information or collusion between consortia.

Bonding. Bidders are sometimes required to provide bid bonds to the Contracting Authority from their bankers, as security for their proceeding with the bid once it has been made. The bond is released when the contract documentation is signed, or when construction of the project begins. The amount of the bond may be quite significant in absolute terms (*e.g.* 1–2% of the project value). This helps to deal with the problem of deliverability (*i.e.* presentation of an aggressive bid that cannot be financed, or where the bidders hope to improve their position once they are the Preferred Bidder). However genuine bidders may be discouraged from bidding by a fear that the bond may be called unfairly, and the cost will eventually be borne by the Contracting Authority.[29]

Compensation for Cancellation. The corollary of bonding for bidders is an agreement by the Contracting Authority conducting the bid that if the process is canceled at any stage bidders should be compensated for the costs they have incurred, perhaps up to a certain limit. Losing bidders may even be given some compensation for their costs in any case, to encourage competition in a complex project, where bid costs can be very high.

Legal Challenge. A bidder who is unfairly treated in the procurement process may have the right to sue the Contracting Authority for damages (*e.g.* loss of profit), or in some cases even have the PPP Contract canceled. For example, the Contracting Authority may decide, late in the procurement process, that the only way to make the project viable is to provide a capital grant (*cf.* §15.10) to its Preferred Bidder. If this support was not available to other eliminated bidders, they may challenge the contract award on the grounds that they could also have modified their bids in a similar way but were not given the opportunity to do so. Therefore lenders may not be willing to allow drawings on their finance commitment until the time period for such a legal challenge is over.

It must also be borne in mind that significant changes to the winning bid cannot be agreed without the risk of the losing bidder legally challenging the decision on the grounds that it could also have modified its bid in a similar way but was not given the opportunity to do so.

State Aid. This is an issue in public procurements in the European Union. E.U. law does not allow a member state to give financial support to private-sector companies on terms which distort competition, *e.g.* providing Gap Financing (*cf.* §15.7) on below-market terms, where the Project Company would be in competition with other companies which have not benefited from this assistance. This is especially liable to happen in negotiations with a single Preferred Bidder (*cf.* §3.7.7). So again lenders will want to be sure the project cannot be attacked on the grounds that it has received state aid.

§3.7.10 COMPETITIVE BIDDING FOR SUB-CONTRACTS

As to the Sub-Contracts, under European Union procurement law a Project Company does not have to go through a competitive bidding procedure where it is signing a contract for services with a controlling shareholder, but may have to do so in other cases.

---

[29] N.B.: The term 'bond' as used here has no connection with the bond as a method of financing described in §4.3. *Cf.* §7.5, §14.8.1.

Under the World Bank's procurement rules, if the Project Company itself (or its Sponsors) has gone through a competitive bid to secure the PPP Contract, then the Project Company does not have to put its own Sub-Contracts out for bidding, but if not, any Project Contracts to be financed by the World Bank have to go through a bidding procedure.

§3.7.11 UNSOLICITED BIDS

Sponsors may make a proposal to a Contracting Authority to construct and operate a PPP project without any previous call for tenders. Generally speaking awarding a PPP Contract against an unsolicited bid is undesirable:

- There is no guarantee that the pricing of the proposal is competitive, and so the Contracting Authority could end up paying more than would have been the case in a full procurement.
- Procurement of PPP projects should be part of an overall infrastructure investment plan by the Contracting Authority—therefore unsolicited bids may distort the priorities in this plan.
- Dealing with unsolicited bids may use up the limited people resources available to a Contracting Authority, and so again distort its priorities.
- Unsolicited bids are often linked to corruption.

Such proposals may seem attractive because the Contracting Authority does not have to incur the expense of developing the project itself, but in reality such proposals still have to be reviewed in much the same way as a project procured by the Contracting Authority.

If, for whatever reason, the unsolicited proposal is considered worth pursuing, competition should still be introduced, *e.g.*:

- *BAFO.* The bid process always includes a BAFO, and the original unsolicited bidder is automatically qualified to be included in this stage.
- *Development fee.* The unsolicited bidder competes against other bidders in the usual way, but if it does not win the tender it is paid a development fee to reimburse costs, or provide a return on these costs (*cf.* §9.5.6). The fee should also include a payment for any intellectual property rights which the unsolicited bidder has in its original proposal. Alternatively, the winning bidder may pay the development fee (but this will then be included by this bidder as a project cost, so the Contracting Authority will pay it in the end).
- *Bid bonus.* The unsolicited bidder is given extra marks in the bid evaluation (*cf.* §3.7.8).
- *Swiss Challenge.* The unsolicited bid is published, and an open public procurement takes place. The bidder that offers the best terms, if better than

the unsolicited bid (hence the 'challenge), will win. Alternatively the unsolicited bidder may be given the right to match bids procured in an open procurement.

One key issue with the above is how much time new bidders are given to make their bid. Obviously the unsolicited bidder has an advantage in this respect.[30]

§3.7.12 RELATIONSHIP WITH THE LENDERS

Ensuring that the Preferred Bidder will in fact be able to raise project-finance debt is obviously another key issue for the Contracting Authority. This issue is discussed in §5.6.

§3.7.13 CONTRACT MANAGEMENT

Contract management (*i.e.* after Financial Close) by a Contracting Authority is discussed in §7.4.

---

[30] *Cf.* John T. Hodges & Georgina Dellacha, *Unsolicited Infrastructure Proposals: How Some Countries Introduce Competition and Transparency* (Working Paper No. 1, PPIAF, Washington DC, 2007)* for a more detailed examination of these options.

Chapter 4

THE PROJECT-FINANCE MARKETS

§4.1 INTRODUCTION

Private-sector project-finance debt has traditionally been mainly provided from two sources—commercial banks (§4.2) and bonds (§4.3). Commercial banks provide long-term loans to Project Companies; bondholders (typically life-insurance companies and pension funds, which need long-term cash flows) purchase long-term bonds (tradable debt instruments) issued by Project Companies. Recently these non-bank lenders have also begun to make direct loans to projects, and participate in debt funds (§4.4). Other types of private-sector finance are sometimes also used in projects (§4.5).

Although the financial and legal structures and procedures are different, the criteria under which debt is raised in each of these markets are much the same. (So 'lender' is used in this book to mean either a bank lender, bondholder, non-bank lender or debt fund.)

61

Principles of Project Finance. DOI: http://dx.doi.org/10.1016/B978-0-12-391058-5.00004-7

Sources of finance for developing countries, including DFIs (such as the World Bank) and ECAs such as U.S. Eximbank, and particular issues which arise when considering project finance in such markets, are discussed in Chapter 16.

The effects of recent market developments and the long-term prospects for project finance are discussed in Chapter 17.

§4.2 COMMERCIAL BANKS

Commercial banks are the largest providers of project-finance—nearly 90% of the private-sector project finance debt raised in 2012. The division between different market sectors set out in Table 2.1 for the private-sector funding market as a whole is broadly reflected *pro rata* in the banking market.

§4.2.1 AREAS OF ACTIVITY

Table 4.1 sets out the geographical split of bank-provided project-finance debt.[1]

Various broad trends can be seen in these figures:

- The most conspicuous feature is the almost incredible rise of the Indian project-finance market. Starting from a negligible level in 2000, by 2010 the total volume of project financing in India was almost equal to that in the two next-largest markets (Australia and U.S.A.). This was based on very high levels of private investment in infrastructure PPPs, power generation and natural resources projects. In 2011–12 the market fell back, primarily because banks could not continue to fund on the scale required.[2] However the Indian project-finance market is distorted by the debt for Concessions being 100% guaranteed (*cf.* §15.14).[3]
- Elsewhere in Asia-Pacific the Australian market has also shown high growth, based mainly on major natural-resources projects aimed at the Chinese and Japanese markets. Just two LNG (liquid natural gas) deals formed a large proportion of the total Australian project-finance market in 2012.
- In 2012 the European market had not fully recovered from the effects of the 2008 financial crisis (*cf.* §17.2). The Americas market recovered somewhat better but was still below its 2008 peak.

---

[1] Market sectors broadly reflect those set out in Table 2.1, which combines banks and bonds.

[2] *Cf.* Clive Harris and Sri Kumar Tadimalla, *Financing the boom in public-private partnerships in Indian infrastructure: Trends and Policy Implications* (Gridlines Note No. 45, PPIAF, Washington DC, 2008)*.

[3] Under these circumstances there is a strong possibility that the Indian road program may end in tears, like Mexico's in the 1990s. *Cf.* Jeff Ruster, *A Retrospective on the Mexican Toll Road Program (1989–94)* (Public Policy for the Private Sector Note No. 125, World Bank, Washington DC, 1997)*.

Table 4.1 Commercial Bank Project-Finance Loan Commitments, 2000–2012.

($ millions)	2000	2007	2008	2009	2010	2011	2012
Americas	52,795	44,476	42,086	20,058	25,535	38,383	39,321
—of which:							
U.S.A.	33,573	25,887	21,602	9,335	13,424	18,489	18,427
Canada	2,526	3,799	4,747	1,540	4,318	5,134	4,135
Brazil	9,217	3,178	7,257	5,548	3,059	8,278	3,505
Chile	1,618	810	2,814	1,619	120	1,118	2,861
Mexico	2,153	5,078	2,345	839	1,710	1,351	7,167
Asia-Pacific—	12,085	44,842	70,741	56,614	98,708	91,764	91,523
of which:							
Australia	3,806	13,088	21,170	12,284	14,592	24,814	43,042
China		8,381	865	88	154	240	1,935
India	129	10,882	19,246	29,944	54,802	44,933	21,219
Indonesia	303	913	2,727	1,652	2,405	1,886	1,838
Japan	131	589	2,737	1,226	682	1,524	2,366
Philippines	1,510	1,538	819	377	1,174	538	420
Singapore	1,857	3,041	5,412	1,322	2,715	6,479	7,666
South Korea	718	3,041	5,412	1,322	2,715	4,612	6,015
Thailand	1,718	665	1,423	875	2,818	2,736	2,593
Europe	36,123	73,485	91,317	38,565	60,726	51,763	37,838
—of which:							
Belgium		2,966	2,122	1,314	2,402	718	1,106
Britain	11,490	17,399	21,582	8,186	13,021	10,318	12,019
France	49	8,372	5,913	2,013	5,351	11,290	9,162
Germany	12,806	2,859	6,839	2,340	2,133	4,039	4,196
Italy	5,310					7,118	3,409
Greece		6,535	208	251	376	36	
Netherlands	300	2,176	4,238	1,113	1,437	354	774
Portugal	1,537	1,603	11,947	4,117	4,639	509	107
Spain	567	12,207	22,152	10,105	17,376	10,342	3,069
CIS (former Soviet Union)	2,077	3,498	11,037	3,121	2,754	11,962	8,010
—of which:							
Russia	2,077	2,114	8,877	3,001	2,754	11,302	5,096
Uzbekistan							2,914
Middle East & North Africa	7,255	44,524	31,399	15,042	16,774	13,829	13,142
—of which:							
Egypt		4,051	2,111		1,013		2,600
Oman	513	3,317	446	802	1,361	1,502	43
Qatar		9,547	4,396	949		4,184	
Saudi Arabia	852	8,080	10,310	1,900	10,000	3,280	3,647
Turkey	2,834	4,295	5,673	2,730	1,720	2,745	3,110
UAE		11,718	4,214	5,433	1,650	987	269
Sub-Saharan Africa	550	9,161	4,347	5,787	3,678	5,786	8,913
—of which:							
Ghana				2,750	1,002	3,085	3,830
Nigeria		4,405	915	355	777	749	
South Africa	127	959		1,138	510	235	2,706
Total	**110,885**	**219,986**	**250,928**	**139,186**	**208,174**	**213,487**	**198,746**

Source: As for Table 2.1.

- In North Africa and the Middle East, project finance is used for petrochemical, LNG, power-generation and desalination projects, and tends to fluctuate from year to year based on relatively few large projects.
- In sub-Saharan Africa the project-finance market remains relatively small, and mainly concentrates on natural-resources projects.

§4.2.2 BANKS IN THE MARKET

Traditionally there has been an inner circle of some 20 major banks that put together project finance transactions as lead arrangers on a worldwide basis, with reasonably large project-finance operations concentrated in key locations around the world. At a minimum, a leading international project-finance bank would have one project finance office in the United States (covering the Americas), one in Europe (covering Europe, the Middle East, and Africa), and one in Asia/Australasia, and perhaps 50 professional staff (at least) in these offices. These banks built up a strong position through their relationships with foreign investors, their structuring skills, and using their experience from other markets. Another factor favoring the international project-finance banks is that in some Asian markets raising a loan in $ and then swapping into the local currency (*cf.* §10.5.2) produces a lower cost of finance than direct lending in that local currency.

However, over the last ten years or so there has been a shift in the main players in the bank project-finance market. This is illustrated by comparing Table 4.2 and Table 4.3, which set out the 'top 20' project-finance banks in 2000 and 2012.

Bearing in mind that modern project finance was largely invented by American banks, it is surprising to see that although prominent in 2000, by 2012 they had disappeared from the list. There seem to be two main reasons for this—firstly that project finance is expensive in staffing terms, with an unpredictable income stream (income comes in lumps as projects are signed, rather than a steady stream), and secondly because U.S. banks are not natural long-term lenders, which is a key requirement for project finance.

It can also be seen that while European banks formed a large part of the market in 2000, their involvement was reduced by 2012. This reflects the major funding problems which these banks had after 2008 (*cf.* §17.2). Apart from the French banks, the most consistent players in the market over this period have been the Japanese, who continue to benefit from a strong market in Asia.

Not surprisingly, the big new players on the block are the Indian banks. However it should be noted that State Bank of India, by far the largest of these, is a majority state-owned bank. So although it is a commercial bank it is questionable if it should be on this list as compiled by *Project Finance International*—the issue of public-sector bank lending is discussed in §15.8. Similarly, given the size of the Australian market, it is not surprising to see that two Australian banks are in the top 20.

Table 4.2 Top 20 Lead Arrangers of Bank Project-Finance Loans, 2000*.

Lead Arranger	Country	Amount ($ millions)	Number of Loans	Average Loan ($ millions)
Citigroup	U.S.A.	11,927	51	234
Société Générale	France	9,616	30	321
Bank of America	U.S.A.	9,370	33	284
ABN AMRO	Netherlands	7,875	31	254
JP Morgan	U.S.A.	7,472	24	311
Credit Suisse First Boston	U.S.A.	6,719	10	672
Westdeutsche Landesbank	Germany	6,716	37	182
Deutsche Bank	Germany	6,487	22	295
BNP Paribas	France	3,712	24	155
Barclays Capital	Britain	3,423	23	149
Dresdner Kleinwort Wasserstein	Britain	3,155	24	131
Merrill Lynch & Co Inc	U.S.A.	2,631	4	658
Bank of Nova Scotia	Canada	2,165	6	361
Mizuho	Japan	1,976	14	141
Goldman Sachs	U.S.A.	1,832	3	611
HSBC Bank	Britain	1,464	1	1464
Crédit Lyonnais	France	1,339	9	149
Bank of Tokyo-Mitsubishi	Japan	1,272	7	182
Abbey National	Britain	1,200	7	171
Bank of Montreal	Canada	1,040	5	208

Source: As for Table 2.1.
*These are banks which arranged and underwrote loans (*cf.* §5.2), sub-underwriters and participating banks are not included; loans with more than one original lead arranger are divided *pro rata*.

Table 4.3 Top 20 Lead Arrangers of Bank Project-Finance Loans, 2012.

Lead Arranger	Country	Amount ($ millions)	No. of Loans	Average Loan ($ millions)
Bank of Tokyo-Mitsubishi UFJ	Japan	11,618	96	121
State Bank of India	India	10,948	32	342
Sumitomo Mitsui Banking Corp.	Japan	7,576	68	111
Mizuho Financial	Japan	6,234	51	122
Korea Development Bank*	Korea	5,411	27	200
HSBC	Britain	4,394	34	129
Crédit Agricole	France	4,159	36	116
Société Générale	France	4,084	35	117
BNP Paribas	France	3,793	35	108
Banco Bilbao Viscaya Argentaria	Spain	3,521	45	78
Lloyds TSB	Britain	3,251	25	130
Commonwealth Bank of Australia	Australia	3,158	21	150
Standard Chartered	Britain	3,035	19	160
ING	Netherlands	2,946	29	102
National Australia Bank	Australia	2,920	20	146
ICICI	India	2,796	13	215
UniCredit	Italy	2,789	29	96
IDFC	India	2,679	22	122
Axis Bank	India	2,645	9	294
ANZ	Australia	2,457	19	129

Source: As for Table 2.1.
Cf. §16.4.2.

Major international project-finance banks (such as the British, French and Japanese banks in Table 4.2) are involved in the complete range of project-finance products and arrange:

- domestic project finance in their own countries (*e.g.* a loan for a French project in €, lent from the Paris branch of a French bank);
- domestic project finance in other countries in which they have branch or subsidiary operations (*e.g.* a loan for an Australian project in Australian $, lent from the Sydney branch of a French bank);
- cross-border loans (*e.g.* a loan for an Australian project in US$, lent from the Paris branch of a French bank).

It is usually preferable for a project in a particular country to raise its funding from banks operating in that country, firstly because they have the best understanding of local conditions, and secondly because the funding can be provided in the currency of the country, so avoiding foreign exchange risks (*cf.* §10.5). Thus in developed countries projects are normally financed by local banks or foreign banks with branch or subsidiary operations in the country concerned. Such financing constitutes the largest proportion of the project finance market.

In some developing countries, however, this approach may not be possible. There may be no market for long-term loans in the domestic banking market, or the domestic banks may have no experience in project finance. Loans in foreign currency may not be feasible. In some developing countries (such as India and Brazil), there are public-sector development banks that can help to fill the gap if the local commercial banks are not able to provide the funding needed, but their capacity is also limited (*cf.* §15.8). Approaches to project finance in developing countries are discussed in detail in Chapter 15 and Chapter 16.

Other banks participate in the project-finance market at the next level down as sub-underwriters or participants in syndicated loans. These generally participate in syndications of domestic loans in their own countries, though others may join a wider range of loans around the world originally arranged and underwritten by the larger players in the market. As discussed in §5.2.8, however, loan syndication has greatly reduced in the Americas and European markets.

Recent market developments, and prospects for the future of bank project finance, are discussed in Chapter 17.

§4.3 BONDS

A bond issued by a Project Company is basically similar to a loan from the borrower's point of view, but it is aimed mainly at the non-banking market and takes the form of a tradable debt instrument, originally evidenced by a paper certificate, but now generally superseded by electronic registration.[4] The issuer (*i.e.* the Project Company) agrees to repay to the bond holder the amount of the bond plus interest on fixed future installment dates. Buyers of project-finance bonds are investors who require a good long-term fixed-rate return without taking equity risk, *e.g.* insurance companies and pension funds, which have matching long-term liabilities. The market for project-finance bonds is far narrower in scope than that for bank loans, but significant in certain countries. Pricing is usually based on the yield on government debt for the same term, plus a margin for extra risk.

Bonds may either be public issues (*i.e.* quoted on a stock exchange and—at least theoretically—quite widely traded), or private placements, which are not quoted and are sold to a limited number of large investors. It is possible for a private placement to take place without the intervention of an investment bank (*i.e.* the Sponsors deal directly with bond lenders), although this is not common.

Since project-finance bonds are a natural fit for insurance companies' and pension funds' businesses, as well as private investors investing through bond funds, this relative lack of development perhaps seems strange. But project-finance bonds have a number of disadvantages for such investors:

- Usually a 20-year bond is repaid in one amount at the end of 20 years; a 20-year project-finance bond is repaid in irregular installments over the 20-year period, beginning at the end of the project's construction phase of say 2 years, which makes it a less attractive investment to an investor who is looking for a long-term return. (This irregular cash flow also makes it difficult to compare one bond with another.)
- Analyzing the credit risks in a project-finance bond, as well as monitoring the project's performance, is complex, and if project-finance bonds only form a small part of the investor's portfolio, it is not cost-effective for the investor to pay for qualified staff to do this.
- Project-finance bonds are normally rated at the bottom end of investment grade (*cf.* §5.3.1), which is too risky for many bond funds.
- The latter disadvantages were overcome in some countries by bond insurance, but as discussed in §4.3.2 this is now difficult to obtain.
- Initiatives to increase the market for project-finance bonds are discussed in Chapter 15.

§4.3.1 THE U.S. BOND MARKET

There is a long history of issuing bonds for infrastructure (much longer than the history of bank project finance), but the U.S. bond market has been the main model

---

[4] Note that a bond in this context has nothing to do with 'bonding' or 'bonds' issued as security, *e.g.* in a Construction Contract—*cf.* §8.2.9. Bonds may also be referred to as 'securities', 'notes', or 'debentures.'

Table 4.4 U.S. Bond Market—New Issues

(US$ billions)	2011	2012
U.S. Treasury	2,103	2,309
Federal agencies	839	677
Corporate*	1,012	1,360
Mortgage-related	1,660	2,056
Municipal	295	379
Asset-backed (securitizations)	126	199
Total	**6,036**	**6,979**

Source: Securities Industry and Financial Markets Association website
(www.sifma.org.)
*Includes project finance in this context.

for the development of today's project-finance bond markets. The U.S. market is by far the world's largest.[5] Table 4.4 sets out the main types of issuer in this market. (It is worth noting that bonds account for 53% of U.S. corporate debt, and bank loans 47%, compared to the Eurozone and Britain, where bank loans account for 85% of corporate debt.)[6]

There are two categories of bonds in the U.S. which are relevant to project finance—the municipal bond market discussed further below, whose investors until recently often relied on insurance to cover credit risks (§4.3.2) and the corporate bond market (which in this context includes private-sector project-finance bonds), the latter being similar to bond markets for raising project finance in other countries (§4.3.3).

The U.S. municipal bond ('muni') market is more than a century old; a key element in its development was a U.S. Supreme Court judgment in 1895 that Federal taxes cannot be levied on bonds issued by state and local-government entities. Investors in these tax-free bonds are therefore usually individuals sheltering their taxes (mainly through muni bond funds), rather than insurance companies or pension funds, whose income is generally tax-exempt anyway.[7]

---

[5] Statistics in this section other than those for Table 4.4 are from *The Bond Buyer's 2011 in Statistics* (*The Bond Buyer*, February 13, 2012)* and *The Bond Buyer's 2012 in Statistics* (*The Bond Buyer*, February 11, 2013)*. There are some slight discrepancies in the figures for total municipal bond issues from SIFMA in Table 4.4 and those from *The Bond Buyer*.

[6] European Commission Staff Working Document, *Long-Term Financing of the European Economy* (SWD(2013) 76 final, Brussels, 2013), p. 14*.

[7] The U.S. Inland Revenue Service ('IRS') imposes an Alternative Minimum Tax whereby the amount of tax that an individual can shelter in munis and other tax-free investments or tax-deductible expenses is limited. However there have been various temporary suspensions of these rules since 2009 to encourage infrastructure investment.

In 2012 a total of $376 billion of long-term muni bonds were issued, of which 88% were tax-exempt. Only a small proportion of munis could be called project-finance bonds—but this is a small proportion of a very large market.

Muni bonds are divided into two main categories:

General Obligation Bonds ($136 billion in 2012): These are bonds backed by the 'full faith and credit' of the issuer, a state or local government. Obviously these do not provide a project-finance form of financing.

Revenue Bonds ($240 billion in 2012): These are backed only by the revenue of the issuing entity, which may be an education board, water and sewage utility, transportation authority, and so on (*i.e.* a public-sector entity). These are akin to corporate bonds in risk rather than project-finance based since the borrowers often already have an established cash flow. But it is also possible for a new project, *e.g.* a toll road, to issue Revenue Bonds, in which case the buyer of the bond is taking a project finance-type risk on a specific public-sector project.

A sub-set of Revenue Bonds, which are important for private-sector project finance, especially PPPs, are **Private Activity Bonds** ('PABs'). These are revenue bonds issued through a public-sector entity but on-lent to a private-sector Project Company, relying only on the project's cash flows for repayment. Municipal bonds are classified as PABs under section 141 of the IRS Code if:

- more than 10% of the bond proceeds are used to support private business activities; and
- more than 10% of the bond debt service is secured by payments from private business.

PABs qualify for federal tax exemption if more than 95% of the bond proceeds are used for the purposes set out in Section 142 of the IRS Code, namely, airports, docks and wharves, mass commuting facilities, facilities for the furnishing of water, sewage facilities, solid waste disposal facilities, qualified residential rental projects, facilities for the furnishing of local electric energy or gas, local district heating or cooling facilities, qualified hazardous waste facilities, high-speed intercity rail facilities, environmental enhancements of hydro-electric generating facilities, and qualified public educational facilities. Clearly most of these can be structured as project financings.

Tax-exempt PABs are subject to volume caps limiting the total amounts of bonds issued in a jurisdiction: however these caps do not apply to 'exempt facilities', namely: airports, docks and wharves, environmental enhancements of hydro-electric generating facilities, qualified public educational facilities, governmentally owned solid waste disposal facilities, governmentally owned high-speed intercity rail facilities, privately owned high-speed intercity rail facilities (only 75% of the bond proceeds). (Also, to qualify for tax exemption, generally not more than 25% of the bond proceeds may be used for acquisition of real property.)

The 2005 Safe, Accountable, Flexible, Efficient Transportation Equity Act: A Legacy for Users (SAFETEA-LU) allowed up to $15 billion of tax-exempt PABs to be issued for transportation projects until 2015, outside the volume caps.

Some other quasi-project finance structures exist in the U.S. market, in particular '**63–20' Bonds** (issued by a not-for-profit corporation and also tax-exempt)— the number refers to that of an Internal Revenue Services ruling—can also be used in a project-finance context. However such bonds obviously have to be issued by a company with no equity investment, which creates a hole in the structure which has to be filled by some other means, *e.g.* by borrowing less against the cash-flow stream to give lenders the required cash-flow cushion (*cf.* §12.3), which is likely to leave a financing gap which may have to be filled by public-sector provision of mezzanine debt (*cf.* §4.5.1).[8]

Tax Increment Finance is another sub-set of muni bonds, discussed in §17.6.4.

§4.3.2 WRAPPED BONDS

A key element of the muni bond market until recently was that a large proportion of the bonds, including PABs, were 'wrapped', or guaranteed by 'monoline' insurance companies. These insurers are called monolines because they specialize in bond insurance (*i.e.* they have only one line of business).

With monoline-insurance cover, bondholders needed to pay little attention to the background or risks of the borrower or (if relevant) the project itself—at least theoretically—and could rely on the credit rating of the insurance company itself. This deals with the problem of private investors not having the capacity to assess the risks on individual bond issues. Before 2007 around half of all munis were monoline-insured.

However the monoline insurers also became heavily involved in insuring 'subprime' mortgage bonds in the U.S., and incurred such heavy losses on this after 2008 that most of them effectively went out of business. As of 2012 only one monoline insurer was covering new business in the muni market. As a result, only $13 billion of bonds were insured in that year, and the market remains skeptical

---

[8] For fuller information and a comparison between muni bonds and other instruments available in public-sector and PPP projects in the United States, including the TIFIA program (*cf.* §15.4), *cf.* Federal Highway Administration, *Project Finance Primer* (US Department of Transport, Washington DC, 2010)*, and E.R. Yescombe, "Project Finance", in John R. Bartle, W. Bartley Hildreth & Justin Marlowe (eds.), *Management Policies in Local Government Finance*, (ICMA [International City/County Management Association], 6th edition, 2012), Chapter 17.

about the value of such insurance. To a certain extent, *e.g.* in major project financings issuing PABs, the gap caused by the disappearance of the monolines is being
filled by commercial-bank guarantees (but primarily from European and Japanese
banks rather than U.S. banks).

§4.3.3 THE INTERNATIONAL BOND MARKET

As can be seen from Table 4.5, the international project-finance bond market is a
far less significant source of project finance than the commercial-bank market, and

Table 4.5 Project-Finance Bond Issues, 2001–2011.

($ millions)	2000	2007	2008	2009	2010	2011	2012
Americas —of which:	16,099	11,710	7,902	4,462	9,822	13,220	17,059
U.S.A.	11,313	7,055	5,266	3,385	4,905	4,264	7,111
Canada	489	3,002	1,738	877	4,521	4,131	2,076
Brazil	875					3,324	3,642
Chile	430						
Mexico	1,831	259	700			552	2,070
Asia-Pacific —of which:	1,384	4,605	1,015	327	6,432	2,628	2,932
Australia	1,293	4,359	300	188	4,550	935	
Malaysia			473				2,406
South Korea			164	139			
Western Europe —of which:	2,790	10,508	2,968		3,536	5,432	2,642
Britain	2,498	4,355	2,968		3,276	4,732	2,538
France		5,500					
Central Europe and CIS	363						
Middle East and N. Africa —of which				3,477		999	1,300
Qatar				1,248			
UAE				2,229			1,300
Sub-Saharan Africa							174
Total	**25,003**	**26,823**	**11,885**	**8,266**	**19,790**	**22,279**	**24,127**

Adapted from *Project Finance International* (for references see Table 2.1).

concentrated in a few countries.[9] 'International' may be a rather a misnomer here, as most project bonds are issued and traded in the country of the project, although there is some cross-border finance in $ as discussed below: project-finance bonds are mainly issued in the Americas, with smaller markets in Europe, the Middle East and Asia. This market does not rely on tax exemption in the countries where bonds are issued. This is a factor behind the relatively small size of the U.S. (non-muni) project-finance bond market shown in the table: in effect this is 'crowded out' by the market for tax-free bonds.[10]

The U.S. market for project-finance bond issues is based on rule 144a, adopted by the Securities and Exchange Commission ('SEC') in 1990. A private placement of a bond issue does not have to go through the SEC's complex registration procedure,[11] but under normal SEC rules such a private placement cannot be sold on to another party for two years.[12] This lack of liquidity is generally not acceptable to U.S. bondholders. Rule 144a allows secondary trading (*i.e.* reselling) of private placements of debt securities, provided sales are to 'qualified institutional buyers' (QIBs). The latter are defined as entities that have a portfolio of at least $100 million in securities. Thus Rule 144a is the main basis on which project-finance bonds are issued in the U.S.A., whether they are limited private placements or more widely-traded issues.

$ bonds are also issued in markets outside the U.S.A., especially in Latin America. So long as all the parties involved are outside the U.S.A., and the bonds are not traded in the U.S.A., Regulation S under the 1933 Securities and Exchange Act provides that the SEC does not have any jurisdiction or control over such bonds.

The U.S.-based project-finance bonds shown in Table 4.5 were primarily for the oil and gas, and renewable power industries, and do not include tax-exempt bonds issued as PABs in the muni market (*cf.* §4.3.1); taxable infrastructure bonds have been largely (but not entirely) 'crowded out' by the tax-exempt market.

Monoline insurers (*cf.* §4.3.2) also played a major part in developing the international project-finance bond markets, *inter alia* in Australia, Britain and Canada; they made bonds competitive with bank pricing by charging around half of what

---

[9] Market sectors broadly reflect those set out in Table 2.1, which combines banks and bonds.

[10] Build America Bonds, a temporary program in 2009-10 for the issuance of taxable municipal bonds with either a federal subsidy for 35% of the interest payments, or a federal tax credit for 35% of the interest, shows the extent of potential demand from tax-exempt entities. $181 billion of such bonds were issued. (The subsidy was generally chosen as it widened the pool of potential investors to tax-exempt entities.)

[11] *E.g.* requiring the issuer to produce financial statements following U.S. generally accepted accounting principles.

[12] Muni bonds are not regulated by the SEC: the Municipal Securities Regulation Board (MSRB) supervises the muni market, and has rules to ensure adequate disclosure, *e.g.* publication of prospectuses.

the banks charged for taking the credit risk. However this differentiation in price meant that either the banks or the insurers were mispricing the risk, and there was always a question whether bondholders should rely on this guarantee—for 25 years or more—without considering the underlying project being guaranteed. Now most monoline guarantees on existing bonds have little value, and the investors are forced to rely on the underlying project alone for repayment. However one monoline not affected by the problems discussed in §4.3.2 (Assured Guaranty) has resumed providing cover for international project-finance bonds.

The British market was primarily based on PFI bonds with monoline insurance: most larger PFI projects were financed in this way until 2008 because the bond market offered greater liquidity and competitive cost, and indeed in 2005 Britain was the largest project-finance bond market ($17 billion *versus* $13 billion in the U.S.A). But the disappearance of the monolines brought this market to an abrupt end, although bonds are still being issued in other sectors than PFI. The issues in 2010/11 were for railway rolling-stock companies and privatized infrastructure, which although technically project finance are more akin to corporate bonds, and 2012's bonds were for port and high-speed rail projects. (The first monoline-insured PFI bond since 2008 was placed in 2013.)

The Canadian bonds in 2012 were primarily for PPP transportation projects, and the Brazilian bonds primarily for oil and gas projects.

Table 4.6 sets out the main project-finance bond arrangers: as can be seen these are nearly all major international banks. HSBC, for example, arranged bonds in

Table 4.6 Top 10 Lead Arrangers of Project-Finance Bond Issues, 2012.

Lead Arranger	Country	$ million	No. of Issues
HSBC	Britain	2,584	9
BoA Merrill Lynch	U.S.A.	1,932	6
Barclays	Britain	1,442	8
Crédit Suisse	Switzerland	1,279	4
Royal Bank of Scotland	Britain	1,130	5
Bank of Montreal	Canada	1,058	6
JP Morgan	U.S.A.	1,023	3
BNP Paribas	France	1,015	4
Maybank	Malaysia	1,020	2
Royal Bank of Canada	Canada	1,011	6

Adapted from *Project Finance International* (for references see Table 2.1). Shows all lead arrangers with total underwritings over US$1 billion.

Malaysia, Mexico, Brazil, Panama and U.S.A., in the power, infrastructure and oil and gas sectors.[13]

§4.4 OTHER NON-BANK LENDERS

Non-bank lenders (primarily life-insurance companies or pension funds) are beginning to become a significant source of debt in particular project-finance markets, especially Australia, Britain, Canada, France, and the U.S. Life-insurance companies are also well-established as lenders in the Korean PPP market. The key difference between lending directly, rather than by purchasing bonds, is that the lenders can exercise control and supervision of a project in the same way as a bank (for which *cf.* Chapter 14).

Project-finance debt funds, which enable smaller pension funds to invest directly but leaving the detailed monitoring and control in the hands of a fund manager experienced in project finance, are also beginning to develop.

§17.4 discusses the prospects for expansion of such sources of project-finance debt.

§4.5 OTHER SOURCES OF PRIVATE-SECTOR DEBT

§4.5.1 MEZZANINE DEBT

Subordinated debt is debt whose repayment ranks after repayments to bank lenders or bondholders (*i.e.* 'senior lenders', whose finance is referred to as 'senior debt), but before payments of profits to investors, and if the project goes into default and is liquidated, subordinated debt will only be paid off once the senior lenders have been fully repaid. It is usually provided at a fixed rate of interest higher than the cost of senior debt.

Subordinated debt may be provided by investors as part of their equity investment (for the reasons set out in §12.2.2); as between lenders and investors, such debt is treated in the same way as equity.

Other subordinated debt may be provided by third parties, usually non-bank investors, such as insurance companies or specialized funds (*i.e.* infrastructure-debt funds concentrating on this sector), in cases where either there is a gap between the amount that senior lenders are willing to provide and the total debt requirements of the project, or in lieu of part of the equity if this produces more competitive pricing for the Project Company's output or service (*cf.* §17.5.2), or to improve the return

---

[13] *Cf.* European PPP Expertise Centre, *Capital Markets in PPP financing: Where we were and where are we going?* (EIB, Luxemburg, 2010)*.

for investors in the equity itself. Such third-party subordinated debt is often referred to as 'mezzanine debt', to make it clear that it comes from sources other than the investors.

As discussed in §15.4, mezzanine debt may also be provided by the public sector in some cases.

Bringing subordinated or mezzanine debt into the financing package obviously creates issues of repayment priority and control over the project between the different levels of lenders (*cf.* §14.14.5).

§4.5.2 LEASE FINANCE

In a lease finance structure, the equipment being financed is owned by the lessor (Lender) rather than the lessee (borrower). The lessee pays lease rentals instead of interest and principal payments (debt service) on a loan, but other things being equal (*e.g.* assuming the implied interest rate for the financing included in the lease rental payments is the same as the loan interest rate), payments under a lease or a loan should be the same.

It should be noted that in this context leasing means a lease of equipment to the Project Company as a way of raising finance. This has to be distinguished from a property (real estate) lease in a BLT/BLOT structure, which as already mentioned is one way of giving the Project Company control of the project instead of full ownership, but does not imply the provision of any finance (*cf.* §6.2).

Leasing is most commonly used for financing vehicles, factory machinery, and similar equipment, and it tends either to offer finance to clients who cannot otherwise raise funding, based on the security offered by the value of the equipment (this is known as a 'finance lease'), or allows the lessee to use the equipment for a short period of time and then return it, with the lessor taking the residual-value risk (operating lease). Both of these types of finance are expensive compared to direct loans, and neither of them are normally relevant to a project-finance situation. Leasing may also be used in vendor finance as discussed below.

Any merit from linking lease finance with project finance is likely to be only from the use of tax benefits. In some countries lessors can take advantage of accelerated tax depreciation through their ownership of the equipment that is the subject of the project finance. Accelerated tax depreciation is only useful if the owner of the equipment has taxable profits that this depreciation can be used to reduce, but in the early years of a project's operation this may not be the case (*cf.* §13.7.1). If so, it may be better for the equipment to be owned by a lessor who can take advantage of the tax depreciation by offsetting it against its other taxable revenue, and pass part of this benefit back to the Project Company (as lessee), in the form of a reduced cost of finance (*i.e.* the lease rentals are lower than debt-service payments would be under a loan). In deciding whether to use lease finance, the Project

Company has to assess whether the benefit of this reduced financing cost outweighs the loss of the tax depreciation. However in most countries the tax benefit and hence the reduced cost from leasing has either been greatly reduced or eliminated altogether, and leasing therefore does not now play a significant rôle in project finance.

Even if lease finance is available, it will be normally just be a 'bolt-on' to the basic finance structure, and does not change the fundamental approach to the finance by either Sponsors or lenders.

§4.5.3 VENDOR FINANCE

In some cases, finance may be offered by a seller of equipment, an Construction Contractor, or a supplier of other services to the project (a vendor in this context). An equipment supplier, for example, may have a better understanding of the technical risks of the project, or of the industry concerned, than a commercial Lender, and therefore be willing to take risks unacceptable to the financial markets. Vendor finance may thus enable a supplier to increase sales and open up new markets.

Vendor finance may take the form of a loan (*i.e.* selling the equipment on credit), a lease of equipment, or even a guarantee of a bank financing. A vendor just introducing banks to provide finance to the project (without any guarantee) is not providing vendor finance, which in this context means finance provided at the vendor's risk, not the banks' risk.

It has to be said, however, that finance is sometimes offered by the vendor as part of a bid to secure a contract, with little understanding of the real risks and difficulties involved, and time may be wasted by the Sponsors pursuing a financing plan that turns out not to be viable when the vendor has a fuller understanding of the project structure and risks.

Therefore the security structure and risk analysis for any vendor finance should largely mirror that provided by the bank and bond financing markets, to ensure that:

- A coherent financial structure is achieved.
- The vendor is not taking excessive or unexpected risks that could affect the ability or willingness to perform under the contract.
- The vendor finance can be refinanced in due course in the general financing markets, so relieving pressure on the vendor's balance sheet.

The vendor-finance option is often examined by Sponsors when looking at financing alternatives, but its rôle in the project-finance market has been limited, being primarily confined to finance for construction of mobile-phone networks.

§4.5.4 Islamic Finance

The key foundation for Islamic finance is the Koranic prohibition on charging interest (but there is no objection to making a profit on an investment). Islamic finance has come to play a significant part in projects in areas such as the Middle East and Malaysia. In summary, the main structures used in this market are:

- *Istisna'a.* Typically the Lender enters into an agreement with the Project Company under which the latter undertakes to construct the project assets. The agreement allows the Project Company to sub-contract this obligation to the D&B/EPC Sub-Contractor. On Project Completion the asset may be the subject of an *ijara*.
- *Ijara* (Islamic lease). Basically similar to leasing elsewhere in the world (*i.e.* allowing use of equipment for a period of time against fixed rental payments—*cf.* §4.5.2).
- *Mudaraba* (installment sale), with a 'mark up' on the price that provides the profit margin to the lender.
- *Sukuk* (Islamic bonds). These give a partial ownership share and entitle the holder to a fixed share in the revenue generated by the assets.

These various modes of financing, provided both by Islamic banks and Islamic finance departments of international banks, can be provided as part of a project-finance package, in parallel with banks lending on a conventional basis.

Chapter 5

WORKING WITH LENDERS

§5.1 INTRODUCTION

This chapter covers the procedures for raising project finance from private-sector lenders, in particular commercial banks (§5.2) and bondholders (§5.3), with a comparison between the two (§5.4). Lenders' 'due diligence' processes, and the rôles of their various external advisors are also discussed (§5.5). §5.6 covers the ways in which a Contracting Authority interacts with bidders' lenders in a public-procurement process.

§5.2 COMMERCIAL BANKS

§5.2.1 ORGANIZATIONAL STRUCTURE

Most commercial banks in the project-finance field have specialist departments that work on putting project-finance deals together. There are three main approaches to organizing such departments:

> **Project-Finance Department.** The longest-standing approach is to have a department purely specializing in project-finance transactions. Larger departments

79

Principles of Project Finance. DOI: http://dx.doi.org/10.1016/B978-0-12-391058-5.00005-9

are divided into industry teams, covering sectors such as infrastructure, energy and natural resources. Concentrating all the project-finance expertise in one department ensures an efficient use of resources and good cross-fertilization, using experience of project finance for different industries; however, it may not offer clients the best range of services.

Structured-Finance Department. As mentioned in §5.2.2, the divisions between project finance and other types of structured finance have become increasingly blurred, and therefore project finance often forms part of a larger structured-finance operation. Again there may be a division into industry teams. This approach may offer a more sophisticated range of products, but there is some danger that project finance may not fit easily into the operation if other business is based on a much shorter time horizon—*e.g.* if LBOs (see below) are also dealt with in the same department.

Industry-Based Departments. Another approach is to combine all financing for a particular industry sector (*e.g.* electricity, natural resources, or infrastructure) in one department; if this industry makes regular use of project finance, project-finance experts form part of the team. This provides one-stop services to the bank's clients in that particular industry, but obviously may diminish cross-fertilization between project-finance experience and different industries.

In the end good communication and cooperation within the bank are probably more important than the formal organization.

In general, the project-finance personnel in these departments have banking or finance backgrounds, although banks may also employ in-house engineers and other specialists, including people with relevant industry experience. Even though most of the personnel are not experts in construction, engineering, or other non-financial disciplines, by working on a variety of transactions over time they develop experience and expertise in various industries and the technical and practical issues that can affect the *via*bility of a project; however, banks also rely extensively on specialized external advisors (*cf.* §5.5).

Project finance is a time-consuming process for banks and uses well-qualified and therefore expensive staff; some past market leaders have withdrawn from the business because the bank has come to the decision that a better return on capital can be obtained from other types of structured finance or from concentrating on corporate lending or retail banking (*cf.* §4.2.2).

Projects need to be of a reasonable minimum size to provide banks with enough revenue to make the time spent on them worthwhile. Arranging debt for a project much under, say, $25 million, is unlikely to be economic (unless it is part of a production line of very similar projects for which the same template can be used, or, preferably, if several smaller projects can be bundled together and the financing for all them procured at the same time), and most major banks would prefer to work on projects of, say, $100 million or more.

§5.2.2 PROJECT FINANCE AND STRUCTURED FINANCE

There is no precise boundary between project finance and other types of financing in which a relatively high level of leveraged debt is raised to fund a business. The boundaries are also blurred when transactions that began as new projects become established and then are refinanced, with such refinancing taking on more of the characteristics of a corporate loan.

Banks themselves draw the boundaries between project finance and other types of lending based on convenience rather than theory, taking into account that skills used by loan officers in project finance may also be used in similar types of financing. Many banks deal with project finance as part of their 'structured finance' operations, covering any kind of finance where an SPV like a Project Company (*i.e.* one specially set up to undertake the financing) has to be put in place as the borrower to raise the funding, with an equity and debt structure to fit the cash flow, unlike corporate loans, which are made to a borrower already in existence. This is another reason why project-finance market statistics have to be treated with some caution, as they may be affected by inclusion or exclusion of large deals on the borderline between project finance and other types of structured finance.

Examples of other types of structured finance and their differences from project finance include the following:

Receivables Financing. This is based on lending against the established cash flow of a business and involves raising funds through an SPV similar to a Project Company (but normally off the balance sheet of the true beneficiary of the cash flow). The cash flow may be derived from the general business (*e.g.* a hotel chain) or specific contracts that give rise to this cash flow (*e.g.* credit-card loans, other consumer loans, sales contracts, *etc.*). The key difference with project finance is that the latter is based on a projection of cash flow from a project yet to be established. Receivable portfolios may be 'sold off' by banks using the collateralized loan obligation structures described in §5.2.10.

Network Development. This would include projects such as development of utility distribution, cable TV, mobile phone, or internet-access networks, where demand cannot normally be established until the system is able to offer the service. These types of project could be said to come halfway between receivables financing and 'true' project finance, in that the financing may be used towards construction of a project, but loans are normally not drawn until the initial revenues have been established.

The usual approach to financing such projects is to establish the initial usage, usually by the first stage of development of the project being funded by investors' equity rather than debt; once an initial level of penetration into the market, and revenues from usage, has been established part of the debt is advanced for further expansion of the network, and releases of debt continue in this way as successive penetration, usage and revenue targets are met. This is known as the 'borrowing base' model. A more liberal approach is for lenders to lend based on the progress of similar projects elsewhere, and their rate of growth in usage and revenues. (The borrowing base model can also be used for developing oil and gas reserves.)

Leveraged Buyout ('LBO') or Management Buyout ('MBO') Financing. This highly-leveraged financing provides for the acquisition of an existing business by portfolio investors, *e.g.* in a 'private equity' fund (LBO) or its own management (MBO), or a combination of the two. It is usually based on a mixture of the cash flow of the business and the value of its assets. It does not normally involve finance for construction of a new project, nor does this type of financing use contracts as security as does project finance. The risks involved in this type of finance are much higher than those for a typical project-finance transaction (*cf.* §17.3).

Acquisition Finance. Acquisition finance enables company A to acquire company B using highly leveraged debt. In that sense it is similar to LBO and MBO financing, but based on the combined business of the two companies.

Asset Finance. Asset finance[1] is based on lending against the value of assets easily saleable in the open market, *e.g.* ships, aircraft or real estate (property), whereas project-finance lending is against the cash flow produced by the asset, which may have little open-market value of itself. (Of course the market value of such assets does assume a capacity to generate revenues.)

Leasing. Leasing is a form of asset finance, in which ownership of the asset financed remains with the lessor (*i.e.* lender) (*cf.* §4.5.2).

§5.2.3 LEAD ARRANGERS

A standard approach to arranging a project-finance loan is to appoint a bank, which will ultimately underwrite the debt, as 'lead arranger'.[2] As with a financial advisor (*cf.* §3.4.1), experience of lending to the type of project and in the country concerned are key factors in selecting a lead arranger; a wider banking relationship with one or more of the Sponsors is often another element in the decision. Lead arrangers' fees are predominately based on a successful conclusion of the financing, although there may be a small retainer, and advisors' and other out-of-pocket costs, such as travel, are usually covered by the Sponsors.

Larger loans may require more than one bank to underwrite the financing. This has become more common since 2008 as a result of pressures on bank balance sheets, and the decline in the syndication market (*cf.* §5.2.8), resulting in Sponsors

---

[1] Also known as 'object finance'.

[2] Other terms are used for this rôle, such as 'lead manager'.

having to appoint several lead arrangers who will underwrite the debt on a 'club' basis, which is in effect a pre-syndication of the loan (*cf.* §5.2.8). The result may be the appointment of some or all of these banks as joint lead arrangers.

One of the first questions Sponsors have to consider on the financing side is when the lead arranger should be brought into the transaction. Ideally, to ensure the maximum competition between banks on the financing terms, the whole of the project package should be finalized (including all the Project Contracts) and a number of banks then invited to bid in a competition to underwrite and provide the loan as lead arranger. This implies either that the Sponsors make use of a financial advisor to put this package together (*cf.* §3.4.1), or do it themselves if they have the experience (*cf.* §5.5.7).

An alternative approach is to agree with a bank at an early stage of the project-development process that it will act both as financial advisor and lead arranger. This should reduce the cost of the combined financial advisory and banking underwriting fees, and also ensure that the advice given is based on what the bank itself is willing to do, and therefore that the project should be financeable.

The obvious problem with this approach is that the banks are not in a competitive position (even if there may have originally been some kind of bidding process for the mandate[3]), and therefore the Sponsors will probably not get the most aggressive final terms for the financing. However, this may be a reasonable price to pay for the greater efficiency of the process and greater certainty of obtaining finance that this method affords. Clearly the general relationship between the Sponsors and the banks concerned, and the Sponsors' own experience in the financial market, may also affect this decision.

It is also possible for the Sponsors to stipulate that they will have the right to 'market test' the final financing package by asking for competitive bids from other banks,[4] and if the original lead arranger(s) are found not to be competitive, the financing will be moved to new banks. However, this may hold up conclusion of the financing and therefore not be practical unless the original lead arranger(s) have become so out of line with the market that it is worth the loss of time and extra legal and other costs that are likely to be involved in going elsewhere.

In major projects, both a financial advisor and lead arranger(s) may be appointed separately at an early stage to provide more balanced advice, although obviously this adds to development costs.

The financial advisor (or lead arranger(s) acting as financial advisor) plays an active rôle in the negotiation of Project Contracts, to ensure that financing

---

[3] *i.e.* the lead-arranger position (*cf.* §5.2.3).

[4] This is known as a 'funding competition', and may be a requirement in PPP projects, or process-plant projects with a Contracting Authority as Offtaker. The benefit of any lower costs would normally be at least partially reflected in a reduction in the Contract Payments. *Cf.* §12.2.5 for equity funding competitions.

implications of these contracts are taken into account. Any changes in the Project Contracts that are good for the Sponsors are generally good for the banks too, and so lead arrangers are also sometimes used by Sponsors to improve their commercial position in these negotiations.

§5.2.4 LETTERS OF INTENT

Banks commonly provide letters of intent (or letters of interest) to Sponsors early in the development of a project. These are usually short—1–2 pages long—and confirm the banks' basic interest in getting involved in the project. If the letter requires the Sponsors to deal exclusively with the banks concerned, this may amount to a lead arrangers' mandate letter as described in §5.2.2. Alternatively, the Sponsors may collect a number of such letters from different banks. Letters of this nature provide the Sponsors with initial reassurance that the financing market is interested in their project, and help to give the Sponsors credibility with other prospective Project Contract counterparts, such as fuel suppliers, product purchasers, Contracting Authorities (*cf.* §5.6), *etc.*

Such letters should not be regarded as a legal commitment on the banks' part. They are primarily used by banks to ensure they keep their foot in the door of the project, but on the other a bank does not issue such a letter frivolously.

A mandate letter is normally signed between the Sponsors and the selected lead arranger(s), which expresses the banks' intention—subject to due diligence, credit clearance, and agreement on detailed terms—to underwrite the debt required; some indication of pricing and other debt terms may also be given, although this may be difficult at an early stage of the transaction. This mandate letter does not (and realistically cannot) impose a legal obligation on the bank(s) to underwrite or lend money for the project. If the lead arranger(s) are also appointed as financial advisor, the mandate letter will also provide for services similar to those of the financial advisor (*cf.* §3.4.1). The mandate may be combined with a term sheet (*cf.* §5.2.7), depending on how advanced the project development is at the time.

§5.2.5 BANK RÔLES

When several banks are involved as lead arrangers, they normally divide up responsibilities for due diligence and other aspects of the transaction, which enables them to use their resources more effectively. Typical divisions of rôles between the banks are:

- *documentation*, in conjunction with the banks' lawyers (*cf.* §5.5.2), perhaps with banks subdividing between Project Contracts and the financing documentation; however, unless there are a lot of banks involved, all the banks in the transaction normally want to be closely involved in this area;

- *engineering*, in liaison with the Lenders' Engineer (*cf.* §5.5.3);
- *insurance* (in liaison with the insurance advisor (*cf.* §5.5.4);
- *financial modeling* (*cf.* §5.2.6), and dealing with the Model Auditor (*cf.* §5.5.5);
- *market or traffic review*, in liaison with the banks' market or traffic advisors (*cf.* §5.5.6);
- preparation of the *information memorandum* (*cf.* §5.2.8);
- *syndication* (*cf.* §5.2.8);
- *loan agency* (*cf.* §5.2.9);
- *account bank* (*cf.* §14.4.1), managing the Project Accounts (often combined with loan agency).

There are varying degrees of perceived prestige (and in some cases division of the arrangement fees) involved with these rôles, and the Sponsors may have to intervene to decide who is doing what if the banks cannot agree between themselves. However banks are used to working in teams in this way in the project-finance market, which is more 'cooperative' than some other forms of financing—banks that compete against each other in one deal may be working together in the next, and people from different banks working together on a deal for a prolonged period of time may well get to know each other better than they do their fellow employees in their own banks. Thus the banks should be able to work together smoothly without too much intervention from the Sponsors. The Sponsors should of course try to ensure that the banks with the best experience in the relevant field undertake the work.

§5.2.6 FINANCIAL MODEL

Throughout the due-diligence process, the financial advisor or lead arranger develops a financial model for the project (if it is developed by a financial advisor, it is normally passed on to the banks for their use). The structure and inputs required for a financial model, and the ways in which its output is used, are discussed in detail in Chapter 13.

The development of the financial model should ideally be a joint operation between the Sponsors and the financial advisor or lead arranger, probably with each assigning one or two people to work in a joint team. Although the Sponsors should have already developed their own model at an early stage of the project's development to assess its basic feasibility, it is usually better for there to be one model for the project so all concerned are working from the same base. This may make it more efficient to abandon the development model and start again when the banks come into the picture.

Similarly, in a public procurement the Contracting Authority will also develop its own financial model before approaching the market for bids (*cf.* §3.7.3), in order to assess the project's financial viability from its point of view. Bidders may be required to layer a common inputs/results template provided by the Contracting Authority on top of their own financial models to ensure that bids can be properly compared.

§5.2.7 TERM SHEET, UNDERWRITING, AND DOCUMENTATION

As the financing structure develops, a term sheet is drawn up, setting out in summary form the basis on which the finance will be provided (*cf.* §14.2).[5] This can develop into quite an elaborate document, especially if the bank lawyers are involved in drawing it up, which can add substantially to the Sponsors' legal costs. It is preferable for term-sheet discussions to concentrate on commercial rather than legal issues, although the dividing line may be difficult to draw.

The final term sheet should provide the basis for lead arrangers to complete their internal credit proposals and obtain the necessary approvals to go ahead with the loan. The work of a bank's project-finance team, and the consequent proposal for a loan, is normally reviewed by a separate credit department, and may be presented to a formal credit committee for approval. Banks must have a well-organized interface between the credit team and the project-finance team, especially where a bank is acting as a lead arranger: it may take a long time to develop a project-finance transaction, and if the loan is turned down at the end of that process on credit grounds, this obviously has serious consequences for the Sponsors (and does not help the bank's project-finance team very much). On the other hand, a bank cannot obtain credit approval at the beginning of the development process, because the structure of the transaction will probably not be sufficiently finalized. The Sponsors therefore need to have confidence that a lead arranger has the experience and credibility to manage this internal review process.

In recent years, given the pressure on balance sheets and liquidity (*cf.* §17.3) many banks have inserted a requirement for an 'investment approval' before the project moves on to credit approval. This considers the merits of the project's use of the bank's balance sheet, compared to other (non-project finance) business which is also available.

After obtaining their credit approval, lead arrangers 'underwrite' the debt, usually by signing the agreed term sheet. The term sheet sets out pricing and key terms

---

[5] A term sheet may also be used by the Financial Advisor in a PIM (*cf.* §5.2.8) as a basis for requesting financing bids from prospective lead arrangers, or at a later stage for the lead arrangers to crystallize their commitment to the financing. It may also be used by an investment bank setting out the terms for a bond issue (*cf.* §5.3.1).

for the loan, and provides for a final date by which documentation should be signed (*i.e.* a validity period), as banks usually have to reapply for internal credit approval if their loan is not signed within a reasonable period.

This signature of a term sheet is still normally no more than a moral obligation, as the commitment by the banks is usually subject to further detailed due diligence of the Project Contracts and associated documentation, and signature of financing and security documentation. Nonetheless, a term sheet is treated seriously, and banks normally only withdraw from an underwriting if there is a major change of circumstances, either in relation to the project itself, the country in which it is situated, or the market in general.

If credit in the project-finance market is especially tight, banks may require a 'market flex' clause. This will provide that, even though the banks have underwritten the debt, its terms must be improved if they become out of line with the market. This is obviously something which the Sponsors will only agree to if there is no realistic alternative, and is a case where independent advice from a financial advisor rather than a lead arranger is useful. In the case of a public procurement, the extra cost is likely to be passed on to the Contracting Authority, to whom it will also be unwelcome.

The next phase in the financing is the negotiation of financing documentation, typical terms for which are discussed in Chapter 14, and, based on the necessary due diligence, securing the bank's agreement to the Project Contracts which provide its security. It is quite likely that as a result of these detailed negotiations, changes in the lending terms or risk profile may arise, which will again require credit approval.

Even when the financing documents and the Project Contracts are signed (this should ideally be simultaneous) the Sponsors have not yet finally obtained committed financing for the Project Company. Even at this stage, the bank(s) may not actually provide the finance as there are numerous conditions precedent that have to be fulfilled, before allowing a drawing to be made (*cf.* §14.8). When the project has reached this stage—*i.e.* conditions precedent have been fulfilled, and the Project Company is able to begin drawing funds for construction, the project has finally achieved 'Financial Close'.

It is evident from this description that arranging project finance is not a quick process. If the project is presented to potential lead arrangers as a completed package, with no bankability problems and all the Project Contracts in place, it is likely to take a minimum of three months before signature of the loan documentation by the lead arrangers. But there is clearly a lengthy process to go through before such a package can be completed, and thereafter issues may well arise during banks' due diligence that further slow down the matter, and it is not uncommon for banks to work for a year or more on the financing side of a major project. Finance can thus be a key critical-path item for the project.

§5.2.8 INFORMATION MEMORANDUM AND SYNDICATION

The lead arrangers (and any sub-underwriters they may bring in) may wish to reduce their own exposure by placing (syndicating) part of the financing with other banks in the market.

The lead arrangers prepare a package of information to facilitate this syndication process, at the heart of which is an Information Memorandum. This Final Information Memorandum (FIM) used for syndication may be based on a Preliminary Information Memorandum (PIM) originally prepared by the Sponsors or their financial advisor to present the project to prospective lead arrangers. The bank in charge of the syndication process is generally known as the 'book runner'.

The FIM should provide a detailed summary of the transaction, including:

- a summary overview of the project, its general background, and *raison d'être*;
- the term sheet;
- the Project Company, its ownership, organization, and management;
- financial and other information on Sponsors and other major project parties, including their experience in similar projects and the nature of their involvement in and support for the current project;
- technical description of the construction and operation of the project;
- market situation (the commercial basis for the project), where relevant, covering aspects such as supply and demand, competition, *etc.* (*cf.* §9.4);
- summary of the Project Contracts (*cf.* §5.6, Chapter 7 and Chapter 8);
- project costs and financing plan (*cf.* §13.44);
- risk analysis (*cf.* Chapter 9, Chapter 10, and Chapter 11);
- financial analysis, including the Base Case financial model (*cf.* §13.10) and sensitivity analyses (*cf.* §13.9).

In other words, the Information Memorandum provides a synopsis of the structure of the project and the whole due-diligence process, which speeds up the credit analysis by prospective participant banks. (If well organized and written, it also provides the Project Company's staff with a useful long-term reference manual on the project financing.)

The Information Memorandum is accompanied by supplementary reports and information, which may include:

- the legal advisors (*cf.* §5.5.2) may provide a summary of legal aspects of the project;
- a technical report from the Lenders' Engineer (*cf.* §5.5.3), summarizing their due diligence review;
- a report on insurances from the insurance advisor (*cf.* §5.5.4);
- a copy of the financial model, with the Model Auditor's report (*cf.* §5.5.5);

- advisor's report on the market in which the project is operating (*cf.* §5.5.6), and its revenue projections (if sales of its product or services are not covered by a long term Project Agreement or Offtake Contract—even if they are, background information on the market is useful);
- a similar market report on fuel or raw material input supplies may be relevant;
- the environmental impact assessment (*cf.* §9.10);
- annual reports and other financial information on the various parties to the project.

The Sponsors and the Project Company are actively involved in the production of the information memorandum, which is normally subject to their approval and confirmation of its accuracy (but *cf.* §14.9).

A formal presentation may be made to prospective participant banks by lead arrangers, the Sponsors, and other relevant project parties, sometimes through a 'road show' in different financial centers.

Prospective participant banks are usually given three to four weeks to absorb this information and come to a decision whether to participate in the financing. They are generally given the documentation to review after they have taken this decision in principle to participate, and may sign up for the financing two to three weeks after receiving this. The lead arranger(s) usually reallow part of their arrangement fee to the participating banks; their residual fee after this reallowance is known as the *præcipium*.

The Project Company does not usually take any direct risk on whether the syndication is successful or not; by then the loan should have been signed and thus fully underwritten by the lead arrangers. Sponsors should resist delay tactics by lead arrangers, who try to avoid signing the financing documentation until after they have syndicated the loan and thus eliminated their underwriting risk.

After the 2008 financial crisis, this bank syndication market almost disappeared, especially in Europe, and the Americas, meaning that more underwriting banks were often needed for each loan on the basis that there will be no syndication and they must expect to keep what they underwrite on their own books—this is known as a 'club' loan arrangement. In this case there may be an initial lead arranger, who later brings other banks into the 'club', or all 'club' banks may be appointed as joint lead arrangers.

§5.2.9 LOAN AGENCY

In cases where the loan is being provided by a syndicate of banks, whether lead arrangers, participating banks or a bank 'club', once the financing documentation has been signed one of the lead arrangers acts as agent for the bank syndicate as a whole: this agent bank[6] acts as a channel between the Project Company and the banks, as

---

[6] Also known as the facility agent.

otherwise the Project Company could find it is spending an excessive amount of time communicating with individual banks. The agent bank performs various tasks:

- collects the funds from the syndicate when drawings are made and passes these on to the Project Company;
- holds the project security on behalf of the lenders (§14.7); however, this function may be carried out by a separate security trustee, acting on the instructions of the agent bank;
- calculates interest rates, interest payments and principal repayments;
- receives these debt-service payments from the Project Company and passes their respective shares on to the individual syndicate banks;
- gathers information about the progress of the project, in liaison with the banks' advisors, and distributes this to the syndicate at regular intervals;
- monitors the Project Company's compliance with the requirements of the financing documentation and provides information on this to the syndicate banks;
- arranges meetings and site visits as necessary for the Project Company and the Sponsors to make more formal presentations to the syndicate banks on the project's progress;
- organizes discussions with and voting by the syndicate if the Project Company needs to obtain an amendment or waiver of some term of the financing;
- takes enforcement action against the Project Company or the security after a default.

The agent bank seldom has any discretion to make decisions about the project finance (for example, as to placing the Project Company in default), but acts as directed by a defined majority of the banks (*cf.* §14.13). Requiring collective voting by the banks in this way helps to ensure that one rogue bank cannot hold the rest of the syndicate (and the Project Company) for ransom.

§5.2.10 COLLATERALIZED LOAN OBLIGATIONS (CLOS)

CLOs are a method of effectively syndicating bank loans to non-bank lenders (*e.g.* life-insurance companies or pension funds)—the process is also known as securitization. A bank 'packages' up a portfolio of its project-finance loans (usually of a similar type, *e.g.* PPPs) and 'sells' these off. There are two types of CLO:

- *Synthetic CLOs*: here the bank just transfers the risk to the new lenders (who thus provide the bank with a guarantee against its portfolio), but continues to fund and manage the portfolio, and keep a share of the credit margin.
- *Cash CLOs*: here the bank (or banks—more than one may be involved) actually sells its portfolio to the new lenders but continues to manage it on their behalf, for which it is paid a fee.

Synthetic CLOs are generally more complex than a simple transfer of all the portfolio risks: usually the bank retains part of the risk for its own account. There is an obvious potential conflict of interest when the bank is selling off its own loans, and retaining part of the risk for its own account helps to mitigate this (*cf.* §17.4.2).

CLOs have not been used extensively in the project-finance market, but a few banks have reduced their exposure to project finance portfolios in this way. CLOs are more commonly used to sell off receivables such as credit-card outstandings (*cf.* §5.2.2). CLOs were also one way in which 'sub-prime' mortgages were sold to investors—hence they were at the heart of the 2008 financial crisis, and fell out of favor thereafter.

§5.3 BONDS

As has been seen (*cf.* §4.3), bonds have provided an important source of project finance in certain specific markets.

The key difference in nature between loans and bonds is that bonds are tradable instruments and therefore have at least a theoretical liquidity, which loans do not. This difference is not as great as it at first appears, because many bonds are sold on a 'private placement' basis, to investors who do not intend to trade them in the market, whereas loans are in fact traded on an *ad hoc* basis between banks.

Bonds are purchased by investors looking for long-term, fixed-rate income—typically life-insurance companies and pension funds, or individual investors (usually investing *via* bond funds).[7]

§5.3.1 THE INVESTMENT BANK AND THE CREDIT RATING AGENCIES

Investors in bonds generally do not get directly involved in the due-diligence process to the extent that banks do, and rely more on the project's investment bank and a credit rating agency to carry out this work.[8]

An investment bank (*i.e.* a bank that arranges and underwrites financing but does not normally provide the financing itself, except on a temporary basis) is appointed as lead arranger and assists in structuring the project in a similar way to a financial advisor on a bank loan (*cf.* §3.4.1).

The investment bank then makes a presentation on the project to a credit rating agency (the leaders in the field as far as project-finance bonds are concerned are Standard & Poor's and Moody's Investors Services), which assigns the bond a credit rating based on its independent review of the risks of the project, including

---

[7] Inflation-linked bonds are also issued for some projects (*cf.* §10.4.3).

[8] *Cf.* European PPP Expertise Centre, *Financing PPPs with Project Bonds* (EIB, Luxemburg, 2012)* for a more detailed description of the bond-issue process.

legal documentation and independent advisors' reports. This review considers the same risk issues that a commercial bank would do.

Gradations of credit ratings by Standard & Poor's and Moody's from the prime credit level of AAA/Aaa down to the minimum 'investment grade' rating of BBB–/ Baa3 (below which most major bondholders will not purchase a bond issue) are as listed in Table 5.1. Most project finance ratings are at the lower end of this range. (Below the investment grade level the ratings continue from BB + /Ba1, *etc.*)[9]

The investment bank then prepares a preliminary bond prospectus that covers similar ground to an information memorandum for a bank syndication (*cf.* §5.2.8), but usually in more summary form. The work done by the investment bank and the credit rating agency reduces the need for detailed due diligence by bondholders; provided the bond rating fits the bondholder's maximum risk profile, such investors can just decide to buy it without having to do a lot of work. Major bondholders, however, do carry out their own review of the project information in the prospectus besides relying on the credit rating, and may even participate in bank loans, or act as sole lenders (*cf.* §17.4).

After any necessary preliminary testing of the market (which may include a road-show of presentations to investors), the investment bank issues the final bond prospectus and underwrites the bond issue through a subscription agreement. The coupon (interest rate)[10] and other key conditions of the bond are fixed based

Table 5.1 Investment-Grade Ratings

Standard & Poor's	Moody's
AAA	Aaa
AA+	Aa1
AA	Aa2
AA–	Aa3
A+	A1
A	A2
A–	A3
BBB+	Baa1
BBB	Baa2
BBB–	Baa3

[9] Bank loans are also sometimes rated by the rating agencies, to assist in a wider syndication. Such a rating may also be relevant to placement of loans with non-bank lenders, *e.g.* through CLOs as discussed in §5.2.10. However, this is not a widespread practice in the bank project-finance market.

[10] The term coupon is used for interest payments on a bond because paper bond certificates often had detachable coupons which were presented for payment on each interest payment date.

on the market at the time of underwriting, and the bond proceeds are paid over to the Project Company a few days later (obviously the project must have reached Financial Close by then). The investment bank places (or resells) the bonds with investors, and may also maintain a liquid market by trading in the bond.

§5.3.2 PAYING AGENT, TRUSTEES AND CONTROLLING CREDITOR

Separate parties are appointed to manage various aspects of the bond administration through its life (except in a private placement to a single bondholder), in a similar way to the agent bank in a bank syndicate (*cf.* §5.2.9):

- The *paying agent* pays over the proceeds of the bond to the borrower and collects payments due to the bondholders.
- The *bond trustee*[11] holds the security on behalf of the investors. Traditionally the bond trustee also calls meetings of the bondholders where decisions are required, *e.g.* to waive a condition of the bond (*cf.* §14.11).[12] However given the complexity of project bonds, a bond trustee is not the ideal party to manage such issues, and also bondholders generally do not want to get involved in relatively the minor but complex changes which are often required.
- Therefore a *Controlling Creditor* may also be appointed to make decisions on such issues on behalf of the bondholders and instruct the bond trustee accordingly. Obviously the Controlling Creditor needs project-finance expertise, so the ideal party from the bond holders' point of view is a project-finance bank. This can be achieved if the bank is also a lender to the Project Company, but otherwise a bank is unlikely to take on this rôle. Where there is monoline insurance (*cf.* §4.3.2) the insurer will take on this rôle as it is the party at risk anyway. A subordinated lender can also be appointed as the Controlling Creditor, but its decisions will be limited to matters which will not affect the bondholders' debt-service payments. Failing all this there will be a voting system to enable bondholders to instruct the bond trustee.

§5.4 BANK LOANS VERSUS BONDS

Assuming that bond finance is one option for a particular project, various factors affect whether a project should use commercial bank loans or bonds (or a combination of the two) for its financing, as set out in Table 5.2.

---

[11] Also known as fiscal agent. The rôles of bond trustee and paying agent may be combined.

[12] This rôle may be further split into a security trustee holding the security, and the bond trustee dealing with bondholders.

Table 5.2 Bank Loans versus Bonds

Bank Loans	Bonds
Banks can be involved in the project from an early stage to help ensure its bankability (cf. §5.2.3)	Bondholders only come in at a late stage (but the investment bank and rating agency act on their behalf—cf. §5.3.1)
The Sponsors' corporate-banking lines may be used up in project-finance loans (but cf. §2.6.1)	Bonds rely on a different investor base, thus avoiding the need to tie up bank credit lines
May be provided (either on a domestic or cross-border basis) to any credit-worthy market	Only available in certain markets (cf. §4.3)
Project Contracts kept confidential	The terms of Project Contracts may have to be published in listing particulars or a bond prospectus: this may not be acceptable to the Sponsors for reasons of commercial confidentiality (e.g. they may not wish to reveal the terms of a fuel-supply contract)
In some markets banks will not offer long-term maturities	May offer a longer repayment term
Although banks do not formally commit to loan terms (such as their credit margin) in advance, they are more likely to stand by the terms they offer at an early stage (cf. §5.2.7). However the underlying interest rate may not be fixed until Financial Close (cf. §10.3.5)	The terms for the bond and the market appetite for it are only finally known at a late stage in the process, when the underwriting takes place (cf. §5.3.1)
Generally only offer fixed interest rates through hedging arrangements (cf. §10.3.1)	Fixed rates of interest
Funds from the loan drawn only when needed	Funds from the bond usually have to be drawn all at once and then redeposited until required to pay for project capital costs—there may be a loss of interest caused by the redeposit rate being lower than the coupon (interest rate) on the bond (cf. §10.3.4)
Banks can offer flexible loan repayment schedules (cf. §12.5.4), and short-term working capital loans	Bond loan repayment schedules are inflexible and cannot offer short-term funding
Banks exercise control over all changes to Project Contracts and impose tight controls on the Project Company	Bondholders only control matters that significantly affect their cash flow cover or security; Events of Default leading to acceleration of the financing are more limited in bond issues
Banks tightly control the addition of any new debt and are unlikely to agree the basis for this in advance.	It may be easier to add new debt (e.g. for a project expansion) to bond financing as bondholders can agree the terms for this in advance through 'variation bonds' (cf. §7.6.3)

(Continued)

Table 5.2 (Continued)

Bank Loans	Bonds
Low penalties for prepayment (*e.g.* because the debt can be prepaid, or refinanced on more favorable terms—*cf.* §14.6.2), but potential swap-breakage costs (*cf.* §10.3.1)	High penalties for prepayment (*cf.* §10.3.4)
Decisions on waivers and amendments to loan terms (*cf.* §14.13) are taken on a case-by-case basis by banks; this is more flexible, especially during the construction phase.	Bondholders cannot easily take complex decisions (because of the wide spread and number of investors), and so rely mainly on mechanical tests such as Cover Ratios (*cf.* §12.3); this may be less flexible if amendments to these ratios are required (although bond holders may allow any parallel bank lenders or a Controlling Creditor to take decisions on their behalf)
It is easier to negotiate with banks if the project gets into difficulty.	Bonds may be less flexible if major changes in terms are required (*e.g.* if the project gets into serious trouble), as it can be difficult to have direct dialogue with bond holders, who are more passive in nature than a bank syndicate; banks may be wary of lending in partnership with bond holders for this reason.
If a project gets into difficulty, negotiations with banks should remain private.	Negotiations with bond holders may be publicized.

In general, bonds are suitable for developed markets and 'standard' projects. They are also especially suitable if a project is being refinanced after it has been built and has operated successfully for a period. Conversely, the greater flexibility of bank loans tends to make them more suitable for the construction and early operation phases of a project, projects which require long-term financial flexibility, more complex projects, or projects in more difficult markets.

§5.5 LENDERS' DUE-DILIGENCE AND EXTERNAL ADVISORS

§5.5.1 Due Diligence

A key element in the success of project finance as a sound method of lending, despite the apparent risk of highly-leveraged projects, is the due diligence carried out by lenders (or the investment bank and credit rating agency on their behalf in the bond market).

Lenders use their own external advisors, largely paralleling and checking the work done by the Sponsors' external advisors (*cf.* §3.4). The costs of all these advisors are payable by the Sponsors, and can add considerably to the total development costs—they may be payable (at least in part) whether or not the financing is concluded. It follows from this that the terms of reference and fees for these advisors must be approved by the Sponsors.

Advisors appointed by the lenders may include legal advisors, Lenders' Engineers, insurance advisors, model auditors, and others.

§5.5.2 Legal Advisors

The lenders' legal advisors carry out due diligence on the Project Contracts, and in due course they assist the banks in negotiating the financing documentation. Both local and international lawyers may be engaged for this purpose.

§5.5.3 Lenders' Engineer

One of the major international engineering firms, which are now well used to providing this type of advice, is appointed as Lenders' Engineer.[13] Its work is in several stages:

Due Diligence. The Lenders' Engineer reviews and reports to the lenders on matters such as:

- suitability of project site;
- project technology and design;
- experience and suitability of the Construction Contractor;
- technical aspects of the Construction Contract;
- construction cost estimates;
- construction schedule;
- construction and operating Permits;
- technical aspects of any Project Agreement, Input-Supply Contract or Offtake Contract;
- suitability of the Project Company's management structure and personnel for construction and operation;
- any particular technical issues or risks in operation of the project;
- projections of operating assumptions (output, likely availability, *etc.*);
- projections of operating, maintenance and lifecycle costs;[14]
- for process-plant projects such as an oil refinery, an engineering company may also carry out a 'hazop' (hazard and operations) study for the lenders, which looks at the possibilities for damage caused by the processes used in the plant and the effect of the layout of the plant on its safety.

---

[13] Also known as the Technical Advisor (TA).

[14] *Cf.* §9.7.5 for a discussion of lifecycle costs.

Construction Monitoring. Once the project construction is under way, the Lenders' Engineer is provided with regular information on progress by the Project Company, the Owner's Engineer, and the Construction Contractor, and provides regular reports to the lenders, highlighting any particular problems. The Lenders' Engineer may also be required to certify that claims for payment by the Construction Contractor have been properly made, and that the required performance tests on Project Completion have been passed (*cf.* §8.2.7), but otherwise is not in any way supervising or controlling the construction process, which remains the responsibility of the Project Company. (N.B. This certification rôle may be carried out by an Independent Engineer, for which *cf.* §7.4.1.)

Operation Phase. When construction is complete and the project is operating, the Lenders' Engineer continues to monitor and report on operating performance and maintenance.

§5.5.4 INSURANCE ADVISOR

The insurance advisor (usually a department of a major international insurance broker, specializing in providing this service for lenders) reviews and reports on the adequacy of insurance provisions in the Project Contracts, the proposed insurance package for the construction phase of the project, and renewals of insurances during operation (*cf.* §8.6). If any claims are made, the insurance advisor monitors these on behalf of the lenders.

§5.5.5 MODEL AUDITOR

When the financial model (*cf.* §5.2.6 and Chapter 13) is virtually complete, a Model Auditor (one of the major firms of accountants, or a specialist modeling firm) is appointed to review the model, including tax and accounting assumptions, and confirm that it properly reflects the Project Contracts and financing documentation and can calculate the effect of various sensitivity scenarios.

§5.5.6 OTHER ADVISORS

Depending on the needs of the project, various other advisors may be appointed in areas such as:

Market. If the product produced by the Project Company is not being sold on a long-term contract, or if it is a commodity whose sale price is dependent on market conditions, market advisors are appointed to review the reasonableness of the projections for the sale volume and price.

Fuel or Raw Material. The same principle applies if fuel or raw material required for the project is not being purchased on a long-term contract, or at a price that can be passed on to the product Offtaker.

Traffic. Traffic advisors are needed for an infrastructure project where revenues are dependent on traffic flows.

Natural Resources. In a project that depends on the extraction of natural resources, whether as an input to or output from the project, lenders require a reserve report (for a mining project) or a reservoir report (for a hydrocarbon project), together with an engineering report that confirms the feasibility, timing, and costs of extracting the reserves. Similarly, lenders to a wind power generation project need advice on wind patterns, and on water supply for a hydropower project.

Environmental Advisor. In cases where environmental issues are potentially significant, an environmental advisor may be engaged to confirm the work that should have already been done as part of an environment impact assessment (*cf.* §9.10).

§5.5.7 PRE-APPOINTMENT OF LENDERS' ADVISORS

It is possible for Sponsors to appoint lenders' advisors before there are any lenders, *i.e.* if it is intended that there will be competitive bids from prospective lead arrangers after the Project Contracts have been negotiated and project structuring is largely complete (*cf.* §5.2.3). In this case the lenders' advisors act as 'devil's advocates' in checking the project specifications and documentation, to ensure that issues normally raised by lenders are adequately covered, and prepare due-diligence reports for prospective lenders. Once the lead arrangers have been appointed, they continue to work with these advisors on a normal basis. The benefits of this procedure are that it helps to ensure the project remains financeable as it is being developed, and it reduces the amount of time spent on due diligence by lenders when they finally bid for the finance, although it may increase Sponsors' development costs if the lead arrangers are not satisfied with the due diligence and ask for further work.

§5.5.8 USE OF ADVISORS' TIME

Lenders work primarily on fixed fees (*cf.* §12.6), whereas their advisors are more likely to work on time-based fees. The lenders therefore have every incentive to try to shift due-diligence work to their advisors to get a better return on the time of their staff involved in the project. Typical examples of this are the use of lawyers to act as secretaries of meetings that are primarily discussing commercial or financial (rather than legal) issues, or to draw up the term sheet (*cf.* §5.2.7).

Sponsors should therefore review and agree to the lenders' advisors' scope of work and carefully supervise time spent to keep these costs under control.

§5.6 LENDERS AND THE PUBLIC-PROCUREMENT PROCESS

The process of public procurement by a Contracting Authority is described in §3.7. It might be thought that there is no need for the Contracting Authority's project team to concern itself with the lenders, as it is the private-sector bidder who is responsible for arranging whatever debt finance is needed to develop the project. However debt finance is a key element of a PPP or process-plant project, and it serves no purpose for the project team to negotiate an agreement with the private party which is not acceptable to its lenders. Similarly, it is bad practice to sign a Project Agreement without the finance also being signed up at the same time, since this is highly likely to mean that when financing is being negotiated, the lenders will require changes in the Project Agreement, typically increasing the level of risk taken by the Contracting Authority in a situation where the latter has little negotiating power. This is another form of deal creep (*cf.* §3.7.7).

§5.6.1 BANK DEBT

Therefore, throughout the procurement and negotiation processes, evidence of sufficient debt commitment by lenders is necessary, becoming firmer as the procurement develops, *e.g.*:

Readiness for Market. As already mentioned (*cf.* §3.7.3), preparing the project for the market should include evidence that the project is likely to be 'bankable'. Direct discussions with potential lenders is one way to help establish this.

Pre-Qualification. Again as already mentioned, initial letters of support from potential lenders should be required as part of the pre-qualification (*cf.* §3.7.5). These letters will not imply any legal commitment on the lenders' part, since they would not have enough information about the project to make such a commitment, but serious lenders will only write such a letter if they believe that the project has a reasonable prospect of being bankable.

Initial Bid. The initial bids based on the RfP should also include evidence of bank support, and a term sheet setting out their detailed terms. (The Contracting Authority's financial advisor should review this to ensure that there are no unduly onerous requirements which would affect the project's financial viability.) If a bidder is using a separate financial advisor is used, this advisor normally also provides a support letter for the bid, confirming that in its view the project can be successfully financed.

Negotiations. Bidders can use the lenders as an excuse for not agreeing to something in the negotiations which is not actually a lender issue. The Contracting Authority's financial and legal advisors should be able to make a reasonable judgment whether or not conceding a particular issue to the bidder is necessary for the latter to obtain bank financing. However the project team may have to negotiate some aspects of the agreement directly with potential lenders as well as the bidders, to ensure their continued support.

Final Bid (BAFO). At this stage lenders should ideally confirm that their due diligence (*cf.* §5.5) is complete, the terms of their loan have been agreed and are embodied in an agreed loan agreement (*cf.* Chapter 14), and they have received the necessary credit and other approvals (*cf.* §5.2.7). The disadvantage of this requirement is that such a full commitment by lenders may involve fee payments (and higher legal costs), and bidders may be unwilling to pay for this with no certainty that they will win the bid—in such cases the Contracting Authority may agree to cover losing bidders' costs up to an agreed level.

Debt Funding Competition. It is also possible to separate the bid for the project from the bid for the financing—*i.e.* the bid process is carried out on preset common financing assumptions, and once the Preferred Bidder has been appointed and the Project Contracts agreed to, the financing itself is put out to lenders for competitive bidding (*i.e.* market testing—*cf.* §5.2.3). The payments under the PPP Contract are then adjusted from the bid pricing to take account of the actual financing costs and structure.

The benefit of this is that it deals with the problem of a bidder having a good technical and financial bid (which the Contracting Authority would like to accept), but the bidder's financing is not on the best terms available in the market. But there is a risk that the lenders may then require aspects of the Project Contracts to be reopened, to the possible disadvantage of both the Preferred Bidder and the Contracting Authority, but especially the latter.

§5.6.2 BONDS

If it is proposed to finance the project through a bond rather than bank debt (*cf.* §4.3; §5.3) it is more difficult to be sure of its 'deliverability' since bonds cannot be underwritten in advance. Nonetheless there are a number of actions which the Contracting Authority can take to provide comfort that bond finance can be raised:

Readiness for Market. The suitability of bond finance should be considered at this stage. The Contracting Authority's financial advisor should also start preliminary discussion on a credit rating.

Initial Bid. If the bidder intends to consider using bond financing its financial advisor should provide a letter of support indicating the feasibility of doing this. The Contracting Authority's own financial advisor should also review this.

Final Bid (BAFO). By this stage a credit rating should have been obtained. Typically a rating of not less than A–/A3 will be required (*cf.* §17.5), and the bidder may be required to take the risk that its proposed structure will not fall below this level and hence increase costs (and maybe jeopardize the financing). If the bidder has appointed an investment bank to lead manage the bond issue, the latter should provide evidence of the deliverability of the bond finance and its likely coupon (*cf.* §12.6.1).

Bond Arranger Competition. There may be a competition for the rôle of bond lead arranger, similar to that in a bank debt funding competition. Here the issues for evaluation are both the cost (arrangement fee), and the relative placing capacity of prospective arrangers.

Chapter 6

TYPES OF PROJECT AGREEMENT

§6.1 INTRODUCTION

The Project Contracts provide a basis for the Project Company's construction and operation of the project (*cf.* §2.4). The most important of these is the Project Agreement (*i.e.* the contract that provides the framework under which the Project Company obtains its revenues).[1] The Sub-Contracts which make up the rest of the Project Contracts are discussed in Chapter 8.

A preliminary clarification: expressions such as BOT, DBFO, and so on are rather confusing, and overlap with each other. There is no need to use these terms (§6.2).

---

[1] However, as noted in §2.5.3, not all projects have Project Agreements.

Principles of Project Finance. DOI: http://dx.doi.org/10.1016/B978-0-12-391058-5.00006-0

There are three main models for a Project Agreement:[2]

- an *Offtake Contract* (*i.e.* a process-plant project), under which the Project Company produces a product and sells it to an Offtaker (§6.3);
- an *Availability-based Contract* (*i.e.* one based on the PFI Model—*cf.* §2.5.2), where a Contracting Authority pays a Project Company for making the project available for use (§6.4);
- a *Concession Agreement*, under which the Project Company provides a public service, and collects User Charges for doing so (§6.5).

These models have many characteristics in common, which are discussed in Chapter 7. The confusing list of 'PPP-like' contracts, which are often counted as PPPs, but most of which do not require project finance, is reviewed in §6.6.

It should be said that although many legal issues are discussed in these chapters, they are not intended as a commentary on all the legal ramifications of Project Contracts and the associated financing documentation, but concentrate on the key issues likely to emerge in commercial negotiations between the Offtaker/ Contracting Authority, Project Company and the lenders. The effect of various risk issues on the structuring of Contract Documents, as discussed in Chapters 9–11 should also be taken into account.

§6.2 BOT, BTO *ET AL.*

Process-plant or PPP projects are sometimes classified with reference to who owns the project at various stages of its life:

Build-Operate-Transfer ('BOT') Projects.[3] In this type of project, the Project Company never owns the assets used to provide the project services. However the Project Company constructs the project and has the right to earn

---

[2] For some standard forms of Project Agreements and their legal framework, *cf.* United Nations Industrial Development Organization: *Guidelines for Infrastructure Development through Build-Operate-Transfer (BOT) Projects* (UNIDO, Vienna, 1996)*; United Nations Economic Commission for Europe: *Negotiation Platform for Public-Private Partnerships in Infrastructure Projects* (UN ECE, Geneva, 2000)*; United Nations Commission on International Trade Law: *UNCITRAL egislative Guide on Privately Financed Infrastructure Projects* (United Nations, New York, 2001)*; South African National Treasury PPP Unit, *Standardised Public-Private Partnership Provisions* (Pretoria, 2004)*; Infrastructure Australia, *National PPP Guidelines*, Vol. 3: "Commercial Principles for Social Infrastructure" (Canberra, 2008)* and Vol. 7: "Commercial Principles for Economic Infrastructure" (Canberra, 2011)*; H.M. Treasury, *Standardisation of PF2 Contracts*, Version 5 (London, 2012)*— referred to hereafter as 'SoPC'; website of the World Bank's PPP in Infrastructure Resource Center for Contracts, Laws, and Regulation (PPPIRC)—http://www.worldbank.org/ppp.

[3] Also known as design-build-finance-operate ('DBFO') projects.

revenues from its operation of the project, under a Project Agreement with a Contracting Authority. (The Project Company may also be granted a lease of the project site and the associated buildings and equipment during the term of the project—this is known as build-lease-transfer ('BLT') or build-lease-operate-transfer ('BLOT').) This structure is used where the public nature of the project makes it inappropriate for it to be owned by a private-sector company—for example, a road, bridge, or tunnel—and therefore ownership remains with the public sector. Hence it is primarily used for PPPs.

Build-Transfer-Operate ('BTO') Projects. These are similar to a BOT project, except that the Contracting Authority does not take over the ownership of the project until construction is completed.

Build-Own-Operate-Transfer ('BOOT') Projects. The Project Company constructs the project and owns and operates it for a set period of time, earning the revenues from the project in this period, at the end of which ownership is transferred back to the Offtaker/Contracting Authority. For example, the Project Company may build a power station, own it for 20 years during which time the power generated is sold to an Offtaker (*e.g.* a state-owned electricity distribution company), and at the end of that time ownership is transferred back to the Offtaker.

Build-Own-Operate ('BOO') Projects. These are projects whose ownership remains with the Project Company throughout its life—for example, a power station in a privatized electricity industry or a mobile phone network. The Project Company therefore gets the benefit of any residual value in the project. (Project Agreements with the private sector also normally fall into this category.)

There are many other variations on these acronyms for different project structures, and the project-finance market does not always use them consistently—for example, 'BOT' is often used to mean 'Build-Own-Transfer,' *i.e.* the same as 'BOOT.' [4]

It makes little difference from the project-finance point of view whether or not the ownership of the project is transferred to an Offtaker/Contracting Authority in the short or the long term, or remains indefinitely with the Project Company, or is never held by the Project Company. This is because the real value in a project financed in this way is not in the ownership of its assets, but in the right to receive cash flows from the project. But although these different ownership structures are of limited importance to lenders, any long-term residual value in the project is obviously important for an Offtaker/Contracting Authority, and to the investors in assessing their likely return, and may also be relevant to lenders from the security point of view.

---

[4] *Cf.* Jeffrey Delmon, *Understanding Options for Public-Private Partnerships in Infrastructure: Sorting out the forest from the trees: BOT, DBFO, DCMF, concession, lease...* (Policy Research Working Paper 5173, World Bank, Washington DC, 2010).

Since this 'alphabet soup' terminology is confusing, and as the key question is whether the project assets revert to the Offtaker/Contracting Authority's ownership and control at latest by the end of the Project Agreement, these terms will not be used hereafter. In lieu of this, where the residual value issue is relevant, this will be referred to as a 'Reverting Asset' Contract (*i.e.* the facility reverts to the Offtaker/ Contracting Authority's control at the end of the contract) or 'Non-Reverting Asset' Contract (ownership and control remains with the Project Company at the end of the contract), as the case may be.

§6.3 OFFTAKE CONTRACT

An Offtake Contract is typically used on process-plant projects (*cf.* §2.5.1)—*i.e.* a project that produces a product. Such agreements provide the Offtaker (*e.g.* a power purchaser) with a secure supply of the required product and the Project Company with the ability to sell its products on a pre-agreed basis. (It should be noted that an Offtake Contract can be signed with a Contracting Authority—*e.g.* a state power distribution company, or a private-sector counterparty—*e.g.* a private-sector power-distribution company.)

Going back to first principles, if a high ratio of project-finance debt is to be raised, the risks taken by the Project Company in selling its product must be limited; an Offtake Contract is one of the easiest ways of limiting these risks.

§6.3.1 Types of Offtake Contract

Offtake Contracts can take various forms:

Take-or-Pay Contract. This provides that the Offtaker (*i.e.* the purchaser of the project's product) must take (*i.e.* purchase) the project's product or make a payment to the Project Company in lieu of purchase. The price for the product is based on an agreed Tariff (*cf.* §6.3.5).

It should be noted that such contracts are seldom on a 'hell-or-high-water' basis, where the Offtaker is always obliged to make payments whatever happens to the Project Company. The Project Company is normally only paid if it performs its side of the deal; in general, if it is capable of delivering the product.

Process-plant projects (*cf.* §2.5.1) involving sale of a product, such as a power-purchase agreement, are usually on a take-or-pay basis.

Take-and-Pay Contract. In this case the Offtaker only pays for the product taken, on an agreed price basis. Clearly this is of limited use as an Offtake Contract in a project financing, as it provides no long-term certainty that the product will be purchased. It may be found, however, in Input-Supply Contracts for fuel or other raw materials (*cf.* §8.5).

Long-Term Sales Contract. In this case the Offtaker agrees to take agreed-upon quantities of product from the project, but the price paid is based on market prices at the time of purchase or an agreed market index. The Project Company thus does not take the risk of demand for the project's product, but takes the market risk on the price. This type of contract is commonly used in, for example, mining, oil and gas, and petrochemical projects, where the Project Company wants to ensure that its product can easily be sold in international markets, but Offtakers would not be willing to take the commodity-price risk.

This type of contract may have a 'floor' (minimum) price for the commodity, as has been the case in some LNG projects—if so, the end result equates to a take-or-pay contract at this floor price and has the same effect as a hedging contract.

Hedging Contract. Hedging contracts are found in the commodity markets; it is possible to enter into various kinds of hedging contracts with market traders, such as:

- a long term forward sale of the commodity at a fixed price (this is effectively the same as a take-or-pay agreement);
- an agreement that if the commodity's price falls below a certain floor level the product can be sold at this floor price; if the price does not fall to this level the product is sold in the open market;
- an agreement similar to this, but also establishing a ceiling price for the commodity, so that if the market price rises above this level the product will also be sold at this ceiling level; if the price is below the ceiling or above the floor, the product is sold in the open market.

Thus, for example, an oilfield project may enter into an agreement to hedge its expected production such that if the oil price is below $100/bbl, it can sell its production at $100 to the hedging counterpart, and if it is above $125/bbl, the hedging counterpart can buy it at $125. In this way the project knows that its oil can always be sold for at least $100; however, if the price goes over $125 the project will not benefit from this.[5]

These types of hedging contracts should be distinguished from financial hedging described in Chapter 10, although similar principles are involved.

Contract for Differences (C*f*D). Under a C*f*D structure the Project Company sells its product into the market and not to the Offtaker. If however, the market price is below an agreed level, the Offtaker pays the Project Company the difference, and *vice-versa* if it is above an agreed level. The effect of

---

[5] This is similar in concept to an interest-rate collar (*cf.* §10.3.2).

this is that both the Project Company and the Offtaker have hedged their respective sale and purchase prices against market movements; however, a Contract for Differences differs from a hedging contract in that the product is always sold in the market and not to the hedging counterpart; it is thus purely a financial contract.[6] The end result is a contract with a similar practical effect as a take-or-pay contract with an agreed Tariff.

Long-term *Cf*Ds are especially used in the electricity market: in fact, in some countries these contracts have to be used rather than a PPA (see below) because all power produced has to be sold into the country's electricity pool rather than to end-users.

Throughput Contract.[7] This is used, for example, in pipeline financings. Under this agreement a user of the pipeline agrees to use it to carry not less than a certain volume of product, and to pay a minimum price for this.

Input-Processing Contract. Certain types of process-plant project are really created to deal with an input rather than produce an output. Examples of this would include:

- a solid-waste incinerator, which takes waste from a Contracting Authority and burns it; the outputs (not usually linked to any Offtake Contract) are heat, which can be used to generate electricity, and ash residue, which has to be disposed of;
- a sewage plant, which takes raw sewage from a Contracting Authority, and processes this into clean water and a residue which may be used as fertilizer.

As can be seen, in these cases the Contracting Authority is not an Offtaker, but is providing an input.

It should be noted that there is considerable confusion of terminology in the project-finance market, especially on the definition of take-and-pay and take-or-pay contracts; in this book the terms are used as set out above.

In §6.3.2–§6.3.6, typical provisions in a take-or-pay Offtake Contract are discussed. A power-purchase agreement ('PPA') is used as an example, as it is a common type of Offtake Contract in the project-finance context, and other contracts tend to follow the PPA model. PPAs were also used as the model for PFI-Model Project Agreements (*cf.* §6.4).

The effect of the lesser coverage from a take-and-pay or long-term sales contract is considered in the context of more general risk analysis in §9.6.1, and projects where there are no long-term sales arrangements are discussed in §9.6.2.

---

[6] This is similar in concept to an interest-rate swap (*cf.* §10.3.1).

[7] Also known as a transportation contract.

§6.3.2 PPA Structure

A PPA is a type of Offtake Contract used for a project generating electricity. The place of a PPA in the structure for an IPP project (for a gas-fired power plant) is set out in Figure 2.1.

A PPA provides for the Project Company to construct a power station, with agreed technical characteristics as to:

- output (in megawatts [MW]);
- heat rate (the amount of fuel required to produce a set amount of power);
- emissions or other environmental requirements.

The PPA requires the plant to be constructed by an agreed-upon date (§6.3.3) and to be operated on an agreed-upon basis (§6.3.4). The power from the completed plant is sold based on a long-term Tariff (§6.3.5) paid by the power purchaser, who may be a public- or private-sector electricity transmission and distribution company, a local distribution company, or a direct end-user of the power (*e.g.* an industrial plant). It also sets out the penalties for failure to meet the contractual requirements (§6.3.6).

The Offtaker (power purchaser) needs to be satisfied that the Project Company and its Sponsors have the necessary technical and financial capacity to construct and operate the plant as required, have an appropriate EPC Contractor and a secure fuel supply, and that the terms of the project finance do not indirectly expose the power purchaser to undue risks. The Offtaker may therefore restrict the ability of the Sponsors to sell their shares to ensure the continuing involvement of appropriate parties in the project (*cf.* §3.2.1; §7.11).

§6.3.3 Construction Phase

An EPC Contract will normally be signed by the Project Company: this passes the risks of delay, cost overrun, and performance to the EPC Contractor (*cf.* §8.2).

Project Completion under a PPA is known as the 'Commercial Operation Date' (COD).[8] To reach COD the Project Company has to demonstrate Project Completion to the Offtaker by undertaking performance tests. These performance tests will—at least—demonstrate the actual output the plant can achieve (since as will be seen the Tariff is based on the output capacity). In a Reverting Asset-based Contract (*cf.* §6.2; §7.10.7), the Offtaker, as the eventual owner of the plant, may

---

[8] Also referred to as the 'Completion Date' or 'Substantial Completion' (*cf.* §8.2.7).

also be concerned to ensure that other technical and performance requirements are fulfilled. The Offtaker's representative may join the performance tests being carried out under the EPC Contract, or the PPA performance tests may be carried out separately. (Obviously the PPA tests should not be more stringent than those under the EPC Contract—*cf.* §8.2.8.)

The Project Company may be required to fulfill other conditions to achieve COD, such as:

- obtaining operating Permits;
- confirmation that emissions requirements are met;
- confirmation that operating-phase insurances are in place on the agreed basis;
- demonstrating reserve stocks of fuel are in place.

§6.3.4 OPERATION OF THE PLANT

The parties agree detailed operating procedures; for example, the Offtaker notifies the Project Company in advance of its expected requirements for power, and the Project Company advises the Offtaker of any changes in output or availability, for example, due to routine maintenance or an emergency shutdown, and as far as possible carries out maintenance in times of low demand. This does not imply that the Offtaker has any right to intervene directly in the operation or maintenance of the plant, except in the case of a default by the Project Company (*cf.* §7.9).

The dispatch risk (*i.e.* the risk of whether or not the power station's electricity is required by the Offtaker—either directly or through the grid-transmission system) is the responsibility of the Offtaker. The Project Company only has to ensure that it is ready and available to produce power when required; as will be seen, the Tariff that the Offtaker pays provides an adequate return to the Project Company whether the plant is dispatched (generates power) or not. Since the Offtaker is taking the dispatch risk, it follows that it has the right to decide when the plant actually produces power.

In the case of a Contract for Differences (*cf.* §6.3.1), the Project Company may not get paid unless it actually sells its electricity into the market (*i.e.* the dispatch risk remains with the Project Company). In such cases the Project Company has to bid an appropriate price into the market to ensure that it always sells its power.

§6.3.5 TARIFF

The Tariff payable under the PPA is based on the minimum required availability of the power plant (*i.e.* the number of days in a year the plant will be able to operate at the specified output, after making allowances for routine maintenance and unexpected plant outages) and deductions are made or penalties paid if the plant does not meet minimum availability or output requirements (*cf.* §6.3.6).

The Tariff is usually paid on a monthly basis by the Offtaker to the Project Company and generally consists of two main elements: a fixed Capacity Charge,[9] and an Energy Charge[10] which varies with usage of the plant. In addition, certain other charges may be payable.

Capacity Charge. The Capacity Charge element of the Tariff is paid even if a plant is not dispatched, since it represents the fixed costs that the Project Company incurs just by building the plant and making it available to the Offtaker.

This element of the Tariff is thus intended to cover:

- *Fixed operating costs*, *e.g.* land rental, staff costs, insurance premiums, scheduled maintenance and replacement of spare parts, fixed (or capacity) payments to a fuel supplier for a fuel pipeline, taxes, *etc.* Accounting depreciation of the plant (*cf.* §13.7.1) is not a fixed operating cost for this purpose, nor is it taken into account in calculating the equity return, as it is not a cash-flow item; however, the debt service and equity return elements cover this and the other capital costs of the project.
- *Debt service* (interest payments and principal repayments), usually based on pre-agreed assumptions as to the level of debt to be incurred by the Project Company and the interest rate on the debt.
- *Equity return*, *i.e.* the Project Company's free cash flow after debt service and fixed operating costs, and taxes, again based on a pre-agreed assumption about the level of equity required.

The Capacity Charge may be split into three elements as above, or two, combining the debt service and equity elements, thus leaving the Project Company to decide the best financial structure for funding the project or even combined as one payment. (The extent to which the Capacity Charge is split is affected by the extent to which these different elements are inflation-indexed—*cf.* §7.3.3.)

The Capacity Charge is normally fixed when the PPA is signed, which means that the Project Company takes the risk of the costs of the project being higher than the original costs assumed when the Tariff was calculated). Sometimes there are exceptions to this, *e.g.* the Project Company may be compensated for the actual costs of insurances during the operation phase (*cf.* §9.9.2).

Energy Charge. This element of the Tariff is intended to cover a project's variable costs, of which the most important is fuel. The Energy Charge takes into account:

- the quantity of fuel that should have been used (on pre-agreed heat-rate assumptions) to generate the electricity actually produced by the plant;

---

[9] Also known as Availability Charge, or Fixed Charge.
[10] Also known as Variable Charge, or Usage Charge.

- the actual cost of this fuel to the Project Company (or the cost based on an index of fuel costs);
- any other O&M costs that vary with usage of the plant.

The Energy Charge makes an allowance for the degradation in performance (and hence gradual increase in fuel consumption) that takes place between each major maintenance of the plant (*cf.* §9.7.3).

In general, if the plant is not dispatched the Energy Charge is not payable, but if the Project Company has take-or-pay obligations for fuel, and it does not need the expected level of fuel because of a low level of dispatch of the plant, the Offtaker would need to cover this cost (unless the low level of dispatch is because the plant has not been available).

In other types of process-plant projects, the cost of raw materials being processed is dealt with through a Variable Charge in a similar way to the Energy Charge.

Other Charges. Various other charges may be payable as part of the Tariff, *e.g.* costs for more than a certain number of start-ups of the plant every year—which use extra fuel and cause higher maintenance costs (*cf.* §9.7.3), or the extra costs of running on a partial load.

Under a combined heat and power ('CHP') project, payments may also be received for the sale of waste steam from the plant for use in industrial processes at an adjacent site or for district heating. (In some countries steam from power generation is used for water desalination, to the extent that this is the main reason for constructing the plant.)

Tariff charges may take account of the Offtaker's varying requirements for power, so that in a northern location more may be paid for power generated in winter evenings.

Measurement of the power produced is through meters at the plant controlled by both parties.

If this type of 'fixed/variable' Tariff structure is used, the Project Company may be obliged to sell the whole of the power output to the Offtaker, even if this output turns out to be greater than originally anticipated (*e.g.* because the project operates at above its design capacity).

This Tariff structure thus leaves various key risks with the Project Company (*cf.* §9.3), for example:

Project-Cost Overrun. If the project costs more to construct than expected, and as a result incurs more debt and equity financing, this is not taken into account in the Tariff calculations.

Availability. If the plant is not able to operate so as to produce the quantity of power required over time, revenue is lost (or penalties are paid) (*cf.* §6.3.6).

Operating Costs. If the plant does not operate as well as expected, and, for example, it takes more fuel to generate the electricity, or maintenance costs are higher than expected, this also does not change the Tariff payment.

§6.3.6 PENALTIES

The Tariff as set out above is only paid by the Offtaker if the Project Company's power plant performs as required under the PPA. If it does not, the Project Company will be liable to penalties, which may be deducted from Tariff payments or paid separately by the Project Company to the Offtaker.

These penalties are liquidated damages ('LDs'), *i.e.* they are the pre-agreed level of loss for the Offtaker, and therefore the only damages that can be recovered. In this sense the use of the expression 'penalties' is misleading, as contractual penalties that are not calculated to cover a real loss generally cannot be recovered in many legal systems (*cf.* §8.2.8).

Typical penalties include:

Late Completion. The Offtaker should bear in mind that the Project Company has every incentive to reach Project Completion on time whether or not penalties are payable: the ability of any highly-geared Project Company to sustain a prolonged delay in Project Completion is limited, because the loss of revenue from such a delay is significant (obviously no Tariff payment is made if the project is not complete). If the Offtaker suffers no loss from the delay, payment of penalties by the Project Company is not appropriate, may not be legally enforceable, and will only add to project costs as the Offtaker will, if possible, pass on this extra risk to the EPC Contractor, who will build it into the contract price and timing.

If, however, the plant is completed later than the agreed-upon date, and as a result the Offtaker expects to have to generate or buy in power from another more expensive source, the Project Company may be made liable to a penalty payment reflecting this loss, at an appropriate rate for each day of delay. The Project Company will of course try to ensure that this penalty is mirrored in the LDs under the EPC Contract, and that there is a cap on the PPA penalties that also reflects the position in the EPC Contract (*cf.* §8.2.8).

To avoid a prolonged period of uncertainty about whether the project is ever going to happen or not, there is normally also a final termination date by which if COD has not taken place the Offtaker has the right to terminate the PPA, typically around one year after the expected Project Completion.

If the Offtaker is also the transmission-grid owner, it must ensure that the grid connection to the plant is provided. If the connection is not provided, and the construction of the plant is complete but it cannot be tested for performance without a grid connection, this cannot be used as a basis for charging penalties for late Project Completion, and the Offtaker is obliged to begin paying the Capacity Charge element of the Tariff (*cf.* §9.5.9).

Provision may also be made for a bonus to be paid to the Project Company for early Project Completion, if this would be beneficial to the Offtaker.

Low Initial Output. If the plant is supposed to have an output of x MW, and when completed it actually produces $(x-y)$ MW, a lump-sum penalty is payable, or the Capacity Charge reduced, to allow for this. Again this penalty should be taken into account in the LDs under the EPC Contract.

High Initial Heat Rate. If at the performance tests the plant uses more fuel than expected to produce a given amount of electricity, this can be dealt with in two ways: either the difference in heat rate is ignored in the Energy Charge calculations, and the Project Company bears the cost of the extra fuel required, or the Energy Charge assumptions for fuel consumption can be adjusted, and an initial penalty paid to the Offtaker to compensate for this. In either case the EPC Contract LDs should cover the cost of the extra fuel consumption or the initial penalty.

Low Availability. If the plant is required to be available to produce, say, 100 MW for 90% of the year (*i.e.* 329 days), this means that the plant must produce 32,900 MWh in a year. Therefore if the plant is not capable of producing this total output level, whether because the plant is unavailable, or the output of the plant deteriorates below the agreed level, the Project Company is liable for a penalty payment (or the Capacity Charge is reduced).

In setting the original availability and output requirements, allowance is made for routine maintenance, and an agreed level of unexpected shutdowns (outages) in calculating the period for which the plant is to be made available each year, and for the natural deterioration in output that takes place between major maintenance overhauls. These allowances are translated into detailed availability and production schedules agreed to in advance, usually on a broad annual basis, adjusted as necessary on a shorter term basis. Penalties may be greater when the power is most needed (*e.g.* during the winter evenings in a northern country), and similarly the Project Company is required to undertake routine maintenance in a period of low demand for power.

To a certain extent it may be possible to pass these penalties on to the O&M Contractor (*cf.* §8.3.4).

The Offtaker may require security for penalty payments through a bank guarantee, which is often provided by the lenders as part of the total financing package for the project.

There may also be a bonus payable to the Project Company if either the availability of the plant or the actual amount of power produced are above certain levels.

§6.4 AVAILABILITY-BASED CONTRACT

This section will deal with the structure of Availability-based Contracts, which are the most widely used type of PFI-Model projects.[11] The place of a Project Agreement in the PFI Model is set out in Figure 2.3.

Examples of Availability-based PFI-Model projects, all of which would relate to public infrastructure (and hence are forms of PPP), include:

- public-sector buildings such as schools, hospitals, prisons, social housing or government offices, where payments are made by the Contracting Authority for availability of the building;[12]
- a transportation facility such as a road, tunnel or bridge, or parts of the system, such as trains or signaling for a railway line, where payments are made by a public-sector system operator (as Contracting Authority) for availability of the system, rather than by the public (or a Contracting Authority) for usage.

Significant elements of Availability-based PFI-Model Project Agreements are directly derived from PPAs, since in the 1990s, when PFI projects were first undertaken, the market was very familiar with PPAs, and it made sense to try to use an existing model rather than start from scratch.[13] In summary, a typical PPA, as described above, has three basic requirements:

- *output*: can the power station generate x MW of power?
- *availability*: can the power station produce its full output as and when required (*i.e.* is it available)?
- *throughput*: the Energy Charge payment for fuel use (usually not relevant in this case).

A PPA does not tell the Project Company how to design, build or maintain the power station—these are matters for the Project Company and its investors to decide. As far as the Offtaker is concerned, the power station just needs to be available, when required, to produce the agreed output in MW.

---

[11] This type of PPP is also known as an 'Annuity Contract', because of its level payment stream (*cf.* §7.3.2).

[12] Availability-based PFI-Model Contracts relating to these types of buildings are often referred to collectively as 'Accommodation Projects', since the Project-Agreement requirements are quite similar for all of them.

[13] However although Availability is a key issue in both types of contract, process-plant projects are not included as Availability-based Contracts in this book—the term will be used only for PFI-Model Contracts.

These principles are applied in an Availability-based Project Agreement through the provisions relating to the Service Fee (§6.4.1), Output Specification (§6.4.2), availability requirements (§6.4.3), and performance penalties (§6.4.4). Some of the Service-Fee costs may be calibrated against market changes (§6.4.5).

§6.4.6 considers the other main type of PFI-Model project, that of a transport project with 'Shadow Tolls'.

§6.4.1 SERVICE FEE

Unlike a process plant, a split between a fixed Capacity Charge and a variable Energy Charge (*cf.* §6.3.5) is not appropriate, and one 'Service Fee' payment is made for provision of the facility.[14] However, the Service Fee is calculated based on sub-elements which include cover for fixed costs (including debt service and equity return) and variable costs (*e.g.* operation & maintenance costs). This calculation is fixed when the Project Agreement is signed, so that if actual costs differ the Service Fee is not normally changed. Payments usually begin on Project Completion (*cf.* §7.3.1).[15]

The Service Fee is reduced for any periods of non-availability, and if the services provided are not at the required standard. But although output and availability are easy to measure for a power station, but how can they be measured for, say, a PFI-Model school? The Output Specification cannot be a single measure (*e.g.* a number of MW), and availability is not 'on-off' like a power station? As will be seen below, calculation of various adjustments/penalties to the Service Fee are therefore more complex than under a PPA.

§6.4.2 OUTPUT SPECIFICATION

The Output Specification is a complex but key element of a PFI-Model Project Agreement. It can be split into two basic elements:

---

[14] The British term for this is a 'Unitary Charge'. The choice of this term was partly for public-sector accounting reasons: if the Service Fee was clearly divided into a fixed and variable element, with the fixed element covering the debt service and equity return on the original capital cost (and with the Contracting Authority taking over the facility at the end of the contract), accounting rules required the facility to be treated as the Contracting Authority's own asset, meaning that the debt and equity financing should appear as liabilities in government accounts. Thus the term Unitary Charge emphasizes that the Service Fee cannot be split in this way. This particular accounting treatment no longer applies, but the term has continued to be used in Britain and some other countries.

[15] Also known as the 'Service Commencement Date', 'Service Availability Date' or 'Commercial Acceptance'.

- *Design & construction*: a school, say, must have *x* classrooms of a certain size, a dining hall, sports facilities, and so on. The Contracting Authority does not usually specify the detailed design of the school beyond these basic requirements, and it is for the Project Company to come up with what it considers to be the best and most cost-effective way of meeting the requirements, a driver for this being that this type of contract is usually the subject of a competitive bidding process (*cf.* §3.7). This means that if there is a defect in the design which requires remedy after the school has been built, the Project Company has to sort out any resulting problems.
- *Performance/services*: Similarly the Project Agreement will not specify how maintenance needs to be carried out, or how day-to-day services such as security, cleaning and catering (if part of the contract) are to be organized. It is up to the Project Company to ensure that these are done so as to meet the performance requirements.

The Output Specification needs to specify *what* is to be achieved, but not *how* it is to be achieved. A useful mnemonic is that the Output Specification must be 'SMART', *i.e.*

S*pecific* – **M***easurable* – **A***chievable* – **R***ealistic* – **T***imely.*[16]

Table 6.1 gives an example of how this works in the context of a PPP school.

The reason for this 'output' approach is that if the Contracting Authority designed the facility and told the Project Company everything it had to do (an 'input' approach—commonly used in normal public procurement not involving PPPs), but the design is flawed, or the instructions create extra costs, the Project Company would claim for these against the Contracting Authority, which obviously means that the Contracting Authority would not be effectively transferring these risks to the private sector.

§6.4.3 AVAILABILITY

Availability is relatively easy to measure if a specific piece of equipment or service is being provided—(*e.g.* a transportation system, an air-traffic control system, or flight-training simulator) but more difficult to measure, for a public-service building such as a prison, hospital, or school, or a number of buildings such as

---

[16] Edward Farquharson, Clemencia Torres de Mästle & E.R. Yescombe with Javier Encinas, *How to Engage with the Private Sector in Public-Private Partnerships in Emerging Markets* (World Bank/ PPIAF, Washington DC, 2011),* p. 34 and Table 4.1.

Table 6.1 SMART Output Specification

	SMART	Not SMART
Specific	Build school to conform to Ministry of Education standard	Build school to good standard
Measurable	Ensure school is structurally sound, with adequate ventilation, lighting and thermal comfort	Ensure school is suitable for teaching
Achievable	Ensure school can maintain internal temperature at X° when outside temperature is between Y° and Z°	Ensure internal temperature is always maintained at X°
Realistic	Ensure faults with heating system are rectified within 8 hours in school hours and 16 hours outside school hours	Ensure faults with heating system are rectified within 2 hours
Timely	Maintain log of faults and report every month	Provide annual report on performance

accommodation units. There are a variety of reasons which could cause all or part of a building to be considered unavailable, such as:

- lack of heating, lighting, water, or other utilities;
- failure of key equipment, communications, or information technology (IT) infrastructure;
- failure to provide any other specified element required to keep the building or facility in operation;
- non-compliance with legal obligations (*e.g.* health and safety regulations);
- any other inability to use any part of the building or facility.

Calculation of the *pro rata* share of this loss of Availability and hence the penalty payable is complex (and very project-specific) if part of the building or facility provided may still be available or usable for part of its required purposes, and if some parts of the building or facility are more important than others.

Table 6.2 is a simplified example of this kind of calculation for a PFI school. The first column sets out the various different types of space within the school; the second column shows the number of spaces of this type (so there are 20 standard classrooms, for example); the third column shows the weighting to be attributed to each type of space so that, for example, a classroom has twice the weighting of the staff room, and four times the weighting of a storage room. The 'number' and 'weighting' columns are multiplied together to derive the number of 'Service Units' for the project as a whole, and the latter are added up to give the total number of Service Units in a school. Penalties—deductions from the Service Fee[17]—are based

---

[17] Also known as abatements.

Table 6.2 Availability Weighting for a PFI School

Area	Number	Weighting	Service Units
Storage rooms	5	1	5
Staff room	1	2	2
Standard classrooms	20	4	80
Laboratories, art rooms, *etc.*	3	6	18
Sports facilities	2	6	12
Assembly hall	1	10	10
Kitchen, dining hall	2	10	20
		Total	**147**

on the number of Service Units affected—thus if a classroom is out of action for one day, the deduction for it not being Available could be 1/365th of the annual Service Fee ÷ 147 × 4.

It is possible to go beyond this system and have a system of Service Units which could theoretically lead to more than 100% deduction from the Service Fee. So in Table 6.2 a classroom could have a weighting of 5, but the number of Service Units remains 147. Similar increases could apply to other weightings considered to be crucial to the operation of the school. This is to incentivize the Project Company to remedy the problem quickly. Also there may be different weightings for availability during term time and school holidays, the former obviously being more important.

§6.4.4 PERFORMANCE

In addition to the basic availability requirements, there will also be requirements for a certain quality of service (*i.e.* a performance régime). Broadly speaking, availability relates to the fundamental core of the service requirements, whereas performance measurement deals with issues which are not covered by the basic availability requirements. There may be an overlap between availability and performance: double-counting is obviously not appropriate so particular failures need to be allocated under only one category.

As with availability, measurement of service performance may be highly complex, with a requirement to specify standards of performance in great detail. These specifications are often called Key Performance Indicators ('KPIs'). KPIs are normally monitored through a Performance Management System ('PMS'), under which the Project Company has to report performance against KPIs on a regular basis. Examples of KPIs which relate to a Availability-based Contract for a road could include:

- safety (based on number of injury crashes per vehicle kilometer);
- surface texture depth; roughness; rutting; skid resistance, patching *etc.*;
- dirt on highway;
- litter and debris;
- landscaping;
- incident management/responsiveness (*e.g.* how quickly the road is cleared after an accident).

The KPI requirements usually involve reaching a measurable standard, *e.g.* for a building:

- accommodation is available during set time periods;
- repair/maintenance requests are actioned within a set time limit;
- lifts operate when the accommodation is available;
- cleaning is carried out to a set standard at agreed intervals;
- fire and other safety equipment is maintained and regularly tested.

A 'help desk' usually has to be made available by the Project Company as a point of contact for the building's users to report problems. Poor service will incur 'Performance Points' based on the KPI weightings, rather than an immediate deduction from the PPP Contract as for Unavailability. There is often a 'ratcheting' mechanism whereby:

- more Performance Points may be imposed, *pro rata*, the longer the problem persists or the more frequently it occurs;
- accumulation of Performance Points eventually leads to a Service Fee deduction;
- deductions typically will be calibrated to cost slightly more than the cost of keeping to the required KPI standard; and
- if this accumulation passes a very high level such that there is a persistent failure of service, the PPP Contract may be terminated (*cf.* §7.10.1).

There is usually a self-reporting régime, *i.e.* the Project Company has to report PMS failures by the Building-Services Sub-Contractor to the Contracting Authority (*cf.* §7.4.3), with this reporting system being audited by the Contracting Authority as felt necessary. This is because it would be too expensive for the Contracting Authority to keep people on site constantly monitoring what is going on.

But it has to be borne in mind that Maintenance or Building-Services Sub-Contractors, who are likely to be the main parties whose actions affect performance standards, earn limited fees and cannot fund large penalties—a cleaner cannot pay for the whole school being unavailable due to bad cleaning—and the Project

Company is not normally in a financial position to assume a greater liability than its Sub-Contractor. Typically the maximum penalties for performance failures amount to two years'-worth of the relevant Sub-Contractor's fees. If this point is reached, the Project Company may be required to replace the Sub-Contractor to avoid a default under the Project Agreement.

In some cases Contract Payments may be made for achieving performance objectives, rather than deducted for failing to achieve them, *e.g.* congestion-management payments for an Availability-based Contract for a road.

§6.4.5 BENCHMARKING AND MARKET-TESTING BUILDING-SERVICES COSTS

If the operating costs are higher than expected, this does not usually result in any change in the Service Fee. Having said this, however, a process of review of Building-Services costs against the market ('benchmarking'), or direct 'market-testing' of the costs by calling for competitive bids, may take place at intervals (say every 5 years). Insofar as the costs that emerge from this review are higher or lower than the originally agreed base costs, the Service Fee is adjusted accordingly.

The main argument for this procedure is that service providers are reluctant to sign up to long-term agreements, since their main costs are likely to relate to staff, and these costs do not necessarily go up with CPI indexing (*cf.* §7.3.3); conversely, working methods may change over time so the that service can be delivered more efficiently at a lower cost.

It follows that under these procedures either adequate data must be available for benchmarking (which it may not be) or other companies in the market must be prepared to bid even though the current incumbent is in a preferred position and (if also one of the Project Company's investors) may seek to impose undue risk transfer or other onerous terms on its Sub-Contractor. (The cost of the services concerned also obviously has to be separately identifiable in the financial model—*cf.* §13.6.)

This procedure is unlikely to be appropriate in relation to maintaining long-life assets under a Maintenance Contract, as it encourages a short-term view of maintenance of such assets (*cf.* §9.7.5). One of the key benefits of a PPP is that it transfers long-term maintenance risks to the private sector (and also ensures that maintenance is in fact carried out, which is often not the case in public-sector buildings). This leaves the Project Company's investors able to make choices such as incurring more capital cost in construction to reduce long-term maintenance costs, and so stimulates innovation by the private sector.

The alternative approach to Building Services is for the Contracting Authority to exclude them from the Project Agreement and sign separate short-term outsourcing contracts (*cf.* §6.6; §8.4). However this may create 'interface' issues, since, for example, how a facility is cleaned on a day-to-day basis is also likely to affect its long-term maintenance requirements.

§6.4.6 SHADOW TOLLS

Apart from Availability-based Contracts, the PFI Model also include projects in which usage risk is taken by the Project Company, a common example of this being that of the Contracting Authority paying 'Shadow' Tolls (or fares). Payment by the Contracting Authority instead of the end-users (payments by the latter being known as 'real' tolls in this context), is used in cases where:

- direct levying of tolls would be too complex because, for example, of the layout of connecting roads;
- traffic flows would be distorted by drivers using unsuitable roads to avoid paying the tolls;
- traffic flows are too small to produce an adequate level of toll payments;
- there is public opposition to payment of tolls;
- the project involves part of an integrated transport system (*e.g.* a mass transit system) and therefore usage of the part of the system provided by the Project Company cannot be directly charged for separately;
- it is considered inappropriate to transfer the full usage (traffic) risk to the private sector.

In this case the Project Company is paid according to usage (*e.g.* so much per passenger or car kilometer). The payment formula is often on a diminishing sliding scale (*i.e.* the highest rate is paid for the first x car kilometers, then a lower rate for the next y car kilometers, and eventually payment may be zero for the top band of usage). This structure serves two purposes:

- The first band of payment, which is based on a relatively low level of usage risk, covers the Project Company's operating costs and debt service (this may be split into two bands).
- The second band of payment provides the equity return to the investors (again this may be split into bands providing a basic return and a bonus return).
- Once usage has exceeded the level from which payments cover operating costs, debt service and equity return the government's liability is capped (*i.e.* the marginal cost to the public sector above this level is zero).

The problem with this methodology, however, is that very little traffic risk is typically taken by the investors and lenders—*i.e.* bidders tend to link most of the Shadow-Toll payments to vehicles in the lower band levels.[18] Balanced against this, since the risks are lower the Contract Payments will also be lower than

---

[18] *Cf.* §9.6.2 for a further discussion on transferring traffic risk to the private sector.

a Concession toll road. But given the limited risk transfer, Availability-based Contracts more commonly used for PFI-Model transport projects.

Note that this structure does not prevent 'real' tolls being charged to users (perhaps as part of a general system of tolling involving other roads in the public sector): these can be collected by the Project Company on behalf of the Contracting Authority, within the scope of a Shadow Toll-based Project Agreement. Shadow-Toll Project Agreements often give the Contracting Authority to impose real tolls on the road.

§6.5 CONCESSION AGREEMENT

A Concession Agreement is a Project Agreement between a Project Company and a Contracting Authority, under which, in return for designing, building, financing and operating a project to provide or upgrade public infrastructure, the Project Company may levy User Charges, *i.e.* tolls, fares, or other payments by users of the project. Ownership of the project remains in the public sector, with the Project Company having a license or lease to use it for the term of the Concession Agreement, after which it is to be returned to the Contracting Authority.

Examples of Concession Agreements include projects for construction (or upgrade) and operation of:

- a toll road, bridge, or tunnel for which the public pays tolls;
- a transportation system (*e.g.* a railway or metro) for which the public pays fares;
- ports and airports, usually with payments made by airlines or shipping companies.

The nexus of Project Contracts surrounding a Concession Agreement, which is a long-established PPP structure, is set out in Figure 2.2. The key difference from the PFI Model is that in the case of a Concession the Project Company is taking the usage risk (but *cf.* §6.4.6).

§6.5.1 USER CHARGES

User Charges are based on the estimated revenues required to cover the project's fixed and variable costs, in a similar way to the Service Fee for a PFI-Model project (*cf.* §6.4.1). The key difference is of course that the total revenue is not fixed, but will vary with usage.

A maximum User Charge is often set, with indexation for inflation (*cf.* §7.3.3; §10.4) and currency movements if appropriate (*cf.* §10.5), within which the Project Company has flexibility to fix User Charges, but subject to provisions preventing discrimination against any particular class of user. But this would not prevent, say, higher tolls being charged for a truck than a car in a toll highway: such differentials may also be set out in the Concession Agreement. Similarly tolls may vary by time of day—*e.g.* a road toll may be higher during rush hours.

The Concession Agreement has to make provision for enforcement of payment of User Charges: this may require the police to stop and arrest drivers who have not paid the tolls, or give the Project Company the right to pursue offenders in the courts. (Note that the Project Company may have to pay for the cost of policing the concession.)

§6.5.2 COMPETITION

Some Concession Agreements may not fix the User Charges in advance, but rely on competition to ensure that they remain reasonable. Obviously there has to be real competition for this to work, as could be the case, for example, where there is a parallel free road of reasonable quality, or another seaport which can be used instead of a port which is the subject of a Concession Agreement.

On the other hand if the tolls are fixed, competition from competing modes of transport is often an issue in Concession Agreements. For example if the Contracting Authority builds a new (free) road which takes vehicles away from a concession road, it may have to compensate the Project Company for loss of revenue. The problem with this is that it may inhibit the Contracting Authority's long-term planning for the road or other transportation network, and in the worst case the Contracting Authority may have to buy back the concession (*cf.* §9.6.3).

§6.5.3 REVENUE SHARING

If traffic is well above the originally agreed projections, the Contracting Authority may require a share of the excess revenue derived from this. This principle is especially important if the Contracting Authority is providing any financial support for the project (*cf.* §15.18).

Such 'upside sharing' should be based on gross revenues, rather than other measures such as the investors' rate of return, since it is rather easy for the latter to be manipulated to the Contracting Authority's disadvantage (*e.g.* by inflating costs and so reducing the apparent rate of return).

§6.5.4 USER ISSUES

'Customer service' is somewhat more important in a Concession, since users are paying for their use of the facility and therefore expect more of it. Service standards are of course included in the Concession Agreement, with penalties for failure to achieve these. There also needs to be a mechanism to resolve disputes (*e.g.*

on electronic billing) between a user and the Project Company. 'Customer satisfaction', measured by surveys as well as more objective measures (*e.g.* *x*% of calls should be answered in *y* minutes) will be one of the KPIs.

§6.5.5 Other Terms

Matters such as Service Commencement, the Output Specification, availability and performance requirements, are dealt with in a similar way to an Availability-based Project Agreement, save that instead of deductions from payments by the Contracting Authority, penalties are payable by the Project Company from its User-Charge revenue.

§6.6 OTHER 'PPP-LIKE' CONTRACTS

There is no fixed definition of a PPP. Typically the definitions vary between a 'narrow' meaning, as used in this book—*i.e.* a long-term contract in which the private sector designs, builds, finances and operates the project—and a 'wide' meaning which includes other types of contract between the public and private sector.[19] The narrow meaning may cover both Concessions and PFI-Model PPPs, or the term PPP may only be used for PFI-Model Contracts, with Concessions used for all user-paid contracts. Examples of contracts which may be included in the 'wide' meaning are:

> **Franchise-*Affermage-Lease*.** A Franchise contract[20] is similar to a Concession in many respects, the key difference being that existing public infrastructure, for example a toll road, or parking facilities, is transferred to a Project Company which then becomes responsible for operating and maintenance project, and collects the tolls or fares for its own account. Thus a Franchise does not involve construction of new infrastructure (although there may be a requirement for upgrading it over time). The Project Company, as Franchisee, usually pays an up-front lump sum to the Contracting Authority, which represents its view of the net present value (*cf.* §10.2.1) of the future cash flow of the project, and which may be covered by a project-finance loan. An example of a Franchise is the 'privatization' of a toll road—*i.e.* the Contracting Authority allows a Project Company to operate the road

---

[19] To add to the confusion, the term PPP is also used for aid-related programs, *e.g.* PPPs for malaria control. The PPPs discussed here are sometimes known as 'PPPs for infrastructure' ('PPPI') to reduce this confusion.

[20] The distinctions in usage of the terms Franchise, *Affermage* and Lease are very confused.

and collect tolls for a period years in the same way as in a Concession Agreement, in return for a lump-sum payment.[21]

An *Affermage* contract[22] is similar to a Franchise: contracts have been used in France since the 19th century, *e.g.* for water provision; the term of such contracts varies between around 7 to 14 years, *i.e.* much shorter than a PPP Contract, and would not normally involve any new investment.

Affermage contracts often include a requirement for the Project Company to set aside funds from its income for future investment and hand these over to the Contracting Authority.

A lease contract, in this context (which differs from a financial lease—*cf.* §4.5.2), again gives the lessee the right to generate income from an asset over a period of years—but in some cases income is not generated from users but from annual payments by the Contracting Authority.

These types of project are a less risky form of Concession, as there are no construction-phase risks, but there is demand and/or risk (and the Project Company has to meet output targets, *e.g.* to reduce losses from water pipes).

Forfaiting. This structure is used in some European countries, *e.g.* Germany, Italy and Spain. Either 100% of the construction cost is repaid by the Contracting Authority after Project Completion, or it is paid over a period of years, so that in either case finance is only needed for the construction phase. In cases where the construction cost is not repaid immediately, the Construction Contractor (who will be the sole Sponsor—there is usually no equity since this type of contract is akin to normal public procurement) can transfer these claims on the Contracting Authority to a lender and so recover its costs and profit. Obviously the project then goes on the public-sector balance sheet, and there is no long-term capital at risk (although the Project Company may continue to take risks on operating costs). This structure is adopted when the government wishes to defer taking the project into the public accounts (and hence showing the related debt) until it is completed.

Institutional PPPs.[23] These are contracts for the operation of existing public infrastructure in which both the Contracting Authority and private-sector investors invest in the Project Company's equity, and the latter is actively involved in the management of the Project Company. The private-sector

---

[21] However if the service provided under the project cannot produce a positive cash flow then the reverse would be the case—the Contracting Authority pays the Project Company (*cf.* §15.10).

[22] There is no modern English equivalent for the French word *affermage* (the old English meaning of 'farming' as in 'tax farming' is equivalent to the French). It is sometimes translated as a 'delegated service contract', which is a direct translation into English of a French legal term for this contract.

[23] May be described as a joint venture.

investors usually bid to purchase part of the equity of the Project Company from the Contracting Authority. This is typically seen in cases where the project has already been built, and so is similar to a Franchise, the differences being that the Contracting Authority remains a shareholder, and debt may also not be required or already be in place.

Provision of Public Property. This may be used, *e.g.* where a developer builds a new school in return for being allowed to build apartments on part or all of the site occupied by the old school. Here there is no long-term contractual arrangement—once construction is complete the contract end. Similarly public land may be provided to a private developer, *e.g.* for construction of a tourist hotel, with the revenues from the hotel being shred between the public and private sector. Here the developer will typically require finance but on a real-estate rather than project-finance basis. Another variant of this would be the developer upgrading public property, *e.g.* a railway station, in return for being able to include shops and other commercial space in the new station.

Service Contract.[24] This takes place when the public sector contracts with a private-sector party to carry out a service function on its behalf. This may include building or other services which might otherwise form part of a PPP Contract (*cf.* §6.4.5; §8.4).

Management Contract. This relates to private-sector management of an already-completed facility, typically in the social infrastructure sector. There is no private-sector capital at risk in this type of contract (although the management fee may include incentive payments), and hence no project finance is required.

A further development of this is a 'GOCO'—government-owned, (private-sector) contractor-operated Project Company. This does not involve project finance or capital at risk for the private sector, as the contractor in this case is paid a management fee, albeit with some incentives based on efficiency.

Design and Build Contract. Even a D&B Contract may be called a PPP, on the grounds that it transfers risk to the private sector.

The term 'performance-based contracting' is sometimes used to cover both the narrow PPP definition and some or all of the other types of contract above. The key point for the purposes of this book is that none of these contracts involve project finance (and are usually much shorter-term than PPPs), other than some cases of Franchise-*Affermage-Lease*.

---

[24] Also known as outsourcing.

COMMON ASPECTS OF PROJECT AGREEMENTS

§7.1 INTRODUCTION

Chapter 6 having dealt with the particular features of an Offtake Contract, Availability-based Contract and Concession Agreement, this Chapter covers issues which are common to any of these types of Project Agreement, namely:

- Contract Term (§7.2);
- Payment Mechanism (§7.3);
- Contract monitoring by the Offtaker/Contracting Authority (§7.4);
- Performance bonding and other guarantees (§7.5);
- Compensation Events (§7.6);
- Excusing Causes (§7.7);
- Relief Events (§7.8);
- Step-In by the Offtaker/Contracting Authority (§7.9);
- Termination (§7.10);
- Change of ownership (§7.11);
- Dispute resolution (§7.12).

129

Principles of Project Finance. DOI: http://dx.doi.org/10.1016/B978-0-12-391058-5.00007-2

In some civil-law countries (*e.g.* Spain, Portugal or in Latin America), some aspects of Project Agreements with a Contracting Authority are not set out in the Project Agreement itself, as they are covered by the general law. This can apply, for example, to provisions for early termination (*cf.* §7.10).

§7.2 TERM

The term (*i.e.* duration) of the Project Agreement is normally a fixed period from signature, leaving the Project Company to bear the risk of loss of revenue from a later Project Completion but take the benefit, if any, of an earlier one. However it may sometimes be measured from Project Completion, subject to a back-stop date (*i.e.* the term is calculated from this back-stop date even if the project is completed later).

Various factors influence the term of the Project Agreement, as set out below.

§7.2.1 USEFUL LIFE OF THE PROJECT

Clearly there is little value in continuing to pay for a product or service from a project that can no longer operate safely, effectively, or efficiently, and so the useful life of the project sets the maximum term of the Project Agreement. If the project mainly involves provision of equipment, such as a PPA this is likely to be a limiting factor.

However many infrastructure projects do not relate to an asset which has a limited life—a road for example. In such cases the useful life of the project is not relevant.

§7.2.2 AFFORDABILITY

If the Project Agreement runs for a comparatively short period, the debt must be repaid and the investors must secure their return over this shorter period, which could force up the cost of the product or service from the project to an uneconomic level *i.e.* the 'Affordability' of the Contract Payments is affected by the term. Conversely, if the Project Agreement has a longer term, the cost of the product or service should be lower. For example, to repay an investment of 1000 over 15 years at 7% costs 109.8 *p.a.*, but to repay 1000 over 25 years costs 85.8 *p.a.*

§7.2.3 TERM OF THE DEBT

The debt term is obviously a product, first of all, of how long the lenders are willing to lend for (*cf.* §12.5.1). Some debt markets may not offer very long-term loans.

Also, if the Project Agreement runs for much longer than the debt the investors may make windfall profits at the Offtaker/Contracting Authority's expense from refinancing the debt already paid for in the Contract Payments (*cf.* §14.16.1).

Therefore the ideal term is probably about 1–2 years longer than the expected term of the debt, to leave lenders with a 'Debt Tail' (*cf.* §12.3.4).

§7.2.4 EQUITY RETURN

The period over which the investors recover their investment is also relevant. Investors usually look not only at their rate of return, but also the period over which they make this return on investment (*cf.* §12.2.4). Clearly if the investors want to recover their return over 15 years there is likely to be little point in signing a 25-year contract. There needs to be a continuing financial incentive for investors over the whole life of the project: if most of their return is earned in the early years this incentive obviously does not exist in the later years.

§7.2.5 RESIDUAL VALUE

In a Reverting Asset-based Contract, the Offtaker/Contracting Authority may be happy with a shorter term for the Project Agreement since the project is taken over at the end of the term and the Offtaker/Contracting Authority can thus benefit from its residual value (*i.e.* ability to continue to operate efficiently and profitably) at that time. However the project still has to be paid for, and a shorter term may make the payments unaffordable (*cf.* §7.2.2).

Conversely, in a Non-Reverting Asset-based Contract, the Offtaker/Contracting Authority loses this residual value, and a longer-term contract may therefore be preferable; alternatively the Project Company may build an assumed residual value into the Contract Payments and so reduce them below a level that fully recovers debt service and the investors' return, thus producing a lower level of Contract Payments than would otherwise have been the case, while taking the risk that the project assets cannot be redeployed or sold at the end of the Project Agreement (*cf.* §7.10.9).

§7.2.6 FLEXIBILITY

Making major changes in a Project Agreement is a difficult and expensive process (*cf.* §7.6.3), and the longer its term the more difficult it is for the Offtaker/Contracting Authority to be sure that its requirements will not change. For example, possible future changes in technology may make it inefficient to have a very long term in certain types of a Project Agreement for provision of IT services, unless the Project Agreement allows for upgrading and renewal of the technology concerned (which is quite difficult to document). Similarly, a school or hospital may need to be expanded with construction of a new building. So the need for long-term flexibility in relation to the project also needs to be considered.

§7.2.7 'Whole-life' Benefits

If the term of the Project Agreement is too short, the Offtaker/Contracting Authority may lose its whole-life benefits, *i.e.* the risk transfer of maintenance and renewal costs to the Project Company (*cf.* §9.7.5). It clearly would not be beneficial for the Project Agreement to terminate just before a major maintenance or lifecycle renewal is due.

§7.2.8 Tax Efficiency

The term of a Project Agreement may be affected by a desire on the Project Company's (or its investors) part to take advantage of tax depreciation. In the U.S., Franchises of highways have had terms of 75–99 years—much longer than would be desirable based on the issues set out above—because this gives the Project Company ownership of the highway for tax purposes, so allowing its cost to be written off against tax on an accelerated basis over 15 years (*cf.* §13.7.1). The effect of this is to greatly reduce tax liabilities in the early years of the project, so improving the investors' return.

§7.2.9 Variable Term

Another approach is to fix a maximum term for the Project Agreement, but if the debt is repaid and the investors have attained an agreed rate of return, the Project Agreement may be terminated at that point. If traffic growth, for example, is well over the original projections, this is probably not due to the merit of the individual project but a factor of growth in the whole regional and national economy; therefore investors should not earn excessive profits from this.[1]

§7.3 PAYMENT MECHANISM

Again there are several key principles which generally apply to the Payment Mechanism, as set out below.

§7.3.1 Payment on Project Completion

Usually no payments are due under the Payment Mechanism until Project Completion is completed, in conformity with the requirements of the Project Agreement. There can be exceptions to this, however, *e.g.* if a project is being built in stages then *pro rata* Contract Payments may be payable as each stage is complete.

---

[1] In this context *cf.* §9.6.2 for the 'Present Value of Revenues' model.

§7.3.2 Level Payments

There may be a temptation to make the Contract Payments lower in the early years of the Project Agreement, and raise them later, especially if an Offtaker/Contracting Authority has short-term budget constraints. However this is generally undesirable, since it would make the next generation pay an unfairly large share of the project's costs. Moreover, it will probably not fit in with the kind of debt-service schedule required by lenders (*cf.* §12.5.2).

Conversely, Sponsors may try to 'front load' the Contract Payments to recover their equity return faster. This is also generally undesirable as it leaves the Offtaker/ Contracting Authority potentially exposed to the Project Company's investors having a much lower commitment to the operation of the project in the later years of the Project Agreement, by which time the lenders' involvement will also have reduced.

Similarly, as the Contract Payments reflect, *inter alia*, the debt that the Project Company has raised, it might be thought that they could be allowed to reduce sharply in the later years of the contract, reflecting the repayment of the debt, but the same issues of long-term commitment and capital at risk by investors and lenders also apply here.

In principle, therefore, Contract Payments should remain the same—*i.e.* there should be 'level' payments—over the life of the Project Agreement, subject to indexation for inflation (see below).

§7.3.3 Inflation Indexation

However a proportion of the Contract Payments are normally indexed (*i.e.* increased over time against an agreed inflation index), so that in this respect Contract Payments are not level (but *cf.* §10.4.1).

For example, in a PPA, Capacity Charge payments are dealt with as follows:

- *Fixed operating costs*: indexed as appropriate against the consumer price index (CPI) or industry price indices in the country where the relevant costs are to be incurred, or in limited respects may be based on actual costs (*e.g.* for insurance);
- *Debt service*: not normally indexed;
- *Equity return*: may be fixed or indexed against CPI.

If any of the fixed operating costs are to be incurred in a foreign currency, or if the equity or debt is raised in a foreign currency, calculations of the Contract Payments may be made in that currency to that extent. In such cases payments normally continue to be made in the local currency, but are indexed against the exchange rate with the foreign currency concerned (*cf.* §10.5.1).

In a PPP, and similar types of contract where there is an Energy Charge, and this is calculated based on actual fuel costs, no further indexation is required. In some cases the Energy Charge may be based on a published index for the cost of the fuel concerned, and in which case the Project Company takes the risk of not being able to obtain fuel at this price.

Similar principles apply to other types of Project Agreement—inflation indexation of Contract Payments should only relate to the proportion of total project costs which are themselves subject to inflation, *i.e.* primarily operating costs (*cf.* §10.4).

There can be some timing problems with indexation, since economic indices are often published after a considerable lag, and hence there may be a need for retrospective adjustment of Contract Payments to catch up with such indices. If foreign-currency adjustments are being made, it may be also necessary to take account of the exchange-rate movements between the time the monthly Contract Payment bill is calculated and presented, and when it is finally paid.

Other adjustments that may be made to the Contract Payments are discussed in §7.6.

§7.3.4 THIRD-PARTY REVENUE

Some projects may also generate revenue from sources other than Contract Payments:

- A CHP project may sell steam (*i.e.* heat) to an industrial company.
- A waste-incineration project may generate electricity for sale, and also sell steam, in addition to charging a Contracting Authority for disposal of its waste.
- A school may hire out its buildings to community users outside school hours or in school holidays.
- A hospital may charge for visitors' car parking, and generate income from visitors to its canteen.

This can be beneficial for an Offtaker/Contracting Authority since these other revenues may be used to subsidize its Contract Payments, or at least third-party income above an agreed level may be divided between the Project Company and the Offtaker/Contracting Authority.

But in general lenders are reluctant to attribute much value to an income source which cannot be predicted, and so would only include this in their cash-flow projections on a conservative basis, meaning that they would not lend much against such elements of the overall cash flow.

In the case of CHP projects there is also a risk that the steam offtaker may close down its plant, so leaving no customer for the steam. In this case lenders generally take the view that this waste steam can be converted into electricity, and thus will take into account a minimum revenue level based on their view of long-term electricity prices.

In some types of project, typically Concessions, there may be surplus land which should increase in value when the project is complete, *e.g.* property adjacent to a new road. Contracting Authorities sometimes try to realize value from this surplus land in advance by including it in the Concession and allowing the Project Company to build facilities for fuel sales, restaurants, shops, offices, *etc.* on this adjacent land, the revenues from which can subsidize the User Fess in the Concession. Even assuming the Sponsors are willing to assume the risk of such ancillary projects, the lenders are unlikely to attribute much value to them in their cash-flow projections, and hence it is generally better for the Contracting Authority to deal with such land separately.

§7.4 CONTRACT MONITORING BY THE OFFTAKER/ CONTRACTING AUTHORITY

An Offtaker/Contracting Authority has to put an appropriate contract monitoring place after Financial Close, bearing in mind that it is the Project Company that actually manages the project. This obviously needs to change over time as the project develops. Issues to be taken into account in setting up this system include:

- design and construction (§7.4.1);
- operation (§7.4.2);
- relationship with Sub-Contractors (§7.4.3);
- relationship with lenders (§7.4.4).

§7.4.1 DESIGN AND CONSTRUCTION

The Project Company is fully responsible for designing the project to meet the required specifications, arranging construction to meet the required Project Completion date, and ensuring that the construction meets the Output Specifications. The Offtaker/Contracting Authority must specify the product or service required in sufficient detail to ensure what is required is constructed but the way in which it is constructed is primarily the Project Company's responsibility; the Offtaker/Contracting Authority should satisfy itself that the way proposed is viable before signing the Project Agreement.

Having said this, the Offtaker/Contracting Authority's experience elsewhere may be helpful when detailed design or construction issues are being considered, and it is therefore not unreasonable for the Offtaker/Contracting Authority to have the right to review designs, visit the site, inspect the works, and be kept informed on progress, since the Offtaker/Contracting Authority clearly has an interest in ensuring that the project is designed and constructed to the agreed specifications.[2] A 'project committee' may be set up with representatives from the Offtaker/Contracting Authority and the Project Company, as a forum for such issues (but this committee must be just a forum, not a decision-making body). However it is up to the Project Company whether it takes any comments or suggestions by the Offtaker/Contracting Authority into account or not. If these comments or suggestions were transformed into an approval process, or if the Offtaker/Contracting Authority were to insist on approval of any aspect of the design or construction, it follows that the Project Company should not be penalized if, after relying on such approvals, things later go wrong, so the Offtaker/Contracting Authority would have to take back some of the construction risk (*cf.* §9.5).

In some cases an Independent Engineer[3] may be appointed jointly by the Project Company and the Offtaker/Contracting Authority, to approve and certify each stage of design and construction. This is more common in Concessions, *i.e.* where the Contracting Authority will not use the site itself, as in the latter case the Contracting Authority will want to have some say in the acceptance process on completion. (*cf.* §5.5.3 for the rôle during construction of the Lenders' Engineer, and §8.2.4 for that of the Project Company.)

§7.4.2 OPERATION

The nature of contact monitoring at this stage obviously varies greatly depending on the type of project. In the case of a process-plant project this is a relatively simple exercise, whereas monitoring performance in as Accommodation-based Contract is far more complex. As a first step the Offtaker/Contracting Authority procurement team should put together an 'operating manual' for the contract monitoring team (*cf.* §3.6.3 for the similar exercise by the Project Company).

The monitoring system needs to be set out in the Project Agreement—monitoring availability should be straightforward because the Contracting Authority is directly affected by lack of availability; but monitoring performance is likely to be more complex. Typically a complex performance régime is monitored by the Project Company, which reports to the Contracting Authority, with the latter having the right to receive and review all data. A significant element of performance monitoring may involve reports by the users of the project, rather than measurements by the Project Company. The project Company may have the right to make its won spot checks both on actual

---

[2] *Cf.* §8.2.4 for the Project Company's own rôle *vis-à-vis* the Construction Contractor.

[3] Also known as an independent reviewer or certifier, or *maître d'œuvre*.

performance and how this is reported by the Project Company, and clearly failure to monitor performance accurately would itself be a KPI.

§7.4.3 Sub-Contracts

Similarly, while the Offtaker/Contracting Authority should review the terms of other Project Contracts to check that they will enable the Project Company to deliver what is required under the Project Agreement,[4] and monitor their activities thereafter (*cf.* §6.4.4), the Offtaker/Contracting Authority cannot give direct instructions to the Sub-Contractors.

In some cases of early termination of the Project Agreement, compensation may be due to Sub-Contractors (*cf.* §7.10.2): the Offtaker/Contracting Authority needs to ensure that this is reasonable.

The Offtaker/Contracting Authority usually signs Direct Agreements with all major Sub-Contractors, which allow it to take over their contracts and related security if the Project Company defaults (*cf.* §8.11).

§7.4.4 Financing

The same principle applies to financing arrangements, where the primary concern of the Offtaker/Contracting Authority should be to ensure that a credible financing plan is in place that ensures the project is completed (*cf.* §5.6). Otherwise one issue which may affect the viability of the project is the provisions for Project Accounts, such as the amounts required to be held in a Maintenance Reserve Account (*cf.* §14.4.1).

However it may be necessary to control some aspects of the financing, *e.g.* increasing the debt burden, which could jeopardize the viability of the financing (*cf.* §14.16.1) or increasing the Offtaker/Contracting Authority's termination liabilities (*cf.* §7.10).

§7.5 PERFORMANCE BONDING AND OTHER GUARANTEES

The Offtaker/Contracting Authority may require a performance bond[5] from the Project Company as security for Project Completion. However this would normally duplicate what the lenders require the Project Company to obtain from the Construction Contractor (*cf.* §8.2.9), to which the Offtaker/Contracting Authority

---

[4] The adequacy of LDs in the Sub-Contracts (*cf.* §8.2.8) should also be reviewed.

[5] *Cf.* §3.7.9 for bid bonds, and §14.8.1 for conditions-precedent bonds: the same issues apply to these.

has access through the relevant Direct Agreement (*cf.* §8.11), and of course the extra cost would be passed on to the Offtaker/Contracting Authority. Moreover, in most cases the Project Company's main incentive to complete the project on time is that if it does not do so it will lose revenue (*cf.* §7.2). And as mentioned in §7.4.3, if the Project Agreement is terminated early and the lenders do not step in to remedy the situation, the Offtaker/Contracting Authority can take over the security provided to the Project Company by the Construction Contractor though its Direct Agreement.

The same principle applies to requiring a performance bond during the operating phase of the project. Performance bonds are not usually required by lenders for the operating phase of a project. However there may in some cases be an argument for the Offtaker/Contracting Authority requiring a maintenance bond from the Project Company in the last years of the Project Agreement (*cf.* §7.10.7), as the lenders will normally be out of the picture by then.

The Offtaker/Contracting Authority may require a parent-company guarantee for the performance of major Sub-Contractors, assuming they are not substantial enough in their own right—but again this is something best dealt with by the lenders through the Project Company, and there is little point in duplicating such guarantees.

§7.6 COMPENSATION EVENTS

'Compensation Events' give the Project Company a right to reimbursement by an Offtaker/Contracting Authority of additional costs or losses resulting from these events. Insofar as projects risks are retained by the Offtaker/Contracting Authority, then the corollary of this is that the Offtaker/Contracting Authority will have to compensate the Project Company if the risks occur. Typical categories of Compensation Events are:

- breach of obligation by the Offtaker/Contracting Authority (§7.6.1);
- delays in construction (§7.6.2);
- Contract Variations (§7.6.3);
- changes in law (§7.6.4).

Compensation is calculated in such cases on the principle of 'Financial Equilibrium' (§7.6.5).

It should be noted that an adverse change in market conditions (*e.g.* making the cost of labor or equipment much higher than expected) is not normally a Compensation Event, but such costs are usually indexed against inflation during the operating phase of the project (*cf.* §10.4).

§7.6.1 Breach of Obligation

If the Offtaker/Contracting Authority is obliged, *e.g.* to provide access to the site or build a connecting road, and does not do so, and the Project Company suffers a loss of revenue or extra cost caused by the delay, compensation would be payable.

In a similar way, if the Offtaker/Contracting Authority does something which affects the Project Company's revenues—*e.g.* builds a new free road which competes with a Concession road (*cf.* §6.5.2)—again compensation may be payable.

§7.6.2 Delays in Construction

If obtaining key Permits (*cf.* §8.8.1), especially planning permits (*i.e.* permission for the construction of the project to go ahead) is delayed, *e.g.* by an appeal to the courts against the grant of a Permit, the resulting delay in starting construction of the project may be treated wholly or partially as a Compensation Event.

Similarly, discovery of archæological or fossil remains, which holds up construction, may also be treated as a Compensation Event (*cf.* §9.5.2).

§7.6.3 Contract Variations

The Offtaker/Contracting Authority usually has a right to make changes in the specification of the project ('Contract Variations').[6] Some Project Agreements may give a specific right to make a Contract Variation, *e.g.* to convert an oil-fired power plant to gas firing. But usually there are just generic provisions for any kind of variation.

Contract Variations may result in loss of revenue, increased operating costs, or capital expenditure, for which compensation will be due; a Contract Variation can also reduce the Contract Payments, *e.g.* if it results in more efficient working.

A number of key issues arise when discussing Contract Variations and other Compensation Events:

Limitations of the Right to Make Contract Variations. There has to be some reasonable limit on the Offtaker/Contracting Authority's right to make Contract Variations, as both the Project Company and its lenders will have concerns which need to be addressed.
- A Contract Variation may increase the risk inherent in the project in some way, or reduce usage (in the case of a Concession): if so this can only be done with Project Company (and Lender) consent.

---

[6] Also called modifications, Contract Changes or change orders.

- The Contract Variation has to be reasonable in scale—*e.g.* it would not be reasonable for the Offtaker/Contracting Authority to ask for a power station's capacity to be doubled, which is in effect a new project. This is dealt with by restricting the maximum cost of any Contract Variation (or series of Contract Variations), *e.g.* to 10% of the original project cost.

Cost. Capital expenditure arising from a Compensation Event raises some problems of ensuring that the costs which are to be paid by the Offtaker/Contracting Authority are fair and reasonable. If the Project Company's relevant Sub-Contractor is the only party submitting proposals for the required works, there is clearly a problem with ensuring that the price is competitive. There are ways of trying to get round this:

- The price can be 'benchmarked' by comparing it with other comparable projects, costs, in a similar way to Building-Services costs (*cf.* §6.4.5), but this may be quite difficult to do.
- The Project Company may be required to conduct a transparent bidding process for the works—but the existing Sub-Contractor may have such an obvious advantage from its prior knowledge of the project that other bidders may not be interested.

It is also possible for the Project Agreement to lay out in advance the margin over cost to be earned by the Project Company and its Sub-Contractor in carrying out changes. This is then linked to transparency on costs—but lack of competition for the work may still be an issue.

Financing. If extra capital cost is incurred, it will obviously not have been taken into account in the original financing plan—one approach is to require the Project Company to raise additional finance and adjust the Contract Payments accordingly. However there is another monopoly problem here: the existing lenders have to agree to the terms of any new financing, and to any new lenders sharing in their security as this will create intercreditor problems (*cf.* §14.14). *De facto*, therefore, the Project Company can only raise new finance through its existing lenders.

If the lenders are not prepared to provide additional finance, or the Offtaker/Contracting Authority is not happy with the effect the terms offered have on the Contract Payments, then the Offtaker/Contracting Authority has to choose between dropping the Contract Variation proposal, replacing the lenders (an expensive option), or financing the Contract Variation itself.

But even if the lenders do not provide additional financing a Contract Variation may still require their approval (as it may affect their risks), which puts the Offtaker/Contracting Authority at a further disadvantage.

However if bond financing is being used, and a Contract Variation is foreseeable (*e.g.* building an extra lane if the traffic increases), it may be possible to incorporate a right to issue further 'variation bonds' into the financing terms (and subject to the project meeting pre-agreed financial targets at the time). If so, the variation bonds would be issued on the same terms as the original bonds, but initially held by Project Company and when required can be placed in the market on the best available terms (which may mean selling them at a discount, and hence having to issue more than 100 of bonds to cover 100 of expenditure).

'**Small Works' Variations.** The fairly elaborate Contract Variation procedure set out above is obviously overkill if the Contract Variation is fairly minor, *e.g.* to put up a new notice-board in a school, or a coat hook on a door. Therefore if 'small works' changes are likely to be required a quicker and simpler procedure is desirable. This 'small works' procedure would apply to Contract Variations costing less than x, the cost being based on the cost of the item, labor at an agreed hourly rate, and a percentage profit margin for the Project Company. The Offtaker/Contracting Authority then just pays for such Contract Variations as they are made.

Changes during the construction phase should be discouraged—the Offtaker/Contracting Authority should say what it wants and stick to it—but if Contract Variations can be made in this phase, the Project Company needs to ensure that it has a corresponding right to make changes in the Construction Contract specifications.

As can be seen from the above, it is not easy for the Offtaker/Contracting Authority to ensure that significant Contract Variations are carried out and financed in the most cost-effective way. This illustrates the lack of flexibility in a long-term Project Agreement which needs to be considered carefully when deciding its optimum term (*cf.* §7.2.6).

§7.6.4 CHANGES IN LAW

A change in the law or regulations relating to the Project Company's business may involve the Project Company in additional capital or operating costs for which compensation may be payable by the Offtaker/Contracting Authority (*cf.* §11.3).

§7.6.5 FINANCIAL EQUILIBRIUM

The compensation payable to the Project Company by the Offtaker/Contracting Authority for Compensation Events is based on the principle of 'Financial Equilibrium',[7] *i.e.* putting the Project Company and its investors and lenders in a 'no better no worse' position then they were before the Compensation Event happened.

---

[7] Also referred to as 'Financial Balance'.

If the Compensation Event affects revenues or operating costs, the Contract Payments can simply be increased to cover the resulting reduction in the Project Company's net income. Alternatively the term of the Project Agreement may be extended (although it is difficult to do this is a way which retains Financial Equilibrium and is fair to both parties).

If the Compensation Event requires capital investment this can be dealt with in several ways (cf. §7.6.3):

- It can just be financed directly by the Offtaker/Contracting Authority making a lump-sum payment to the Project Company.
- It can be financed by the Project Company raising more debt, covered by a change to the Contract Payments: this can be calculated by changing the Contract Payments in the Base-Case financial model (cf. §13.10) so as to give the investors with the same return as they had originally expected (cf. §12.2), but with respect to the new investment only, and also to leave the lenders with the same cash-flow cover (cf. §12.3).[8]
- Again an extension in the term of the Project Agreement can also be considered but is difficult to quantify in a way which respects Financial Equilibrium—e.g. if the lenders do not extend the term of their loan (which they would not usually do), this distorts the calculation, and can give rise to a windfall profit on refinancing later with a longer term (cf. §14.16).
- For more minor capital costs (but bigger than 'Small Works'), it may be sufficient to agree that they will be repaid through the Contract Payments on an annuity basis (cf. §12.5.3) at an agreed interest rate over the balance of the term of the Project Agreement, if this does not result in a significant payment mismatch between the Project Company and its relevant Sub-Contractor (cf. §9.12) or debt service—or again a lump-sum payment may be the simplest route.

The above applies to a Reverting Asset-based Contract, but the issue becomes more complex where there is a Non-Reverting Asset-based Contract. A full Financial Equilibrium payment as set out above assumes that the Offtaker/Contracting Authority will be the ultimate owner of the project. If this is not the case, the payments set out for capital expenditure above have to be adjusted in proportion between the remaining life of the Project Agreement and the remaining economic life of the relevant project asset, which may be much longer.

---

[8] However the model may not be adequately designed to carry out this calculation, as it will be difficult to provide for all possible permutations of events in advance, and there may be disagreement about how the calculation is to be done in practice. Also in the less-usual situation where the Offtaker/Contracting Authority does not have access to the financial model and the Project Company does not want it to have details of the operating costs and profit (which should be discouraged—cf. §3.7.6) there may be a need to go to arbitration to settle the matter.

§7.7 EXCUSING CAUSES

An 'Excusing Cause' protects the Project Company against penalties or deductions under the Project Agreement (as well as termination). The list of such events is normally very limited, but could include:

- temporary closure of the project facility by agreement with the Offtaker/ Contracting Authority;
- implementation of a Contract Variation or a change in law (*cf.* §7.6.3; §11.3);
- following instructions from the Offtaker/Contracting Authority in an emergency.

§7.8 RELIEF EVENTS

A 'Relief Event' is one which is not the fault of, and cannot be controlled by, any party. In effect, it is a temporary *force majeure* event.[9] Once any damage is repaired or obstruction to construction or operation removed, the project should be able to pick up where it had left off. Designating an event as a Relief Event therefore give the Project Company protection against the termination of the Project Agreement for Project Company default (*cf.* §7.10.1), *e.g.* for failure to complete on time, but does not relieve the Project Company from any loss of income, penalties or deductions under the Project Agreement. (Note that Relief Events are far more common than Excusing Causes.)

Compensation Events (*cf.* §7.6) are said to give the Project Company 'time and money'—*i.e.* time to remedy the problem plus financing to maintain the Financial Equilibrium, whereas Relief Events are said to give the Project Company 'time but no money'—*i.e.* there is no compensation from the Offtaker/Contracting Authority, no Contract Payments will be due if the service is not being provided, and the normal penalties and deductions under the Project Agreement will continue to apply—but the Project Company is not placed in default, and is given extra time to sort the problem out.

However many Relief Events should be covered by insurance, which should put the Project Company back in a position of Financial Equilibrium (*cf.* §8.6).

The coverage of Relief Events is usually much discussed in the negotiations on the various Project Contracts: the Sponsors naturally prefer where possible to have

---

[9] *Force majeure* is French for 'superior force'. (The Latin term meaning the same thing—*vis major*—is also sometimes used.) There is no direct English equivalent to this term. ('Act of God' is more narrow in meaning, as can be seen below.) The term *force majeure* will only be used hereafter for permanent *force majeure* (*cf.* §7.10.4), which has a permanent effect; Relief Event will be used for temporary *force majeure*.

these types of events classified as Compensation Events, but some typical categories of Relief Events are:

- damage to the project by fire, flood, storm, *etc.*
- accidental damage to the project;
- unforeseen ground conditions or discoveries during construction (*cf.* §9.5.2);
- unforeseeable weather conditions;
- delay in obtaining Permits or licenses (*cf.* §9.5.3);
- failure to carry out works by, or relating to, utility suppliers (*cf.* §9.5.9);
- failures in power or other utility supplies;
- national strikes, or strikes at suppliers' plants.

Relief Events in the Project Agreement may or may not be reflected in the Sub-Contracts, depending on the overall risk allocation (*cf.* §8.2.6). If Relief Events delay the required Project Completion date (*cf.* §7.10.1), an extension may be given.

A further twist when considering Relief Events is the possibility that insurance which the parties had originally agreed was appropriate to deal with such events becomes unavailable, or only available on unduly onerous terms. Although this is generally unlikely, this can be a problem in specialist sectors—*e.g.* PPP prisons. In this situation the Offtaker/Contracting Authority usually has a choice—either to act as insurer of last report (deducting the insurance premiums that would otherwise have been paid from the Contract Payments), or terminating the Project Agreement (*cf.* §7.10.4).

Temporary problems affecting an Offtaker/Contracting Authority (*e.g.* Offtaker's grid line going down) do not relieve it from the obligation to pay the Tariff or Service Fee, since the project is obviously still available even if unusable.

§7.9 STEP-IN BY THE OFFTAKER/CONTRACTING AUTHORITY

As an interim measure on a default by the Project Company, the Offtaker/Contracting Authority may also have the right to step in and operate the project itself to ensure continuity of supply or service. A Contracting Authority may also have this right in the case of an national emergency, or on grounds of safety or public security even if the Project Company is not in default (*cf.* §11.4.2).

If the Offtaker/Contracting Authority operates the project, whether the Project Company is in default or not, the Contract Payments normally continue to be payable (after deducting reasonable costs incurred, and any penalties or deductions which apply), and the Offtaker/Contracting Authority must indemnify the Project Company for any damage.

Clearly both investors and lenders will be uneasy about the terms on which such a Step-In right can be allowed, and it has to be coordinated with the lenders' Step-In rights (*cf.* §8.11).

§7.10 TERMINATION OF THE PROJECT AGREEMENT

The Project Agreement may be terminated before the end of its normal term because of a default by the Project Company (§7.10.1) or the Offtaker/Contracting Authority (§7.10.2). The Offtaker/Contracting Authority usually also has an option to terminate the Project Agreement early (§7.10.3). Early termination may also be necessary because a *force majeure* event has made it impossible to complete or continue operating the project (§7.10.4). If the Project Agreement is with a Contracting Authority, provisions for termination for corruption or fraud are also usually required (§7.10.5). Allowance may have to be made for the tax status of any payments on early termination (§7.10.6). Provisions also need to be agreed to for the handover of the project at the end of a contract (§7.10.7).

The issues to be discussed as above assume that the Project Agreement relates to a Reverting Asset-based Contract. In such projects, at the end of the Project Agreement's term the project is transferred to the Offtaker/Contracting Authority for no or a nominal payment. If such a Project Agreement is terminated early, the transfer of ownership[10] is also likely take to place early, because the Offtaker/Contracting Authority will probably wish to take over operation of the project, assuming it can sort out the problems that caused the default.

Therefore, the positions on early termination of a Non-Reverting Asset-based Contract need separate consideration (§7.10.8), as do the various possibilities on the final maturity of such projects (§7.10.9).

§7.10.1 EARLY TERMINATION: DEFAULT BY THE PROJECT COMPANY

Events of default by the Project Company that give the Offtaker/Contracting Authority the right to terminate the Project Agreement should clearly only be of so fundamental a nature that the project is really no longer delivering the product or service required. A short-term failure of availability or performance can generally be dealt with by deductions or penalties rather than a termination. Events that come under the 'fundamental' heading may include:

- failure to develop the project or to operate it for prolonged periods of time (abandonment);
- a Drawstop by the lenders (*cf.* §14.12); this is to ensure that the Offtaker/Contracting Authority will have a relatively early seat at the table if the project is going seriously wrong, but may face lender resistance if the lenders want the ability to sort out the problem by themselves;

---

[10] Or of control, if the Offtaker/Contracting Authority is already the owner of the asset, as would normally be the case in a PPP.

- Project Completion does not take place by an agreed backstop date (typically one year after the scheduled Project Completion),[11] or the Independent Engineer decides that it is not possible for Project Completion to be achieved by this date;
- the project cannot meet minimum required specifications;
- non-payment of penalties;
- penalties or deductions for lack of availability reach more than a certain percentage of the Contract Payments over a period of x months;
- accumulated Performance Points exceed a trigger level;
- other minor breaches (which do not incur Performance Points) keep occurring and the problems have not been rectified despite warning notices from the Public Authority—this is known as 'Persistent Breach' (and is typically very difficult to negotiate);
- breach of any other provisions of the PPP Contract, *e.g.* not taking out insurance, or a major failure to maintain health and safety of the users of the facility subject to a reasonable grace period to remedy the default (unless the failure is a deliberate act by the Project Company);
- insolvency of the Project Company;
- change in the ownership/control of the Project Company without Offtaker/ Contracting Authority consent (*cf.* §7.11).

Default by the Project Company's Sub-Contractors should not be a default under the Project Agreement unless it creates one of the defaults above: basically this is the Project Company's (and its investors' and lenders) problem and they should be left to sort it out—this is result of their having 'capital at risk' (*cf.* §2.6.2).

A key issue in negotiating Project Agreements relating to a Reverting Asset-based Contract is the provisions concerning what happens after a early termination when the Project Company is in default, in particular whether a compensation payment (known as a 'Termination Sum') should be made by the Offtaker/Contracting Authority in all circumstances (as it usually inherits the project), and if so, how this should be calculated. Not surprisingly, lenders have strong views on the matter and may be more concerned about it than the Sponsors, who may take the view that if the Project Company goes into default there will be little or no equity value left in the project anyway. Therefore, even though the lenders are not parties to the Project Agreement, negotiation on this issue may become a dialogue between the lenders and the Offtaker/Contracting Authority, with the Sponsors on the sidelines. Note also that the lenders will normally have Step-In and cure period rights under their Direct Agreement (*cf.* §8.11).

---

[11] This is sometimes called the 'Sunset Date'.

Dealing first with termination for default by the Project Company after the project has started operating, the possibilities of how to deal with this include:

- compensation payable to the Offtaker/Contracting Authority for its loss;
- 'walk away' by the Offtaker/Contracting Authority;
- transfer of the project to the Offtaker/Contracting Authority without payment of any Termination Sum;
- payment by the Offtaker/Contracting Authority of a Termination Sum equal to the outstanding debt;
- sale of the project with its Project Agreement in the open market;
- payment by the Offtaker/Contracting Authority of a Termination Sum based on the estimated value that would be achieved by a market sale as above.

To look at these in more detail:[12]

Compensation for the Offtaker/Contracting Authority's Loss. This might seem the obvious structure if the Project Company has defaulted, and as can be seen below (*cf.* §7.10.8) it may be the first choice for a Non-Reverting Asset project, but since the Project Company is unlikely to have any funds to make this payment it is not usually a practical course of action. Furthermore, how would the Offtaker/Contracting Authority's loss be calculated?

Walk-away by the Offtaker/Contracting Authority. The Offtaker/Contracting Authority may have the right to 'walk away' as for a Non-Reverting Asset project, so it is then up to the Project Company and its lenders to realize some value from the project—but this is unlikely to be an option if the project is providing an essential public service.

No Termination Sum. Default by a Project Company under its Project Agreement once it has begun operations is actually very rare. The most likely scenario is a position where, because of low revenues, the investors have lost hope of any equity return and therefore walk away from their investment and the project. This is probably most likely to apply in the case of a Concession, as a result of over-optimistic usage forecasts. (Thus this approach is taken in Australia, for example, with respect to Concessions, together with a claim for compensation for the Authority.[13])

The argument for a transfer of the project to the Offtaker/Contracting Authority with no Termination Sum payment is that even if the problem that caused the Project Company to default is serious enough to eliminate the equity return and therefore the investors' continuing interest in a solution, the

---

[12] Variants on some of the above are discussed in Chapter 15.

[13] Infrastructure Australia, *National PPP Guidelines*, Vol. 7: "Commercial Principles for Economic Infrastructure" (Canberra, 2011), §24.3; §25.1*.

project can be taken over by the lenders (*e.g.* by exercising their substitution right under the Direct Agreement—*cf.* §8.11), who will do their best to sort it out to protect their loan. Thus since the Project Agreement should never actually terminate, a formula that involves the Offtaker/Contracting Authority in the problem is unnecessary.

The argument against this, given that even a poorly-operating project should have some value, is that it appears unreasonable for the Offtaker/Contracting Authority to get the project for nothing after a default, if this results in a windfall gain at the expense of lenders and investors, however unlikely the possibility.

Payment Equal to Outstanding Debt. A simple approach is for transfer of the project to the Offtaker/Contracting Authority on payment of a Termination Sum equal to the outstanding debt, but with no payment to be made for the equity investment. This of course leaves the investors at risk of losing the whole of their equity investment.

Investors may find this acceptable on the grounds that if the project goes into default there is likely to be little equity value left anyway (and it is preferable in such cases that this debt guarantee should only apply once the project is completed to the required standard). This approach is quite common for projects in developing countries; *e.g.* it was the basis on which the first generation of BOT projects in Turkey (where the term BOT was invented in the 1980s) were undertaken.

It is evident that if outstanding debt is automatically repaid on a Project Company default, the lenders' due diligence, control and general monitoring of the project will be very limited since they are not taking a risk on its failure (*cf.* §15.14).

How Much Debt Should be Repaid? A problem that applies to any Termination-Sum formula involving repayment of debt (see other early Termination scenarios below) is what level of debt should be covered by this payment—the debt originally scheduled to be outstanding at the time of the default, or the actual level at that time? If the project has been having problems it may have failed to repay debt as expected and so have more debt outstanding than expected. Should the Offtaker/Contracting Authority have any responsibility for this? The issue becomes even more acute if extra debt has been incurred through refinancing (*cf.* §14.16), either because the project had done well and so was able to borrow more debt before the termination, or because it had done badly and the lenders had injected more debt to try to save it.

An Offtaker/Contracting Authority expected to cover this extra debt may want the ability to approve it, which both investors and lenders may feel inhibits their ability to deal flexibly with problems should they arise (*cf.* §14.16.4). A compromise may be to allow extra debt up to an agreed limit (say 110% of the originally scheduled amounts), and for amounts above this to be subject to the Offtaker's/Contracting Authority's approval. (If the approval is not given, the debt may be increased anyway, but the Offtaker/Contracting Authority should have no liability for the extra amount on early termination of the Project Agreement, except perhaps in the case of its own default or optional termination—see below.)

Other payments also need to be added to or subtracted from the debt outstanding when this is being repaid by the Offtaker/Contracting Authority:

Accrued unpaid interest (but not any extra penalty interest payable on default);

plus breakage costs for interest rate swaps, fixed-rate debt, or repayment of a floating-rate loan before the interest date (*cf.* §10.3.1, §10.3.4),[14] insofar as these represent real costs to the lenders (*i.e.* prepayment fees or other penalties of this type should not be covered);

minus any breakage profits;

minus any amounts held in Project Accounts (*cf.* §14.4.1) including insurance proceeds—the lenders can recover these amounts directly as they have security over them;

minus the value of any other security held by the lenders (unless this is transferred to the Offtaker/Contracting Authority).

In cases such as this where the Offtaker/Contracting Authority is repaying debt, it may wish to have the option to make the repayment over time, at pricing which reflects the transfer of risk away from the project, so avoiding an immediate and unexpected call on its budget.

Sale in the Market. In the 'market value' approach, the Project Agreement is offered for sale 'as is' for new investors to take over the project, deal with the problems which caused default, and run it as required by the Project Agreement.[15] The sales proceeds, less the cost of organizing the sale, are paid to the Project Company. This obviously assumes that a new owner of the project can sort out whatever caused the Project Company to default.

This clearly exposes both lenders and investors to a much higher risk, and it is quite possible that when the time comes there may not be a real market for the project. Lenders in particular may be concerned that if nobody bids for the project they will recover zero. So this provision may have to be subject to a 'Liquid Market' clause, *i.e.* if there are no potential bidders (or less than *x*—say 3) the sale will not take place and the provisions set out below will apply.

---

[14] This means that any interest rate hedging or fixed-rate borrowing has to be agreed to in advance by the Offtaker/Contracting Authority, as it is responsible for the breakage costs.

[15] This concept was introduced in the first version of SoPC in 1999—again it is now widely used.

Estimated Market Value. As an alternative to market sale, therefore, a formula which tries to replicate what the market value of the project would be can be used, *e.g.*:

The total future Contract Payments, assuming no deductions or penalties; *minus* the originally projected Base Case (*cf.* §13.10) costs of operating the project;[16]

minus the costs to remedy the problem which caused the default, or any other loss suffered as a result of the default (*e.g.* obtaining products or services from elsewhere);

all discounted at the Base Case Project IRR (*cf.* §12.2.4)—thus removing the equity return and financing costs elements from these future revenues, and giving the current equity and debt outstandings).

This formula is one which, on the whole, is preferable for lenders, but it does not really establish the actual market value—which it should do, given that it is a substitute for a market sale. The main problem is the use of the Base Case Project IRR (*cf.* §10.2.2, §12.2.4) as a discount rate, as by the time the default takes place it may not be a true market discount rate that a buyer would use in valuing the project. There are two ways of dealing with this:

- The Base Case Project IRR can be adjusted so as to align it better with current market rates by changing it in proportion to the change in a comparable government bond with the same average life (*cf.* §12.5.2) as the cash-flow stream. So if such a bond initially had a return of 6%, and now yields 4%, the Base Case Project IRR should be adjusted by $(1 + (4 \div 6))$—thus if the Base Case Project IRR was 10%, 6.7% should be the rate used in the default calculation. The problems with this are two-fold:

  - If the costs to remedy the default, or other losses, are discounted at the Project IRR, and assuming these costs are spread over some time into the future, the NPV sum received to spend on remedying the default may not be sufficient, because it probably cannot be invested at a rate as high as the Base Case Project IRR.

  - In any case adjusting the Project IRR does not mean that this is a true market discount rate, which is a function of other things, such as the supply and demand for failed projects of this type. In fact it is highly likely that a market bidder would bid a discount rate higher than the adjusted Project IRR, reflecting the fact that the project has obviously had major problems.

---

[16] This assumes there is a transparent Base Case financial model which has been agreed between the parties. (*cf.* §3.7.6).

- Reinforcing the above argument, if the costs to remedy are not adjusted (increased) to allow for the risk that the outturn costs in such a situation are highly-likely to be higher, then clearly the discount rate has to be adjusted (*i.e.* increased) for risk.

  - Therefore there is a strong argument for an independent appraiser to decide an appropriate discount rate to use in valuing the Project Company. (This appraiser is needed anyway to give an independent view on the costs to remedy the default.)

  - On the other hand the parties may not want to leave this to an appraiser who may have great difficulty making a decision, and stick to the formula above as at least enabling them to know in advance what discount rate will be used.

Default before Project Completion. If the Project Company default occurs before Project Completion, the choice is normally between:

- no payment if the Offtaker/Contracting Authority chooses not to take over the project assets; or

- paying the cost incurred on the project to date, less an amount by which this cost and the NPV of the cost to complete exceed the Base-Case budget (*cf.* §13.5.1)—*e.g.* suppose the Base-Case construction cost is 100, 70 has been spent so far, and the cost to complete is now a further 50, the Project Company would be paid 50 [100–50] and so lose 20); or

- one of the systems above; however it seems excessive for the Project Company to be paid the NPV of future income from a project which they have not even succeeded in constructing, as in the Estimated Market Value formula.

Relationship with Lenders. The lenders will take security over project assets as far as possible (*cf.* §14.7.1). However this should not be allowed to limit or obstruct the transfer of project assets to the Offtaker/Contracting Authority on a default termination as discussed above.

§7.10.2 EARLY TERMINATION: DEFAULT BY THE OFFTAKER/CONTRACTING AUTHORITY

The most likely cause of default by the Offtaker/Contracting Authority is an inability to pay the Tariff/Service Fee, so it might be thought that negotiating a Termination Sum payment is a waste of time. The Termination Sum may, however, be guaranteed (*e.g.* by the government guaranteeing the Offtaker/Contracting Authority's liability), and even if it is not, a large Termination Sum will still discourage the Offtaker/Contracting Authority from default. A Termination Sum payment also discourages other fundamental breaches of obligations under the Project

Agreement, which make it impossible for the project to be constructed or to operate as intended (*e.g.* providing site access or rights of way); this is the only way in which a Contracting Authority can default in a Concession, assuming that it is not paying any subsidy or providing any other finance.

The Termination Sum payable by the Offtaker/Contracting Authority will usually include several elements:[17]

The Outstanding Debt. Clearly if the outstanding debt is not repayable in this situation, the lenders are unlikely to lend in the first place. Payment of outstanding debt as defined as in §7.10.1 is a reasonable approach, although in Australian Concession Agreements, for example, the level of debt (excluding breakage costs) repayable is the lower of the debt forecast to be outstanding in the Base Case financial model, and the actual debt outstanding on the termination date.[18]

Sub-Contract Liabilities. Early termination of the Project Agreement would normally lead to termination of the Sub-Contracts as well. These contracts themselves will have penalties for early termination, payable by the Project Company, (*cf.* §8.2.10; §8.3.4) which have to be covered by the Offtaker/Contracting Authority (*cf.* §8.9). (For O&M/Maintenance or Building-Services Sub-Contracts the typical termination penalty is two years' fees.)

The Project Company's Loss of Profit. If loss of future profit were not taken into account, the Offtaker/Contracting Authority could default shortly after Project Completion as a way of purchasing it at cost, leaving the investors with little monetary return for their risk. Where there is third-party revenue (*cf.* §7.3.4) this also has to be taken into account (typically on the basis of the lower of Base-Case projections and actual revenues over the last few years).

While the outstanding debt and Sub-Contract liabilities are easily to calculate, loss of profit is more complex, but loss of profit on the equity is more complex. There are various possibilities here, some of which are shown in Table 7.1, which is based on termination of a 20-year project, with a Base-Case Equity IRR of 15% (*cf.* §12.2.1), at the beginning of year 10 (project revenues are assumed to increase by 2.5% *p.a.*):

---

[17] It could be argued that a single payment equal to the value of the Project Company, assuming the Project Agreement had not been terminated, should cover all these elements, and indeed it might do so, but it is theoretically possible it might not (if the project had been going badly and the Offtaker/Contracting Authority defaulted at that time), and the lenders will therefore generally insist that their debt is specifically covered.

[18] Note that subordinated debt provided by investors (*cf.* §12.2.2) should not be included in debt for this purpose, but treated as equity.

Table 7.1 Compensation for Loss of Profit

Base Case

Years:	0	1	2	3	4	5	6	7	8	9	10	20
Cash flow	−700.0	100.0	102.5	105.1	107.7	110.4	113.1	116.0	118.9	121.8	124.9	159.9
Base Case Equity IRR	15%											

Termination at year 10

1. Method 1 – Equity IRR to Termination Date

Years:	0	1	2	3	4	5	6	7	8	9	10
Cash flow	−700	100.0	102.5	105.1	107.7	110.4	113.1	116.0	118.9	121.8	124.9
Equity IRR to year 10	15%										

2. Method 2 – Future Cash Flow discounted at Base Case Equity IRR

Years:	10	11	12	13	14	15	16	17	18	19	20
Cash flow	745.0	128.0	131.2	134.5	137.9	141.3	144.8	148.5	152.2	156.0	159.9
	124.9										

NPV 812.1

3. Method 3 – Market Value of Equity

Secondary equity return	10%										
Years:	10	11	12	13	14	15	16	17	18	19	20
	124.9	128.0	131.2	134.5	137.9	141.3	144.8	148.5	152.2	156.0	159.9

NPV 989.3

- *Method 1*: A payment sufficient to ensure that the investors receive the Base-Case Equity IRR to the date of payment (taking account of past equity cash flows). In the example in Table 7.1 this comes to 745. The danger of this formula is that it may encourage default or an optional termination of the Project Agreement (*cf.* §7.10.3) soon after the project has begun operations, thus enabling the Offtaker/Contracting Authority to buy out the project more or less at cost without paying very much for the construction risk taken by the investors.
- *Method 2*: The future projected Base-Case equity cash flows, discounted at the Base-Case Equity IRR, which comes to 812 in Table 7.1; this has the same problem as discussed in respect of the Estimated Market Value payment in §7.10.1; or
- *Method 3*: An independent valuation of what the market value of the investors' equity would have been if there had been no default; this would normally be based on an estimate of future equity cash flow discounted at a secondary-equity return (*cf.* §14.17); as this implies a lower discount rate, the result is a payment of 989, and not surprisingly this is what investors tend to choose.[19]

If these payments are made the project is transferred to the Offtaker/Contracting Authority.

§7.10.3 Optional Termination by the Offtaker/Contracting Authority

The Offtaker/Contracting Authority may also have an option to terminate 'for convenience', *i.e.* because it wants to take over the project, perhaps because of a policy change.[20]

In this case the same Termination-Sum formula applies as that payable on default by the Offtaker/Contracting Authority.

§7.10.4 Early Termination: *Force Majeure*[21]

A *Force Majeure* event is something that makes it impossible for one party to fulfill its contract, but which is not the fault of, and could not reasonably have

---

[19] These methods can be further refined:
- The projected cash flows can be adjusted to reflect the performance of the project—if the project is doing well this is obviously beneficial to the investors, and vice-versa.
- The Base-Case Equity IRR can be adjusted for changes in underlying long-term government bond rates, to reflect current market rates (as illustrated in §7.10.1 for the Project IRR0.

[20] This is also known as 'Voluntary Termination', or 'Unilateral Termination'.

[21] Also known as 'no fault' termination.

been foreseen by, that party. *Force Majeure* provisions are found in most Project Agreements: the general contractual treatment for *Force Majeure* is to leave each party to bear its own losses, but this is not always the case in contracts with an Offtaker/Contracting Authority, as discussed below. Coordination between the provisions of the different Project Contracts in this respect is important (*cf.* §9.12).

Force Majeure events can be divided into two main classes:

- **Natural *Force Majeure*** (also known as 'Act of God')—*e.g.* fire, explosion, flood, unusual weather conditions, *etc.*;
- **Political *Force Majeure***—*e.g.* war, terrorism, or civil unrest (*cf.* §11.4.3).[22]

Various *Force Majeure* events may lead to termination of the Project Agreement because it is no longer possible to complete or to operate the project.

Natural *Force Majeure*. A Natural *Force Majeure* event may destroy the project, but this should be covered by insurance and so should not automatically lead to a termination of the Project Agreement as the insurance proceeds can be used to rebuild the project. However if restoration is not financially viable, even taking account of insurance (*cf.* §8.6.5), the usual approach is to treat this as a default by the Project Company (*cf.* §7.10.1). The lenders should be repaid by the insurance proceeds (but *cf.* §9.9.1), and investors' losses may also be covered, depending on the level of insurance cover.

Political *Force Majeure*. Especially when the project is Reverting Asset-based, which means that the Offtaker/Contracting Authority will be the ultimate owner, and so arguably should be taking long-term ownership risks, the most equitable approach if political *Force Majeure* permanently prevents the project operating, is for the Offtaker/Contracting Authority to pay a Termination Sum which will repay the debt, less any insurance receipts, plus some compensation for the equity investment.

As to the equity investment, payment of compensation for loss of future profits is too much to expect in these circumstances. One approach is to repay the net equity investment—*i.e.* the total equity investment, less Distributions (*cf.* §14.4.2) received by the investors to the termination date. An alternative approach is to pay a proportion (*e.g.* half) of the equity investment shown in the Project Company's accounts at the time of termination.

In developing countries, however, the approach may be to repay outstanding debt (as defined above), plus loss of future profits, *i.e.* to treat this in the same way as default by the Offtaker/Contracting Authority.

---

[22] Also known as 'political violence'.

Having paid the relevant Termination Sum as above, the Offtaker/Contracting Authority would acquire the project 'as is'.

Action by the Host Government itself (*e.g.* expropriation of the project, or blocking the transfer or exchange of currency—*cf.* §11.4.1; §11.4.2) would normally be treated as a default by a public-sector Offtaker or a Contracting Authority.

§7.10.5 EARLY TERMINATION: CORRUPTION OR FRAUD

Where a Project Agreement is with a Contracting Authority—*i.e.* it is a public-sector contract—it will probably be necessary to include provisions to cover any corruption or fraud which occurs during the procurement process. The simplest approach here is that the Project Agreement is terminated, and the Contracting Authority acquires the project against repayment of the debt, but with no payment to the investors (on the grounds that investors rather than lenders are likely to benefit from corruption or fraud).

§7.10.6 TAX IMPLICATIONS OF A TERMINATION SUM PAYMENT

Finally, the tax implications of any Termination Sum need to be considered; if the Termination Sum is taxable the amount received by the investors and lenders may be insufficient to compensate them as intended, and it therefore needs to be 'grossed up' (*i.e.* increased as necessary to produce the net amount required after tax). This would always apply to any element of a Termination Sum which is being used to repay debt (*i.e.* default or optional termination by the Offtaker/Contracting Authority, or for *Force Majeure* or corruption). Such a gross-up provision would not apply, however, if the Termination Payment relates to a Project Company default where there is no liability on the part of the Offtaker/Contracting Authority for repayment of debt, or where the calculation of the project's value for Termination-Sum purposes is based on pre-tax cash flows.

As to equity compensation, insofar as investors would be liable for tax on the amounts received, there should be no need for a gross-up payment, but this may not always be the case, *e.g.* where investors provide subordinated debt rather than equity (*cf.* §12.2.2).[23]

§7.10.7 FINAL MATURITY OF A REVERTING ASSET-BASED PROJECT AGREEMENT

In a Reverting Asset-based Project Agreement, provisions are required for 'handback', *i.e.* the 'transfer of the project to the Offtaker/Contracting Authority at the end of the contract (assuming it still has some remaining useful life). So first of all an

---

[23] *Cf.* Jonathan S. Shefftz, "Taxation Considerations in Economic Damages Calculations", *Litigation Economics Review* Vol. 6 No. 2 (National Association of Forensic Economics, 2004), p. 45*.

'Asset Register' needs to be created (usually at Project Completion), which sets out all the assets which are required to operate the project, and which will be handed back at the end of the Project Agreement. These may include:

- land or buildings;
- plant and equipment;
- books and records (including operating, maintenance and health and safety manuals);
- as-built drawings;
- spare parts, tools and other assets;
- any continuing contracts;
- any intellectual property (*cf.* §9.5.12);
- Permits (*cf.* §8.8).

An 'Asset Management Plan' may be drawn up which sets out the requirements for maintenance, refurbishment, and lifecycle replacements for the project. There is an obvious temptation for the Project Company to neglect maintenance and renewals during the final years of operation. An Asset Management Plan may be included in the Project Agreement and monitored in good time before the end of the contract, but still, by that time, the Project Company may have paid over all its remaining cash to its shareholders, and ceased to have any financial substance to pay compensation for poor maintenance.

Therefore if the Offtaker/Contracting Authority wishes to ensure that maintenance is properly carried out in the latter years of the Project Agreement, this can be achieved by:

- a right to survey the condition of the project, and require outstanding maintenance work to be carried out; and
- part of the Contract Payments are paid for the last few years into a maintenance reserve or retention account under the control of both the Project Company and the Offtaker/Contracting Authority; this fund is used for maintenance as required, and any final surplus is returned to the Project Company; or
- the Offtaker/Contracting Authority has the right to carry out maintenance, if not done by the Project Company, during, say, the last two years of the contract, and withhold Contract Payments to cover the costs; or
- the Project Company provides security—a Sponsor or bank guarantee, or a maintenance bond (*cf.* §7.5)—to ensure that the final maintenance obligations are carried out.

Provisions are also needed for the transfer of operating information, manuals, *etc.*

§7.10.8 Early Termination of a Non-Reverting Asset-based Project Agreement

Each of the early termination scenarios discussed above also needs to be reconsidered for a Non-Reverting Asset-based Contract. In the case of Reverting Asset-based Contracts the Offtaker/Contracting Authority's gets the project assets back, but ideally does not pay any more than they are worth (though this may not always be the case, as discussed above). Therefore short of a guarantee from investors, the Offtaker/Contracting is as well secured in such a case as it can reasonably expect. This position clearly has to apply to any case where public infrastructure (with no alternative use) is the object of the Project Agreement.[24]

As will be seen from the discussion below, matters are not so clear-cut where the Project Agreement relates to a Non-Reverting Asset-based Contract. This is most likely to apply in process-plant projects, such as a power plant, waste-incineration plant, or sewage-treatment plant, where the project could continue to operate in a private-sector market, but could also apply, *e.g.* to public housing or government office buildings which also have an alternative use.

> **Project Company Default.** As ownership of the project remains with the Project Company, the Offtaker/Contracting Authority should ideally be able to just terminate the Project Agreement if it goes into default and pursue a claim for damages (being the additional cost of obtaining the product or service elsewhere), or for a pre-agreed LD sum. However the problem here is that the Project Company is unlikely to have the cash available to pay such damages.
>
> The only way to cover this issue is for the Sponsor(s) to provide guarantees for the Termination Sum—but the credit risk of such a contingent long-term liability is difficult to assess, meaning that the Offtaker/Contracting Authority cannot be sure that the Sponsor(s) will actually be able to pay the Termination Sum when the default occurs, and anyway such a guarantee obviously means that the project has become one with recourse to the Sponsors, which is not normally the case.
>
> Given these problems, the same formula as for a Reverting Asset-based Contract, as set out in §7.10.1, may have to be used as a fall-back should damages not be paid by the Project Company. However a further issue here is that the Contract Payments may have been reduced to take account of the residual value (*cf.* §7.10.9), so if the Project Company is now going to lose the residual value the Termination Sum may have to take this into account.

---

[24] Also even if the project has no residual value at the end of the Project Agreement, the Contracting Authority will probably still want to retrieve the project site.

Finally, if the Offtaker/Contracting Authority originally provided the land for the project site, care needs to be taken that the Project Company has no incentive to go into default and sell the land rather than continue with the project. Further adjustment to the Termination Sum may be needed to ensure this, as well as appropriate drafting in any lease of the land (*cf.* §8.7).

Offtaker/Contracting Authority Default, or Optional Termination. Here again the ideal approach—namely the Offtaker/Contracting Authority paying the Project Company the losses it incurs as a result of the Project Agreement terminating early—also may not work.

The problem with just paying loss of profit is that this is unlikely to pay off the lenders—and the lenders will have come into the project on the basis of there being a Project Agreement with the Offtaker/Contracting Authority. The compensation payment from the Offtaker/Contracting Authority might be used to prepay some of the debt, leaving a reduced amount of debt at risk as against a project which now has a higher risk, which may be acceptable to the lenders. However the lenders may not want to continue lending to a project which does not have an assured income from the Offtaker/Contracting Authority, or at least may not be willing to commit to this in advance.

Again, this may mean that one of the Reverting Asset provisions set out above have to be used as a fallback in this case.

Force Majeure. The usual contractual approach to *Force Majeure* is that the contract is terminated and the losses 'remain where they fall', *i.e.* neither party pays anything to the other (and the Project Company would keep the assets and do the best it can with them). But here, too, however, the lenders may want to see a position similar to that for a Reverting Asset-based Contract.

Corruption or Fraud. In this case using the same provisions as for a Reverting Asset is probably the simplest approach—the equity is penalized but the debt is not. The alternative is a simple cancellation of the Project Agreement, with no payments either way, and no transfer of the asset.

§7.10.9 Final Maturity of a Non-Reverting Asset-based Contract

In principle, on final maturity of a Non-Reverting Asset-based Contract, the Project Company continues to use the project assets as it sees best, and the Offtaker/Contracting Authority fades out of the picture. However this would only be acceptable if the Offtaker/Contracting Authority has not in fact paid for the whole project's costs through the Contract Payments, *i.e.* the Contract Payments have been reduced to take account of the residual value (*cf.* §7.2.5).

If the residual value has been reflected in the Contract Payments, it is still possible for options to be built into the Project Agreement for the Offtaker/Contracting

Authority to acquire the project in a way which reflects the residual value which now belongs to the Project Company, *e.g.*:

- an option to purchase the project for a pre-agreed fixed sum; or
- an option to purchase the project for its then current market value; or
- an option to extend the Project Agreement on then current market terms; or
- an option to put a renewal contract out for a new competitive bid (in which the existing Project Company may participate); the winner of the bid may purchase the facilities provided by the Project Company (on a pre-agreed price formula).

If the residual value is not taken into account in the initial Contract Payments, the Offtaker/Contracting Authority should normally try to ensure that the commercial benefit of the residual value mainly accrues to it and not to the Project Company (because it has probably paid off the full capital cost of the project by then), *e.g.*:

- an option to purchase the project for a nominal sum (which effectively turns the project back into a Non-Reverting Asset-based Contract, meaning that the provisions for final maturity of a Reverting Asset-based Contract must apply here too); or
- an option to extend the Project Agreement for the remaining economic life of the project assets, on terms which reflect the fact that the Project Company's investors have already secured their required return; hence the extension would be on a 'cost-plus' basis, giving the Project Company an agreed profit margin over its operating and maintenance costs only.[25]

§7.11 CHANGE OF OWNERSHIP

The Offtaker/Contracting Authority may wish to restrict the sale of any of the Sponsors' shares to another party, to ensure they remain committed to the project rather than walk away with a quick profit (*cf.* §3.2.1). In general this restriction would be applied during the construction phase, so that once Project Completion has taken place—which is when sales are most likely (*cf.* §14.17)—it would be lifted. However if the project depends on a particular technology supplied by one of the Sponsors, it may be required to retain its shareholding for a longer period.

---

[25] Where public-procurement rules apply, this extension may have to be treated as a new procurement: this can be managed by requiring the Project Company to bid in the new procurement at no more than this price formula.

§7.12 DISPUTE RESOLUTION

It is generally considered preferable for legal disputes in complex contracts of this type to be dealt with, at least initially, by arbitration either by an expert or in a generally-recognized arbitration tribunal.

Another minor issue that may arise in this context is the language in which Project Contracts and financing documentation are to be prepared. Generally, a Project Company seeking financing from the international market should try to ensure Project Contracts are prepared in English, as this will make it easier to access the widest range of potential lenders; Project Contracts or financing documentation governed by English or New York law should also preferably be drafted in English.

Issues that arise in cross-border investment and lending, where there is a public-sector Offtaker, Contracting Authority, or other Project Contract counterpart (*e.g.* an Input Supplier), are discussed in §11.5.1.

SUB-CONTRACTS AND OTHER RELATED AGREEMENTS

§8.1 INTRODUCTION

This chapter summarizes the key provisions usually found in the major Sub-Contracts, *i.e.* the Project Contracts that may be signed by the Project Company, apart from the Project Agreement discussed in the last chapter, as well as other related Agreements, namely:

- Construction Contract (§8.2);[1]
- O&M/Maintenance Contract(s) (§8.3);
- Building-Services Contract (§8.4);
- Fuel or other Input-Supply Contract (§8.5);
- Insurance (§8.6);
- Site lease (§8.7);
- Permits and other rights—not contracts as such but an important underpinning for all the Project Contracts (§8.8);
- Parent-company guarantees for Sub-Contractors (§8.10);

---

[1] Strictly speaking individual Sub-Contracts should be referred to as Construction Sub-Contract, O&M Sub-Contract and so on, but for the sake of brevity the 'Sub-' will generally be omitted.

163

Principles of Project Finance. DOI: http://dx.doi.org/10.1016/B978-0-12-391058-5.00008-4

- Direct Agreements, which link the lenders (and the Offtaker/Contracting Authority) to the Project Contracts (§8.11).

As already mentioned (*cf.* §2.5.3), all of these contractual building blocks are not found in every project financing, but one or more of them usually are, and it is important to understand their general scope, purpose, and structure as they usually form a major element of the foundation on which the project financing is built.

Changes in any Project Contracts normally require the lenders' consent.

§8.2 CONSTRUCTION CONTRACT

In the conventional contracting procedure for a major project, the project developer, or a Contracting Authority uses an architect and/or consulting engineer to draw up the design for the project, with detailed drawings, bill of quantities, *etc.*, based on which a bid for the construction is invited; any specific equipment required is procured separately. But even if the Sponsors or Contracting Authority have the experience to arrange the work under separate contracts and coordinate different responsibilities between different parties, this is not usually acceptable to lenders in project finance who want there to be 'one-stop' responsibility for completing the project satisfactorily, since they do not want the Project Company to be caught in the middle of disputes as to who is responsible for a failure to the do the job correctly.

Therefore the Construction Contract in a project-financed project is usually in the form of a contract to design/engineer the project, procure or manufacture any plant or equipment required, and construct the project, so creating a 'turnkey' responsibility to deliver a complete project fully equipped and ready for operation—*i.e.* a D&B or EPC Contract.

Another approach to contracting for major projects is to appoint a contracting or engineering company as construction manager, with the responsibility of handling all aspects of the construction of the project, against payment of a management fee. The fee may vary according to the final outcome of the construction costs. Although this may be an economically efficient way of handling major projects, a variable construction cost is not acceptable to lenders because of the risk of a cost overrun for which there may not be sufficient funding, or which adds so much to the costs that the project cannot operate economically (*cf.* §9.5.4). The Construction Contract therefore also provides for the work to be done by the Construction Contractor at a fixed price.

Finally Project Completion has to match the requirements of the Project Agreement for the project to be complete by a fixed date. So the Construction Contract also provides for a fixed Project Completion date.

Such a turnkey, fixed-price, date-certain Construction Contract transfers a significant amount of responsibility (and thus risk) to the Construction Contractor. Moreover the Construction Contractor has to 'wrap' (*i.e.* guarantee) the performance of its own sub-contractors, and is taking extra risk in this respect. These extra risks are clearly likely to cause the Construction Contractor to build more contingencies into the contract costings, and hence a higher contract price than the price if the work were done on a cost-plus basis. Typically the extra cost of such a Construction Contract adds 20% to the estimated cost of a contract which is not on a turnkey, fixed-price, date-certain basis, but the outturn cost of the latter kind of contract may easily increase by 20%, hence producing the same result.[2]

Fixed-price, date-certain Construction Contracts are standard in most process-plant and infrastructure projects. Sponsors who want to adopt a different approach normally have to give lenders a Project Completion guarantee, thus diluting the non-recourse nature of the transaction (*cf.* §9.13). Certain types of projects do not or cannot usually use such contracts—for example mining and oil and gas extraction projects, as well as projects involving a gradual investment in a network, influenced by changing demand, such as in telecommunications projects (*cf.* §9.5.12).

Another exception to the turnkey responsibility of the Construction Contractor arises where the project is being constructed using technology licensed by a third party, which is commonly the case in refinery or petrochemical plant projects. The Construction Contractor does not take responsibility for the performance of the plant insofar as this depends on such a third-party license.

It should be noted that standard forms of Construction Contracts, such as those produced by the International Federation of Consulting Engineers (FIDIC) are generally not suitable for project finance, first because they tend to be too 'contractor friendly,' and second because there are some differences of structure compared to project finance requirements.[3]

Key aspects of a Construction Contract from the project-finance point of view are:

- contract scope (§8.2.1);
- commencement of the works (§8.2.2);
- contract price, payments, and variations (§8.2.3);
- construction supervision (§8.2.4);
- Owner's Risks (Compensation Events) (§8.2.5);

---

[2] *Cf.* Frédéric Blanc-Brude, Hugh Goldsmith & Timo Välilä, "Ex Ante Construction Costs in the European Road Sector: A Comparison of Public-Private Partnerships and Traditional Public Procurement", *Economic and Financial Report* (EIB, Luxemburg, 2006)*, which gives the *ex-ante* capital costs for European PPP roads as 24% higher than *ex-ante* costs for public procurements, but the *ex-post* costs for PPP roads did not differ greatly from the *ex-ante* costs whereas studies of publicly-procured roads showed an optimism bias of about 22%. In other words, the risk and the outcome is similar whatever the method of construction—in the PPP case risk is retained by the D&C Contractor, who prices accordingly.

[3] A useful detailed commentary on EPC Contracts can be found in United Nations Commission on International Trade Law: *UNCITRAL Legal Guide on Drawing up International Contracts for the Construction of Industrial Works* (United Nations, New York, 1988)*.

- Relief Events (§8.2.6);
- definition of Project Completion (§8.2.7);
- liquidated damages and termination (§8.2.8);
- security (§8.2.9);
- suspension and termination by the Construction Contractor (§8.2.10);
- dispute resolution (§8.2.11).

§8.2.1 SCOPE OF CONTRACT

The Construction Contract sets out the design, technical specifications, and performance criteria for the project, and may offer a 'fast-track' route to construction of the project, since the contract can be signed and construction can begin before all the detailed design work is complete. Nonetheless the Construction Contractor remains responsible for constructing a project that is capable of performing as specified, even if something has been omitted from the detailed description. The Project Company may also have the right to object to detailed designs as these are produced by the Construction Contractor. (Its position here is different to that of an Offtaker/Contracting Authority—*cf.* §7.4.1.)

The Construction Contractor is responsible for employing (and paying) its own subcontractors or equipment suppliers, although the Project Company may have a right of prior approval over major subcontractors or equipment suppliers, to ensure that appropriately qualified subcontractors or suppliers with relevant technology are being used.

Construction insurance should normally be excluded from the scope of the Construction Contract price (*cf.* §8.6.1).

For tax reasons Construction Contracts with international contractors are sometimes broken into separate parallel contracts, *e.g.* for provision of services (such as design) and equipment, or into an 'offshore' contract for work outside the country of the project, and an 'onshore' contract for the rest (which would probably be mainly carried out by a local construction company as sub-contractor to the Construction Contractor). This is acceptable provided the contracts are clearly linked together and effectively form one whole.

§8.2.2 COMMENCEMENT OF THE WORKS

There may be a gap between the time the Construction Contract is signed and the point at which Financial Close has been reached, and usually the Construction Contractor does not begin work until the latter date, when there is assurance that the financing is available. The Construction Contract therefore often provides for a Notice to Proceed (NTP), *i.e.* a formal notice to begin the works, which can be issued by the Project Company at Financial Close. In such cases the required Project Completion date is calculated as a date that is a period of time after the NTP is issued, rather than a fixed date.

A delay in reaching Financial Close may affect the Construction Contract price—there is likely to be a final date for NTP, after which the Construction Contractor may increase the price (or there is an automatic increase based on an inflation index) or is no longer bound to undertake the works. Similarly, a delay in starting the work will lead to a delay in Project Completion, which could jeopardize the project as a whole. In such cases, the Sponsors may be willing to take the risk of asking the Construction Contractor to begin work under their guarantee, based on the assumption that Financial Close will catch up with events, enabling the guarantee to be canceled at that point. For this purpose, an optional procedure for 'pre-NTP' works may be included in the Construction Contract: this work may cover just the (relatively low cost) preliminary design work, or allow the Construction Contractor to place orders for (high-cost) long lead-time equipment.[4]

The Project Company should have the right to terminate the Construction Contract if at any time a decision is taken not to proceed further with the project (this is known as a 'termination for convenience'), against an agreed formula for paying compensation to the Construction Contractor.

§8.2.3 Contract Price, Payments, and Variations

Payment of the contract price is normally made in stages: after an initial deposit, payments are made against the Construction Contractor reaching pre-agreed milestones, relating to items such as completing a major stage of the works or delivery of a major piece of equipment, or alternatively against the overall value of the work performed as a proportion of the total contract value.

Payments may be made directly by the lenders to the Construction Contractor, rather than passing the funds through the Project Company's bank account (*cf.* §14.3.2).

If export credits or other tied funding (*cf.* §16.2; §16.4) are being used, the Construction Contractor cannot change the arrangements for sourcing of equipment or services (as otherwise the Project Company may not have enough finance available).

Although in principle the Construction Contract price is fixed, there are some exceptions to this that usually allow the Construction Contractor to increase the price, *e.g.*:

- if the Project Company changes the required design or performance of the plant, or adds other new elements to the contract;

---

[4] If the Construction Contract (and/or other major Sub-Contracts) is signed before Financial Close, this is known as 'Commercial Close' (whether or not a NTP is issued). Obviously Commercial Close has little value if Financial Close cannot take place quite soon thereafter, but it may be necessary to ensure the Construction Contractor's pricing cannot be increased.

- if Owner's Risks cause additional costs, including the cost of delays to the construction program (*cf.* §8.2.5; §9.5);
- if changes in law require the design or construction of the project to be changed (*cf.* §11.3).

The Construction Contractor normally remains responsible for any problems with the geology of the site that cause extra costs, although the Construction Contractor may not accept liability for problems with projects being built in locations where mining has taken place and underground site conditions are uncertain.

The way in which the Construction Contract price is made up has in principle nothing to do with the Project Company, which is just paying a lump-sum price; however, it is sometimes necessary for the price to be broken up by the Construction Contractor for the Project Company's tax purposes (*cf.* §13.7.1).

§8.2.4 CONSTRUCTION SUPERVISION

Although the Construction Contractor is responsible for completing the project as agreed, the Project Company still supervises the construction process closely to ensure that it is built to the agreed specifications (*cf.* §7.4.1; §5.5.3 for the rôle of the Lenders' Engineer, and for that of an Offtaker/Contracting Authority in this respect).

An outside engineering firm is often employed as Owner's Engineer to draw up the specifications for the project plant, to assist in the process of calling for bids for and negotiating the Construction Contract, to supervise the Construction Contractor's work construction of the plant, and to certify that claims for payment are in order. (The Lenders' Engineer may also be required to certify payments.)

The Construction Contract may also provide for an Independent Engineer to certify that the various stages of the works have been properly completed, who may also perform the same function under the Project Agreement (*cf.* §7.4.1).

Key Construction Contractor personnel working on the project are also designated and cannot be changed without the Project Company's consent.

§8.2.5 OWNER'S RISKS

Apart from making payments under the Construction Contract when these fall due, the Project Company (often called the 'owner' in the context of the Construction Contract) is responsible for matters such as:

- making the project site available (*cf.* §9.5.1);*
- ensuring access to the site;*
- obtaining construction and similar Permits (where these have to be obtained by the Project Company rather than the Construction Contractor—*cf.* §9.5.3);

- providing access to utilities needed for construction (such as electricity and water);
- providing fuel or other materials required for testing the plant;
- work 'outside the fence,' such as fuel and grid connections for a power station, or road or rail connections being built by the Offtaker/Contracting Authority under the Project Agreement, or by a third party (cf. §9.5.9).*

These are generally known as Owner's Risks—and are in effect Compensation Events (cf. §7.6) as between the Project Company and the Construction Contractor. The items marked with an asterisk are normally Compensation Events under the Project Agreement, and so ultimately the responsibility of the Offtaker/Contracting Authority, but as far as the Construction Contractor is concerned the Project Company is still responsible.

Allocation of other risks related to the condition of the site are discussed in §9.5.2, and those related to the environmental effect of the project in §9.10.

§8.2.6 RELIEF EVENTS

A Relief Event in the context of a Construction Contract is an event which could not reasonably have been anticipated by and is outside the control of a prudent and experienced Construction Contractor, and which therefore excuses the Construction Contractor from liability for delay in completing the project. However, the Construction Contractor cannot normally claim compensation for extra costs caused by a Relief Event.

Relief Events under the Construction Contract will should, as far as possible, mirror those under the Project Agreement (cf. §7.8; §9.12).

§8.2.7 PROJECT COMPLETION

The Construction Contract sets out the basis on which the project will be accepted by the Project Company as complete. Project Completion may take place in several stages:[5]

Mechanical Completion, under an EPC Contract, when the project is ready for start-up and testing, including performance tests; these tests would include confirmation that the project can meet the required performance and operating criteria (or liquidated damages—cf. §8.2.8—have been paid).

---

[5] Unless it is necessary to distinguish between these stages, Project Completion will be used hereafter. It should be noted that Project Completion does just mean that the project can begin operating, as Permits, for example, may be required to do this (and hence obtaining Permits may also be a completion test).

Substantial Completion,[6] when the project meets the basic requirements of the Construction Contract (or liquidated damages have been paid), at which point the project is handed over to the Project Company.

Final Completion,[7] which is dependent on resolution of 'punch list' or 'snagging' items, which are part of the agreed scope of the Construction Contract but do not prevent the project operating (*e.g.* landscaping). The Lenders' Engineer (*cf.* §5.5.3) is usually involved in the process of certifying that the works are complete.

A final date for Mechanical or Substantial Completion (to match the Sunset Date in the project Agreement) is set out in the Construction Contract and can only be extended in limited circumstances, *e.g.* if delays are caused to the Construction Contractor's work by Owner's Risks (*cf.* §8.2.5).

Title to the equipment or works usually passes from the Construction Contractor to the Project Company when it is delivered or paid for, but the Construction Contractor remains responsible for any losses of equipment or other damage at the site until Substantial Completion, although such losses should usually be covered by insurance (*cf.* §8.6.1).

The Lenders' Engineer is usually required to certify the completion: *i.e.* a certificate from the Owner's Engineer will probably not be sufficient given the importance of this stage.

§8.2.8 LIQUIDATED DAMAGES AND TERMINATION

LDs are fixed amounts that both sides agree are sufficient to cover the Project Company's financial losses resulting from late Project Completion or failure of the project to perform as specified (where the Construction Contractor is at fault). If specific amounts are not agreed to in this way there would be lengthy disputes about the quantum of loss in each case: the uncertainty involved in this would not be acceptable to lenders, and the time spent in dispute could be financially disastrous for the Project Company.[8]

LDs are not intended as a penalty (indeed, many legal systems make a penalty payment of this type unenforceable), but a fair compensation for the loss suffered.

Apart from the LD amounts, the Project Company cannot make claims against the Construction Contractor for loss of profits or extra costs, except on termination of the Construction Contract. LDs are important for lenders, who tend to require

---

[6] Also known as 'initial acceptance'.

[7] Also known as 'final acceptance'.

[8] LDs are also referred to as 'buy-down payments', *i.e.* they represent the payments which have to be made for the project to be accepted despite its poor performance.

higher levels of LDs than might be found in a construction contract that is not being project financed. LDs may also be needed to cover loss of income or penalties payable under the Project Agreement. Obviously the Construction Contractor takes the risk of providing high levels of LDs into account when proposing a construction schedule and pricing the contract.

Delay LDs. LDs for delay in Project Completion, unless caused by Owner's Risks or Relief Events, are standard in most Construction Contracts.

Delay LDs are calculated on a daily basis, at a rate that is a matter for negotiation but should at the minimum be sufficient to cover the Project Company's debt interest costs and fixed overheads, plus any penalties payable to an Offtaker/Contracting Authority for late Project Completion (*cf.* §6.3.6)—*i.e.* the costs incurred by the Project Company as a result of the delay; ideally they should be high enough to cover the total loss of revenue (less any variable overheads, *e.g.* for fuel).

The total sum payable as delay LDs is usually capped; lenders expect this cap to be at a high enough level to cover at least 6 months of delay in Project Completion. A typical cap for delay LDs would be 15–20% of the Construction Contract value.

Performance LDs. Performance LDs are appropriate where the project involves a process plant (*e.g.* a power station, refinery or petrochemical plant), or the performance of a system. For example a PPA will specify that the project must produce at least x megawatts of power, and should not burn more than y units of fuel for each z megawatts of power production.

The calculation of LDs in such cases is done by projecting the loss of revenue or increase in operating costs resulting from failure to meet the specification over the life of the project. These amounts are then discounted to an NPV (*cf.* §10.2.1), which is the level of the LDs. Again there will be an overall cap on the performance LDs of say 10% for each particular requirement.

Overall LD Cap. An overall cap is established for LDs for all types, typically around 25–30% of the contract value for an EPC Contract (rather lower for a D&B Contract), again a figure that is higher than that usually found in non-project financed Construction Contracts. It is important to note, therefore, that LDs do not provide compensation for a complete inability by the Construction Contractor to complete the contract: termination of the contract (see below) may provide further remedies in this case.

Environmental Guarantees. The Construction Contractor may also provide guarantees of the environmental effect of the project (*e.g.* emissions from a plant). If meeting emissions limits is a legal requirement, LDs are usually not relevant—the standards have to be met or the Construction Contract cannot pass performance tests.

Bonus. The Construction Contractor may also be paid a bonus for completing the project ahead of schedule: this should divide the benefit of earlier revenue (if the Project Agreement allows for this) between the Project Company and the Construction Contractor.

Termination by the Project Company. LDs alone may not cover the Project Company against poor performance by the Construction Contractor, especially as these are limited in amount: the Project Company therefore also has the right to terminate the contract if the Construction Contractor fails to complete the project by an agreed long-stop date. In this context exhaustion of the LD cap(s), or failure to meet environmental requirements would be a failure to complete the project.

In such cases the Project Company has the right to terminate the contract and to employ another contractor to finish the project, in which case any extra costs of doing so would be payable by the original Construction Contractor. (This is also subject to a cap, but at a much higher level, *e.g.* 100% of the contract price) Alternatively the Project Company may require the Construction Contractor to restore the site to its original condition, and repay all sums the Project Company has paid under the Construction Contract.

Position of the Offtaker/Contracting Authority. An Offtaker/Contracting Authority may wish to charge LDs to the Project Company, *e.g.* for late completion of the project. However it is likely to be difficult to increase the LDs required by the lenders to cover this further payment. The main incentive to ensure on-time completion is that the Project Company cannot earn any revenues until then (*cf.* §7.3.1; §9.14).

§8.2.9 SECURITY

The Construction Contractor usually provides the Project Company with various types of security for fulfillment of the obligations under the Construction Contract (known generally as 'bonding'[9]):

Retainage. A percentage (usually around 5–10%) of each contract payment is retained by the Project Company until satisfactory final Project Completion. This ensures that the Construction Contractor will deal expeditiously with outstanding smaller items of work at the end of the contract. Alternatively, the Construction Contractor may be paid this 'retainage'[10] and instead provide a retention bond for the same amount.

---

[9] N.B.: This has nothing to do with the bonds as financial instruments discussed in §4.3.
[10] Also known as 'retention amount'.

Performance Bond.[11] The Construction Contractor is usually required to provide a bond for around 10–15% of contract value as further security to cover the obligation to pay LDs, insofar as the retention amount is not sufficient for this purpose.

Advance-Payment Guarantee. If any payments have been made in advance of the work being done (for example, an initial deposit of say 10%, which is quite common) the Construction Contractor provides an advance-payment guarantee, under which the amounts concerned will be repaid *pro rata* if the contract is terminated before the work is complete.

Warranties. After Project Completion, the Construction Contractor usually provides warranties, *e.g.* against poor construction or failure of equipment, running for several years (the 'defects liability period').[12]

These obligations should be secured by bank letters of credit or insurance-company bonds that enable the Project Company to make an immediate drawing of cash rather than having to go through a dispute procedure or legal action before being paid anything (if they are not covered by cash retainage). If this is not the case the Project Company may face a cash crisis if the events being covered by the security arise and payment cannot be obtained immediately.

§8.2.10 SUSPENSION AND TERMINATION BY THE CONSTRUCTION CONTRACTOR

The Construction Contractor has the right to terminate the contract and obtain compensation for any losses if the Project Company defaults by failing to pay amounts due under the contract, or in any other fundamental way under the contract (*e.g.* by failing to give access to the project site).

As an interim measure, the Construction Contractor is normally required to suspend work for a period of time before finally terminating the contract. For example, if the Project Company defaults in a payment, the Construction Contractor may suspend work 30 days after the payment was due, but not terminate the Construction Contract for another three months. This suspension period is normally extended further under the terms of the Direct Agreement with the lenders (*cf.* §8.11).

If work resumes because the Project Company has cured the default, the suspension period is added on to the end-date for Project Completion, and the Project Company may also have to pay costs incurred in keeping the project in suspension (*e.g.* personnel costs or storage of equipment).

---

[11] Also known as a completion bond, or a construction bond.

[12] Also known as a maintenance bond.

§8.2.11 Dispute Resolution

As with Project Agreements (*cf.* §7.12), resolution of disputes in a Construction Contract is often by an arbitration procedure rather than court action, which is preferable on grounds of getting a quick resolution of the issue. Smaller issues in dispute may be dealt with by an expert agreed by both sides.

Even if there is a dispute, the Construction Contractor is usually required to keep working on the project.

§8.3 O&M/MAINTENANCE CONTRACT(S)

An O&M/Maintenance Contract (depending on the type of project) helps to ensure that project operating costs stay within budget and that the project operates as projected. Because the Project Company has no track record of operating at the beginning of a project, lenders often prefer established companies, with the necessary experience of similar projects as well as more financial substance, to take this responsibility.

Even if the project is going to be operated by one of its Sponsors, a separate agreement for this purpose is necessary, to define the scope of the Sponsor's involvement.

§8.3.1 Scope of Contract

O&M or maintenance may be dealt with under one contract with a single contractor, if this is appropriate to the type of project (*e.g.* a power station). Alternatively, the responsibilities may be split (*e.g.* for a toll road, where toll operations involve one type of expertise and road maintenance another). Another approach is for the EPC Contractor or equipment supplier to provide long-term major maintenance (*cf.* §8.3.5), while minor maintenance and general operations are undertaken by an O&M Contractor. Maintenance is usually dealt with by one contractor, but Building Services may be dealt with separately (*cf.* §8.4).

§8.3.2 Services

The scope of work needs to be clearly defined to ensure that the division of responsibility with the Project Company is clear. The Project Company must have an adequate ability to monitor what the O&M/Maintenance Contractor should be doing; corporate functions should normally remain under the control of the Project Company rather than the Sub-Contractor. In summary, the O&M/Maintenance Contractor should deal only with the project and the Project Company at least with general administration, finance, insurance, and personnel issues (other than O&M/Maintenance Contract personnel).

Under a standard O&M Contract, the O&M Contractor provides the key staff (*e.g.* a plant manager). Other more junior staff may be employed by the Project Company or the O&M Contractor. The O&M Contractor may also make further staff available from its own organization to provide initial training and help in starting up the project (in liaison with the Construction Contractor, who may also have responsibilities in this respect), and to deal with operating problems as they arise. A Maintenance Contract for an Accommodation Project would normally also be carried out by the Sub-Contractor's own staff.

Services are usually divided into three phases:

Planning. The O&M/Maintenance Contractor provides input into the design of the project on operational issues and projections of operating parameters and costs.

Mobilization. An O&M Contractor is responsible for a smooth handover from the EPC Contractor and transition into operation when the project has reached the end of construction, and may therefore provide support during the start-up and testing of the project.

Operation. The O&M/Maintenance Contract obviously comes into full effect when the project is ready to begin operations. Responsibilities thereafter obviously vary greatly depending on the type of project, but may include:

- securing operating Permits;
- general maintenance of the project (*e.g.* painting the walls every *x* years);
- operating the project to general industry standards, and on a day-to-day basis as required under the Project Agreement;
- annual budgeting;
- ordering and handling input supplies;
- maintaining a stock of spare parts;
- keeping operating costs within the annual budget;
- maintaining health and safety standards;
- keeping operating, maintenance, and personnel records;
- keeping the operating manuals up-to-date (the original manual will probably have been prepared by the Construction Contractor);
- scheduling and carrying out routine and major maintenance, taking account of the Construction Contractor's warranty obligations (*cf.* §8.2.9);
- replacement of lifecycle equipment (*cf.* §9.7.5);
- carrying out emergency repairs.

§8.3.3 FEE BASIS

The O&M/Maintenance Contractor's fees may be on a fixed or a 'cost plus' basis plus a profit margin.

Fixed fees tend to apply for a Maintenance Contractor looking after a building, road, or similar civil works, fixed fees are normally indexed against CPI or an industry price index. Thus the Maintenance Contractor is taking the long-term risk of unpredictable maintenance and lifecycle costs away from the Project Company (*cf.* §9.7.5).

Cost-plus fees tend to apply to an O&M Contractor looking after a process plant. The O&M Contractor may be paid fixed fees to cover staff costs and a profit margin, with other costs (*e.g.* materials or replacement parts) reimbursed by the Project Company as incurred.

§8.3.4 INCENTIVES AND PENALTIES

In a process-plant project the O&M Contractor may be paid a bonus if the project operates at better than initially agreed levels, and conversely may suffer penalties (*i.e.* LDs) if it operates below agreed levels. Any bonus is calculated so as to share the extra revenue from better operation between the Project Company and the O&M Contractor. Bonuses do not normally apply to a Maintenance or Building-Services Contract.

Penalties payable to the Project Company in O&M/Maintenance Contracts are normally limited to the equivalent of one or two year's fees (*cf.* §6.4.4, §9.7.2). Exceptions from penalties, including relief against termination, will normally mirror those in the Project Agreement (*cf.* §7.6–§7.8).

§8.3.5 MAJOR MAINTENANCE CONTRACT

In some cases the manufacturer may be willing to assume responsibility for performance and maintenance of major elements of the project in a project (*e.g.* for the turbines in a power station) against payment of fixed maintenance fees over a period of time.

The benefit of this type of arrangement is that it fixes maintenance costs for such items (*cf.* §9.7.5), and so helps in long-term budgeting. However, as with any O&M Contract, the manufacturer may be unwilling to compensate the Project Company for consequential loss (*i.e.* loss of revenue or payment of penalties) if the plant is not maintained adequately. There may also be difficulty in establishing whose fault it is that the project did not work if part of it is being maintained separately.

§8.4 BUILDING-SERVICES CONTRACT

A Building-Services Contract applies to Accommodation Projects, primarily in the PPP sector, and covers services such as cleaning, mail, laundry, catering, waste, parking, reception and security, telephones, *etc*. This Sub-Contract may be combined with the Maintenance Contract so that all these services are the obligation of one supplier. The requirements are set out in detailed Service Specifications in the contract.

As discussed in §6.4.5 this Sub-Contract may be subject to benchmarking or market testing at regular intervals. Performance will be measured against the KPIs in the Project Agreement (*cf.* §6.4.4), and again LDs are usually limited to around two years' fees.

Alternatively the Contracting Authority may consider it better VfM (*cf.* §9.2) to contract separately (*i.e.* outside the Project Agreement) for building services on a short-term basis (*e.g.* annually, or for a limited number of years).[14] The Contracting Authority can even retain responsibility for some aspects of the building maintenance which do not affect the fundamental fabric of the building, *e.g.* internal decoration and floor covering, window cleaning and replacement of broken windows, ground maintenance, *etc*. If the Contracting Authority takes this approach there may be a need for an interface agreement setting out how these short-term service providers will liaise with the Project Company and its Sub-Contractors, and making it clear that if, for example, the project becomes Unavailable as a result of actions by the short-term service provider this will not affect the Contract Payments (*i.e.* this is an Excusing Cause), but on the other hand making a deduction from the Contract Payments if the short-term service provider is prevented from carrying out its work. Such interface issues can be quite complex.

§8.5 FUEL OR OTHER INPUT-SUPPLY CONTRACT

Fuel or raw materials (referred to below as 'input supplies) are likely to be the main operating cost for a process-plant project selling an output product (as opposed to providing a service), whether under an Offtake Contract or into the open market. Security of the input supplies, on an appropriate pricing basis, is therefore an important building block for this type of project finance, usually achieved through a long-term Input-Supply Contract.

In some cases input supplies may create revenue for the Project Company, rather than incur a cost—examples include a municipal solid waste incinerator, or a water-treatment (sewage) plant, where the Project Company is paid to dispose of the waste or clean the sewage.

If a Project Company has an Offtake Contract, an Input-Supply Contract is usually signed which, as far as possible, matches the terms of the Offtake Contract,

---

[14] However there are some types of accommodation contract—prisons are an obvious case—where these services cannot be contracted separately.

such as the pricing basis, length of the contract, *force majeure, etc*. In the absence of an Offtake Contract, the Input-Supply Contract should normally run for at least the term of the debt.

Of course an Input-Supply Contract for the Project Company is an Offtake Contract for the Input Supplier, and therefore it may share many of the characteristics of an Offtake Contract.

§8.5.1 SUPPLY BASIS

The Project Company normally purchases its input supplies on an exclusive basis from the seller. The Input-Supply Contract sets out the technical specifications for the input supplies, with metering or other methods for measuring delivery volumes and quality, and a right to reject supplies if they do not meet the required standard.

The start-up date for supply is generally COD. This date should have some flexibility to allow for delays in Project Completion. (Provision may also be needed for input supplies to be made available to the project before Project Completion when required for testing purposes. Volumes and timing are obviously likely to be uncertain, and therefore arrangements for this have to be flexible.)

The volume of input supplies required by the Project Company is linked to the project's output. The Project Company may not be in control of that output, since demand for its product may depend on a long-term Offtake Contract, such as a PPA where an Offtaker who does not require power can tell the Project Company to shut down the power plant and continue to pay the Capacity Charge—in such cases the Project Company needs to ensure that its obligations to buy fuel can be reduced in parallel.

An Input Supplier who fails to deliver as contracted is liable to penalties (subject to being excused because of *force majeure*); however, in an arm's-length Input-Supply Contract (*i.e.* where there is no relationship between the Input Supplier and the Offtaker), these penalties may be limited to the extra cost of obtaining alternative supplies rather than any loss of revenue for the Project Company.

Since an Input-Supply Contract is an Offtake Contract for the Input Supplier, as with Offtake Contracts (*cf.* §6.3.1) different contractual approaches are used, involving different levels of commitment by the Project Company to purchase input supplies:

Take-or-Pay Contract. (Also called a Put-or-Pay Contract, to distinguish it from a Take-or-Pay contract signed with an Offtaker.) A Take-or-Pay Contract requires the Project Company to buy a specified minimum volume of input supplies. If the Project Company does not require the input supplies, they may be sold in the open market by the Project Company or the Input Supplier, where this is possible, but of course this may lead to a loss if the price paid by the Project Company is higher than the current market.

Take-and-Pay Contract. In this case the Project Company pays only for input supplies actually needed. Here the risk of disposing of unwanted input supplies remains with the Input Supplier.

Tolling Contract. In a Tolling Contract the input supplies are provided at no cost. In effect, the Project Company is paid a 'toll' (through a Capacity Charge) for processing the raw material into another product (whether or not the raw material is delivered). There are two types of tolling contracts:

- *Pull tolling.* The Offtaker prefers to handle and take the risk of securing input supplies, (*e.g.* a power purchaser may provide the gas for the Project Company's power plant); here, since the raw material supplier and the Offtaker are the same person, there is no benefit in this person paying for the product while charging for the raw material, since this is just moving money from one pocket to the other.
- *Push tolling.* The product is sold into a competitive market, and the Input Supplier is willing to take the price risk. In this case the Capacity Charge is paid by the Input Supplier rather than an Offtaker, and sales revenues flow directly to the Input Supplier (*e.g.* an oil company paying a refinery project to refine crude oil, or a metal company paying a smelter project to smelt copper).

The degree of commitment by the Input Supplier can also vary:

Fixed or Variable Supply. The Input Supplier agrees to provide a fixed quantity of supplies to the Project Company, on an agreed schedule (which may have some flexibility in timing), or a variable supply between an agreed maximum and minimum, as required by the Project Company. In either case the Input Supplier is responsible for ensuring it has enough supplies, and the supply may be under a take-or-pay or take-and-pay arrangement.

Output Dedication.[15] The Input Supplier dedicates the entire output from a specific source to the Project Company (*e.g.* all production from its own plant, or a Contracting Authority may send all its municipal solid waste to an incinerator); again, this can be under a take-or-pay or take-and-pay arrangement. It should be noted that the Input Supplier may have no obligation (other than a general requirement to act in good faith) to produce any output, unless agreed otherwise with the Project Company.

Reserve Dedication. This is similar to output dedication—the Input Supplier owns, say, a coal mine, and dedicates the entire output of the mine to the Project Company. Again the Input Supplier may have no more than a good faith obligation to produce anything, but anything that is produced

---

[15] Also known as 'sole supplier'.

cannot be sold to anyone other than the Project Company without the latter's agreement.

Interruptible Supply. Some input supplies, such as gas, are offered on a lower-cost 'interruptible' basis—often *via* a pipeline supplying other users. If the Project Company agrees that input supplies can be interrupted for specified maximum periods each year, the price for the supplies is reduced. So long as these arrangements can be kept parallel with Offtake Contract requirements for the operation of the project, they are beneficial to both Project Company and Offtaker.

Tolling Contract. In a Tolling Contract the Input Supplier has no commitment to supply at all, and may choose not to do so if the supplies can be used more profitably elsewhere. However, whether supplies are provided or not, a Capacity Charge must be paid to the Project Company.

§8.5.2 Physical Delivery Risks

Title and therefore risk of loss on the input supplies normally passes to the Project Company on delivery to the project site.

If the Input Supplier has to build a physical connection (*e.g.* a pipeline) to the project site, the Project Company may be required to pay a capacity payment to cover the cost of construction of the pipeline, in a similar way to the Capacity Charge under an Offtake Contract (*i.e.* irrespective of whether it takes the input supplies or not). This payment normally begins on the expected Project Completion date, subject to extensions for Compensation Events or Relief Events.

If the connection is not completed on time, the Input Supplier may provide compensation to the Project Company for the extra cost of obtaining supplies elsewhere.

Relief Events under the Input-Supply Contract may include problems with third-party connections (*e.g.* a railway line) used to make deliveries to the project site, meaning that the Input Supplier will be penalized if this prevents deliveries, but the Input Supply Contract cannot be terminated for default.

§8.5.3 Pricing Basis

Where there is an Offtake Contract, the pricing for the input supplies is normally linked to it:

either   the product price under the Offtake Contract is based on the cost of the input supplies (*e.g.* in the Energy Charge under a PPA); this approach is more likely where the input supplies are a widely traded commodity such as oil or gas;

or   the price under the Input-Supply Contract is based on the price at which the product is sold under the Offtake Contract. This approach is more likely either where the input supplies are a more specialized commodity such as petrochemicals, or if there is no Offtake Contract and risk is being passed back to the Input Supplier.

If there is no Offtake Contract the input supply price may be linked to the product sale price, based on a negotiated price, or simply based on the open-market price for the product.

Obviously if a Tolling Contract is used there is no price to be paid.

§8.5.4 SECURITY

The Input Supplier may require security from the Project Company for:

Project Completion. If the Input Supplier incurs costs in building connecting facilities such as a pipeline, the lenders or Sponsors may have to guarantee a penalty payment that enables the Input Supplier to recover these costs if their project is not completed. (Clearly a guarantee from the Project Company would have little value in such circumstances.)

Payment for Input Supplies. Input supplies are usually sold on credit, with payment being made at, say, monthly intervals in arrears. Again, lenders may be required to guarantee outstanding payments. As an alternative, the Input Supplier may be given security over stocks of input supplies at the plant (if these would normally be sufficient to cover the amounts due), or a first mortgage over the plant itself, ahead of the lenders. Although lenders would not normally allow anyone else to have security ahead of them, this leaves them in the same position as if they had guaranteed the amounts due and so should not be objectionable in principle. This alternative approach also saves the Project Company having to pay the lenders for giving a guarantee.

§8.5.5 RELIEF EVENTS AND CHANGE IN LAW

Relief Events (temporary *force majeure*) normally excuse the Input Supplier from making deliveries; Relief Events preventing completion or operation of the project excuse the Project Company from taking them.

A change in law could increase the Input Supplier's cost of fulfilling the contract, either because transportation costs are increased (*e.g.* because there are stricter rules on how the product is to be transported), or because a change in law (*e.g.* a new tax) affects the profit margin under the Input-Supply Contract. The Project Company can accept these risks if it is able to pass them on to an Offtaker (*cf.* §11.3).

§8.5.6 DEFAULT AND TERMINATION

The events which allow the Input Supplier to terminate the Input-Supply Contract must be limited or too much uncertainty may be created for the project financing. Typical events of default that could give rise to termination by the Input Supplier are:

- failure by the Project Company to pay for supplies;
- abandonment of the project, sale of the project assets, or failure to complete the project by an agreed long-stop date (subject to Relief or Compensation Event extensions);
- insolvency of the Project Company or acceleration of its debt.

Termination by the Project Company could be for:

- failure of the Input Supplier to make deliveries (subject to Relief Event exemptions);
- insolvency of the Input Supplier or acceleration of its debt;
- default by a guarantor of the Input-Supply Contract.

Permanent *force majeure* making continued deliveries impossible also gives rise to a mutual right to terminate the contract.

Rather than termination for failure to make deliveries, and a claim for a loss that may or may not be recovered, the Project Company may wish to enforce specific performance of the contract (*i.e.* obtain a court order requiring delivery of input supplies as contracted). Whether such a remedy is available varies between different countries. It may also be possible to make provision in the Input-Supply Contract for the Input Supplier to be required to obtain supplies from another source.

§8.6 INSURANCE

The extent to which insurance, and failing this a Project Agreement, covers *force majeure* risks is discussed in §9.9.

While not strictly a Sub-Contract, insurance is a key element in the network of contracts for a project financing. Insurance requirements in project finance are demanding, and as a result insurance costs are high, but this tends to be a neglected area of project development. This can lead to an underestimation of project costs because all required insurances have not been taken into account or to the financing being held up because the insurances required by the lenders are not in place. At an early stage of the project's development, therefore, the Sponsors need to appoint an insurance broker with specific experience both in insurance for project finance in general, and in insuring major projects in the country concerned, to advise on and eventually place the insurance program.

The broker also plays an important rôle in communicating information about the project to the insurance company. This is important because in some jurisdictions insurance is an *uberrimæ fidei* (of the utmost good faith) contract; if any material information is not disclosed to the insurer there is no obligation to pay under the policy (*cf.* comments on non-vitiation cover in §8.6.5). The broker must therefore work with the Project Company and the Sponsors to ensure that this does not happen.

Brokers are often paid a percentage of the insurance premiums, but this is obviously not an incentive to keep premiums down, and it is preferable to negotiate a fixed fee for their work.

The insurance is arranged in two phases: first, the insurance covering the whole of the construction phase of the project (including start-up and testing), and second, annual renewal of insurances when the project is in operation. It should be noted that the operating phase insurances (other than perhaps the first year) cannot be arranged or their premiums fixed in advance (*cf.* §9.9.2).

In addition, normal insurances required by law, such as public liability, employer's liability, vehicle insurances, *etc.*, have to be taken out by the Project Company or the Construction Contractor, as appropriate.

§8.6.1 CONSTRUCTION-PHASE INSURANCES

In construction contracts that are not being project-financed, it is common for the contractor to arrange the main insurances for the construction phase of the project and to include this as part of the contract price. This is logical, because under a standard construction contract the contractor is at risk of loss from insurable events: if part of the project is destroyed in a fire, the contractor is required to replace it, whether it is insured or not.

However, contractor-arranged insurance is not always suitable in project finance for several reasons:

- As will be seen, lenders require Delay in Start-Up insurance, which cannot easily be obtained by the Construction Contractor, who is not at risk of loss in this respect (although there may be liability for the consequences of the delay—*cf.* §8.2.8). If the Project Company takes out a separate insurance for this purpose, there is a risk that the two policies will not match properly.
- It is quite common in project finance to arrange insurance for the first year of operation as part of the package of construction-phase insurances, to ensure that there are no problems of transition between the two phases; again this could not be done in the name of the Construction Contractor.
- Projects that complete construction in phases (*e.g.* two production lines in a process plant) have construction and operation insurances in place at the same time; these have to be handled as one package and therefore have to

be arranged by the Project Company as the Construction Contractor has no interest in operating insurances.

- Lenders wish to exercise a close control on the terms of the insurance and on any claims, working through the Project Company, rather than leaving this to the Construction Contractor.
- There are a number of specific Lender requirements on insurance policies that may be difficult to accommodate if the policy is not in the Project Company's name (*cf.* §8.6.5).
- Lenders normally control application of the insurance proceeds.

Construction Contractor-sourced insurance may appear cheaper, but this is usually because the coverage is less comprehensive than that required by lenders.

But lender-controlled insurances may cause problems for the Construction Contractor. The Construction Contractor takes the risk of physical loss or damage before Project Completion and is thus responsible for making it good. The Construction Contractor would not be excused for a delay caused by waiting for an insurance claim to be settled, since this delay would not constitute a Relief Event under the Construction Contract, and may therefore have to order and pay for replacement equipment, even though it is still unclear whether the claim will be met in full by the insurance company (the Construction Contractor may have no direct knowledge of the progress of the insurance claim), or the proceeds disbursed by the lenders (rather than used to prepay debt—*cf.* §8.6.5). This is likely to be an area for delicate tripartite negotiation between the Project Company, Construction Contractor, and lenders.

The main insurances required for the construction phase of a project (and which usually cover the whole of the construction phase, rather than being annually renewable) are:

Construction and Erection All Risks ('CEAR').[16] This covers physical loss or damage to works, materials, and equipment at the project site. Where appropriate cover should include mechanical and electrical breakdown. The level of coverage is normally on a replacement-cost basis, including any extra import duties and costs of erection. Insured events include most *force majeure* risks, such as acts of war, fire, and natural disaster, as well as damage caused by defective design, material, or workmanship, or incorrect procedures in start-up and testing.

The main exception for the requirement for replacement-cost coverage is if it is inconceivable that the whole construction site could be destroyed at once (*e.g.* a road or a long pipeline). In such cases 'first loss' coverage may be effected—a level of coverage sufficient to cover the largest possible individual loss which could occur.

---

[16] Also known as Construction All Risks ('CAR') or Builder's All Risks.

Marine Cargo. This covers physical loss or damage to equipment in the course of transportation to the project site or in storage prior to delivery. The level of coverage should be sufficient to deal with the largest possible loss in one shipment. The scope of coverage is similar to CEAR insurance.

Public Liability.[17] This is usually bundled up with CEAR and covers all those involved in the project from third-party damage claims. As this insurance is relatively inexpensive, the levels of coverage are usually high.

Employer's Liability. In a similar way, this provides cover against injury to employees on the project site.

Contractor's Pollution Liability. Where appropriate, insurance may be required against third-party claims resulting from the Construction Contractor aggravating pre-existing pollution, or causing new pollution.

Environmental. Insurance may also be required to cover the risk of finding hidden pollution or hazardous waste on the construction site (*cf.* §9.10.3).

Delay in Start-Up ('DSU').[18] This compensates the Project Company for loss of profit or additional costs (or at least the cost of the debt interest and fixed operating costs, plus any penalties payable for late Project Completion of the project), resulting from a delay in start of operations of the project caused by a loss insured under the CEAR policy. The DSU coverage pays an agreed amount per day of delay, for an agreed maximum period of time. The level of coverage should be sufficient to deal with the longest possible delay caused by loss or damage to a crucial element of the project at the worst possible time. In a power project, for example, coverage for around 18 months of delay is normally required to allow for the delivery time for a replacement turbine, whereas a shorter period of say a year might be acceptable for a school building. DSU cover is expensive—roughly speaking it may double the cost of the construction-phase insurances, and the scale of coverage can be a matter of considerable discussion between the Sponsors and the lenders.

Marine DSU. Marine DSU covers the same scope as DSU in relation to delays caused by loss or damage to equipment being shipped to the project.

Force Majeure. The cover provided by *force-majeure* insurance is to enable the Project Company to pay its debt-service obligations if the project is completed late or otherwise affected by temporary *force-majeure* events that do not cause direct damage to the project (which should be covered by DSU) such as:

- Natural *Force-Majeure* events away from the project site, including damage in transit and at a supplier's premises (to the extent this is not covered under the DSU insurance);

---

[17] Also known as Third-Party Liability.

[18] Also known as Advance Loss of Profits ('ALOP'), although as mentioned the insurance may not actually cover loss of profits.

- strikes, *etc.*, but not between the Project Company and its employees;
- any other cause beyond the control of any project participants (*e.g.* damage affecting third-party connections), but not including a loss caused by financial default or insolvency.

In effect, *force-majeure* insurance may be used to cover any significant gaps in the DSU cover.

Liquidated Damages. The Construction Contractor may take out 'efficacy' insurance, which covers the liability to pay LDs for delay or poor performance (*cf.* §8.2.8).

§8.6.2 OPERATING-PHASE INSURANCES

In the operating phase, the insurance cover is similar in nature, but typically renewed on an annual basis, which creates a risk of uncontrollable changes in the premiums (*cf.* §9.9.2):

All Risks. Covers the project against physical damage. The level of coverage is normally the replacement cost of the project or relevant equipment (except where first loss cover as described above would be relevant). This coverage may be split into Property (or Material Damage) insurance and Machinery Breakdown (also known as Boiler and Machinery) insurance.

Public Liability/Employer's Liability/Pollution Liability. Similar to the coverage during the construction phase.

Business Interruption ('BI'). This is the equivalent of DSU insurance, once the project is operating. Again, the scale of coverage should be sufficient to cover losses (or at least interest, penalties, and fixed operating costs) during the maximum period of interruption that could be caused by having to replace a key element of the project.

Force Majeure. Similar in scope to the construction-phase insurance, covering debt service if the project cannot operate.

Environmental. Again insurance cover may still be needed for hidden pollution, or any new pollution resulting from the project (*cf.* §9.10.3; §9.10.4).

§8.6.3 DEDUCTIBLES

All these insurances are subject to deductibles (*i.e.* the loss to be borne by the Project Company before payments are made under the insurance cover). The Project Company may try to make these relatively large, since this cuts the cost of the insurance premiums. The Construction Contractor will try to make the CEAR and Marine Cargo deductibles as low as possible, to limit liability for such uninsured losses. The lenders will also try to keep all deductibles low to reduce their risk.

§8.6.4 SUPPLIER'S OR BUYER'S EXTENSIONS

These are an exception to the normal rule that loss of revenue will only be covered where it relates to damage at the insurer's own facility. A Supplier's Extension covers for loss of revenue for the Project Company caused by an Input Supplier failing to deliver the product required because of an insurable loss at its plant. Similar, a Buyer's Extension covers loss of revenue if the Buyer is unable to take the project's product because of its insurable loss.

These types of insurances may be useful in filling a gap in the risk-allocation structure (*cf.* §9.9.1), but as with DSU and BI insurances, they are fairly expensive.

§8.6.5 LENDER REQUIREMENTS

As the insurance forms an important part of the security package, the detailed terms of the policies and the insurance company's credit standing must be acceptable to the lenders.

There are also a number of specific requirements some or all of which lenders generally require to be included in insurance policies to ensure that they are properly protected (known as 'bankers' clauses):

Additional Insured. The lenders' agent bank or security trustee is named as an additional insured (or co-insured) party on the policies. (Apart from the Project Company, parties with an interest in the project such as the Offtaker/Contracting Authority, Construction Contractor, and O&M/Maintenance Contractor may also be named as additional insured.) As an additional insured party, the lenders are treated as if they were separately covered under the insurance policy, but have no obligations under the policy (*e.g.* to pay premiums).

Severability. The policies are stated to operate as providing separate instances for each of the insured parties.

Changes in and Cancellation of the Policy. The insurer is required to give the lenders prior notice of any proposed cancellation of, or material change proposed in the policies, and agrees that the policies cannot be amended without the lenders' consent.

Non-payment of Premiums. The insurer agrees to give the lenders notice of any non-payment of a premium. As additional insured, the lenders have the option, but not the obligation, to pay premiums if these are not paid by the Project Company.

Loss Payee. The lenders' agent bank or security trustee is named as sole loss payee on policies covering loss or damage, or sole loss payee for amounts above an agreed figure, with smaller amounts payable to the Project Company. (However, payments for third-party liability are made direct to the affected party.) This may also give the lenders the right to take action directly against the insurance company in some jurisdictions, but in any case assignment of the insurance policies forms part of the lenders' security package (*cf.* §14.7.1). In general being named as additional insured (see above) is preferable if being loss payee does not give the lenders the right to take direct action under the policy.

Waiver of Subrogation. The insurer waives the right of subrogation against the lenders; in general insurance law, an insurer who makes payment under a policy claim may be entitled to any share in a later recovery that is made by the lenders, such a repayment to the insurance company is not acceptable to the lenders until the debt is fully repaid.

Non-Vitiation. Lenders prefer to have a non-vitiation clause[19] included in the insurance policies. This provides that even if another insured party does something to vitiate (*i.e.* invalidate) the insurances (*e.g.* failure to disclose material information), this will not affect the coverage provided to the lenders. This can be a very difficult area to negotiate with the insurer, as it may add to their potential liability in a way that is not usual. In fact, in tighter insurance market conditions, it may not be possible to get the insurer to agree, and in such circumstances—if their insurance advisor advises there is no choice—lenders have to live without it.

It is sometimes possible to obtain separate coverage for this risk, and in some jurisdictions it may be dealt with by naming the lenders as additional insured parties and including a severability clause, and thus giving lenders their own direct rights that cannot be affected by the actions of others.

'Head for the Hills' *vs.* Reinstatement. The lenders often wish to have the option of using the proceeds of an insurance claim for physical damage to repay the debt rather than restore the project—the so-called 'head for the hills' option. This is unlikely to be realistic, given that even a project on one site (such as a process plant) is unlikely to be a total loss, and it is evident that will not be the case for a project on several sites, or a 'linear' infrastructure project such as a road (*cf.* §8.6.9): therefore, the insurance claim would normally not be enough to repay all the debt unless it came at a late stage in the project life. Also, the insurance company may require restoration of the project as a condition for paying out under the claim. Similarly, the Construction Contractor—if the project is still under construction—may wish to ensure that insurance proceeds are automatically applied to restoration of the project, rather than used to reduce debt, as would an Offtaker/ Contracting Authority if there is a Project Agreement. Nonetheless, the lenders may want to keep the option open, in case the project is no longer

---

[19] Also known as a 'breach of provision' or 'breach of warranty' clause.

economically viable when a claim is made. This then means that a definition of 'economic viability' needs to be included in the insurance provisions of the Project Agreement: typically this will relate to the ability of a restored project to cover the debt-service requirements. At the very least the lenders control how the insurance proceeds are disbursed (*cf.* §14.4.1).

Any payment covering loss of revenue (*i.e.* claims on DSU, BI, or *force majeure* policies) is controlled by the lenders in the same way as they control the application of the general revenues of the Project Company (*cf.* §14.4.2).

An Offtaker/Contracting Authority will also be concerned that adequate insurance is maintained, both to ensure continuity in the project, and to cover, as far as possible, any Termination Sum payment on termination of the Project Agreement for *force majeure* (*cf.* §7.10.4), so that similar requirements to those of the lenders would also apply in the Project Agreement.

§8.6.6 REINSURANCE

Most insurance companies insuring a large project will reinsure some of their liability in the reinsurance market. This is usually of no concern to lenders, as they rely on the primary liability (and credit standing) of the original insurance company. (Clearly the credit standing of the insurer must be acceptable to the lenders.)

However, in some countries local law may require that the insurances are all placed with domestic insurance companies. In developing countries these local insurance companies may have neither the credit standing nor the capacity to take on the insurance requirements for a major project.

The local insurance companies therefore normally reinsure the risk on the international market: this reinsurance can provide the route to dealing with investors' and lenders' credit problems with the local insurers, by allowing a 'cut-through' to the reinsurance (*i.e.* the local insurer instructs the reinsurers to pay any claims directly to the Project Company or the lenders), hence reducing the local credit risk issue (although there could still be a problem if the local insurance company, as the person to whom the reinsurance payments are legally due, goes bankrupt—this may be avoided by the local insurer executing a legal assignment of these proceeds to the lenders).

§8.6.7 CONTROL OF LITIGATION

In general the insurer will want to control any litigation which may change the amount payable under its policies. There may be cases when an Offtaker/Contracting Authority, for reasons of general policy and precedent, wants to pursue a legal claim when the insurance company may be willing to settle the claim. This can be dealt with by the Offtaker/Contracting Authority agreeing to cover the additional legal costs, and any increase in the claim compared to that which would have applied had there been a settlement without litigation.

§8.6.8 INSURANCE PREMIUM/UNINSURABLE RISK

Insurance-premium risk is discussed in §9.9.2, and unavailability of insurance in §9.9.3.

§8.6.9 LINEAR OR MULTI-SITE PROJECTS

It may not be necessary to insure for the full replacement cost of a project, if that project is a 'linear' project, such as a road (*cf.* §8.6.10), or is on multiple separate sites. In these cases the chances of a total loss of the whole project are almost negligible, so the sum insured may be based on the highest reasonably conceivable loss.

§8.6.10 PORTFOLIO INSURANCE/SELF-INSURANCE

If the Sponsors have a large portfolio of similar projects, they may find it more cost-effective to insure the portfolio as a whole, rather than the individual project. This may be acceptable to lenders if their interests can be protected as set out above.

Alternatively, an Offtaker/Contracting Authority may prefer to self-insure the project and compensate the Project Company for any losses accordingly. This could be the case where the Offtaker/Contracting Authority has a large portfolio of similar assets, so the risk is widely spread and thus occurrences of loss as a percentage of the total value of the assets would be similar to the insurance premiums which would otherwise have been paid. Similarly, road and transportation projects may not take out operating insurances for physical damage through the Project Company. In these cases the public sector has again traditionally self-insured (*i.e.* taken the risks on without any insurances, a reasonable approach given the widespread nature of the risks involved).

Also there may not be a suitable insurance market for some types of project—*e.g.* lack of insurance for prisons may be a problem for a PPP prison project, and insurance may not be available for some types of defense project. In such cases self-insurance by the Offtaker/Contracting Authority is the only solution.

§8.7 SITE LEASE AND OTHER USAGE RIGHTS

In projects where there is a public-sector Offtaker, or a Contracting Authority, this party often provides the site for the project, especially where a Reverting Asset is involved. The Project Company is given the right to use the site for the project, for the term of the Project Agreement. This right may take the form of a lease, or some other form of permit, depending on the relevant legal environment.

The main concern of the Project Company and its lenders will be to ensure that the property-law structure does not increase the Project Company's obligations, nor reduce the rights, which it has under the Project Agreement.

The Offtaker/Contracting Authority needs to ensure that there is no incentive for the Project Company to separate the lease from the project and then sell the lease without completing the project (*cf.* §7.10.7).

§8.8 PERMITS AND OTHER RIGHTS

The Permits and other rights required for construction and operation of the project are not separate contracts, but obtaining or providing for these is usually both a key condition precedent to the effectiveness of the Project Contracts and to Financial Close.

Permits divide into two main categories: firstly those required for construction and operation of the project (§8.8.1), including rights of way or easements (§8.8.2), and agreements to use common facilities with another party (§8.8.3). Secondly, in some countries, Permits may be required for investment in and financing of the Project Company (§8.8.4).

§8.8.1 PROJECT PERMITS

Permits vary greatly from country to country and from project to project. They may be granted by central government departments or regional or local authorities. If there is a Project Agreement with a public-sector Offtaker, or with a Contracting Authority, this may automatically grant the project some of the required Permits, or it may give assurances that the government will provide support in obtaining them.

Major projects are likely to require a lot of Permits, and failure to obtain Permits in good time can seriously affect progress. The Sponsors and the Project Company need to ensure that their organization includes people dealing with Permits, in close liaison with the legal advisors.

Construction Permits. A wide variety of specific Permits for construction may be required. Responsibility for obtaining such Permits should generally lie with the Construction Contractor, who should be experienced in this area, and should take the risk of delays caused by Permits not being obtained in time. Some Permits may only be issued on application by the Project Company rather than the Construction Contractor, but the Construction Contractor should where possible be responsible for preparing the permit applications on the Project Company's behalf.

Permits may also be needed for the import of equipment for the project and the temporary import of construction equipment.

Operating Permits. Permits to operate the project are also likely to be required. These may relate to the operation of particular types of industrial plant, emissions or noise levels from the project, or cover matters such as health and safety in the project. They may also be needed for the import of fuel or raw materials. It may not be possible to obtain such Permits until the project is complete, because for example it may be necessary to demonstrate the actual emissions, noise levels, *etc.* of the project (*cf.* §9.5.3).

§8.8.2 Rights of Way and Easements

In addition to these official Permits, the Project Company may also need to obtain rights of way (*e.g.* access to the site for construction or operation or to lay a pipeline for delivery of fuel) or easements (*e.g.* a right to discharge water) from parties owning adjacent land, who may have no other connection with the project.

§8.8.3 Shared Facilities

Some projects may be built in two phases and raise finance separately for each phase (*e.g.* a process plant or power station with two separate production or power-generation lines). In such cases the construction of the first phase of the project usually includes provision for the common facilities required by both lines such as water intake and outlet.

Similarly, a cogeneration project, in which a power plant sells steam to an industrial user, may also share facilities with the steam buyer, such as a demineralized water supply, water discharge, and other utilities.

In such cases the rights of each party have to be clearly documented, including:

- access for construction of the new project;
- rights to use the common facilities (including priority of use);
- obligations to maintain the common facilities;
- provision for the protection of the dependent project if the other project is abandoned or foreclosed.

§8.8.4 Investment and Financing Permits

Specific Permits for the investment in or financing of the Project Company are unlikely to be required in developed countries, but in developing countries investment and exchange controls are likely to be applied to the Project Company.

Investment Permits. Permits may be required for foreign investors (including the Sponsors) investing in the Project Company and for remitting dividends or other payments by the Project Company to investors overseas.

Tax Exemptions may also be given (*e.g.* exempting dividends and interest paid to overseas investors, or interest paid to lenders, from withholding tax).

Exchange Controls. Countries with exchange-control systems restrict the ability of companies to undertake foreign-currency exchange and payment transactions. Exchange controls may prevent the Project Company from:

- holding bank accounts in foreign currencies;
- holding bank accounts outside the country;
- borrowing foreign currency or amending the terms of foreign currency loans;
- making payments to suppliers outside the country.

In such cases specific approvals are required from the country's central bank or ministry of finance to undertake these transactions where they are required for the project financing.

§8.9 AMENDMENTS TO AND REPLACEMENT OF SUB-CONTRACTS

An Offtaker/Contracting Authority will normally wish to exercise some control over amendments to Sub-Contracts, bearing in mind that the review of these contracts, and of the particular Sub-Contractors, will have been part of its due diligence when entering into the Project Agreement. On the other hand, the Project Company will want to deal with its own Sub-Contractors without interference, especially if there is a problem with the project. The usual compromise here is that amendments which may increase the Offtaker/Contracting Authority's liability (*e.g.* for payments on early termination—*cf.* §7.10.2), or affect obligations under the Project Agreement require its approval. Other issues can be dealt with in the Payment Mechanism.

Similarly the Project Company will usually want to have the freedom to replace any Sub-Contractors who are not performing as required, and since the Project Company is taking the risk on this performance the Offtaker/Contracting Authority should normally have limited rights (*e.g.* based on an objective view of the Sub-Contractor's financial strength and technical capacity) to control this.

§8.10 PARENT-COMPANY GUARANTEES

If, as is commonly the case, a Sub-Contractor is a subsidiary of a much larger company, lenders may require that the former's obligations in its Sub-Contract are guaranteed by its parent company (*cf.* §9.5.4). For example, if the O&M/maintenance is being dealt with by an SPV set up for the purposes of this contract with no other source of funds, the transfer of risks such as excess maintenance costs from the Project Company may be compromised. The solution may be for the SPV to provide a parent-company guarantee ('PCG') of its LD or other obligations.[20]

§8.11 DIRECT AGREEMENTS

The Offtaker/Contracting Authority, Construction Contractor, O&M/Maintenance Contractor, Building-Services Contractor, Input Supplier, and other key Project Contract counterparties are all normally required to sign Direct Agreements with the lenders (to which the Project Company may also be a party).[21]

Similar agreements will be signed between the Offtaker/Contracting Authority and these parties, to give the former the right to take over the Project Contracts if there is an early termination and the lenders do not step in.[22]

Whether Direct Agreements should be classified as Project Contracts or financing documentation is a moot point, but they are usually negotiated at the same time as the Project Contracts, and the form of Direct Agreement is set out as an annex to the relevant Project Contract.[23]

Under these Direct Agreements:

- The lenders' security interests in the underlying Project Contracts are acknowledged.
- Contract Payments by the Offtaker/Contracting Authority are to be made to specific bank accounts (over which the lenders have security) or as notified by the lenders.
- The Offtaker/Contracting Authority agrees that amendments will not be made to the contract concerned without the lenders' consent.

---

[20] The same is true for any other Project Contract being carried out by an SPV, but maintenance costs are the main long-term concern in this respect. But a PCG may also be required for the Construction Contractor's obligations, even though these are shorter term.

[21] Also known as 'acknowledgments and consents,' since they acknowledge the position of the lenders, and consent to their taking an assignment of the contracts as security, and as 'tripartite deeds' because there are usually three parties (the lenders, the Project Company and the relevant Sub-Contractor).

[22] A Direct Agreement is also known as a 'consent to assignment' if this is the main purpose of the agreement.

[23] It can be difficult to 'retrofit' a Direct Agreement onto a Project Contract which has already been negotiated, which is why it is advisable to include the form of Direct Agreement in the Project Contract itself.

- The lenders are notified if the Project Company is in default under the underlying contract and have the right to join in any discussions the Offtaker/Contracting Authority at that time.
- The lenders are given 'cure periods,' (*i.e.* extra time to take action to remedy the Project Company's default, in addition to that already given to the Project Company) before the contract is terminated. These cure periods are limited in length—perhaps only a week or two—where the Project Company has failed to pay money when due (except under the Construction Contract where a suspension period applies—*cf.* §8.2.9), but substantially longer for non-financial default (*e.g.* failure to operate the project to the required minimum performance level)—usually around 6 months—if the lenders are taking active steps to find a solution to the problem.
- The Offtaker/Contracting Authority is obliged to continue to perform its obligations during the cure period, so long as payments of money (*e.g.* for fuel deliveries) during this time are made when due.
- The lenders have the right to 'Step-In' to the contract during the sure period. This means that they can appoint a nominee to undertake the Project Company's rights in parallel with the Project Company; the nominee is effectively in charge of the project, but the Project Company remains liable for all the obligations. The period of Step-In is at the lenders' discretion, and they can 'step-out' again whenever they wish.
- Alternatively, the lenders have the right to 'Substitution,' *i.e.* appointment of a new obligor in the place of the Project Company, who then ceases to have any further involvement with the project (other than the right to any cash or perhaps a retransfer of the relevant Project Contract, after the loans have been repaid). The technical and financial capacity of the lenders' nominee or substitute obligor may have to be acceptable to the Project Contract counterpart.
- The lenders themselves will not assume any additional liability as a result of Step-In or substitution.
- Neither Step-In nor substitution extends the lenders' cure period; they have to take place before the end of the cure period, and any defaults must have been remedied by that time.
- The lenders may also be given the right to step in because there is a default under the financing, even if the Project Contract concerned is not in default.
- The Project Company undertakes (either in the Direct Agreement itself or in the financing documentation) not to obstruct the lenders' exercise of their Step-In and substitution rights provided an Event of Default under the financing documentation has occurred.
- In the case of a Project Agreement with a Termination Sum on Project Company default (*cf.* §7.10.1), the Offtaker/Contracting Authority may

agree that if the lenders enforce their security, the Project Agreement will automatically be terminated, thus ensuring the Termination Sum is paid. (In return, the Offtaker/Contracting Authority may also want the right to terminate the Project Agreement if the lenders cease to make funds available for construction of the project.)

- Additional assurances may also be given to the lenders under a Direct Agreement, *e.g.* the Host Government may confirm that the lenders will be allowed to remove project assets or proceeds from sale of assets out of the country if they terminate their loan and enforce their security.
- In general, additional provisions may be negotiated through the lenders in a Direct Agreement as an indirect way for the Project Company to improve the terms of the relevant Project Contract, *e.g.*:
- Extra financial guarantees may be provided by the Host Government for performance of Project Contract counterparties.
- A Host Government may give further assurances on policy matters affecting the project (*e.g.* privatization of an Offtaker).

A public-sector Offtaker, or a Contracting Authority, may also receive some additional assurances or benefits, for example, a right of pre-emption if the lenders exercise their security.

Some of these provisions may be covered in a Government Support Agreement (*cf.* §11.7), with the benefit transferred to lenders *via* a Direct Agreement relating to this Government Support Agreement.

It could be argued that the practical value to the lenders of many of the provisions of Direct Agreements is questionable. (Moreover, third parties, especially in the public sector, may be reluctant to sign such agreements.) The Project Company clearly has little interest in them (unless they indirectly improve the terms of the underlying Project Contracts), since the Direct Agreements effectively cut the Project Company out of the picture once it is in default and create a direct relationship between the lenders and the Project Contract counterparts. In practice, if a project is going wrong, all parties have to sit around the table and try to find a solution, whether there is a Direct Agreement or not. However, from the lenders' point of view probably the most important point is that the real value of their security lies in the Project Contracts, and Direct Agreements may help them to step rapidly into the picture after a Project Company default to preserve these contracts and find another party to take them over (*cf.* §14.7).

The lenders may also obtain 'collateral warranties' with respect to construction or operation of the project from, *e.g.* the Construction Contractor, or other person performing a service for the Project Company, under which direct liability is accepted for the performance of this service (to the extent agreed in the contract with the Project Company) *vis-à-vis* the lenders.

Chapter 9

COMMERCIAL RISKS

§9.1 INTRODUCTION

Project-finance risks can be divided into four main categories (which from a lender's point of view can be described collectively as credit risks[1]):

Commercial Risks (also known as project risks) are those inherent in the project itself, or the market in which it operates, as summarized in §9.3 and discussed in this chapter.[2]

Macro-Economic Risks (also known as financial risks) relate to external economic effects not directly related to the project (*i.e.* inflation, interest rates, and currency-exchange rates); these risks are considered in Chapter 10.

---

[1] *Cf.* Marco Sorge, "The Nature of Credit Risk in Project Finance", *BIS Quarterly Review* (Bank for International Settlements, Basel) December 2004, p.91*.

[2] It should be noted that the classifications of commercial risks set out in the remainder of this chapter are inevitably only a guide to the issues that may have to be considered in any particular case, as each project has its own characteristics.

197

Principles of Project Finance. DOI: http://dx.doi.org/10.1016/B978-0-12-391058-5.00009-6

Regulatory and Political Risks, *i.e.* changes in law, or risks which relate to the effects of government action or Political *Force Majeure* events such as war and civil disturbance (the latter are also known as country risks, and are especially, but not exclusively, relevant if the project involves cross-border financing or investment); these risks are considered in Chapter 11.

§9.2 RISK EVALUATION AND ALLOCATION

Risk evaluation is at the heart of project finance. Project-finance risk analysis is based on:

- a due-diligence process intended to ensure that all the necessary information about the project is available;
- identification of project risks, based on this due diligence;
- allocation of risks (to the extent possible) to appropriate parties to the project through provisions in the Project Contracts;
- quantifying and considering the acceptability of the residual risks that remain with the Project Company, and hence with its lenders.

Of course, due diligence and risk assessment are not procedures peculiar to project finance, and all financing involves risk in some way. But the process of contractual risk allocation, and raising finance based on this, are particular characteristics of project finance.

The theoretical principle of risk allocation in project finance is that risks should be borne by those who are best able to control or manage them, and to bear their financial consequences: for example, the risk of late Project Completion and its financial consequences for the project should ultimately be borne by the Construction Contractor, unless this late Project Completion arises from events outside the Construction Contractor's control, in which case insurance may step in to take such risks.

Risk and the Project Company. Other parties to Project Contracts have to recognize that the Project Company's ability to absorb risk is limited if it wishes to raise highly-leveraged project finance: it is no use allocating risk to a party who cannot sustain the financial consequences if the risk materializes. Similarly, if the Offtaker/Contracting Authority wishes to achieve the lowest possible Contract Payments, this usually implies that it must absorb a higher level of risk (*cf.* §2.6.2). A common error in the early development and negotiation of Project Contracts is to leave too much risk with the Project Company, which causes problems later when raising the finance. On the other hand, transfer of all risk away from the Project Company to other parties is not viable; if other parties are asked to assume too much of the risk, they will also expect the appropriate equity return for doing so, with obvious consequences for investors in the Project Company.

Risk and Value for Money. When an Offtaker/Contracting Authority is considering the extent to which risks should be transferred to a Project Company, a key issue is whether such risk transfer can be considered 'Value for Money' ('VfM'). Almost any risk can be transferred at a price, but if the Offtaker/ the Contracting Authority tries to push risks onto the shoulders of the Project Company which the latter cannot easily manage, the Project Company will include a large safety margin to cover such risks in its Contract Payment proposals. Paying for this safety margin may be a wasted expense for the Offtaker/Contracting Authority, and so it may therefore be better VfM for the Offtaker/Contracting Authority to retain the risk itself.

Risk and the Lenders. As to risk allocation between Sponsors and lenders, one basic fact has to be kept in mind: the Sponsors and other investors have 'upside' and 'downside', *i.e.* if the project goes well, they will earn a better return on their investment, but if it goes badly they may lose money. Lenders only have 'downside': if the project goes well they don't benefit, as their loan terms are fixed, whereas if it goes badly they may lose money. It follows from this that risk minimization is a key principle for the lenders—so, as the saying goes, 'a banker is a man who lends you his umbrella when it's not raining.'[3]

Thus the lenders are not 'investors' in the project, although Sponsors may use this expression in the heat of negotiation. If the lenders were investors they would get an equity rate of return, but they do not; typically in a successful project, the gross rate of return on the equity is at least twice that on the debt, which reflects the different risks taken by investors and lenders. As the ability of the Project Company itself to absorb risk is limited by the low level of its equity, this may mean in some cases transfer of risk from the Project Company to the Sponsors (*cf.* §9.13).

It should be noted that risk assessment by lenders is based as much on the financial impact that a particular risk may have on the project's viability as on the likelihood of it actually happening: so a 'low probability/ high impact' risk is one that will usually concern the lenders.[4] As a result, Sponsors may feel that lenders concentrate on risks that are unlikely to arise and therefore of little commercial importance.

Although the process of due diligence and risk evaluation may be thought of as primarily one to be undertaken by lenders, it is evident that if the Sponsors, and an

---

[3] This has been attributed to Mark Twain, but there seems to be no evidence that he actually said or wrote it.

[4] This is the reason that Monte-Carlo simulation (*cf.* §12.2.4) is not relevant for lenders.

Offtaker/Contracting Authority, if any, do not go through the same process first, they will not be able to develop a financeable project.

§9.3 ANALYSIS OF COMMERCIAL RISKS

The main questions to be considered in the commercial risk-analysis process can be summarized as:

- *Commercial viability*: does the project make overall commercial sense for all parties (§9.4)?
- *Construction risks*: can the project be built on time and on budget (§9.5)?
- *Revenue risks*: will its operating revenues be as projected (§9.6)?
- *Operating risks*: is the project capable of operating at the projected performance level and cost (§9.7)?
- *Input supply risks*: can raw materials or other inputs be obtained at the projected costs (§9.8)?
- *Uninsured risks*: are there significant risks not covered by insurance? (§9.9)?
- *Environmental risks*: what effect will the project have on its surrounding environment (§9.10)?
- *Residual-value risk*: what happens to the project after the end of the Project Agreement (§9.11)?
- *Contract mismatch*: do the Project Contracts fit together properly (§9.12)?
- *Sponsor support*: is there a need for more recourse to the Sponsors (§9.13)?
- *Risks for the Offtaker/Contracting Authority*: are these reasonable (§9.14)?
- *Reasons for failure*: does the project display any of the common reasons for failure (§9.15)?
- *Loss on default*: what level of loss can a lender expect if the project does in fact default (§9.16)?

The due-diligence process therefore examines the risks inherent in the project under these different headings, the extent to which these are covered or mitigated by contractual arrangements, and whether remaining risks left with the Project Company are reasonable and acceptable to lenders. One standard approach to this is to produce a 'risk matrix' table,[5] which sets out in columns:

- what the risk is;
- whether it is covered in the Project Contracts;
- what other mitigation there is for risks not covered contractually (*e.g.* through guarantees or insurance);
- what impact the risk that remains would have on the Project Company (and hence effectively the lenders).

---

[5] Also known as a 'risk register'.

The final effect of risk allocation within the Project Agreement will be reflected in the classification of risks as Compensation Events (*cf.* §7.6), Excusing Causes (*cf.* §7.7), or Relief Events (*cf.* §7.8). Insofar as they are not listed in the Project Agreement within any of these categories, risks will lie with the Project Company. However the Project Company may transfer these risks to a Sub-Contractor, by dealing with their effect in the relevant Sub-Contract. So for example a risk which is not covered by the Project Agreement—such as late Project Completion—may give rise to a claim against the Construction Contractor (*cf.* §8.2.8), *i.e.* the Construction Contractor will have to compensate the Project Company, should the risk crystallize. In some cases risks may be taken on by the Sponsors (*cf.* §9.13).[6]

§9.4 COMMERCIAL VIABILITY

The first step in due diligence for any project is to consider its basic commercial viability (*i.e.* is there a sound market for the product or service provided by the Project Company?). This initial question has nothing to do with the terms of any contracts signed by the Project Company. Project finance is a long-term business, and long-term contracts that give an undue advantage to one side are vulnerable; it is impossible to provide in advance for every event that may affect a Project Contract in the future, and an aggrieved party will obviously take advantage of any flaw to get out of an onerous obligation. Therefore the deal underlying any Project Contract should make good long-term commercial sense for both parties.

Questions that may be considered in examining commercial viability include:

- Is there an established market for the project's product or service?
- What competition exists or may exist in this market in the future?
- Is the price at which the product or service is being sold reasonable in relation to the existing market, and does it take adequate account of future competition?
- Is the technology proven?
- Can any major structural changes in the market (*e.g.* deregulation or new technology) be foreseen, and what might the effect of these be?
- Is the project affordable within the Offtaker/Contracting Authority's long-term budget, or can the prospective end-users of the product or service afford to pay for it (and would they willing to do so)?
- Are other players in the same market facing any particular difficulties?
- Are the prices quoted by the Construction Contractor or the Input Supplier(s) realistic?

---

[6] For another useful classification of project risks (in relation to a power project), *cf.* Jeff Ruster, "Mitigating Commercial Risks in Project Finance", *Public Policy for the Private Sector, Note 69* (World Bank, Washington DC, 1996).*

- Is there anything that would prevent the project operating normally when complete (*e.g.* grid connections for a power station, connecting roads for a bridge, input-supply delivery) and have arrangements been made to ensure that this is dealt with?

The following are some examples of types of projects that have an apparently sound contractual structure, but which are not commercially viable:

- The Construction Contractor has quoted too low a price, perhaps because of insufficient experience of this sector. A Construction Contractor who finds that there is going to be a loss on the Construction Contract will use every loophole which can be found in the contract terms and specifications to claim more money for the job. Such disputes may seriously delay the project and affect its overall viability.
- The cost of the product or service sold under a Project Agreement is not competitive (or is likely to become uncompetitive) with current prices for the same product or service, or too high in relation to the ability of end-users to pay for it. The Offtaker/Contracting Authority, squeezed between the Project Company and the end-users, will inevitably try to find a way out of the contract.
- A power station project depends on the state power company as Offtaker connecting the plant to the national grid system; the Offtaker is obliged to pay the Capacity Charge even if the grid connection is not made. Although this is a reasonable provision for a PPA, a 'white elephant' plant is of no use to the Offtaker, who will try to find any way to get out of the PPA if the grid connection cannot be funded or completed.
- An Input Supplier, relying on the open market to source supplies, faces a large increase in the free-market price for the product concerned, which is not reflected in the long-term sales price in the Input-Supply Contract, because the contract price is not linked to the free-market price. Disputes or even default on the Input-Supply Contract are highly likely.
- A hospital provided under the PFI Model is built and operated as required in the project Agreement, but the Contracting Authority's annual budget is lower than projected, and the Service Fees take up such a large part of the actual budget that the other health services provided by the Contracting Authority, which are not based on any long-term contracts, have to be reduced in scope (and hence cost) to balance the budget—*i.e.* the Project Agreement is not 'affordable'. This situation is likely to lead to political problems for the project.

Incomplete Contract. As mentioned above there is a high risk that something will happen over the life of the Project Agreement which the parties have not thought of, *i.e.* that it may be what lawyers call an 'incomplete contract'.[7] An incomplete contract is one with gaps, missing provisions, or ambiguities which may have to be dealt with either by renegotiation or through a court. The more complex the contract the higher the possibility that this may be the case. This can obviously result in a Project Agreement which becomes commercially unviable. There is no real answer to this, other than to be aware of the risk and try to ensure that due diligence and risk analysis is as thorough as possible.

Project Company Management. Lenders also review the proposed management structure of the Project Company itself, to ensure that the required skills are available, either through the Project Company's own staff, or through a management contract (*cf.* §3.6.3).

§9.5 CONSTRUCTION RISKS

The first detailed due-diligence question is whether the project can be completed on time, on budget and to the required specification—this question obviously mainly revolves around the risks inherent in the construction process.

The key construction-phase risks[8] include:

- site acquisition and access (§9.5.1);
- site condition (§9.5.2);
- Permits (§9.5.3);
- risks relating to the Construction Contractor (§9.5.4);
- Construction Contract-related cost overruns (§9.5.5);
- other construction-phase cost overruns (§9.5.6);
- revenue during construction (§9.5.7);
- delay in Project Completion (§9.5.8);
- third-party risks (§9.5.9).
- inadequate performance on Project Completion (§9.5.10).

The Construction Contractor will have its own concerns about the financial risks it is taking in contracting with a Project Company (§9.5.11).

---

[7] There is also a 'principal/agent' problem with many types of project, *i.e.* the agent (in this case the investors) controls the project on a day-to-day basis, and has more information and is better resourced than the principal (here the Contracting Authority). So the agent can make money at the expense of the principal, even though it is the principal's project. A simpler example of this is that the board directors of a company (the agents) can pay themselves high salaries because it is difficult for the shareholders (the principals) to control this.

[8] Also known as completion risks. *Cf.* Robert Bain & Jan Willem Plantagie, *The Anatomy Of Construction Risk: Lessons From A Millennium of PPP Experience* (Standard & Poor's, 2007)*.

The position where there is no fixed-price, date-certain, turnkey Construction Contract also needs to be considered (§9.5.12).

§9.5.1 SITE ACQUISITION AND ACCESS

Lenders will not normally take on this risk, and therefore only lend when the Project Company has clear title[9] and access to the project site, and any additional land needed during construction. This is mainly likely to be a problem in a linear infrastructure project, *e.g.* where land has to be acquired for a road or a railway line, and acquisition is not complete at the time construction on one part of the project begins.

In PPPs, it is common for site acquisition to be the responsibility of the Offtaker/Contracting Authority, since this often involves acquiring large areas of land in multiple ownership, for which public-sector compulsory-purchase powers may be needed.

§9.5.2 SITE CONDITION

There are a variety of ways in which the condition of the project site may affect construction, either by increasing the costs of construction or causing delays in Project Completion (or both):

Geological Structure. Generally speaking the Construction Contractor should accept the risk of problems with the geology (*e.g.* affecting foundation or piling costs). Test borings before the Construction Contract is signed—perhaps carried out by the Project Company or the Offtaker/Contracting Authority—can be helpful in this respect, although this can never provide 100% certainty that there is not a problem that has not been picked up by the survey. The problem can be especially acute in linear projects—*i.e.* projects not occupying one site, but being built over a long stretch of land where detailed site investigation may be impossible, such as a road, pipeline or electricity gridline.

Previous Use. The way in which a project site has been used in the past may create risks for construction on the site (*cf.* §9.10.3). Lenders certainly prefer to see projects being built on 'greenfield' rather than 'brownfield' sites. Previous heavy commercial or industrial use is one warning sign. Conversely, land which has been used for farming, residential property, offices or warehouses would usually be considered low risk. A high risk may have to be treated as a Compensation Event under both the Project Agreement and the Construction Contract.

---

[9] This may consist of a license from the Offtaker/Contracting Authority to use the land, rather than an ownership interest, if it is public-sector owned land.

Latent Defects. The same principle applies to structures which will form part of the project and so remain on the site. In some cases the condition of the assets cannot be easily ascertained (*e.g.* there may be latent defects in old buildings, bridges, or tunnels), and clearly the lenders will not wish the Project Company to take on unknown risks of this type.

Pre-Existing Contamination. *Cf.* §9.10.3.

Discoveries at the Site. Extra costs may be caused by delays due to the discovery of fossils, archæological remains, human remains, and so on; again this is a risk which would normally be assumed by the Construction Contractor.

If such problems are unexpected, and therefore have not been dealt with in the Project Contracts, the main mitigation from the lenders' point of view is that risks of this nature should be apparent at an early stage of construction, when project costs have probably not yet exceeded the amount of the equity investment; therefore, they can stop advancing funds if any major issues of this type arise (*cf.* §14.3.2; §14.12), with their risk covered by the equity.

In any case delays resulting from these issues of site condition would generally be treated as Relief Events in both the Project Agreement and the Construction Contract.

§9.5.3 PERMITS

Lenders generally require construction Permits (*cf.* §8.8.1) to be obtained before any funds are advanced, to ensure that failure to obtain such permits does not delay Project Completion. If, for good reason, such Permits cannot be obtained at this stage, a specific timetable for obtaining them is normally established with the lenders. Where possible lenders prefer the risk of obtaining these later Permits to be placed on the Construction Contractor, who thus becomes responsible for any delay caused by failure to obtain them.

Rights of way, easements, *etc.* (*cf.* §8.8.2) may be more difficult where these involve parties not otherwise connected with the project, and the Construction Contractor is unlikely to take the risk of obtaining these; lenders will be uncomfortable if these are not obtained prior to Financial Close.

Investment and financing permits (*cf.* §8.8.4) must be obtained before the financing can become effective. In some countries the final approval for the financing is not granted by the central bank until after the loan has been signed and registered with them, which means there is an inevitable gap between the loan signing and Financial Close.

Final Project Completion may also be dependent on obtaining operating Permits that confirm that the project meets emissions or other environmental requirements (*cf.* §9.10) or health and safety regulations. Often these cannot be obtained in advance, but obtaining such Permits (or meeting the requirements to obtain them) should where possible be an obligation of the Construction Contractor: if this is made a condition to reaching Project Completion under the Construction Contract (*cf.* §8.2.5), the risk of failure to obtain operating Permits is thus transferred to the Construction Contractor.

A Government Support Agreement (*cf.* §11.7) can be helpful in reducing the risk of problems with Permits; although it may not eliminate the need for Permits, it can provide a basis for the cooperation of the government in obtaining the permits from ministries and other agencies. The central government may not be willing to take responsibility for ensuring permits are obtained from provincial, state, or local governments, over which it has no control. In projects in developing countries, the Offtaker/Contracting Authority may take the risk of permits not being obtained as required, provided the Project Company can demonstrate that it has applied for them diligently.

§9.5.4 THE CONSTRUCTION CONTRACTOR

The 'counterparty risks' in projects need to be identified and analyzed. These risks—mainly related to technical and financial capacity—relate to all parties with which the Project Company has contracts or Sub-Contracts: these could include the Construction Contractor, Contracting Authority (especially if it is not part of central government—*cf.* §11.6), Input Supplier (*cf.* §9.8.1) and O&M Contractor (*cf.* §9.7.2). The risk related to a project counterparty is less if that party can be replaced easily, which may be the case with an O&M Contractor but not with a Construction Contractor. It may be necessary to obtain a parent-company guarantee (*cf.* §8.10) for private-sector project counterparties' obligations.

Counterparty risk analysis of the Construction Contractor[10] takes account of:

- competence to undertake the work;
- technology risk;
- position as a Sponsor (if relevant);
- level of direct involvement in the Construction Contract;
- whether the pricing for the work is appropriate;
- the scale of the Construction Contract in relation to the size of the Construction Contractor;
- the Construction Contractor's overall credit standing.

This type of counterparty review is a fundamental first step before considering risk allocation in the Construction Contract itself.

---

[10] A similar type of review should also be applied to other key project counterparties.

Competence. The Construction Contractor plays a vital rôle in most projects, and therefore the first step in risk assessment is to consider whether the Construction Contractor is adequately qualified for this, with sufficient experienced personnel to undertake the job. It is unlikely that finance could be raised for any project where lenders are not convinced that the Construction Contractor has a good record in similar projects. Clearly the more complex the construction of the project, the more this becomes an issue: there would be less concern about the ability to build a school, compared with the ability to build a power station.

The right to claim LDs, bonding, and other security provided under the Construction Contract (*cf.* §8.2.8; §8.2.9) cannot substitute for the competence of the Construction Contractor. Even a default termination payment that recovers all the money spent on the Construction Contract will not adequately compensate the Project Company for losses if the project is not built, since the Construction Contract price only covers about 60–75% of typical project costs (let alone loss of future profits).

Therefore a potential Construction Contractor who is not already well-known to the Sponsors is normally required to go through a pre-qualification process, demonstrating the experience to build the type of project required successfully. This would include providing references for similar projects already built, including, where appropriate, references for the technology being employed in the project. The Lenders' Engineer reviews such references in depth, as well as making checks on the general reputation of the Construction Contractor in the market. Similar references may be required for its major sub-contractors, and the Construction Contract should provide the Project Company a list of approved sub-contractors, or the right to veto them (and may give some rights of approval over the terms of these sub-contracts, although sub-contract prices are not usually revealed).

If the Construction Contractor is working overseas, experience in the country of the project, and good relationships with strong local sub-contractors, are also relevant.

Finally the expertise of the Construction Contractor's key personnel who are actually working on the construction should be examined.

The Owner's Engineer (*cf.* §8.2.4) and the Project Company's own staff also mitigate this risk by supervising the activities of the Construction Contractor. Although construction is the Construction Contractor's job, lenders will also wish to ensure that there is adequate supervision of the works, and therefore that the combination of the Project Company's own personnel and the Owner's Engineer have the qualifications and experience for this rôle. Also the Lenders' Engineer provides a further layer of supervision.

Technology Risk. This is may be an issue, typically with an EPC Contract, for which *cf.* §9.7.1.

The Construction Contractor as Sponsor. A Sponsor that is also the Construction Contractor has an obvious conflict of interest between this rôle and that of an investor in the Project Company (*cf.* §3.2). The risk of inappropriate contractual arrangements, or a less than rigorous supervision of the Construction Contract, is evident, and lenders therefore have to be satisfied that the EPC relationship is on an arm's-length basis.

This risk may be mitigated in several ways:

- Other Sponsors not involved in the Construction Contract may specify the work and negotiate the Construction Contract, assuming they have the relevant expertise to do so.
- Supervision of the Construction Contract should be carried out by Project Company personnel who are not connected with the Construction Contractor, with the assistance of an independent Owner's Engineer.
- The Construction Contractor's directors on the Project Company's board should absent themselves from discussions on the Construction Contract.
- The Lenders' Engineer is likely to play a more prominent checking rôle.

But if the Construction Contractor is a major Sponsor of the project, which is inevitably often the case with infrastructure projects, there is a limit to the extent that the Construction Contractor can be isolated from the Sponsor side of discussions on the Construction Contract. In such cases, the Construction Contractor must at least convince the lenders that the investment and construction rôles are adequately separated internally.

Limited Involvement in the Contract. A Construction Contractor normally subcontracts a significant part of the contract; for example, a lead contractor whose primary business is that of equipment supply will normally subcontract the civil works (charging LDs and taking security from the subcontractors that parallel the terms of the main EPC Contract).

This process, however, can be carried too far, if the Construction Contractor is not a significant supplier of either equipment or civil works to the project, but just provides an 'envelope' for a contract largely carried out by sub-contractors. The Construction Contractor may have insufficient experienced personnel 'in house' and rely too much on the sub-contractors.

In such a situation, the risk of poor overall control of the project may be reduced by requiring the Construction Contractor to work in joint venture with one or more companies that would otherwise have been sub-contractors.

Construction Contract Price too Low or too High. The risk of the Construction Contractor offering too low a price, however attractive this might seem at first sight, has already been mentioned in the general discussion on commercial viability (*cf.* §9.4). The Owner's Engineer should check the commercial viability of the Construction Contractor's price, which will also be reviewed by the Lenders' Engineer.

Conversely, a price that is too high (even if the higher cost can be covered by project revenues) suggests, at best, that there is not an arm's-length relationship with the Construction Contractor, which is likely to leave the Project Company's lenders in a weak position if something goes wrong, and, at worst, that corruption is involved.

Scale of Construction Contract. The Construction Contract should not be excessively large in relation to the Construction Contractor's other business, as otherwise there is a risk that if the Construction Contract gets into trouble, the Construction Contractor may not be able to deal with such problems because of their financial effect on the business as a whole. The scale of the Construction Contract should therefore be compared with the Construction Contractor's annual turnover; if it is more than, say, 10% of this figure, the Construction Contract may be too big for the Construction Contractor to handle alone, and a joint-venture approach with a larger contractor may be preferable.

Credit Risk. Allocating project risk to the Construction Contractor is not worthwhile if the contractor is not creditworthy. If the Construction Contractor's wider business gets into financial difficulties, the project is likely to suffer. The credit standing of the Construction Contractor therefore needs to be reviewed to assess whether it could cause any risk to the project.

If the Construction Contractor is part of a larger group of companies, guarantees of its obligations by its ultimate parent company may also be necessary to support the credit risk.

The risk of nonpayment of LDs, warranty claims, *etc.*, can be mitigated by bank bonding, but, for the reasons mentioned above, this security is not a substitute for a good general credit standing.

§9.5.5 CONSTRUCTION CONTRACT-RELATED COST OVERRUNS

The effects of an overrun in construction-phase costs against the budget on which the funding structure has been based are:

- There may be insufficient funding available to complete the project, thus forcing the Sponsors to invest funds for which they have made no commitment, to avoid a loss of their investment, or putting them at a severe disadvantage (and therefore liable to higher borrowing costs or other disadvantageous changes in loan terms) by having to ask the lenders to advance further funds or to agree to new financing arrangements.

- Even if additional funding is available, the project's cost base, and hence debt-service costs, will thus be increased, with no corresponding increase in revenue: therefore, the investors' return will inevitably be reduced. In the worst case, it could lead to the Sponsors abandoning the project because the increased costs destroy its viability.
- From the lenders' point of view, any increase in the debt reduces their Cover Ratios (*cf.* §12.3) and thus makes the loan more risky.

To control construction-phase costs a budget is agreed with the lenders, and any actual or projected excesses over the amounts set out in the major cost categories normally need to be approved by them as they occur or are projected, even if there is still enough overall funding to complete the project (*cf.* §14.3.2). However Lenders should be discouraged from trying to set up too detailed a 'line-item' control of the budget; most of the construction-cost budget is contractually fixed, or represents financing costs, and some flexibility needs to be given to the Project Company to manage remaining minor variations in cost categories, especially if the overall project cost is not significantly affected.

The risk analysis therefore needs to identify the main cost headings in the construction budget (*cf.* §13.5.1), how these costs are controlled, and the likelihood of overruns under each heading.

The Construction Contract is normally by far the largest cost item in the budget—perhaps 60–75% of the total. (Other budget items are discussed in §9.5.6.) Therefore it is evident that this is the most important item to control, and the relevance of a fixed-price turnkey contract in this connection is clear. If a fixed-price contract is not in place, this adds a major dimension of extra risk to the project.

But a so-called fixed-price contract is never 100% fixed, and the risk of the Construction Contractor making claims for additional payments under various contract provisions has to be considered. These claims come under several categories:

Delay in Commencement of Works. The actual start-up of the Construction Contract may be delayed after signature, perhaps because of difficulties obtain the necessary Permits, or in raising the finance, or satisfying all the lenders' conditions precedent (*cf.* §8.2.2; §14.8). The Construction Contractor cannot be expected to keep the price fixed indefinitely, and therefore a cut-off date for the fixed price is normally established. Thereafter the Construction Contractor may be willing to agree to a formula for adjusting the final fixed price against CPI or another index after the cut-off date: this may be manageable by adjusting the financing plan. If no formula is agreed to lenders may be reluctant to continue with work on the financing, as one of the main cost elements is no longer fixed.

Site Risks. As set out in §9.5.2, if site risks are not the responsibility of the Construction Contractor, the additional costs of such a risk crystallizing will be for the account of the Project Company, which may in turn be covered by funding from the Offtaker/Contracting Authority (as a Compensation Event), or by the Sponsors.

Design Risk. Applies to most projects: the issues here are firstly, has the design been sufficiently completed so that the project's costing are not subject to changes required when more detailed design is undertaken; and secondly, is the design unusually complex, which could obviously cause problems during construction. The Construction Contractor normally carries out detailed design after signature of the Construction Contract, but this should not lead to changes in the Construction Contract price. There remains a high risk, however, in any project where the overall design and specifications are not fully settled in advance in the Construction Contract, which is not likely to be acceptable to lenders.

Owner's Risks. As set out in §8.2.5, the Project Company has responsibilities under the Construction Contract, and if these are not fulfilled, and therefore the Construction Contractor incurs extra costs, a claim can be made for these. The main mitigation here is to ensure that Owner's Risks under the Construction Contract are kept to a minimum.

Changes in Contract Specifications. All such changes, unless *de minimis* in amount, must be approved by the lenders, who will have to be convinced that there is enough funding available to cover the cost, and that the benefits of the changes (*e.g.* in reducing operating costs) outweigh their capital costs, or will be covered by increases in Contract Payments (*cf.* §7.6.3).

Change in Law (*e.g.* requiring lower emissions standards) may add unavoidably to the construction costs of the project; as with any change in specifications, the risk remains with the Project Company as far as the Construction Contractor is concerned (*cf.* §8.2.3), but may be covered by the Project Agreement (*cf.* §11.3).

Spare Parts. If an initial stock of spare parts for the project is required, this may not be included in an EPC price, so the cost of these may be higher than budgeted; however, the amounts should be relatively small.

Having said all this, there is strong evidence that the level of overruns and other problems with properly-structured Construction Contracts which meet project-finance lender requirements is quite low, despite construction often being considered the 'high risk' phase of a project.[11]

---

[11] *Cf.* Frederic Blanc-Brudé & Dejan Makovsek, *Construction Risk in Infrastructure Project Finance* (EDHEC Business School, Lille/Nice, 2013)*.

§9.5.6 Other Construction-Phase Costs

Other construction-phase costs[12] which may lead to cost overruns include:

- development costs;
- mobilization costs;
- insurance premiums;
- other Project Company costs;
- advisory costs;
- contingency reserve;
- financing costs—usually the second biggest budget item after the Construction Contract payments (*cf.* §13.4.1); and of course cost increases under the headings above themselves give rise to increases in the financing costs.

These are discussed below.

Development Costs. A project's development costs (*cf.* §3.5; §12.2.5) are those incurred by Sponsors before Financial Close, so it might seem that there cannot be an overrun on these costs during the construction phase. However, there is often a time gap between when the construction budget is agreed to with the lenders, and Financial Close, and during that time there is a risk that legal and similar costs may mount up more than budgeted.

Development costs are normally reimbursed to the Sponsors (if they are not being treated as an initial equity investment) at Financial Close, but if they are finally above budget by that time, lenders may require reimbursement of the excess to be deferred until the end of the construction phase, at which time reimbursement may be allowed if sufficient funds are then available.

Mobilization of O&M Contract. Mobilization costs—the costs of training staff to operate the project—are often covered by the Construction Contractor or the O&M Contractor on a fixed-price basis, and therefore should not pose an undue risk.

Insurance Premiums. The insurance premiums for the construction phase are fixed (and usually paid) at the beginning of the period; therefore, they should not cause any cost overrun, unless there is a gap in time between the final budget and Financial Close. Even in this case, the Project Company's insurance brokers should be able to get good indications of premiums from the market to reduce this risk. Extra insurance premiums will be incurred if there is a delay in Project Completion, as a longer period of cover has to be paid for. There may also be a problem with the premiums for the first year of

---

[12] Sometimes referred to as 'soft costs', in contrast to the 'hard cost' of the Construction Contract.

operation, which may need to be paid just before the end of the construction phase, and therefore form part of the construction budget: it is preferable for these to be fixed in advance as part of an insurance package.

Advisory Costs. The Project Company's own advisors (*cf.* §3.4), such as the Owner's Engineer, will continue to work during the construction phase, and other advisors may be called back to give advice on any specific problems which arise during this time. In addition the lenders' advisors (*cf.* §5.5), especially the Lenders' Engineer, will also continue to work. These routine costs should be fixed, and not that substantial in relation to the overall budget. Having said this, if changes in any of the Project Contracts are become necessary, so that lawyers and financial advisors are brought back into the picture, this is likely to add considerably to advisory costs during this phase of the project.

Project Company's Own Costs. These are any remaining categories of costs not covered above, and which continue after Financial Close. The main items are likely to be the costs of the Project Company's offices, office equipment and staff, and continuing payments to advisors such as the Owner's Engineer. The amounts should be relatively small in the context of overall project costs, and it should not be difficult to ensure that such items remain close to budget.

Contingency Reserve. However well-managed the budget, there is always a risk of unexpected events causing a cost overrun. Despite all the risk mitigations set out above, a contingency reserve covered by matching funding is also often required by lenders. As a rough rule of thumb, a contingency of around 10% of the Construction Contract cost, or 7–8% of total project costs, may be needed. The contingency is also intended to cover the effects of delays in Project Completion, where delay LDs are not payable by the Construction Contractor.

This contingency amount is funded within the total financing package (*cf.* §12.4.2). Note that such contingency funding is intended to cover construction-phase cost overruns and the effect of a delay in Project Completion (*cf.* §9.5.8), not financial risks relating to interest-rate, inflation and currency-exchange rate movements which must be covered in other ways (*cf.* §10.3–§10.5).

§9.5.7 Revenue During Construction

In some projects, part of the construction costs may be funded not just by equity and debt financing, but also partially by revenues earned from a part of the project already operating. For example, revenue from an existing toll bridge or tunnel may be paid to a Project Company to fund part of the cost of building a new bridge or tunnel in parallel to expand the traffic capacity. Similarly, a project may be constructed in phases, with revenues from the early phases covering part of the construction costs of the later phases.

Unless this construction-phase revenue is very stable in nature, there is an extra dimension of risk that the revenues will not be enough to provide the proportion of the funding required. In such cases projections of revenues during construction have to be conservative, and there may be a need to increase the level of contingency funding to allow for this extra uncertainty. Moreover, if a large part of the 'equity' is derived from income during construction rather than new investment, this could leave the investors with very little actual investment at risk, which will clearly make lenders uneasy. One way to deal with this, at least in part, is to require the Sponsors to guarantee the level of income during construction. A similar issue applies if part of the construction cost is being financed by a sale of surplus land (*cf.* §15.10).

An Offtaker/Contracting Authority may provide various kinds of finance towards the capital cost of a PPP project, for which *cf.* Chapter 15.

§9.5.8 Delay in Project Completion

A delay in Project Completion may be caused by:

- failure of the Construction Contractor to perform under the Construction Contract;
- Compensation or Relief Events affecting the Construction Contractor (*cf.* §7.6, §7.8, §8.2.5 and §8.2.6);
- failure of third parties to provide necessary connections to the project (*cf.* §9.5.9).

A delay in Project Completion of the project may have several consequences:

- Financing costs, in particular interest during construction (*cf.* §10.3) will be higher because the construction debt is outstanding for a longer period: this is, in effect, another form of construction cost overrun.
- Revenues from operating the project will be deferred or lost.
- Penalties may be payable to the Offtaker or Input Supplier.

The effect of delays is thus to increase costs, in a similar way to other cost overruns (*cf.* §9.5.5).

To consider these delay risks in more detail:

Delay by Construction Contractor. A date-certain turnkey Construction Contract is the main protection against the risk of late Project Completion; the Construction Contractor is liable for delay LDs, which should be sufficient to keep the project financially whole, at least for some time (*cf.* §8.2.8). LDs provide an incentive for the Construction Contractor to take any necessary action to deal with prospective problems. But if the delay extends beyond 6–12 months, it is likely that delay LDs will run out, and the pressure on the Construction Contractor then reduces considerably.

Unless caused by last-minute performance problems, a delay in reaching Project Completion by the Construction Contractor is often quite predictable if detailed programming for the project is in place, as it will become evident that critical-path items (*i.e.* aspects of the project which, if delayed, will delay the final Project Completion) are falling behind schedule. The Project Company and the Owner's Engineer should be supervising progress sufficiently closely to ensure that they are aware of potential delays in the critical path and assist (or put pressure on) the Construction Contractor to catch up. The Lenders' Engineer also monitors this process (*cf.* §14.3.2).

Relief Events. Since Relief Events provide extra time (*cf.* §8.2.6), it is evident that they may cause delays in completing the project.

Definition of Project Completion. Project Completion is a concept that may appear in various different contracts—the Construction Contract, the Project Agreement, the Input-Supply Contract (if any), and as a required milestone date in the financing documentation. It is therefore important to ensure that the definitions of Project Completion between all these different contracts fit together from the Project Company's point of view. If the Project Company is subject to penalties for late Project Completion (*e.g.* in an Offtake Contract), the definition in that contract should be as 'loose' as possible so Project Completion can easily be achieved. On the other hand, the Project Company may impose a much higher Project Completion hurdle on the Construction Contractor.

Lenders may be concerned about a rushed Project Completion (*i.e.* the Offtaker and the Project Company agreeing that the project is complete when problems remain, and allowing the Construction Contractor off the hook too easily): as a result lenders may require that the Project Company cannot agree that Project Completion has taken achieved until the Lenders' Engineer signs off in agreement. Furthermore, the definition of Project Completion from the Lender point of view is likely to be wider than just completion under the Construction Contract (*e.g.* completion of any third-party connections—see below).

§9.5.9 THIRD-PARTY RISKS

Various risks related to the performance of third parties may also delay Project Completion: these are often treated as Relief Events under the Project Agreement (*cf.* §7.8).

Connections and Utilities Required for the Project. The Construction Contractor may be dependent on third parties, such as an Input Supplier or Offtaker, to provide connections to the site that enable the project to be completed. Similarly, such links may be needed before the project can begin operation. For example, a fuel pipeline or water supply may have to be linked to the site, a rail link may be needed to bring in fuel, or a grid connection to export electricity from a power plant, or a connecting road may be needed to enable traffic to use a toll road or bridge. The third party providing the connection may themselves be dependent on others (*e.g.* for rights of way).

If the connections are being provided by a party to a Project Contract, such as an Offtaker/Contracting Authority, or an Input Supplier, this party should normally be responsible for the loss or penalties that the Project Company suffers from their delay.

If the third party providing these connections is not otherwise involved with the project, they may have no particular incentive to keep to the project timetable, and the damage to the project caused by late connection may be disproportionate to the cost of the connection. In such cases the Project Company can only assess the degree of risk by looking at the record of the third party in similar situations, and try to control the risk by close coordination with and monitoring of the third party. The Construction Contractor's relationship and experience with such third parties may also be relevant.

Relocation of Utilities. In a similar vein, projects such as construction of a road need to arrange for diversion or relocation of utilities (*e.g.* a gas, water, or sewage pipeline may need to be moved under a road). The utility concerned will probably have control of this procedure, and their cooperation is needed. Again, because they have no particular incentive to keep to the project's construction timetable, there is a risk that this could delay progress. However this risk may be passed on from the Project Company to the Construction Contractor, as it is a relatively routine requirement in construction.

Protesters. Projects involving the construction of public infrastructure (*e.g.* a road) may also be the subject of public protest, which may seriously affect the construction schedule. In the worst case this may turn into politically motivated violence (*cf.* §11.4.3) rather than just obstruction of the Construction Contractor's work.

In general, if a project involves the construction of public infrastructure, the public sector should take responsibility for delays of this kind, first by providing appropriate police protection for the Construction Contractor to carry out the work, and second (in the case of PPPs) by treating delays caused in this way at least as Relief Events, thus sheltering the Project Company from a default caused by the delay in Project Completion, if not also compensating the Project Company for loss of revenue.

Project Dependent on Another Project. The worst kind of third-party risk—often fatal to the development of a project—is where one project depends on another. For example, a gas-fired power station may be dependent on delivery of gas through a pipeline that is itself being project financed. If the completion of the pipeline cannot be guaranteed, the power station project will probably not be able to get project financing; conversely, if the completion of the power station cannot be guaranteed, the gas pipeline will probably not be able to get project financing. Financing the two projects as one may be a way out of this impasse, but the Sponsors of one project may be different from the Sponsors of the other, and each side may have no interest in investing in or guaranteeing the other's project. In such cases a Contracting Authority may have to stand in the middle and take on these interface risks.

§9.5.10 INADEQUATE PERFORMANCE ON PROJECT COMPLETION

Performance risks (*e.g.* because of problems of poor design or inadequate technology) may affect the ability of the project to perform as expected on Project Completion. This relates primarily to process-plant projects rather than buildings or civil works, since any problems with the latter would normally arise quite a long time after Project Completion.

If performance requirements are not achieved, performance LDs will become payable by the EPC Contractor, which should have originally been calculated as sufficient to cover the NPV of the financial loss from this poor performance for the life of the project (*cf.* §8.2.8). Performance LDs are normally used to reduce the debt so as to leave the lenders with the same Cover Ratios (*cf.* §12.3; §14.6) as they would have had if the project had performed as expected. (Any surplus should be paid as a special distribution to investors to compensate them for their reduced equity return.)

But some of the assumptions made during the original LD calculation may also prove incorrect; for example, if the project uses a higher volume of input supplies to operate than originally anticipated, the extra cost of this should be covered by the LDs, but the assumption of the unit cost of the input supplies may itself be proved incorrect by events; if this unit cost turns out to be higher than projected, the LDs will not fully cover the economic loss.

Furthermore, the performance measurements of the project on Project Completion are only a snapshot taken over a limited period of time, and there may still be further variations in performance as time goes on which will not produce further LDs.

Thus the calculation used to fix the performance LDs may be little more than a rough projection, and there is also no opportunity (unless claims can be made under warranty) to go back to the EPC Contractor several years after Project Completion if performance gets worse. The Project Company should be aware of the uncertainty of these assumptions and allow a margin for this in negotiating the LD calculations with the EPC Contractor.

Finally, performance LDs alone may not be sufficient if the project involves new technology: it may be acceptable to lenders for the EPC Contractor to provide higher levels of performance LDs than normal for upgrades of existing technology, but this would not be adequate for something totally new in concept (*cf.* §9.7.1).

§9.5.11 THE CONSTRUCTION CONTRACTOR'S SECURITY

A Construction Contractor might reasonably ask what security is offered that its required payments will be made by the Project Company—which could be the biggest risk from its point of view. Lenders have first security over the project assets, and therefore these are not available to the Construction Contractor. Neither the Sponsors nor the lenders will normally provide the Construction Contractor with guarantees. (Of course, one of the Sponsors may be the Construction Contractor, so then such a guarantee would not be needed.)

Normally the Construction Contractor's only security is the existence of the financing arrangements, and the fact that it is seldom in the lenders' interests to cut off funding for construction of the project. Therefore the Construction Contractor will not normally begin work until:

- all other project and financing contracts are in place;
- when satisfied that sufficient funding has been made available by Sponsors and lenders on terms that should ensure that payments due under the Construction Contract can be made, and that the financing will not be withdrawn by the lenders on an arbitrary basis;
- Financial Close has been reached.

Sometimes the Sponsors may wish the Construction Contractor to begin work earlier than Financial Close, and therefore provide the Construction Contractor with temporary guarantees against which the work can progress until Financial Close has been reached (*cf.* §8.2.2).

The Construction Contractor should also ensure that the Construction Contract's payment schedule is linked as closely as possible to its own financial exposure to direct costs and payments to its sub-contractors and equipment suppliers, so that if the Project Company does collapse the Construction Contractor's losses can be limited.

§9.5.12 PROJECTS WITHOUT A FIXED-PRICE, DATE-CERTAIN, TURNKEY CONSTRUCTION CONTRACT

The fixed-price, date-certain, turnkey Construction Contract is a major mitigation of risk in project finance. There are some types of project, however, for which such a contract is not available or appropriate, for example:

Mining and Other Extraction Projects. The development of a mine or an oil field tends to suffer from higher than average construction risk because of delays due to bad weather, an inaccessible location, and geological, technical, and labor problems. Even if a fixed-price, date-certain Construction Contract is in place, LDs may be insufficient to cover these risks, and the more common approach is for the Sponsors undertake the construction of the facility themselves, with appropriate sub-contractors.

Oil Refinery/Petrochemical Plants. These often depend using patented processes (intellectual property, or 'IP) controlled by existing operators, The Project Company buys the right to use a particular process. This means that the EPC Contractor is not supplying a key element of the IP required for the project, and therefore cannot offer a full turnkey contract. Again it is more common in such cases for the Sponsors to undertake the construction.

Systems Installations. A project may involve installation of a system over a period of time (*e.g.* a cable-TV or mobile-phone network) where the speed of installation of the system depends on demand. The lenders may specify that if revenues from customers for the system come in faster their debt can be drawn faster, so construction will speed up, and vice versa. Given the uncertainty of the construction timetable, a Construction Contractor cannot easily offer a fixed price, and clearly a fixed Project Completion date is not relevant.

In such cases lenders may require a Project Completion guarantee from the Sponsors to reduce their risks (*i.e.* the financing becomes limited-recourse rather than non-recourse—*cf.* §9.13). If the Sponsors guarantee to complete the project, it necessarily follows that:

- The Sponsors must be responsible for any shortage of funding to complete.
- If the project is not completed, the Sponsors will have repay the debt or cover the debt service.

Thus, the additional financial liability that Sponsors incur may become very significant in the absence of a project finance-friendly Construction Contract. Furthermore, the definition of Project Completion in such cases has to be carefully considered. Depending on the type of project, it may involve not just physical completion of the facility, but a demonstrated ability to operate as projected over a sustained period of time.

§9.6 REVENUE RISKS

The risk that the Project Company may not earn sufficient revenue to service its operating costs and debt, and produce an adequate return for investors, is at the heart of project finance.

If the project is producing a product (which would apply to both process-plant and natural-resources projects), the risks are whether—assuming it is able to operate as projected—the Project Company can achieve:

- the volume of unit sales projected—the volume risk;
- at the projected unit-sales price—the price risk.

These risks may be covered by an Offtake Contract or other similar arrangements (§9.6.1), or the Project Company may take the risk of sales into a competitive market (§9.6.2).

In the case of an infrastructure project—either privatized or a PPP Concession—the key revenue risk is typically whether the Project Company can achieve the volume of usage of the service projected at the projected toll, fare, or other usage charge—the usage risk (§9.6.3).

In Availability-based Project Agreements the usage risk is most commonly taken by the Contracting Authority, so that the primary revenue risk is the ability of the Contracting Authority to make the Contract Payments when due (§9.6.4).

The risks of penalties or deductions from PPP Contract revenues related to availability or performance are discussed under operating risks below (§9.7).

§9.6.1 Offtake and Similar Contracts

This section reviews the risks on Offtake Contracts, and three variants of this type of contract—hedging contracts, contracts for differences and long-term sales contracts. Each of these has similar characteristics, but different risk issues:

- an Offtake Contract covers both volume and price risk;
- a hedging contract may cover volume and price, or just price risk;
- a Contract for Differences covers price risk;
- a long-term sales contract covers volume but not price risk.

To the extent that volume and sales risks are covered contractually, it is primarily the operating risks (*cf.* §9.7) that are left with the Project Company.

Offtake Contract. In a take-or-pay Offtake Contract (*cf.* §6.3.1) both the volume and price risks are transferred to the Offtaker. In principle, then, no significant revenue risk is left with the Project Company. It follows from this that a process-plant project with this type of contract can achieve the highest debt leverage and hence offer a lower product price.

The main remaining risk for the Project Company with an Offtake Contract is the ability of the Offtaker to pay for the product. The Project Company and its lenders are in fact taking a very long-term credit risk on the Offtaker. Although conventional balance sheet-based corporate credit analysis is the first step in assessing this risk, this alone is not necessarily appropriate to determine whether the Offtaker's credit risk is acceptable. The term of the risk (say for 15–25 years) runs well beyond the limits of conventional bank lending to most companies, because no really reliable credit assessment can be carried out on any company so far into the future—however strong its credit appears to be. (However it should be noted that corporate-bond issues can have such longer maturities, and credit-rating agencies will assign a long-term rating to such bonds.)

The risk assessment here therefore also has to look at the commercial viability of the project (as described in §9.4). If the project makes long-term commercial sense—for example if the cost of its product is less than the average for the industry concerned—it is likely to survive even if the Offtaker has problems elsewhere. Indeed, one school of thought holds that it is preferable for projects not to have long-term Offtake Contracts because these reduce the need for an assessment of the project's fundamental viability, which is the real security for lenders. Most lenders, however, would rather have an Offtake Contract in the structure if it is available.

A further issue is whether the Offtaker itself—if a private-sector company—is operating in a stable environment or whether its own business may be vulnerable to long-term problems. For example, a project selling power to an industrial plant is obviously taking a risk on the long-term market for the output of that plant.

There may be different long-term credit risk issues if the Offtaker is a public-sector entity. In the short term, lenders will take comfort from the public ownership and may assume that the government will provide financial support if needed, even if there is no formal government guarantee. However if the Host Government owns the Offtaker and regulates its industry, there is a strong case for the Host Government also guaranteeing the long-term credit risk of the Offtaker, on the grounds that they are best able to control this risk.

There is always a possibility that a government's decision to privatize a public-sector Offtaker (or part of its business) may seriously affect its credit. No government will agree to fetter future governments by contracting not to privatize the Offtaker, but there are various possible approaches to this issue:

- If the Host Government guarantees the Offtaker's liability this guarantee should not be affected by privatization or any other restructuring of the Offtaker.
- The Host Government may be required to provide a guarantee on privatization unless the Offtaker meets an agreed credit rating at that time.
- The lenders may take the view that no privatization will be successful unless the privatized company has a strong balance sheet and a sound basis for its business; a state-owned company's real credit standing may

therefore get better rather than worse after privatization and so the lenders may not be concerned so long as the project fundamentals are sound.

If the Offtaker is a weaker credit risk, there may be ways of taking security over its own revenues to strengthen the position of the Project Company. For example, the Offtaker under a PPA may be a local electricity-distribution company; if there is some question about its credit risk, it may be possible for arrangements to be made for the revenues it collects from its customers to be paid into an escrow account for the benefit of the Project Company and applied to ensure that payments are made under the PPA.

Hedging Contracts (*cf.* §6.3.1). These are normally concluded with market intermediaries rather than end-users of the product. The risks that remain with the Project Company are:

- Credit risk on the intermediary, *e.g.* a commodity-trading company.
- Generally, as these are standard market instruments, they are not as flexible as, for example, contracts for differences that are individually negotiated.

The main problem with hedging contracts of this type is that the term available in the commodity markets may be limited, and therefore the later years of the project may be left exposed to market price movements.

One type of hedging arrangement can be undertaken directly with lenders, namely, commodity-denominated loans. Gold loans, for example, have been used to finance gold mine projects. In this structure of financing, the lenders lend gold rather than a currency to the Project Company; the latter then sells the gold and uses the proceeds to finance the mine development; the gold produced is then used to repay the gold loan.

The disadvantage of any form of product-price hedging for the Sponsors is that the Project Company may have to undertake the hedging at a time of low commodity prices (this is when lenders will be most anxious about the project economics) and then not benefit from later price rises.

Contracts for Differences (*cf.* §6.3.1). CfDs are commonly used in the electricity industry. Because such contracts are primarily used because power cannot be sold directly to the end-user, the risks involved are very similar to those of an Offtake Contract.

The main additional risk that the Project Company may still be taking under such an agreement is that it has to sell the power produced to the grid or electricity pool system. This is less of a problem so long as the pool works on a marginal pricing basis (*i.e.* the price paid by the pool is equal to the highest price bid at which enough electricity is supplied by all bidders to meet demand). In such cases the Project Company merely has to bid a low price to ensure that its power is sold at the price paid to the pool as a whole. But if the pool works on the basis of only paying the price bid by each bidder, the bidding risk will probably have to be passed to the counterpart under the *CfD*, because they will wish to control more closely the price that is being bid by the Project Company to ensure they do not have to pay further amounts to the Project Company to compensate for too low a bid price.

Long-Term Sales Contracts. A long-term sales contract (*cf.* §6.3.1) removes the volume risk from the Project Company, but leaves it with the price risk. Such a contract may be appropriate if:

- The product produced by the project is a commodity that is not sold in widely traded markets and requires a sales organization to sell the product (as is the case with petrochemical products, for example); or
- If the end-user is willing to contract for the product on a long-term basis, but wishes to index the price to a commodity market (*e.g.* in long-term contracts for the sale of LNG, where is price is often linked to that of oil).

In such cases, lenders will wish to ensure that there is a clearly defined pricing basis for the product, so that the extent of the price risk can be measured. It is clearly preferable for pricing to be based on some widely-traded index such as oil prices, since price projections are easier for such commodity markets. However it is apparent that the risk for the Project Company remains much higher than under the other offtake arrangements described above, and therefore the debt leverage that can be achieved for projects where the price risk is being taken by the Project Company is lower.

If a Project Company takes the price risk, the lenders' main concern is the extent of cash-flow cover for the debt (*cf.* §12.3); obviously the higher the cover the less the risk of loss caused by fluctuations in the market price for the project's product. The extent of this risk can also be measured by looking at the product price required to enable the Project Company to break even (*i.e.* a combination of a unit price and unit sales just sufficient to cover the Project Company's operating costs and debt service, but providing no return to shareholders). This break-even price should be low in relation to historical and projected prices, and take account of likely price volatility.

§9.6.2 PROJECTS WITHOUT PRICE OR VOLUME RISK MITIGATION

Adding the volume risk to the price risk (*i.e.* if the Project Company has not got a long-term sales contract of any kind) can be acceptable to lenders where the product concerned is a commodity that is widely traded in a market.

The two main types of projects in which lenders may be willing to lend to Project Companies taking the price risk (and volume risk, if necessary) on their products are natural-resources projects, and 'merchant' power projects in the electricity market.

Natural-Resources Projects. The volume risk is not significant in hydrocarbon and minerals projects because the product concerned can easily be sold on widely-traded commodity markets.

The price risk is obviously very significant, however, and lenders take a cautious attitude in this respect. Commodity prices are affected by the economic cycles: lenders therefore base their projections for the Project Company and hence the viability of the project on the lower range of historic prices for the commodity over a long period of time. Factors that might lead to a growth in supply need to be considered (*e.g.* opening of new mines elsewhere or developments of new mining technology) as well as anything that could lead to a drop in demand in future (*e.g.* because another commodity can be substituted, such as plastic bottles instead of aluminum cans).

Lenders and their advisors also look at the cost competitiveness of the project in the market as a whole and would normally expect the project to be able to produce at a cost placing it in the lowest quartile of world production costs for the product, based on the assumption that if 75% of the world's production is being sold below cost, this is not a sustainable position over the long term. Even then, unless some form of commodity price hedging is in place, the leverage of the project will be relatively low (*i.e.* lenders require high Debt-Cover Ratios—*cf.* §12.3).

Merchant Power-Plant Projects. With the development in a number of countries such as the United Kingdom, Australia, and the United States (in certain states) of market trading in electricity, lenders have provided financing for merchant power plants that do not have long-term power purchase agreements.

Again the volume risk is relatively small, since the existence of a pool or similar market trading system should ensure that power produced can be sold at a market price, so long as transmission or other constraints do not inhibit this.

Price risk is much more difficult to assess; these markets generally may not have long enough trading data to assess clearly the factors affecting electricity prices, and in some cases a few large generators may be able to manipulate market prices, thus making past prices meaningless as a basis for future projections. Although demand for electricity is relatively stable, unlike the markets for oil and minerals, it is difficult to predict the future supply of electricity to a market, since this is affected by investors' decisions on whether to keep older more inefficient plant in existence, and new investors' changing perceptions of whether it is worthwhile to build new plant. Most Lender risk analyses therefore concentrates on the cost competitiveness of the Project Company's plant and hence its break-even unit price by comparison with other plants, which is a factor of:

- capital cost (*i.e.* the EPC price);
- funding structure (more debt and a longer term make the project's unit prices more competitive, but also increases the credit risk for lenders);
- efficiency (*i.e.* output and fuel consumption);
- fuel cost.

If a project is cost-competitive against others in the market, the presumption is often made by lenders that it is unlikely to have to operate at a loss for a sustained period of time, and therefore although it may have temporary problems, in the medium term it should make enough money to service its debt. This, however, may not adequately address issues of over capacity from construction of too much new plant with a similar cost base. It also does not address the effect of a change in the costs of different types of fuel (*e.g.* coal *vs.* gas) causing a major change in the cost base between different types of plants, or a drop in the price of fuel making a long-term fuel-supply contract uncompetitive compared to other plants using short-term contracts (or *vice versa* if the project is using short-term fuel supply contracts).

In general lenders are likely to require some kind of risk mitigation in such projects, *e.g.*:

- hedging arrangements or a Contract for Differences (perhaps not for all the plant's output or the full term of the loan, but covering a significant proportion of both);
- signing a PPA with an 'anchor tenant' (*e.g.* a large industrial plant), which will purchase a significant proportion of the plant's output;
- the fuel supplier taking on some of the risks by:
- indexing the cost of the fuel to the market price of the electricity, so reducing the price risk; or
- subordinating fuel payments to the lenders, so if there is a shortage of cash flow because of adverse market conditions the lenders get paid ahead of the fuel supplier; or
- a Tolling Contract (*cf.* §8.5.1), whereby the fuel supplier pays the plant to process its fuel into electricity, and takes upon itself the risk of selling that electricity;
- financing a mixed portfolio of plants rather than an individual plant, thus spreading the risk.

There is an obvious relationship between this spectrum of risk and the amount of debt that can be raised against a project; at one end of the scale a full Contract for Differences or a Tolling Contract gives much the same protection to lenders as a PPA, and so the amount of debt raised (*i.e.* the debt:equity ratio) will be similar, whereas at the other end of the scale the pure market risk of selling into a power pool will greatly reduce the proportion of debt to equity in the project.

§9.6.3 Concession Agreements and Privatized Infrastructure

Usage is the main risk in a Concession Agreement or private-sector infrastructure project, *i.e.* whether users will use the project in sufficient numbers, and thus create the revenues projected for the project. Similar principles apply to privatized infrastructure such as ports and airports.[13]

The most common projects of this type are Concessions involving roads (including bridges and tunnels, often financed as a separate project to improve an existing road), so this issue will be discussed here in the context of a toll road.

Finance can only be raised for a toll project where there is a clearly established demand. For example, a project may consist of building a tolled bridge alongside an existing one to add capacity: the established traffic flows make projections of future toll revenues relatively easy. The risk assessment is more difficult if, for example, a toll road is to be built near to other roads with no toll. Similarly there may be competing transport modes such as rail. In these cases, however, if the current demand is clearly demonstrated by congestion on the roads, and the cost of tolls or fares is reasonable in relation to the cost of existing transport modes, lenders are willing to take the usage risk.

Usage projections for transportation projects are based on complex financial modeling by the Project Company's traffic consultants, which in turn is reviewed by the lenders' traffic advisors. Modeling of usage is based on projections that take into account factors such as:

- overall population growth, distribution, and movement;
- general and local economic activity;
- land use around the area of the project;
- travel at different times of the day or different seasons;
- distribution of travel (*i.e.* the split between local and long-distance travel);
- origins and destinations of trips;
- split between commercial and private traffic (the former being more willing to pay tolls);
- split between modes of travel such as bus, car, or train;
- the value of time saved by users, compared to the toll.

These and other factors combine to produce a model of current traffic patterns, which it should be possible to validate by using it to project traffic growth from a date in the past up to the present and comparing the results with the actual growth figures.

---

[13] *Cf.* Patrick Boeuf, *Public-Private Partnerships for Transport Infrastructure Projects* (EIB, Luxemburg, 2003)*; Antonio Estache, Ellis Juan & Lourdes Trujillo, *Public-Private Partnerships in Transport* (Policy Research Working Paper 4436, World Bank, Washington DC, 2007)*.

Future projections of traffic growth for project finance purposes are based on macro-economic factors such as growth in the national and regional economy leading to growth in private and commercial vehicle ownership, and generally do not take into account extra traffic that may be created by the construction of the project itself (but *cf.* §14.3.3).

Any project involving traffic risk also has to take into account the effect of government policies on usage. These policies may be local to the project (*e.g.* competition from untolled roads or construction of other roads that take traffic from a toll road) or national, but affect the project (*e.g.* an increase in fuel prices that reduces road traffic volume in general). Lenders often require some protection against some of the risks of this type to be built into the Concession Agreement (*cf.* §6.5.2).

Does Transfer of Traffic Risk Make Sense? The basic principle of risk allocation set out above (§9.2), is that risks should be borne by those who are best able to control or manage them, and to bear their financial consequences. But it is clear that a Project Company with a toll-road Concession can actually do very little to influence its usage (other than reduce the tolls, which may destroy the project's viability).[14] For example, quality of service on the part of the Project Company is also unlikely to affect traffic flows very much.

Quality of Traffic Forecasts. The first problem here is that the record of traffic consultants forecasting usage, and hence revenues, for toll projects is quite poor.[15] There are a variety of reasons for this:

- The data on historical and current traffic flows may be inadequate.
- 'Willingness to pay'—*i.e.* whether users will in fact be prepared to use the toll road rather than take a slower route—is very difficult to estimate. Such projections are based on an estimate of the 'time value of money'— *i.e.* the value of the time saved by using the road is greater than the toll charge. But road users are often not entirely rational about this—truck drivers in particular, who usually have to pay a significantly higher toll than car drivers, as they do about 10 times as much damage to the road surface as a car, will take quite large deviations over often unsuitable roads rather than pay the toll.
- From the public-sector point of view, it is prudent to over-estimate traffic (or at least to use the upper range of projections) to ensure that the road which is built will be large enough to cover a high traffic growth scenario.

---

[14] Having said this, revenue projections for toll roads often show two peak scenarios—a high toll with a low level of traffic, or a low toll with a high volume of traffic, and bidders for such projects need to decide which strategy to pursue.

[15] Robert Bain, *Review of Lessons from Completed PPP Projects Financed by the EIB* (EIB, Luxemburg, 2009)* notes that half of EIB's toll-road projects failed to meet their early year forecasts, in some cases with errors of 50-70%. This is said to be similar to other studies on traffic forecasting accuracy.

The traffic consultants will inevitably be influenced by these optimistic traffic projections made by the Contracting Authority, even if they shade them down to some extent.

- Then there is the 'winner's curse'—*i.e.* the adrenalin of competition causes bidders to get too enthusiastic and assume too high a rate of traffic growth. This may be further encouraged by the bidder's staff being paid a bonus if they win the project, and possibly losing their jobs if they don't. The final result is that the bidder wins, but then soon wishes it hadn't.

- Projects of this type are very much affected by 'ramp up'—*i.e.* the period of time it takes for drivers to get to know about the new alterative route and begin using it, such that the traffic builds up to its long-term 'steady state'. If the ramp-up takes, say, four years instead of two, the Project Company can very quickly find itself in financial difficulty (*cf.* §17.5.3 for the use of standby finance to address this risk).

Network Risks. But there are also external effects on the project which will lie largely outside the Project Company's control, collectively known as 'network risks':

- Traffic growth is a factor of general growth in the economy, local development, and the local and national road network; it is also affected by things such as fuel prices and taxes. There is obviously nothing the Project Company can do about this.

- The Project Company's projections may be based on the assumption that some new road will be build elsewhere in the road network, which will cause an increase in the flow of the traffic on the Concession road. But— especially if the new road is to come out of the public-sector budget—the new road may not be built, or be delayed, seriously impacting the Project Company's projected revenues.

- Conversely, the public-sector may build a competing free road: this may seem a bit perverse at first sight, but it is often the result of different parts of the public sector having responsibility for different roads—so, for example, a free competing road could be built by a municipality to solve a local traffic problem, but this also affects a national toll road nearby as it is no longer used by the local traffic.

- Because of this latter risk, the Concession Agreement may include a clause which prevents a competing road being built, or provides for compensation if it is. The problem with this from the Contracting Authority's point of view is that it inhibits the natural long-term development of the road network as a whole, by either making it pay compensation to the Project Company, or in the worst case the Contracting Authority may have to 'buy out' the Concession, which is likely to be extremely expensive (*cf.* §7.10.3).

Conclusion. So what is the result of all this? Firstly, the rate of failure in toll-roads is significantly higher than in other infrastructure projects.[16] Secondly, in many cases the Contracting Authority recognizes that transfer of usage (traffic) risk is inappropriate: various solutions can be adopted for bringing in private capital:[17]

- The Contracting Authority may provide *partial finance or a guaranty*, to reduce the usage risk, as discussed in Chapter 15.
- *Shadow Tolls* (*cf.* §6.4.6) may be applied to the project, which tends to reduce, although not eliminate, the traffic risk.
- The more common solution is to switch to using an *Availability-based Contract*, as discussed below. Tolls may still be charged but the revenues from these go to the Contracting Authority to help offset the Availability-based Contract Payments.

Present Value of Revenues. Another solution to the traffic-risk issue, but which has not been widely adopted, is the 'Present of Revenues' system which originated in Chile. In this structure bidders bid for a Concession Agreement which will not terminate on a fixed date, but when the NPV (*cf.* §10.2.1) of the toll revenues reaches a certain figure. This means that if traffic is lower than projections the Concession term will be longer, and *vice-versa.*[18] This system therefore substantially reduces traffic risk, although there is still some risk, *e.g.* because greater volumes of traffic will lead to higher maintenance costs which may not be fully recovered if the project terminates earlier than expected. Also although helpful to investors, a contract extension is unattractive to lenders, as they will not usually want to be forced to extend the term of their debt.

§9.6.4 Availability-based Contracts

The Contracting Authority takes the usage, and hence the revenue risk on this type of project, just as in a PPA the Offtaker has to pay the Capacity Charge whether or not it needs any electricity to be generated. So if the demand for school places, or the number of prisoners in a prison, is lower than projected, the Service Fee is still payable, and the

---

[16] 'Failure' does not mean that the project is not built, as these problems usually do not become apparent until after Completion. The investors, and possibly the lenders, will suffer losses, but from the Contracting Authority's point of view that should not matter as the road has been built anyway, so it has got what it wanted. In reality, however, political pressures often mean that the public sector has to step in and rescue the project in some way. *Cf.* Jeff Ruster, *A Retrospective on the Mexican Toll Road Program (1989–94)* (Public Policy for the Private Sector Note No. 125, World Bank, Washington DC, 1997)* for a succinct summary of how this program got everything possible wrong.

[17] *Cf.* Chapter 15 for more complex forms of public-sector support for transport and other projects.

[18] Eduardo Engel, Ronald Fischer & Alexander Galetovic, "A New Approach to Private Roads", *Regulation* (Cato Institute, Washington DC, Fall 2002), p. 18*.

Project Company does not suffer. This is logical because if the Contracting Authority controls the usage of the service provided by a PPP project, directly or indirectly, it should clearly take this risk in the same way as an Offtaker under an Offtake Contract.

But long-term usage risk can produce problems for the Contracting Authority. The need for a PPP school for example, may be reduced by population movements in the local area, or changes in medical treatment may reduce the long-term need for a PPP hospital (or reduce the size of hospital required, *e.g.* because of a shift to using local clinics or treating patients at home). Termination of a Project Agreement because the project is no longer required, or needs to be reduced in scope, is a very expensive process (*cf.* §7.10.3). As discussed in §7.2.6, reduced long-term flexibility can be a issue in a PPP Contract, although it should be borne in mind that even if a Contracting Authority builds a new hospital using its own tax resources or debt, it cannot realistically decide it does not want the project a few years later and walk away.

From the Project Company's point of view, the risk issues are similar to those for an Offtake Contract, as discussed in §9.6.1 above. In this case, however, the Contracting Authority is less likely to be an entity which could be privatized in future, so the main issue is likely to be the effect on the Contracting Authority's budget of the long-term Contract Payments, *i.e.* whether the project is 'Affordable' (*cf.* §7.2.2; §9.4).

§9.7 OPERATING RISKS

Once the project has been completed and is demonstrated to be operating to specification, a new risk phase begins, that of long-term operation. Even if the Project Company has hedged many of its risks through a Project Agreement, some level of operating risk is likely to be left with the Project Company, and therefore this aspect of the risks, and their cost consequences, are closely reviewed by lenders.

Preliminary issues that will concern lenders include how the Project Company's operations will be managed, what are the track record and skills of those involved, and to what extent it will be able to receive technical or similar support from the Sponsors (*cf.* §3.6.3).

Otherwise, although there are some common issues, the key operating risks tend to differ between different types of project. As an example, the issues for process-plant and Availability-based projects are considered separately below, reflecting the differing 'drivers' for such projects. (Obviously there are other types of project to which neither of these analyses would be entirely relevant.)

Operating-risk issues relating to process-plant projects (whether with or without an Offtake Contract) would include:

- technology (§9.7.1);
- general operation of the project (§9.7.2);

- performance degradation (§9.7.3);

while those relating to infrastructure, especially PPPs, would include availability and performance (§9.7.4).

There are also a number of risks relating to potential overruns in the Project Company's own costs which need to be taken into account, and are dealt with separately as examples of common issues for different types of contract:

- maintenance (§9.7.5);
- utilities (§9.7.6); and
- the Project Company's other operating costs (§9.7.7).

Also, risks relating to insurance coverage are discussed in §8.6.8.

§9.7.1 PROCESS-PLANT PROJECTS—TECHNOLOGY RISK

Lenders are always reluctant to lend against a project that is using new and untried technology, whose performance cannot be checked against existing references. The problem is that the new technology risk is unquantifiable and cannot be covered by performance LDs from the EPC Contractor because these do not cover a future deterioration in performance. In this context, new technology has a wide definition: it includes major improvements to existing technology, for example, a gas turbine for a power plant that is supposed to deliver significantly greater efficiency than the manufacturer's current model. (It is also worth noting that insurance companies charge higher premiums for new technology plants because of the increased uncertainty in their risks.)

If new technology is being used, this risk can be mitigated in various ways:

- The EPC Contractor may give a long-term performance guarantee, rather than the warranties normally provided, which are limited both in amount and to a term of 2–3 years (*cf.* §8.2.9). The problem with this approach, however, is deciding whether a problem with the plant in several years' time is caused by a defect in design or construction (the EPC Contractor's fault) or in the way it has been operated (the Project Company's fault).
- The Sponsors may provide a long-term performance guarantee, perhaps counter-guaranteed by the EPC Contractor or the manufacturer of the plant.

In summary, however, project finance is more suitable for established technologies.

The converse of this is the risk that the technology used in the project may become obsolescent and thus uncompetitive in the market in which the Project Company is operating. This should be considered when reviewing the basic commercial viability of the project (*cf.* §9.4), but it may be of particular concern in, *e.g.* projects with a high IT component.

§9.7.2 PROCESS-PLANT PROJECTS—PROJECT OPERATION

If a process-plant project is not able to operate as projected due to poor management (*e.g.* negligent operation, failure to maintain plant, *etc.*), there is likely to be a loss of revenue (Capacity Charge or Energy Charge) or higher operating costs. An O&M Contract with an experienced operator provides the greatest comfort to lenders in this respect, especially if this is with a Sponsor.

However the O&M Contractor does not guarantee the revenues or costs of the project, and penalties are usually capped at around 1–2 years' fees (*cf.* §8.3.4). The total level of fees paid to an O&M Contractor (and hence the penalties the O&M Contractor would be willing to pay) is small in relation to both the total revenues or the costs (including finance) of projects, and it would not make economic sense for the O&M Contractor to cover the Project Company's loss of revenue by accepting liability to pay penalties many times greater than the fees that could be earned.

The main sanction against a poorly performing O&M Contractor is thus not penalties but the termination of the O&M Contract, which is always available if performance falls below the minimum required standard. In this respect the O&M Contract differs from other major Project Contracts, because replacement of other Sub-Contractors is seldom a realistic possibility.

Coupled with this, however, lenders have a strong preference for O&M Contractors to be investors in the project, because an O&M Contractor who has an equity investment stands to lose more than just the penalties for poor performance.

§9.7.3 PROCESS-PLANT PROJECTS—DEGRADATION

In many process-plant projects, an allowance has to be made for operating degradation (*i.e.* the gradual decline in operating efficiency between maintenance of the plant). In a power plant, for example, this will cause a decline in output and increase in heat rate (fuel consumption), which should be largely but not entirely reversed after each major overhaul of the plant. Again assuming the plant is using established technology, it should be possible to assess the degree of this risk and build it into operating and hence financial projections, based on the experience of similar plants elsewhere.

Similarly, the way in which a process plant is used affects degradation and the maintenance cycle. For example, if a power plant is constantly stopping and restarting, or being kept on hot standby by the Offtaker, this causes a much more rapid degradation in performance and requirement for maintenance than if it is operating constantly. Therefore the PPA needs to establish a separate category of Tariff costs that take this kind of flexibility of use into account (*e.g.* if the plant is started up more than a certain number of times in a year, the Offtaker will pay so much per start-up—*cf.* §6.3.5).

§9.7.4 Concession Agreements and Availability-based Contracts—Availability and Performance

The risks relating to availability in PFI-Model Contracts are generally somewhat less than for a process-plant project, since most of such projects relate to buildings or other infrastructure assets which cannot 'break down' in the same way as a machinery-based project. Moreover, as can be seen from §6.4.3, 100% Unavailability of a project—and hence a total loss of revenue—is quite unlikely. Penalties for Unavailability in a Concession Agreement operate in a similar way.

Poor performance in such contracts, *e.g.* by a Building-Services Sub-Contractor, also gives rise to penalties, as described in §6.4.4.

§9.7.5 Maintenance and Lifecycle Costs

Compared to most other project operating costs, maintenance costs are irregular in nature since they are likely to fall outside an annual cycle. Broadly speaking, up to three different types of maintenance can be distinguished, although they are not all found in every project:

- *Routine maintenance*: As the term implies this is maintenance carried out on a regular basis, perhaps almost continuously, so this is a cost which may not vary much from year to year. So in the case of a road this might include removing leaves in the Fall, filling in potholes or repainting road markings.
- *Major maintenance*: This occurs when a significant part of the project requires major refurbishment work. An example of this would be that a turbine in a power station has to be shut down completely for major maintenance over some weeks, once every 5–7 years. Obviously while this type of maintenance is going on the project will probably lose revenue, but estimates of the lost revenue should have been factored into cash-flow projections.
- *Renewal/lifecycle costs*: These are costs to replace a major item of equipment, or some other key aspect of the project when it has come to the end of its useful life. So in the case of a building this might mean replacing the heating boiler after 15 years, or in the case of a road this might mean replacing the surface after 15–20 years.

Collectively these are known as 'scheduled maintenance'.[19] Assumptions for scheduled maintenance are built into Base Case projections (*cf.* §13.6), and allowed for in any Project Agreement. The main risks related to maintenance are:

---

[19] Also known as 'planned maintenance', or 'planned outage' (for process plant).

- It may take longer than expected, and so affect availability.
- It may cost more then expected.
- Insufficient cash flow may be retained to meet maintenance costs.
- Higher than expected usage may increase maintenance costs.
- Unexpected maintenance requirements may reduce availability,[20] although some allowance for this is often included in the Project Agreement's availability formula.

Whether the project has an assured revenue through an Offtake Contract, or relies on selling its project or service into the market, it is evident that if the project is not available to operate it will lose revenue (and may incur penalties—*cf.* §6.3.6).

The importance of using established technology for the project is again evident; the past record of similar projects should enable the Project Company to produce conservative estimates of scheduled and unscheduled downtime. This is an aspect of project risk where the experience of the operator of the project (whether the Project Company or an O&M Contractors) is important to satisfy lenders of the viability of the downtime estimates.

The longer the maintenance cycle, the greater the risk that the major maintenance costs may be higher than expected. It may be possible for the major maintenance or lifecycle cost risks to be passed on to a O&M/Maintenance Contractor, or to sign an agreement with an equipment supplier to provide maintenance for this equipment on an agreed formula (*cf.* §8.3.5).

In a long maintenance cycle there is a risk that the Project Company may fall short of cash flow when these costs are to be paid. This is dealt with by the establishment of a Maintenance Reserve Account, in which the Project Company (under the lenders' control) builds up a cash reserve for major maintenance during the maintenance cycle period (*cf.* §14.4.1). But if this cycle is very long—as would be the case in a road project—lenders may agree that the Maintenance Reserve Account only needs to be built up in the latter part of this period.

However, the more a project is used (*e.g.* by operating a plant or by traffic using a road) the more frequently it is likely to require maintenance. If the Project Company's revenue increases as usage increases, more frequent maintenance may not cause any problems, but this is not always the case. For example, in road projects where Shadow Tolls are being paid, the level of toll per vehicle may decline as usage increases, and perhaps go down to zero above a maximum usage level (*cf.* §6.4.6), to ensure that the payments the Contracting Authority makes for the road are capped. In such cases, paradoxically, high usage of the project is bad from the lenders' and investors' point of view, since it increases

---

[20] Also known as 'forced outage' in a process plant.

the frequency of maintenance without any corresponding revenue. By definition in such cases the risk is left with the Project Company, and therefore lenders will have to assess the effect of being too successful. In an Availability-based Contract the Contracting Authority may pay compensation for an unexpectedly high level of usage, *e.g.* on a road.

An Offtaker/Contracting Authority who will take over the project at the end of the Project Agreement will be concerned about maintenance in the latter years of the control, by which time the lenders may have been fully paid off and are no longer supervising the project (*cf.* §7.10.7).

§9.7.6 UTILITY COSTS

Utility costs—electricity, water, gas—may be a significant in a project's budget, either because utilities are needed for a process plant to operate, or in an infrastructure project involving one or more buildings. There are two risks associated with such costs: firstly, will the utility consumption be greater than projected, and secondly, will the unit costs of utilities be higher than projected?

This raises a particular issue in PPP projects in which a Contracting Authority occupies a building, such as a school or hospital. The use of electricity, for example, can be largely determined by the behavior of the Contracting Authority's own staff—windows left open when the heating is on, lights not switched off at night, PCs left running, and so on. Clearly the Project Company may not be able to exercise control over such wastage.

This is also a case, like maintenance, in which level of usage affects the Project Company, even though it is not taking the usage risk. There is a difficult balance to be struck here: the Project Company should design the building to be energy-efficient, for example, and the behavior of the Contracting Authority's staff should not negate this requirement. One approach to the use of utilities is to allow the building to 'bed down' over its first year, and then to take this level of utility use as the baseline, with increases in use being payable by the Contracting Authority. As to the unit cost of utilities, this is obviously not usually a risk which can be controlled by the Project Company, and if the Project Company is to take the risk, lenders will want to see extra Contract Payments being set as a reserve to meet fluctuating costs, the effect of which is to increase the cash flow required from the project, and hence the cost to a Contracting Authority: it is therefore better VfM for the Contracting Authority to retain this risk.

In general in process-plant projects, on the other hand, utility cost risks are left to the Project Company unless they are significant enough to operating costs to require indexation (assuming there is no long-term Input Supply Contract covering such costs).

§9.7.7 OTHER OPERATING COSTS

The largest continuing costs for any project are likely to be those for input supplies (if any, for which *cf.* §9.8), debt service, O&M/Maintenance Contract fees and Building-Services Contract fees (if any). It is inappropriate for lenders to restrict the Project Company's ability to fulfill its obligations under its Project Contracts, and therefore such payments (*e.g.* for fuel under an Input-Supply Contract) should be outside any budgetary controls.

However lenders will wish to set limits on any other variable operating costs that are within the budgetary control of the Project Company in a similar way that they control construction-cost budgeting (*cf.* §9.5.5).

One approach to budgetary controls over items that the Project Company does control (*e.g.* its own office and personnel costs, capital expenditure after the end of the construction phase, *etc.*) is to agree to a budget for these costs over the life of the financing as part of the Base-Case financial projections at Financial Close (*cf.* §13.6), including provision for adjustment for the general rate of inflation (*cf.* §13.4.1). The Project Company (or the O&M/Maintenance Contractor, if there is one) then produces an annual operating budget before each operating year, which is automatically approved by the lenders if it is within an agreed-upon margin of tolerance of the original budget (say a 10% variation, depending on how significant these Project Company-controlled budget figures are). If the Project Company wishes to make greater changes in the budget, Lender approval is required.

Similarly, a degree of tolerance between the annual budget and actual expenditure may be required so as not to impose unnecessary constraints on the Project Company's day-to-day operations. This actual expenditure is also controlled through the lenders' controls on the application of operating cash flow (*cf.* §14.4.2).

§9.8 INPUT-SUPPLY RISKS

In a process-plant project, a reliable supply of fuel or other raw materials, on an appropriate pricing basis, is essential. Lenders are unlikely to accept the Project Company taking an open risk on the availability of its main fuel or raw material supplies. Unless it can be clearly shown that the fuel or raw material concerned is a widely available commodity, a long-term Input-Supply Contract is required, even if the project has not got an Offtake Contract (*e.g.* in the case of a merchant power plant project).

Similarly, some form of hedging or other protection is needed against the risk that the price of the fuel or raw material increases so much that the project becomes unable to operate. This can be achieved by:

- Passing the risk through to the Offtaker (*e.g.* through an Energy Charge in a PPA (*cf.* §6.3.5; §8.5.3).

- Linking the price paid to the Input Supplier to the market price for the project's product (*cf.* §8.5.3).
- Long-term hedging of supply requirements in the commodity market (*cf.* §6.3.1).

The risks involved in Input-Supply Contracts are further discussed in §9.8.1, and the acceptability of doing without them in §9.8.2.

Certain other inputs may be free, but still represent a risk for the Project Company, for example, water for a hydroelectric power project, or wind for a wind power project (§9.8.3). Similarly, the 'reserve risk' has to be assessed for projects extracting oil, gas, or minerals—*i.e.* the risk of whether the oil or gas field or mine has the volume of reserves projected (§9.8.4). Risks involved in the supply of other utilities are discussed in §9.8.5.

§9.8.1 INPUT-SUPPLY CONTRACTS

An Input-Supply Contract provides the Project Company with defined volumes of fuel or other raw materials on an agreed-upon cost basis. The contract therefore should eliminate supply or price risks for the Project Company, but there remain some risk issues that require examination in the due-diligence process:

Credit of Supplier. As with Offtake Contracts, the credit risk of the supplier has to be considered, not just in the context of a corporate credit analysis, but also taking into account the place of the supply arrangements in the supplier's business. The supplier's experience, ability, and resources to manage its side of the project must also be considered.

Issues of direct or indirect political risk on the supplier may arise in some markets (*e.g.* the European gas market, where a significant proportion of the supply is from one supplier in Russia).

Source of Supply. If the inputs are traded commodities such as oil, the Project Company does not normally need to be concerned where the supplier is securing them. If the Input Supplier is a major oil or gas company, they are normally willing to take the input supply risk. If, however, the inputs are being supplied from, say, a particular oil or gas field, the issue is who will take the reserve risk (*cf.* §9.8.4). If the risk is taken by the Project Company, this may fall into the trap similar to that of one project being dependent on another to succeed (*cf.* §9.5.9). However, lenders are willing to take this risk if it is clear that the reserves are well in excess of what is required for the project.

Viability of Pricing. The pricing basis for the supply must, as with all Project Contracts, be viable for both sides. The price must be one at which the Input Supplier can continue to make a reasonable return. The price paid by the Project Company should also be reasonable in relationship to the market into which it is selling its product (even if the price risk is being taken by the Offtaker), for similar reasons of commercial viability.

Quantity and Timing of Supply. The quantity and timing of supply must match the needs of the project, with some flexibility to allow, for example, for delays in Project Completion. In a few cases a Project Company may take some risk on the quantity of supply: for example in a municipal waste-incineration project the Contracting Authority, rather than agreeing to supply fixed quantities of waste, can give exclusivity to the Project Company, meaning that all its available waste will be sent to this project. Lenders may find this acceptable if the current and projected level of waste available is reasonable in relation to the capacity of the plant (bearing in mind that waste may also be available from other sources).

Quality of Supply. Obviously most Input-Supply Contracts place the risk of the quality of the input product on the supplier, which can be complex in some cases. For example, a municipal waste-incineration project will require the Contracting Authority to deliver waste with certain defined characteristics such as calorific value, within a certain range of measurement. This may cause problems for the Contracting Authority if, for example, more waste is recycled, which may mean that high calorific-value waste such as paper and plastics are removed from the general waste before delivery to the incinerator.

Take-or-Pay Risk. Lenders are unlikely to accept the Project Company entering into a Take-or-Pay Contract for input supplies unless:

- The Project Company has passed this risk onto the Offtaker under the Project Agreement; or
- The Project Company can easily dispose of any surplus, without taking an undue sale price risk; or
- The contract is structured on a Take-or-Pay basis for a quantity reasonably smaller than the project's expected needs and Take-and-Pay for the balance of the expected needs.

Effect of Failure to Supply. If the Input Supplier fails to supply, the Project Company may lose revenue, incur extra cost by securing supplies from elsewhere, or incur penalties from an Offtaker (unless the Offtaker takes this risk). If the Input Supplier is under the same ownership as the Offtaker (*e.g.* both owned by the government) it or the Offtaker may compensate for this loss of revenue. The Input Supplier may be willing to compensate for any more than the cost of obtaining alternative sources of supply if possible (*i.e.* not the Project Company's loss of revenue). If not, this may be dealt with by:

- Storage of supplies at the project site, or the use of an alternative back-up supply (*e.g.* diesel oil in lieu of a supply of natural gas to a power station); these approaches normally cover 30–60 days' interruption of supply, but are unlikely to provide a long-term substitute.

- A provision in the Offtake Contract that if the Project Company cannot operate because of non-delivery of input supplies it remains 'available' for the purposes of the Offtake Contract, and therefore can continue to earn its Capacity Charge, although the Project Company may have an obligation under the Offtake Contract to operate with reserve stocks (to an agreed extent), or obtain alternative input supplies where this is possible.

- *Force majeure* insurance where physical damage to the connections is involved (*cf.* §8.6.2).

Failure to Complete Connections. Similarly, the Project Company may suffer loss of revenues or have to pay penalties to its Offtaker for its inability to start operations if connections being constructed by the Input Supplier (*e.g.* a gas pipeline) are not completed in time, but again the Input Supplier is unlikely to agree to a compensating penalty payment on an adequate scale, unless the Input Supplier is under common ownership with the Offtaker. This may be treated as a Relief Event under the Offtake Contract, thus extending its start date so the Project Company at least does not suffer penalties for the late start-up, or again be covered by *force majeure* insurance.

Third-Party Delivery Risks. A further problem arises if delivery is not through the Input Supplier's own facilities, but by road, rail, or through a port for which the Input Supplier has neither control nor responsibility. The Input Supplier could reasonably claim that if the national rail system does not deliver on time, or the nearby port is not able to berth or unload ships carrying input supplies, this is *force majeure* for which the Input Supplier should not be responsible.

The third party providing transport is very unlikely to accept liability for the consequences of the failure to supply; lenders therefore have to be shown that this party has a good record and experience in delivering similar supplies in the area in order to be convinced that they should allow the Project Company to accept the risk. If the Project Company or the lenders are uneasy about the capacity or capability of the delivery system, and if adequate guarantees for this are not available, this may be a major obstacle to the project finance.

The Input Supplier may rely on being able to bring the product through another country (*e.g.* in a pipeline). The risk of interruption of this supply—perhaps for political reasons—needs to be considered, as does allocation of liability for this risk.

Risk for the Input Supplier. Mitigation of risks from the Input Supplier's point of view is discussed in §8.5.4.

§9.8.2 WHEN IS AN INPUT-SUPPLY CONTRACT NOT NEEDED?

In some circumstances, lenders will accept that a Project Company requiring fuel or raw material inputs does not need to rely on an Input-Supply Contract, if the project is using supplies of a commodity that is easily available and can be transported to the project site without special arrangements, and if price fluctuations are passed on to the Offtaker. This would be the case for, say, a coal-fired power plant, situated close to good transportation connections, which can buy its coal from the international markets. (The plant would also store sufficient quantities of coal on site to guard against temporary interruptions in supply.)

Similarly, a wood-chip burning power plant situated in the middle of an area with an active forest products industry may not need a long-term contract for wood-chip supplies, since these are a waste product of the local industry with limited other uses. If in the longer term the local wood industry declines, the plant may be in danger, but in that case a long-term supply contract would not provide the lenders with much real security, since the supplier will probably default anyway.

§9.8.3 WATER AND WIND

Many process plant projects depend on significant quantities of water from rivers, lakes, or canals, as do hydroelectric power plants and, of course, water-supply projects. The availability of this water may vary significantly during the year or from year to year. To enable them to accept this kind of water risk, lenders need to be provided with long-term statistics demonstrating the volume, quality, and reliability of the water supply.

The same principle applies to projects using wind for power generation: the Sponsors need to provide statistics on wind volume, direction, and so on, at the project site over a number of years as a basis for the projected assumptions in this respect.

§9.8.4 MINERAL RESERVES

Both in a project that involves the extraction and sale of natural resources, and in a project that depends on the supply of natural resources from a specific source as an input fuel or raw material, there is a risk that these natural resources may not be extracted as expected.

Lenders commonly ask their advisors to classify the estimated hydrocarbons or minerals reserves in the ground into 'proven' reserves, which also have to be economically recoverable—further classified into 'P90' and 'P50' (*i.e.* reserves that have a 90% possibility of recovery, and those that have a 50% possibility)—and 'possible' reserves. Lending is only against proven reserves (and hence is known as 'reserve-based' lending), and primarily against the P90 reserves, taking into account the geology of the project and hence the difficulty of extraction.

Lenders also only take into account a proportion of the proven reserves, and require a reserve 'tail' (*cf.* §12.3.5), *i.e.* lenders usually do not lend to the end of expected life of the reserves, but to a date on which 25–30% of the original proven reserves are expected to be left. This allows for difficulty in recovering reserves as they become more depleted and the eventual costs of closing down the project.

§9.8.5 OTHER UTILITIES

The Project Company needs to demonstrate that it has a reliable supply of any general utilities needed for the project, such as electricity, telephone, water, and sewerage.

§9.9 UNINSURED RISKS AND RELATED ISSUES

Force majeure is a difficult area in negotiating Project Contracts: by definition *force majeure* is nobody's fault, but someone has to suffer the consequences. The position where *force majeure* has made it impossible to finish constructing or to operate the project, so leading to a termination of the Project Agreement, is discussed in §7.10.4 (for Reverting Asset-based Contracts) and §7.10.9 (for Non-Reverting Asset-based Contracts).

As to temporary *force majeure*, *i.e.* Relief Events (*cf.* §7.8), a number of risk issues arise:

- Insurance may cover most but not all of the problem, and a way of filling the insurance gaps is needed. Lenders will be concerned if the Project Company is left with temporary *force majeure* risks which could affect its ability to service the debt (§9.9.1).
- Insurance costs may increase considerably over the original estimates, so causing an operating-cost overrun for the Project Company (§9.9.2).
- Insurance may become unavailable (§9.9.3).

Also a Relief Event in the Project Agreement will probably also have an effect on the different Project Contracts, and so the provisions of these contracts need to be coordinated in this respect (*cf.* §9.12).

§9.9.1 *FORCE MAJEURE* AND INSURANCE

The purpose of insurance is to cover the Project Company against unpredictable losses, and so it might be thought that the Project Company and its lenders should therefore not be at risk from *force-majeure* events. There may be gaps, however, between the scope of insurance coverage (*cf.* §8.6) and the potential for *force-majeure* losses.

First of all, insurance generally only covers loss caused by physical damage to the project (the cost of repair or replacement), or economic loss deriving from this (delay in start-up of the project or loss of revenue), caused by the same physical damage. Thus an event such as a national strike delaying completion or operation of the plant would not be covered by standard DSU or BI insurance. *Force majeure* insurance may be available to cover this type of risk (*cf.* §8.6.1), but issues of cost or scope of the cover may arise.)

Second, Political *Force Majeure* events (*cf.* §7.10.4) cannot be covered by general insurance unless physical damage (*e.g.* from war), as opposed to just economic loss, is involved, and in some cases (*e.g.* coverage for terrorism) the cover may be theoretically available but at a cost that is commercially unattractive.

Third, certain risks of physical damage cannot be covered by insurance:

- All insurance policies have deductibles (*i.e.* limits below which the loss must be suffered by the insured party rather than the insurance company). The higher the deductible the lower the insurance premiums will be. The Project Company may wish to reduce costs by increasing deductibles, whereas the Construction Contractor (in relation to construction insurances) and the lenders will prefer to have a fuller coverage.
- If there is a fire in a facility next to that operated by the Project Company, and as a result the latter has to close down, the BI cover would not apply as the Project Company's facility has not suffered any physical damage.
- Certain risks, such as damage caused by a nuclear explosion, cannot be insured. Lenders accept these standard exclusions.

§9.9.2 INSURANCE COSTS

The Project Company's insurance premiums are usually fixed for the whole of the construction phase, but thereafter the insurance cover is typically on an annual basis (*cf.* §8.6.2), which of course means that the annual insurance premiums may change. In fact insurances premiums may vary enormously over several years, a doubling (or halving) of costs being not unusual. The cost of insurance is a product of two factors—historical losses in the insurance market concerned, and the state of the stock markets. The reason that the latter is important is that the insurance companies invest the premiums they receive into the stock market, which subsidizes the cost of the insurance. After

9/11, for example, insurance costs rose sharply, but this was mainly caused by the drop in the stock markets rather than an expectation of greatly-increased levels of terrorism.

This is another case where VfM suggests that in projects where there is an Offtaker/ Contracting Authority it may not make good sense to pass on the full insurance-cost risk to the Project Company. One approach is use a 'cap and floor' system:

- A baseline for operating-phase insurance costs is agreed.
- The Project Company's insurance broker obtains competitive quotes on each renewal date.
- If costs increase by more than $x\%$, the Offtaker/Contracting Authority pays 90% of the excess.
- If costs decrease by more than $x\%$, the Offtaker/Contracting Authority receives 90% of the excess.
- Note that these cost increases/decreases relate to general insurance market costs: if the Project Company has a bad claims record, and this is the reason for an increase in insurance costs, such cost increases would be ignored.
- Insurance mainly required by the lenders, such as DSU/BI and non-vitiation cover, may not be covered by these arrangements (but this is likely to mean that the lenders will want reserves to be set up, again raising VfM issues for an Offtaker/Contracting Authority).

For other types of project, the cost of operating insurances is an open risk for lenders and investors; it is not possible to obtain long-term operating insurance coverage at the beginning of the construction phase (although coverage for the first year of operation may be possible). Lenders have generally been willing to allow the Project Company to assume this risk without requiring Sponsor support.

Thus even though the Project Company is required, both by Project Contracts and by lenders, to cover *force-majeure* risks through insurance as far as possible, the risks to the Project Company of additional costs or loss of revenue caused by a Relief Event cannot be completely mitigated in this way.

§9.9.3 UNAVAILABILITY OF INSURANCE

Finally, changes in the insurance market may leave the project exposed to uninsured *force majeure*. This relates to insurance during the operation phase (as noted above, construction-phase insurances are fixed at Financial Close). An estimate for cost of this insurance is agreed to with lenders in advance as part of the operating-cost budget, but market fluctuations may affect the actual costs considerably. The lenders will generally wish the agreed-upon levels and terms of insurance coverage to be obtained even at a higher cost, but there may come a point when the insurance market has changed so much as to make this commercially unattractive, and, for example, deductibles have to be higher than originally expected.

In the worst case, actual availability of the required insurance may be a problem, perhaps because the insurance market has had a recent poor claims record in the industry or with the equipment concerned.

Therefore while the financing documentation may set out detailed provisions for what the Project Company is obliged to do in respect to operating insurances, such provisions must be qualified by a 'market out' provision. There are two possible approaches here:

- If the insurances are not available, or not available at reasonable cost, the Project Company is permitted to take out the insurances on the best basis reasonably available on the market.

- Unavailability of insurance (or availability only on punitive terms) may also be considered an event analogous to Political *Force Majeure*. In such cases the Offtaker/Contracting Authority may be willing to act as insurer of last resort, and assume the uninsurable risks. Failing this, the Project Agreement may be terminated in the same way as for Political *Force Majeure* (*cf.* §7.10.4; §7.10.8).

§9.10 ENVIRONMENTAL RISKS

The project's impact on the surrounding environment, during both the construction and operation phases, may need to be considered. An Environmental Impact Assessment (EIA) may be needed for this purpose (§9.10.1).

Sponsors cannot rely only on keeping within environmental laws and regulations; they need to consider whether any environmental aspects of the project leave them at risk of opposition to construction or operation of the project indirectly discouraging lenders from getting involved with it.

Even if the Project Company is acting within the law, it may still be at risk on wider political grounds. Public opposition to the project may cause the Host Government to reconsider its obligations under a Project Agreement. Similarly, the lenders themselves may find themselves under attack for supporting a project that is perceived to be environmentally damaging.

Most DFIs have their own environmental standards mandated by their members (*i.e.* state shareholders) and may require these to apply to projects even if local law does not require this. In the worst case this could put the Project Company into default under the financing if it violates these standards, even though it is not breaking the law in the country in which the project is situated. These standards have increasingly been taken up by private-sector lenders, in particular through the set of guidelines known as the 'Equator Principles' (§9.10.2).

Pre-existing environmental pollution of the project site may create a significant obstacle to progressing a project (§9.10.3). Waste products from the project may also have to be dealt with (§9.10.4). It may be possible to cover off some of these risks using environmental insurance (*cf.* §8.6.2). Some types of project are also vulnerable to changes in environmental laws (§9.10.5).

§9.10.1 ENVIRONMENTAL IMPACT ASSESSMENT

The first stage in obtaining both construction and operating Permits is often to prepare an EIA for the project. The EIA examines the environmental impact of the project in a variety of ways such as:

- the effect of construction and operation of the project on the surrounding natural environment (plant and animal habitats, landscape, *etc.*);
- the effect of construction on any historical remains;
- the effect of construction on local communities, including noise, dust, other pollution, and construction traffic;
- the level of emissions into the atmosphere caused by operation of the project;
- water abstraction and discharge;
- disposal of waste products (*e.g.* 'tailings' from a mine or ash from a coal-fired power station);
- long-term effects of the project on local traffic, transportation, and utilities;
- other long-term effects of the project on local communities or the natural environment.

Following this assessment, which at a minimum must clearly demonstrate that the project complies with legal requirements on such environmental issues, an environmental Permit may be obtained.

§9.10.2 THE EQUATOR PRINCIPLES

The Equator Principles were launched by a group of leading project-finance banks in 2003. (They were revised in 2006, and again in 2012).[21] The financial institutions that adhere to the Equator Principles pledge to maintain these standards in their project-finance lending, and hence not to finance projects which do not meet these standards. As of mid-2013, 78 financial institutions had adopted the Principles. There are ten Principles:

---

[21] The full text of the Principles can be found at www.equator-principles.com.

Principle 1: Review and Categorization. New project proposals will be categorized based on the International Finance Corporation's ('IFC'—*cf.* §16.5.2) environmental and social screening criteria. These categories are:

- Category A – Projects with potential significant adverse social or environmental impacts that are diverse, irreversible or unprecedented;
- Category B – Projects with potential limited adverse social or environmental impacts that are few in number, generally site-specific, largely reversible and readily addressed through mitigation measures; and
- Category C – Projects with minimal or no social or environmental impacts.

    The Principles relate primarily to Category A projects, or B projects in non-OECD (*cf.* §16.2.3) or OECD low-income countries.

Principle 2: Environmental and Environmental Assessment. To be carried out for all Category A and B projects.

Principle 3: Applicable Social and Environmental Standards. Projects must adhere to the IFC's standards. Those in high-income OECD countries should adhere to national laws in this respect.

Principle 4: Environmental and Social Management System ('ESMS') and Equator Principles Action Plan. Project Sponsors are required to prepare an ESMS, and an Environmental and Social Management Plan ('ESMP') to comply with applicable standards, or if required by the lender, an Action Plan which conforms to the Equator Principles.

Principle 5: Stakeholder Engagement. For all Category A and B Projects, the lender will require the client to demonstrate effective Stakeholder Engagement as an ongoing process in a structured and culturally appropriate manner.

Principle 6: Grievance Mechanism. This must enable the borrower to receive and facilitate resolution of concerns and grievances about the project's social and environmental performance raised by individuals or groups from among project-affected communities.

Principle 7: Independent Review. An independent social or environmental expert not directly associated with the borrower will review the processes set out above and assess Equator Principles compliance.

Principle 8: Covenants. The financing documentation will include covenants (*cf.* §14.10):

- to comply with all relevant social and environmental laws, regulations and permits, and for Category A and B Projects:
- to comply with the ESMP and any Equator Principles Action Plan during the construction and operation of the project;
- to report periodically on the above requirements;
- to decommission the project in accordance with a pre-agreed plan.

Principle 9: Independent Monitoring and Reporting. This is done through appointment of an Independent Environmental and Social Consultant.

Principle 10: Reporting and Transparency. Institutions are to make annual reports on their application of the principles.

§9.10.3 PRE-EXISTING SITE CONTAMINATION

As part of the EIA process an 'environmental audit' of the project site may also be carried out, which examines the site for potential existing pollution, taking account of its previous uses (*cf.* §9.5.2). If site contamination is discovered, a program for containing or removing it is required, and one of the parties must take responsibility for this, including the extra costs caused by having to remove pollution or hazardous waste from the site, other than any pollution caused by the Construction Contractor (this is known as 'site-legacy' risk).

If there is known to be pollution or hazardous waste on the site, or past history suggests there may be, this is likely to be a major issue with lenders, even if removal is included in the project budget.

- Firstly it may be difficult to estimate the costs of cleaning up, so the lenders will usually require someone other than the Project Company to be responsible for this—meaning either the Offtaker/Contracting Authority or the Construction Contractor.

- Secondly, in some countries (*e.g.* U.S.A.), lenders have may liability for damage caused by pollution from a site over which they take security; even if this is not the case, if the lenders do have security over the project site, and foreclose on this security, they may become the owners of the site, and thus have to take on liability in this respect. In general lenders feel vulnerable, as the parties with 'deep pockets,' to the problem proving more difficult than expected or to long-term damage caused from site pollution. Insurance may be available to mitigate these risks.

If the site is provided by an Offtaker/Contracting Authority, there is a case for the Offtaker/Contracting Authority taking responsibility for site condition, and hence treating the issues above as Compensation Events; if the Construction Contractor is not willing to assume such risks. A further possibility is to split the costs resulting from crystallization of such risks between the Construction Contractor and the Offtaker/Contracting Authority, so that the former assumes risks costing up to x, with the Offtaker/Contracting Authority compensating thereafter *via* a Compensation Event under the Project Agreement which is mirrored in the Construction Contract.

Insurance may also help to deal with risk issues arising from pollution (*cf.* §8.6.1).

§9.10.4 WASTE DISPOSAL

Disposal of waste products such as ash or mineral 'tailings' is obviously an environmental issue, but may also be a financial and contractual one. If it is necessary to dispose of such waste products off-site, the Project Company must normally have long-term contracts in place for this purpose, and if they are dealt with onsite this needs to be done in an appropriate and legal manner.

Again, the lenders have to take care to ensure they are not held liable for pollution from such sources.

§9.10.5 CHANGE IN LAW

Even if the Project Company has obtained the necessary Permits to construct and operate the project, it may still remain at risk from changes in law relating to environmental aspects of the project (*e.g.* emissions) that require extra capital expenditure (*cf.* §11.3).

§9.11 RESIDUAL-VALUE RISK

In Project Agreements with an Offtaker/Contracting Authority, either it or the Project Company's investors may be taking a risk on the residual value of the project (*cf.* §6.2; §7.2.5; §7.10.7; §7.10.9).

§9.12 CONTRACT MISMATCH

When the due-diligence process is being undertaken, it is easy to get bogged down in the details of individual Project Contracts, and as a result miss risks that may arise from incompatible provisions in different Project Contracts.[22] Each Project Contract is not self-contained, but affects the others, and the contracting structure of the project must be reviewed as a whole. This has already been illustrated in the discussion on Relief Events above (*cf.* §8.2.6). Other Examples of areas where contract mismatches may arise could include:

- differences between Project Completion requirements under the Construction Contract and under the Project Agreement (*cf.* §9.5.8);
- differences between the first date for deliveries under the Input-Supply Contract and under the Offtake Contract;

---

[22] This issue is also known as 'structural risk'.

- a different procedure for fixing the cost of a Contract Variation in the project during the construction phase under the Project Agreement (*cf.* §7.6.3), and for fixing the cost of the same variation in the Construction Contract, so that the cost of the variation payable to the Construction Contractor may not be fully passed through to the Offtaker/Contracting Authority;
- a similar issue arises with extra costs caused by a change in law (*cf.* §11.3);
- differences in the pricing formula for fuel or other input supplies between the Input Supply and Offtake Contracts;
- timing differences between revenue receipts, payment for input supplies, and loan payments;
- different definitions of *force majeure* in different Project Contracts.

This interplay between the Project Agreement, and other Project Contracts including the Construction Contract and insurance can be illustrated in more detail by reviewing the effect of Relief Events, as below.

Relief Event Causing a Delay in Project Completion. Physical damage to the project site or equipment in the course of delivery that delays in Project Completion should be covered by the CEAR or Marine Cargo insurances, and loss of revenue by the DSU or Marine DSU insurances (*cf.* §8.6.1), unless the event concerned falls outside the scope of coverage. Obviously, if insurance payments are made to the Project Company it should not receive any windfall payments or relief under the Project Contracts.

It should be noted that one of the main purposes of the contingency reserve included in the project budget (*cf.* §9.5.6) is to cover the possibility of a *force majeure* delay in Project Completion or additional cost for which insurance is not available.

The effects of this Relief Event have to be tracked through the various Project Contracts.

- *Construction Contract*: Relief Events relieve the Construction Contractor from liability for LDs for delay in Project Completion (*cf.* §8.2.6), but do not create any right to additional payments. However, the Construction Contractor may try to get some events designated as Owner's Risks (*cf.* §8.2.5) rather than Relief Events, *e.g.* strikes at the project site or at a supplier's factory; this is not usually acceptable to a Project Company— only general (national) strikes should be included—but may be agreed to if it can be reflected in the Project Agreement (so avoiding penalties for late Project Completion) or Input-Supply Contract (so avoiding fuel or other input supplies having to be paid for before they are needed).
- *Project Agreement*: This same delay from a Relief Event affecting the Construction Contractor should also relieve the Project Company of any penalties for delay in reaching Project Completion, but because the

project is not available it does not usually receive any revenue; temporary *force majeure* that prevents the Offtaker/Contracting Authority completing any necessary connections to the project site does not generally relieve them from having to paying the Capacity Charge or Service Fee (or to compensate for loss of Tariff) following the general principle set out above.

- *Input Supply Agreement*: Following the same general principle, if *force majeure* prevents Project Completion, the Project Company should still have to make any minimum payments required under the Input-Supply Contract; however, this risk may remain with the Input Supplier, or be passed on to the Offtaker under the Offtake Contract.

Relief Event Causing an Interruption in Availability. As with delay in Project Completion, the effect of a Relief Event affecting availability has to be tracked through the various Project Contracts:

- *Project Agreement*: The Project Company is relieved from penalties but does not receive the Capacity Charge or Service Fee; on the other hand, the Offtaker/Contracting Authority must continue to make Availability payments if *force majeure* events affect its ability to continue taking the Project Company's product or service.

- *Input-Supply Contract*: *Force majeure* generally does not excuse the Project Company for paying for input supplies for a process-plant project, but the risk may be passed on to the Offtaker under the Project Agreement; *force majeure* will excuse the Input Supplier from making deliveries, but again the effect of this may be passed on under the Project Agreement. If *force majeure* prevents the Input Supplier from completing its connections to the project site, the Input Supplier may not have to pay any penalties for this, but again the risk may be passed on to the Offtaker who thus has to start paying the Capacity Charge. (It may also be feasible for the Project Company to store back-up supplies of fuel or raw materials, and so use these to start operation.)

A Debt-Service Reserve Account (*cf.* §14.4.1) provides some protection against a temporary interruption of revenue not covered by insurance.

§9.13 RECOURSE TO THE SPONSORS

Lenders are unlikely to spend time on detailed due-diligence work on the project if the parties behind it are not credible. A project that appears entirely commercially *via*ble will still probably not find financing without appropriate Sponsors, with arm's-length relationships with the Project Company (*cf.* §3.2).

Similarly, lenders wish to see Sponsors earning an adequate rate of return on their investment, to encourage their continuing commitment to and involvement in the project. If the Sponsors appear to be only earning a low rate of return, this may also suggest that they are compensating themselves in another way (at the expense of the lenders' cash-flow cover)—*e.g.* by a high-cost Construction Contract if the Construction Contractor is a Sponsor, or by the provision of O&M or other services to the Project Company.

Finally, if a commercial risk involved in the project is not adequately mitigated by other means, the Sponsors may have to step in to fill this gap. 'Comfort letters' are sometimes offered to lenders as a risk mitigation in place of formal guarantees; for example, a Sponsor may state that it owns the shares in the Project Company, that it presently intends to maintain this ownership and keep the Project Company in a sound financial condition, and that it provides management support. Such undertakings seldom have effective legal force, and while helpful in some circumstances are unlikely to eliminate risks that are otherwise unacceptable.

The only financial obligation that Sponsors have in all project financings is to subscribe their equity share in the Project Company (*i.e.* the lenders provide a loan to the Project Company with no guarantee of repayment from the Sponsors, thus the loan is non-recourse to the Sponsors). Also they are often required to hold their shareholding for a period of time—at least until Project Completion, to ensure their continued commitment to the project.

While in principle Sponsors do not provide loan guarantees to the Project Company's lenders, limited guarantees may sometimes be provided to cover a risk that proves to be unacceptable to lenders[23]. Examples of such limited-recourse guarantees are:

- *Contingent equity commitment*: The Sponsors agree to inject a specific additional amount as equity into the Project Company to meet specified cash-flow requirements.
- *Cost-overrun guarantee*: The Sponsors agree to inject additional equity up to a certain limit to cover any cost overruns during construction (or operating-cost overruns).
- *Completion guarantee*: The Sponsors undertake to inject extra funding if necessary to ensure that construction of the project is completed by a certain date, thus taking on the risk that more funding for construction or initial debt payments may be required (*cf.* §9.5.12).

---

[23] *Cf.* Stephen Arbogast. "Quantifying contingent support in project financings", *Project Finance* (Euromoney, London, July 2013) p. 136, for a discussion of how projects should be dealt with in balance-sheet terms.

- *Financial-completion guarantee*: The Sponsors provide a guarantee not only that the project will be physically completed, but that it will achieve a minimum level of operating revenues or cash flow.
- *Sales-completion guarantee*: Similar to a financial-completion guarantee, but with the guarantee only covering an undertaking that the project will achieve a certain level of sales after physical completion.
- *Input-supply undertaking*: The Sponsors agree to secure supplies of the fuel or raw material required for the project, at a fixed or maximum price, if these cannot be obtained elsewhere.
- *Payment subordination*: If a Sponsor is a supplier of fuel or raw material to the project, payments for these supplies are deferred in favor of paying the lenders if the Project Company is short of cash.
- *Performance guarantee*: The Sponsors agree to provide additional funding for debt service if the cash flow is reduced by the project not operating to a minimum performance standard (*cf.* §9.5.10).
- *Product-price guarantee*: The Sponsors guarantee to make up any deficit if the product produced by the Project Company sells below an agreed-upon floor price, or to buy the product at the floor price (*cf.* §9.6.2).
- *Claw-back guarantee*: The Sponsors agree to make up any deficiency in the Project Company's cash flow for debt service, to the extent they have received Distributions from the Project Company (*cf.* §14.4.2).
- *Interest guarantee*: The Sponsors agree to pay the interest on the loan if the Project Company cannot do so (in practical terms this is very close to a full guarantee of the loan; if it is not paid back the Sponsors will have to keep paying interest indefinitely).
- *Interest make-up guarantee*: The Sponsors agree to pay interest above a certain level.
- *Deficiency guarantee*: The Sponsors agree to make up any debt service that cannot be paid because of a lack of cash in the Project Company (this is, of course, virtually a full financial guarantee).
- *Shortfall guarantee*: A guarantee to pay any sums remaining due to lenders after termination of the loan and realization of other security.

If Sponsors have contractual relationships with the Project Company other than their obligation to invest their equity, non-recourse project finance is more likely to be diluted into limited-recourse; for example, a Sponsor acting as a fuel supplier is likely to have to take liability for the financial consequences if the fuel is not delivered. (*Cf.* §8.10 for parent company guarantees for Sub-Contractors.)

Even if limited-recourse financial support is not being provided, Sponsors may agree to provide management or other technical support to the Project Company (*cf.* §3.6.3).

§9.14 RISKS FOR AN OFFTAKER/CONTRACTING AUTHORITY

An Offtaker/Contracting Authority is of course taking the risk that the Project Company may not succeed in constructing and operating the project as expected, and as a result a public service may not be provided, or the Offtaker/Contracting Authority has to buy the product or service more expensively from elsewhere. The Sponsors will not usually provide any support in this respect, as any such guarantees would destroy the non-recourse structure of the project finance. (As noted in §9.5.11, the Construction Contractor is in a similar position.) The Offtaker/ Contracting Authority can take various steps to mitigate this risk by ensuring that:

- The project has credible Sponsors (*cf.* §3.2).
- The project is technically sound.
- The Sub-Contracts are to be signed with appropriate parties. Although the Offtaker/Contracting Authority should not normally get involved in negotiating the Sub-Contracts (*cf.* §7.4.3), it may be prudent to ensure that there are reasonable levels of LDs (*cf.* §8.2.8) and bonding (*cf.* §8.2.9).
- The project is financially sound, with appropriate costings, a sensible financial structure, and reasonable returns for the Sponsors. The Offtaker/ Contracting Authority's bid evaluation process (*cf.* §3.7.8) is very important in this respect.
- The lenders are experienced in project finance, committed to the project (*cf.* §5.6), and have carried out a sound and independent due diligence (*cf.* §5.5).
- The Contract Payment structure ensures that there is long-term capital at risk (*cf.* §7.3.2).
- Payments on termination for the Project Company's default are structured to ensure that the Offtaker/Contracting Authority does not pay more than the project is worth if it takes over a Reverting Asset-based Contract (*cf.* §7.10.1), or is at least compensated for its losses in the case of a Non-Reverting Asset-based Contract (§7.10.8).[24]

§9.15 WHY DO PROJECTS FAIL?

The rating agency Standard & Poor's (*cf.* §5.3.1) rated 510 project-finance debt issues from 1991 to 2102, 34 of which defaulted on their debt. S&P calculate the annual default rate as 1.5%. 65% of the defaults originally received 'speculative

---

[24] However, there are cases where this may not be possible because the Offtaker/Contracting Authority has wholly or partially guaranteed the debt—*cf.* §15.4.

grade' ratings, *i.e.* below investment grade. There were two defaults annually in 2008–2010, three in 2012, and five in 2012. In recent years the highest level of defaults has been seen in the U.S. market, which is linked to the fact that a higher than average proportion of U.S. rated deals are speculative grade. Seven of the eight defaults were in the power sector, and according to S&P occurred because of issues such as:

- "technology or design failures that led to failed construction or chronic underperformance during operations;
- operational performance consistently below projections;
- poor hedging and commodity exposure to variation in fuel and other input prices;
- market exposure on project outputs, such as electricity sold in the merchant power market;
- structural and financial weaknesses, which were heightened by accidents, court judgments, or an unexpected need for sizable capital spending. Often an event will only be terminal for a project that is already vulnerable for other reasons and lacks applicable insurance or adequate liquidity reasons and lacks applicable insurance or adequate liquidity."[25]

S&P commented "Some of the lower rated power projects were structured with exposure to market or fuel risk, which partially explains the number of power projects in the list of defaults. Construction overruns on projects in a sector with complex technology was another reason. The transport sector defaults are generally volume-based projects (ones that rely on usage, such as a toll road) that failed due to lower-than-expected demand."[26] Most defaults occurred during the construction and early years of the project.

S&P also maintains the much larger S&P Capital IQ Project Finance Consortium database, containing data on portfolio performance from the majority of major project-finance lenders (*cf.* §17.3). In 2012 there were 6,862 projects in this database, of which 512 had defaulted.

Other reasons for failure (besides those listed by S&P above) would include:

- Sponsors' inability to raise finance (*e.g.* because the terms of the project Agreement or the cash flows make the project unbankable);
- 'low ball' bids by Sponsors (especially if they are Construction Contractors), which assume that in due course extra cost claims against the Offtaker/ Contracting Authority will make the project viable;

---

[25] *Project Finance Default and Recovery: Shale Gas Fuels Rise In U.S. Defaults* (Standard & Poor's Ratings Direct, New York NY/Los Angeles CA, 2013).
[26] Particular reasons for default in traffic-related concessions are discussed in §9.6.3.

- political interference (examples of which would include requiring a particular bidder to be chosen on a non-transparent basis, or trying to prevent the Project Company's using its contractual right to raise tolls);
- lack of experience by the Sponsors, Contracting Authority or other parties, leading to the drafting of poorly-worded Project Contracts;
- in the case of natural-resources projects, especially in developing countries, there is a high risk of expropriation by the Host Government (*cf.* §11.4.2).

Very similar results can be found from a database of 4,067 project-finance loans entered into between 1983 and 2011, maintained by the other major rating agency, Moody's.[27] 302 (7.4%) of these projects went into default. Like S&P, Moody's found that defaults generally occur during the construction or early operation phase of projects. Average default rates in the first three years from Financial Close were 1.7%, declining thereafter, illustrating that construction risk is usually the main cause of default.

The rate of default within industries, which as stated above is 7.4% on average, can be broken down further. Here it can be seen that the high-risk industries are manufacturing (17% of loans defaulted), metals & mining (12%), and media & telecoms (12%). The lowest-risk industry was infrastructure (4%), followed by oil & gas (8%) and power (8%).

Within infrastructure there were 954 projects classified as PFI/PPPs (although given unclear boundary lines this number is rather fuzzy). Their default rates (2.6%) were lower than those for infrastructure as a whole, illustrating that this sector is probably the safest for project-finance lending.

Within power, about ⅓ of projects were in the U.S.A., with an average default rate of 11%, and ⅔ in the rest of the world, with an average default rate of 6%. This mainly reflects the higher level of merchant power plants in the U.S.A. Incidence of such defaults peaked in 2001–2004, reflecting the losses in the power industry after the collapse of Enron.

§9.16 LOSS ON DEFAULT

However, the fact that a project has defaulted does not mean that the lenders' financing has been wholly lost (*cf.* §7.10.1—hence lenders will analyze both 'probability of default' and 'probable loss on default').

S&P has also calculated the recoveries made by lenders against the defaulted projects in its rated-debt database. The average recovery was 75% of the outstanding

---

[27] *Special Comment: Default and Recovery Rates for Project Finance Bank Loans, 1983–2011* (Moody's Investors Service, New York NY/London, 2013)*

debt, but it should be noted that the loss rates are concentrated at either end of the scale, *i.e.* lenders either recovered all or almost all of their debt, or the recoveries were very low (25% or less). The latter low-recovery cases were mainly in the natural-resources sector. Similar results appear in the wider Project Finance Consortium database, where actually 100% recovery was achieved from 356 of the 512 defaulted projects.

Again similar figures are found in the Moody's database: the 302 defaulted projects are further split down into 102 still at the work-out stage, so there are no final figures on lenders' losses, 34 where a distress sale has taken place (*i.e.* the banks exercised their security without any debt restructuring), and 161 on which recoveries have been made and the project has emerged from default. 105 of these latter 161 projects had emerged from default with no losses for lenders. The levels of losses for the remaining projects were spread fairly evenly between 0–24% and 75–99%.

The average recovery rate for projects which defaulted during the construction phase was 65%, and during the operation phase was 83%, obviously confirming the higher-risk nature of the former. The average recovery rate for PPP/PFI projects (in both phases) was 84%.

Overall these figures confirm that project-finance is a low-risk business for lenders if organized and structured following market best practices (*cf.* §17.2).

Chapter 10

MACRO-ECONOMIC RISKS

§10.1 INTRODUCTION

External macro-economic risks (also known as financial risks), namely changes in interest rates (§10.3), inflation (§10.4), and currency exchange-rates (§10.5), do not relate to the project in particular, but to the economic environment in which it operates. These risks need to be analyzed and mitigated (hedged) in the same way as the specific commercial risks discussed in the previous chapter. Also, a mismatch between a short-term loan and a long-term project is another form of macro-economic risk (§10.6).

However before looking at these macro-economic risks in detail, some basic financial concepts which lie behind calculations of the effect of these risks, as well as other cash-flow related issues in following chapters, are reviewed. In summary, these all relate to adjusting cash-flow calculations for the time value of money (§10.2).

257

Principles of Project Finance. DOI: http://dx.doi.org/10.1016/B978-0-12-391058-5.00010-2

§10.2 THE TIME VALUE OF MONEY

To have $1 in a year's time is obviously not as beneficial as having $1 today. But is it beneficial to have $1.50 in a year's time instead of $1 today? To answer this question a calculation is needed to show how much $1.50 in a year's time is worth in terms of today's money, which will then enable a comparison to be made with $1 today, and hence to decide which would be the better choice. This is called a discounted cash flow (DCF) calculation (§10.2.1).

Similarly, project finance is based on an investment being made today, in return for which a cash flow is received over a period of years. Obviously it is necessary to calculate what return on this investment the investor is receiving. This is called an internal rate of return (IRR) calculation (§10.2.2).

However there are some problems with these measures, and results have to be treated with care (§10.2.3).

§10.2.1 DISCOUNTED CASH FLOW

A DCF calculation produces the value in today's money of a sum or sums of money due in the future, taking account of the cost of money, known as the discount rate. The result was known as the net present value (NPV) of the cash flow concerned.

The formula for an NPV calculation is: $\dfrac{C}{(1+i)^n}$ where C is the future cash sum, i is the interest or discount rate, and n is the number of periods. (The discount rate may be an annual, or, say, semi-annual rate corresponding to the period.)

Thus if the discount rate or cost of money is 10% p.a., and a sum of 1000 is due in a year's time, the NPV of that sum is: $\dfrac{1000}{(1+0.10)}$ or 909.1. To turn the calculation the other way round, if 909.1 is invested for a year at 10%, 1000 (*i.e.* 909.1 × 1.10) will be repaid at the end of the year. Similarly, the NPV of a sum of 1000 due in two years' time, at a discount rate of 10% p.a. calculated semiannually (*i.e.* 5% per half year) is: $\dfrac{1000}{(1+0.05)^4}$ or 822.7.

The NPV of a cash flow calculates the present value of a series of future cash sums. It is calculated as:

$$\sum_n \frac{C^n}{(1+i)^n}$$ *i.e.* the sum of the net cash flow for each future period (usually semi-annually in project-finance calculations), each period's cash flow being discounted to its NPV at the discount rate. (There is no need to use formulae or books of tables to work out NPV calculations—this can easily be done using financial calculators or spread-sheet software.)

The use of DCF calculations can be illustrated by the two contrasting investment cash flows set out in Table 10.1. Both have an initial investment of 1000, and

Table 10.1 DCF Calculation

(a) Year	(b) Discount Factor $[(1 + 10\%)^{(a)}]$	Investment A		Investment B	
		(c) Cash Flow	NPV $[(c) \div (b)]$	(d) Cash Flow	NPV $[(d) \div (b)]$
0	1.0000	−1000	−1000	−1000	−1000
1	1.1000	340	309	200	182
2	1.2100	305	252	235	194
3	1.3310	270	203	270	203
4	1.4641	235	161	305	208
5	1.6105	200	124	340	211
Total		**350**	**49**	**350**	**−2**

cash flows over 5 years of 1350, producing a return (net of the initial investment) of 350. The cash flow for each annual period has been discounted to its NPV at 10% *p.a.*, using the discount factor in column (b). Year 0 is the first day, when the investment is made; the remaining cash flows take place at annual intervals thereafter.

It will be seen that although the undiscounted cash flows come to the same amount over the 5-year period, the NPV of Investment A is 49 (*i.e.* discounted cash flows from years 1–5 of 1049, less the original investment of 1000), whereas that of Investment B is − 2.

The discount rate used by an investor when considering a new investment is the required minimum rate of return on the investment (the 'hurdle rate'), which is usually derived from a variety of factors including the investor's cost of capital (*cf.* §12.2.1). If the NPV using this discount rate is a positive figure, the investment has met the minimum requirements; if not, the investment should not be made. In Table 10.1, if 10% is the investor's required minimum rate of return, it is evident that Investment A meets the minimum requirements as the result is positive, but not Investment B. An NPV calculation may also be used to calculate which is the better of two projects with different cash flows (but *cf.* §10.2.3)—clearly in the case above Investment A is the better project. These differences in the NPV calculations illustrate the importance to investors of the timing of cash flows.

DCF calculations are used in a project-finance context in a number of different circumstances, *e.g.*:

- As a hurdle rate by Sponsors in reviewing financial viability of a new project (*cf.* §12.2.4);
- by a Contracting Authority comparing different bids for a project (*cf.* §3.7.8);

- in calculating early termination payments under a Project Agreement (*cf.* §7.10);
- in calculating Performance LDs under a Construction Contract (*cf.* §8.2.8);
- by interest-swap providers and fixed-rate lenders in calculating early-termination payments (*cf.* §10.3.1);
- by lenders in calculating Debt-Cover Ratios (*cf.* §12.2.3);
- by investors calculating the value of a project which is up for sale (*cf.* §14.17).

§10.2.2 INTERNAL RATE OF RETURN

The IRR measures the return on the investment over its life. It is the discount rate at which the NPV of the cash flow is zero. Thus in the examples in Table 10.1, the IRR of Investment A is 12.08% and Investment B is 9.94%, so again showing that Investment A is the better of the two; the calculation can be checked by discounting the two cash flows at these respective rates (Table 10.2).

Again IRR calculations are used in a project-finance context in a number of different circumstances, *e.g.*:

- in calculating the overall return on the project, or in valuing it, before taking account of its financing structure, *i.e.* the 'Project IRR' (*cf.* §7.10.1; §12.2.4);
- in calculating the investors' return on investment in a project (*cf.* §12.2.1);
- in calculating Compensation Sums under a Project Agreement (*cf.* §7.6.5);
- in calculating early termination payments under a Project Agreement (*cf.* §7.10);
- in calculating the benefit of a Refinancing (*cf.* §14.16.3).

Table 10.2 IRR Calculation

End Year	Investment A		Investment B	
	Cash Flow	NPV @ 12.08%	Cash Flow	NPV @ 9.94%
0	−1000	−1000	−1000	−1000
1	340	303	200	182
2	305	243	235	194
3	270	192	270	203
4	235	149	305	209
5	200	113	340	212
Total	350	0	350	0

§10.2.3 Problems in Using DCF and IRR Calculations

These measures have to be used with some caution, and an understanding how the calculations work. There are several issues in this respect:

DCF and Different-Sized Projects. It is misleading to use an NPV comparison when comparing two projects where the initial investment is different. This is illustrated by Table 10.3. The NPV of Investment D is greater than that of Investment C, but this is simply because Investment D is larger than Investment C. The greater IRR of Investment C demonstrates that it is indeed a better investment (unless the investor has no use for the 1000 difference between Investment C and Investment D, in which case Investment D's greater cash-flow return may be attractive).

   When making a comparison of this type, it has to be extended to include a cost: benefit analysis, as shown in the lower part of Table 10.3. In this analysis the NPVs of both the costs (the original investment) and the benefits (the return on that investment) of the projects need to be calculated, and then the ratio between the two is compared for each project. On this basis the cost: benefit ratio of Investment C is 1.27, and Investment D is 1.18. The higher the ratio the better the project, so Investment C is again shown as the better project.

   Note that this is not a problem when a Contracting Authority has to compare the NPV of two different PPP bids (cf. §3.7.8), as in that case its initial investment is zero. However Sponsors bidding for such a project, and considering alternative investments as a way of doing do, do need to be careful on this point—but as they usually use IRR as a measure of their investment return, this should deal with the problem. (Also cf. §12.2.4 for the similar calculation of the profit: investment ratio.)

Table 10.3 DCF and Different-Sized Projects

	Investment C	Investment D
Original investment	−1000	−2000
Cash flow 1 year later	1400	2600
NPV @ 10%	273	364
IRR	**40%**	**30%**
Cost–benefit analysis		
(a) NPV of benefits	1273	2364
(b) NPV of costs	1000	2000
Cost–benefit ratio [(a) ÷ (b)]	**1.27**	**1.18**

Overstatement of IRR Returns. This can be illustrated by the two cash flows in Table 10.4. It is evident that Investment E gives a better return, and the NPV calculation supports this, but the IRRs of the two investments are the same. This is because the standard IRR calculation assumes that cash taken out of the project is reinvested at the IRR rate until the end of the calculation period. Thus, as shown in the fourth column of Table 10.4, if the Investment F's cash flow in years 1–4 is reinvested at 15% *p.a.*, the total amounts to 2011 at the end of year 5, the same as Investment E, which is why they have the same IRR. Clearly some account should be taken of Investment F generating cash more quickly, but the assumption that this cash can be reinvested at 15% double-counts the return on another investment. Thus an IRR calculation overvalues early cash flows—the longer the cash flow period, the more the IRR is exaggerated by using a high reinvestment rate, which is especially relevant for project finance cash flows which may extend to 25 years or more.

The scale of this exaggeration is illustrated in Table 10.4: the actual net revenue earned from Investment F is 492. But as can be seen in the last column, a further 520 of revenue is added as a result of reinvesting the cash flow, *e.g.* in year 1 the actual cash flow from the investment is 298 but the IRR calculation assumes that this year 1 cash flow generates 522 over the life of the project, or 223 more (522–298) than the year 1 cash flow.[1] So 520 (51%) out of the total

Table 10.4 Overstatement of IRR

			Investment F—Annual Cash Flow	
End-Year	Investment E Cash Flow	Investment F Cash Flow	Reinvested @ 15% to Year 5	Reinvestment Income
0	−1000	−1000		
1	0	298	522	223
2	0	298	454	155
3	0	298	395	97
4	0	298	343	45
5	2011	298	298	0
Total	1011	492	2011	520
IRR	15%	15%		
NPV @ 12%	141	75		

---

[1] Note there is some rounding of numbers.

'return' of 1011 depends on reinvestment in another project—and in a typical much longer project-finance transactions cash-flow reinvestment may account for as much as 80% of the total return.

A way of alleviating this problem—although this is not widely-used by project finance investors—is a 'modified IRR' ('MIRR') calculation. The MIRR calculation assumes a lower reinvestment rate for cash taken out of the project (*e.g.* the investor's marginal cost of capital, instead of the IRR rate, because this is the saving which the investor makes from redeploying this cash flow). The periodical cash flows are then reinvested at this lower rate until the end of the cash flow period in the same way as for an IRR calculation. The MIRR will show a lower (but more accurate) return than the IRR, which is a better representation of the real world. Table 10.5 shows the effect of this on Investment F, assuming a reinvestment rate of 12% instead of 15%. (The MIRR for Investment E is the same as the IRR in Table 10.4, since there are no payments being 'reinvested' at 15%.) Based on this it can be seen that the MIRR or 'true' IRR of Investment F is 13.6%, not 15%. Having said this, the investor still has a risk, unconnected with the project being evaluated, that the cash flow cannot be successfully reinvested at 12%.

IRR and Different Cash-Flow Periods. IRR is not an appropriate measure for projects with different lives, as illustrated in Table 10.6. The table shows two investments of 1000 each: Investment G produces a cash flow of 200 *p.a.* for 8 years, while Investment H produces a cash flow of 145 *p.a.* for 15

Table 10.5 IRR and MIRR

End-Year	Investment F Cash Flow	Reinvestment of Cash Flow		MIRR Calculation
		15.0%	12.0%	
0	−1,000			−1,000
1	298	522	469	0
2	298	454	419	0
3	298	395	374	0
4	298	343	334	0
5	298	298	298	1,895
Total	492	2,011	1,895	895
NPV	75			
IRR	15.0%			13.6%
MIRR	13.6%			

Table 10.6 IRR and Different Cash-Flow Periods

Year	Investment G	Investment J
0	−1000	−1000
1	200	145
2	200	145
3	200	145
4	200	145
5	200	145
6	200	145
7	200	145
8	200	145
9		145
10		145
11		145
12		145
13		145
14		145
15		145
Total	600	1180
IRR	12%	12%
NPV*	67	105

*Discount rate of 10%.

years. The IRR of each is the same, at 12%. But it is clear that Investment H is the better choice (assuming the risks of each investment are the same, and subject to the point that the timing of the cash flows is not irrelevant— *cf.* §12.2.4). Investment G has a better IRR simply because the cash flow is received earlier. A DCF calculation, at a discount rate of 10%, does show Investment H as the better choice.

This and the other examples above illustrate the general problem with IRR calculations, which is that they prioritize the 'quick win', something which is not helpful to project finance.

Cash Flow Changes from Negative to Positive to Negative. A further quirk of IRR is that it is not a reliable measure of return if the cash flow starts negative, becomes positive, and then flips back to negative. This could happen, for

Table 10.7 Cash Flow –ve/ +ve/–ve

Period	Cash Flow	10% Discount		20% Discount	
		Factor	NPV	Factor	NPV
0	–50,000	1.0000	–50,000	1.0000	–50,000
1	115,000	0.9091	104,545	0.8333	95,833
2	–66,000	0.8264	–54,545	0.6944	–45,833
		NPV =	0		0
	Excel calculation:				
	Guess rate:	5%	15%		
	IRR =	10%	20%		

example, in a project involving an industrial process, where the project site has to be decontaminated, or otherwise cleaned up, at the end of the project. The problem is illustrated in Table 10.7. This shows two IRR calculations on the same cash flow, one discounting to zero at 10% and one at 20%. If an Excel spread sheet is used for this cash flow, there is no indication that there are two answers, except that if different 'guess rates' are included in the function, different answers are received as shown in the table. If no guess rate is included Excel only shows an IRR of 10%.

§10.3 INTEREST-RATE RISKS

If the project is being financed with fixed-rate bonds or loans from lenders providing fixed-rate funding, then, in principle, the Project Company has no interest-rate risk.

In many markets, however, bank lenders do not provide long-term loans at fixed rates because their deposit base is short-term, and fixed-rate long-term funding is either unavailable or uneconomic. The base interest rate on project finance loans is thus often adjusted at intervals (say six monthly) to the then current wholesale market rate at which the lenders raise their funding, and is therefore on a 'floating' (variable) rate rather than a fixed-rate basis. In the international market, the most important floating rate is the London inter-bank offered rate (LIBOR),[2] in which interest rates are quoted by banks for borrowing from and lending to each other in the major international currencies. Banks basing their lending on LIBOR quote the interest rate for the financing as a margin over the LIBOR rate, with the

---

[2] There are separate arrangements for some currencies, *e.g.* Euribor for the €, and Tibor (Tokyo inter-bank offered rate) for the Yen.

base interest rate usually re-fixed against the then current LIBOR rate every 3 or 6 months.[3] These are known as 'rate-fixing dates' or 'interest dates.'

Construction-Phase Interest-Rate Risks. Interest is not paid in cash on the financing until the project is in operation. During the construction phase the accrued interest is normally capitalized (*i.e.* added to the loan amount) or paid by making a new drawing on the loan. Thus interest during construction ('IDC') becomes part of the project's capital budget (*cf.* §13.5.1), and if the interest rate for the IDC is not fixed, and is eventually higher than originally projected, this is a construction cost overrun (*cf.* §9.5.6). Lenders do not normally allow the general construction-cost contingency to be used to cover this risk, as it is primarily intended to cover overruns in the 'hard' costs (mainly the Construction Contract), or the effect of a delay causing higher total interest costs.

Operating-Phase Interest-Rate Risks. During the operation phase, a higher interest rate leads to a lower project cash flow, and hence reduction in lenders' Cover Ratios (*cf.* §12.3) and lower returns for investors.

One simple method of dealing with the interest-rate risk during the operation phase, which can be used by projects with an Offtake Contract including a Capacity Charge, or an Availability-based Contract, is for the Contract Payments to be changed as the underlying market interest rate on the Project Company's debt changes. This of course means that the long-term interest-rate risk is taken by the Offtaker/Contracting Authority. The latter is really in a better position to take the risk, as it can probably obtain an interest-rate swap or other hedging instrument (see below) on better terms than the Project Company. In the case of a public-sector Offtaker, or a Contracting Authority, the national treasury can take over this risk and deal with it as part of its overall interest-rate management of government debt.

There is also an argument that if a project's revenue is inflation-linked, the interest rate on its financing should also be based on short-term interest rates, which tend to move with inflation (*cf.* §13.4.3). This view has not received much support among project-finance lenders: while it is true that the overall trend is for the two rates to move together, it can take a considerable time before interest rates catch up with a high rate of inflation.

Interest-rate hedging arrangements therefore will probably need to be put in place to mitigate the interest-rate risk when floating-rate loans are used. The

---

[3] In 2012 a number of banks paid fines to regulatory authorities for manipulating LIBOR and similar market interest rates, which had become increasingly artificial because of the shrinkage of the inter-bank market after the credit crisis of 2008. Some change in the system will probably take place, but financial regulators will probably reform rather than abolish the LIBOR system, as there seems to be no viable alternative.

commonest type of hedging used in project finance is interest-rate swaps (§10.3.1); to a lesser extent interest rate caps, collars, and other instruments are used (§10.3.2); 100% of the risk may not need to be covered (§10.3.3). Alternatively, finance may be provided at a fixed rate, typically through a bond, but a number of issues arise in this case (§10.3.4). Sponsors may face particular problems with interest rate movements prior to Financial Close (§10.3.5).

§10.3.1 INTEREST-RATE SWAPS

Under an interest-rate swap agreement[4] one party exchanges an obligation for payment of interest on a floating-rate basis to one for payment at a fixed rate, and the other party does the opposite. Banks in the capital markets run large books of such interest-rate swaps.

In a project financing, a Project Company that has an obligation to pay interest at a floating rate under its loan agrees to pay its counterpart (a bank or banks—the 'swap provider) the difference between the floating rate and the agreed-upon fixed rate if the floating rate is below this fixed rate, or will be paid by the swap provider if the floating rate is above the fixed rate.

Calculation of Interest-Rate Swap Payments. The calculation of the net payment amounts between the Project Company and the swap provider is based on the 'notional principal amount' for each period (*i.e.* the amount of the loan on which the interest is being calculated), although in a swap agreement neither side lends the other any money but simply pays over the difference in the two interest rates.

Table 10.8 shows how an interest-rate swap between 6-month LIBOR and a fixed rate might work in practice, assuming that the Project Company borrows 1000 (*i.e.* this is the notional principal amount), at LIBOR re-fixed 6-monthly, swaps this floating interest rate against a fixed rate of 6% and repays the loan in one installment at the end of 3 years. Thus the Project Company has turned its floating rate LIBOR interest payments into a fixed rate of 6%, and the swap provider has done the reverse.

Interest-Swap-Breakage Costs and Credit Risk. If the Project Company prepays the debt, or defaults on its debt, the swap arrangement has to be canceled (or 'broken'). The swap provider then enters into another swap for the balance of the term (*i.e.* another party takes over the obligations of the Project Company). But if long-term fixed-interest rates have gone down since the swap was originally signed, the new counterpart will not be willing to pay the same high rate of fixed interest as the Project Company. The difference

---

[4] Also known as a 'coupon swap'.

Table 10.8 Interest-Rate Swap

		6-Month Period					
		1	2	3	4	5	6
(a) Notional principal amount		1000	1000	1000	1000	1000	1000
(b) LIBOR		4%	5%	6%	7%	8%	9%
(c) Swap fixed rate		6%	6%	6%	6%	6%	6%
(d) LIBOR interest	[((a) × (b)) ÷ 2]	20	25	30	35	40	45
(e) Fixed-rate interest	[((a) × (c)) ÷ 2]	30	30	30	30	30	30
(f) Difference	[(d) − (e)]	−10	−5	0	5	10	15
Project Company position:							
Interest on loan	[= (d)]	20	25	30	35	40	45
Swap payment/(− receipt)	[= −(f)]	10	5	0	−5	−10	−15
Net interest cost	[= (e)]	30	30	30	30	30	30
Swap provider position:							
Interest on notional principal	[= (e)]	30	30	30	30	30	30
Swap payment/(− receipt)	[= (f)]	−10	−5	0	5	10	15
Net interest cost	[= (d)]	20	25	30	35	40	45

between the original fixed rate and the new fixed rate represents a loss to the original swap provider. This is known as the 'breakage' cost.[5] So although the swap provider is not lending any money, it is taking a credit risk on the Project Company equal to any breakage cost which is due to it. This risk is not a fixed number, as it can only be determined at the time of the breakage, and so the credit risk which the swap provider is taking cannot be precisely quantified when it enters into the swap contract.

Of course if, when the default takes place, the long-term fixed rate for the remainder of the swap term is higher than the original rate, there is no breakage cost to the swap provider—on the contrary, there is a profit, which should be paid to the Project Company.

Table 10.9 demonstrates how the swap-breakage cost is calculated, based on the assumptions:

- loan of 1000, repaid in one installment;
- term: 15 years;
- swap fixed rate: 6%;

---

[5] This is also referred to 'unwinding' the swap, so creating an 'unwind' cost or profit.

Table 10.9 Calculation of Interest-Rate Swap-Breakage Cost

	Year													
Fixed-rate payment	3	4	5	6	7	8	9	10	11	12	13	14	15
Original amount	60	60	60	60	60	60	60	60	60	60	60	60	60
Revised amount	30	30	30	30	30	30	30	30	30	30	30	30	30
Swap provider's loss:	30	30	30	30	30	30	30	30	30	30	30	30	30

NPV of loss (@ 3% discount rate) = 319.

Table 10.10 Interest-Rate Swap—Breakage Cost over Time

Year:	1	2	3	4	5	6	7	8	9	10
(a) Notional principal	1000	900	800	700	600	500	400	300	200	100
Fixed-rate payment:										
(b) Original amount [(a) × 6%]	54	48	42	36	30	24	18	12	6	60
(c) Reinvestment [(a) × 3%]	27	24	21	18	15	12	9	6	3	30
(d) Running loss [(b) − (c)]	27	24	21	18	15	12	9	6	3	30
(e) **NPV of loss** [NPV of (d)]	121	98	77	58	42	28	17	9	3	147
Loss as % of loan [(e) ÷ (a)]	15%	13%	12%	11%	10%	8%	7%	6%	4%	3%

- swap broken after: 2 years;
- reinvestment rate: 3%.

As can be seen, the swap provider's loss on termination is therefore not the same as the notional principal amount, but amounts to 20 *p.a.* for the remaining 13 years. The NPV of this cash flow is the swap-breakage cost—in this case this is 32% of the notional principal amount—so this is the credit risk on the Project Company in these particular circumstances at this particular time. However this is an unusually high figure because the loan is not being repaid. So Table 10.10 sets out the swap-breakage costs for a more typical loan cash flow, calculated year by year during the loan, assuming:

- loan of 1000, repaid in 10 equal annual installments of 100;
- swap fixed rate: 6%;
- reinvestment rate (after default on the swap): 3%.

Thus if the Project Company goes into default just after the time the loan and swap are signed, and long-term interest rates have also gone down from 6% to 3% at that time, the loss to the swap provider is 121.[6] If the default occurs at the beginning of Year 2 the loss is 98, at the beginning of Year 3, 77, and so on.

This potential loss is the credit risk that the swap provider is taking on the Project Company, but unlike the credit risk of a loan, this is not a fixed figure, but depends on:

- the remaining length of the swap;
- the way market rates have changed, when the default takes place;
- whether the original swap is at a historically high or low rate (if at a low rate, the likelihood of a breakage cost is less because long-term rates are less likely to go even lower, and *vice versa*).

A swap provider entering into a swap with the Project Company therefore has to make an initial assessment of the level of the credit risk, which cannot be more than an educated guess at that stage. As can be seen, using the particular assumptions for Table 10.10, the maximum credit exposure is 15% of the initial loan amount, reducing thereafter both in absolute terms, and as a percentage of the loan outstanding. Very roughly speaking (as there are many variables), for a 20-year interest-rate swap based on an amortizing loan repayment, banks might assume an initial credit risk of 15% of the maximum notional principal amount.

Of course, in Table 10.10, if the reinvestment rate is higher than 6%, there is a profit—which benefits the Project Company—rather than a loss on the breakage. The calculation of the profit or loss on a swap if it is broken at any point is known as 'mark-to-market'; a swap that shows a profit on being broken is said to be 'in the money,' and one which shows a loss is 'out of the money.'

For the swap-provider bank, arranging a matching swap in the market, to cover its interest-rate exposure in the swap with the Project Company, is far easier than raising long-term fixed rate funding and on-lending this to the Project Company, since its own market counterparts take a much lower credit risk in providing a swap than making a long-term loan, whereas the bank providing a swap to the Project Company has easy access to short-term floating rate funding and assumes this will always be renewed.

A floating-rate Lender also may have a small additional breakage cost if the Project Company defaults between the two interest-rate fixing dates.

How Interest-Rate Swap Rates are Determined. The swap market works on the basis of 'bullet' repayments of notional principal—*i.e.* the type of loan

---

[6] N.B.: Project Company default is not the only reason that a swap might be broken—other reasons could include early termination by an Offtaker/Contracting Authority (*cf.* §7.10.3), or a debt refinancing (*cf.* §14.16). Whenever an Offtaker/Contracting Authority has an obligation to repay the debt, this obligation will include payment of any swap-breakage costs (or receipt of positive breakage costs), and similarly if the debt is refinanced the swap must be broken unless it is taken over by the new lenders. However from a credit-risk point of view the swap provider is obviously mainly concerned about Project Company default.

repayment schedule shown in Table 10.9, which assumes none of the notional principal of 1000 is repaid until the end of the 15-year schedule shown. However, a project-finance loan cash flow, and hence notional principal repayment, is like that set out in Table 10.10 *i.e.* repayment in installments over a period of time, so the swap cash flow has to match this. The way the market deals with this is to quote a weighted average rate for a series of swaps covering each repayment date (known as an 'amortizing swap'), and thus on the schedule in Table 10.10 the swap provider would quote the weighted rate for the swaps based on 100 notional principal repaid after 1 year, 100 after 2 years, 100 after 3 years, and so on.

The swap quotation also has to take into account that the notional principal is not drawn all at once; most projects have a drawing period of 2–3 years or so during construction, and so are quoted swap rates in advance for an increasing notional principal amount during the construction/drawing period. This is known as a 'accreting swap', as opposed to the operating phase of the project where the notional principal is decreasing, when it becomes an 'amortizing swap'.

The fixed rate quoted by the swap provider is based on three elements:

- *Government bond rates for the relevant period in the relevant currency*: These provide the 'base rate' for the swap; for example, a swap in US$ for 7 years would be based on the current yield of a U.S. Treasury bond for the same period.
- *The swap market premium*: This is the difference between government bond rates and the swap rates, which reflects supply and demand in the swap market and also in the fixed-rate corporate-bond market, since corporate-bond issuers can arbitrage between the fixed-rate market and the floating-rate market with a swap. (Swap market rates—*i.e.* the total of the government bond rate and the swap market premium—are quoted in the financial press and on dealing screens.)
- The swap credit premium (see below).

Swap Credit Premium. The swap credit premium is the margin charged by the swap provider is the charge for the credit risk of the Project Company: If the swap provider assumes that the level of risk (based on a similar calculation to that set out in Table 10.10) is, say, 15% of the initial notional principal amount, and the credit margin on the loan to the Project Company is, say, 1.5%, then the swap credit premium should be 15% of 1.5% (*i.e.* 0.225% *p.a.*).

Swap Structures. The simplest way for the Project Company to cover its interest rate risk through a swap is to have the syndicate of banks providing the floating-rate loan also provide the swap *pro rata* to their share of the loan; however, the problems with this are:

- The final syndication of the loan to banks may not be completed until after Financial Close (*cf.* §5.2.8), and swap arrangements have to be concluded at or shortly after Financial Close, in order to fix the project's interest costs.

- Some of the syndicate banks may be less competitive than others in their swap pricing, and the Project Company may end up having to pay the swap rate of the most expensive bank.
- It leaves the syndicate banks with no competition, and therefore the Project Company may not get the best rates for the swap.

It is not normally possible for the Project Company to go directly to other banks in the market and ask them to quote for the swap, because a bank not already involved in lending is unlikely to want to spend the time bringing in its project-finance department to analyze the risk involved. Moreover if the swap providers are not lenders this creates an intercreditor problem between swap providers and other lenders (*cf.* §14.14.1).

If there are several banks in a lending syndicate, they can be asked to compete with each other for the swap business, rather than each bank providing a swap to cover its share of the loan. (Each bank in the syndicate may then provide a *pro rata* guarantee for the swap to the swap provider, or the latter may be willing to take the whole of the risk on its own books.) But if there are only one or two banks in the syndicate, which may be the case if the loan has been underwritten but not syndicated before Financial Close, competition in this way may not work.

A structure that gives the Project Company access to the best market rates is for one or more of the banks in the lending syndicate to act as a 'fronting bank.' The Project Company goes into the swap market for quotations, based on the swap provider entering into a swap with the fronting bank; the Project Company then enters into an identical 'back-to-back' swap with the fronting bank. (The fronting bank itself can still quote in competition for the market swap.) The fronting bank charges the swap credit premium or is counter-guaranteed by the syndicate banks and charges a smaller premium reflecting this.

A further benefit from the fronting bank structure relates to the swap credit premium, which can cause a problem if there is a swap breakage. The swap documentation (see below) just quotes a gross rate, including the credit premium. So in the case of Table 10.10, the swap rate of 6% would in fact be a rate of say 5.775% plus a premium of 0.225%. The calculation as shown in Table 10.10 is the way in which the swap-breakage cost would be calculated in this case—meaning that the Project Company has to pay the NPV of the whole of the swap credit premium for the rest of the loan term, even though there is no longer any risk on the project for the swap provider. An alternative way to deal with this problem is to pay the swap credit premium under a separate agreement, rather than as part of the swap agreement. However in some markets swap providers are very resistant to giving up the swap credit premiums in these ways. In fact banks in some markets have relied to a surprising extent on swap income, both from uncompetitive rates and retention of swap premiums, to subsidize their project-finance lending.

Rollover Risk. The notional principal schedule used as a basis for the swap is based on estimates of when drawings on the loan will be made during construction, and when loan repayments will be made (beginning when the project is completed). These estimates may prove incorrect; *e.g.* a delay in the construction program affects the timing of drawings, or Project Completion is delayed, which may affect the repayment schedule, as this is normally calculated from the Project Completion date.

If the shift in timing is a relatively short period of a month or so, this does not matter, and the swap can be left to run on the original schedule (assuming that the Project Company will have funds available to make any net payment that is due) since any extra loss in a one-month period is likely to be compensated by a profit in another. If a significant shift in the schedule takes place—say 6 months—because of a delay in Project Completion, it is preferable to 'roll over' the swap (*i.e.* terminate the original swap and enter into a new one on the new schedule). Any breakage cost on termination would be largely matched by the benefit of a lower long-term fixed rate, and any profit would compensate for a higher fixed rate.

However the Project Company may face some difficulty with the swap provider:

- The swap provider may no longer wish to provide the swap and try to use the rollover request as a way of getting out of it.
- If there is no competition on the rate for the rollover, the Project Company could pay too much for the rollover swap.

If the fronting bank structure described above has been used, rollover of the swap should be less of an issue; in other cases it may be possible to agree to a competitive approach in advance. If not the Project Company (and its lenders) may just have to take this risk as one of the inevitable adverse consequences of a delay in Project Completion.

A similar issue arises if the loan amount is increased (*e.g.* by drawing on contingent funding because of a delay in Project Completion), and the swap needs to be increased correspondingly.

Swap-Breakage Costs and Refinancing. The issue of breakage costs also arises if the Project Company wants to refinance its debt (*cf.* §14.16). The normal procedure here is for the new lender, if a bank, to become the counter-party to the original swap in place of the Project Company, and then enter into its own swap agreement (which may also have a somewhat different repayment schedule) with the Project Company. However this does mean that the Project Company ends up paying the swap premium twice, *i.e.* the premium charged by the original swap provider remains unchanged even though the risk is now on another bank and not the Project Company, and the new swap provider charges its swap premium for the risk on the Project Company.

Documentation. Interest rate swaps are documented in a standard form, based on documentation produced by ISDA (International Swap and Derivatives Association), and on which there is limited room for negotiation. This is necessary because swap dealers want to be able to trade their entire swap book on the basis of standard terms. The actual swap cash flows and payments are annexed in a schedule to the standard form.

§10.3.2 INTEREST-RATE CAPS AND OTHER INSTRUMENTS

Under an interest-rate cap, the cap provider (again usually a bank) agrees to pay the Project Company if floating interest rates go above a certain level. For example, the current floating rate may be 3%, and the cap rate set at 5%. So long as the floating rate remains below 5% the Project Company just pays the floating rate. If the floating rate goes above 5%, the cap provider pays the Project Company the difference between the two in the same way as in an interest-rate swap. For budget purposes the Project Company can thus assume an interest cost of 5% fixed, and insofar as the floating rate cost comes out below this level, this is a bonus.

Interest-rate caps may provide a short-term solution to interest-rate hedging, for example, if a floating-rate loan during the construction phase is to be refinanced by a fixed-rate loan after Project Completion. They have the advantage that the provider does not take a credit risk on the Project Company, and so can be obtained from any provider in the market, but the disadvantage is that there is an upfront fee payable that adds to the project's development costs. They are therefore seldom used for long-term hedging. However a cap can be used to put an absolute limit on the level of breakage costs for an interest-rate swap, which may be useful for some projects where there is concern about the level of such contingent liabilities.

Other more sophisticated instruments may be useful for some projects; a 'swaption' (or 'contingent swap) is the right to enter into a swap at a future date, which may give some flexibility in timing.

'Collar' arrangements combine an interest-rate cap with a floor rate (*i.e.* the maximum rate is fixed with a cap as above, while if the floating rate goes below a floor rate of say 2% the Project Company pays the difference to the provider). Interest-rate collars may be done at no cost (*i.e.* without a front-end fee), because the cost of the cap is offset by the fee received from selling the floor rate. However the taker of the floor rate has a credit risk on the Project Company, albeit usually a lower level of risk than that for an interest-rate swap provider.

§10.3.3 Scale and Timing of Interest-Rate Hedging

At the time of arranging the financing, the Sponsors may take the view that it is more likely that interest rates will go down than up; therefore, they prefer to finance on a floating interest-rate basis for the time being. This is unlikely to be acceptable to lenders, who will not support the Project Company taking unnecessary financial risks, however small these risks may appear at the time.

But lenders normally accept that the Project Company does not have to hedge 100% of its interest rate risk. Firstly, some flexibility needs to be left for the draw-down and repayment timing differences mentioned above; secondly, the interest-rate risk on contingent funding, which may never be drawn at all, need not be hedged at the beginning of construction. The Project Company may agree with the lenders that initially it should hedge not less than, say, 90% of its interest-rate risk, ignoring contingent funding. Subject to the rollover risk point discussed above, finance documentation can be left sufficiently flexible for a higher level of interest-rate hedging to be added later if contingent finance is drawn or if the Project Company wants to increase the hedging percentage.

The hedging transaction is normally carried out at or shortly after Financial Close, to ensure the budget costs are fixed as quickly as possible. A window of up to a month after Financial Close may be left for concluding the swap, to ensure that the Project Company does not have to go into the swap market on a bad day.

§10.3.4 Fixed-Rate Loans or Bonds

A Lender providing a fixed-rate loan or buying a bond also has a breakage cost if the Project Company defaults, for exactly the same reason as the swap provider: if the rate at which the fixed-rate funds can be re-lent has gone down when the Project Company defaults, the fixed-rate Lender makes a loss by re-lending at this lower rate. However in some markets the breakage cost on early termination of a bond issue (or a fixed-rate loan) can be substantially higher than the breakage cost for an interest-rate swap.

Payment of Future Profit Margin. When a loan is repaid early for whatever reason, a floating-rate lender usually loses the future profit margin (although a small prepayment fee may be charged). However, fixed-rate lenders or bondholders may require payment of some or all of their future profit margin. This is done at the termination date by discounting the future loan or bond debt-service payments at the current yield on a government bond (or some other agreed comparison) for the same average life. Obviously a government bond is a lower credit risk than a Project Company's bond so it will have a lower yield; hence using this lower discount rate will result in the Project

Company owing more than the outstanding principal sum due on its fixed-rate loan or bond. The result is that the Project Company effectively has to pay some or all of the future credit margin on the fixed-rate loan or bond, so leading to a similar result to the payment of the future swap premium on early termination (*cf.* §10.3.1).

'Par Floor'. Furthermore, the breakage calculation for a bond may be one way—*i.e.* if interest rates have gone down the bond holder is compensated by the borrower, but if they have gone up the bond holder does not pay over this profit to the Project Company (as would be the case in an interest-rate swap). The reason is that the breakage profit would offset against the capital repayment of the bond, meaning that the bondholder would get less than 100% of its capital investment back. Even though there would not be any loss over the original life of the bond, bondholders do not want to suffer an immediate capital loss in this way, and so often require a 'par floor'.[7] *i.e.* 100% of the outstanding amount of the bond must be paid on termination, with no deductions for a breakage gain.

Table 10.11 shows the effect of the par-floor requirement on the prepayment (*i.e.* breakage) cost for a bond. The assumptions for the calculations are:
- bond issue amount: 1000.
- government bond rate: 5.25% (at time of issue).
- credit margin: 0.75%.
- bond coupon: 6.00% (= government bond rate + credit margin).
- term: 20 years, annuity repayment (*cf.* §12.5.3).
- government bond rate: 8.00% (on termination).

As can be seen in the table, the make-whole clause can result in a substantial extra breakage cost for a bond, compared to a loan with an interest-rate swap which does not have such a clause (and so broadly speaking the breakage cost plus the loan outstanding for a swap would be the same as the termination payment without par floor in Table 10.11).

Guaranteed Investment Contract (GIC). As mentioned in §5.4, one of the disadvantages of bonds compared to loans is that the funding cannot be drawn as and when required, but must all be drawn at once, and any funding temporarily surplus to requirements kept on deposit until needed. The interest earned on this deposit is itself a source of funds for construction of the project, but if the deposit is at a floating rate, this exposes the Project Company to a short-term interest rate risk during the construction phase, until the financing has all been spent on project costs, because if the rate of interest earned on these redeposited funds is lower than projected, the Project Company may be short of funds to complete the project.

---

[7] Also known as a 'make-whole' clause, and in Britain as a 'Spens clause'.

Table 10.11 Bond Prepayment Cost

Year	0	1	2	3	4	5	15	16	17	18	19	20
(a) Interest payment		60	58	57	55	53	26	22	18	14	10	5
(b) Principal repayment		27	29	31	32	34	61	65	69	73	78	82
(c) Total debt service		87	87	87	87	87	87	87	87	87	87	87
(d) Bond principal O/S [= Previous balance – (b)]	1,000	973	944	913	881	847	367	302	233	160	82	0
Termination payment												
– without par floor [= NPV of (a) @ 8%]		837	817	795	772	746	348	289	225	155	81	
– with par floor [= (d)]		973	944	913	881	847	367	302	233	160	82	

This can be dealt with by taking out an interest-rate swap covering the construction phase only, but this time the other way round; the Project Company agrees to receive a fixed rate of interest in return for paying the same floating rate as it is receiving on the deposit. Alternatively a bank may offer a fixed rate for the deposit, and carry out the swap internally; this is known as a 'guaranteed investment contract'.

Under normal circumstances the short-term fixed interest rate for the GIC will be lower than the long-term coupon on the bond, *i.e.* this requirement to draw all the funds at Financial Close creates a loss for the Project Company (known as 'negative arbitrage), which has to be taken into account when comparing the cost of a loan to that for a bond.

There is a potential intercreditor issue (*cf.* §14.14): if there is a parallel loan from a bank: who should have security over the funds in the GIC—do they go into the general pool of security, to be shared by all lenders, or are they security for the bondholders alone? The latter solution seems more equitable.

§10.3.5 INTEREST-RATE HEDGING BEFORE FINANCIAL CLOSE

A particular problem for Sponsors is how to deal with interest rate risk during the development period of the project. The Sponsors may have originally put in a bid for a project with Contract Payments covering debt service on a fixed basis, thus leaving the Project Company rather than the Offtaker or Contracting Authority with the interest-rate risk, and there may be a substantial period of time between the original bid and Financial Close. If interest rates go up before Financial Close has been reached and no interest-rate hedging is in place, the investors' returns, and the financing as a whole, may be jeopardized.

One answer to this problem is for the Sponsors to take up the long-term interest-rate hedging arrangements themselves in advance of Financial Close, and then transfer the hedging to the Project Company at Financial Close—but they are then taking on an extra risk if the project, for whatever reason, does not reach Financial Close. If long-term interest rates go down, there will be a loss in breaking a long-term interest-rate swap as discussed above. (Of course the reverse is true if rates go up.) The calculation is also affected by the difference between short-term and long-term interest rates, as this difference has to be covered before Financial Close (*i.e.* if short-term redeposit rates are lower than long-term lending rates the Sponsors will be out of pocket before Financial Close in a similar way to a GIC, and *vice versa*). Sponsors therefore need to be confident that Financial Close can be reached, and realistic about the schedule for doing so, before taking on interest-rate hedging in this way. Similarly, a swaption (*cf.* §10.3.2) can be used, but may involve a cost that will be lost if the bid does not succeed.

In some cases a public-sector Offtaker or a Contracting Authority may be willing to take the risk (or benefit) of any changes in interest rates between agreement on terms with the Sponsors and the hedging finally being undertaken at Financial Close, and adjust the Contract Payments accordingly. If so, the Offtaker or Contracting Authority will wish to control the process of fixing the interest rate in due course, since the Sponsors have little incentive to get the best pricing in this situation. (The Offtaker/Contracting Authority will probably need to use its financial advisor, or a specialist advisor, to check the pricing when the interest rate is fixed.)

The argument for an Offtaker/Contracting Authority taking this risk is that if there is a program of such procurements by the public sector, the latter will 'win some and lose some', *i.e.* some deals will be closed at interest rates lower than expected, while others have to pay more. Overall the public sector is likely to be better off than leaving the risk with bidders, as if bidders do have to take this risk they will build in a safety margin on the assumed long-term interest rate, which may not be needed, but the Offtaker/Contracting Authority will still have to pay for it – as with other risk-transfer issues this comes down to a VfM issue (*cf.* §9.2).

If there is no Offtake or Availability-based Contract the Sponsors obviously have no choice but to take the risk of interest-rate movements while they develop the project, but if they are not in a bidding situation, they may be more willing and able to take on some long-term hedging before Financial Close as discussed above.

Market Stabilization. In general it is not prudent for a Contracting Authority to take responsibility before Financial Close for hedging interest rates, any more than any other part of the PPP Contract arrangements should be activated before everything is signed and effective. However there is one aspect of interest-rate hedging where this may be necessary. If a very large bond issue is to be placed in the market, the effect may be to push up market rates and so also the Contract Payments. The investment bank placing the bond issue may therefore undertake a 'market stabilization' exercise in advance of the bond issue—in effect hedging against a future rise in rates by selling government bonds forward. If market rates do go up when the bond is placed, the profit on the forward sale of the government bonds will offset this. A similar exercise can be carried out if a large interest-rate swap is to be placed in the market. In such cases the Contracting Authority has to underwrite any loss which arises from this exercise, *i.e.* if rates go down, but this stabilization will still have effectively fixed the price of the bond in advance of its issue.

§10.3.6 SHOULD INTEREST-RATE RISK BE THE PROJECT COMPANY'S PROBLEM?

At least in process-plant and Availability-based Contracts, there is an argument that it does not make sense to transfer interest-rate risks to the Project Company. The risk can be managed with the approaches set out above, but this is not always very cost-effective, especially when interest-rate swaps are used. There is an argument that the Payment Mechanism should be based on a floating-interest rate, and the Offtaker/Contracting Authority can just do its own interest-rate hedging to cover the interest-rate risk. This will certainly reduce the swap credit premium as the swap can now be procured on a fully competitive basis since the swap providers are taking a risk on the Offtaker/Contracting Authority and not the Project Company. The Offtaker/Contracting Authority may also benefit from further economies of scale if it has a portfolio of projects to hedge. The risk from the Offtaker/Contracting Authority's point of view is that if the project goes into default, and there is a swap-breakage cost, it may not be able to recover this (and in any case any recovery would have to be subordinated to the lenders, not *pari-passu*—*cf.* §14.14.1).

§10.4 INFLATION

Depending on its timing, inflation may be either a risk or a benefit to the Project Company.

During the construction phase, if price inflation is higher than projected, this may lead to a cost overrun, with the consequences set out in §9.5.5. (And *vice-versa* if price inflation is lower than projected.) Most of the construction-phase costs should not be vulnerable to inflation-based increases: the two major line items—the Construction Contract price, and financing costs, should both be fixed. In preparing the construction-phase budget, however, an allowance has to be made for inflation over the construction phase in costs that are not fixed, such as the

Project Company's general personnel costs, and purchase of any items (such as spare parts) not included in the scope of the Construction Contract.

During the operation phase, if inflation leads to higher operating costs than projected, the level of lenders' Cover Ratios (*cf.* §12.3), and the return for investors, may be reduced, unless this risk is hedged as discussed below. But if the project is just selling into a commodity market, the commodity price is likely to reflect the level of inflation and so provide a 'natural hedge'.

Just to deal with a point of terminology before looking at inflation risks in more detail—a 'nominal' cash flow or other calculation is based on figures which include the effect of inflation, whereas a 'real' cash flow excludes inflation. To put it another way, a nominal cash flow is what is actually received in money, while a real cash flow reduces these payments by the rate of inflation to money of today.

- So if 100 is payable in a year's time, and the rate of inflation is 5%, in nominal terms 100 will be received, but in real terms this is worth 95.23 [100 × (1.00 ÷ 1.05)].
- Similarly, if 1050 is payable in a year's time, and the rate of inflation is 5%, the nominal payment will be 105, but in real terms this is worth 100 [105 × (1.00 × 1.05)].

§10.4.1 Inflation Indexation of Contract Payments

If the Project Company has a long-term Project Agreement under which revenues are received on the basis of agreed Contract Payments, some elements of the Contract Payments may be indexed against inflation (*cf.* §7.3.3), thus substantially reducing any inflation-risk mismatch between revenues and costs. But—paradoxical as it may seem—if revenues are fully indexed against inflation, the Project Company still faces an inflation risk. This is because a key element of its operating costs, namely debt service, is not normally inflation-linked.

Table 10.12, which assumes a 1000 loan repaid in 5 equal annual debt-service payments, at an interest rate of 6%, illustrates this:

Case (A) assumes nil inflation:
- This produces an overall return to investors of 811.
- Given that inflation is zero, this cash flow can be discounted at 0%, so producing a real NPV of 811.

Case (B) assumes 5% inflation of 100% of both revenues and operating costs.

As can be seen Case (B) leaves the investors better off, so that instead of a net cash flow of 813 at 0% inflation, the net cash flow becomes 1023. This is because although 100% of their revenues are going up at 5%, only 72% of the operating costs (237 ÷ [600 + 237]) are doing so—because the debt-service payments are fixed and so not subject to inflation.

Table 10.12 Effect of Inflation on Project Cash Flow

Year:	1	2	3	4	5	Total
(A) 0% inflation						
Revenues	1000	1000	1000	1000	1000	5000
Operating costs	−600	−600	−600	−600	−600	−3000
Debt interest	−60	−49	−38	−26	−13	−187
Debt repayment	−177	−188	−199	−211	−224	−1000
Net cash flow	163	163	163	163	163	813
(B) 5% inflation						
Revenues	1000	1050	1103	1158	1216	5526
Operating costs	−600	−630	−662	−695	−729	−3315
Debt interest	−60	−49	−38	−26	−13	−187
Debt repayment	−177	−188	−199	−211	−224	−1000
Net cash flow	163	183	204	226	249	1023
NPV @ 5% discount	877					
(C) 2.5% inflation						
Revenues	1000	1025	1051	1077	1104	5256
Operating costs	−600	−615	−630	−646	−662	−3154
Debt interest	−60	−49	−38	−26	−13	−187
Debt repayment	−177	−188	−199	−211	−224	−1000
Net cash flow	163	173	183	193	204	916
NPV @ 2.5% discount	848					
(D) 5% inflation + 60% revenue indexation						
Revenues	1000	1030	1061	1093	1126	5309
Operating costs	−600	−630	−662	−695	−729	−3315
Debt interest	−60	−49	−38	−26	−13	−187
Debt repayment	−177	−188	−199	−211	−224	−1000
Net cash flow	163	163	162	161	159	807
NPV @ 5% discount	699					
(E) 2.5% inflation + 60% revenue indexation						
Revenues	1000	1015	1030	1046	1061	5152
Operating costs	−600	−615	−630	−646	−662	−3154
Debt interest	−60	−49	−38	−26	−13	−187
Debt repayment	−177	−188	−199	−211	−224	−1000
Net cash flow	163	163	162	162	162	811
NPV % 2.5% discount	754					

To reflect the investors' real return, the net cash flow can be discounted at the 5% rate of inflation, which produces a real (net of inflation) NPV of 877, which again leaves the investors better off than in Case (A).

Case (C) assumes that instead of the projected rate of inflation of 5%, the actual outturn inflation rate is 2.5%.

- Now it can be seen that if they were counting on inflation remaining at 5%, the investors and lenders are worse off—they receive only 916 instead of 1023 in nominal terms as a result of the inflation only being 2.5%.
- The investors are also worse off in real terms, with an NPV of 848, because the higher the rate of inflation the more beneficial this is when part of the costs—the debt service—are not subject to inflation.

So for investors and lenders, inflation is a two-edged sword—with fully-indexed Contract Payments, inflation higher than projected is a friend, but inflation lower than projected is an enemy. (From the point of view of an Offtaker/Contracting Authority, the reverse is the case.)

The remaining part of Table 10.12 shows how inflation risk can be hedged by an appropriate level of indexation in the Contract Payments:

Case (D) and *Case (E)* are the same as *Case (B)* and *Case (C)*, but assume that revenues are only 60% indexed against inflation, to match the operating costs. As can be seen the result is that the cash flow is almost the same in both cases—so the inflation risk has been substantially hedged.[8] However in both nominal and real terms the investors are worse off and the Offtaker/Contracting Authority better off than if the revenues had been indexed 100%.

These calculations show that it is not possible to produce a financial model using real figures (*i.e.* ignoring inflation); for the purposes of project-finance cash flows, nominal figures (which take projected inflation into account where relevant) should be used, and then if desired these figures can be adjusted afterwards for inflation.

So based on the above, the best choice for the Offtaker/Contracting Authority is to index the Contract Payments against inflation in proportion to the operating costs which are subject to inflation. This cannot be done precisely (as can be seen by comparing Case D and Case E) because the ratio of operating costs to revenues in Table 10.12 is fixed at 60%. In fact the operating costs are 60% of revenues in year 1, but this percentage gradually climbs as time goes on (and increases faster the higher the inflation rate). It is not normal practice to change the indexation percentage for each year.

Furthermore, operating costs usually vary from period to period, *e.g.* because of bulges in expenditure due to maintenance; also inflation has an effect on the calculation of tax payments (*cf.* §13.6.8).

---

[8] If the investors, who will receive the net cash flow, also want an inflation-indexed return, the proportion of indexation will have to be increased.

Therefore the correct way to determine the optimum level of inflation indexation is to run a series of scenarios with the financial model using different proportions of indexation and different inflation rates, to find the level of indexation which is least affected by changes in the inflation rate.

§10.4.2 'OVER-INDEXATION'

However this ideal practice is not always followed, and the results shown in Table 10.12 are misleading in one respect—'over-indexation, *i.e.* 100% inflation indexation of revenues, actually results in a lower initial cost for the Offtaker/Contracting Authority, as illustrated in Table 10.13. These calculations assume that the Contract Payments are already inflation-indexed in the proportion required to against operating costs, as in Table 10.12. So what Table 10.13 concentrates on is the effect of inflation indexing the rest of the Contract Payments, which would be used to cover the debt service and investor's return. The key assumptions for the table are:

- operating costs: nil (*i.e.* this table only deals with debt service and investors' return, assuming that the operating costs have already been hedged by inflation-indexed Contract Payments);
- loan amount: 1000;

Table 10.13 Effect of 'Over-Indexation' on Contract Payments

Year:	1	2	3	4	10	11	12	24	25	Total
(X) Fixed Contract Payments										
Contract Payments	94	94	94	94	94	94	94	94	94	2,347
Opening loan O/S	1,000	982	962	942	791	760	727	143	74	0
Interest	60	59	58	57	47	46	44	9	4	956
Loan repayment	18	19	20	22	31	33	35	70	74	1,000
Total debt service	78	78	78	78	78	78	78	78	78	1,956
(Y) Inflation-Indexed Contract Payments (2.5%)										
Contract Payments	74	76	78	80	92	95	97	130	134	2,526
Opening loan O/S	1,000	998	995	990	914	892	866	202	105	0
Interest	60	60	60	59	55	54	52	12	6	1,105
Loan repayment	2	3	5	7	22	25	29	97	105	1,000
Total debt service	62	63	65	66	77	79	81	109	111	2,105
(Z) Inflation-Indexed Contract Payments (5%)										
Contract Payments	75	79	83	87	117	123	129	232	243	3,597

- term: 25 years (note that years 13–23 are omitted from the table for reasons of space);
- interest rate: 6%;
- lenders' required Cover Ratio (*cf.* §12.3.1): 1.2.

Looking at the results in the table:

- *Case (X)* assumes no indexation of the Contract Payments covering debt service and equity return. So these payments remain at 95 throughout the term of the Project Agreement.
- *Case (Y)* assumes 100% indexation of these Contract Payments, and an inflation rate of 2.5% throughout the life of the Project Agreement. The debt is at the same cost, but repayments are structured to maintain the Cover Ratio (*cf.* §12.3). As can be seen the effect of this is to reduce the initial Contract Payment from 94 to 74, which is obviously a substantial change from the point of view of the Offtaker/Contracting Authority. However as time goes on the Contract Payments increase, and end up 27% higher than in Case (X).
- *Case (Z)* assumes that the actual outturn inflation rate is 5% instead of 2.5%, while the debt service remains fixed as in Case (Y). As can be seen the effect on the Contract Payments which the Offtaker/Contracting Authority has to make is substantial (and this increase would produce a considerable windfall for the investors).

If the Offtaker/Contracting Authority assumes that its own budget will rise by the rate of inflation, or in the case of a Concession, that the willingness of users to pay will also rise with inflation, then choosing 100% inflation indexation of the Contract Payments is not unreasonable, since in real terms they are no worse off, and the payments are more affordable in the early years anyway (compared to Case (X)). But in the world of public finance—where sooner or later there are cuts in budgets rather than constant inflation-linked increases—it would clearly be imprudent to make such an assumption.

In effect, 100% inflation indexation is a way of 'back-ending' Contract Payments and is generally not desirable (*cf.* §7.3.2).

§10.4.3 INFLATION-INDEXED FINANCING

But if, despite these arguments, 100% inflation indexation of Contract Payments is felt to be necessary to reduce the initial Contract Payments and so make the project more affordable, at least in the short term, this may cause a problem for the lenders. As is evident from the tables above, if the inflation outturn is below the rate projected, the Project Company is going to be short of cash flow. Even if there is enough cash flow left to cover the debt service, the investors will clearly be worse off.

Not surprisingly, therefore, lenders want to see this risk hedged. This can be achieved by linking part of the debt to inflation, which would mean that if inflation outturn is below the projected level, the debt service would also be lower and hence the net effect would be small, if any. Inflation-indexed financing can be raised in countries where the government issues inflation-indexed bonds, which provides a floor for private-sector inflation bonds, in a similar way that fixed-rate government bonds does for private-sector fixed-rate bonds (*cf.* §4.3).

Table 10.14 sets out how a typical inflation-indexed bond works. The assumptions are:

- loan amount: 1000.
- term: 20 years (years 5–16 from the table).

Table 10.14 Inflation-Indexed Bond

	0	1	2	3	4	17	18	19	20	Total
(A) Real cash flow										
Interest		20	19	18	17	5	4	2	1	223
Principal repayment		41	42	43	44	56	58	59	60	1,000
Total debt service	−1,000	**61**	**61**	**61**	**61**	**61**	**61**	**61**	**61**	**1,223**
Loan balance	1,000	959	917	874	830	176	119	60	0	
(B) Nominal cash flow										
Inflation index	1.000	1.025	1.051	1.077	1.104	1.522	1.560	1.599	1.639	
Interest		21	20	20	19	7	6	4	2	271
Principal repayment		42	44	46	48	86	90	94	98	1,330
Total debt service	−1,000	**63**	**64**	**66**	**68**	**93**	**95**	**98**	**100**	**1,601**
Loan balance	1,000	983	963	941	917	268	185	96	0	
(C) Nominal cash flow @ 5% inflation										
Inflation index	1.000	1.050	1.103	1.158	1.216	2.292	2.407	2.527	2.653	
Interest		21	21	21	21	11	8	6	3	332
Principal repayment		43	46	50	53	129	139	149	159	1,791
Total debt service	−1,000	**64**	**67**	**71**	**74**	**140**	**147**	**155**	**162**	**2,123**
Loan balance	1,000	1,007	1,011	1,012	1,009	404	286	152	0	

- real interest rate: 2.00%.
- inflation: 2.50% (throughout loan term).

The repayment structure for the bond is based on a real cash-flow calculation, *i.e.* assuming inflation is nil, as in (A). This shows that the loan of 1000 is paid off over 20 years with annual debt-service payments of 61. (B) Then shows how this cash flow is adjusted for inflation, based on the a projected inflation index (*i.e.* an estimate of future inflation made on day 1), which increases 2.5% *p.a.* Note that both principal and interest payments are adjusted for inflation by multiplying the real figures in (A) by the inflation index amount. The end result is that in nominal terms the loan increases from 1000 to 1330 over 20 years, and total nominal interest payments increase from 223 to 271. As can also be seen the breakage cost (assuming no changes in real interest rate and no credit margin), *i.e.* the loan outstanding, is higher in (B) throughout the term of the loan.

(C) then assumes that outturn inflation goes up to 5% and remains at this level throughout the loan term. The effect of this on the debt service can be seen, and compared to (B). Here the Project Company may be surprised to find that even though it is making annual debt-service payments, its loan amount actually increases from 1000 to 1012 in year 3, and only gets back below 1000 in year 5.

It is also possible in some markets to enter into an inflation swap,[9] so instead of swapping a floating interest rate for a fixed rate, the Project Company swaps a variable rate of inflation for a fixed rate of inflation, which would produce the same net effect as the inflation-indexed loan above.

But it must again be emphasized that this complex inflation-linked financing would not be necessary (or appropriate) if the Contract Payments were properly hedged against operating-cost inflation in the first place.

§10.5 FOREIGN-EXCHANGE RISKS

Foreign-exchange risks are those risks resulting from movements in the exchange rate between one currency and another.[10] There are a number of different issues to be considered when considering such risks:

- managing foreign-exchange risks (§10.5.1);
- hedging of foreign-exchange risks (§10.5.2);
- local-currency debt (§10.5.3);
- liquidity support (§10.5.4);

---

[9] Known in Britain as an 'RPI swap' (RPI = Retail Prices Index)
[10] *Cf.* Philip Gray and Timothy Irwin, "Exchange Rate Risk: Allocating Exchange Rate Risk in Private Infrastructure Projects" *Public Policy for the Private Sector*, Note 226 (World Bank, Washington DC, 2003)*.

- catastrophic devaluation (§10.5.5);
- finance in more than one currency (§10.5.6);
- conversion of local-currency revenues (§10.5.7);
- fixing of security in local currency (§10.5.8).

§10.5.1 MANAGING FOREIGN-EXCHANGE RISKS

As with interest-rate risks, lenders will not accept the Project Company taking foreign-exchange risks in its financing, however much of a 'safe bet' this may appear to be. Lenders wish such risks to be minimized or eliminated wherever possible.[11]

There are two interlinked approaches to dealing with the issue:

Construction Phase. During the construction phase, if costs are in one currency and funding in another, the Project Company is exposed to the risk that the currency in which the costs are being incurred may appreciate (become stronger). For example, if the Construction Contract costs $100, and €100 of funding for this has been arranged when the €:$ exchange rate is €1.00:$1.00, and the Euro subsequently depreciates to €1.20:$1.00, the funding is then only enough to pay for $83.33 (€100 ÷ 1.20) of EPC costs, and in effect the project has a construction-cost overrun (or a funding deficit) of $16.67.

To deal with these construction-cost foreign-exchange risks, either the costs have to be redesignated into the currency of the funding or the funding currency has to be changed into the currency of the costs, whichever is easier and is also in line with the approach to long-term (operation phase) foreign-exchange risk discussed below.

The largest item of construction costs is likely to be the Construction Contract; if the Construction Contractor can be persuaded to fix the price in the currency of the funding, most of the problem disappears, as the next largest costs during construction is likely to relate to the financing (IDC and fees), which will automatically be in the funding currency.

However this transfers the foreign-exchange exposure to the Construction Contractor, who may be reluctant to quote a price in another currency without a cost base in that currency. The Construction Contractor could cover this exposure with forward foreign-exchange cover as discussed below (§10.5.2), but the Construction Contractor may not be prepared to quote a price in this way at the time of bidding for the Construction

---

[11] Using offshore-currency long-term debt to finance a project in a country where revenues are in local currency but long-term local-currency debt is not available (*e.g.* using $ to finance a road project in Nigeria where the tolls are paid in Nigerian naira) is sometimes referred to as 'the original sin'.

Contract, since there is no certainty of being awarded the contract or of the schedule for construction and thus payment. If the Construction Contractor takes out forward-exchange cover and is not awarded the contract or the timing changes, this could result in a heavy loss.

In such cases the Construction Contractor may be prepared to quote the initial price in the home currency, but enter into forward-exchange contracts with the Project Company at Financial Close (*i.e.* when the Construction Contract is signed and financed: and so the schedule for construction and payment is then fixed) to convert the price into the foreign currency (probably with hedging on a back-to-back basis with the Construction Contractor's bankers). Alternatively the price itself can be converted into the foreign currency using this hedging. But in either case this leaves the Sponsors and the Project Company with this risk until Financial Close.

Operation Phase. During the operating phase, if the Project Company's revenues are in one currency and its financing or other costs are in another, movements in the exchange rate will affect its net revenues, and hence ability to repay debt. Ideally, finance should be arranged in the local currency, hence eliminating such long-term exchange-rate risks, but in practice this may not be possible in developing countries where the domestic financial markets are not able to provide long-term project-finance debt. The currency of the revenues therefore dictates the currency of the financing, or *vice-versa*:

- If revenues are earned in a currency in which financing can be provided (*e.g.* $ or €), the financing should be in that currency.
- If funding for a project in a developing country can only be arranged in $, then any payments from an Offtaker/Contracting Authority under a Project Agreement must also be in $, or paid in local currency but indexed against $ (*cf.* §6.3.5, but also *cf.* §10.5.5).
- If the project is producing a commodity whose price is $-based (*e.g.* oil), then funding should be in $ (*cf.* discussion of Enclave projects in §11.4.1).
- If the project has a major input cost in $ (*e.g.* a Gas Supply Agreement for a power station), then its revenues should also be fixed in $.[12]

Similarly, continuing operating costs need to match the revenue currency as far as possible.

It follows from this that if the funding has to be in, say, $ to match revenues, the construction costs, especially the Construction Contract, also have to be in this currency. As discussed in §13.7.7, an inherent exchange-rate risk related to the tax position may also remain.

---

[12] Local operating costs—offices, staff—may not be incurred in this revenue currency, but the degree of currency risk here is usually not significant.

§10.5.2 Exchange-Rate Hedging

It is theoretically possible for forward foreign-exchange contracts (currency swaps) to be used to cover currency exchange-rate risks: in this type of contract a Project Company that had construction costs in € but funding in $ could agree at Financial Close to sell $ and buy € on the estimated loan drawdown dates, thus fixing the exchange rate at which the € costs are being funded in $.

Similarly a Project Company that had costs and revenues in $ but funding in € could agree:

- to sell $ and buy € on the estimated loan-drawdown dates;
- to sell the same amount of € and buy $ on the estimated loan-repayment dates, which would fix the exchange rate at which the loan is being repaid.

Currency swaps between local financial institutions, and DFIs or other lenders (rather than the Project Company), are therefore used in some developing countries as a way of providing the former with long-term project-finance funding in local currency which can then be used for the benefit of the Project Company. But such long-term currency swaps (*i.e.* 20 years or so) cannot be arranged in many developing countries because there is no market for such transactions.

If the currency swap is entered into with the Project Company directly, the credit risk assumed by lenders providing such a swap is significantly greater than for an interest-rate swap: a movement on the exchange rate of 20% increases loan principal payments and hence the level of risk by 20%, whereas a movement in the interest rate of 20% affects the interest payment only, and (assuming an interest rate of 10%) equates only to an additional 2% *p.a.* of the (declining) loan-principal outstandings. However, as mentioned in §4.2.2, this structure does work in some Asian countries, and produces a lower cost of finance for local projects.

An alternative approach is for the Host Country's central bank to agree to enter into the currency swap with the Project Company. This means that the foreign-currency risk is dealt with as part of the overall pool of foreign debt, for which the central bank is more suited than an individual project. This could of course mean that the central bank is taking a credit risk on the Project Company as discussed above.

§10.5.3 Local-Currency Debt

If the local currency loan market can offer the amount and term of financing required in local currency, this clearly eliminates any long-term currency risk although there may be a construction-phase problem where equipment is being imported, as discussed above.

If the local market can prove the debt but is not willing to take project-finance risks, then using an offshore guarantee may help to square this circle. Foreign commercial banks could provide such a guarantee, thus dividing the financing of the project from its credit risk. Guarantees of this type can also be provided by other parties such as DFIs; these are known as Partial-Credit Guarantees (*cf.* §16.5.1).

§10.5.4 LIQUIDITY SUPPORT

DFIs may be able to provide a standby loan to support a project where its revenues are in a local currency but financing costs are in an offshore currency such as $. This may take the form of a revolving loan,[13] or a guarantee to the lenders who would provide an extra liquidity tranche, to cover the time lapse between a devaluation of the local currency and the subsequent increase in inflation that should, over time, be sufficient to compensate the Project Company (with Contract Payments indexed against local inflation) for the effect of this devaluation on its ability to service foreign-currency debt. Thus additional mezzanine debt (*cf.* §4.5.1) may be made available to the Project Company equal to a maximum of, say, 10% of the Project Company's foreign-currency debt if, as a consequence of a devaluation, the Project Company cannot generate sufficient foreign currency to sustain its debt-service payments. Repayment would have to be made on a subordinated basis (*cf.* §14.14.5), but perhaps with a *pari-passu* claim on security.

§10.5.5 CATASTROPHIC DEVALUATION

'Catastrophic devaluation' (*i.e.* a sudden major devaluation of the local currency) is now recognized as one of the most serious risks in providing project finance in foreign currencies to developing countries, where the project is not a natural generator of foreign-exchange revenues.

The currency-hedging techniques described in §10.5.2, or liquidity support, may enable the Project Company to deal with the risk of normal market movements in exchange rates, but if economic mismanagement in the Host Country leads to a major currency devaluation, these techniques are liable to break down. An Offtaker/ Contracting Authority who is taking the exchange-rate risk by indexing the Contract Payments against a foreign currency probably cannot pass on the greatly increased cost of this indexation after a major devaluation to the local end-users of the product or service, and if the Offtaker's or Contracting Authority's exchange risk has been hedged in the local banking system, these banks may not be able to sustain any consequent losses.

The effect of this was seen, for example, in the Asian crisis of 1997, and in Turkey in 2001, where power purchasers under long-term PPAs had linked Tariff payments to foreign currencies. When the power purchasers' home currencies

---

[13] *i.e* a loan that can be drawn repaid, and reborrowed.

suffered huge devaluations, they had an obligation under the PPA to increase the Tariff payments accordingly. However, it was simply not economically or politically realistic for the charges to their own end-users of electricity to be increased immediately to a similar extent, to enable the required payments to be made to foreign lenders and investors. Thus in practice the protection supposedly given by currency indexation in the Tariff did not work and the PPAs of course fell into default.

Paradoxically, there is an argument that in this situation it is better for the Project Company's revenues to be derived from Contract Payments indexed not against a foreign currency, but against local inflation. In this way, if a product such as electricity suddenly becomes cheaper for the end-user after a devaluation (when measured in foreign currency), this will only be a temporary phenomenon—in due course the rate of inflation will increase correspondingly. So a devaluation of 40% should lead to an increase in inflation of 40%, and Contract Payments based on local inflation will thus increase by 40% to compensate for the devaluation. (This is based on the purchasing-power parity assumption set out in §13.4.4.)

This approach is likely to be politically far more acceptable in the Host Country, and hence more sustainable during an economic crisis. The main problem, however, even in a completely free market without Host Government interference with prices, is that it takes time for the adjustment in prices to take place; in the meantime the Project Company with Contract Payments based on inflation may not have enough revenues to cover its debt service.

§10.5.6 FINANCE IN MORE THAN ONE CURRENCY

If the debt or equity is being provided in more than one currency (and the currencies concerned are not each provided *pro rata* by debt and equity), the exchange rate between these currencies at Financial Close should be used to fix the relationship between the currencies for the debt:equity calculation (*cf.* §12.4.1). If this is not done, it is impossible to provide the correct amounts of funding in advance, as illustrated by in Table 10.15.

Table 10.15 Debt:Equity Ratio and Changing Exchange Rates

	At Financial Close	At Project Completion
(a) Current exchange rate	$1 = €1.3	$1 = €1.5
(b) Equity	€200	€200
(c) Debt	$615	$615
(d) Debt in € equivalent [(c) × (a)]	€800	€923
(e) Debt:equity ratio [(d) ÷ ((b) + (d))]	80:20	92:20

Table 10.16 Mixed Funding Currencies and Debt:Equity Ratio

	At Financial Close (£1 = €1.3)			At Project Completion (£1 = €1.5)		
	€	£	€ equivalent	€	£	€ equivalent
Debt	€640	$208	€800	€640	$208	€952
Equity	€160	$52	€200	€160	$52	€238
Debt:equity ratio			80:20			80:20

The table shows that if the Project Company is required to maintain a debt:equity ratio of no more than 80:20, and if the exchange rate at Project Completion is used, the project will be in default. There is no way of foreseeing in advance what the exchange rate will be: no form of hedging is appropriate because the mixed financing currencies will have been used to reflect the Project Company's construction-phase costs as discussed above, and hedging back into, say, $ will undo this.

The problem can also be avoided by arranging for both equity and debt to be contributed *pro rata* between $ and € (*i.e.* 80 of $ to each 20 of € in the case above), with the amounts in each currency fixed at the exchange rates at Financial Close. This gives the result shown in Table 10.16. However, this split in the currencies still leaves a long-term problem if the operating-phase costs and revenues are not split in the same proportions.

§10.5.7 CONVERSION OF LOCAL CURRENCY REVENUES

Although a Project Company's exposure to foreign-currency debt may be hedged by indexing its local currency revenues under a Project Agreement to the foreign currency concerned, this may not provide complete hedging because of timing differences on conversion:

Gap Between Billing and Payment. There is inevitably a gap between the time the Project Company calculates the amount due from the Offtaker/Contracting Authority, including currency indexation, and the time payment of the bill is made (perhaps a month or more). The Project Company is thus exposed to further exchange-rate movements in that time, although obviously the risk is limited as only one month's payments are involved at any one time. The risk can be covered by short-term hedging in the local financial market if this is possible, or by adjusting the next month's bill to reflect the actual indexed rate at the time the previous month's bill was paid.

Timing of Currency Conversions. Host Country exchange-control regulations may specify that local currency can only be changed into foreign currency when the payment is due to be made. If revenues indexed to foreign currency that are intended for foreign currency costs, debt service or dividends cannot be converted until payment of these is due, an unacceptably long period of risk may result (up to six months for the typical half-yearly debt-service and dividend payments). If forward-exchange cover is not available in the local market (or credit risks in this market are not acceptable to the lenders, which is quite likely), the Host Country's central bank or ministry of finance has to be persuaded to allow a more liberal interpretation of the rules to allow immediate conversion.

§10.5.8 FIXING OF SECURITY IN LOCAL CURRENCY

When the lenders register their mortgage (or other security) over the Project Company's assets in the Host Country, local law may require that the amount of the mortgage be fixed, and stated in local currency even if the debt is in foreign currency (*cf.* §14.7.1). This leaves the lenders exposed if the local currency depreciates, and the Project Company has other unsecured creditors, who may have a *pari-passu* claim for any amounts not covered by the mortgage. It may be possible to register the mortgage for an amount larger than the loan at the current exchange rate, to leave room for maneuver, but if not the increase in the loan amount in local-currency terms will have to added to the mortgage at intervals (which besides being cumbersome and involving the Project Company in extra costs, may not be wholly secure against other creditors for a period of time).

§10.6 REFINANCING RISK

In some markets it has not been the universal practice to arrange long-term loans for projects. In the United States, for example, banks may provide short-term construction loans, which are refinanced by long-term (so called 'permanent') loans from insurance companies or pension funds, or by bond issues, after Project Completion. The initial loan is usually arranged to mature in a 'bullet' repayment 2–3 years after Project Completion (making it what is known as a 'Mini Perm'[14]) to allow flexibility of timing for the refinancing.[15]

This approach may at first sight seem attractive but it carries major macro-economic related risks:

- The first macro-economic risk is that long-term interest rates may have gone up above the assumptions originally used in the financial model, making it

---

[14] For the distinction between a 'Hard' Mini-Perm and a 'Soft' Mini-Perm, *cf.* §14.4.4.

[15] *Cf.* §14.16 for the different situation where there is refinancing of an existing long-term loan.

impossible for the project to carry the whole of the debt that needs to be refinanced. Investors could obviously lose heavily in this situation. Interest-rate hedging (*cf.* §10.3) is unlikely to work in this situation, since if banks won't lend for a long term they are unlikely to provide hedging for a long term either.

- A further macro-economic risk is that there may be a lack of liquidity in the loan or bond market at the time of the refinancing (*cf.* §17.2), making it actually impossible to obtain long-term finance when needed.

Lenders might also have a concern that the project could be going badly at the end of the Mini-Perm debt term, and so cannot be refinanced even though the issues above do not arise. Logically, however, either the project will go well, in which case it can be refinanced, or it will go badly, in which case there will be a problem anyway, so this should not be as great a concern as the macro-economic points discussed above.

This issue is further discussed in §17.5.1 in the context of new approaches to project finance.

Chapter 11

REGULATORY AND POLITICAL RISKS

§11.1 INTRODUCTION

All major projects have political aspects (§11.2). The Project Company may therefore be subject to political risks relating to the project's presence in a particular country and its relationship with the Host Government, rather than to the more general commercial and macro-economic risk aspects of the project covered in Chapter 9 and Chapter 10. These political risks are discussed in detail in this chapter.

There are two main areas of risk relating to government actions: firstly 'regulatory' or 'change in law' risks (§11.3), which affect all projects to some extent, and secondly 'investment' risks (§11.4), which mainly affect cross-border project investments, primarily in developing countries. Linked to the latter are 'quasi-political' risks, which relate to government taking indirect action against the project (§11.5).

This chapter also deals with the particular issues arising from 'sub-sovereign' risks—*i.e.* where the Offtaker/Contracting Authority is a state or local government instead of the central government (§11.6).

295

Principles of Project Finance. DOI: http://dx.doi.org/10.1016/B978-0-12-391058-5.00011-4

Finally the terms for a Government Support Agreement, which may help to deal with the issues covered in §11.3–§11.6, are described (§11.7).

Political-risk insurance may be available to cover these risks (§11.8).

§11.2 PROJECTS AND POLITICS

Governments play a very important rôle in project finance. Projects financed in this way are usually major long-term investments, for which political will and sustained political support are needed. They may also form part of a government policy of privatization or the provision of public infrastructure through PPPs, whose success or failure will have considerable political consequences.

In fact, few major projects can be structured and financed without political backing. Political support from a high level is often necessary to enable a project to be completed successfully; for example, if a PPA is being negotiated with a state-owned power company, the latter's management may consider that such a contract is not in their interests, and it would be better if they developed the power station themselves as they have done in the past. Thus the power purchaser has no incentive to negotiate constructively. The only way to break this impasse is for the power purchaser to be given a strong direction from the Host Government that they must not take this attitude.

Once the project is operating, continued political support is needed. The project will be weakened if it becomes a political football because it provides a handle for the opposition to attack the government, or for a new government to try to undo the deal agreed by the previous government, perhaps because it did not go through a transparent (competitive) public-procurement process (*cf.* §3.7) or it produces very high returns for the investors, and so is open to charges, at best, of having been favored unfairly, or, at worst, of corruption. Once a project is complete it cannot be taken out of the country again, and the Project Company's position inevitably becomes weaker than it was when the Host Government first wanted to attract the investment.

This links to the concept of the 'obsolescing bargain', which reflects the way in which the relationship between a major foreign investor and the Host Government, especially in a developing country, changes as the project progresses.[1] Initially the Host Government is anxious to attract foreign investment, and so the foreign investor has the upper hand, but once the investment has been made, the foreign investor becomes less necessary and so a lot more vulnerable to pressure by the Host Government.[2] Hence the original bargain between the two becomes obsolescent.

---

[1] First set out in Raymond Vernon, *Sovereignty at Bay: The multinational spread of U.S. enterprises* (Basic Books, New York, 1971).

[2] This could be regarded as a variant of the old saying that if you owe the bank $1,000 you are in trouble, but if you owe the bank $1,000,000 the bank is in trouble.

Similarly if there is no consensus on the benefits of the project, this gives rise to problems such as the 'willingness to pay' issue for toll roads (§9.6.2), which quickly become very political, and can lead to the Contracting Authority putting pressure on the Project Company not to charge the full tolls to which it is entitled.

Project-financed investments are especially vulnerable in this respect. The high leverage means that there is little room for the Project Company to adjust to short-term macro-economic or other problems in the Host Country—a fixed amount of foreign-currency debt service always has to be paid irrespective of how difficult this might be for the Host Country, whereas a project with a much lower leverage has the option to reduce its dividends and hence relieve some of the stress on the Host Country's economy. Clearly this lays a project-financed investment open to accusations of just being run for the benefit of foreign investors.

So just as a project has to be commercially viable (*cf.* §9.4), it must also be politically viable. The fundamental issue is whether the project is seen as 'fair' and beneficial to its users; if it is not, *e.g.* because the cost of its product or service is out of line with local costs or comparable projects, investors and lenders cannot just rely on Project Contracts and ignore this political aspect. And a high rate of return, which is meant to compensate for risk, may paradoxically increase the risk if it becomes politically unacceptable.

The project also has to be set up in a way that leaves the Host Government in a position to make future changes in the market in which it operates. For example, if the state-owned power distributor is to sign a long term PPA, the Host Government will have to consider whether this contract could be an impediment to a future privatization of the electricity industry, and if so how it can be structured to leave future flexibility in this respect. Similarly, when signing a toll-road Concession the Host Government should consider whether it is subject to provisions such as non-competition (*cf.* §6.5.2) which could prevent the normal evolution of the road network.

§11.3 CHANGE IN LAW

In general terms, the Project Company must operate in a stable legal and regulatory environment—this requires:

- general legislation that allows for private ownership or control of the project and adequately protects private investment;
- a clear legal and regulatory framework for the project's operation;
- consistency of legal and regulatory policies;
- straightforward procedures for obtaining construction, operation, and financing Permits (*cf.* §8.8);
- the ability for the lenders to take and enforce security (*cf.* §14.7).

This may not be wholly feasible if the type of project is new to the country concerned; in such cases, especially in developing countries, a Government Support Agreement (*cf.* §11.7) may be required. But, however stable the legal framework, the risk of a change in law affecting the project cannot be eliminated. Moreover, a Contracting Authority or its Host Government can never bind itself not to change the law in future. It is not possible for a government to bind its successors in this way.

§11.3.1 CHANGE IN LAW RISK

The risk of a change in law ('regulatory risk') therefore needs to be considered for any project, wherever it is located. In this context, 'law' includes anything having the force of law, and so would include, for example, industry regulations. An adverse decision by a court affecting the Project Company's costs, rights, or revenues may lie outside this definition, because it could be argued that the court decision does not change the law, but only correctly interprets the law as it stands, and indeed most courts would present their decision in this way. Including 'changes in the interpretation of the law' in the contractual definition of change in law may provide some protection in this respect (but *cf.* §11.5.1).

The overall issue here is one of Value for Money (*cf.* §9.2): if the Offtaker/Contracting Authority does not pay for the cost of a change in law, bidders will probably have to create a reserve from the cash flow to provide finance if and when required (although it nobody knows how much finance might be required, if any, and when). This will add a cost to the Contract Payments even if the reserve is never used, so arguably it is better VfM for the Offtaker/Contracting Authority to pay for these costs. Also, if the Offtaker/Contracting Authority is a public-sector body, it is evidently in a better position to assess and control this risk—directly or indirectly—than the Project Company.

Changes in law also have to be tracked, and kept consistent, between the various Project Contracts (*cf.* §9.12). Thus under the Construction Contract, the Project Company may be responsible for paying for any extra cost that the Construction Contractor faces from having to modify the specifications of the project to comply with changes in the law (*e.g.* additional investment to reduce emissions), and cannot penalize the Construction Contractor for delays caused by having to make these modifications. This risk may then be passed by the Project Company to an Offtaker/Contracting Authority, who would again be responsible for extra costs or loss of revenue caused by the change in law. In Concessions there may be a right to pass such costs through directly to the User Fees.

§11.3.2 CATEGORIES OF CHANGE IN LAW

Changes in Law can be placed in three categories:

- *General Change in Law*: applies to the country as a whole, rather than a particular industry or type of project. One example would be an increase in company tax rates. Another might be new regulations for disabled access to buildings, requiring modification of existing buildings. Another might be giving employees new pension or sick-pay rights.

- *Specific Change in Law*: this covers the industry in which the Project Company is operating, or the services which it is providing. This could include, for example, higher taxes on emissions by power stations, or reduced emissions limits requiring new investment to meet these limits.
- *Discriminatory Change in Law*: this relates to laws or regulations which are specifically aimed at the Project Company, the particular project, or all projects of this particular type (*e.g.* PPP toll-road Concessions).

General Change in Law. It could be said that this is a normal cost of doing business in the country concerned, and the person paying for the product or service under a Project Contract should take the risk—and thus pay for—a change in law. The further argument for this is that a change in law affecting the country as a whole will affect all types of projects, and any extra costs will normally be passed on to the all end-users of the product or service provided, whether or not these relate to project-financed projects; therefore an Offtaker (whether a public- or private-sector entity) or Contracting Authority who does not cover this cost will be earning a windfall profit at the expense of the Project Company. However a full assumption of General Change in Law risk by the Offtaker/Contracting Authority is not common.

In relation to changes in tax rates, the market practice tends to vary between developing countries, where any change in taxes is compensated, and developed countries, where the risk of a change in general taxes tends to remain with the Project Company. In Construction Contracts (whatever the location of the project), the Construction Contractor generally bears the risk of changes in taxes on its own business (*i.e.* direct corporate taxes), but not in indirect taxes such as value-added tax ('VAT'), goods & services tax ('GST') or sales tax, or in import duties. Similarly, an Input-Supply Contract normally passes on the costs of any extra taxes directly levied on the product being supplied.

A separate issue with taxes relates to withholding taxes on dividend payments to foreign investors (which reduces their return), or interest payments to foreign lenders (the cost of which usually has to be borne by the Project Company. These tend to be treated in the same way as corporate-tax increases, but the issue may be complicated by a double-tax treaty between the investors' or lenders country and the Host Country, which should allow the investors or lenders to offset this foreign tax against their domestic tax liability. (but *cf.* §12.7.1).

In the case of Reverting Asset-based Contracts (*cf.* §6.2), the Offtaker/ Contracting Authority will of course take over the project at the end of the contract term, and so benefit from any capital expenditure on the plant. There is therefore an argument, in this case, that the Offtaker/Contracting Authority should at least pay for capital expenditure required by a General Change in Law, for example a relatively small proportion in the early stages of the Project Agreement, and more as the Agreement nears the end of its term. Alternatively there can be an arrangement whereby the Project Company pays the first $x of costs, and the Offtaker/Contracting Authority the rest, which sets a clear cap on the Project Company's (and its lenders) exposure.

Discriminatory Change in Law. At the other end of the scale, it is much more difficult to argue that the Project Company should have to cover costs arising from a Discriminatory Change in Law, and it would be normal to pass these on to the Offtaker/Contracting Authority, or to end-users.

Specific Change in Law. This obviously lies within the two extremes, but again the general practice is to pass on such costs to the Offtaker/Contracting Authority, or to end-users.

If the costs of a change in law are to be covered by the Offtaker/Contracting Authority, this is treated as a Compensation Event (*cf.* §7.6). There is no need for change in law provisions for a Building-Services Contract, if such changes are automatically covered by benchmarking/market-testing arrangements (*cf.* §6.4.5).

If the Project Agreement does not contain adequate Change in Law provisions, the project's risk in this respect can be substantial. An example of a Change in Law of this type occurred in Spain, where the government announced in 2012 that the tariffs payable for power generated by solar or wind-energy projects was not sustainable and that it intended to cap the profits made by such projects. In such cases foreign investors and lenders may get some protection from bilateral investment-protection treaties between their home country and the Host Government.

§11.4 INVESTMENT RISKS

The standard 'investment' risks are:

- currency convertibility and transfer (*cf.* §11.4.1);
- expropriation of the project by the state (*cf.* §11.4.2);
- political violence (*i.e.* war, terrorism and civil unrest—*i.e.* Political *Force Majeure*) (*cf.* §11.4.3).

Investors and lenders into the country where the project is situated (the 'Host Country'[3]) are likely to be concerned about these issues if the project is located in a developing country that is politically unstable or has a lower credit rating.

These risks may be passed on by the Project Company to the Offtaker/Contracting Authority by requiring compensation to the Project Company for losses caused by them. However when the time comes the Host Government may simply be unwilling or unable to fulfill this obligation, and political-risk guarantees or insurance may be required to cover these risks (*cf.* §11.8, Chapter 16).

§11.4.1 CURRENCY CONVERTIBILITY AND TRANSFER

Following on from the macro-economic issues relating to exchange-rate risks (*cf.* §10.5), this section deals with the risks of currency convertibility and transfer. Two processes have to be carried out in this respect:

- sufficient revenues have to be converted into the foreign-currency amounts required by lenders and investors; and
- these foreign-currency amounts have to be transferred out of the Host Country to lenders and investors. (Foreign currency may also be required to pay for fuel or other operating costs.)

If a project is able to rely on the free international financial markets that exist in developed countries, the only real currency risk is that of an adverse movement of the exchange rate between the domestic and foreign currencies (*i.e.* devaluation of the local currency, discussed in §10.5). However, if a country gets into economic difficulties and so runs short of foreign-currency reserves, it may totally forbid either the conversion of local currency amounts to foreign currencies or the transmission of these foreign currencies out of the country. In effect, at this point the Host Country has defaulted on its foreign-currency debt. One of the standard provisions of a Government Support Agreement (*cf.* §11.7) is a Host Government or central bank guarantee of foreign-exchange availability and transfer, but if the Host Country has no foreign-exchange reserves this guarantee will be of little value.

Apart from complete unavailability of foreign currency, the worst problem of this nature likely to be faced by a project in a developing country is a catastrophic devaluation of the Host Country's currency (*cf.* §10.5.5). A Host Government guarantee of an Offtaker's/Contracting Authority's payment liabilities may also be of limited value in this situation.

---

[3] This expression is normally used where the investors and lenders are in a different country to the project.

Lenders assess the degree of these risks by examining the macro-economic position, balance of payments, and foreign debt levels of the Host Country. If the country has a well-managed and sound economy, then lenders may find the risk acceptable, but if not mitigation of these risks is required.

Apart from political risk guarantees or insurance (*cf.* Chapter 16), there are some other possible ways of mitigating the risks (but seldom entirely eliminating them):

- Enclave Projects;
- offshore reserve accounts;
- the 'Angola Model'.

Enclave Projects. If a project's revenues are paid in foreign currencies from a source outside the Host Country, in principle the project can thus be insulated against both currency exchange and transfer risks. Because the foreign currency never arrives in the country, it cannot be restricted from leaving it, and the foreign-currency revenues can be retained to service foreign-currency debt raised outside the country. This may be a feasible approach if the project involves production of a commodity for export, for example, oil, gas, or minerals, or the sale of electricity across a border.

Lenders find generally Enclave Projects in developing countries more attractive than those that do not generate their own foreign currency earnings from outside the Host Country. As the term implies, they are relatively isolated from what lenders consider to be one of the main risks of lending to developing countries—that of failure to pay foreign-currency debt—and this approach can mean that a developing country may be able to raise foreign currency for development of its resources that would not be otherwise possible. In a similar way, rating agencies may give a higher credit rating to a bond issued by an Enclave Project than to the sovereign debt of the country in which the project is located.

Typical factors that would create a feasible Enclave Project are:

- importance of the sale of the commodity to the country's economy and balance of payments;
- a limited market for the commodity inside the country (so it is unlikely to be diverted for domestic use);
- an infrastructure oriented towards exports (pipelines, ports, *etc.*), again to avoid diversion;
- sales through a third party with a good credit standing, located outside the jurisdiction or control of the Host Country;
- direct payment of revenues to an SPV or escrow account outside the Host Country;
- difficulty of diverting payments elsewhere.

The issue with Enclave Projects from the Host Country point of view is that they lose control over what may be their most important export earnings, and so are less able to manage their foreign currency reserves and balance of payments situation in the way they consider appropriate, which they may consider a form of economic colonialism. Enclave projects, however, are a way of raising development finance on more attractive terms for a project in a country with a poor credit rating.

Use of Offshore Reserve Accounts. Even if the Project Company's revenues are not being generated in foreign currencies and held outside the Host Country, the currency-exchange and transfer risk can be mitigated for a limited period by the use of offshore Reserve Accounts. As described in §14.4.1, lenders normally require a Debt-Service Reserve Account (DSRA) to be built up so that these funds can be used to deal with temporary problems in debt payments. If the DSRA is maintained in foreign currency outside the Host Country, it can also be used to cover temporary problems in obtaining foreign currency for debt service. Other Reserve Accounts to accumulate cash for specific purposes can also be set up offshore.

Lenders therefore prefer overseas Reserve Accounts for projects in countries with poor credit ratings, but this may be difficult in countries with strict exchange controls, where domestic companies are not allowed to have such accounts (*cf.* §8.8.4).

The 'Angola Model'. The Project Company could enter into an arrangement under which it barters its product or services in exchange for a commodity that can then be exported and produce foreign currency, thus creating an Enclave Project in two stages. This procedure is known as counter-trade.

Counter-trade played a limited part in projects for developing countries until the creation of what is now called the 'Angola Model' first provided by the Export-Import Bank of China (*cf.* §16.4.3) in Angola in 2004.[4] This has now been applied by China Exim in various African countries. It is in effect a counter-trade transaction—the bank provides finance for infrastructure development (*e.g.* a road, which would be built by a Chinese contractor), but is repaid from the proceeds of a natural-resources project being undertaken by Chinese investors. This approach does raise some issues, in particular the linkage between the two projects (what happens if the natural resources project fails?), and how changes in commodity prices affect the transaction. However it has brought infrastructure development, at least in a limited way, to African countries which would otherwise not have been able to make such investments.

---

[4] *Cf.* Vivien Foster, William Butterfield, Chuan Chen & Nataliya Pushak, *Building Bridges: China's Growing Role as Infrastructure Financier for Sub-Saharan Africa* (World Bank/PPIAF, Washington DC, 2009)*; Martyn Davies, *How China Is Influencing Africa's Development* (OECD Development Centre, Paris, 2010)*.

§11.4.2 EXPROPRIATION

A government always has the power and right to take over privately-owned assets temporarily where this is necessary for reasons of national security (for example, states requisition ships and aircraft in time of war). Many countries have also legislation that gives powers to take over or direct the actions of privately-controlled utilities, or divert oil or other fuel supplies, to maintain essential services. Any investor or lender takes this risk, and in any case the government usually provides compensation for such actions (*cf.* §7.9).

Expropriation goes beyond this; it is the seizure by the Host Government of the Project Company or its physical or financial assets without payment of just compensation (which is illegal under international law). This is a risk that concerns lenders and investors involved in projects in less politically stable countries. It is greatest in high-profile projects that might otherwise be in public ownership, such as power plants or transportation projects, or projects related to a country's natural resources, such as oil or minerals (where such expropriations have been common in the past, but less so in recent times). Technically the Host Government does not even need to deprive the Project Company of its assets or the investors of their shares; for example, it could pass a law giving it the right to appoint a majority of the directors of the Project Company and so gain control in that way.

Expropriation of private assets for political reasons does not just affect cross-border investors and lenders, but is primarily considered to be a risk affecting cross-border investments and loans to developing countries.

A Project Agreement should treat expropriation as a default by the Offtaker/ Contracting Authority, and therefore provide for compensation accordingly (*cf.* §7.10.2). Expropriation should be defined as widely as possible to include not just taking over the assets of the project, but also actions that give the Host Government control of the Project Company. This may provide some deterrent to the Host Government acting arbitrarily against the project. However, it does not deal with the issue of 'creeping expropriation' discussed in §11.5.2.

It should be noted that there can be an overlap between expropriation and the currency conversion and transfer risk discussed above, because the reason for the Project Company being unable to convert or transfer its revenues in the host currency may be that its bank accounts have been expropriated (or frozen) by the Host Government.

Another related risk which may need to be considered in this context is 'deprivation', *i.e.* the inability to export products from the project.

§11.4.3 WAR AND CIVIL DISTURBANCE

Investors and lenders have to face the risk of internal political instability, including civil unrest, sabotage or terrorism, or a war against the Host Country causing physical damage to the project, or preventing its operation, and so causing additional capital costs or a loss of revenue, *i.e.* Political *Force Majeure*'. (*cf.* §7.10.4)

There is also the possibility of a blockade or other sanctions against the Host Country that do not cause physical damage to the project, but prevent its completion because equipment cannot be imported, or prevent its operation because its products cannot be exported or its input supplies imported. A war outside the Host Country may have a similar effect.

Physical damage and consequent loss of revenue caused by this type of Political *Force Majeure* may be covered by insurance; in the absence of this, a Project Agreement may provide for compensation to the Project Company, but there is an obvious risk that when the time comes the Offtaker/Contracting Authority may not be able to fulfill this obligation. Again, therefore, mitigation in the form of political-risk guarantees or insurance may be required by lenders.

Another related risk in this context is forced abandonment, *i.e.* the project itself is not damaged but local conditions make it impossible for it to continue construction or operation.

§11.5 WIDER POLITICAL RISKS

This risk category includes issues such as contract disputes, which may have a political or commercial background; it illustrates that the dividing line between commercial risks and political risks is not a precise one. This is relevant to obtaining political-risk cover through insurance or guarantees (*cf.* §11.8, Chapter 16); if the boundaries of risk cannot be defined, the cover cannot be obtained.

It might be thought that incorporating the Project Company outside the Host Country could mitigate some of these political risks, but this is seldom a workable solution. The project itself obviously cannot leave the country, and most of the risks relate to the project itself rather than its ownership. Furthermore, investment laws of the Host Country may not allow the project to be owned by a foreign company, and even if they do the activities of the foreign company inside the Host Country in running the project are subject to the same laws and risks as a domestic company.

Issues that arise in this context are:

- contract repudiation (§11.5.1);
- creeping expropriation (§11.5.2).

§11.5.1 CONTRACT REPUDIATION/LEGAL PROCESS

Contract repudiation is the deliberate failure by a public-sector Offtaker, Contracting Authority, or other Project Contract counterpart (*e.g.* an Input Supplier) to fulfill its obligations (especially payment obligations) under the relevant Project Contract, or by a Host Government to fulfill its obligations to compensate for this under a Government Support Agreement (*cf.* §11.7).[5]

Clearly a distinction should be made between a genuine commercial dispute about contract terms or liability, and a deliberate refusal on the part of the Host Government or its agencies to honor their obligations, often on obviously spurious grounds, the former being a commercial and the latter a political risk. Matters can be made more complex by the Host Government claiming that corruption was involved in the procurement process, which may be difficult to prove or disprove.

But even if the reasons given are spurious, and an attempt to hide the fact that the contract is actually being repudiated, the only objective way to determine who is in the right is to resort to a court, and if the Host Country's court system is unused to dealing with disputes of this type, or subject to political pressures, the judgment on an action brought by the Project Company against the Host Government or other public-sector counterpart may not be on objective legal grounds.

Where there is concern about the possibility of arbitrary behavior by the Host Government or its courts, some protection may be obtained by specifying that Project Contracts are to be governed by the law of a country other than the Host Country, and that disputes about the contracts are to be litigated or arbitrated in a forum outside the Host Country (*i.e.* both the governing law and the jurisdiction are outside the Host Country). The forum used may be the courts of another country or an international arbitration tribunal. These provisions are fairly standard in Project Contracts signed in developing countries.

Apart from giving protection against arbitrary decisions in the Host Country's courts, if the Project Agreement is governed by a foreign law, this also means that the Host Country cannot easily change the law to affect the Project Contracts themselves. The issue is especially acute in Project Agreements with a government department, since the government obviously has an ability to change the law to its own direct benefit. But this approach may run into opposition with the Host Government, and can easily be translated into a claim that the Project Company is acting like a 19th-century great power, securing extraterritorial rights in the Host Country.

It also may not prevent action being taken in a court in the Host Country on a claim that the Project Agreement or other Project Contract is not valid under the laws of that country (*e.g.* as to ownership or control of public infrastructure), and therefore, for example, payments should not be made by parties in the Host Country to the Project Company. Such cases may be brought by individuals, non-governmental organizations, or other parties with a genuine interest in the matter, but they may also be brought by a 'front man' for the Host Government itself if it is trying to evade its liabilities (or by opponents of the government for political reasons).

---

[5] The less emotive term 'breach of contract' may be used instead of 'contract repudiation', although the latter may also have a wider meaning.

Alternatively, local courts may prevent the Project Company from using international arbitration even if this is a term of the Project Agreement or other Project Contract, on the grounds that the relevant contract provisions are not valid under local law.

So decisions by local courts which were not supposed to have jurisdiction over the Project Agreement, or which are made on unreasonable grounds, would also fall under the heading of contract repudiation. (This issue is also referred to as 'denial of justice'.)

Even if the Project Contracts remain governed by local law and jurisdiction, it is standard practice for financing contracts with offshore lenders (other than security documentation—*cf.* §14.7.1) to be governed by the law and jurisdiction of a developed country if the borrower is located in a developing country. (English or New York law are recognized as the most creditor-friendly.) This also ensures, for example, that a change in law preventing payment of loans in foreign currency would not prevent lenders from maintaining their claim for such payment.

§11.5.2 CREEPING EXPROPRIATION

A government has many ways to take action against a Project Company without specifically repudiating contractual obligations. The cumulative effect of such actions may be to deprive the Project Company or its investors of the real benefit of the project, even though each action, taken by itself, would not necessarily have this result. This is a 'creeping expropriation' of the project—very difficult to define in advance, or to recognize until it has actually taken place, although some potential issues (such as Permits) may be addressed in a Government Support Agreement. Obviously Discriminatory Changes in Law provisions in the Project Agreement (*cf.* §11.3.2) may help in dealing with such issues, but are unlikely to cover all possible eventualities.

A complex project must rely on the good faith and fairness of the state, but the government may use political pressure in bad faith and unfairly as a way of obtaining commercial concessions from the Project Company, or even taking the project over. There is no clear boundary between a legitimate use of state power and deliberate harassment of the project. Moreover, it may be difficult to prove that the Project Company would not have defaulted on its debt or failed to pay dividends to the investors if these acts of creeping expropriation had not taken place, and hence to make a claim on any political risk cover. Examples of the misuse of government power to put pressure on the Project Company (and which would probably not be caught by Discriminatory Change in Law provisions) include:

- state agencies being slow and obstructive in issuing Permits, including work permits for foreign personnel without whom the project cannot operate;
- imports or exports being held up at the docks;
- politically-motivated strikes;

- the Project Company being accused of tax offenses and subjected to lengthy investigations, and possibly also freezing of its bank accounts;
- Project Company personnel being accused of criminal offenses such as corruption, or harassed generally;
- arbitrary amendment or withdrawal of the Project Company's or its Sub-Contractors' construction or operating Permits.

Projects without a Project Agreement, such as those involved in natural-resources extraction, are especially vulnerable in this respect, since they would not have the standard Discriminatory Change in Law protection (although there may be an investment-protection treaty between the investors' or lenders' country and the Host Government which may provide some support to the Project Company). Arbitrarily changing tax rates or production-sharing arrangements for the particular resource sector are not that uncommon.

Creeping expropriation is one of the most difficult problems in political-risk insurance, and political-risk insurers are still struggling to draw precise boundaries for this risk.

§11.6 'SUB-SOVEREIGN' RISK

Political risk has been analyzed so far as if it is always a risk on the central government of a country; however, the risks on a Project Contract, and of political action, may not just lie with the central government. A regional, provincial or local government may have the right to pass its own legislation and raise its own taxes, and contract as Offtaker/Contracting Authority under a Project Agreement. If it gets into financial difficulty, the central government may have no obligation (or political will) to support it, and municipal bankruptcies are not unknown.

State-owned enterprises ('SOEs'), whether established under special legislation or general company law, come into a similar category. The state electricity utility may have been established by the Host Government under such a special law, and its board may all be appointed by the government, but the government does not necessarily have any liability for its obligations under a PPA unless this is specifically agreed to. Similarly it is evident that the government does not automatically have any liability for a limited company that happens to be owned by the state.

The behavior of sub-sovereign and SOE obligors under Project Contracts may be more difficult to predict than that of the government, because such obligors may be less concerned with overall considerations on the credit-worthiness of the country, or its attractiveness to foreign investors, compared to their own local or industry problems.

Lenders therefore make a careful distinction between the sovereign risk of a country (*i.e.* a risk carrying the 'full faith and credit' of the country) that may be acceptable, and public-sector risks below this level—known as 'sub-sovereign' risks—that may not. Lenders may therefore require a central-government guarantee to support the regional or local government's obligations, which may cause difficulties because if the central government is giving a guarantee it may wish to get actively involved in the project to ensure that its guarantee is not called—which will be an interference in the powers which have been devolved to the regional or local government. In the absence of a central government guarantee, it may be possible to obtain external political-risk guarantees or insurance for sub-sovereign risks.

§11.7 GOVERNMENT SUPPORT AGREEMENT

The purpose of a Government Support Agreement is to facilitate the completion and operation of the project by providing government support for any aspect of the project where the parties agree this is required.

This type of Project Contract has a wide variety of names, such as 'stability agreement,' 'implementation agreement,' 'coordination agreement,' 'cooperation agreement' or—confusingly—'concession agreement.' It is usually supplementary to an Offtake Contract signed with another state entity purchasing the product of the project (*e.g.* a PPA with the state power company) or to a Project Agreement that is not signed with the central government, but with another Contracting Authority, such as a public agency, or a regional or local government. (If signed with the central government, these provisions are included in the Project Agreement itself.)

In most projects there is no need for a Government Support Agreement—the general law of the country sets up the framework for a project. This would be the case, for example, in a country with a fully privatized electricity sector, where once general permitting conditions are fulfilled there is no need for specific contracts with the public sector regarding a particular power station. Similarly, where a project is based on a license to operate (*e.g.* a telephone network), no other project-specific contract with the government is required.

But where there is no clear legal framework for the project, as is likely to be the case when particular sectors of the economy are using private-sector finance for the first time, or where there are particular local risks to be considered, a Support Agreement with the government of the country where the project is located (the 'Host Government') reduces risk and thus encourages development that would otherwise not take place.

The scope of a Government Support Agreement varies according to the particular project, but some typical provisions may include:

- The Agreement sets the general framework for the project and gives permission for construction and operation of the project on an exclusive basis.

- The financing structure for the Project Company (*e.g.* the debt:equity ratio) or the sources or currency of the financing is specified (usually in a country with strict exchange controls or rules on foreign investment).
- The Sponsors are required to retain their shareholdings for specified periods.
- The Project Company is given the right (*e.g.* through a lease) to use the project site, if it is public-sector land or if there are restrictions on foreign ownership of land in the country.
- The form of Direct Agreement with the lenders (*cf.* §8.11) is agreed.

Undertakings given by the Host Government may include:

- non-discrimination against the project (*cf.* §11.3.2);
- guarantees for the performance of the Input Supplier, the Offtaker/ Contracting Authority, or other parties under the Project Contracts, including a guarantee of payment of the Termination Sum under the Project Agreement (*cf.* §7.10.2);
- exemption of the Project Company from obtaining Permits required for imports of equipment, construction and operation of the project, or undertaking to ensure that all Permits required are granted provided applications are properly submitted (or to provide assistance in this respect), and that they will not be revoked without good cause;
- to ensure that imports of equipment, *etc.*, are cleared promptly through customs;
- assurances on availability of work permits for expatriate employees of the Project Company, Construction Contractor, and O&M Contractor;
- guarantees for the provision of utilities for the project, such as water, telephones, and electricity, and connecting road, rail, or other links;
- guarantees that port, rail, or other transportation connections will deliver input supplies or take away the product of the project as needed;
- guarantees of the availability of foreign exchange for debt service and dividend repatriation (*cf.* §11.4.1);
- compensation for expropriation of the project (usually calculated in the same way as default by the Offtaker/Contracting Authority under the Project Agreement—*cf.* §11.4.2; §7.10.2);
- tax concessions (*e.g.* exemption from import duties, sales taxes, or value-added taxes, corporate taxes—including taxes levied on the Construction Contractor—or withholding taxes on dividends).
- waiver of sovereign immunity in relation to any claims under the Project Agreement or the Support Agreement.

Default under the Government Support Agreement will be treated as a default under the Project Agreement (to allow a claim for the Termination Sum). Disputes will be litigated outside the country, in an agreed jurisdiction or arbitration tribunal (*cf.* §7.12; §11.5.1).

A contract of this type may obviously be highly political in nature, so the Sponsors need to ensure that the Host Government has followed appropriate constitutional procedures to make it effective.

█ §11.8 POLITICAL-RISK INSURANCE AND GUARANTEES

Political-risk insurance and guarantees provided by ECAs and DFIs are discussed in Chapter 16.

§11.8.1 Private-Sector Insurance

The private-sector insurance market has been playing an increasing rôle in the provision of political-risk insurance (though no overall statistics are available it is thought that private insurers cover about half of the total market, with ECA/DFI insurance not surprisingly concentrated in the highest-risk countries). This has been helped by cooperation with the public sector, such as through MIGA's CUP program (*cf.* §16.5.4) or coinsurance with OPIC (§16.4.4). Major insurers in the market include AIG, various Lloyds syndicates, and Zurich; overall, more than 20 insurance companies offer political risk coverage of up to $150 million per project, in some cases for terms of up to 15 years.[6] The nature of the coverage reflects that offered by DFIs and ECAs to both investors and lenders. Private-sector insurers may, like some ECAs, require the investor to retain, say, 10% of the insured risk.

The private sector may also offer 'bridging' cover, if it would take too much time until the necessary procedures for ECAs or DFIs to provide coverage have been completed; if the ECA or DFI coverage is never provided, the private-sector coverage continues.

It should be noted that whereas public-sector insurers of political risk, whether of equity or debt, generally require that their presence in the transaction is publicly known (and often require the Host Government to counter indemnify them— *cf.* §16.5.1), private insurers may make it a condition of their insurance's validity that its existence is not revealed, so as avoid any party behaving badly in the knowledge that insurers will pick up the loss.

---

[6] Gallagher London, *Credit and Political Risk: PRI Report & Market Update* (London, January 2013)*

Chapter 12

FINANCIAL STRUCTURING

█ §12.1 INTRODUCTION

This chapter examines some of the main financial-structuring issues likely to arise once the commercial fundamentals and risks of the project have been reviewed as set out in previous Chapters. The chapter is written on the assumption that financing is being provided by commercial banks, but, for the most part, similar principles are followed by the bond market, as well as the other types of private- and public-sector lenders or guarantors discussed in Chapters 15 and 16. Financial structuring would normally proceed in parallel with the financial-modeling process set out in Chapter 13.

Since the Sponsors are the drivers for any project, the investors' point of view is discussed first (§12.2). Then the main elements likely to be dealt with in the negotiations between the Project Company and its lenders on the overall financing structure and terms are reviewed. These are usually include:

- debt-cover ratios (§12.3);
- debt:equity ratio (§12.4);

313

Principles of Project Finance. DOI: http://dx.doi.org/10.1016/B978-0-12-391058-5.00012-6

- debt-service profile (§12.5);
- interest rate and fees (§12.6);
- additional costs (§12.7).

These are all inter-related, so that a change in one requirement will usually lead to a change in one or more of the others. Therefore these interrelated effects need to be taken into account through further 'optimization' of the financial model to produce the most efficient financial structure (§12.8).

It should be borne in mind that there is no merit in innovation for the sake of it in project finance. As is evident, this is a highly complex form of financing, and innovative financing structures may just add to the time and cost of putting the deal together, or be too rigid if something goes wrong, or add extra risks that cannot be foreseen at the beginning. The financial structure should therefore be kept as simple as possible; for example, several different sources of debt should not be used if sufficient finance can be raised from one source, as it is far quicker and easier to deal with one group of lenders (so avoiding intercreditor problems—*cf.* §14.14).

§12.2 INVESTORS' ANALYSIS AND EQUITY STRUCTURE

A minimum Equity IRR is the most usual measure used by Sponsors and other investors to determine whether a project investment is viable from their point of view (§12.2.1). However 'equity' in this context is usually a blend of share capital and subordinated debt (§12.2.2). The timing of the equity investment is important as it affects the investors' return calculations (§12.2.3). Other measures of return on investment may also be used in parallel with the Equity IRR (§12.2.4). The Sponsors may bring in other investors on or before Financial Close (§12.2.5).

§12.2.1 EQUITY IRR

The Equity IRR is calculated based on the cash return on the cash equity investment. So if the equity is invested, say, over a two-year construction period, each sum invested is taken into the IRR calculation (*cf.* §10.2.2) as and when this investment is made.

Similarly, it is not when the Project Company generates cash that matters for this IRR calculation, but when that cash is paid out to investors: there may be a considerable gap between these two points, because the lenders typically require cash to be held back in Reserve Accounts with payments to investors twice a year, based on the half-yearly cash-flow results (*cf.* §14.4.3).

Project-finance investors use the return on their equity investment in the Project Company as their main measure. Investors usually have hurdle rates for their Equity

IRR, above which an investment is acceptable, and below which it is not.[1] The hurdle rate is generally fixed based on:

- *the investor's own weighted cost of capital*;
- *the additional return over cost of capital required for particular types of risk* (which would be influenced by, *e.g.* type of project, location, extent to which risks are hedged by Project Agreements, extent to which the investment adds to or diminishes the spread of risk in the investor's portfolio, *etc.*);
- *market competition*, in cases where the prospective Sponsors are bidding for a project in a public procurement (*cf.* §3.7);[2]
- *project viability*: even if the project is not subject to a competitive bid, the product or service provided should itself be competitive (*cf.* §9.4), which would not be the case if the Equity IRR is too high.

Setting a required return for the risk based on the Project Company's Equity IRR is circular in nature, because the Equity IRR is dependent on the level of leverage, which is itself dependent on the risk: indeed it could be argued that the Equity IRR is simply an arithmetic product of the lenders' Debt Cover Ratios (*cf.* §12.3).

Market rates for Equity IRRs have developed in industries where projects are frequently put out to investors for bidding by governments or Offtakers (*cf.* §3.7), especially process-plant and PPP projects. Equity IRRs in projects with moderate risk, such as a power project with a PPA or an infrastructure project with limited usage risk (such as a Availability-based PPP project), located in low-risk countries, tend to be in the range of 12–15% *p.a.* (pre-tax, and on a nominal basis, *i.e.* including inflation in the cash-flow projections). This is relatively low compared to returns on some other types of equity investment in new ventures, reflecting the lower level of risk: arguably, however, the return is still high considering the limited risk (*cf.* §14.17.1). Higher returns (up to 20% *p.a.*) may be seen in projects with higher risks (*e.g.* traffic risk), in developing countries, or in new project-finance markets generally.

§12.2.2 BLENDED EQUITY IRR

In many projects the shareholders' investment is mainly made by way of a subordinated loan, rather than in share capital. In fact the Project Company's share capital

---

[1] For a discussion on whether a single hurdle/discount rate is appropriate in project finance, *cf.* Benjamin C. Esty, "Improved Techniques for Valuing Large-Scale Projects", *The Journal of Project Finance* (Institutional Investor, New York NY, 1999), Spring 1999 p. 9.

[2] Bid pricing for competitive procurements also has to include recovery of costs on other losing bids— *e.g.* a bidder may assume that it will win one bid in four, which means the costs of the three losing bids will have to be covered by the return on the winning bid.

may be quite minimal, say \$100, with the rest provided as subordinated debt at an interest rate close to the required Equity IRR. The subordinated debt is normally 'stapled' to the equity shares, *i.e.* the proportion in which they are both held cannot be changed and if one is sold the other must also be sold *pro rata*.

This is done for two reasons:

- to avoid the 'Dividend Trap' (*cf.* §13.7.2);
- because interest payments on shareholder-provided debt are tax-deductible for the Project Company, whereas dividend payments on share capital are not (in most countries).

So the normal measurement for investors is actually not the simple Equity IRR, but the 'Blended Equity IRR', *i.e.* the return taking both the return on their shareholding and on their subordinated debt together.

If this structure is used, typically in the early years of the project the Investors receive their return mainly by way of debt service on the subordinated debt, and only in the latter years of the project are substantial dividends paid.

The payment of dividends and debt service on the subordinated debt are collectively known as 'Distributions'. Lenders generally do not concern themselves whether the equity is subscribed in shares or subordinated debt—all Distributions are controlled in the same way (*cf.* §14.4.2).[3]

Because subordinated debt is so common in projects, the lenders are often called the 'senior lenders' to distinguish them from the investors as subordinated lenders (*cf.* §14.14.5).

The Blended Equity IRR is typically calculated post-tax, *i.e.* after allowing for tax paid by the Project Company, but not taking any account of the investors' individual tax positions. However if most of the equity is subscribed as tax-deductible subordinated debt the pre- and post-tax IRRs will be quite similar.

The financial model for the project should not assume that cash is retained if it could be paid out as Distributions. If this is done it will distort the Blended Equity IRR calculation, and any payments based on this (*e.g.* related to Financial Equilibrium—*cf.* §7.6.5). Similarly, if the investors later choose to leave cash in the Project Company rather than pay it out as Distributions this should also be disregarded for calculation purposes.

§12.2.3 TIMING OF EQUITY INVESTMENT

There are several possibilities as to the timing of the equity investment, *i.e.* when the investors' share of the total funding is drawn:

---

[3] Therefore 'Equity IRR' will be used hereafter, even if most of the 'equity' is in fact shareholder subordinated debt.

- before any drawings on the debt finance (*i.e.* at the beginning of the construction phase);
- *pro rata* with drawings on the debt finance (*i.e.* spread throughout the construction phase);
- after any drawings on the debt finance (*i.e.* towards the end of the construction phase).

Most investors calculate their Equity IRR based on cash investment, not on the funds they have at risk but have not yet invested in cash. This means that the later the equity is invested, the higher the Equity IRR, because the investment is being repaid over a shorter period (*cf.* §10.2.3), which makes investment at the end of the construction phase the most attractive in IRR terms.

The only disadvantage of not contributing the equity before debt is that project costs are increased because of the need to fund more IDC. If there is any difficulty in raising the marginal amount of debt funding required for this (*e.g.* because the total funding available is limited, or because only tied funding that does not fund IDC is available), the Sponsors may have to go first.

Lenders would obviously prefer the equity to be invested first, but will not normally object to the debt being drawn first (or *pro rata*) so long as the Sponsors are legally committed to invest the equity, through an Equity Subscription Agreement (*cf.* §3.6.2) and will do so immediately if the project goes into default. Bank guarantees or letters of credit may need to be provided as security for this uncalled equity. Thus the investors' risk is the same whether the equity is invested early or late.

However, certain types of projects do require equity to be invested before any debt is advanced:

- If equity is to be obtained from a public issue of shares, lenders would also not consider it prudent to rely on a future public issue, even if this is underwritten, because such underwriting commitments are likely to have unacceptable qualifications (*e.g.* a provision that the underwriting can fall away in certain market conditions).
- In a project where revenue is being built up gradually as investment is being made in the system (*e.g.* a mobile-phone network), lenders set targets for how much of the system has to be built out with equity funding, and what minimum revenue levels have to be achieved, before any part of the debt is advanced. This approach is suitable when the project does not consist of building one plant, but is a continuous process of investment.

Equity-Bridge Loan. For investors who want to squeeze the maximum IRR benefit out of the timing of their cash equity investment, an 'Equity-Bridge Loan' can be provided by the lenders. This is a loan to the Project Company for the amount of the equity, secured by corporate guarantees from the

Sponsors (so no risk is being taken on the project by the Equity-Bridge Loan lenders). This loan is used to cover the equity share of the project costs, and at the end of the construction phase the real equity is finally paid in and used to repay the bridge facility. If there is an Equity-Bridge Loan this is usually drawn before any senior debt (because it is cheaper).

For example, in the annuity repayment structure financing in Table 12.6 below, it is assumed that the equity is invested at the end of the construction phase, with loan repayments and dividends beginning one year later. In fact, the Equity IRR would only have been as high as the 19% shown in the table if an Equity-Bridge Loan had been used, as otherwise the equity would have to have been invested to cover project costs before the end of the construction phase. If, on the other hand, the equity is assumed to be invested 50% at the start of a 2-year construction phase, and 50% one year into construction, the Equity IRR reduces from 19% to 14%.

Undrawn equity can be taken into the Equity IRR calculation quite easily, by assuming for calculation purposes that it is drawn on day one of the project, and earns a cash return equivalent to the investors' cost of capital until it is in fact drawn by the Project Company. This more accurately measures the return on the investor's real risk—but is not generally used by investors, just as the more accurate MIRR calculation is not used either (*cf.* §10.2.3). The result is that when the boards of Sponsors approve equity investments in projects, this may be based on an exaggerated idea of the equity return.

§12.2.4 OTHER EQUITY-RETURN MEASUREMENTS

Given the problems with using Equity IRR, many investors do not use it as the sole measure of whether an investment should be made in a project-financed transaction. Other measures are used as further checks to ensure that the IRR measure does not recommend an unsuitable investment.

Net Present Value. The investor's 'hurdle rate' of return (as discussed in §12.2.1) can be applied to the cash flows as a discount rate, and if the result is a positive NPV the investment can proceed.

NPV at Risk. It could however be argued that adjusting for risk in the NPV discount rate is an over-simplified approach. Many factors affect the investor's risks, and therefore looking at a range of outcomes could be more realistic. So rather than increasing the hurdle rate for risk it would make more sense to use a 'risk-free' hurdle rate—the investor's own cost of capital—and apply this to a range of risk-based cash-flow scenarios for the project, which can be calculated using Monte-Carlo simulation.[4] This approach, known as 'NPV at Risk', produces a range of probabilities for the NPV outcome, and the investment would be made if the range of highest probability outcomes have an NPV over zero.[5]

Payback Period. In the final analysis 'cash is king' for any investor. So it is relevant to know how fast the investment will be paid back (the 'payback period'). Investors may require that any equity investment also has a maximum payback period of not more than a certain number of years (*i.e.* the length of time that it takes to recover the original cash investment). This is a crude measure—in particular it does not take account of returns after the end of the payback period. None the less, it still provides a useful check against projects which offer a high Equity IRR, but do not produce adequate cash Distributions for a long time.

A refinement of the payback-period calculation is the 'discounted payback' period. This calculates the period of time it takes to recover the original investment, based on the NPV of the future cash flows being discounted at the investor's cost of capital. This takes the time value of money into account as part of the calculation, which the simple method does not.

Table 12.1 gives an example of both methods of calculation. For the payback period calculation, it can be seen that in year 4 the cumulative total of the cash flow become positive. The payback period is therefore $(4 + ((450–200) \div 450)) = 4.6$ years. (Note that a *pro rata* calculation works out the payback timing in year 4.) For the discounted payback calculation the cash flows are discounted at the investor's cost of capital—in this case 8%—and then the payback period is worked out in the same way, producing a discounted payback period of 5.1 years.

---

[4] This is nothing to do with gambling on roulette tables: a Monte-Carlo simulation involves performing a large number of calculations simulating a wide range of possible outcomes to particular risks. The best and worst outcomes of, say, 30 key project variables are defined, and then many different scenarios (*e.g.* up to 10,000) are run in the financial model. The end result will give a range of probabilities of a particular risk occurring, *e.g.* a 90% chance that construction would not be delayed more than 3 months. But of course the calculations still depends on assumptions of the range of outcomes for each scenario. Monte-Carlo simulation may be appropriate for investors when evaluating their equity investment, or for an Offtaker/Contracting Authority to assess its risks. However it is not normally used by lenders, since they are concerned about low-probability high-impact risks (*cf.* §9.2).Specialist software is usually used: *cf.* Mansoor Dailami, Ilya Lipkovich & John Van Dyck, *INFRISK: A computer simulation approach to risk management in infrastructure project finance transactions* (Policy Research Working Paper 2083, World Bank, Washington DC, 1999)*.

[5] S. Ye & R. Tiong. "NPV-at-Risk Method in Infrastructure Project Investment Evaluation" *Journal of Construction Engineering Management*, Vol. 126(3) (American Society of Civil Engineers, 2000), p.227–233.

Table 12.1 Payback and Discounted Payback

	Payback		Discounted Payback (@ 8% discount)	
Year	Cash flow	Cumulative Total	Discounted Cash Flow	Cumulative Total
0	−1,000	−1,000	−1,000	−1,000
1	150	−850	139	−861
2	250	−600	214	−647
3	350	−250	278	−369
4	450	200	331	−38
5	500	700	340	302
6	500	1,200	315	617
	Payback period: 4.6 years		**Discounted payback period: 5.1 years**	

Profit:Investment Ratio.[6] This follows the same methodology as the cost:benefit ratio (*cf.* §10.2.3). It compares the NPV of future cash flows with the initial investment. So in Table 12.1 the NPV of the future cash flows (discounted at 8%) is 1617, and the initial investment is 1000, giving a profit:investment ratio of 1.6:1. An investor can therefore establish a minimum profit:investment ratio as another investment measure, which is more useful than the NPV calculation discussed above for the reasons discussed in §10.2.3.

Operating Margin. As noted in §13.7, companies also inevitably look at how their investment in a project will appear in their published accounts as well as these cash flow-based calculations. A standard measure here is the operating margin, *i.e.* net profit as a percentage of revenues. An investor may therefore require a minimum annual operating margin of, say, 12%, as well as a minimum Equity IRR.

Project IRR. The Project IRR is calculated from the cash flow of the project before debt service and Distributions,[7] measured as a return on the cash investment required (whether debt or equity). This is sometimes done at the early stage of development of a project to check its robustness without taking account of its particular financing structure.

Otherwise, the Project IRR has limited relevance in the project-finance context, where one of the main points of leveraging the project with debt

---

[6] Also known as the 'profitability index'.

[7] Often two calculations are performed, pre- and post-tax.

is to improve the equity return, and so a measurement of the return on the project without leverage is not that relevant. However it can be used as a discount rate to value the project, *e.g.* on early termination (*cf.* §7.10.1). It may also be used by investors who have a portfolio of corporate-financed and project-financed projects, to compare one project with another.

§12.2.5 BRINGING IN NEW INVESTORS AT FINANCIAL CLOSE

A Sponsor developing a project who brings in another investor to commit the required balance of the equity shortly before Financial Close (*cf.* §3.2)[8] expects to be compensated for having assumed the highest risk—*i.e.* having incurred substantial development or bid costs with no certainty of recovery. This can be achieved by requiring the new investor to pay a premium for its shares (a higher price per share than that paid by the Sponsor, or higher than its par value), or crediting the Sponsor with a notional high rate of interest on cash already spent on the project, which is taken into account when calculating the Sponsor's development costs, and allocating shares based on this. The premium will be kept by the Sponsor.

Alternatively, the Sponsor may take money out of the project by charging the Project Company a development fee, which is usually payable at Financial Close. This is in effect an early return on investment. A development fee can thus also be used as an alternative way for one Sponsor to compensate another for taking the development risk. Development fees may be contentious with lenders, but can be acceptable, provided that the original Sponsor's real cash investment has not been effectively reduced to an unacceptably low level by doing this, and obviously also provided that the project can support the corresponding increase in debt.[9]

Equity Funding Competition. In PPP projects, and process-plant projects with a Contracting Authority as Offtaker, an 'Equity Funding Competition' may be held shortly before Financial Close. New investors bid for some of the shares, and the winning bidder will the one paying the highest price over the par value.[10] The benefit of this (*i.e.* the amount paid for the shares over their par value) would either accrue wholly to the Contracting Authority, or be split between the Project Company and the Contracting Authority. (*Cf.* §5.2.3 for debt funding competitions.)

---

[8] For a 'secondary' equity sale after Project Completion, *cf.* §14.17.

[9] Note that the same methods (share allocation or development fee) may be used where there is more than one Sponsor to take account of their differing costs during the development phase.

[10] Alternatively, the competition can be based on the lowest bid for the Equity IRR required by these new shareholders, but this is more complex to implement. In either case the result for the new investors will be an Equity IRR lower than that of the original Sponsors. Also where there is only one Sponsor it can take out a development fee if the lenders are willing to finance this as part of construction costs.

§12.3 DEBT COVER RATIOS

The level of debt that can be raised for a project is based primarily on its projected ability to pay interest and repay loan principal installments as they fall due, with a comfortable margin of safety. To assess this margin of safety, lenders calculate 'Cover Ratios', *i.e.* various ratios between operating cash flow and the level of debt or debt service, namely:

- Annual Debt Service Cover Ratio ('ADSCR') (§12.3.1).
- Loan-Life Cover Ratio ('LLCR') (§12.3.2).
- The averages of the ADSCR and LLCR over the term of the debt (§12.3.3).
- The project-life Cover Ratio ('PLCR') (§12.3.4), or the Reserve Cover Ratio for a natural resources project (§12.3.5).

The higher the Cover Ratios, the greater the margin of safety for lenders. Calculations of Cover Ratios for a typical project are set out in §12.3.6. It should be noted that none of these Cover Ratios can be calculated for a period before the Project Company begins operating, and that the calculations are based on cash flow nor accruals (*e.g.* for tax payments—*cf.* §13.7.4).

§12.3.1 ANNUAL DEBT-SERVICE COVER RATIO

The ADSCR assesses the Project Company's ability to service its debt from its annual cash flow, and is calculated as:

- *Net operating cash flow* of the project over the year—*i.e.* operating revenues less operating expenses—taking account of any Maintenance Reserve Account or similar Reserve Accounts covering anything other than debt service (*cf.* §14.4.1), and ignoring any non-cash items such as accounting depreciation;[11] *divided by*
- *Debt service* of the project over the year—*i.e.* interest payments and principal repayments, ignoring transfers to or from Debt-Service Reserve Accounts.

Thus if operating cash flow for the year is 120, interest payments are 55, and loan repayments are 45, the ADSCR would be 1.2:1 (120 ÷ (55 + 45)).

The ADSCR is usually calculated semiannually, on a rolling annual basis. The ratio can obviously only be calculated when the project has been in operation for a year, although because it may affect the ability to pay dividends (*cf.* §14.4.3), it

---

[11] This looks similar to the 'EBITDA' (earnings before interest, depreciation, and tax) measure used in corporate financing, but is based on cash flow rather than accounting results.

may be calculated for the previous 6 months only for the first period after the project begins operation.

In their initial Base-Case projections (*cf.* §13.9.10), the lenders look at the projected ADSCR for each period throughout the term of the loan and check that this does not fall below their required minimum at any time. The actual ADSCRs are reviewed (and projections of the future ADSCRs may be recalculated) once the project is in operation (*cf.* §14.4.3).

The minimum ADSCR requirement obviously varies between projects, higher-risk projects requiring a high ADSCR, and *vice-versa.* Very approximate levels for standard projects could be:

- 1.20:1 for an Accommodation-based Contract;
- 1.25:1 for a process-plant project with an Offtake Contract;
- 1.50:1 for a natural-resources project with no Offtake Contract;
- 1.75:1 for a transport Concession;
- 2.00:1 for a 'merchant' power plant project with no Offtake Contract or price hedging.

Higher cover levels would be required for a project with non-standard risks, or located in a country with a poor credit risk.

§12.3.2 LOAN-LIFE COVER RATIO

The LLCR is based on a similar calculation, but taken over the whole term of the loan:

- *Projected net operating cash flow* (calculated as for the ADSCR), from the date on which the project is projected to begin operations, to the date on which the loan is repaid, discounted to its NPV at the same interest rate as that assumed for the debt (taking account of any interest swap or other hedging); *divided by*
- *Debt outstanding* on the calculation date, less the balance of Debt-Service Reserve Accounts (*cf.* §14.4.1); other Reserve Accounts should not normally be included in the calculation.

It may be argued that free cash balances (*i.e.* not in any Reserve Accounts) should either be deducted from the debt in the LLCR calculation, or added to the NPV of cash flow. (The former is better for the Project Company and the latter for the lenders.) But if these balances are intended to be used for Distributions, it is doubtful whether they should be counted in.

The minimum initial LLCR requirement in Banking Case projections for 'standard' projects is around 10% higher than the figures shown above for minimum ADSCR.

Apart from the initial LLCR on Project Completion, the LLCR may be recalculated throughout the rest of the project life, comparing the projected operating cash flow for the remainder of the loan terms with the remaining loan outstanding on the calculation date.

LLCR is a useful measure for the initial assessment of a project's ability to service its debt as a whole and for continuing to look at it over its remaining life, but clearly it is not so useful if there are likely to be significant cash flow fluctuations from year to year. ADSCR is thus a more significant measure of a Project Company's ability to service its debt as it falls due.

§12.3.3 AVERAGE ADSCR AND LLCR

If the projected ADSCR from year to year is at the same level, the average ADSCR will be the same as the LLCR. However, if the ADSCR is higher in the earlier years, the average ADSCR will be higher than the LLCR, and *vice-versa*. Therefore, average ADSCR is sometimes given more weight by lenders than LLCR as a long-term measure of coverage; if so, the minimum requirements are likely to be similar to those for the LLCR.

The average LLCR (*i.e.* recalculating the LLCR every 6 months for the remainder of the loan, and then taking the average of these figures) is also used as a measure by some lenders, although its usefulness is perhaps questionable.

§12.3.4 PROJECT-LIFE COVER RATIO

Another point that lenders check is whether the project has capacity to make repayments after the original final maturity of the debt, in case there have been difficulties in repaying all of the debt in time. This extra debt-service capacity is known as the debt 'Tail',[12] and lenders normally expect at least a year or two of cash-flow cover in this way. This is achieved by ensuring that the Project Agreement runs for a period of x years after the scheduled final debt-repayment date, so providing a Debt Tail of x, during which the cash flow continues to provide the lenders with extra security.

The extra security to lenders provided by the Debt Tail can be calculated using the Project-Life Cover Ratio ('PLCR'); here the net operating cash flow before debt service for the whole life of the project (not just the term of the debt as for the LLCR) is discounted to its NPV, and this figure is divided by the debt outstanding. Obviously the PLCR will be higher than the LLCR; lenders may wish to see it around 15–20% higher than the minimum ADSCR.

---

[12] Also known as the Residual Cushion.

§12.3.5 RESERVE-COVER RATIO

In natural-resources projects, the PLCR (in this context usually called the Reserve-Cover Ratio) is of more importance, because of the specific requirement in such projects for a Reserve Tail (*i.e.* proven reserves of the commodity concerned that remain to be extracted over a period after the loan term—*cf.* §9.8.4).

A standard rule of thumb is that the Reserve-Cover ratio should be 2:1, based on the lenders' conservative projection of commodity prices, and obviously not less than 1:1 in a downside price projection.

§12.3.6 CALCULATING COVER RATIOS

Table 12.2 sets out cover-ratio calculations for a typical project, with:

- a level annual cash flow before debt service of 220;
- 1000 loan, repaid in equal annual principal installments over 10 years;
- interest rate on the loan of 10% *p.a.* (= NPV discount rate).

If it is assumed that the project generates 200 *p.a.* of cash for a further 3 years' 'tail' period after the end of the loan (*i.e.* years 11–13), the NPV of the total 12 year cash flow is 1499, and so the initial PLCR is 1.50:1 (1499 ÷ 1000).

Table 12.2 Cover-Ratio Calculations

Year:	0	1	2	3	4	5	6	7	8	9	10
(a) Operating cash flow		220	220	220	220	220	220	220	220	220	220
(b) NPV of (a) @ 10% discount	1352	1267	1174	1071	958	834	697	547	382	200	
(c) Loan repayments		100	100	100	100	100	100	100	100	100	100
(d) Loan outstanding	1000	900	800	700	600	500	400	300	200	100	0
(e) Interest payments		100	90	80	70	60	50	40	30	20	10
(f) Total debt service [(c) + (e)]		200	190	180	170	160	150	140	130	120	110
ADSCR [(a) ÷ (f)]		*1.10*	*1.16*	*1.22*	*1.29*	*1.38*	*1.47*	*1.57*	*1.69*	*1.83*	*2.00*
Average ADSCR		*1.47*	*1.51*	*1.56*	*1.60*	*1.66*	*1.71*	*1.77*	*1.84*	*1.92*	
LLCR [(b) ÷ (d)]	*1.35*	*1.41*	*1.47*	*1.53*	*1.60*	*1.67*	*1.74*	*1.82*	*1.91*	*2.00*	
Average LLCR	*1.65*	*1.68*	*1.72*	*1.75*	*1.79*	*1.83*	*1.87*	*1.91*	*1.95*	*2.00*	

Effect of Taxes. One issue in calculation of these ratios is whether tax payments should be deducted from the net cash flow before debt service, especially when calculating the ADSCR, since a variation in interest payments also affects the tax payments. It may be prudent to do this if there are wide variations in taxes paid between one year and another (for example, because of the effect of accelerated tax depreciation allowances), which should be taken into account. The argument against this is that taxes are only paid after deductions for interest costs, which are not included in the operating cash-flow figure; also, significant fluctuations in tax between one year and the next can be dealt with by placing cash in a Tax Reserve Account (*cf.* §14.4.1). However, so long as the inclusion or exclusion of taxes is taken into account when deciding what the ratio level should be, and dealt with consistently, the choice of approach is not too important.[13]

Project Finance *vs*. Corporate Finance. It should be noted that, unlike in corporate loans, the cash-flow Cover Ratio for annual interest[14] (as opposed to total Debt Service) is not generally considered a significant measurement. This is because corporate loans are often renewed, whereas project finance loans have to be repaid because the project has a finite life; therefore, the Project Company must be able to reduce its debt each year as scheduled, and payment of interest alone is generally not adequate. Similarly, corporate-finance 'accounting' ratios such as the current or liquid ratio are generally not used in project finance—short-term liquidity is dealt with through the establishment of Reserve Accounts (*cf.* §14.4.1).

§12.3.7 Minimum Cover Ratios and Debt Amount

Cover Ratios are often a key factor in determining how much debt a project can raise. This is illustrated in Table 12.3. This assumes that a project produces 1,000 *p.a.* of net cash flow before debt service, over a 25-year period. If the lenders require a minimum 1.50:1 ADSCR, this means that debt service cannot be more than 667 (1,000 ÷ 1.50) *p.a.* This means that, assuming the debt service is repaid on an annuity basis (*cf.* §12.5.3), at an interest rate of 6% *p.a.*, 8,522 of debt can be raised against this project cash flow (*i.e.* paying back 8,522 of debt on an annuity basis over 25 years at an interest rate of 6% costs 667 *p.a.*). However if the required ADSCR is reduced to 1.25, this means that the maximum annual debt service increases to 800, and thus the debt can also be increased to 10,227 while still observing the required minimum ADSCR.

---

[13] *Cf.* §12.2.4 for a similar issue on calculating the Project IRR.

[14] Known as 'interest cover', *i.e.* the ratio of EBITDA to interest payable.

Table 12.3 Minimum Cover Ratio—Effect on Maximum Debt

Debt Term		25 years	
Interest Rate		6%	
(a) Annual project cash flow (pre-debt service)		1,000 *p.a.*	
(b) **Annual Debt-Service Cover Ratio**		**1.50**	**1.25**
Maximum annual debt service	[(a) ÷ (b)]	667	800
Maximum debt		**8,522**	**10,227**

§12.4 DEBT:EQUITY RATIO

As already discussed, a high ratio of debt is the essence of project finance. Within prudent limits, therefore, Sponsors wish to limit the amount of equity they invest in a project, and thus to raise the maximum level of debt.

The Cover Ratios discussed above, especially ADSCR, are a key factor in determining how much debt a project can raise (and hence how much equity will be required if there is no other source of finance for the project's costs), and therefore lenders typically work backwards from the Cover-Ratio calculations to set the debt:equity ratio, rather than pre-fixed debt:equity ratio.

Having said this, the debt:equity ratios which result from Cover-Ratio calculations reflect the risks of the project (the higher the required Cover Ratio the greater the safety margin for lenders, but as Table 12.3 illustrates the lower the amount of debt which can be raised), and so projects with greater risk have lower debt:equity ratios, *e.g.*:

- 90:10 for an Accommodation-based Contract;
- 85:15 for a process-plant project with an Offtake Contract;
- 80:20 for a transport Concession;
- 70:30 for a 'merchant' power plant project with no Offtake Contract or price hedging
- 50:50 for a natural resources project.

It should also be borne in mind that the debt:equity ratio is not a constant figure. In fact the set ratios above only apply at one time in the project's life, *i.e.* on Project Completion. Thereafter the debt is being regularly repaid (more slowly than the equity, which is 'repaid' over the full term of the Project Agreement, including the Debt Tail period), and so the proportion of debt will reduce over the project life, eventually reaching zero—all being well—at the beginning of the 'Debt Tail' period.

§12.4.1 CALCULATION OF DEBT:EQUITY RATIO

Once the debt:equity ratio has been fixed, the lenders will require this ratio to be adhered to. The point at which the Project Company is normally required to demonstrate that it has met this required debt:equity ratio (assuming that debt and equity are not being drawn down *pro rata—cf.* §12.2.3) is the later of Project Completion, or the date on which no further drawings can be made on the debt (which may be up to 6 months after Project Completion).

The calculation is based on the cash injections of debt and equity, not whatever appears on the balance sheet, and if more than one currency is being used for funding, the calculation should be based on the exchange rate between these currencies at Financial Close (*cf.* §10.5.6).

§12.4.2 CONTINGENCY FINANCING

It is preferable for the Project Company to have contingency financing available to cover any unexpected additional project costs during the construction phase (*cf.* §9.5.6). This is normally provided as additional equity and debt, usually in the same ratio as the Base-Case equity and debt. If this contingency financing is needed, it is drawn after the Base-Case equity and debt is fully drawn.

Sponsors normally have no liability to invest any further funds in addition to the contingent equity if the project gets into trouble; that is what non-recourse funding to the Project Company implies.

Contingent debt and equity finance usually remains available for drawing only until shortly after Project Completion. Contingent risks during operations are covered by Reserve Accounts (*cf.* §14.4.1).

§12.4.3 100% CONTINGENT EQUITY

Taking the principle of an Equity-Bridge Loan (*cf.* §12.2.3) further, funding beyond the construction phase might continue to be provided only as debt, with the equity committed purely on a contingent basis (*i.e.* to be drawn if required). Such a use of contingent equity:

- reduces the Project Company's cost of funding, assuming that investors are willing to accept a lower level of IRR or NPV than they would have obtained from a cash investment of equity (logically this would be the 'hurdle rate' Equity IRR (*cf.* §12.2.1), less the investors' cost of capital);
- avoids the need for the Project Company to be capitalized with equity at a level to meet the worst conceivable scenario—which may never occur—and so again makes its financial cost base more competitive.

This approach has only been used in a limited way in the project finance market to date. It should be noted that cash-based IRR and NPV calculations are not appropriate for investors in this scenario as they do not take account of amounts that are at risk but not drawn in cash (*cf.* §12.2.3), and the Cover-Ratio problem discussed in §12.4.4 would apply in such cases. Similarly, if the investors provide a standby commitment to invest equity if there are cost overruns or the Project Company's cash flow is inadequate (*cf.* §9.13), this is not reflected in a IRR calculation. One key issue would be what security is offered to lenders that the equity will in fact be invested when called upon—this may require the backing of a bank letter of credit.

§12.4.4 PROJECTS WITHOUT EQUITY

If a project has a high degree of certainty in its cash flow (thanks to a Project Agreement that transfers the price and demand risks) and high ADSCRs and LLCR, arithmetically it might need no equity at all and still have enough cash flow to support 100% debt financing. Generally however, lenders wish the Sponsors to be at risk with a reasonable amount of equity in the project, and—given the requirement for Cover Ratios—arithmetically speaking there must always be surplus cash flow above that required for debt service, that must be used somehow—and the obvious use is paying an equity return. Moreover it is important that the Sponsors have an investment at risk during the construction phase, and if there are no Sponsors, who is to manage the project?

Some projects have been financed with 'pinpoint' equity (*i.e.* a nominal amount of equity), but these are exceptional. One example is not-for-profit projects using the U.S. 63–20 bonds (*cf.* §4.3.1). They usually arise when an existing cash flow is being fed into a new PPP project—*e.g.* construction of a new bridge alongside an existing one, where the Project Company has the benefit of already established cash flow from traffic tolls on the old bridge, as well as charging tolls on the new one. In effect, the existing cash flow is the equity in the project. In such cases the surplus cash required for the Cover Ratios (*cf.* §12.8) may be used for debt prepayment, with the project being transferred back to the Contracting Authority when the debt has all been paid off.

§12.5 DEBT SERVICE PROFILE

Debt service (*i.e.* loan interest payments and principal repayments) is one of the biggest factors in the financing structure that influences an investor's rate of return.

The faster investors in a Project Company are paid dividends and other Distributions, the better their rate of return. Investors therefore do not wish too much cash flow from operation of the project to be devoted to repayments to lenders, at the expense of these Distributions. Lenders, on the other hand, generally wish to be repaid as rapidly as possible. Striking a reasonable balance between these conflicting demands is an important part of the loan negotiations.

The issues that come up in negotiating the debt repayment schedule are:

- the term of the financing (§12.5.1);
- its average life (§12.5.2);
- the repayment schedule (§12.5.3);
- flexibility in repayment (§12.5.4).

§12.5.1 TERM OF FINANCING

In general, project-finance debt is much longer in term (repayment period) than normal bank loans;[15] a power project may have a 2- to 3-year drawdown period during construction, and then 15 years of repayment, giving a total term of 17–18 years; an infrastructure project finance may be for 25 years or more. Financing for natural resources and telecommunications projects is usually shorter in term, however, taking account of the shorter life cycle of such projects: *e.g.* a mining loan may be as short as five years (but another factor here is that the leverage is usually around 50:50, so there is less debt to pay off). Of course this depends on there being a financing market which is able and willing to provide the necessary term of debt (*cf.* §17.2).

The term of the financing depends mainly on the long-term certainty of the cash flow of the project, taking into account the need for a Debt Tail (*cf.* §7.2.3; §12.3.4): thus a Project Company with a 20-year Project Agreement may aim to raise debt for 17–19 years.

The Cover Ratios are of course affected by the debt-service schedule; the shorter the term the higher the debt-service payments, and the lower the ADSCRs and LLCR will become, and so if the debt is made too short-term it cannot be supported by the cash flow.

Another factor that may affect the financing term is the location of the project; if it is in a high-risk country, the term of the financing will usually be shorter than the same project in a low-risk country.

The notional term of the financing may be lengthened by the use of a 'Cash Sweep' arrangement (*cf.* §14.4.3).

---

[15] The term of a loan, or a contract, is also referred to as its 'tenor'.

§12.5.2 AVERAGE LIFE

Apart from the overall term of the loan, lenders also look at the repayment schedule to assess how rapidly their risk reduces over the term. There is obviously a considerable difference in risk between a loan of 1000 repaid in 100 installments over 10 years, and a loan of 1000 repaid in one bullet installment at the end of 10 years.

Lenders may have an average-life limitation (*i.e.* maximum average life) as part of their overall credit policy towards project-finance loans, and so it may be necessary for investors' Distributions to be slowed down, and debt service speeded up, to maintain the required average life.

The average life is measured by looking at the loan's average life, which is used by lenders in a similar way to the payback-period calculation by investors (*cf.* §12.2.4), *i.e.* a check to ensure that the repayment schedule is not overextended. This can be calculated in a variety of ways:

- based on the period of time until half the loan has been repaid; thus if a loan of 4 is repaid over 4 years in annual installments of 1, the average life would be 2 years, because at that point half the loan has been repaid; or
- weighting the loan principal outstanding for each year, by adding these together, and then dividing by the original loan amount; thus for the same loan the average life on this basis would be 2½ years ($[4 + 3 + 2 + 1] \div 4$); or
- weighting the repayments, by multiplying each installment by the number of years outstanding, and dividing by the loan amount; for the same loan this calculation would be $[((1 \times 1) + (1 \times 2) + (1 \times 3) + (1 \times 4)) \div 4]$ which of course produces the same result.

A weighting calculation is more appropriate because it takes account of the repayment schedule. Suppose the loan of 4 was repaid as 2 at the end of year 2, and 2 at the end of year 4: the simple calculation would still give this an average life of 2 years, the same as with 4 annual repayments of 1, but the weighted calculation would give an average life of 3 years $[((2 \times 2) + (2 \times 4)) \div 4]$, so making it clear that it has a longer weighted average life than the loan repaid by equal annual installments.

However, this calculation is made more complex in a project-finance context, as project finance loans are drawn down over a period of time, during the project's construction phase—so in such a case how long is each drawing outstanding, and how can this be averaged?

There are three ways of dealing with this:

- Ignore the drawdown period and look only at the average life of the repayment (which is how ECAs calculate it under the OECD Consensus—*cf.* §16.2.3).

Table 12.4 Average Life with Construction Period

	Drawing	Loan Outstanding
Year 1	2.0	2.0
Year 2	2.0	4.0
Year 3	–1.0	3.0
Year 4	–1.0	2.0
Year 5	–1.0	1.0
Year 6	–1.0	0.0
Total loan outstandings		12.0
Average life (12.0 ÷ 4)		**3 years**

- Add the whole drawdown period onto the calculation of the average life of the repayment period, the argument for this being that the lenders are on risk for the whole of their loan during the drawdown period. Thus if the loan of 4, with annual repayments of 1, were drawn down over 2 years and then repaid in equal installments over the following 4, its weighted average life would be 4½ years (2 years' drawdown plus the 2½ years' weighted average life for the repayment as calculated above).
- Using the weighted loan-principal outstanding method, with the denominator of the calculation being the peak loan principal outstanding (though this becomes rather problematical if the loan principal outstandings revolve, *i.e.* go up and down because they are being drawn, repaid from some other cash flow source, and then drawn again). So if the loan of 4 is drawn over a 2-year construction phase in 2 installments at the end of each year, and is repaid in 4 annual installments of 1, the average life is 3 years, as shown in Table 12.4 (which can be compared to 4½ years calculated as above, based on the whole drawdown period).

§12.5.3 REPAYMENT SCHEDULE

Loan repayments usually begin around 6 months after the construction of the project is complete,[16] and are usually made at 6-monthly intervals. Where bond financing is used, a sinking fund may be built up to repay the whole amount of the bond on its

---

[16] The period from the signing of the loan until repayments are due is known as the 'grace period', so the lenders may offer, say, a 20 year loan with 3 years' grace, this grace period being normally calculated to cover the construction period and 6 months thereafter, as indicated above.

final maturity rather than making repayments in installments, but this obviously adds to the financing cost and is not common in the project-finance bond market. Hence project-finance bonds are normally amortized (repaid) in a similar way to loans.

As to the repayment structure, it might be thought that the fairest way to deal with lenders, assuming the project's cash flow is reasonably even over time (*cf.* §7.3.2), would be to repay the financing in equal installments (*e.g.* if the debt is 1000, and it is being repaid over 10 years, repayments would be 100 *p.a.* In fact, this repayment structure, although not uncommon, is disadvantageous to the investors in the Project Company, as far more of the cash flow is being paid out to the lenders in the early years of the loan because the interest payments are relatively high at this stage. It also leaves the project with lower ADSCRs in the early years, just at the time when project cash flow is more likely to be affected by start-up problems. The standard approach is therefore to use an annuity repayment structure, which keeps principal and interest payments level throughout the loan term.

This can be illustrated by the simplified examples in Table 12.5 and Table 12.6, which have the following common assumptions:

- project cost: 1250;
- debt:equity ratio: 80:20;
- loan amount: 1000;
- repayment: 10 years, annually in arrears;
- interest rate: 10% *p.a.*;
- equity amount: 250;
- cash flow before debt service and dividend payments: 220 *p.a.*;
- cash flow after debt service is all paid out to investors;
- residual value of the project: nil;
- investors' NPV discount rate (cost of capital): 12%;
- investors' reinvestment rate (for MIRR calculation): 12% *p.a.*;
- the calculation ignores any construction period.

An immediate and obvious problem with the level principal payment structure is that the annual debt service in year 1 (200) is almost double that of year 10 (110), and correspondingly the ADSCR is 1.10:1 (too low for comfort) in year 1, and 2.00:1 (much higher than needed) in year 10.

Investors' Distributions, on the other hand, are heavily back-ended, with dividends increasing by 5½ times between year 1 and year 10; it takes nearly 6 years to pay back the original investment.

The benefits from the change in repayment to an annuity structure are self-evident: the ADSCR is a comfortable 1.35:1 throughout, thanks to the level debt service payments, the same as the LLCR.

The dividends are also level throughout, and although the total dividends received by the investors over the life of project reduce from 650 to 573 (because more interest

Table 12.5 Effect of Level Principal Payments

Year:	0	1	2	3	4	5	6	7	8	9	10
(a) Project cash flow		220	220	220	220	220	220	220	220	220	220
Lenders' viewpoint											
(b) Loan repayments		100	100	100	100	100	100	100	100	100	100
(c) Loan outstanding (year end)	1000	900	800	700	600	500	400	300	200	100	0
(d) Interest payments		100	90	80	70	60	50	40	30	20	10
(e) Total debt service [(b) + (d)]		200	190	180	170	160	150	140	130	120	110
ADSCR [(a) ÷ (e)]		1.10	1.16	1.22	1.29	1.38	1.47	1.57	1.69	1.83	2.00
Average ADSCR		1.47	1.51	1.56	1.60	1.66	1.71	1.77	1.84	1.92	
LLCR [NPV((a) ÷ (c))]	1.35	1.41	1.47	1.53	1.60	1.67	1.74	1.82	1.91	2.00	
Average life of loan	5½ years										
Investors' viewpoint											
Equity investment:	250										
Dividends [(a) – (e)]		20	30	40	50	60	70	80	90	100	110
NPV of investment	66										
Equity IRR	16.6%										
Equity MIRR	14.6%										
Payback period	c. 6 years										

Table 12.6 Effect of Annuity Repayments

Year:	0	1	2	3	4	5	6	7	8	9	10
(a) Project cash flow		220	220	220	220	220	220	220	220	220	220
Lenders' viewpoint											
(b) loan repayments		63	69	76	84	92	101	111	122	134	148
(c) Loan outstanding (year end)	1000	937	868	792	709	617	516	405	282	148	0
(d) Interest payments		100	94	87	79	71	62	52	40	28	15
(e) Total debt service [(b) + (d)]		163	163	163	163	163	163	163	163	163	163
ADSCR [(a) ÷ (e)]		1.35	1.35	1.35	1.35	1.35	1.35	1.35	1.35	1.35	1.35
Average ADSCR		1.35	1.35	1.35	1.35	1.35	1.35	1.35	1.35	1.35	
LLCR [NPV((a) ÷ (c))]	1.35	1.35	1.35	1.35	1.35	1.35	1.35	1.35	1.35	1.35	
Average life of loan	6¼ years										
Investors' viewpoint											
Equity investment:	250										
Dividends [(a) − (e)]		57	57	57	57	57	57	57	57	57	57
NPV of investment	74										
Equity IRR	18.8%										
Equity MIRR	14.9%										
Payback period	4½ years										

is being paid to lenders), the investors' IRR improves from 16.6% to 18.8%; however, the improvement in MIRR (a fairer reflection of the picture) is more limited, from 14.6% to 14.9%. The payback period reduces significantly, to within 4½ years.

The repayment structure is relatively more important to the investors than the interest rate on the debt. If, in this example, the lenders offered to reduce their interest rate by 0.25% in return for a level principal payment structure instead of an annuity repayment, the IRR benefit of this to the investors would be 0.6% *p.a.*, whereas in the annuity-repayment structure it is worth an extra 2.2% *p.a.* Similarly, it is likely to be worth paying a higher rate of interest to obtain longer term financing, if there is sufficient cash flow 'tail' to allow this.

However, an annuity repayment structure considerably increases the debt service payments and so reduces the ADSCR in the later years of the project. It also increases the average life of the debt: in Table 12.5, it is 5½ years, whereas in Table 12.6 it is just over 6¼ years.

If there is more uncertainty about the later cash flows from the project, lenders may look for higher Cover Ratios and a shorter average life than can be achieved with an annuity repayment. A compromise between level principal payments and annuity repayments may need to be agreed to in such cases.

On the other hand, if the project is projected to produce higher cash flows in the later years, a repayment schedule with loan installments being paid even more slowly than an annuity structure but with adequate annual Cover Ratios could be feasible, although lenders resist too much back-ending of repayments and hence an unduly long average life for their loan.

If irregular cash flows are projected, the loan repayments can also be structured on an irregular schedule such that the same level of ADSCRs are maintained throughout the loan term (this is known as a 'sculptured' repayment schedule). This may be necessary, for example, if there is a large maintenance cost in one year, or if after-tax cash flows in later years decrease because deferred taxes start becoming payable if the Project Company has benefited from accelerated tax depreciation on its assets in the early years of operation, assuming that these 'blips' are not smoothed out by advance payments in Reserve Accounts (*cf.* §14.4.1).

These considerations are not only relevant to the investors: the debt repayment structure clearly affects the cost of the Project Company's products or services and may be a crucial factor if Sponsors are in a competitive-bidding situation for a prospective project.

§12.5.4 FLEXIBLE REPAYMENT

To provide the Project Company with some room to maneuver if a temporary cash-flow problem occurs (especially when the project is just beginning operations), lenders may agree to a 'target and minimum' repayment structure. Two repayment schedules are agreed to: one is the level that the lenders actually wish to achieve if

Table 12.7 Target and Minimum Repayments

Repayment No	Target Repayments		Minimum Repayments		Difference
	Repayment	Loan Outstanding	Repayment	Loan Outstanding	
0	—	1000	—	1000.0	0.0
1	50	950	—	1000.0	50.0
2	50	900	52.6	947.4	47.4
3	50	850	52.6	894.7	44.7
4	50	800	52.6	842.1	42.1
5	50	750	52.6	789.5	39.5
... etc.					
18	50	100	52.6	105.3	5.3
19	50	50	52.6	52.6	2.6
20	50	0	52.6	0.0	0.0

the project operates as expected (*i.e.* the 'target repayments'), and one is the minimum level of repayment required to avoid a default by the Project Company. For example, if the target repayments for a 10-year loan of 1000 are 20 equal semi-annual installments, the minimum schedule could be calculated as in Table 12.7.

If the Project Company has cash flow available, it must make a repayment sufficient to bring the loan outstanding down to the target schedule, but if not, it must at least achieve the minimum schedule. As can be seen in Table 12.7, the two schedules differ by one loan repayment (50) to begin with, this loan repayment being spread over the remaining 19 payments in the minimum schedule. The loan outstanding in each schedule becomes closer and closer to the original schedule as time goes on so that final repayment is achieved at the same time on both schedules; thus at the end of the first 6 months the whole 50 of repayment can be deferred, while only 2.6 of the penultimate repayment can be deferred. This gives the Project Company 6 months' room to maneuver at the beginning of the project's operation, when things are likely to go wrong because of so-called 'teething troubles'.

§12.6 INTEREST RATE AND FEES

The main financing costs payable by the Project Company are:

- if the loan is on a floating interest-rate basis, the base interest rate (*e.g.* LIBOR) plus the interest margin (§12.6.1), together with net payments under an interest-rate swap (*cf.* §10.3.1); or

- if the loan (or bond) is on a fixed rate basis, the interest rate (§12.6.1); and
- advisory, arranging and underwriting fees (§12.6.2);
- commitment fees (§12.6.3);
- agency and security trustee fees (§12.6.4);
- lenders advisors' fees (*cf.* §9.5.6);
- credit rating agency's fees if the debt is rated (*cf.* §5.3.1).

§12.6.1 INTEREST RATE

International project-finance loans at a floating rate based on LIBOR typically have interest margins in the range of 2–3.5% over LIBOR.[17] Pricing is usually higher until Project Completion, reflecting the higher risk of this stage of the project, then drops down, and then gradually climbs back again over time. Thus in a project with a loan covering a 2-year construction and 15-year operation phase, the margin might be 2.5% for years 1–2, 2% for years 3–7, 2.25% for years 8–13, and 2.5% for years 14–17.[18] (This is known as a 'margin ratchet'.) Where a floating-rate margin applies, interest-rate hedging will also be put in place (*cf.* §10.3).

Many banks now split the quoted margin internally between two factors—the balance sheet/liquidity effect of the loan (*cf.* §17.3), and the charge for the credit risk. The latter is retained by the project-finance department while the former is paid to the bank's treasury department (which deals with raising the necessary finance for the loan portfolio).

If fixed-rate lending is being provided by an ECA or DFI on a subsidized or noncommercial basis (*cf.* Chapter 16), the rate may reflect the cost of funds for a AAA borrower plus a small margin to cover administration costs, and a further margin to cover risk.,

The coupon rates for other types of fixed-rate lending, including bonds, are based on similar factors to those that affect the pricing of interest-rate swaps (*cf.* §10.3.1). Bond coupon pricing is usually quoted as a margin over the current yield of a government bond with a similar maturity to the average life of the debt, and reflecting the current yields at which similar bonds are already trading in the market.

§12.6.2 ARRANGING AND UNDERWRITING FEES

Arranging and underwriting fees charged by bank lead arrangers are derived from several factors:

- the size and complexity of the financing;
- the time and work involved in structuring the financing;

---

[17] Margins increased substantially (by around a factor of 2–3 times) after the financial crisis of 2008 (*cf.* §17.2).

[18] Margins are sometimes quoted in 'basis points', *i.e.* 1/100th of a percent (0.01%). So a margin of 2.5% would be 250 basis points.

- the risk that a success-based fee may not be earned because the project does not go ahead. So that, to some extent, the successful deals subsidize the failed ones);
- the bank's overall return targets for work of this kind (bearing competitive pressure in mind), taking into account both the fees earned and the return on the loan balance that it keeps on its own books;
- the length of time the underwriting bank has to carry any syndication risk (*cf.* §5.2.8)—for a variety of reasons there can often be a considerable time lag between the signing of loan documentation and hence underwriting, and syndication to other participating banks in the project finance market;
- the proportion of the fee that has to be reallowed to sub-underwriting, 'club' or participating banks to induce them to join the financing (which is itself a function of the time the participating bank spends reviewing it, the overall return the market requires for the risk, taking interest margin and fees together into account, and perhaps competition from other transactions in the market at the same time).

Roughly speaking, the overall level of fees is about the same percentage as the interest margin. If the arranging bank is also acting as financial advisor, this may increase the fees by around 1%.

The considerations affecting bond arranging and underwriting fees are much the same, except that the investment bank underwriting the transaction does not usually intend to retain the bonds in its own portfolio and therefore does not take this into account in assessing return; also, the period of risk on the bond underwriting is much shorter than for a bank syndication (*cf.* §5.3.1). Bond underwriting fees are therefore significantly lower than those for comparable loans.

§12.6.3 COMMITMENT FEES

Commitment fees are paid on the available but undrawn portion of bank debt during the construction phase (*i.e.* so long as drawings may be made on the loan). In project-finance loans commitment fees are usually around half the interest margin. As most project-finance loans are drawn very slowly (taking 2–3 years in most cases) banks need the commitment fee to give them a reasonable rate of return on their risk during the construction of the project. (Commitment fees do not apply to bonds or a loan drawn immediately after it is signed.)

§12.6.4 AGENCY FEES

Finally there are the agency fees payable to the agent bank or security trustee (*cf.* §5.2.9). The time that a bank has to spend on agency work can be quite considerable, and it is in the Project Company's interests to ensure that a reasonable annual agency fee covers this work adequately, but this fee should be based on a fair assessment of costs, not a major source of extra profit for the agent.

§12.7 ADDITIONAL COSTS

Lenders are also exposed to the possibility of additional lending costs, the risk of which is generally passed to the Project Company, arising from:

- withholding tax on interest payments (§12.7.1);
- additional regulatory costs (§12.7.2);
- market disruption (§12.7.3).

§12.7.1 WITHHOLDING TAX ON INTEREST PAYMENTS

The Project Company may be required to deduct local income taxes on payments of interest to lenders outside the country. In this situation banks normally require the Project Company to 'gross up' its interest payments (*i.e.* increase them by an amount sufficient to produce the amount of net interest payment to the bank after deduction of tax, so for example if the interest payment is 100, and the withholding tax is 10%, the Project Company has to increase the interest payment to 111, then deduct 11 as the 10% withholding tax, so paying 100 net to the bank).

A bank may agree that if it can able to offset this amount of tax against its other tax liabilities in its country of operations (where there is a relevant tax treaty with the Project Company's country), the withholding will be refunded to the Project Company. However, banks are not prepared to get into debates about how they manage their tax affairs (*i.e.* they may use other tax offsets and so can't use the tax credit that would arise from the withholding tax), and therefore any refund relies entirely on a bank's good faith.

This issue is not peculiar to the project-finance market, and withholding tax is treated the same on all types of bank loan; however interest payments should only be increased to cover the banks actually affected, not the whole syndicate. Similar issues apply with respect to bonds.

Withholding tax on investors' dividends or subordinated loan interest is discussed in §13.7.6.

§12.7.2 MANDATORY COSTS

A further sum is often payable to commercial-bank lenders for the 'mandatory costs' which they incur by making the loan.[19] These payments are specific to the particular market in which the lender concerned operates: to take London as an example, these consist of:

---

[19] Also known as minimum liquidity requirements (MLRs) or minimum liquid asset requirements (MLAs)—not to be confused with the different meaning of MLAs in §16.5. However these terms are not appropriate in cases where the costs do not just relate to the bank maintaining liquidity.

- *Bank of England costs*: The Bank of England requires banks to place a non interest-bearing deposit equal (in mid-2012) to 0.18% of their 'eligible liabilities', which include net interbank borrowing. So loans are charged a proportional cost equal to the opportunity cost of having to place a further deposit when the loan is drawn. (There are similar provisions for banks lending from the Eurozone in relation to deposits they have to place with the European Central Bank.)
- *FSA fee*: Banks were charged a fee to cover the cost of running the Financial Services Authority (now abolished and partially merged into the Bank of England), and again the *pro rata* cost of this was added to the interest cost.

The extra sums payable resulting from these provisions should be very small, *e.g.* a 0.02% addition to the interest rate. The provisions also require payment of any future increased or additional costs resulting from changes in regulations affecting the lenders.[20]

§12.7.3 MARKET DISRUPTION

Commercial-bank lenders also require standard 'market disruption' provisions in their long-term floating-rate loans. This could arise if lenders cannot renew their short-term (*e.g.* LIBOR-based) funding due to disruption in the market—which could mean that if, say, LIBOR is no longer quoted another pricing basis has to be used, or if the lenders cannot fund at all, that the loan must (in theory) be repaid.

If one or two lenders get into trouble because of their own rather than general market problems, these provisions do not apply, but the intercreditor documentation may include provisions to cover a 'Defaulting Lender', *i.e.* a bank which does not fund its participation in the loan when a drawing is made (*cf.* §14.14.6).

§12.8 OPTIMIZING THE FINANCIAL STRUCTURE

The various financial structuring activities set out above are not independent of each other. A process of 'optimization' of the financial model is carried out by the Sponsors' financial advisor, to find the best possible structuring combination to produce the best equity IRR, or the best bid in a public procurement.

This process is illustrated, in simplified form, in Table 12.8.

Case 1 assumes a project cost of 1,000, that the lenders will lend up to 95% of the cost, but also require a 1.35:1 ADSCR. The loan bears an interest rate of 7% and is repayable (on an annuity basis) over 25 years.

---

[20] See §17.3 for the more serious effect of the 'Basel III' provisions.

Table 12.8 The Optimization Process

	Case 1	Case 2	Case 3	Case 4
	Maximum Debt	Lower Leverage	Lower Cover	Higher equity
Project cost	1,000	1,000	1,000	1,000
Debt:equity ratio	95:5	82:18	86:14	75:25
Debt interest rate	7%	7%	7%	6.5%
Debt repayment term	25 years	25 years	25 years	25 years
Lenders' required ADSCR	1.35:1	1.35:1	1.25:1	1.35:1
Investors' required Equity IRR	13%	13%	13%	11%
Annual Payments				
Debt service (annuity repayment)	81	70	74	61
Distributions to provide Equity IRR	7	25	18	30
Contract Payment to cover debt service + Equity IRR	88	95	93	91
Contract Payment to satisfy ADSCR	109	95	93	77

Given these assumptions, the annual debt service is 81, and the annual Distributions to investors would be 7, so Contracts Payments of 88 *p.a.* would be needed to pay these sums to lenders and investors. However the project also has to satisfy the lenders' requirement for a 1.35:1 ADSCR. Since the annual debt service is 81, the Contract Payments have to be 109 (*i.e.* 81 × 1.35). So even though the lenders and investors would be receive their required debt service and Distributions with an annual Contract Payment of 88, the Contract Payment is forced up to 109 because of the Cover Ratio requirement.

Case 2 therefore assumes that the leverage has been reduced to 85%, and all other assumptions are the same. Counter-intuitive as it may seem, this reduces the required Contract Payments. The total of annual debt service and Distributions is now 95. The Contract Payment to satisfy the ADSCR requirement is also 95 (*i.e.* 70 × 1.35). So now the Cover Ratio is no more than is needed to meet the required annual debt and equity payments.

Case 3 assumes that the lenders are willing to reduce their ADSCR to 1.25:1. This also enables the leverage to increase to 86%. The total of annual debt service and Distributions is now 93. The Contract Payment to satisfy the ADSCR requirement is also 93 (*i.e.* 74 × 1.25). So a reduction in Cover Ratio produces lower Contract Payments—in fact, it may be more beneficial for the Sponsors to negotiate a lower Cover Ratio than a lower debt interest rate.

Case 4 assumes that the investors are willing to provide more equity (25%), and also to reduce their required equity IRR. Similarly the debt interest rate is reduced to 6.5%, reflecting the lower risk now there is more equity.[21] (This is logical because each $ invested now has a lower risk in proportion to cases with higher leverage.) The total of annual debt service and Distributions is now 91, below the previous Case. (In this case the ADSCR requirement would only require an annual Contract Payment of 77, but this does not affect the answer.) So, again quite paradoxically, a substantial reduction of the leverage may reduce the Contract Payments. Therefore there has to be some qualification of the statement in §2.6 that higher leverage necessarily produces a lower cost for the project's product or service. However one problem with this approach for an Offtaker/Contracting Authority is that this structure makes it easy for the investors to refinance the project with higher leverage early in the project life (*cf.* §14.16), which is financially inefficient from the former's point of view.[22]

In summary the objective is not necessarily to produce the lowest cost of debt finance for the Project Company, but to arrive at its lowest weighted average cost of capital ('WACC'), *i.e.* the total financing costs taking debt-finance terms and costs and equity-return requirements into account.

These illustrations of model optimization are highly simplified. The calculations ignore operating revenues and costs—which can be assumed to be the same in all the Cases—as well as inflation and tax, and the lenders' requirement for a project 'tail'. And other factors which may affect the cash flows, such as maintenance 'spikes' (*cf.* §9.7.5) are also ignored.

---

[21] Reducing the interest rate if there is more equity in the project is known as 'interest buy-down'.

[22] *Cf.* §17.5.5 for a brief experiment by the British government in increasing the equity ratio for PFI projects.

Chapter 13

THE FINANCIAL MODEL

§13.1 INTRODUCTION

This chapter reviews the main functions of a financial model (§13.2), and the main building blocks of information and assumptions used for projections that are assembled to create inputs for a project's financial model (§13.2), namely:

- macro-economic assumptions (§13.4);
- project costs and funding (§13.5);
- operating revenues and costs (§13.6);
- accounting and taxation assumptions (§13.7).

The final model outputs (§13.8) will confirm the viability (or otherwise) of the project from the point of view of investors (and in the case of a process-plant or infrastructure project the costs to the Offtaker/Contracting Authority, or users). Lenders use the model to carry out sensitivity calculations to ensure that their loan is not unduly at risk in downside scenarios (§13.8). The final version of the

345

Principles of Project Finance. DOI: http://dx.doi.org/10.1016/B978-0-12-391058-5.00013-8

model is normally fixed Financial Close (§13.10), but continues to be used thereafter (§13.11).[1]

§13.2 FUNCTIONS OF THE FINANCIAL MODEL

A financial model is an essential tool for any project financing. It serves a variety of purposes:

Pre-Financial Close. During the development phase a financial model is needed for:
- initial evaluation and reevaluation of the project's financial aspects and returns for the Sponsors (*cf.* §12.2);
- structuring the finance and reviewing the benefits to the Sponsors of different financial terms (*cf.* §12.8);
- formulating the financial provisions of the Project Contracts, including LD calculations (*cf.* §8.2.8);
- as part of the lenders' due-diligence process (*cf.* §5.5.5);
- quantifying critical issues in the finance negotiations.

An Offtaker/Contracting Authority also needs to develop a financial model during the development phase (*cf.* §3.7):
- to confirm the financial viability and Affordability of the project (*cf.* §3.7.3);
- to compare and evaluate bids from prospective Sponsors (*cf.* §3.7.8).

Post-Financial Close. The financial model continues to have a rôle after Financial Close:
- as a budgeting tool (although the Project Company is likely to develop a separate model for this purpose);
- enabling lenders to review the changing long-term prospects for the project and thus their continuing exposure (*cf.* §14.4.3);
- enabling investors to calculate the value of their investment (*cf.* §14.17).

Where there is an Offtaker/Contracting Authority the financial model is also used:
- to calculate Compensation-Event payments (*cf.* §7.6.5);
- to calculate any refinancing gain (*cf.* §14.16.3);
- to calculate the Termination Sum for some early-termination scenarios (*cf.* §7.10.2).

---

[1] This chapter does not pretend to turn the reader into an expert financial modeler, but is just aimed at setting out the key aspects of modeling that are relevant for parties involved in a project. Penelope Lynch, *Financial Modelling for Project Finance* (Euromoney Institutional Investor, London, 2010 [2nd ed.]) provides detailed guidance.

Although separate and parallel financial models may be developed by the Sponsors and the lenders, as discussed in §5.2.6 it is often more efficient for a single model to be developed jointly. This may mean that the Sponsors develop the model initially and then work on it jointly with the lenders, depending on the timing of the lenders' involvement in the project. The Sponsors may then use the model to calculate their own returns, taking into account the ownership structure of the Project Company, the results of which are not of concern to the lenders. However by Financial Close there needs to be one model agreed between the Project Company and the lenders, for the purposes outlined above.

As also mentioned in §5.2.6, an Offtaker/Contracting Authority will develop its own model for evaluation of the project and bids, but by Financial Close there also needs to be a single model which has been agreed with the Project Company for use thereafter as outlined above, meaning that the Project Company, the Offtaker/Contracting Authority and the lenders are usually all using one model, although some inputs used by each party may differ.

§13.3 MODEL INPUTS

The input assumptions for the financial model for the Project Company can be classified into five main areas:

- macro-economic assumptions (§13.4);
- project costs and funding structure (§13.5);
- operating revenues and costs (§13.6);
- loan drawings and debt service (§12.5; §14.3);
- taxation and accounting (§13.7).

These inputs need to take account of the terms of the Project Contracts, including expected and required Project Completion, timing of payments or receipts, and calculation of penalties or bonuses.

The basis for the inputs must be clearly documented; the standard way of doing this is for an 'assumptions book' to be compiled. This takes each line of the financial model and sets out the source for the input or calculation of that line, with copies of (or references to) the documentation to back this up.

The main categories of inputs are usually entered in separate input sheets (*e.g.* one for specific assumptions such as project costs, and one for long-term macroeconomic and operating assumptions that cover the life of the project). Inputs should not be scattered throughout the model, as someone not familiar with it will find it much harder to understand what is going on.

To calculate the investors' returns correctly the financial model should cover the whole period from when the initial development costs on the project are incurred to the end of the project life, although for the purposes of the lenders the model is only needed from Financial Close, with past expenditure on project development being 'day 0' figures. The project life is either the term of the Project Agreement or the expected economic life of the project if it is not operating with such a contract. A residual value of zero, with the whole of the Sponsors' equity having been repaid by the end of the project life, is normally assumed unless there is good reason to the contrary (*cf.* §7.10.9).

The model is usually prepared on the basis of 6-month periods. During construction, where this may not be detailed enough (*e.g.* including interest calculations, the precise timing of payments to the Construction Contractor, *etc.*), separate projections may be made on a monthly basis and consolidated in the main model.

§13.4 MACRO-ECONOMIC ASSUMPTIONS

Macro-economic input assumptions are those that are not directly related to the project, but that affect its financial results (*cf.* Chapter 10). Such assumptions may include:

- inflation (§13.4.1);
- commodity prices (§13.4.2);
- interest rates (§13.4.3);
- exchange rates (§13.4.4);
- economic growth (§13.4.5).

Ideally, macro-economic assumptions for modeling projections should be taken from an objective source; for example, most major banks produce general economic research with generic projections that can be used for this purpose, although it is unlikely to extend for the full term of a model (*cf.* §13.11).

§13.4.1 INFLATION

Inflation should be taken into account in the financial model, as it may be misleading to draw up projections on a 'real' basis (*cf.* §10.4.1).

Different indices may need to be used as a basis for projections of inflation in different types of revenue or cost, for example:

- Consumer Price Inflation (CPI) in the Host Country, for general operating costs;
- indices of employment costs in the country of suppliers or providers of services to the project, in relation to these costs;
- industrial price inflation for the cost of spare parts or lifecycle renewals;

- specific price indices for commodities produced by or purchased by the project (supply and demand in the commodity's own market may affect its price more than general inflation).

Care should be taken to ensure that an artificial result is not produced by using higher inflation rates for revenues than for costs.

If the Project Company has a Project Agreement in which revenues are indexed against inflation (*cf.* §7.3.3), the financial model should also reflect this.

§13.4.2 COMMODITY PRICES

It is usually inappropriate to treat commodity prices in the same way as inflation (*i.e.* to assume that they will keep going up). The vulnerability of the project to cyclical movements in commodity prices, which are normal for most commodities, needs to be examined in the financial modeling.

One of the key problems of project finance in the natural resources sector is that projects are often developed when commodity prices are high, and assume that these high prices will continue, underestimating the effect of the development of the project itself, and others like it, on the market for the commodity. (Or conversely, if a project is developed using a commodity as a fuel or raw material when it is at a low price, it is assuming that this low price will continue.)

Commodity-price movements may be very violent on a short-term basis, whereas project finance is inevitably a long-term business; therefore, it must be demonstrated that the project is robust enough to deal with significant fluctuations in commodity prices (*cf.* §9.6.2).

§13.4.3 INTEREST RATES

If the interest rate on the debt is to be fixed throughout the term of the debt (*cf.* §10.2.1) the assumption for this rate should be used for projections. However, even in such cases, another floating (short term) interest rate will probably have to be projected for earnings on surplus funds held by the Project Company as security for lenders or prior to distribution to investors (*cf.* §14.4).

There are two approaches to projecting short term interest rates: either an assumption can be made as to the rate itself, or 'real' interest rates (*i.e.* the interest rate after allowing for inflation) can be used for this purpose, and the actual interest rate is determined by the assumed CPI rate. In the latter case, as shown in Table 13.1, if a real interest rate of, say, 4% is used, the projected nominal interest rate is the real interest rate adjusted for the projected rate of inflation, using the 'Fisher formula'.

Table 13.1 Interest-Rate Projections—Fisher Formula

	Year 1	Year 2	Year 3
(a) Projected real interest	4.00%	4.00%	4.00%
(b) Projected inflation rate	5.00%	4.00%	3.00%
Nominal interest rate [((1 + (a)) × (1 + (b)) − 1]:	9.20%	8.16%	7.12%

Similarly, if the discount rate for an NPV evaluation, *e.g.* of bids for a PPP project (§3.7.8), is based on the projected real interest rate plus inflation, the Fisher formula is also used to calculate the discount rate.

§13.4.4 EXCHANGE RATES AND CURRENCY OF THE MODEL

If a Project Company raises debt and equity funding in its Host Country's currency, and all its construction and operating costs and revenues are in that currency, the question of exchange rates becomes irrelevant.

If this is not the case, the financial model should still be prepared in the Host Country's currency, with the ability to make assumptions about exchange-rate movements between this currency and other currencies used for the costs or funding of the project. Overseas investors and lenders may feel it preferable to have the model in their home currency, but this is likely to give inaccurate or misleading results (*e.g.* because of the effect of exchange rate movements on tax payments—*cf.* §13.7.7), and because some costs will inevitably be in the Host Country's currency). It is not difficult for the model to generate reports that translate the results of projections in the Host Country's currency to the relevant foreign currency based on assumed exchange rates, thus maintaining the accuracy of the calculations.

There are two approaches to projecting exchange rates between currencies, similar to those for projecting interest rates: either specific assumptions can be made as to the future exchange rates, or 'purchasing-power parity' rates can be used.[2] The latter calculation takes the difference in projected inflation rates between the two currencies and adjusts the exchange rate accordingly, based on the assumption that the future exchange rate between the two currencies will move in line with their inflation differential. This can be seen in Table 13.2: in year 1, with a difference between the two inflation rates of 6% in favor of Currency B, Currency A depreciates against Currency B by 6%, and so on.

---

[2] Purchasing power parity is often referred to as 'PPP' but this has nothing to do with the public-private partnerships discussed elsewhere; in this book 'PPP' refers only to the latter.

Table 13.2 Purchasing-Power Parity

	Now	Year 1	Year 2	Year 3
Projected inflation rates				
– Currency A		9%	10%	9%
– Currency B		3%	4%	3%
Projected exchange rates				
Currency A/Currency B	10.00	10.60	11.24	11.80

§13.4.5 ECONOMIC GROWTH

Infrastructure projects may be affected by the general growth rate of the economy, which translates itself, for example, into traffic for the project (*cf.* §9.6.2). For instance, there has been a fairly consistent ratio between the rate of long-term growth in air travel and GDP, with air travel's growth at twice that of GDP. Thus assumptions in the GDP growth rate are crucial for an airport project. A similar situation is likely to apply for a project involving other forms of transportation.

§13.5 PROJECT COSTS AND FINANCING

The next stage in the detailed modeling process is the preparation of a budget for the construction costs from the Project Company's point of view (§13.5.1), and determining how these are to be financed (§13.5.2) and how this finance is to be drawn down.

§13.5.1 CONSTRUCTION-PHASE COSTS

The cost budget takes into account costs incurred since the beginning of the project development and covers the period until the project is complete and ready to operate. A typical budget for a process plant or infrastructure project (*cf.* §9.5.5; §9.5.6) is likely to include:

Development Costs. These are the costs incurred by the Sponsors (and charged on to the Project Company), or by the Project Company itself, in the period prior to Financial Close. Sponsors need to agree among themselves to a methodology for allocating their own costs to the project, including staff overheads and travel costs, which are likely to be significant over a long development period (*cf.* §3.3). Costs of the Sponsors' and lenders' advisors also need to be taken into account. If development costs are included as part of the project costs (*cf.* §3.5), these can be treated as part of an initial equity investment, or refinanced by debt if equity is being injected last.

Development Fees. Project economics may allow one or more Sponsors to take out an initial fee from the Project Company for developing the project (in addition to the development costs), and thus realize an upfront profit (*cf.* §12.2.5). This figure may fluctuate (or be eliminated entirely) as the financial evaluation of the project, and hence the ability to finance such a fee, develops.

Project Company Costs. These are the Project Company's direct costs incurred by the Project Company after Financial Close (rather than those payable to Sub-Contractors, advisors, insurers, or lenders) such as:

* personnel costs;
* office and equipment;
* costs for Permits and licenses;
* Owner's Engineer's costs for construction supervision (*cf.* §7.4.1);
* training and mobilization costs (including any payments to an O&M Contractor for its training and mobilization).

Construction Contract Price. (*cf.* §8.2.3).

Construction-Phase Insurance Premiums. (*cf.* §8.6.1).

Start-Up Costs. These are costs for any fuel or raw materials used by the Construction Contractor during the testing and start-up of the project, before Project Completion; in some projects it may also be possible to earn some revenue from the project's output during this period to offset these costs.

Initial Spares. These are costs for initial stocks of spare parts (if these are not included in the Construction Contract).

Initial Working Capital. The working capital required for operation of the project is the amount of money required to cover the time difference over the Project Company's invoicing cycle between payment of operating costs and receipt of revenues in cash. In effect it is the short-term (usually 30–60-day) cash flow cycle of the project, which cannot be calculated directly in a financial model that runs for six monthly periods during the operating phase of the project. The initial working capital requirement can be calculated as the non-construction-related costs that the Project Company has to incur until it receives its first revenues. These costs may include:

* initial inventories of fuel or other raw materials;
* the first operating insurance premium;
* any timing differences between payments for input supplies and product outputs.

Thereafter changes in the amount of working capital required are usually a product of major movements in sales or purchases of input supplies, which should be reflected in the general cash flow.

Taxes. These include taxes payable during construction on the various project costs, such as VAT, GST or other sales taxes, and import duties (*cf.* §13.7.5).

Financing Costs. These include:

- IDC (*cf.* §10.3);
- loan arrangement and underwriting fees (*cf.* §12.6.2);
- commitment fees (*cf.* §12.6.3);
- loan agency fees (*cf.* §12.6.4);
- additional debt-related costs (§12.7);
- funding of Reserve Accounts (*cf.* §14.4.1);
- security registration costs (*cf.* §14.7.1);
- costs of lenders' advisors (*cf.* §5.5.1).

Contingency. Any contingency reserve (*cf.* §9.5.6) needs to be added to the project costs.

§13.5.2 Construction-Phase Financing

Based on the cost plan, the financing plan is drawn up to cover the total amount of finance required, divided into debt and equity (*cf.* Chapter 12 for particular issues that need to be considered in this respect, including the calculation of how much debt can be raised), and any other sources of finance.

During the construction phase the financial model should show drawings on the financing to meet the costs set out above, but also taking into account:

- the required ratio between equity and debt (*cf.* §12.4);
- the priority of drawing between equity and debt (*cf.* §12.2.3);
- any limitations on the use of debt (*e.g.* ECA loans (*cf.* §16.2) can only be used for exported equipment and limited local costs—thus if project costs of 100 include equipment of 70 under the export contract, a financing plan that uses ECA funding for 80 and other financing for 20 is not going to work);
- requirement for costs in one currency to be financed in that currency;

—and having done so calculates the drawdown schedule for both equity and debt.

Drawings on the debt give rise to IDC payments, which also need to be financed.

The Project Company should not use a short-term loan to finance initial working capital (*cf.* §13.5.1); this is a permanent requirement, which should be covered by the long-term project finance. However it may be useful to have part of the project finance in the form of a revolving credit for working capital (*i.e.* allowing the Project Company to repay some of this financing when it has surplus cash, and borrow it again when cash is short). This may reduce the required level of Sponsors' equity and thus also be advantageous for this reason.

Separate short-term funding may be required for VAT, GST or other taxes payable during construction that are recovered later, from offsetting against taxes on revenues once operations begin (*cf.* §13.7.5).

§13.6 OPERATING REVENUES AND COSTS

The first stage in projecting the operating revenues and costs in the model is to identify the key operating assumptions—*e.g.*, for a process plant:

- What is the initial output?
- How does this output change over time?
- How much time is needed for maintenance?
- How much time should also be allowed for unexpected downtime?
- What is the rate of consumption of fuel or raw materials?
- How does this consumption change over time?

The net operating revenues are the product of these operating assumptions, combined with the terms of the Project Agreement, and any relevant Sub-Contracts such as Offtake prices (or assumptions about market prices in the absence of such contracts).

Based on this, the main elements of operating cash flow may include:

- operating revenues from sales of products;
  minus
- cost of fuel or raw materials (*cf.* §8.5.3);
- the Project Company's own operating costs (personnel, office, *etc.*) (*cf.* §9.7.7);
- maintenance and lifecycle renewal costs (*cf.* §9.7.5);
- O&M/Maintenance Contract costs (*cf.* §8.3.3);
- insurance premiums (*cf.* §8.6.2).

Having determined the net operating cash flow as above, the model then calculates the interest payments and other sums due to the lenders (*cf.* §12.6), allowing for hedging contracts (*cf.* §10.3).

§13.7 ACCOUNTING AND TAXATION ISSUES

Although the decision to invest in a project should be based primarily on cash flow evaluation (*cf.* §12.2), the accounting results are important to the Sponsors, who will not wish to show an accounting loss from investment in a Project Company affiliate (*cf.* §12.2.4).

Thus although a financial model for a project financing is concerned with cash flows rather than accounting results, it is usually necessary to add accounting sheets to the model, *i.e.* a profit and loss account ('P&L account')[3] and balance sheet for each calculation period.

Apart from the need to check the effect on a Sponsor's reported earnings, there are a number of reasons why accounting results are needed in the financial model for the Project Company:

- tax payments are based on accounting results rather than cash flow (§13.7.1).
- the accounting results may affect a company's ability to pay dividends (§13.7.2) or even its ability to keep trading (§13.7.3).
- an accounting balance sheet is a good way of checking for errors in the model: if the balance sheet does not balance, there is a mistake somewhere.

Further issues relating to taxation are:

- timing of tax payments (§13.7.4);
- Value-Added Tax (§13.7.5);
- withholding tax (§13.7.6);
- exchange rates and tax (§13.7.7);
- inflation and tax (§13.7.8).

§13.7.1 CAPITALIZATION AND DEPRECIATION OF PROJECT COSTS

The most important difference between accounting and cash-flow calculations on a project relate to the capitalization and later depreciation of the project costs.

If the Project Company had to charge off the costs of the project as they were incurred, the result would be an enormous loss in the construction phase of the project, followed by enormous profits in the operating phase. This obviously does not represent the real situation of the project.

In most countries, the project's capital costs are capitalized (*i.e.* added to the asset side of the balance sheet), instead of being written off immediately. 'Cost' in this context includes not only the EPC construction cost (or the 'hard' cost) but also the 'soft' costs incurred until the project is in operation, *i.e.* development and financing costs (including IDC), payments to advisors, *etc.*

Thereafter, the capitalized cost is depreciated (written down) against revenues. A standard straight-line accounting depreciation of a project might allow the Project Company to write off the project asset, over, say, a 20-year life. Thus the depreciation on a project costing 1000 would be 5% of its original cost (or 50) *p.a.*

---

[3] Also known as the 'income statement'.

If this depreciation is offset against taxable income, assuming a tax rate of 50%, the depreciation allowance will reduce the tax by 25 *p.a.* for 20 years.

The Project Company may benefit from greater initial tax deferrals because its investment in fixed assets is eligible for an accelerated tax-depreciation allowance. If, for example, the tax depreciation allowance on the project cost is 25% of the declining balance—a pattern of 'accelerated' depreciation allowances that is a typical investment incentive—this means that the depreciation allowance on an investment of 1000 is:

- Year 1: 25% of cost, or 250;
- Year 2: 25% of (cost minus Year 1 depreciation) 188, or 438 in total;
- Year 3: 25% of (cost minus depreciation from Year 1 to Year 2) = 141, or 578 in total;
- Year 4: 25% of (cost minus depreciation from Year 1 to Year 3) = 105, or 684 in total;
- Year 5: 25% of (cost minus depreciation from Year 1 to Year 4) = 79, or 763 in total;
- … *etc.*

Thus over the first 5 years more than 75% of the project costs can be written off against tax, compared to 25% on the 20-year straight-line depreciation schedule mentioned above. In the later years of the project, tax payments where there has been accelerated depreciation increase as the cost of the project has already been written off against tax, and so by the end of 20 years the total reduction in tax through the depreciation allowance (assuming no changes in tax rate) will be the same as for a straight-line tax depreciation.

Another common type of tax depreciation is that of 'double depreciation'—if the normal rate of depreciation for an asset is, say, 10% *p.a.* straight line, double depreciation allows depreciation at the rate of 20% *p.a.* for say the first 3 years, and then 10% *p.a.* thereafter. Thus, to compare with the declining balance method set out above, by the end of year 5, on this basis 80% of the cost would have been written off against tax.

In some countries (*e.g.* the U.S. and Britain) depreciation is dealt with in different ways for accounting and tax purposes: for accounting purposes, the project asset is depreciated over its useful life, thus spreading the cost of the asset against the earnings it generates and increasing the reported profits in the early years of the project, whereas for tax purposes accelerated depreciation is used. The difference between the two is taken directly to (or later deducted from) a tax reserve on the liability side of the balance sheet. In other countries (*e.g.* France and Germany), the accounting and tax depreciation must be the same.

Different depreciation rates may apply to different parts of the project (*e.g.* buildings and equipment). In such cases the Construction Contractor will have to break up the lump-sum Construction Contract price into these components for tax-classification purposes (*cf.* §8.2.3). In some cases buildings (especially non-industrial buildings) may not be depreciated against tax (since they are assumed to hold their value): this can lead to a high *de facto* tax rate for the project since its taxable profits will be higher as a result of not being able to set the expense of the building against the revenues derived from it.

A similar issue may arise in the case of PPPs, where the project may not be in the legal ownership of the Project Company—again this may mean that a large part of the capital cost of the project cannot be offset against tax. There are various ways of dealing with the problem, such as 'finance debtor' accounting in Britain, where the Contract Payments are separated between operating revenues and notional repayments of a loan, the former being taxable and the latter not being taxable. In Spain a reserve equal to the capital cost of the asset, *e.g.* a Concession road is built up over the life of the Concession, and offset against tax each year: at the end of the Concession this reserve is written off against the capital cost, reducing both to zero.

§13.7.2 THE DIVIDEND TRAP

As discussed in §12.2.2, the 'equity' provided by the Sponsors may not be in the form of ordinary share capital, but a combination of share capital and subordinated debt, one reason for this being that interest on shareholder subordinated debt may be tax-deductible, unlike dividends on ordinary shares.

Another reason that shareholder equity is often provided as a combination of share capital and shareholder subordinated loans is the possibility of falling into what is known as the 'dividend trap,' whereby the Project Company has cash flow but cannot pay a dividend to the investors because of a negative cumulative balance on its P&L account. In many countries if a company has a cumulative negative P&L account balance, it cannot pay dividends. (So if there is a loss of 50 in year one, and a profit of 25 in year 2, the company cannot pay dividends even in year two as the cumulative loss is 25. If the company makes a profit of 30 in year 3, it can pay a dividend of 5, so leaving a cumulative profit of zero.)

This is illustrated by Table 13.3. The assumptions for the calculations are:

- project cost is 1500, funded 1200 by debt and 300 by equity;
- income and expenditure are constant at 475 and 175 *p.a.*, respectively;
- the tax depreciation allowance on the project cost is 25% of the declining balance (see above);
- accounting depreciation is the same as tax depreciation;
- the tax rate is 30%;
- if the Project Company makes a tax loss, a tax credit of 30% of the loss is carried forward, and applied against future taxes payable;

Table 13.3 The Dividend Trap

Year	1	2	3	4	5	6	Total
(a) Revenues	475	475	475	475	475	475	2375
(b) Expenditure (including interest)	−175	−175	−175	−175	−175	−175	−875
(c) Tax depreciation	−375	−281	−211	−158	−119	−89	−1144
(d) **Taxable income/loss** [(a) + (b) + (c)]	−75	19	89	142	181	211	567
(e) Tax credit/due [(d) × 30%]	23	−6	−27	−43	−54	−63	
(f) Tax credit used		6	17	0	0	0	
Tax credit carried forward	23	17	0	0	0	0	
(g) Tax payable [(e) + (f)]			−10	−43	−54	−63	−170
(h) **Net income** [(d) − (g)]	−75	19	79	99	127	148	397
(i) Loan repayments	−200	−200	−200	−200	−200	−200	−1200
(j) Dividend paid			−23	−99	−127	−148	−397
(k) **Cash flow** [(h) − (c) + (i) + (j)]	100	100	67	−42	−81	−111	33
Cash balance	100	200	267	225	144	33	
Opening Profit & Loss Account	0	−75	−56	0	0	0	
(l) **Year-end Profit & Loss Account**	−75	−56	0	0	0	0	0

- loan principal repayments are 200 *p.a.*;
- the figures run for 6 years to illustrate the point, although the project life is longer than this.

The calculations show that the Project Company has a positive cash flow available for payments to investors from Year 1, but it would still not be able to pay a dividend, because its balance sheet shows a cumulative loss of 75, caused by the accelerated tax depreciation, which creates an accounting loss in Year 1. Not until Year 3 is this negative balance eliminated, so the Project Company would not be able to pay dividends until then. Even by Year 6 the cash surplus has not been fully paid out to the investors, and the considerable delay in receiving these payments will substantially reduce their rate of return.

In effect, the dividend trap in this case is a function of the difference between tax depreciation and debt principal repayment; if the former is much greater than the latter a trap develops, which disappears as the situation is reversed. (This is clearly less of an issue in countries where the accounting depreciation does not have to mirror the tax depreciation.)

If the investors' equity is partly paid in as subordinated debt, with the balance in share capital, payments to the investors in the early years when dividends cannot be paid can be made as repayments of subordinated debt. It should thus be possible for the Project Company to pay out the whole of the surplus cash balance.

A further point about these figures is that a portion of the benefit of the accelerated depreciation is in effect being wasted—tax credits of 23 in Year 1 cannot be fully offset against taxes payable until Year 3. In such a case the Project Company may consider:

- not taking advantage of the accelerated depreciation allowance in full (*i.e.* writing off the cost of the project against tax at a slower rate), which many countries will allow, and thus not creating a negative profit, so also enabling earlier payment of dividends; or
- using tax-based leasing (*cf.* §4.5.2) and passing on the allowances to a leasing company that can make immediate use of them and pass on the benefit to the Project Company through a lower funding cost.

The other advantage of mainly using shareholder subordinated debt rather than share capital to finance the Project Company's equity requirement is that it is much easier to return these funds to investors if a refinancing takes place and the senior debt is increased, or in the later years of the project when the investors may wish to have their equity investment gradually paid back. (It may also be beneficial from a capital-gains tax point of view.)

§13.7.3 NEGATIVE EQUITY

But the Project Company has to ensure that by avoiding the Scylla (rock) of the dividend trap it does not fall into the Charybdis (hard place) of wiping out the whole of its equity. If a large part of the Project Company's funding is through subordinated debt, and the company makes large accounting losses in its early years, the end result may be to eliminate its equity completely. In many countries a company with negative equity (*i.e.* its share capital is less than the negative balance on the profit and loss account) has to cease trading and go into liquidation.

In the case in Table 13.3, if the 1500 of project cost is funded with 20% equity (*i.e.* 300), of which 267 is subordinated debt and thus 33 is share capital, the subordinated debt could be repaid first, and hence repayments of 267 of subordinated debt would be made over the first 3 years, with dividend payments beginning thereafter. The Project Company has made an accounting loss of 75 in Year 1 (even ignoring any interest on the subordinated debt), which is already greater than this share capital of 33, and so this split between share capital and subordinated debt is not feasible. (In this case the Project Company probably has to look at the possibility of a slower rate of tax depreciation.)

A similar result could arise even with straight-line tax depreciation, but a lower level of profitability in the early years of the project (*e.g.* from high interest charges, including the subordinated debt).

Therefore, because of the low level of equity inherent in project finance, the accounting results of the Project Company in the financial model need to be carefully checked to ensure that even if cash flow is available, it can legally be paid over out to the investors, and the Project Company maintains a positive equity.

§13.7.4 TIMING OF TAX PAYMENTS

Corporate-tax payments are often paid in arrears, which means that there is a gap between the time the tax payment accrues and the time it is paid. The financial model must therefore show the tax calculation in the P&L account, and the actual payments in the cash-flow calculations, at these different times.

§13.7.5 VALUE-ADDED TAX

In some countries (*e.g.* in the European Union), VAT is payable by the Project Company on the construction cost of the project, but the amount paid can in due course be offset by VAT chargeable on sales by the Project Company once it begins operations. The lenders may provide a separate VAT loan to deal with this short-term financing requirement.

§13.7.6 WITHHOLDING TAX

If interest payments to lenders have to be grossed-up as discussed in §12.7.1, the model will have to reflect this.

Withholding tax may also apply to offshore investors' dividends or subordinated loan income. A double-tax treaty may allow this to be offset against taxes on other domestic income, but if it cannot be offset investors would usually take this into account in calculating the Equity IRR, even though it does not appear in the Project Company's accounts or cash flow.

§13.7.7 EXCHANGE RATES AND TAX

If the Project Company has debt in a foreign currency, exchange-rate movements against the Host Country's currency affect tax payments and hence the investors'

Table 13.4 Exchange Rates and Tax

Year	0	1	2	3	4	5	Total
$ calculation							
(a) Initial cost	$1000						
(b) Depreciation [(a) × 10%]		$100	$100	$100	$100	$100	$500
(c) Tax deduction [(b) × 30%]		$30	$30	$30	$30	$30	$150
€ calculation							
(d) Initial cost	€1100						
(e) Depreciation [(d) × 10%]		€110	€110	€110	€110	€110	€550
(f) Tax deduction [(e) × 30%]		€33	€33	€33	€33	€33	€165
(g) Exchange rate	€1.10	€1.16	€1.21	€1.27	€1.34	€1.40	
(h) Depreciation in $ [(e) ÷ (g)]		$95	$91	$86	$82	$78	$433
(j) Value of Tax deduction in $ [(f) ÷ (g)]		$29	$27	$26	$25	$24	$130

return on the project, even if revenues and operating costs are all indexed against the foreign currency.

This can be seen in Table 13.4, which again illustrates why the financial model has to be calculated in the Host Country's currency and not in the overseas investors' and lenders' currency.

These calculations look at the return to a $-based investor in a Project Company based in Europe, with its accounts and tax calculations in €. Two calculations are shown: one based on a financial model in $, the other on a financial model in €. The assumptions in the calculations are:

- All project costs, revenues, and expenses (including debt interest and principal repayments) are either denominated in or indexed against $, so that the project theoretically has no exchange exposure.
- The initial €/$ exchange rate is €1.10 = $1.00.
- € depreciates against $ by 5% *p.a.* from the beginning of the project.
- Project cost is $1000, which equates to €1100 at the time the expenditure is incurred.
- The tax depreciation allowance on the project cost is 10% *p.a.* on a straight-line basis.
- The tax rate is 50%.
- The table shows the cash flow for the 1st 5 years of the project.

As can be seen, when the depreciating exchange rate is taken into account, the total tax deduction for depreciation in $ terms is not $150, as would appear in a

$-based model, but $130. Hence a $-based model would not properly reflect this and would overstate the cash flow.

Therefore, in a project with foreign-currency funding, even if this is fully hedged, the effect of a variety of exchange-rate movements—both up and down in the rate and at different stages of the project—should be checked.

§13.7.8 INFLATION AND TAX

Apart from the general effect of inflation on project cash flows (*cf.* §10.4), for much the same reasons as those set out in §13.7.7, a project that operates in an environment of high inflation, and whose revenues and costs are all fully indexed against inflation, will still not produce a return which increases fully with inflation, because the tax depreciation of the project cost is based on the original uninflated cost. (In some countries, however, the cost of the project on the company's balance sheet can also be revalued against the inflation index before calculating the tax depreciation allowance.)

This again illustrates the importance of calculations based on 'nominal' not 'real' figures in a project finance cash flow (*cf.* §10.4).

§13.8 MODEL OUTPUTS

The aims of a financial model will differ, depending on who the model is for (investors, lenders, Offtaker/Contracting Authority), and on the type of project. Investors obviously want to ensure that the model produces the required Equity IRR (*cf.* §12.2), lenders that the required Cover Ratios can be achieved (*cf.* §12.3), an Offtaker/Contracting Authority wants to know what the Contract Payments will be (*cf.* §3.7.8).

The model outputs are a series of calculations:

- construction-phase costs;
- drawdown of equity;
- drawdown and repayment of debt;
- interest calculations;
- operating revenues and costs;
- tax;
- P&L account;
- balance sheet;
- cash flow (source and use of funds);
- lenders' Cover Ratios;
- Contract Payments (if any).

A summary sheet usually sets out the key results on one page, such as:

- summary of project costs and funding;
- cash-flow summary;
- lenders' Cover Ratios;
- Base Case Equity IRR;
- Project IRR;
- first full year's Contract Payments (if any);
- NPV of Contract Payments (*ditto*).

§13.9 SENSITIVITY ANALYSIS

The financial model also needs to be sufficiently flexible to allow both investors and lenders to calculate a series of sensitivities[4] showing the effects of variations in the key input assumptions when initially reviewing the project. Such sensitivities may include calculating the effect on Cover Ratios and the Equity IRR of:

- Construction-cost overrun (usually based on a full drawing of the contingency funding);
- payment of the LDs under the Construction Contract to cover delays or failure of the project to perform as specified;
- delay in Project Completion (say for 6 months) without LDs from the Construction Contractor;
- reduction in performance without LDs from the Construction Contractor;
- higher downtime or lower availability;
- reduced volume of sales or usage of the project; this is a key issue where any kind of usage or market risk is being taken: a typical sensitivity for a toll road might be to reduce traffic by 30% and see if this still maintains an ADSCR of at least 1:1, *i.e.* debt can still be serviced;
- reduced sale prices;
- breakeven sales prices or usage, *i.e.* how low can sales or usage go before the project can no longer service its debt on time;
- higher input costs;
- higher operating costs;
- higher interest rates (where these are not yet fixed);
- higher and lower inflation;
- exchange-rate movements.

---

[4] Also known as 'cases'.

In summary, the sensitivities look at the financial effect of the commercial and macro-economic risk aspects of the project not working out as originally expected.

Lenders also usually run a 'combined downside case' to check the effects of several adverse things happening at once (*e.g.* 3 months' delay in Project Completion, a 10% drop in sale prices, and 10% more downtime). This calculation of several different things happening at once is known as 'scenario analysis.'

§13.10 THE BANKING CASE, BASE CASE AND FINANCIAL CLOSE

Once the lenders, Sponsors and Offtaker/Contracting Authority (if any), and the Model Auditor (*cf.* §5.5.5) agree that the financial model's structure and calculation formulæ reflect the project and its contracts correctly, the basic input assumptions are settled, and the financial structure and terms (*cf.* Chapter 12) are agreed to and also incorporated in the model, the final run of the model on this basis is known as the 'Banking Case' as between Project Company, or 'Base Case' as between the Project Company and an Offtaker/Contracting Authority, if any. It is possible that the lenders may require different assumptions to be made to those used for calculating the Contract Payments, meaning that the Base Case and Banking Case may differ.

This final calculation usually takes place on or just before signing or Financial Close, to enable the lenders to check that, using fully up-to-date assumptions and the final versions of the Project Contracts, the project still provides them with adequate coverage for their loan. The fixed-debt interest rate or the swap rate may also be input into the model at this stage, to fix the calculation of the Contract Payments (*cf.* §10.3.5).

§13.11 USING THE MODEL AFTER FINANCIAL CLOSE

But the project does not stand still after Financial Close, and lenders continue to review their exposure. Adverse changes in the projected ADSCR or LLCR in the future may affect the ability of the Project Company to pay Distributions to its investors (*cf.* §14.4.2), or even put the Project Company into default on the loan (*cf.* §14.12). However, if a new Banking Case projection is to be calculated once the project is under way, someone has to decide how the input assumptions previously used should be changed. If the Project Company is left to decide the assumptions, the lenders may not agree and *vice versa*.

There is no simple answer to this problem, but as far as possible it is usually best to use objective rather than subjective sources for revising projections where this is possible, *e.g.*:

- Macro-economic assumptions (including commodity prices) can be based on an economic review published by one of the lenders or another outside source, so long as this is a general publication, not specific to the project. (However such publications may not provide the long-term projections required for the project.)
- Changes in operating costs or revenue assumptions should generally be based on the actual performance of the Project Company.
- Lenders usually have the greatest weight in the final decision on assumption changes, but where possible investors should ensure that these decisions are based on and are required to follow specific advice from the Lenders' Engineer, or their market, insurance, or other advisors, who should have expertise on the issues involved, rather than leaving it to an arbitrary decision by the lenders.

If there is an Offtaker/Contracting Authority, the Base-Case model may continue to be used in a number of other ways, *e.g.*:

- for calculations of payments due for Compensation Events (*cf.* §7.6.5);
- for changes in benchmarked or market-tested services (§6.4.5; §8.4);
- for some of the Termination-Sum calculations (*cf.* §7.10);
- for Refinancing calculations (*cf.* §14.16.3).

Chapter 14

PROJECT-FINANCE LOAN DOCUMENTATION

§14.1 INTRODUCTION

Apart from the financial structuring and modeling issues discussed in Chapters 12 and 13, the loan documentation also deals with the lenders' additional controls and other requirements which will be imposed on the Project Company, as listed in Table 14.1 below, and dealt with in this chapter. The end result is a loan agreement to which the Project Company and the lenders are parties,[1] and ancillary security documentation.

Drafting for 'boilerplate' terms (*i.e.* those which vary little from one loan agreement to another) is often based on the Loan Market Association ('LMA') standard-form loan documentation. The LMA was formed in 1996, with the aim of standardizing bank loan documentation as far as possible, so that loans can be more easily syndicated (*cf.* §5.2.8) or otherwise transferred in the market. Members

---

[1] Also known as a 'credit agreement', 'financing agreement' or 'facilities agreement'.

367

Principles of Project Finance. DOI: http://dx.doi.org/10.1016/B978-0-12-391058-5.00014-X

(500+) include commercial and investment banks, institutional investors, law firms, service providers and rating agencies, primarily but not entirely in Europe.[2] LMA has not produced any standard-form project-finance loan documentation, but having said this many of the standard corporate-loan clauses are also to be found in a project-finance loan, and hence the LMA documentation is a useful starting point for project-finance loans since it sets out generally-agreed market drafting, so avoiding the need to negotiate 'boilerplate' clauses in a loan agreement from first principles.[3]

This chapter also covers two other key topics for the Project Company's investors, which typically arise once the project is completed and operating—refinancing the Project Company's debt (§14.16) and sale of its equity to secondary investors (§14.17).

§14.2 LENDERS' TERM SHEET

The lenders' term sheet (*cf.* §5.2.7) sets out a summary of the main commercial and financial terms and structure the lenders are offering, and in due course serves as a template for the financial documentation. The terms and conditions usually covered by this term sheet are listed in Table 14.1; references in the table indicate where the relevant topic is discussed.[4]

§14.3 CONSTRUCTION PHASE—DRAWDOWN OF DEBT

The debt is usually available for drawing for a period slightly longer than the construction phase of the project (§14.3.1). The drawing procedure for the debt (§14.3.2) is linked to that for the equity (*cf.* §12.2.3).

---

[2] There are other regional LMAs in the Americas (Loan Syndications and Trading Association—'LSTA'), Asia-Pacific (Asia Pacific Loan Market Association—'APLMA') and Africa (African Loan Market Association—'ALMA').

[3] For discussion of various legal aspects of project finance, *cf.* Scott L. Hoffman, *The Law and Business of International Project Finance* (Cambridge University Press, Cambridge, 2007 [3rd ed.]); Graham D. Vinter and Gareth Pierce, *Practical Project Finance* (Sweet & Maxwell, London, 2006 [3rd ed.]); Philip R. Wood, *Project Finance, Securitisations and Subordinated Debt* (Sweet & Maxwell, London, 2007 [2nd revised ed.]).

[4] The summary terms and conditions in Table 14.1 are follow the key provisions found on a commercial-bank term sheet; substantially similar conditions would be found on term sheets provided by other types of lenders.

Table 14.1 Debt Term Sheet—Key Terms

Borrower	§3.6	Availability period	§14.3.1
Sponsors	§3.2	Drawdown procedure	§14.3.2; §12.2.3
Purpose of loan	§2.5	Project Accounts	§14.3; §14.4
Arrangers/Lender(s)	Chapter 5	Reserve Accounts	§14.4.1
Eligible project costs	§13.5.1	Cash-Flow Cascade	§14.4.2
Loan facilities and amounts	Chapter 12	Distribution Lock-Up	§14.4.2
Cover-Ratio requirements	§12.3	Reporting requirements	§14.5
Maximum debt:equity ratio	§12.4	Cancellation and prepayment	§14.6
Repayment	§12.5	Security	§14.7
Interest basis and margin	§12.6.1	Conditions precedent	§14.8
Arrangement fee	§12.6.2	Representations and warranties	§14.9
Commitment fee	§12.6.3	Covenants	§14.10
Agent/Agency fee	§12.6.4	Waivers and Amendments	§14.11
Other loan costs	§12.7	Events of Default	§14.12
Advisors' costs	§5.5.1	Lenders' decision process	§14.13
Interest-rate hedging	§10.3	Intercreditor arrangements	§14.14
Swap credit premium	§10.3.1	Governing law and jurisdiction	§14.15
		Validity period	§5.2.7

§14.3.1 AVAILABILITY PERIOD

The Availability Period is the period during which the debt is available for drawing—if not fully drawn by the end of the Availability Period the commitment to advance any further debt is terminated. Typically, the Availability Period runs until the earlier of six months after the actual Project Completion (to cover any remaining minor costs such as 'snagging' items under the Construction Contract— cf. §8.2.7), or 12 months after planned Project Completion (to allow time for delays in construction).

§14.3.2 DRAWDOWN PROCEDURE

The procedure for drawing on the loan usually involves the Project Company pre-senting a formal drawdown request several days in advance of the date on which funds are required. There is usually only one drawing a month. The drawdown request:

- attaches a payment request from the Construction Contractor, certified by the Lenders' Engineer;
- summarizes the purpose for which other funds are required;
- sets out how these costs are to be funded—*i.e.* by equity or debt, depending on their priority for drawing (*cf.* §12.2.3) and if there are several loans, which one is to be drawn;
- if tied funding from ECAs or other sources is being used (*cf.* §16.2), provides the certification on the origins of the equipment or services required for this;
- compares the monthly and cumulative project costs with the construction budget (*cf.* §13.5.1);
- demonstrates that enough funds remain available to complete the project (*cf.* §13.5.2);
- demonstrates compliance with any other conditions precedent to drawings (*cf.* §14.8).

Both equity investment and loan drawings are paid into a Disbursement Account in the Project Company's name over which the lenders have a security interest,[5] or they are paid directly to the beneficiaries, especially the Construction Contractor (*cf.* §8.2.3).

Lenders may control all payments from the Disbursement Account, or allow the Project Company to make the payments for the purposes set out in its drawdown requests, only taking control of payments if there is a default. (The latter is a more practical procedure; if a drawdown request procedure as set out above is used, there is no need for lenders to do anything other than monitor payments out of the Disbursement Account.)

An alternative system is to have fixed monthly drawdowns (based on the Banking Case) paid into the Disbursement Account, perhaps variable ±5%. In this system the agent bank has to control the payments out of the Disbursement Account. Similarly the proceeds of a bond issue are all paid into the Disbursement Account and controlled by the Controlling Creditor or bond trustee (*cf.* §5.4; §10.3.4).

§14.3.3 Debt Accretion

In some cases, the Project Company may be able to use a borrowing-base system of drawdown to finance separate tranches of investment, as and when cash flow or other targets have been met (*cf.* §5.2.2).

---

[5] Also known as a Proceeds Account.

Debt Accretion is a drawdown structure closely-related to a borrowing-base system, under which the debt can be drawn during a much longer Availability period than that indicated in §14.3.1. The most common use relates to Concessions. In this type of project lenders usually take a conservative view of the likely build-up of traffic (*cf.* §9.6.3). Therefore if over time the traffic increases above these projections, more debt can be draw on a pre-agreed Cover-Ratio formula based on the growth in User Fees. The Availability Period in such cases may extend to, say, the first 10 years of operation. However a similar result can also be achieved by refinancing the original debt when the traffic growth allows it (*cf.* §14.16).

§14.4 OPERATING PHASE—CONTROL OF CASH FLOW

Just as during the construction phase of the project the lenders only allow drawings to be made and costs to be paid when they are satisfied that these are for the budgeted and approved purposes, similarly, during the operating phase, the lenders normally control the application of the cash flow of the project by controlling the way in which the cash is used. These controls include:

- requirement for the Project Company to establish various Project Accounts, over which the lenders have security and varying degrees of control (§14.4.1);
- an order of priorities in applying cash, known as the Cash-Flow 'Cascade' (§14.4.2);
- control on Distributions of cash to investors (§14.4.3);
- in some cases, Cash Sweep (§14.4.4) or cash clawback requirements (§14.4.5).

§14.4.1 PROJECT ACCOUNTS

The Lenders require various Project Accounts[6] to be set up with the Project Company's bank to ensure that the project's cash flow is allocated as required in the loan documentation.[7] These relate both to the Project Company's revenues and their application to operating and financing costs, as well as to various sums which have to be set aside in Reserve Accounts.

---

[6] Also known as Control Accounts.

[7] These include the requirements during the construction phase set out in §14.3.2.

There are two ways in which the revenues of the Project Company are subject to Lender control and supervision as they accrue:

- Lenders may require the Project Company to segregate funds to cover operating costs in a separate Operating Account under the Project Company's day-to-day control, leaving the other funds in a Revenue Account under the joint control of the agent bank or security trustee and the Project Company until the other payments need to be made as discussed in §14.4.2.
- Alternatively, all revenues may flow into one account, from which payments are made by the Project Company when required.

The latter is obviously preferable for the Project Company and generally more practical for day-to-day operations, but the lenders have to be comfortable with trusting the Project Company not to misapply revenues on a short-term basis.

Lenders also require the Project Company to establish separate Reserve Accounts into which various sums of money are held. Although these are in the Project Company's name, withdrawal of funds from these requires the consent of the agent bank or security trustee, and the balances in these Reserve Accounts form part of the lenders' security.

The Reserve Accounts provide security against short-term cash flow problems and are also established if funds need to be set aside for major expenditure in future. They also segregate funds such as insurance proceeds, which are to be used for a particular purpose.

Insofar as Reserve Accounts are built up, the investors' return decreases, as they prevent or delay distribution of net cash flow. Assuming that the Reserve Accounts are being established anyway, the Sponsors' main concern will be that the Project Company should not be left in the position of having insufficient cash to carry on its normal business, while other cash is trapped in Reserve Accounts.

Some of the standard Reserve Accounts are:

Debt Service Reserve Account ('DSRA'). This account contains sufficient funds to pay the next debt service (principal and interest) installment, usually six months' worth of debt service. If the Project Company cannot pay some or all of the debt service from its normal cash flow (or a Debt Payment Reserve Account, if any), funds are taken out of this account to do so.

The DSRA has to be established at the beginning of the operation phase. There are two ways of doing this:
- including the DSRA as part of the construction cost budget for the project;
- funding the DSRA from operating cash flow under the Cascade (*cf.* §14.4.2), which means that it is not filled up on Project Completion, but as cash flow comes in from initial operations.

The first approach is preferable from the investors' point of view, because most of the funds required for the DSRA are funded by the lenders (*i.e. pro rata* to the debt portion of the debt:equity ratio). It also has the benefit from the lenders' point of view that they know that the DSRA is funded as soon as the project begins operation. As a halfway house between these two alternative approaches, the Project Company may be allowed to draw funds for the DSRA at Project Completion from any unused funding at that time not needed for any other purpose.

Debt Payment Reserve Account. This account may be used to accumulate funds on a month-by-month basis to pay the next installment of principal and interest, instead of leaving the funds in the Project Company's operating account (usually if the Project Company's revenues flow into one account, instead of being split into Operating and Revenue Accounts as described above). If so, the account is emptied at the end of each payment period to pay the interest and principal installment then due. (Note that this is in addition to the DSRA.) This may be coupled with an Interest Payment Reserve Account, building up the next interest payment in the same way, or these two accounts can obviously also be combined.

Maintenance Reserve Account ('MRA'). If a project has a major maintenance cycle (*e.g.* a process plant has to be maintained every five years, with most of the maintenance costs thus being incurred every five years rather than annually), these payments are 'smoothed out' by placing one-fifth of the estimated major maintenance costs in a Maintenance Reserve Account (*i.e.* a kind of sinking fund) every year, and then drawing on the account to pay for the maintenance in year five (*cf.* §9.7.5).

An alternative approach may be used where there is less of a long-term maintenance cycle (*e.g.* in a PPP building such as a school or hospital): in this case the Project Company may be required to place funds in the MRA equal to 100% of the next year's estimated maintenance (and lifecycle) costs, 50% of the next year, and 25% of the next year, to make sure that there are always funds available for maintenance.

Change in Law Reserve Account. If the Project Company is not fully protected against Changes in Law, lenders may require a Reserve Account to be established to provide funds for this purpose. The problem with this is, as discussed in §11.3, there is no way of deciding how much money should be placed in this account.

Tax and Other 'Smoothing' Reserve Accounts. If the Project Company incurs a significant tax liability in one year, but does not have to pay the tax until a later year, a Tax Reserve Account is normally established to set aside the cash for this purpose. Other 'smoothing' Reserve Accounts of this nature may be established to cover significant deferred liabilities or irregular costs.

Insurance Proceeds Account. A separate Reserve Account may be established into which the proceeds of insurance claims are paid, and from which amounts are paid under the lenders' control for restoration of the project or reduction of the debt (*cf.* §8.6.5).

Similar accounts may be used for other types of compensation received by the Project Company, such as LDs from the Construction Contractor. In these accounts, where money has been received for a specific purpose, the cash does not flow through the Cascade discussed in §14.4.2, but directly into the account.

Reserve Accounts and Cover-Ratio Calculations. In calculating the ADSCR (*cf.* §12.3.1) and LLCR (*cf.* §12.3.2), payments to Reserve Accounts other than those for debt service are treated as a deduction from the operating cash flow in the period concerned, and drawings from such accounts (*e.g.* to pay maintenance costs) are added back to the cash flow (and hence offset the actual expenditure).

Payments to and from the DSRA are ignored in the ADSCR calculation (which is intended to show the Project Company's ability to service its debt on a regular basis without using reserves). The balance on the DSRA is normally deducted from the debt outstanding in calculating the LLCR, on the basis that this cash could be used for immediate repayment of the loan. The Project Company may argue that balances on other Reserve Accounts such as that for maintenance should also be deducted in the LLCR calculation for the same reason; lenders may, however, point out that this cash is not intended for debt reduction.

Interest earned on Reserve Accounts is normally added to the operating income when calculating Cover Ratios, unless the balance of the Reserve Account concerned is below the minimum required (which would mean that the interest earned cannot be taken out of the Reserve Account).

To improve their Equity IRR the Sponsors may provide the lenders with a bank letter of credit or, if acceptable, corporate guarantees, for the amount that would otherwise have been placed in a routine Reserve Account such as the DSRA, in return for the lenders allowing this cash to be distributed rather than being trapped in the Project Company.

The Project Company may be given some flexibility to make a limited range of low-risk 'authorized investments' with surplus funds including those in Reserve Accounts, to earn a better return on these deposits, but of course the lenders require their security to include these.

§14.4.2 THE CASH-FLOW CASCADE

The controls for application of cash earned by the Project Company from its revenues are set out in a 'Cash-Flow Cascade',[8] setting out the order of priorities for the use of this cash. A typical order of priorities is:

1. Payment of fuel or raw material and operating costs, including the O&M Contract (based on the agreed budgetary procedures—*cf.* §9.7.7) and taxes (*i.e.* all the costs the Project Company needs to pay to continue operating the project).
2. Fees and expenses due to the agent bank, security trustee, *etc.*
3. Interest on the debt and any swap or other hedging payments.[9]
4. Scheduled debt principal repayments (to the 'target' schedule if there is one—*cf.* §12.5.4).
5. Payments to the Debt Service Reserve Account, and other Reserve Accounts (see above).[10]
6. Distributions to investors (§14.4.3).

Once all the funds required for the first category have been paid, remaining cash available is moved down to the second, and so on (like water flowing down a series of pools—hence the names for this system of cash-flow allocation). It follows that if there is insufficient cash to pay the first five items, no cash is distributed to the investors.

The structure of the cascade is of course rather artificial, in that these cash payments do not all occur on the same day. It may be necessary to ensure that for a particular project the system takes account of situations where the Project Company has received payment for a service but has not yet provided it (*e.g.* advance payments for corporate boxes in a stadium)—an additional Reserve Account may be needed if this cash would otherwise eligible to be used for Distributions.

It should be noted that this Cascade arrangement is largely dormant during the construction of the project, when funds from equity and debt are paid into the Disbursement Account (*cf.* §14.3.2).

---

[8] Also known as the cash-flow 'waterfall'.

[9] These may be accumulated on a month-by-month basis in a Debt Payment Reserve Account (see above).

[10] As mentioned in §14.4.1, funds in specific-purpose Reserve Accounts such as the MRA, or a Tax Reserve Account can be drawn to meet their specific purpose when needed, and so do not go through the Cascade.

§14.4.3 DISTRIBUTIONS TO INVESTORS

The investors come at the bottom of the Cash-Flow Cascade; once operating costs, and all the lenders' repayment and Reserve-Account requirements have been met, in principle Distributions to investors can be made. If the Project Company cannot immediately pay these amounts over to the investors (*e.g.* because there may be a delay before its annual general meeting can be held and a dividend declared), they are paid into a Shareholder Distribution Account in the name of the Project Company (which should be outside the lenders' security package).

But it is seldom quite as simple as seeing if there is any cash left over and paying it to the investors: there are other hurdles to jump.

Distribution Stop. The Project Company obviously has to demonstrate that sufficient cash will remain or be generated in the future to repay debt after the Distributions have been made. This is dealt with by establishing a 'Distribution-Stop' Ratio;[11] for example, if the Banking Case projected average ADSCR was 1.35:1, the lenders may require Distributions to be stopped if the previous year's actual ADSCR was lower than, say, 1.2:1.[12]

The calculation of the Cash-Flow Cascade to determine whether there is sufficient cash to pay Distributions is usually carried out once every six months (and hence Distributions are only made every six months). If cash flow cannot be distributed because Distribution-Stop ratio requirements are not met, any cash available may be used to prepay the debt or held in a special Reserve Account, until the Cover-Ratio calculations again fall on the right side of the line after allowing for the debt reduction or funds held in the special Reserve Account.

An issue in calculating the Distribution-Stop Ratio is whether 'forward-looking' ratios (*e.g.* the projected ADSCR for the next year, or the LLCR or average ADSCR as projected for the rest of the loan) should be also used for this purpose. Once the project is operating, the best way of projecting how it will operate in the future is to look at how it has actually operated in the past, but in that case the actual ADSCRs achieved are what should mainly concern lenders. Especially in a project with a regular assured cash flow under a Project Agreement, it is difficult to conceive why the projections of cash flow for the next year should be much lower than those for the last year (predictable fluctuations, *e.g.* maintenance, should be dealt with using Reserve Accounts). Therefore, although beloved by lenders, forward-looking

---

[11] Also known as a 'Distribution-Block', 'Dividend-Stop' or 'Lock-Up' Ratio, or a 'Cash Trap'.

[12] And *cf.* §14.12 for what happens if the ADSCR goes lower still.

ratios are largely a waste of time in this situation, and doing away with them also eliminates the problem of deciding what assumptions should be used in the financial projections for this purpose (*cf.* §13.11). However there is a case for forward-looking ratios if a Project Company is selling a commodity into the open market or taking full usage risk in a Concession project, *i.e.* cases where the annual cash flow is less predictable.

The Project Company will have to fulfill further requirements before making Distributions, in particular no Event of Default (*cf.* §14.12) should have occurred under the Project Contracts or the financing documentation (*cf.* §14.12).

§14.4.4 CASH SWEEP

There are several circumstances in which lenders may require a 'Cash Sweep', *i.e.* using free cash flow which would otherwise have been used for Distributions to prepay the debt:

Irregular Cash Flow. This approach is normally used if there are likely to be substantial fluctuations in cash flow (*e.g.* because of commodity-price movements), and the lenders wish to ensure that some of the surplus cash generated in good times is used to reduce debt and so provide a buffer against a downturn. Therefore after an agreed-upon level of Distribution to the investors, the balance of the cash flow is used to prepay the debt or split between prepayment and a further Distribution to the investors. Thus if the project performs according to the agreed Banking Case, the investors will receive the Banking Case return, but cash flow from the project above this level is split between investors and debt repayment.[13] A Cash Sweep of this type may also be required because the lenders are concerned about the adequacy of the Debt Tail (*cf.* §12.3.4) or the Reserve Tail (*cf.* §12.3.5).

Standby Finance. §17.5.3 gives an example of the use of a cash sweep to repay standby finance which has been drawn to cover a temporary deficit in the projects cash flow.

Lifecycle Costs. In some projects it may be known that costs have to be incurred a long time in future, which are too substantial to be covered by setting aside spare cash in a Maintenance Reserve Account. For example, a road project may require significant lifecycle expenditure such as a major resurfacing of the road after 15 years. The initial loan may run for 20–25 years (*i.e.* past the date when additional funding will obviously be

---

[13] This is sometimes known as a 'good times sweep' because it applies when the project is performing well, to contrast with other cash sweeps when the project is doing badly.

needed). It is likely to be very difficult to fix the costs of the major works 15 years in advance, and raising debt that would not be used for 15 years is virtually impossible (*cf.* §7.6.3). Again, the solution may be a full (100%) Cash-Sweep (*i.e.* all available cash goes into the sweep and there are no Distributions to investors) beginning several years before the date for the major works, to encourage the Sponsors to refinance the loan and raise the additional debt required when it becomes feasible at that time. In this case the Cash Sweep will apply before any Distributions can be made (and hence the investors will receive nothing unless they refinance the loan).

Soft Mini-Perm. Similarly, a Cash Sweep is also very useful as part of a package of measures dealing with problems that lenders might otherwise have with the total length of the financing, In such cases most or all of the cash flow generated after debt service is not distributed to the investors, but is used for debt prepayment, or placed in a Reserve Account.

For example, suppose the lenders have been asked to provide a 25-year loan, but really only feel comfortable with a 7-year loan for liquidity reasons (*cf.* §17.2). In such a case a 25-year loan repayment schedule is agreed to, but a 100% Cash Sweep (again before any Distributions are made, so the investors receive no cash flow) may be applied from, say, year 5 and cases the debt-interest margin may also increase sharply from year 5. This is known as a 'Soft' Mini-Perm, as opposed to a 'Hard' Mini-Perm which would require repayment of the debt balance at the end of year 7 (*cf.* §10.6), and the aim is to provide 'encouragement' to refinance the debt (*cf.* §17.5.5), but if this cannot be done the loan will continue for up to 25 years.

Similarly, the lenders may not want to lend for more than, say, 12 years in the country where the project is located, whereas the Project Company needs a 15-year repayment to make the project viable. In this case, the Project Company may agree to a Cash Sweep from, say, year 10 of a 12-year loan, whose repayment schedule is based on that of a 15-year loan with a 'balloon' payment of the outstanding balance after 12 years. This is normally done in the expectation that when the time comes the lenders will be prepared to waive the Cash Sweep requirement and lend for a longer term.

It might seem that the Project Company could achieve the same result by just borrowing the funds for the period the lenders are actually prepared to lend for. However, in this case the repayment schedule is likely to make the financing unviable, as the lenders would require a higher level of repayments in the early years of the loan, instead of relying on the Cash Sweep at the end.

Event of Default. The lenders may also impose a full Cash Sweep if there is an Event of Default under the financing agreements (*cf.* §14.12).

§14.4.5 CASH CLAWBACK

If there is some uncertainty about future costs (*e.g.* major maintenance or lifecycle cost) or revenues, lenders may still be prepared to allow investors to take Distributions out of the Project Company, provided a clawback undertaking is given. Under such an undertaking, the Sponsors agree that if the possible future cash-flow problem develops, they will repay or lend to the Project Company up to the amount they have received in Distributions over a set period of time.

§14.5 REPORTING REQUIREMENTS

Throughout the term of the financing, the Project Company will be required to give reports on various aspects of its business to the lenders and their advisors. These requirements fall naturally into two phases—the construction (§14.5.1) and operating (§14.5.2) phases of the project.

It is easy for Sponsors and lenders to get so carried away by the detail of structuring and negotiating the deal that the big picture of what really matters gets buried. Lenders sometimes fall into the trap of requiring an over elaborate system of information flow about the project, which both hinders the Project Company from doing its job of running the project efficiently, and burdens the lenders with information they do not want to read.

The lenders' advisors' costs continue to be for the account of the Project Company, as they are before Financial Close (*cf.* §5.5.1; §13.5.1).

§14.5.1 CONSTRUCTION PHASE

As can be seen from the drawdown procedure set out in §14.3.2, the lenders regularly check the latest information on the project before advancing further tranches of debt. In addition to the information required for certification of drawings, the Lenders' Engineer will expect to be provided with all significant information on the progress of the construction, and to be able to attend all relevant site or other meetings.

§14.5.2 OPERATING PHASE

The lenders typically reduce the Project Company's formal reporting on the project to a quarterly interval once the project has been completed and is seen to be operating smoothly. This reporting would include the Project Company's management accounts (and audited accounts annually), and its report on the key aspects of the project, *e.g.* performance in the case of an Availability-based project, or traffic and toll revenues in the case of a Concession toll-road, any deductions made by an Offtaker or Contracting Authority, significant variations from projections or budget for the period, Cover Ratio calculations, *etc.* This is supplemented by further reports from the relevant Lender's advisors, *e.g.* on trends in traffic volumes. Should a particular problem arise with the project, the lenders may also require further *ad hoc* reports or information.

§14.6 DEBT CANCELLATION AND PREPAYMENT

A Cash Sweep (*cf.* §14.4.4) is a form of mandatory (*i.e.* compulsory) prepayment of the loan by the Project Company. Other mandatory prepayments are normally required:

- if the Project Company realizes cash from the sale of assets (unless the cash is used to replace the asset);
- if insurance proceeds are not applied to the restoration of the project (*cf.* §8.6.5).

In these cases the cash is applied directly to prepayment rather than passed through the Cash-Flow Cascade.

If performance LDs are received from the Construction Contractor (*cf.* §8.2.8), prepayment is made to the extent necessary to maintain the lenders' Cover Ratios; any surplus LDs flow into the Cash-Flow Cascade (and will probably therefore flow out as Distributions, which compensates the investors for the reduction in their Equity IRR caused by the performance failure). Delay LDs, however, all flow straight into the Cascade, since they are in lieu of operating revenue.

A mandatory prepayment of the loan is also required if it becomes illegal for the lenders to continue with it; this is usually meant to cover the possibility of international sanctions against the country in which the Project Company is located. (The obligation may be limited to prepayment insofar as the Project Company has available cash flow.)

The Project Company may also wish to reduce or prepay the loan voluntarily:

- The loan commitment may be reduced because the total funding raised is not all needed (§14.6.1).
- The Project Company may wish to prepay part or all of the loan (§14.6.2).
- The Project Company may wish to prepay the whole loan and refinance it on more attractive terms elsewhere (*cf.* §14.16.1).

§14.6.1 COMMITMENT REDUCTION

As construction of the project progresses, the Project Company may consider that it will not need all the funding raised for the project (including any contingency funding), and it could save commitment fees by reducing the committed amount of the debt, perhaps also reducing its investors' risks (and increasing their return) by reducing the committed equity *pro rata*.

In principle, lenders should not object to this, so long as the Project Company can demonstrate that after the reduction there will be enough funds to complete the project as scheduled, with an adequate remaining safety margin. It is therefore unlikely that lenders would allow reduction in committed funding until quite a late stage in the construction of the project.

§14.6.2 PARTIAL PREPAYMENT

A typical case where the Project Company may want to prepay part of the loan can arise from Distribution restrictions imposed by the lenders (*e.g.* a Distribution Stop). For this or other reasons it may be cost-effective for the investors to prepay part of the debt in order to restore the Cover Ratios to a level above the Distribution Stop, rather than have funds trapped in the Project Company.

In most project financings bank lenders are generally prepared to accept a prepayment after Project Completion, but they may require a prepayment fee (typically 0.5–1.0% of the amount refinanced). Swap-breakage costs also need to be covered (*cf.* §10.3.1). Although bank lenders are flexible on partial prepayment, partial prepayment is not normally allowed in bond issues, or at least partial prepayment of a bond is only likely to be allowed on payment of a substantial penalty (*cf.* §10.3.4). The same principle generally applies to other fixed-rate loans.

The main question with a partial prepayment (whether voluntary or mandatory) is, against which future loan payment installments should it be applied? If, for example, a prepayment of 120 is made on a loan of 500 due to be repaid in five future annual installments, the prepayment could be applied in any of the ways shown in Table 14.2.

Table 14.2 Order of Prepayment

Prepayment of 120		Remaining Loan Payment Installments after Prepayment in:		
	Original Schedule	Order of Maturity	Inverse Order of Maturity	*Pro rata*
Year 1	100	—	100	76
2	100	80	100	76
3	100	100	100	76
4	100	100	80	76
5	100	100	—	76
Total	500	380	380	380

- Provided that surplus cash flow can be distributed, application of prepayments *in order of maturity* is most beneficial to investors, since this reduces the following debt-service payments and so releases the cash for future Distributions more quickly. This approach is the fairest if the Project Company has made a free choice to prepay the loan because of temporary constraints on Distributions to investors.
- Lenders, on the other hand, may wish to reduce the average life of their loan, and hence their risk on the project, by applying prepayments *in inverse order of maturity*.
- Some types of prepayment must be applied *pro rata* if they are going to work (*e.g.* the Construction Contractor's performance LDs are applied *pro rata* to all installments, to maintain the Lender's ADSCRs at an even level).

It may therefore be necessary to specify different applications of partial prepayments depending on the circumstances in which they are made.

§14.7 LENDERS' SECURITY

As already discussed (*cf.* §2.2), lenders do not expect to be able to get their money back by selling the Project Company's assets: in most project financings only the cash flow of a successful continuing operation will provide this repayment. Foreclosure on project assets is seldom a solution to a problem with the project;[14] however, security over the project as a whole remains important:

- to ensure the lenders are involved at an early stage if the project begins to go wrong;
- to ensure that third parties (such as unsecured creditors) do not gain any prior or *pari-passu* rights over the project assets;
- to ensure that project assets are not disposed of without the lenders' agreement;
- to enable the lenders to 'encourage' cooperation by the Project Company if it gets into trouble—*i.e.* the lenders will be able to tell the Project Company what to do.

The lenders' security—which may be held by the agent bank or a security trustee[15]—normally has four layers:

---

[14] Even assuming this is possible, which it is generally not with a PPP project as the project assets belong to the public-sector, and often do not have a alternative private-sector use: *e.g.* it is not possible to foreclose on a road.

[15] The reasons for using a security trustee are, firstly, to make it easier for the agent bank, should it wish to do so, to relinquish that rôle (*e.g.* if it sells its share of the debt), otherwise it could be necessary for all the security to be re-registered to a new agent; and secondly in case the agent bank becomes insolvent, which could jeopardize the lenders' security. Security trustees are also usually used in bond transactions (*cf.* §5.3.2).

- control of cash flow (*cf.* §14.4);
- the ability to Step-In to the project under Direct Agreements (*cf.* §8.11);
- mortgages and assignments of the Project Company's assets and contracts (§14.7.1);
- Security over the Project Company's shares (§14.7.2).

§14.7.1 MORTGAGES AND CONTRACT ASSIGNMENTS

There is seldom any substantial disagreement between Sponsors and lenders about the latter's right to take security over all physical assets, contractual rights, and guarantees, which the Project Company has. The security package therefore includes:

- mortgages or charges over the project site, buildings, and equipment (insofar as they belong to the Project Company and not to a Contracting Authority or another public-sector entity);
- assignment of Project Contracts, including advisory contracts with parties such as the Owner's Engineer, and any bonds or guarantees for these contracts;
- assignment of the Project Company's right to receive payments of equity from the Sponsors (*cf.* §3.6.2; §12.2.3);
- assignment of revenues (linked to the Project Accounts—*cf.* §14.4.1);
- assignment of Permits and licenses;
- charges over Project Accounts, with dual signatures from the Project Company and the agent bank or security trustee required where Lender approval is needed to transfer funds from an account;
- undertaking by the Offtaker/Contracting Authority, if any, to make payments only to the Project Accounts (if this is not covered in a Direct Agreement);
- assignment of insurance policies (*cf.* §8.6.5);
- assignment of the Project Company's right to receive any payment due to it if an interest swap is unwound (*cf.* §10.3.1).

Problems may arise however if third-party cooperation is needed to create or make this security effective:

- Consent to assignments by the other parties to Project Contracts may not be forthcoming. (If possible, this should be covered by ensuring there are appropriate provisions in the original Project Contract documentation for Direct Agreements (*cf.* §8.11).
- It may not be possible to assign Permits or licenses as security; some countries may not allow some types of Permits or licenses to be assigned because they are granted to a specific permit or license holder. (Direct Agreements may provide some support in such cases.)

Where a cross-border project investment is concerned, since the Project Company's assets are in the Host Country the security over them usually has to be governed by local law and jurisdiction, unlike the situation that may apply to the Project Contracts or financing documentation (*cf.* §11.5.1). In developed countries this approach does not normally cause any difficulties, although local legal advisors are of course necessary. However, in some developing countries the lenders may not be able to achieve an ideal security position:

- The local law may prevent foreigners from owning land, and so the lenders cannot take over the Project Company's rights in this respect.
- High levels of stamp duty or similar *ad valorem* taxes may be charged on registration of lenders' loans or security, adding significantly to the financing costs payable by the Project Company.
- There may be preferential creditors (such as tax payments) that automatically rank ahead of the lenders' security.
- Lenders may only be able to register security over assets that already exist, not those that will be acquired or constructed in future.
- Lenders may only be able to register their security for a fixed amount, leaving a risk that the total amount payable on default may be higher when interest, breakage costs, and enforcement costs are included.
- Lenders may only be able to register their security in the local currency, with the risk the lenders may become undersecured if the local currency depreciates against the currency in which they are lending (*cf.* §10.5.8).
- Lenders may be prevented from enforcing their security if insolvency proceedings are taking place against the relevant counterparty.
- The procedures for enforcing security may be inappropriate or too cumbersome for lenders who want to be able to take over control of the project quickly; in particular, lenders may be required to sell the assets in a public auction or after a court action rather than take over their control and operation through an administrator or receiver.
- Exchange controls may hinder the lenders from removing enforcement proceeds from the country.

Security may have to be taken in several different jurisdictions apart from that of the Host Country: if Reserve Accounts are held offshore (*cf.* §11.4.1), then the security must be registered under the law of the country where they are held; the same applies if the shares of an offshore holding company are pledged to the lenders.

In common-law countries such as England and Australia, it is possible to have a 'floating charge' over the Project Company's assets. This does not require registration of security against each specific asset and contract but nonetheless gives security over all of them, which crystallizes when enforcement proceedings are taken.

If for some reason the lenders cannot be granted a security over the project's fixed assets, the Project Company must give a 'negative pledge' undertaking (*i.e.* not to pledge the assets concerned to anyone else). This is obviously of limited value compared to a proper security interest. (Even then, lenders will want security over Project Accounts.)

§14.7.2 SECURITY OVER PROJECT COMPANY'S SHARES

Lenders normally take security over the Sponsors' shares in the Project Company. This is to enable the lenders to step in more quickly to take over management of the Project Company than may be achieved by taking action under mortgages or contract assignments. There may be some difficulties with this:

- A Sponsor's corporate lenders may impose negative-pledge provisions, as discussed above, which may prevent a pledge being given over the Project Company's shares.
- As also discussed above, cumbersome court procedures may make enforcement of a pledge over the shares too slow.
- There is a potential problem if the Sponsors wish to take out political-risk insurance to protect their investment (*cf.* §16.3).
- There could also be a problem if the Sponsors wish to sell their shares, unless the new shareholders are willing to grant the same security.

As for the first issue, it may be necessary for the Sponsor to negotiate a waiver of this provision in the case of its Project Company shares. There are various possible ways of dealing with the second issue:

- Lenders take security over the shares of an offshore holding company, owned by the investors, and in a more creditor-friendly jurisdiction, which owns the shares in the Project Company, thus enabling the lenders to take control of the Project Company quickly through taking control of its only shareholder. (Care needs to be taken that there are no other creditors of the Project Company who could interfere with this process, and that the intermediate holding company has no debt, even to its own shareholders, or these creditors will have first call on its assets, *i.e.* the Project Company's shares, at the expense of the Project Company's lenders.)
- Lenders take a call option over the Project Company's shares (*i.e.* the Sponsors agree to sell the shares to the lenders for a nominal sum if the loan goes into default).
- Sponsors give the lenders a 'golden share' that allows them to appoint directors if the loan is in default.

The latter two approaches may cause regulatory difficulties for banks and may create legal liabilities if the lenders become directly involved in management of the Project Company.

Lenders will also wish to ensure that the Project Company is not affected by financial difficulties or even bankruptcy of a Sponsor or another investor (*i.e.* it is 'bankruptcy remote'). For example, if a Sponsor is made bankrupt this should not result in its Project Company subsidiary or affiliate being made bankrupt as well, or remove the benefit of a pledge of the Project Company's shares. Depending on the location of the project and Project Company, it may be necessary to insert an intermediary company between the Sponsor(s) and the Project Company to reduce this risk.

§14.8 CONDITIONS PRECEDENT

Signature of the financing documentation alone does not mean that the lenders will start advancing funds to the Project Company. In order to draw down any debt at all, the project must first reach Financial Close. This is the date at which all Project Contracts and financing documentation have been signed, and the 'conditions precedent' to the effectiveness of the lenders' commitments have been satisfied or waived. The conditions precedent are effectively a checklist of documents the lenders require as the basis for their financing; when these are provided the lenders are obliged to advance funds. (This does not mean that lenders have no obligations before that date; for example, if the financing documentation requires the lenders to keep information about the project confidential, this is effective on signing.)[16]

§14.8.1 Conditions Precedent to Financial Close

The list of conditions precedent ('CP') documentation for a project-finance loan can be of immense length, often running into several hundred documents and certificates. Typical requirements by lenders (all of which must be satisfactory to them in form and content) include:

- Corporate documentation:
  - corporate documentation, board resolutions, legal opinions, *etc.*, for the Project Company, evidencing that it is properly constituted and able to enter into the financing;

---

[16] It should be noted that all the Project Contracts and related documentation will each have their own conditions precedent which need to be satisfied at the same time.

- similar corporate documentation for any other parties to Project Contracts or financing documentation, and providers of guarantees, bonding, or other security;
- signed copies of the Shareholder Agreement(s) relating to the Project Company (*cf.* §3.6.2).
- Project documentation:
  - evidence of title to (or right to use) the project site;
  - signed copies of all the Project Contracts and evidence that all their CPs have been fulfilled and that they are in full force and effect;
  - contract guarantees, bonds, or other security (*cf.* §8.2.9; §8.10);
  - NTP given to the Construction Contractor (*cf.* §8.2.2);
  - Permits for the financing, construction, and operation of the project (*cf.* §8.8);
  - signed Direct Agreements (*cf.* §8.11);
  - Arrangements for construction of third party facilities and connections (*cf.* §9.5.9).
- Financing documentation:
  - signature of all financing documentation;
  - bank loan agreement, agency agreement, or bond terms and conditions and trust deed;
  - fee letters, covering payment of arranging and underwriting fees;
  - any Sponsor Support Services Agreements (*cf.* §9.7.2) or guarantees (*cf.* §9.13), or parent-company guarantees for Sub-Contractors (*cf.* §8.10);
  - security documentation (*cf.* §14.7);
  - registration of security.
- Financial due diligence:
  - evidence that all investor funding (equity or subordinated debt) has been paid or committed and any security for this is in place;
  - evidence that any other parallel financing arrangements are in place and effective;
  - evidence that interest-swap or other hedging arrangements are in place (*cf.* §10.3), if these have to be concluded immediately at Financial Close;
  - evidence that the Project Accounts and other banking arrangements are in place;
  - evidence that the required insurance is in place (*cf.* §8.6.1);
  - up-to-date financial statements for relevant parties.
- Technical/commercial due diligence:
  - Final reports from the Lenders' Engineer, insurance advisors, and any other advisors (*cf.* §5.5);
  - Model Auditor's report (including report on tax aspects of the project);

- final construction and funding budget and drawdown schedule (*cf.* §13.5);
- Banking Case financial model (*cf.* §13.10).
- Legal due diligence:
  - legal opinions from lenders' lawyers (and in some jurisdictions also from borrowers' lawyers) as to the validity of the documentation;
  - confirmation that no Event of Default (*cf.* §14.12) has occurred;
  - confirmation that the Project Company is not the subject of any litigation.

Some of these CPs are circular in nature (*e.g.* the right to issue a notice to proceed to the Construction Contractor may be dependent on Financial Close having been reached, and Financial Close cannot be reached until the NTP has been issued). In such cases the legal advisors to the various parties arrange a simultaneous closing of the documentation.

Some CPs may not be achievable when the loan documentation or Project Contracts are signed, and so a distinction may be made between CPs, which are available at the signing, and 'conditions subsequent' which have to be fulfilled before Financial Close can be reached. (If this is the case, the original signing may be referred to as a 'dry closing'.)

The period between the signature of loan documentation and finally achieving Financial Close can become very lengthy if not well-managed. It is the Sponsors' responsibility to manage this process effectively, preferably by gathering as much of the CP documentation as possible in advance of the loan signing, to ensure the minimum delay before Financial Close. Agreeing to CP documentation before signing the financing also ensures that there are no unexpected surprises from issues raised by lenders after the loan has been signed.

An Offtaker/Contracting Authority may require the Sponsors to provide a conditions-precedent bond, as security for their satisfying the CPs by a certain date, but the issues with this raised in §3.7.9 and §7.5 also apply in this case.

§14.8.2 CONDITIONS PRECEDENT TO LOAN DRAWDOWNS

There may be further CPs to each individual drawdown of the debt (*cf.* §14.3.2), in particular:

- confirmation by the Project Company and the Lenders' Engineer:
  - that the amounts payable to the Construction Contractor are properly due;
  - that the construction remains on schedule; and
  - that other amounts to be paid from the drawing are within the agreed construction budget;
  - that enough funds remain to complete construction.
- confirmation by the Project Company:
  - that continuing Representations and Warranties (*cf.* §14.9) remain correct;
  - that no Event of Default or potential Event of Default has occurred (*cf.* §14.12).

§14.8.3 MAC CLAUSE

Lenders may also require that no material adverse change ('MAC') to the project should have occurred after the financial documentation was signed, as a condition precedent both to Financial Close and subsequent drawings of the debt (this is known as a 'MAC clause'). The problem with this kind of vague general provision is the Project Company may be left vulnerable to an arbitrary decision by the lenders to stop funding the project. Careful legal drafting is needed to ensure that if a MAC clause is inserted it is reasonably objective and limited in nature.[17]

§14.9 REPRESENTATIONS AND WARRANTIES

The facts that form the basis of the lenders' provision of the project finance are set out and confirmed in 'representations and warranties' given by the Project Company in the financing documentation.[18] As these are the basis for the financing, if any of the representations and warranties are later found to be incorrect this will create an Event of Default (*cf.* §14.12).

In effect, the representations and warranties are a check-list reconfirming the key elements that lenders have reviewed in their due diligence to confirm that they are satisfied with the risks of the financing.[19] Typical representation and warranties provisions in the finance documentation are that the Project Company:

- is duly incorporated and has the power and has taken all necessary corporate actions to undertake the project and the financing;
- is owned by the Sponsors in the proportions approved by the lenders;
- has no business, assets, or subsidiaries, nor any contractual obligations, except those relating to the project (all of which have been disclosed to the lenders);
- has the capacity to enter into the various Project Contracts and other agreements, and that all these are legally valid and in effect, with no defaults outstanding; no event of *force majeure* has occurred affecting the Project Company or any Project Contracts;
- has title to its property (N.B.: may not be the case in a PPP) and all rights required to construct and operate the project;
- has obtained all licenses and Permits required for the project and these are still valid;

---

[17] And *cf.* §14.12 for the use of a MAC clause as an Event of Default.

[18] Also known as 'undertakings'.

[19] The Project Contracts also have extensive Representations and Warranties, *e.g.* from the Construction Contractor, which the lenders also review.

- is in compliance with the law in all respects and has paid all taxes due;
- has not made, nor have the Sponsors nor any other party made, any corrupt payment (this is of particular concern under the U.S. Foreign Corrupt Practices Act of 1977, and in other countries with similar legislation);
- is not in breach of any existing agreements;
- is not insolvent, and there is no litigation outstanding or threatened against it;
- has no other debt (unless agreed otherwise as part of the financing plan), and the lenders have a valid prior charge over the Project Company's assets through their security arrangements; there are no other security claims on project assets;
- has provided complete and accurate information on the project in an information memorandum (*cf.* §5.2.8), or by other means. The Project Company should only take responsibility for information that it provides directly, and not, *e.g.* summaries of the Project Contracts prepared by the lead arranger(s) and their lawyers. (This provision can be a problem if the loan is underwritten by banks who will syndicate it with an information memorandum later; the undertaking may then have to apply to an information memorandum to be issued in the future, which the Project Company has not yet seen: this can be dealt with by giving the Project Company some degree of control over the parts of the information memorandum for which it is takes responsibility.)
- has provided complete and accurate financial statements, and no significant changes have occurred since the date of the statements;
- has prepared budgets and projections in good faith using reasonable assumptions;
- believes that Project Completion will take place by the agreed date.

Insofar as any of these statements are not correct when the representation is to be made, or the Project Company cannot fully subscribe to them, it must notify the lenders accordingly, and the latter may decide to waive the requirement temporarily or permanently (*cf.* §14.13). If requirements are to be fulfilled later (*e.g.* obtaining an operating permit), this may be covered in the covenants (*cf.* §14.10).

For its own protection, the Project Company may wish to exclude responsibility for 'immaterial' errors in its representations and warranties (*e.g.* if a parking ticket for the plant manager's car has not been paid, does this mean the Project Company is not in compliance with the law?). However lenders are unlikely to accept any significant watering down of their requirement for the Project Company to take full responsibility for the basis behind the financing.

The Sponsors themselves may also be required to provide similar representations and warranties directly to the lenders; if so, the debt becomes a limited-recourse loan, in the sense that the Sponsors may be liable for a loss suffered by the lenders relying on a representation that is not correct. The Sponsors should therefore ensure that their liability in this respect relates only to things under their direct control (*e.g.* their ownership of the Project Company).

These representations and warranties are made on signing of the financing documentation and are usually deemed to be repeated at Financial Close; they may also be deemed to be repeated when each drawing is made, and on each interest payment or loan repayment date.

§14.10 COVENANTS

Covenants are undertakings by the Project Company either to take certain actions (positive covenants), or not to do certain things (negative covenants). These undertakings by the Project Company are a characteristic of project finance, being more comprehensive and detailed than usually found in other types of financing. (Covenants are typically less stringent for a bond issue—*cf.* §5.4.) It is through the covenants that the lenders exercise their continuing control over the construction and operation of the project, but they may need to take care that this control does not also make them liable for Project Company obligations to third parties; for example, in Britain, if lenders are deemed to have acted as 'shadow directors' of an insolvent company, this could create liability for them towards other creditors.

The main purposes of the covenants are:

- to ensure that the project is constructed and operated as agreed with the lenders;
- to give lenders advance warning of any problems that might affect the Project Company; and
- to protect the lenders' security.

§14.10.1 POSITIVE COVENANTS

Typical positive covenants[20] by the Project Company include obligations to:

- maintain its corporate existence, make all required corporate filings, and pay taxes when due;
- construct, operate and maintain the project in accordance with the Project Contracts, applicable law, and good industry practice;

---

[20] Also known as 'affirmative covenants'; positive covenants which require the Project Company to maintain something not less than *x*, *e.g.* the debt:equity ratio, are also known as 'maintenance covenants'.

- provide the agent or security trustee and lenders' advisors with reasonable access to the project and its records;
- maintain the management structure agreed with the lenders (*cf.* §3.6.3);
- obtain and maintain the agreed project insurances;
- supply copies of management accounts (usually quarterly) and annual audited financial statements;
- supply reports (usually monthly) on the progress of construction, including achievement of milestone dates, percentage completion, critical-path issues, and expected Project Completion date (these reports are usually produced by, or based on information from, the Construction Contractor—*cf.* §14.5.1);
- apply funding (equity and debt) in the agreed order (*cf.* §12.2.3; §13.5.1) and only for the purposes agreed in the construction and funding budget (*cf.* §13.5.1);
- ensure that Project Completion is achieved by the agreed date (*cf.* §8.2.7);[21]
- achieve the agreed debt:equity ratio at the end of the construction phase (*cf.* §12.4);
- ensure that the required Cover Ratios are achieved (*cf.* §12.3);
- provide annual budgets in advance of each operating year (*cf.* §9.7.7);
- apply all revenues in accordance with the cash-flow Cascade (*cf.* §14.4.2);
- supply revised financial projections, usually every half-year during operation of the project (*cf.* §14.4.3);
- supply reports (usually quarterly) on the operating performance of the project (*cf.* §14.5.2);
- provide the lenders' advisors with reasonable access to the project, and all information reasonably requested;
- notify the agent bank or security trustee of any significant interruption in the operation of the project or supply of fuel, raw materials or other essential utilities;
- notify the agent bank or security trustee of any insurance claims;
- notify the agent bank or security trustee of any Event of Default (*cf.* §14.12), dispute under the Project Contracts, or litigation or other claims;
- enforce all its rights under the Project Contracts;
- indemnify the lenders against any claim arising from environmental liabilities related to the project (*cf.* §9.10.3–§9.10.4);

---

[21] The definition of Completion for this purpose may be wider than that in the Construction Contract, or the Project Agreement, especially if there is a limited-recourse completion guarantee from Sponsors (*cf.* §9.13); in such cases, beside physical completion as required under the Construction Contract, the Project Company may also, *e.g.* have to achieve a minimum ADSCR to demonstrate that it can operate as projected.)

- obtain all Permits required in future for construction and operation of the project (*cf.* §8.8);
- notify the agent bank or security trustee of any change in law affecting the project (*cf.* §11.3) or withdrawal, failure to renew, or amendment of any Permit or license;
- take any action required to maintain the lenders' security interests (*cf.* §14.7);
- pay for the continuing costs of the lenders' advisors.

The Sponsors may also give separate undertakings to the lenders as to the maintenance of their ownership of the Project Company (*cf.* §7.11; §9.13), provision of technical support (*cf.* §3.6.3), *etc.*

If the Project Company is not able to comply with a positive Covenant, for what the lenders consider to be a good reason, a temporary or permanent waiver of the requirement can be given (*cf.* §14.11). Since many lenders have to go through a formal credit-approval procedure for even quite small waivers of this type, the covenants on the Project Company should not be so restrictive that it has to keep requesting such waivers.

§14.10.2 NEGATIVE COVENANTS

Typical negative covenants[22] by the Project Company include undertakings not to:

- undertake any business other than the project;
- amend its constitutional documents;
- merge or consolidate with any other entity;
- exercise any discretion, or agree to any amendment, waiver, or variation in the Project Contracts, or any changes in the project itself (some scope may be given for *de minimis* items);
- enter into any new contracts (other than the agreed Project Contracts), subject to a *de minimis* exception (*e.g.* for leasing a photocopier);
- use its cash balances to make any investment;[23]
- incur any additional debt or issue guarantees for third parties;
- enter into any hedging contracts other than the agreed hedging of interest-rate or exchange-rate risks (*cf.* §10.3; §10.5.2);
- incur any capital expenditure not agreed to by the lenders;[24]

---

[22] Also known as 'protective covenants'.

[23] Surplus funds are normally held in interest-bearing Project Accounts, although in more sophisticated markets the Project Company may be able to invest in an agreed list of short-term money-market instruments if this does not jeopardize the lenders' security.

[24] Even if it is financed with equity—this is to ensure the specifications of the project (and hence its risks) are not changed without Lender consent.

- incur operating costs not provided for in the agreed annual budget (*cf.* §9.7.7);
- give any other party security over any of its assets (this is known as a 'negative pledge'—*cf.* §14.7);
- sell, lease, or otherwise transfer any of its assets (subject to a *de minimis* exception);
- make any Distributions except as allowed by the loan documentation (*cf.* §14.4.3);
- change its financial year-end or auditors.

Should the Project Company wish to do any of these things, it has to seek permission from the lenders.

It can be seen from the above that the difference between positive and negative covenants is often a matter of wording; a positive covenant to maintain the management structure agreed with the lenders is the same as a negative covenant not to change the management structure agreed with the lenders. Moreover covenants overlap with Events of Default (*cf.* §14.12), since a specific Event of Default could be, for example, a reduction in Cover Ratios below *x*, even if there is no covenant to maintain the Cover Ratio above this figure.

§14.11 PERMISSIONS, WAIVERS AND AMENDMENTS

Covenants such as the Project Company agreeing not to amend any Project Contract do not prevent the Project Company asking the lenders for permission to do so anyway. If the situation has changed since Financial Close and the change in terms would be beneficial to the Project Company and its lenders, then the latter should not object to such a change.

The lenders may also agree to give the Project Company a temporary waiver of some of the covenants and other terms set out above, instead of immediately placing it in default for failure to fulfill them.

Similarly, it may be found that an amendment to the loan documentation is needed, perhaps because of changes in the assumptions made at the time it was negotiated, or other changes in circumstances.

The Project Company should be capable of assessing whether a permission, waiver or amendment is needed well in advance, to ensure time for discussion with the lenders. In general, lenders don't like surprises, and their relationship with the Project Company can be seriously affected if the lenders consider that problems are not being identified and dealt with efficiently.

Lenders may require different levels of control over actions by the Project Company:

- no action without lenders' consent;
- action required if the lenders so request;

- lenders' consent not required subject to prior notice by the Project Company;
- Project Company may take action without prior notice.

If the lenders do not agree to give a permission or waiver, or to amend the loan documentation, this may result in an Event of Default.

§14.12 EVENTS OF DEFAULT

Project-finance lenders do not want to have wait to take action until the Project Company has run out of funds to service the debt; they therefore create a defined set of 'triggers' that gives them the right to take action against the Project Company. These are 'Events of Default'—once an Event of Default has occurred, the Project Company is effectively no longer able to manage the project without Lender involvement. Some of these events (such as failure to pay, insolvency, *etc.*) would apply to any corporate financing, but others (such as failure to complete the project) are peculiar to project finance.

Various courses of action are open to the lenders after an Event of Default, partly depending on what stage the project has reached:

- to waive (*i.e.* ignore) the Event of Default;
- to require the Project Company to take a particular course of action—in effect the lenders can take over control over the Project Company's decision-making process;
- if the project is still under construction, to freeze any further drawdowns of funds—known as a 'Drawstop';
- if the project is operating, to require that all net cash flow be applied to reduction of debt (*i.e.* a Cash Sweep—*cf.* §14.4.4) or held in a separate Reserve Account under the lenders' control;
- to 'accelerate' the loan,[25] and enforce their security.

Once the Event of Default has occurred it is entirely within the lenders' discretion which of these actions they choose to take. It should be noted that these events do not of themselves put the project in default—*i.e.* bring the financing to an end and allow the lenders to accelerate the loan and enforce their security:—a positive decision to take this next stage of action has to be made by the lenders after the Event of Default has occurred (*cf.* §14.14). The threat of moving to this next stage gives the lenders a lever that ensures that they can sit at the table with the Project Company and other project counterparts to find a way out of the problem which either exists already or is indicated by the trigger events to be on the horizon.

---

[25] *i.e.* the whole of the debt becomes due at once.

'Default interest', *i.e.* a higher interest margin on the debt, is usually chargeable until an Event of Default is waived or otherwise dealt with.

Typical events of default are:

- The Project Company fails to make any payment under the financing documentation on its due date.
- Any representation or warranty made by the Project Company (or any other party such as a Sponsor) proves to have been incorrect or misleading.
- The Project Company does not fulfill any of its covenants or undertakings under the finance documentation.
- The Sponsors fail to fulfill any of their obligations or undertakings to the lenders or the Project Company.
- There is any change in the ownership or control of the Project Company prior to an agreed date.
- The Project Company, any Project-Contract counterpart, or any Sponsor or other guarantor fails to pay any of its debts when due, or is subject to a court judgment for more than a *de minimis* amount, or to insolvency proceedings that are not discharged within a specified time.
- Project Completion cannot be achieved by an agreed 'long-stop' date.
- Insufficient finance remains to complete construction of the project.
- Any Permit or license is revoked.
- The project is abandoned (for more than a specified period of time) or becomes a total loss for insurance purposes (but *cf.* §8.6.5).
- Any party defaults under a Project Contract, or these contracts cease to be in full force and effect.
- The Project Company loses title (or access, as the case may be) to the project site.
- Any of the lenders' security becomes invalid or unenforceable.
- The latest ADSCR falls below a certain level; thus the initial Banking Case average ADSCR might be 1.35:1, the Distribution-Stop level (*cf.* §14.4.3) 1.2:1, and this 'Default Ratio' level 1.1:1; as with Distribution Stops, there is the issue of whether forward-looking ratios should be used in this context.
- The Host Government expropriates the project, declares a moratorium on its foreign currency debt, or restricts the conversion or transfer of foreign currency (if the Project Company has borrowed in foreign currency).

Grace Periods. The Project Company needs to secure grace periods to remedy the events of default, if remedy is possible. Non-payment is not the kind of default that can be allowed to drift on, and therefore a grace period of more than 2–3 business days (to allow for any technical problems in transfer of the funds through the banking system) is the normal maximum here.

A reasonable period (say 30 days) should be given for other defaults that can be remedied; for example, failure to fulfill an undertaking to provide financial information.

Potential Event of Default. Lenders may wish to include 'potential Events of Default,' *i.e.* an Event of Default that can be foreseen but has not yet occurred, thus allowing early action on the lenders' part. This should be acceptable to the Project Company provided that it is quite clear that the occurrence of the event is only a matter of time.

Material Adverse Change. Lenders may also wish to add a MAC clause as an Event of Default. As already mentioned, a MAC clause may be used as a condition precedent to prevent the project reaching Financial Close, or subsequent drawing on the loan (*cf.* §14.8.3). Adding this to Events of Default widens the uncertainty for the Project Company and its investors; lenders often take the view, however, that they cannot foresee everything that might go wrong with the project, and they need a catch-all provision to fill any gaps. If the Project Company agrees to such a provision, a material adverse change should be carefully defined—*e.g.* a MAC should have a material adverse effect on the ability of any party to the Project Contract to discharge its obligations, or on the Project Company's operations, assets, or financial condition, and materially affect either the Project Company's ability to service its debt or the lenders' security interests.

Materiality. Similarly, some materiality limitation may be reasonable for some of the Events of Default: for example, a representation should have been misleading in a material respect to make it an Event of Default. This is usually an issue of much debate between Project Company and lenders. For example, the latter may argue that the whole loan should not be placed in default just because it does not fulfill the covenant to deliver the management accounts by a certain date; however, the lenders are likely to consider the failure to produce management accounts in a reasonable period of time a symptom of something seriously wrong with the Project Company's operations, and therefore this should give them a basis to intervene. Lenders always make the point that they will not automatically use Events of Default to destroy the project (which is seldom in their interests), and that they are just there to get everybody around the table, but obviously once an Event of Default occurs, the Sponsors and Project Company are at a disadvantage in any discussions that take place with the lenders.

It will be seen that there is considerable potential for overlap between representations and warranties, covenants, and Events of Default, especially as a breach of a representation, warranty, or covenant is itself an Event of Default. There is little merit in duplication between them.

§14.13 LENDERS' DECISION-MAKING PROCESS

If there is a more than one lender providing the loan, there has to be a decision-making process, or one rogue lender could pull the house down by taking individual action against the Project Company while the rest are trying to find a solution. (Indeed, it is not unknown for a small bank lender to blackmail the larger ones by threatening to do this, so that the larger lenders will buy out the smaller lender's loan.) The agent bank or security trustee also needs to have clear instructions from the lenders as a whole on what action is to be taken on their behalf. Voting mechanisms therefore have to be agreed to in advance between lenders; the Project Company also has an interest in these arrangements, to try to ensure that one or two 'hostile' lenders cannot dictate the action taken, against the wishes of the majority.[26]

Voting arrangements need to cover:

- a decision to waive an Event of Default, so that no further action need be taken on the matter;
- an advance waiver (*i.e.* permission to the Project Company to take an action that would otherwise be a default; *e.g.*, to issue a change order to the Construction Contractor, sell an asset above the *de minimis* level set out in the covenants, or amend some aspect of the Project Contracts);
- amendments to the financing documentation, both to correct errors and to change the provisions to avoid future defaults or allow the Project Company to make some change in the project;
- instructions to the agent bank or security trustee (*e.g.* to enforce security after an Event of Default).

Typical voting arrangements on such issues could be:

Waivers and Permissions. These usually require a 'normal' majority, usually 66⅔–75% of the lenders (by value of their participation in the finance), except for 'fundamental' defaults such as non-payment (and possibly fundamental changes to Project Contracts), for which 100% majority would be needed. (Individual banks may, however, retain the right to withhold further draw downs if the Project Company is in default in the construction phase, *i.e.* without a syndicate vote.)

Amendments to Financing Documents. Amendments that amend the lenders' security, repayment dates, repayment amounts, or interest rate require 100% consent; other amendments may be made with a 66⅔–75% vote.

---

[26] As mentioned in §5.3.2 bondholders may leave most decisions to a Controlling Creditor, so the procedures set out here relate mainly to commercial banks, or to other lenders lending in parallel to them, *e.g.* DFIs or ECAs.

Acceleration of the Debt. If the required majority is not achieved for a waiver, the agent bank or security trustee issues a notice of default: the next stage is 'acceleration' of the debt, meaning that it becomes immediately due and payable. There can be a sliding scale of voting for this: 75% of the lenders must vote for acceleration within, say, 90 days of the notice of default, 66⅔% for the next 90 days, and 51% thereafter.

Enforcement. Enforcement action against the project security is the next stage, and follows from the decision to accelerate the debt; however, some lenders may insist on the right to take individual enforcement action if the agent bank or security trustee does not do so once a notice of default has been issued, especially if the default is caused by nonpayment.

The main practical problem with any voting arrangement is that usually a bank lending as a relatively small participant in a syndicate does not want to be bothered with voting on small issues: for most banks, this means the loan officer having to prepare and explain a paper on the issue to the bank's credit department, and for a minor or technical waiver this is not a very productive use of the loan officer's time. Therefore, actually getting banks to vote at all is difficult. (This is likely to be even more of a problem with bondholders, but in this case the Controlling Creditor may be able to deal with issues without a formal vote.) As a result, if the hurdles for voting majorities on day-to-day amendments and waivers are set too high, the Project Company's business can be paralyzed.

Solutions to this problem of inertia in voting include either a 'silence equals consent' rule, or if, for example, a 75% majority is required, this can be achieved by getting a 75% majority of those lenders who actually vote by a defined deadline, not of all lenders.[27] Such approaches are not just beneficial to the Project Company, since paralyzing the Project Company's business through voting inertia is seldom in the interests of the lenders as a whole. The issue becomes even more acute where there are a large number of bondholders involved, hence the use of a Controlling Creditor.

If a commercial bank's loan is mainly or fully guaranteed (*e.g.* by an ECA—*cf.* §16.2.4), the bank has to vote as the guarantor directs, but if there is political-risk cover only, the bank should be free to vote as it wishes because such votes normally deal with commercial issues.

Having said this, however, a guarantor will still expect to have a vote on any change in the project that could affect the risk it has agreed to take on. For example, if a guarantor is relying on private-sector lenders taking on the construction risks, these lenders should have the right to make decisions on issues arising during the construction of the project, but not if these issues may affect the project's operation after Project Completion. Thus drawing precise dividing lines between when

---

[27] Known in the market as the 'you snooze you lose' clause.

the lenders can make their own decision and when the guarantor decision applies in such cases, may be a matter of some debate. The same principle applies if another party has agreed to 'take out' the initial lenders on Project Completion.

§14.14 INTERCREDITOR ISSUES

If the Project Company has one syndicate or 'club' of lenders, they can act as a single block through the voting arrangements described above. But it is quite common to have more than one group of lenders, for example, a bank syndicate and bondholders, an ECA-backed loan and a bank syndicate lending without ECA cover, domestic banks and foreign banks.

Each of these groups will have their own loan agreement with the Project Company, but the lending groups also need to establish machinery for working together, or the Project Company will soon find itself like a bone between two dogs, with the project in pieces after being pulled in different directions by different lenders. Although the Project Company may not be a direct party to these intercreditor arrangements, it has a strong interest in ensuring that they are practical and workable.

As a minimum, the intercreditor arrangements need to establish:

- common arrangements for Financial Close (usually Financial Close cannot be reached in one loan if it is not also simultaneously reached in the other);
- common voting arrangements for waivers, amendments, and enforcement action: voting in such cases is normally by lending group; each group of lenders can still decide on its own voting rules, and then the decision of each group becomes one block of votes (*pro rata* to that group's exposure) in the intercreditor voting, although it should be noted that commercial banks are reluctant to get into a position where their ability to take action can be blocked by public-sector lenders or others who may not be motivated by purely commercial factors.
- sharing of security;
- sharing of recoveries; sharing of recoveries—*e.g.* a bank may recover more than its *pro-rata* share because it holds the Project Accounts: if this happens such a recovery (providing it relates to the project loan and not some other financing) has to be shared *pro-rata* (to their exposure) by all lenders.

It is preferable for the intercreditor arrangements to extend well beyond this, through the signature of a much wider-ranging Common Terms Agreement.[28]

---

[28] The agreement has a variety of other names, such as Project Coordination Agreement or Co-Financing Agreement.

Under this arrangement, the individual loan agreements cover little more than the amount of the loan, fees, the interest rate, and the repayment schedule. All the other provisions are set out in the Common Terms Agreement, *e.g.*:

- CPs to Financial Close and drawdowns;
- agreement on priority of drawdowns on each loan and adjustments between lenders at the end of construction, or if there is a default, to keep the loans on an agreed *pro rata* basis;
- representations and warranties;
- covenants;
- Project Accounts and the Cash-Flow cascade;
- Events of Default, including cross-default—*i.e.* an Event of Default under one loan agreement is automatically an Event of Default under the others;
- appointment of an intercreditor agent as a central conduit for payments and voting;
- security documentation.

If these issues are not covered in a common agreement, the Sponsors will have difficulty negotiating exactly parallel terms in separate financing agreements, and if exactly parallel terms are not negotiated, the Project Company is again likely to have great difficulty keeping the different groups of lenders from moving in different directions, to the detriment of both lenders and investors.

There is also a legal benefit to a Common Terms Agreement, as lending groups may be from different countries and wish their loan documentation to be governed by the laws and jurisdiction of their group's country. Even if the loan documentation is exactly parallel between the different groups, the differing legal systems may produce different interpretations of what it means. This problem is largely solved by signing loan agreements with a limited scope as above, and then signing the Common Terms Agreement based on one convenient law and jurisdiction.

The creditor groups normally also appoint an intercreditor agent, to perform similar coordination functions for the creditors as a whole to the agent bank for a single group of lenders (*cf.* §5.2.9).

Further intercreditor issues arise if particular groups of lenders or other parties to the financing are not on a similar footing:

- interest-rate swap providers (§14.14.1);
- fixed-rate lenders (§14.14.2);
- lenders with different security (§14.14.3);
- Lessors (§14.14.4);
- Subordinated or mezzanine lenders (§14.14.5);
- defaulting lenders (§14.14.6).

§14.14.1 INTEREST-RATE SWAP PROVIDERS

If an interest-rate swap (§10.3.1) is provided *pro rata* by all the banks in a lending syndicate, there is obviously no need for any special intercreditor arrangements to take account of this, but if—as is commonly the case—the swap is being provided just by one or two banks (either for their own account or acting as a fronting bank), their voting and enforcement rights *vis-à-vis* the rest of the syndicate need to be considered. Because their breakage costs at any one time cannot be predicted (and may be zero if rates move the right way), the extent of their risk—if any—on a default by the Project Company cannot be fixed in advance. Theoretically, the swap provider would wish to have a vote in the syndicate equal to whatever proportion the breakage cost at the time of the vote bears to the rest of the debt: this uncertainty is usually not acceptable to the other lenders. The end result is often that:

- The swap provider does not take part in voting on waivers and amendments (the swap provider is usually also a lending bank and thus still has a voice that can be heard in this way).
- The swap provider may terminate the swap independently if the Project Company is in default under a limited number of categories (such as non-payment and insolvency).
- Once the claim has been crystallized by termination of the swap, the swap provider's vote on enforcement is also fixed *pro rata* to this.

However the voting rights are structured, the swap provider shares *pro rata* in any enforcement proceeds based on the crystallized breakage cost.

§14.14.2 FIXED-RATE LENDERS

Fixed-rate lenders are in a similar position to interest-rate swap providers when a default takes place: they may also have a breakage cost (*cf.* §10.3.4). This does not normally give them any extra voting rights, but is taken into account in determining their *pro rata* share of any enforcement proceeds.

A problem may arise, however, if the fixed-rate Lender charges a very large penalty for terminating the loan; for example as discussed in §10.3.4, the amount due on early repayment may include not just the principal and interest amounts outstanding and breakage costs, but also the NPV of the lenders' future profits. Floating-rate lenders usually do not claim future loss of profit in this way, although an interest-rate swap provider may have a similar claim (*cf.* §10.3.1). This may lead to a large discrepancy in the relative size of the claim that the different groups of lenders have on a default. (Similar problems may arise where one group of lenders is lending on an inflation-indexed basis.)

§14.14.3 LENDERS WITH DIFFERENT SECURITY

The lenders usually share the same security over the project. (This is known as 'cross-collateralization'.)

However, if one lender group has, for example, a Sponsor guarantee that another group has not, then it is evident that the former cannot be inhibited by the latter from enforcing their security after a Project Company default, and *vice versa*.[29]

§14.14.4 LESSORS

If the Project Company finances part of the project costs through leasing, the equipment financed is legally owned by the lessor (leasing company), who are likely to be reluctant to share the value of this security *pari-passu* with other lenders. But any other lenders will not wish the lessor to deal separately with key components of the project. Therefore, an agreement will be needed both to coordinate on foreclosure and probably to share the benefits of a sale.

A similar position may arise if the Project Company uses Islamic financing to fund part of the project costs (*cf.* §4.5.4). In such cases the ownership of the asset may remain with the Islamic Lender, giving rise to the same 'sharing' issues as for a lease.

§14.14.5 SUBORDINATED OR MEZZANINE LENDERS

Subordinated debt provided by the investors in lieu of equity (*cf.* §12.2.2) cannot be used to give them any extra rights either before or after a default. The lenders will require them to agree that they have no security rights and cannot take any enforcement action to recover this debt, or otherwise obstruct the senior lenders, until all the senior lenders' debt has been fully repaid.

Mezzanine debt may be provided by third parties unconnected with the Sponsors or other investors (*cf.* §4.5.1), usually secured by a second mortgage or junior position on the senior lenders' security. Such mezzanine lenders are placed in the cash-flow Cascade (*cf.* §14.4.2) above Distributions to investors, and so are repaid if sufficient cash flow is available after prior payments have been made. They accept that if the financing package as a whole is in default, and enforcement action is taken, they will only be repaid if the senior lenders are fully repaid.

But there are a number of potentially difficult issues with mezzanine lenders. In general, these issues revolve around the concern that senior lenders have of 'Samson in the temple' behavior by mezzanine lenders; if the project goes wrong and there is only enough money to repay the senior lenders, if the mezzanine

---

[29] There is a potential issue here with the 'Preferred Creditor' status of MDFIs (*cf.* §16.5.2); ECAs, for example, that do not have this status, may object to any excess recovery by MDFIs via this route.

lenders have nothing to lose (because there is only enough value in the project to pay the senior lenders) they can threaten to pull the whole project to pieces unless the senior lenders share some of the value that their loans still have.

Senior lenders therefore restrict the rights of mezzanine lenders in a number of ways to try to avoid this happening:

Timing of Drawings. Senior lenders may wish mezzanine loans to be drawn first by the Project Company, in a similar way to equity funding; mezzanine lenders may only be willing to fund *pro rata* with senior lenders.

Conditions Precedent to Drawings. If funding is being provided on a *pro rata* basis, senior lenders will want there to be only very limited CPs to drawings from mezzanine lenders.

Amendments to Senior Loan Terms. Senior lenders want freedom to make amendments to their loan terms, including the repayment schedule and interest rate, and the ability to increase the amount of senior debt if the project gets into trouble. Obviously this may make the mezzanine lenders' position worse: a compromise may be to limit the amount of extra debt or other costs that can be added on to the senior debt at various points in the project life, in a similar way to limits which may be placed by an Offtaker/Contracting Authority on additional debt for which it may be responsible on an early termination of the Project Agreement (*cf.* §7.10.1).

Amendment to Project Contracts. Any amendments to the Project Contracts require senior lenders' consent; they normally require freedom to allow such amendments without interference by mezzanine lenders, unless the result is to increase the senior debt amount, as discussed above.

Blocking of Payments. The place of the payments to mezzanine lenders in the cash flow cascade may raise issues: do the senior lenders' DSRA, or the Maintenance Reserve Account, have to be filled up before mezzanine lenders can be paid; can payments to mezzanine lenders be blocked in a similar way to payments to investors (*e.g.* if Cover Ratios fall below certain levels)?

Default. Mezzanine lenders want to have the right to take enforcement action if they are not paid when due. It is difficult for senior lenders to exclude the mezzanine lenders completely from taking action; a common compromise is to require the mezzanine lenders to wait, say, six months after a payment default before they can take action (and of course such action will trigger action by the senior lenders, so ensuring that any enforcement proceeds still accrue to them first).

'Springing Lien'. A particular structure is used in the U.S.A. if TIFIA financing (*cf.* §15.4) is provided for a transportation project. The TIFIA loan is subordinated to other lenders as far as the cash-flow Cascade is concerned, but if the project goes into default, the TIFIA debt becomes *pari-passu* with the senior lenders. This is known as a 'springing lien'.

§14.14.6 DEFAULTING LENDER

After the difficulties that many commercial banks got into after 2008 Sponsors became concerned about the possibility of a bank (a 'Defaulting Lender') failing to provide its committed finance (*cf.* §12.7.3).

The other lenders are likely to fill the gap (or find another bank to do so) to protect their own loan as otherwise the project may collapse, but they will not commit to do this in advance. Provisions are therefore needed to clarify how the rights of a bank which has not fully provided its full loan commitment are limited, *e.g.* in the decision-making process. The remaining banks have various options in this situation, *e.g.* to buy out its participation in the loan, or remove its voting rights. (Similar provisions to cover the agent bank may provide for a new agent to be appointed.)

§14.15 GOVERNING LAW AND JURISDICTION

If a project is entirely 'contained' in a particular country, *i.e.* not only the Project Company and the project, but also the lenders, are situated in that country, then it would be normal for both the Project Contracts and the project-finance documentation to be governed by the law of the country concerned, and subject to the jurisdiction of the country's courts.

However, although arbitration is often used to resolve disputes in the Project Contracts (*cf.* §7.12), this is not normal as far as loan documentation is concerned, *i.e.* lenders usually want to see disputes about their documentation resolved by an appropriate court.

But if the project is a cross-border one—*i.e.* the lenders are outside the Host Country—the lenders will usually prefer the governing law to be that of England or New York, and for jurisdiction to lie with English or New York courts. The main reason for this is that these jurisdictions or experienced in dealing with complex contractual disputes of the type which may develop in project financings. Another key factor is that lenders may have concerns about the impartiality of the Host Country's courts. Also using an offshore law and jurisdiction prevents the Host Government changing the local law to the detriment of the lenders.

§14.16 DEBT REFINANCING

The process of financial structuring does not necessarily stop at Financial Close. Opportunities may be open to refinance the debt, usually once construction is complete and the project is operating normally (§14.16.1). However this raises the issue of 'windfalls' for the investors, which can cause political problems, especially in a PPP program. In such cases it may be thought advisable for Project Agreements to include provisions for the Contracting Authority to share in this 'refinancing gain' (§14.16.2), but calculation of the gain to be shared is complex (§14.16.3), a lot of things have to be excluded from the definition of a refinancing (§14.16.4), and the relevant provisions are difficult to enforce (§14.16.5). So the practical usefulness of such provisions may therefore be questioned (§14.16.6).

§14.16.1 BASIS FOR REFINANCING

Refinancing of the debt, once the project has been completed and is seen to be operating as expected, is a common phenomenon in project finance, reflecting the reduction in risk as the project progresses. While there can be just a simple refinancing which reduces the interest margin or costs, in general debt refinancing involves other changes in the financing structure as well, the aim being to increase the amount of debt the Project Company can borrow (so allowing an immediate cash transfer to the investors). So a combination of some or all the following are found in most refinancings:

- reducing the interest margin;
- changing the type of debt—*e.g.* from a bank loan to a bond (if this reduces the interest rate);
- extending the debt repayment term (so reducing annual debt-service payments);
- releasing guarantees, or standby or contingency finance (*cf.* §8.10; §12.4.2);
- decreasing the Cover-Ratio requirements;
- otherwise improving loan terms (*e.g.* by reducing Reserve Account requirements—*cf.* §14.4.1).

The refinancing may be undertaken by the original lenders, or the original debt may be prepaid (*cf.* §14.6), by new debt raised from other lenders.

Note that a reduction in underlying market interest rates cannot usually provide the basis for a refinancing. Assuming the Project Company has fixed its interest rate, either by using a fixed-rate loan, or an interest-rate swap, the breakage costs of repaying these early (*cf.* §10.3.1; §10.3.4) will equal if not exceed the NPV of the reduction in costs from lower interest rates thereafter. So as part of the structuring of the refinancing, such costs will have to be minimized or the benefit will be eroded. In fact fixed-rate loans (as opposed to floating-rate loans with an interest-rate swap) are seldom refinanced precisely because the breakage costs (including the par floor) are too high to make it worthwhile.

Table 14.3 shows the effect of a refinancing of the debt 2 years into operation (year 4 of the project). The original debt structure is based on the following assumptions:

- term of Project Agreement: 25 years;
- project cost: 1000;

- construction phase: 2 years, with one-third of the cost paid on day 1, and the balance at the end of each following year;
- financing: 85% debt/15% equity, drawn down *pro rata* during the construction phase;
- net operating revenues: 100 *p.a.* before debt service, over the 23-year operating phase;
- loan term: 22 years (2 years' construction and repayment over first 20 years of operation);
- debt service: debt is repaid on an annuity basis;
- interest rate: 6% *p.a.* (N.B. IDC is added to the debt and financed as part of project costs);
- ADSCR: 1.35:1 (from year 3);
- the effects of inflation and tax are ignored;
- figures are rounded to whole numbers.

The refinancing is based on the following changes in terms:

- refinancing takes place at the end of year 2 of operation (year 4 of the project);
- loan term: increased by 2 years to 24 years;
- Interest rate: reduced to 5.8%;
- ADSCR: reduced to 1.25:1 (from year 5);
- loan outstanding at the end of year 4 increased by 130;
- these calculations do not take into account the fees and legal and other costs of the refinancing itself, which may be 1–1.5% of the refinanced amount.

From the investors' point of view, the results of the refinancing are as follows:

- An extra 130 has been taken out of the project at the end of year 4.
- This increases the Equity IRR (over the whole project life) from 15% to 22%.
- The total cash flow to the investors over the life of the project is *reduced* from 668 to 535—this is a reflection of the increased debt service.

So how is a refinancing beneficial to the investors? The debt borrowed against the project has increased—but increasing the amount of money you borrow does not make you richer. In fact, adding debt to the project makes the Project Company worse off and increases the risk for investors. Equally the increase in the Equity IRR is somewhat illusory—the calculation is distorted by the early release of the 130 to the investors (*cf.* §10.2.3). But what the refinancing does do is make a large difference in the payback period for the equity investment (*cf.* §12.2.4). The undiscounted payback before the refinancing is about 8¼ years: after the refinancing it is 4 years, *i.e.* the refinancing at the end of year 4 enables all of the original equity investment to be recovered. From the investors' point of view this early return of the investment enables the capital to be reinvested rapidly in a new project, albeit at the cost of a lower return

Table 14.3 Effect of Debt Refinancing

	Construction							Operation					
Year:	0	1	2	3	4	5	6	21	22	23	24	25	Total
(1) Pre–Refinancing													
(a) Project cost (incl. IDC)	−333	−333	−333										−1,000
(b) Project cash flow				100	100	100	100	100	100	100	100	100	2,300
(c) Debt drawdown [−(a) × 85%]	283	283	283										
(d) Debt interest payments [(h){previous year} × 6%]				−51	−50	−48	−47	−8	−4				−632
(e) Debt principal repayments				−23	−24	−26	−28	−66	−70				−850
(f) Total debt service [(d) + (e)]				−74	−74	−74	−74	−74	−74				
(g) Investors' cash flow [(b) − (f)]	−50	−50	−50	26	26	26	26	26	26	100	100	100	**668**
(h) Year-end debt outstanding [(h){previous year} + (c) + (e)]	283	567	850	827	802	776	749	70	0				
ADSCR [(b) ÷ (f)] 1.35 (from year 3)													
Equity IRR = 15%													
(2) Post–Refinancing													
Project cost (incl. IDC)	−333	−333	−333										−1,000
Project cash flow				100	100	100	100	100	100	100	100	100	2,300
Debt drawdown	283	283	283										
Additional debt					130								130
Debt interest payments				−51	−48	−54	−52	−16	−12	−9	−4		−765
Debt principal repayments				−23	−26	−26	−27	−64	−67	−71	−75		−980
Total debt service	283	283	283	−74	−74	−80	−80	−80	−80	−80	−80		−2,595
Investors' cash flow	−50	−50	−50	26	156	20	20	20	20	20	20	100	**535**
Year-end debt outstanding	283	567	850	827	931	905	878	214	147	75	0		
ADSCR = 1.25 (from year 5)													
Equity IRR = 22%													

on the original project over its remaining life. Taking the two projects together, the investors are obviously better off (assuming they wish to recycle a limited amount of capital), and their capital at risk on the original investment has been reduced.

§14.16.2 Debt Refinancing: The 'Windfall' Issue

If the project involves an Offtaker, or a Contracting Authority, the Sponsors' ability to realize early cash flow by refinancing the debt can raise some issues:

- A refinancing increases the risk of financial problems for the project, simply because the Project Company is carrying more debt.
- A refinancing may increase the amount payable as an early Termination Sum by the Contracting Authority, if this is calculated based on outstanding debt (*cf.* §7.10).
- The Contracting Authority may be concerned that the Sponsors have a limited long-term financial risk in the project (and hence limited interest in its long-term success) if they have taken out their cash investment and a profit at an early stage after Project Completion. In other words the Sponsors then have little capital at risk (*cf.* §2.6.2). However the lenders actually have more capital at risk after the refinancing, which should somewhat alleviate this concern.

It follows from this that the Project Agreement may require the Offtaker/ Contracting Authority's consent to be given before a refinancing can be undertaken. Clearly this consent will not be given if the refinancing provides no benefit to the Contracting Authority, meaning that some sharing of the benefit will have to be agreed, either in advance in the Project Agreement, or at the time by negotiation. The flexibility which lenders have to increase the loan amount (§7.10.1) is only intended to deal with a 'rescue' refinancing (*cf.* §14.16.4).

But in some cases the biggest issue is likely to be a political one: private-sector investors can be portrayed as having made a 'windfall profit' at the expense of a public-sector Offtaker, or a Contracting Authority. This is not beneficial to the particular project as it may increase its general political risk (*cf.* §11.2), and also it can potentially have a serious effect on the political acceptability of a PPP program.

This issue arose during the early development of the British PFI program, where a large refinancing 'gain' on a PFI prison project was the subject of a Parliamentary inquiry.[30]

---

[30] National Audit Office, *The refinancing of the Fazakerley PFI prison contract* (London, 2000)*; House of Commons Public Accounts Committee, *The refinancing of the Fazakerley PFI prison contract* (13th Report, Session 2001–2001, London, 2001)*. This continued to be a major issue for the PFI program— *cf.* National Audit Office, *The Refinancing of the Norfolk and Norwich PFI Hospital: how the deal can be viewed in the light of the refinancing* (London, 2005)*; House of Commons Public Accounts Committee, *The refinancing of the Norfolk and Norwich PFI Hospital* (35th Report, Session 2005-6, London, 2006)*, which described the refinancing as 'the unacceptable face of capitalism' (p. 3).

Many of the older PFI Project Agreements required a consent from the Contracting Authority to any refinancing for the reasons set out above, but the Contracting Authorities had failed to realize that they could extract a price for this consent. This led to a change in the standard form of PFI Project Agreement[31] in 2002, under which a 'refinancing gain' was to be shared 50:50 between the public- and private-sector parties to PFI Project Agreements,[32] a provision which has been widely imitated in other PPP programs elsewhere in the world. (There is no reason why the same provisions could not apply where there is a private-sector Offtaker, but they are not usually found in private-sector Project Agreements.)

There are other arguments for sharing the refinancing gain with the Contracting Authority, apart from this problem of political perception:

- If, as was the case from the mid-1990s to 2007, the project-finance lending market for PPPs keeps improving (*i.e.* lenders offer better and better terms), this is just a 'windfall' for the investors in the Project Company—they have done nothing to improve the market as a whole.
- Furthermore, if lending terms for PPPs keep improving, this is a product of the government having developed a successful pipeline of PPP projects, and also reflects the lower risk of such projects, especially Availability-based PPPs, where usage risk is taken by the Contracting Authority (*cf.* §9.6.4). Again the investors in the Project Company have done nothing to influence this.

But obviously one must balance against this the simple fact that a refinancing cannot take place if the project is not successful (subject to the comments on 'rescue refinancings' below), and also the cash flow to investors can be increased by greater efficiency or other good management on the part of the Project Company. It was the balancing of these market-specific and project-specific factors which produced the theoretical argument in Britain for sharing refinancing gains between the public and private sector.

§14.16.3 CALCULATING THE REFINANCING GAIN

However sharing of refinancing gains raises a number of complex issues:

- How is the gain to be calculated and paid?
- How should the Financial-Close Base-Case financial model (*cf.* §13.10) be adjusted for the calculation?

---

[31] *Cf.* §6.1 footnote 2.

[32] Later versions of SoPC increased the Contracting Authority's share of refinancing gains depending on the size of the gain.

- How can the 'Lazarus rising from the dead' syndrome be covered: *i.e.* the project has been performing badly, but eventually picks up enough to allow a refinancing to take place; should all of the refinancing gain be shared in this case, even though the investors will not recover the past under-performance by the Project Company?

The size of the gain has to be calculated before it can be shared. In Table 14.3, although the investors have taken out 130 of extra cash not in the original Base-Case projections, it cannot be said that they have made a 'gain' of 130, since their cash flow thereafter is lower than in the Base Case. In fact, as already pointed out, it is questionable if they are even better off at all, since all they have done is increase the amount of debt borrowed against the project.

Clearly if there is a 'gain' to investors from a refinancing, it must somehow relate to the early release of cash from the project, which suggests that a DCF or IRR calculation is needed to determine what the benefit is in today's money (*cf.* §10.2). But, as set out in Table 14.4, the best way to do this is not obvious, and the results from different methods vary considerably. Table 14.4 uses the

Table 14.4 Different Methods of Calculating a Refinancing Gain

Year:	4	5	6	21	22	23	24	25	Total
Method 1									
Post-refinancing cash flow	156	20	20	20	20	20	20	100	535
Pre-refinancing cash flow	26	26	26	26	26	100	100	100	668
Difference	130	−6	−6	−6	−6	−80	−80	0	−133
Discounted at Base-Case Equity IRR* 74									
(* 15%—*cf.* Table 14.3)									
∴ **Contracting Authority 50% share = 37**									
Method 2									
Discounted at current market Equity IRR* **55**									
(* 10%—*cf.* §14.17)									
∴ **Contracting Authority 50% share = 27**									
Method 3									
Pre-Refinancing Equity IRR = 15%									
Post-Refinancing Equity IRR = 22%									
∴ adjusted Equity IRR = 19% = (15% + 22%) ÷ 2									
Payment to Contracting Authority = 57									

same refinancing assumptions as Table 14.3 and shows the effect of feeding these assumptions into the following different methods of calculation:

> *Method 1*: Take the difference between the future post-refinancing cash flow and the future pre-refinancing cash flow, and discount difference this to an NPV at the Base-Case Equity IRR; the result is the refinancing gain, of which 50% (or the agreed proportion) is paid to the Contracting Authority, *i.e.* 37 on the assumptions given. This is the method used in SoPC (and in other jurisdictions such as Australia and South Africa whose PPP Contracts have followed SoPC's approach). Perhaps counter-intuitively, the lower the discount rate the lower the refinancing gain—this is because the future cash flows being discounted are negative. But arguably it is inappropriate to use the (relatively high) Base-Case Equity IRR as the discount rate because at the time the refinancing takes place this is no longer the correct discount rate for valuating the equity, which should be lower, reflecting the lower project risk at the time of the refinancing (*cf.* §14.17).
>
> *Method 2*: As for *Method 1*, but using a current-market (therefore lower) Equity IRR discount rate. This has been taken as 10% in the table. This produces a payment of a 50% share of the refinancing gain to the Contracting Authority of 27, illustrating that the lower the discount rate, the lower the refinancing gain. (N.B.: If the discount rate were reduced to 5%, the refinancing gain would be zero.)
>
> *Method 3*: Take the pre- and post-refinancing projected Equity IRRs (over the whole project life—actual figures to the date of the refinancing, and projected thereafter). As seen from Table 14.3 these are 15% and 22% respectively. Then make a payment to the Contracting Authority which has the effect of reducing the post-refinancing Equity IRR to 16% [(15% + 22%) ÷ 2], *i.e.* half the benefit of the IRR increase is paid over (assuming that the refinancing gain is being divided 50:50). As can be seen from Table 14.3 this would result in a payment to the Contracting Authority of 57, considerably higher than the previous two Methods. This is a result of using what amounts to a higher discount rate. It is perhaps not surprising that this apparently simpler calculation has not been used in any market as a basis for calculation of refinancing gains.
>
> *Method 4*: The above methods all assume that the debt amount is increased by the refinancing, and therefore that there is cash available to pay the Contracting Authority's share of the refinancing gain immediately. However if the benefit of the refinancing is in the future—typically because the only change in debt terms is a reduction in the interest cost or margin—then none of the systems above works well. The easiest approach is to treat this type of refinancing gain separately, and use the Contracting Authority's share of

the future benefits to reduce the Contract Payments as and when the benefits occur.

Method 5: However in the *Method 4* situation of sharing future gains, SoPC tries to fit this within the *Method 1* approach.[33] The refinancing gain is calculated in the same way, by discounting the difference between the pre- and post-refinancing cash flows (although in this case the high discount rate is disadvantageous to the Contracting Authority as the future changes in cash flow are positive). Then the NPV sum is applied to reduce Contract Payments over the remaining term of the Project Agreement, including interest on these future reductions,[34] to compensate for them not being paid as a current sum. One problem with this method is that it is circular—reducing the future Contract Payments (although partly offset by the consequent reduction in tax payments) reduces the refinancing gain.

Finally investors might reasonably ask, if the Contracting Authority shares in the 'upside' from a refinancing of a successful project, shouldn't it also take on some of the 'downside' if the project goes badly? This does not happen in practice, but the only real argument against it is that this one-way deal reflects a solution to a political problem rather than commercial balance.

Adjustment to the Financial-Close Base Case. A sensible model to show the effect of a refinancing cannot be produced if it does not properly reflect the current situation of the project. So long as the same financial model is used to reflect the pre- and post-refinancing cash flows (*i.e.* the only change in the model relates to the refinancing) this should not distort the results. It therefore makes sense to update the Financial-Close Base-Case financial model to reflect actual performance of the project to date (and to make assumptions about future projections), as well as updating for macro-economic factors (*cf.* Chapter 10).

The Lazarus Syndrome. If the project has been performing badly but then improves, the better outlook for the future may enable a refinancing to take place, but sharing this apparent gain would be unfair on the investors, who

---

[33] H.M. Treasury, *Guidance Note: Calculation of the Authority's Share of a Refinancing Gain* (London, n.d.)*.
[34] The Guidance Note above suggests an interest rate comparable to the government debt rate for the remaining average life of the project, plus a margin equal to the credit margin. This is of course much lower than the Equity IRR discount rate used in both *Method 1* and *Method 6*, making the latter even more disadvantageous to the Contracting Authority.
SoPC also allows Contracting Authorities to choose *Method 6* even if an immediate payment of the share of the gain as in *Method 1* is possible. This is even more disadvantageous to the Contracting Authority from a financial point of view, and moreover means that the investors will keep the whole of the cash released by the refinancing, and the Contracting Authority will have the risk of never recovering its share if the Project Company has financial problems in future.

should be able to make up their past underperformance before having to share a refinancing gain based on a better future. For example, suppose the project had underperformed for the first 5 years, and then got back to the Base-Case level of cash flow in year 6, and is projected to do so for the remaining term of the Project Agreement. This means that if the refinancing does not take place the project can never achieve the Base-Case Equity IRR over the project life as a whole. A refinancing may be achieved after year 6 based on the brighter prospects for the future, but if the gain from this refinancing is calculated in the usual way, this will not make up for the investor's reduced return in the first 5 years.

The method used to adjust for this situation in SoPC is to make a payment to the investors such that they are projected to achieve their Base-Case Equity IRR (called the 'Threshold Equity IRR' in this context) over the whole life of project. It appears to be intended that this payment is made as a first call on the cash released by the refinancing. However this calculation produces a similar distorted affect to *Method 3* above, this time to the disadvantage of the Contracting Authority. Another way to deal with this is perhaps to compare the actual cash flow up to the refinancing date with the Base-Case figures. Differences (positive or negative) should be compounded up to the date of the refinancing at the Base-Case Equity IRR. If negative, this sum should then be allocated to the investors, before the refinancing gain is calculated.

§14.16.4 What Apparent Refinancings Should be Excluded from Gain-Sharing Provisions?

There are a number of actions which may be taken by the investors or the lenders which at first sight may look like a refinancing as described above, but for one reason or another should not result in any refinancing gain payment to the Contracting Authority:

'Rescue' Refinancing. Refinancing may be necessary because the project has got into trouble, rather than, as above, because it is doing well. The lenders may take the view that their best hope of maximum recovery on their loan to a project in trouble may be to provide additional finance to solve the problem. Clearly this type of 'bad' refinancing is quite different to the 'good' refinancing discussed above.

In this situation the lenders would not want their action to rescue the project to be subject to the Contracting Authority's consent—they are risking their money to solve the problem, which is beneficial to the Contracting Authority. However there still needs to be a limit on how much additional debt may be taken on by the Project Company without consent, for which the Contracting Authority may be liable on a early termination (*cf.* §7.10.1). The lenders may increase the debt above this limit, but the Contracting Authority would have no liability for this amount.

No Refinancing Gain. If a refinancing takes place, but does not produce a refinancing gain as defined in one of the ways above, *e.g.* the Equity IRR goes down rather than up as a result of the refinancing, then of course there is no benefit to share. This is another way of looking at a Rescue Refinancing, which is the most likely case where this may happen. So it is feasible to require that a refinancing which produces a refinancing gain requires the Contracting Authority's consent, but if there is no refinancing gain the lenders may increase the debt without consent.

Changes in Equity structure. If the investors change the equity structure—*e.g.* by reducing the subordinated debt and increasing the share capital (*cf.* §12.2.2), this would not be a refinancing, since it does not relate to the Project Company's external (third-party) financing.

Sale of Equity. This is a separate issue, discussed in §14.17.

Interest-Rate Gains Post-Financial Close. If the Project Company's debt interest rate is fixed for modeling purposes at Financial Close (*cf.* §10.3.5) but is not in fact fully hedged at that point and the Project Company makes a saving on market interest rates compared to the Base Case, this would not be a refinancing gain as the Project Company took this risk and is entitled to benefit from the result.

Refinancing in the Base Case. The investors may take the risk of being able to achieve a refinancing in the Base Case. For example if the lenders require a Hard or Soft Mini-Perm (*cf.* §10.6; §14.4.4) this may not be shown in the financial model used to calculate the Contract Payments where the Sponsors are in a competitive bidding situation, *i.e.* the Base-Case financial model will show the debt service spread over the life of the project, with no accelerated repayment from a Cash Sweep by the lenders (despite this being in the Banking Case), nor a balloon repayment). The effect of not showing it in the model, and hence not taking it into account in the Payment Mechanism, means that the Sponsors are taking on the refinancing risk. So clearly the full benefit of the refinancing is already reflected in the Base Case, which is a far better situation than the Contracting Authority only getting a proportion of this benefit if and when the refinancing occurs. Insofar as the final refinancing produces better terms than assumed in the Base Case, then this extra benefit can be subject to refinancing gain-sharing.

Corporate Finance. A Sponsor may decide to finance the construction phase using its own funds, *i.e.* using non-project specific finance by borrowing against its general balance sheet. Then the aim may be to refinance after

Project Completion with project finance. This may be done because the Sponsor is willing to take the construction risk, without a turnkey Construction Contract, to save the extra costs that such a contract involves (*cf.* §8.2). In effect, the Sponsor is providing a kind of Soft Mini-Perm (*cf.* §14.4.4). Clearly if the Project Company takes on project finance a refinancing has taken place, but assessing the refinancing gain is virtually impossible, as the cost of the original corporate finance is an internal matter for the Sponsor and can be set at any figure. Moreover the initial level of equity may be far less than required for project finance (even zero), since the debt:equity split is meaningless in this case, and so the Base Case Equity IRR is also meaningless.

The one lever the Contracting Authority may have is to refuse to sign any documentation (such as a Direct Agreement—*cf.* §8.11) with the project-finance lenders, or to amend the Financial Equilibrium provisions (*cf.* §7.6.5), or those relating to Termination Sums due on early default (*cf.* §7.10), which may leave the new lenders at risk, *e.g.* of not recovering their swap breakage costs in full. It may therefore be possible for the Contracting Authority to extract a price for cooperating in the switch from project to corporate finance, but in any case this cannot be calculated using any of the Methods set out above.

However this approach should not apply if the Sponsor includes a project finance-based refinancing in the Base-Case model, in which case the provisions for refinancing in the Base Case set out above would apply, and the Contracting Authority should be prepared to agree in advance to amend the Project Agreement to incorporate the normal project-finance lender requirements.

Tax and Accounting. Changes in tax rates, or other changes in tax treatment of the Project Company's revenues or assets, or in the accounting treatment for these, would not be a refinancing the Project Company has assumed these risks (*cf.* §11.3.2).

Loan Syndication. If the lenders syndicate or otherwise place part of the loan with new lenders, any profit which they make from this exercise would not be considered a refinancing gain.

Flexible Debt Service. The lenders may allow some flexibility in the required timing of principal repayments, or vary the interest margin depending on the success of the project. Exercising this type of flexibility would not normally be considered a refinancing.

Waivers and Amendments. A temporary waiver by the lenders of a requirement in their loan documentation would not normally be considered as a refinancing (*cf.* §14.11), but any amendment which has the effect of changing the cash flow to investors (*e.g.* allowing less money to be kept in Reserve Accounts) may be.

§14.16.5 Are refinancing gain-sharing provisions enforceable?

It is evident from the above that dealing with refinancing gains is a surprisingly complex issue. This complexity inevitably means that the Project Company's investors and their advisors will try to find holes in the system which enable them to take out a refinancing gain, without paying any share to the Contracting Authority. Two obvious ways of doing this are:

- A 'synthetic' refinancing structure can be used: the refinancing can be channeled 'behind the curtain' *via* a holding company, while leaving the Project Company's cash flow unchanged and so refinanced. Similarly, an investor or investment fund owning a number of different Project Companies may refinance their collective debt *via* a group holding company. This can also be achieved through the CLO structures discussed in §5.2.10.
- Sponsors' affiliates' Sub-Contracts with the Project Company can be amended to drain out cash at the operating level (so long as Contracting Authority consent is not required—*cf.* §8.9).

This can be illustrated by what happened after the requirement to share refinancing gains was introduced into the British PFI program. Estimates were made of the possible gains from refinancing both past and future projects, but the actual refinancing gains shared with the public sector were well below these estimates.

To address this problem, provisions were introduced into SoPC under which a Contracting Authority could require the Project Company to approach the market for a refinancing at intervals after Project Completion.[35] These provisions have yet to be tested, because by the time they came into effect the project-finance market had deteriorated considerably (*cf.* §17.2) and so the prospects for any refinancing of past projects were reduced considerably. Also although the provisions allow the Contracting Authority to force a refinancing if available in the market, they do not allow the Contracting Authority to increase the senior debt, which is the key aim of any refinancing (*cf.* §14.16.1), so their practical value is likely to be limited.

§14.16.6 Does it Matter?

The Contracting Authority is therefore likely to spend a lot of unproductive time trying to second-guess whether the Sponsors' particular financing structure is intended to avoid sharing any windfall benefits, establishing the 'real' Base-Case return for investors against which to measure any such benefits, distinguishing between windfall benefits and an improved return because of greater efficiency on

---

[35] SoPC §28.9–15.

the part of the Project Company, and trying to stop up any potential holes in the drafting of the Project Agreement to deal with these issues.

Furthermore, the Contracting Authority must take into account the fact that a refinancing may be factored into the pricing proposed by the Sponsors in the first place; the Sponsors may be willing to accept a lower initial return for their original risk than they really require, on the assumption that a higher return will be obtained through a refinancing at a later stage. This is quite likely if the bidding for the Project Agreement has been very competitive. Therefore, if the Contracting Authority insists on sharing in these benefits, the only result may be to increase the original bid pricing under the Project Agreement.

This therefore suggests that it is only necessary for the Contracting Authority to try to share in refinancing gains if:

- Bidding competition for the Project Agreement has been limited.
- There has been 'deal creep' (*i.e.* lengthy negotiation with a preferred bidder, during which contract terms have shifted in the latter's favor).
- The terms of the financing are affected because it is for a new type of project or in a new market, and once the market has become used to the risk an significant improvement in terms can be expected.
- Competition for the financing has been limited (*cf.* §5.2.3).

Also it is not appropriate to use these refinancing provisions in the case of Concessions (although a number of jurisdictions such as Australia and Texas do so), because the future long-term cash flow is much more uncertain than in an Offtake or PFI-Model Contract. In the Concession case, the best way to eliminate windfalls to investors is to have robust excess cash-flow sharing provisions (*cf.* §6.5.3; §15.18).

If the decision is taken not to pursue refinancing gains in the Project Agreement, a Contracting Authority needs to be aware of the potential political impact if such gains arise.

§14.17 SECONDARY EQUITY SALE

The return required by investors also varies depending on when they come into the project. Investors come in to projects at different stages and with different investment strategies. Any project has various different levels of risk over time—as discussed in §12.2.5, the highest-risk position is to be a Sponsor or bidder for a project, and it is possible to bring in investors at Financial Close who will accept a lower return for not having to take the development- or bid-cost risk.

The more common timing for disposing of equity to new investors, however, is about a year after Project Completion; this is considered to be a 'secondary'

Table 14.5 Effect of Secondary Equity Sale

Year:	0	1	2	3	4	5	6	21	22	23	24	25
Primary Investor												
Cash flow	−50	−50	−50	26	26							
Sale of project					250							
Total	**−50**	**−50**	**−50**	**26**	**276**							
Equity IRR 26%												
Secondary Investor												
Purchase of project					−250							
Cash flow						26	26	26	26	100	100	100
Total					**−250**	**26**	**26**	**26**	**26**	**100**	**100**	**100**
Equity IRR 10%												

equity investment, a 'primary' equity investment being at Financial Close (*cf.* §3.2). At this stage the project should have been built successfully and be operating normally, hence a large portion of the initial project risks has been taken away (*cf.* §9.5). As a result, a secondary investor will accept a lower Equity IRR, reflecting this lower risk. So while the primary investors in the project used as an example in Table 14.3 should receive an Equity IRR of 15%, even without any refinancing, a secondary investor may be willing to accept an Equity IRR of, say, 10% *p.a.*

So as an alternative to refinancing,[36] investors may prefer to sell some or all of their equity investment. Using the pre-refinancing cash flow in Table 14.3as an example, Table 14.5 shows the effect of selling the equity 2 years after Project Completion to a secondary investor who is willing to accept an Equity IRR of 10%, reflecting the lower project risk at this stage.

Comparing Table 14.5 to Table 14.3, it can be seen that whereas refinancing produced a cash release of 130 at the end of year 4, if the whole of the equity were sold instead this would produce a cash amount of 250, although of course in the latter case there would be no further income from the project. So in the case of a secondary equity sale, the primary investor has invested 150 in years 1–2, received 26 in year 3, and 276 in year 4, and hence has received roughly double its original investment within a relatively short period of time.

---

[36] Actually it is possible to both refinance the debt and still sell off equity thereafter. There is a trade-off between the two—*e.g.* if the debt is refinanced the equity will be worth less, reflecting the early cash taken out of the project through the refinancing.

There are potential issues for lenders if a secondary equity sale is proposed if as they have lent to the project relying on a long-term commitment from the original Sponsors (*cf.* §3.2). On the other hand, if one of the Sponsors is the Construction Sub-Contractor, for example, it would not be unreasonable for it to be able to sell its shareholding once it has completed its rôle and build the project successfully. Typically lenders require the original Sponsors to hold their shareholdings (this would include any subordinated debt—*cf.* §12.2.2) until around a year after Project Completion (*cf.* §9.13). A similar restriction may be imposed by an Offtaker/Contracting Authority (*cf.* §3.2.1; §7.11).

§14.17.1 SECONDARY EQUITY SALE—THE 'WINDFALL' ISSUE

As will be apparent from the figures discussed above, in PPP projects or process-plant projects with a public-sector Offtaker a secondary equity sale is also open to attack as producing a 'windfall' for the private-sector investors at the apparent expense of the public sector. Sharing of the gain on a secondary equity sale has not, to date, been written into PPP Project Agreements.

One key argument for doing nothing in this case is that the sale should be subject to capital gains tax (if this exists in the country concerned), and so the public sector gets its share of the gain through taxation. However there are usually ways of getting round this, one of the most obvious being to have the Project Company owned by a holding company in another, low-tax, country, and then for the primary investors to sell this company instead of the Project Company.

Furthermore trying to enforce a share of this type of gain is also very difficult.

- Equity may be held *via* an intermediate holding company, and the shares in this holding company sold rather than those in the Project Company.
- The investors may sell warrants to subscribe for shares, or an interest in the revenues of the company, which do not formally count as a sale of their equity.
- The investors may conceal the sale by acting as nominees for the new buyers of the shares.

The bigger question is, why are secondary equity sale profits so large?[37] This is obviously a function of the big gap between the primary Equity IRR of, say 12–15% (*cf.* §12.2.1) and a secondary Equity IRR of say 8–10%. It is this comparatively large difference which creates the large profit from a secondary equity sale.

---

[37] *Cf.* PriceWaterhouseCoopers, *Study into rates of Return in PFI Projects* (Office for Government Commerce, London, 2002)*; National Audit Office, *HM Treasury: Equity investment in privately financed projects* (London, 2012)*.

One argument for the high primary Equity IRRs is that they are simply an arithmetical consequence of the lenders' Cover ratio requirements: if there is a ADSCR requirement of, say, 1.3:1, then after paying debt service there must be free cash of 0.3 for every 1.3 of revenue, and this can only go to the investors as Distributions. This connection can be seen in Table 12.8. But if there were a desire to reduce primary Equity IRRs this could be achieved, as shown on Table 12.8, by decreasing the debt:equity ratio. It could also be achieved by the use of third-party mezzanine debt (*cf.* §4.5.1).

The real issue is that infrastructure investment funds are major Sponsors of projects (*cf.* §3.2). These funds need high primary Equity IRRs to provide a 20%+ IRR to their investors (and pay the fund managers relatively high fees) by selling equity after Project Completion as discussed above. This return requirement has been influenced by putting infrastructure projects in the same risk category as LBO/MBOs (*cf.* §5.2.2).[38] Contractors who come in as primary investors because they will also be Sub-Contractors to the Project Company are not concerned about this issue, and would easily accept a lower equity return since this is not the main motive for their involvement in the project (*cf.* §3.2).

So the way forward here may be for the infrastructure investment-fund market to reflect the risks and returns inherent in a project-finance transaction, which requires a change in thinking by both the funds and their investors.

---

[38] Florian Bitsch, Axel Buchner & Christoph Kaserer, "Risk, return and cash flow characteristics of infrastructure fund investments", *EIB Papers* Vol. 15 No. 1 (EIB, Luxemburg, 2010), p. 106*.

PUBLIC-SECTOR FINANCIAL SUPPORT

Chapter 15

§15.1 INTRODUCTION

This chapter covers financial support to projects from Contracting Authorities or other government entities in the Host Country. Cross-border support provided by ECAs and DFIs is discussed in Chapter 16. Recent developments in public-sector project support as a result of the 2008 financial crisis are discussed further in Chapter 17. Public-sector equity investment is discussed in §3.2.2.

Some form of indirect public-sector financial support is found in many projects (§15.2), but this chapter deals with direct financial support in various ways (§15.3), through public-sector loans (§15.4–§15.9), grants or other funding (§15.10–§15.13), debt guarantees (§15.14–§15.19) and revenue support (§15.18–§15.19), as well as the use of a public-sector Project Company (§15.20).

A government may also set up a guarantee fund, to provide investors and lenders with more certainty that there will be funds available to meet guarantee obligations (§15.21).

423

Principles of Project Finance. DOI: http://dx.doi.org/10.1016/B978-0-12-391058-5.00015-1

§15.2 INDIRECT PUBLIC-SECTOR FINANCIAL SUPPORT

The analysis of project finance so far has assumed that a project financing can stand on its own feet, *i.e.* it is without recourse, either to the Sponsors or to any other party, or perhaps has some limited recourse to the Sponsors (*cf.* §9.13).

Actually, however, some form of indirect public-sector support is found in many project financings. In the power-generation or PPP sectors this may simply consist of a payments for capacity in a PPA or availability in a PPP by a Contracting Authority, which greatly decreases the risks, and hence increases bankability, of a project.

Similarly, where offtake prices are regulated by governments to encourage investments in particular types of project without capacity or availability payments—*e.g.* by ensuring that the price of electricity sold by wind-power projects is not less than $x per MWh—this too makes the difference between projects which are bankable and those which are not.

Even in Concessions, although it is users and not the public sector who pay for services, there are still likely to be contingent liabilities which fall back on the Contracting Authority, and so reduce the risks of lenders and investors, *e.g.*:

- *Retained risks.* Insofar as the Contracting Authority retains certain risks, *e.g.* provision of land or access to the site, if these risks crystallize (*e.g.* the land is not provided on time) the Contracting Authority will have to compensate for their consequences (*cf.* §7.6).
- *Termination payments.* If the Project Company defaults, the Contracting Authority may have to pay fair value for the project (*cf.* §7.10).

§15.3 DIRECT PUBLIC-SECTOR FINANCIAL SUPPORT

There are, broadly speaking, four types of public-sector financial support other than those mentioned in §15.2—loans, grants, guarantees, and revenue support[1]—and these can be provided in various ways to cover part of the capital cost or debt, or to support revenues.

Such financial support may be provided to infrastructure projects, or process-plant projects where the Offtaker is a Contracting Authority, with several different motives:

- *For financial-market reasons*: In such cases the public sector provides finance (or guarantees) to deal with any financing gap caused by private-sector lenders (especially banks) being unable or unwilling to provide the necessary long-term debt. The effect of the credit crisis and the subsequent

---

[1]As will be seen from the examples below, programs for public-sector support often offer a 'menu' of different types of support in the same program.

Basel III regulations, as discussed in Chapter 17, has accelerated the search for other sources of long-term finance essential to maintain investment in some markets. Chapter 17 looks at recent market developments and future prospects in this respect.

- *For financial-viability reasons*: In such cases public-sector support is needed because the project would not be financially viable if all its finance were raised on market terms.
- *For cost reasons*: *i.e.* to reduce the cost of private finance and hence reduce the Contract Payments by an Offtaker/Contracting Authority, or by users. (This obviously overlaps with financial viability issues.)
- *To reduce political risk*: This generally applies to investment in, or loans to, cross-border projects (*cf.* Chapter 11), and relates to support provided by ECAs or DFIs (discussed in Chapter 16).

In providing financial support the Contracting Authority has to consider:

- if it is appropriate for the particular project;
- if the potential cost (for loans or grants) or loss (for guarantees or revenue support) is VfM;
- whether a reserve should be set up to meet any such loss;
- how much (if anything) should be charged for the support.[2]

From the public-sector point of view, the degree of risk or possibility of loss on such support can be classified (in increasing order of risk) as:

- *No project risk—the public sector provides finance but does not take project risk.*
- *Second Loss—'Underpinning'*: The equity and senior debt has to be written off before the public sector makes any loss. So if there investment of $100 in a project, consisting of $20 of debt, $580 of senior debt and $30 of Underpinning, and the project defaults and is worth $60, the $20 of equity and $20 of the $80 of debt will be lost, but the public sector will not suffer any loss.
- *Pari-Passu*. The public-sector finance or guarantee is on a *pari-passu* basis with the senior debt. So in the case above, but with $30 of *pari-passu* support, $20 of equity would still be lost, but the remaining loss of $20 would be suffered *pro rata* by senior lenders and the public sector, so the latter's loss would be $12.50 [20 ÷ (50 + 30) × 30].
- *First Loss—'Credit Enhancement'*: The whole of the public-sector commitment must be lost before the senior lenders suffer any loss. So in the case

---

[2] *Cf.* Chris Marrison, "Risk Measurement for Project Finance Guarantees", *The Journal of Project Finance* (International Investor, New York NY) Summer 2001*; Timothy C. Irwin, *Government Guarantees: Allocating and Valuing Risk in Privately Financed Infrastructure Projects* (World Bank, Washington DC, 2007)*; European PPP Expertise Centre, *State Guarantees in PPPs: A Guide to Better Evaluation, Design, Implementation and Management* (EIB, Luxemburg, 2011)*.

above, but with $30 of public-sector credit enhancement, $20 of equity would be lost, and $20 of the $30 of public-sector finance at risk, and the senior lenders would not suffer any loss.

- *Revenue Support*: In these cases the public-sector will suffer a loss before investors or senior lenders do.

Table 15.1 sets out the examples of these forms of support, categorized by type and risk.[3]

Table 15.1 Forms of Public-Sector Financial Support

	See	First Loss	Pari-Passu	Second Loss	No Project Risk
Public-sector loan:					
● Mezzanine debt	§15.4	×			
● Standby financing	§15.5	×			
● Refinancing after project Completion	§15.6	×			
● Gap financing	§15.7		×		
● Development/public-works banks	§15.8		×		
● Credit guarantee finance	§15.9				×
Public-sector grant or other funding:					
● Capital grant	§15.10			×	
● Viability-gap finance	§15.11			×	
● Part-construction	§15.12			×	
● Complementary investment	§15.13				×
Public-sector debt guarantee:					
● Full debt guarantee	§15.14	×			
● First-loss guarantee	§15.15	×			
● *Pari-passu* debt guarantee	§15.16		×		
● Debt underpinning	§15.17			×	
Public-sector revenue support:					
● Minimum revenue guarantee	§15.18	×			
● Tariff subsidy	§15.19	×			
Public-sector Project Company	§15.20	×			

---

[3] Table 15.1 does not exhaust the possible methods of public-sector support, but concentrates on the main types of support which are in fact being provided. Some of these types of support could also be provided by a private-sector Offtaker, but in practice this does not usually happen.

Private-sector lenders to the project may obviously have some concerns about the potential conflict of interest for the public-sector lender or guarantor, in particular that the latter may use its voting powers (*cf.* §14.13) to obstruct action against the Project Company. The private-sector lenders may seek to have it excluded from voting. This issue applies in cases of financial support where the public sector is taking project risks, especially on a first-loss or *pari-passu* basis. Where a second-loss risk applies the lenders can be presumed to protect the public-sector's interests because they will lose all their loan before the public-sector party does.

§15.4 MEZZANINE DEBT

As discussed in §4.5.1, in risk terms mezzanine debt lies between the senior debt provided by external lenders, and usually be payable at the bottom of the cash-flow Cascade, above Distributions.[4] So if the project does not perform well the mezzanine debt may not be fully repaid and it will have to be written off by the Contracting Authority by the end of the project term. Thus in this case the public sector takes a first-loss risk—it will have to lose all its loan before the private-sector lenders suffer any loss.

This is a widely-used structure in the infrastructure fields, *e.g.* by U.S. State Infrastructure Banks (§15.4.1), the U.S. 'TIFIA' program (§15.4.2), and the European Investment Bank's 'Project Bond Initiative' (§15.4.3).

§15.4.1 U.S. State Infrastructure Banks

State Infrastructure Banks ('SIBs') were first authorized in a pilot program for ten states in the 1995 National Highway System Designation Act ('NHS'), further extended by the 1998 Transportation Equity Act for the 21st Century ('TEA-21'), and, with authorizations under subsequent legislation,[5] are now in operation in many U.S. states.

SIBs may be funded with up to 10% of Federal transportation-related grants. The state has to match any such funding on an 80–20 Federal/non-Federal basis. SIBs can provide a variety of support for private-sector transportation projects including mezzanine debt at subsidized rates. The legislation also allows SIB funds

---

[4] The mezzanine loan repayments may also be deferred until the senior debt has been fully repaid, but at the same time Distributions may also be prohibited until the mezzanine debt is repaid, so encouraging the Project Company to refinance it.

[5] Apart from annual extensions, the key legislation which continued this and the TIFIA program was the 2005 Safe, Accountable, Flexible, Efficient Transportation Equity Act: A Legacy for Users ('SAFETEA-LU'). 'MAP-21' (see below) provided continued appropriations for TIFIA but not for SIBs.

to be used for supporting loan guarantees and bond insurance, as well as standby credits.

The idea behind this is to allow Federal grants to be leveraged by private-sector finance, and recycled into new projects once repayments are received.

§15.4.2 'TIFIA' PROGRAM

The U.S. Transportation Infrastructure Finance and Innovation Act ('TIFIA') of 1998 specifically encouraged the use of private-sector financing for major ($50 million-plus) PPP transportation projects by offering direct federal loans and guarantees covering up to 33% of project costs. TIFIA loans offer low rates based on U.S. Treasury bond rates, and repayments may be made after a long grace period of up to 5 years after Project Completion, and over a much longer period than the senior debt (up to 35 years). The policy behind this TIFIA support (which is managed by the Federal Highway Administration) is that "...*a Federal credit program for projects of national significance can complement existing funding resources by filling market gaps, thereby leveraging substantial private co investment.*"[6]

TIFIA finance is usually provided in the form of a low-cost mezzanine loan, thus reducing the project's risks for senior lenders. (The TIFIA program also offers guarantees and standby financing.) There is considerable flexibility on repayment terms, but if the project goes into default the TIFIA financing ceases to be subordinated and becomes *pari-passu* with the senior debt. (This is known as a 'springing lien'.) The use of TIFIA finance has grown considerably as it has become more difficult to access other financing avenues (*e.g.* municipal bonds and bank loans).

The TIFIA program originally received annual appropriations from the Federal budget of about $122 million *p.a.*, which seems quite small. However, this amount refers to the net anticipated cost to the Federal budget over the life of the project, based mainly on the 'credit risk subsidy'—*i.e.* assumed losses which could be made on TIFIA loans—of around 10% of the amount of the loans. Thus TIFIA provided financing of around $1.2 billion *p.a.* The 2012 Moving Ahead for Progress in the 21st Century Act ('MAP-21') considerably enlarged the TIFIA program, as it allocated $750 million for 2013 and $1 billion for 2014 respectively, which would result in $17.5 billion of TIFIA finance in these years, or an estimated $50 billion of total project investment.

The combination of the TIFIA credit program with PABs (*cf.* §4.3.1) has been a significant source of financing for recent PPP transportation projects in the U.S.

---

[6] US Department of Transportation, *TIFIA Program Guide* (Washington DC, 2011)*, p. 1-1.

§15.4.3 EIB PROJECT BOND INITIATIVE

In 2011 the European Union and the European Investment Bank ('EIB'—*cf.* §16.5.8) jointly launched a 'Europe 2020 Project Bond Initiative', the purpose of which would be to unlock the project bond market for key infrastructure projects (focusing on energy, transport and broadband) after the demise of the monoline insurers (*cf.* §4.3.3). The initial sum available is €230 million, to be used for a series of pilot projects in 2013–14.

However the EIB does not intend to step into the shoes of the insurers—instead it proposes to provide first-loss support, for an amount equal to a maximum of 20% of the senior debt, with the aim of reducing the senior lenders' risks, and hence improving the project's bonds' credit rating (the aim is to improve from BBB to A) to attract bondholders. This can be provided by way of mezzanine debt, first-loss guarantee (*cf.* §15.14; §17.5.2), or a standby facility (*cf.* §15.5; §17.5.3). In the latter case the standby facility can be drawn to cover construction-cost overruns (*cf.* §9.5), or senior debt service, or to deal with cover-ratio defaults (*cf.* §14.12) after completion by partially prepaying senior debt. The scheme is described as 'project bond credit enhancement' ('PBCE').

▌ §15.5 STANDBY FINANCING

As can be seen from the SIB, TIFIA and EIB examples in §15.4, standby finance—*i.e.* mezzanine finance which can be drawn if, *e.g.* traffic is below forecast leading to a cash-flow deficit—is an alternative method of providing financial support at the mezzanine level.

The EIB's Loan Guarantee Instrument for Trans-European Transport Network Projects ('LGTT') is another example of this structure. LGTT is a guarantee for a standby liquidity facility to be provided by the lenders (usually banks in this context). The amount covered is normally 10% of the senior debt, and subject to an absolute maximum of €200 million per project. This standby loan is available for up to 7 years after Project Completion, *i.e.* it is mainly intended to cover 'ramp-up' risk (*cf.* §9.6.2). If it is not repaid at this point, the EIB takes over the loan from the lenders and becomes a mezzanine lender to the project. A cash sweep (*cf.* §14.4.4; §14.12) is then normally applied until the EIB loan is repaid.

▌ §15.6 REFINANCING AFTER PROJECT COMPLETION

The Contracting Authority may refinance part of the debt after Project Completion, but on a basis senior to the private-sector lenders, *i.e.* on a second-loss basis. This has been done, for example by the Queensland Treasury which refinanced 70% of the debt on some PPP projects. In risk terms this is similar to Debt Underpinning (*cf.* §15.17), and the arguments for and against this apply here too, but it also leaves the public sector exposed to interest-rate risk at the time of the refinancing (*cf.* §10.6).

Forfaiting (*cf.* §6.6) is one structure which provides for refinancing of the whole of the debt after Project Completion, and in fact leaves little risk with the private sector. In risk terms this is similar to providing a full debt guarantee at this point, and similar issues apply (*cf.* §15.14). For further discussion on refinancing of the whole of the debt after Project Completion *cf.* §17.5.1.

§15.7 GAP FINANCING

Gap Financing may be required for a very large project if there is a lack of sufficient private-sector finance available, and so the public sector provides part of the debt on a *pari-passu* basis with the lenders. Gap Financing may also be provided by Policy Banks (*cf.* §15.8).

The Treasury Infrastructure Finance Unit ('TIFU'), set up by the British government in 2008 is an example of Gap Financing. It offered banking-style debt finance for loans to PFI projects if sufficient debt could not be raised from the market. Its loans were *pari-passu* with, and on the same terms as the bank lenders.[7] The need for its services proved to be very limited—it only participated in lending for one large PFI contract—but it may also have served to prevent banks unduly exploiting the lack of competition.[8] In 2012, as the improvement in the project-finance banking markets after 2008, which had made it unnecessary to continue with TIFU appeared to be reversing the British government set up a new version of TIFU within the Treasury, Infrastructure Financing Unit Ltd. (IFUL), as well as the UK Guarantees Scheme (*cf.* §15.16), to perform a similar function. However the Treasury may have overreacted again to a temporary market slow-down.

---

[7] This type of support has to be on these open-market terms to conform to the 'state aid' rules in the European Union (*cf.* §3.7.9).

[8] *Cf.* Ed Farquharson & Javier Encinas, *The U.K. Treasury Infrastructure Finance Unit: Supporting PPP Financing During the Global Liquidity Crisis* (World Bank Institute, Washington DC, 2010)*; National Audit Office, *HM Treasury: Financing PFI projects in the credit crisis and the Treasury's response* (London, 2010)*.

▌ §15.8 POLICY BANKS

The general lack of a project-finance market in developing countries can be attributed to several factors:

Short-Term Lending is More Attractive. In many developing countries the level of interest rates is very high, and hence domestic commercial banks can earn a high return from short term-lending. Therefore long-term project finance is not attractive compared to high-return low-risk short-term lending.

Lack of Expertise. It follows that if domestic banks have no expertise in project finance, they cannot easily undertake this type of lending, but this is something which can be remedied quite quickly if interest in project finance increases. For example in recent years large domestic banks in Nigeria have set up project-finance departments headed by expatriate Nigerians returning home after experience in project finance in London and other major project-finance centers.

No Long-Term Government Bond Market. If there is no market for long-term government bonds, a market for long-term project bonds is unlikely to develop, since the former provide the basis for any bond market (*cf.* §12.6.1). However efforts are being made, *e.g.* in Sub-Saharan Africa, to develop the bond markets to a stage where project bonds could be placed in local currencies.

'Policy Banks' is a catch-all name for state-owned banks which are set up to provide long-term finance to a particular sector or aspect of the national economy.[9] In the project-finance sector these would include infrastructure, economic-development and public-works banks, whose rôle was originally to provide finance for domestic projects, especially in the infrastructure field, but traditionally this was only by lending to public-sector entities and so not taking project risk. Examples include Brazil's Banco Nacional de Desenvolvimento Econômico e Social ('BNDES'),[10] China Development Bank ('CDB'—*cf.* §16.4.3), Germany's KfW Bankengruppe ('KfW'—*cf.* §16.4.5), Development Bank of Japan ('DBJ'), Korea Development Bank ('KDB'—*cf.* §16.4.2), Mexico's Banco Nacional de Obras y Servicios Públicos ('BANOBRAS'),[11] and Development Bank of South Africa ('DBSA').[12]

---

[9] The term 'state financial institutions' ('SFIs') may be used for such banks, but its meaning is rather wider as it would include state-owned commercial banks such as State Bank of India.

[10] 'National Bank for Economic and Social Development'.

[11] 'National Bank for Public Works and Services'.

[12] *Cf.* José de Luna-Martínez & Carlos Leonardo Vicente, *Global Survey of Development Banks* (Policy Research Working Paper 5969, World Bank, Washington DC, 2012)*.

In recent years these institutions have moved into project finance, usually for projects where commercial bank financing is not available or is insufficient (*i.e.* Gap Financing in the latter case). In some cases, such as BNDE and BANOBRAS their activities are purely in the domestic market, especially (as far as project finance is concerned) in the infrastructure and process-plant sectors. As will be seen, however, a number of Policy Banks also provide finance to overseas projects on a project-finance basis, *i.e.* they could also be classified as DFIs (*cf.* §16.4).

More recently, countries with active PPP programs have set up infrastructure financing institutions, primarily to refinance the bank debt initially provided to such projects, *e.g.* the Indian Infrastructure Finance Company, established in 2006, which issues tax-free bonds to provide it with resources for refinancing bank debt, as well as running debt funds (*cf.* §17.4.2). Other specialized public-sector financing institutions may also provide project finance as part of their remit. The U.K. Green Investment Bank, which was set up by the British government in 2012, and *inter alia* finances projects in the renewable energy and waste-to-energy sectors in parallel with private-sector lenders, is an example of this. Additionally, state-owned commercial banks may provide project finance as part of their overall business, State Bank of India being an obvious case (*cf.* Table 4.3).

There is an obvious danger that state-owned banks lend to projects because of political pressure, and therefore do not carry out adequate due diligence. This is especially the case if they provide 100% of the debt, *i.e.* there are no other private-sector lenders carrying out due diligence.

§15.9 CREDIT GUARANTEE FINANCE

Under this structure, the Contracting Authority or another public-sector entity lends to the Project Company, on similar terms as to repayment profile, Cover Ratios, security, *etc.*, to private-sector lenders, but at a lower cost because the loan is at or near to the cost of government bonds. Equity is provided by private-sector investors in the usual way. The debt is guaranteed by private-sector parties—banks or insurance companies. So project risks remain with the private sector, but funding is provided by the public sector. Some pilot projects using this scheme were undertaken in 2003–4 by the British Treasury, who gave it the name Credit Guarantee Finance ('CGF'). The scheme was proposed by the monoline insurance companies (*cf.* §4.3.2), to whom it was obviously beneficial, but the guarantees could also be provided by banks.

The aim of CGF was to take advantage of the lower public-sector borrowing costs, *i.e.* the difference between government bond rates and swap rates (*cf.* §10.3.1). There was also a political benefit as it would take the sting out of the argument that public-sector funding is 'cheaper' (*cf.* §3.7.3). The guarantee fees were, as might be expected, the same as the guarantee fees or credit margins that would otherwise have been charged by monoline insurers or lenders. Only 2–3 projects were financed in this way, however, and CGF was then 'mothballed'.

The main reason for abandoning the scheme was that systems and staff are needed to carry out the same due diligence and control as private-sector lenders, and the Treasury was not well-equipped to act like a lender. Someone has to:

- monitor and review policy on exposure to guarantors;
- review financing and other documentation to ensure it follows required principles;
- manage loan disbursements and administration;
- deal with Contract Variations;
- monitor the credit standing of its guarantors; and
- be prepared, in the worst case, take direct control of the underlying loan because the guarantor is no longer acceptable, and is unable to provide alternative security, such as cash collateralization, or a new guarantor to take its place—and of course a few years later most monoline insurer guarantees became worthless (*cf.* §4.3.3).

Having said this, after the 2008 financial crisis the British Treasury again become involved in providing or guaranteeing finance for the PFI program (*cf.* §15.7; §15.16), *i.e.* taking on project risks which it would have to monitor (and had to recruit staff with project-finance expertise to do this).

§15.10 CAPITAL GRANT

The Contracting Authority may pay part of the initial capital cost for an Availability-based or other PFI-Model project. Motives for providing this capital grant[13] are:

- to reduce the Contract Payments, reflecting the fact that the Contracting Authority's own cost of long-term borrowing is less than that for the Project Company; typically the Contracting Authority does not charge the Project Company for this subsidy, but the Tariff or Service Fee is reduced to reflect it—thus the Contracting Authority just pays its own debt costs for the subsidy amount.

---

[13] Also known as a 'Capital Contribution' (in Britain), or capital subsidy.

- to reduce the level of private-sector finance, so making it easier for the Project Company to raise finance in a market where there are market constraints (*cf.* §17.2), especially if the project is a large one.

Effectively the Contracting Authority is paying part of the capital cost in advance: the saving is on the cost of private-sector debt to finance this pre-paid portion. Obviously this is only appropriate for a Reverting Asset-based Contract.

The amount of a capital grant should be limited in relation to the total capital cost. To take the extreme case, if the Contracting Authority provides enough grant to eliminate the need for debt, it has clearly taken on the rôle of a Lender, and the benefit of risk transfer to the private sector is substantially eroded (although equity is still at risk). The benefit of lender due diligence (*cf.* §2.6.2) will also be lost. Moreover, if the Project Company defaults, leading to an early termination of the project (*cf.* §7.10.1), the Contracting Authority would not want to be in a position where the defaulted project is worth less than the amount of its capital grant—otherwise it has clearly lost part of its investment.[14] So, to maintain a second-loss position, typically around 50% of the capital cost would be a reasonable maximum for a capital grant.[15]

It is also preferable for the capital grant to be made after Project Completion, so that the Contracting Authority does not take on any construction-phase risks (*cf.* §9.5). This means that the Project Company would need to raise additional short-term financing to cover this temporary gap.

'Operational Gearing'. A large grant may cause some concern to the lenders, as this has the effect of increasing the 'operational gearing' of the project. This is the ratio in the Service Fee between payments for operations, and payments to cover debt service and equity return. If the latter reduces the result is that the lenders have a relatively larger risk on operating performance, and hence on deductions for poor performance.

Sale of Land. The Contracting Authority may fund its capital grant by selling off some land not required for the project—*e.g.* the old site for a school when the new school is being built on a new site. But someone has to take the risk that the land can be sold when the cash is required, and for the

---

[14] The Contracting Authority needs to examine various termination scenarios (*cf.* §7.10.1) to make sure that if does not lose the subsidy because it is paying too much for the project, so the Termination Sum payable on default by the Project Company should be adjusted to take account of the construction subsidy. This is automatic if the Termination Sum is based on the future cash-flow stream under the Project. Agreement, as this will have been reduced to allow for the construction subsidy.

[15] The Contracting Authority should require that the ratio of debt and equity to the subsidy amount at the end of the construction phase is fixed at Financial Close so that if the debt and equity are not fully drawn the subsidy is reduced *pro rata.*

assumed price (*cf.* §9.5.7 as to revenue during construction, where similar issues may apply). If the school is being moved from the old land to the new land, the sale cannot be finalized until Project Completion, and it is unlikely that the sale can be entered into long before then, *e.g.* at Financial Close. Lenders are unlikely to accept the risk of the capital grant being dependent on this sale, and will therefore require the Contracting Authority to commit to pay the grant irrespective of the position on the land sale, unless the Sponsors are willing to underwrite the sale instead.

100% Debt Repayment. Taking this approach to the extreme, the Contracting Authority can repay the debt after Project Completion, on the grounds that the main risk phase of the project has now passed. However this loses most of the benefit of long-term risk transfer to the private sector, raises additional risk issues, and it may not be attractive for lenders to cover only, or mainly, the construction risk (*cf.* §15.6; §17.5.1).

§15.11 VIABILITY-GAP FUNDING

Viability-Gap Funding ('VGF') plays a similar rôle in Concessions to capital grants in Availability-based projects, insofar as it reduces the cost of the project to the end-user. But VGF may also be provided because the project would not be viable if fully financed by private capital. These two motives for providing VGF are obviously linked, since it is likely to be the high cost to the user if no VGF is provided which makes the project unviable. In a public procurement bidders may be asked to bid for their required level of VGF, with the lowest bidder being awarded the Concession. However the maximum proportion of the capital cost covered by VGF should not be as high as for a capital grant, because a usage-based project has a significantly higher possibility of loss.

There is also a question of whether VGF is used by projects as a substitute for equity, leaving the debt at the same level. While this obviously reduces project costs, it also diminishes investors' risks, and if combined with a full debt guarantee (*cf.* §15.14) there is little incentive for investors or lenders to concern themselves with due diligence.

VGF, like capital grants, is not normally repayable by the Project Company. However in all cases like this, if a Contracting Authority provides support for Concessions, where there is a risk on user payments, it should get a share in any 'upside', *i.e.* if the project is more successful than investors originally projected, excess revenues above a certain level should be shared with the Contracting Authority (*cf.* §6.5.3).

VGF has been a key component of the huge PPP road program in India (*cf.* §4.2.1). The central government may provide up to 20% of capital costs as VGF, and the state government in which the project is situation may provide up to a further 20%, making 40% public-sector support in total. Bidders bid for the level of VGF they require.

§15.12 PART-CONSTRUCTION OF THE PROJECT

Another way for support to be provided for major public projects is to divide the project into two separate but linked projects, and for the Contracting Authority to build one of these projects itself. For example, in a rail project the Contracting Authority may build the track bed and the track using conventional public procurement and funding, and a Project Company will provide signaling and other equipment, and possibly the trains (or the trains could be a third project). Similarly in a road project, the Contracting Authority may build connecting roads to the main project, or build a stretch of the road which is too expensive to be covered by the private finance (*e.g.* where there are a lot of bridges or tunnels).

The main problem with this approach is coordinating the publicly- and privately-financed activities. If the rail track-bed is not built on time, for example, this will delay the Project Company's program, leading to a claim for compensation. There may also be more complex interface issues, where it is not clear which side of the project is at fault, so losing a lot of time in disputes.

§15.13 COMPLEMENTARY INVESTMENT

Complementary investment relates to elements not directly part of the project (and hence differs from part-construction) but there is clearly overlap in these concepts. For example, building a connecting road to a bridge could be considered a complementary investment if the road is assumed to be not part of the project, or part-construction if it is. The same issues arise as those discussed above.

§15.14 FULL DEBT GUARANTEE

Full repayment of debt on termination for a Project Company default has already been discussed in §7.10.1. A 100% debt guarantee (or a very high level of Debt Underpinning, *e.g.* 90% of the debt as is the case in some developing countries), means that the Contracting Authority is no longer in a second-loss position and is effectively providing a full debt guarantee. The lenders have little or no 'capital at risk' (*cf.* §2.6.2), and so a limited incentive to monitor the project, let alone undertake a rescue refinancing if something goes wrong (*cf.* §14.16.4). As a result, the Contracting Authority will have to take a much more active rôle in monitoring and controlling the project than would otherwise be the case, for which it may not be well-equipped. But there may be no choice but to offer 100% cover for loans in developing countries, as a way of getting an infrastructure finance program started.

Further issues may arise from lenders if the construction phase is not covered by the guarantee (*cf.* §17.5.1).

§15.15 FIRST-LOSS DEBT GUARANTEE

This is the guarantee equivalent of providing mezzanine debt, *i.e.* the guarantee will cover the first x% of loss on the senior debt. Hence this type of guarantee is one of the options available in the U.S. SIB (*cf.* §15.4.1) and TIFIA (*cf.* §15.4.2) programs, and EIB's Project Bond Initiative (*cf.* §15.4.3).

§15.16 *PARI-PASSU* DEBT GUARANTEE

In this case the public-sector entity providing the guarantee is taking the same risk on the part of the debt which is guaranteed, as the private-sector lenders on the part of the debt which is not guaranteed. A guarantee of more than 50% of the capital cost of a Concession generally puts the whole debt on the public-sector balance sheet. Therefore a *pari-passu* guarantee is unlikely to exceed this level. So if, say, a 50% guarantee is provided on a loan of $100, and only $60 can be recovered, the lenders and the guarantor will each suffer a loss of $20. The result is the same as if the public-sector entity had lent in a syndicate with other private-sector lenders, as might be done for Gap-Financing reasons or by a national-development Policy Bank, and similar issues on voting control arise for the private-sector lenders.

Moreover the private-sector lenders may still have a long-term liquidity problem—this is a problem which applies to all guarantee structures unless non-bank lenders are attracted to projects by the guarantee (which is unlikely as they would still have to take the risk on the unguaranteed balance).

The UK Guarantees Scheme, announced in 2012, is an example of a *pari-passu* guarantee program.. The Scheme provides for *pari-passu* government guarantees for up to 50% of the cost of major national infrastructure projects (whether PPPs or privatized infrastructure) which are 'shovel-ready', *i.e.* able to begin construction in a relatively short timescale. The Scheme, for up to £40 billion, is intended to be a temporary program, with no further guarantees being issued after 2016, its primary aim being to boost economic recovery by encouraging more rapid development of infrastructure projects.

Similarly in 2012 Italy announced a program of project bonds to be guaranteed by public entities such as SACE (*cf.* §16.4.6). This program can also be used for refinancing debt, *e.g.* after Project Completion.

▌ §15.17 DEBT UNDERPINNING

It could be argued that the risks taken by private-sector lenders in some types of infrastructure finance, especially Availability-based projects, are sufficiently low once the project has been built to the required specification, that the chances of a complete loss on the debt are very low and so if public-sector support is needed for one of the reasons above, a Contracting Authority (or another public-sector entity) can reasonably provide or guarantee some of the finance for such projects for one or more of the reasons set out above. So if the total debt is $100, with 70% guaranteed, but the recovery is only $50, the lenders will lose the whole of their $30 unguaranteed debt, and the Contracting Authority will lose $20 under the guarantee.[16] This type of second-loss guarantee is known as Debt Underpinning.

Logically, therefore, Debt Underpinning should not reduce the total cost of financing. While the cost of the underpinned debt should go down to reflect the public-sector guarantee, the cost of the rest of the debt should go up to reflect the increased risk per $ of unguaranteed debt. However the underpinning is still valuable because the lenders, especially banks, will be required to hold less capital against a loan with a government guarantee. This is its main benefit in developed countries. Also, in cases where it would otherwise be difficult to raise enough private-sector debt, underpinning obviously makes this easier. This is the main reason for its use in developing countries.

Debt Underpinning is found, for example in French PFI-Model projects, where once the project's construction is complete, up to 80% of the debt can become a direct Contracting Authority liability under the administrative-law procedure known as 'Cession de Créance' (transfer of the debt).[17]

▌ §15.18 MINIMUM REVENUE GUARANTEE ('MRG')

Private-sector investors and lenders may consider that the traffic or other usage level in a Concession may not be adequate to support a financing of the whole project; therefore the Contracting Authority provides an MRG (i.e. a guarantee of a minimum level of revenue from users), to ensure that the remaining revenues are sufficient to cover the debt.

An MRG is not really appropriate if it is clear that the project cannot generate enough revenue to be viable. In such cases VGF or mezzanine finance is more appropriate, the principle here being that the project needs to be able to stand on its

---

[16] Note that this excludes equity, which obviously provides the first cushion for losses.

[17] Also known as the 'Dailly tranche' after the law which set up this procedure. The French state-owned bank Caisse des Dépôts et Consignations and EIB (cf. §16.5.8) refinance most of the guaranteed debt.

own feet from day one. If an MRG is provided, investors and lenders will be taking a long-term credit risk on the Contracting Authority to this extent, which may be a problem in some developing countries. It also makes the project more vulnerable to political attacks if it is constantly receiving payments under the MRG, rather than the less conspicuous up-front one-off payment from VGF or mezzanine finance. An MRG should thus be used only to deal with uncertainty about future revenues, not when it is certain that future revenues will be inadequate as a basis for financing the project. As in any case where there is a revenue guarantee, the guarantor should also benefit from revenues significantly above projections, *i.e.* there should be excess-revenue sharing (*cf.* §6.5.3).

A key difference between this approach and a debt guarantee is that the investors may also benefit from an MRG. Clearly if the investors are not guaranteed, even if the lenders are (to some extent), the former still have an incentive to make the project work, but this incentive diminishes if equity income if also guaranteed.

An alternative MRG approach is to grant an extension to the Concession if the MRG traffic level is not reached. This makes the risk profile similar to a contract based on NPV of Revenues (*cf.* §9.6.3).

In Korea, an MRG system was one of the factors in a very large-scale and rapid development of transport infrastructure using Concessions.[18] This went though various phases of development, as set out in Table 15.2:

- In 1995, when the scheme was set up, guarantees were provided for 90% of the projected revenue in solicited projects, and 80% in unsolicited bids (*cf.* §3.7.11). So if revenues were projected at 1000 Won, and the outturn

Table 15.2 Evolution of the Korean MRG Scheme.

		1995–2003	2004–2005			2006		2009
Guarantee period (years)		1–20	1–5	6–10	11–15	1–5	6–10	See text
Solicited bids	Guarantee	90%	90%	80%	70%	75%	65%	
	Sharing	110%	110%	120%	130%	125%	135%	
Unsolicited bids	Guarantee	80%	80%	70%	60%	None		
	Sharing	120%	120%	130%	140%			
			No MRG payment if revenues are below 50% of forecast					

Source: Jay-Hyung Kim, Jungwook Kim, Sunghwsan Shin & Seung-Yeon Lee, *Public–Private Partnership Infrastructure Projects: Case Studies from the Republic of Korea* (Asian Development Bank, Manila, 2011)*.

[18] VGF (*cf.* §15.11) and a guarantee fund (*cf.* §15.21) were other key factors.

was 800 won, on a solicited project, the MRG would cover 100 of this 200 Won deficit, *i.e.* bringing the revenues up to 90% of the projection. The problem about this was that it left very little risk with the private sector, and not surprisingly the MRG was called on heavily, making this a one-way-bet for investors and lenders.

- An excess-revenue sharing arrangement was also put in place, such that if revenues exceeded 110% of the forecast (120% for unsolicited bids) the excess would be shared between the Project Company and the Contracting Authority.

- Key changes were made to the scheme in 2003—the MRG was 'tapered' and cut off entirely after 15 years, and no MRG was payable if a project did not meet 50% of its projected revenues. (During the previous phase projects which were below 50% were quite numerous.) The latter provision was to ensure that projects in which there was no serious study of traffic risk did not just pass this risk back to the MRG. The excess-revenue sharing threshold was also increased in parallel with the reduced guarantee tapering (*i.e.* the higher the degree of tariff risk being taken by the private sector, the higher the volume of traffic until the sharing arrangements took place).

- Then in 2006 the MRG was abolished for unsolicited bids, and the guarantee period and taper reduced for solicited bids. By 2009 35 of the 83 Concessions signed by the central government (*i.e.* excluding local-government projects) had MRGs.

- Finally in 2009 the MRG mechanism was fundamentally changed. (This mechanism only applies to solicited bids.) The revenue is guaranteed to be not to be less than the government's 'share of investment risks', which is calculated based on the project cost, excluding IDC, multiplied by the yield on a government bond. (This means that the most that would be paid by the government in such cases would be what the costs would have been had the project been financed with public debt.) Again this does not apply if the revenue is below 50% of the share of investment risk. Also, if revenue later goes above the guarantee level, any guarantee payments made can be recovered.

§15.19 TARIFF SUBSIDY

User payments in a Concession can be subsidized by the Contracting Authority. This means that the Project Company is still taking usage risk, unlike where an MRG is provided, as the subsidy would normally be paid per user. Some kind of sliding scale for the subsidy payments usually applies, *i.e.* the more users the lower the subsidy, so that the Contracting Authority benefits from the upside as discussed above.

However the same point applies here as discussed for an MRG—it is preferable to use VGF or mezzanine debt instead, although it has to be recognized that in some cases the Contracting Authority will not have the budget to make an up-front payment of this kind, and so the only alternative is payment of subsidies spread over a much longer term.

§15.20 PUBLIC-SECTOR PROJECT COMPANY

In this model the Project Company is owned by the public sector, but debt is provided by private-sector lenders on a normal project-finance basis; the Project Company also enters into the usual Sub-Contracts. This is the model used for Revenue Bonds in the U.S. municipal bond market (*cf.* §4.3.1).[19]

It would also be possible for the Project Company to be Franchised to the private sector once Project Completion takes place. But it is sourcing debt rather than equity which is the main reason for public-sector financial support, which this approach obviously does not help. However this could be used as a method of refinancing after Project Completion (*cf.* §15.6).

A variant of this is a company required by law to act in the public interest. Examples are the Canadian Public Interest Company (PIC), the British Community Interest Company (CIC), and the U.S. not-for-profit corporation (*cf.* §4.3.1), all of which may raise project finance for their investments.

§15.21 GUARANTEE FUNDS

The question might be asked, why is there any need for a guarantee fund to support the various types of government guarantee, especially the MRG discussed above? The problem is one of credibility of such a guarantee—in some countries investors and lenders do not feel confident that the government will remain willing or able to meet MRG claims. The issue is similar to the concern on relying on long-term Tariff subsidies (*cf.* §15.19). A guarantee fund operates independently of government, and has its own sources of funding—the latter may include funds contributed by the government, fees charged for the guarantees, and any upside sharing received in return for revenue or similar guarantees.

For example the Indonesian Infrastructure Guarantee Fund ('IIGF') was established in 2009, funded with equity from the Indonesia government and credit

---

[19] *i.e.* Revenue Bonds other than PABs.

facilities from DFIs. It provides guarantees on behalf of Contracting Authorities, against an indemnity from them, and it undertakes independent due diligence and monitoring of projects. The guarantee can cover a variety of risks such as the Contracting Authority's payment obligations, Termination-Sum payments, Change in Law and the standard investment risks (*cf.* §11.4). Similar funds exist, *inter alia*, in Brazil and Korea.

Chapter 16

EXPORT-CREDIT AGENCIES AND DEVELOPMENT-FINANCE INSTITUTIONS

§16.1 INTRODUCTION

This chapter covers the types of cross-border support which may be available for projects, especially in developing countries.[1] There are three main sources of such support:

- *export-credit agencies*, which provide loans, or financial- or political-risk insurance or guarantees, for exports of capital equipment to projects outside

---

[1] *Cf.* the background discussion on infrastructure in developing countries in Tomoko Matsukawa & Odo Habeck, *Review of Risk Mitigation Instruments for Infrastructure Financing and Recent Trends and Developments*, Trends and Policy Options No. 4 (PPIAF/World Bank, Washington DC, 2007)*; Antonio Estache, 'Infrastructure finance in developing countries: An overview', *EIB Papers* Vol. 15 No.2 (EIB, Luxemburg, 2010), p. 60*; Riham Shendy, Zachary Kaplan & Peter Mousley, *Towards Better Infrastructure Conditions, Constraints, and Opportunities in Financing Public-Private Partnerships: Evidence from Cameroon, Côte d'Ivoire, Ghana, Kenya, Nigeria, and Senegal* (World Bank/PPIAF, Washington DC, 2011).

Principles of Project Finance. DOI: http://dx.doi.org/10.1016/B978-0-12-391058-5.00016-3

the country concerned (§16.2); ECAs also provide political-risk cover for investors—but obviously no cover for commercial risks (§16.3).

- *bilateral DFIs*, which provide 'untied' loans, or political-risk insurance or guarantees, generally for projects outside the country concerned (*i.e.* not linked to specific exports from the country concerned); these frequently work with their national ECAs; these may include both development agencies which also provide aid, as well as development-finance institutions or funds; the various types of support offered by the leading ECAs and bilateral DFIs are discussed in §16.4.
- *multilateral DFIs* ('MDFIs')—these provide support for all types of projects, mainly but not entirely in developing countries (§16.5).[2]

Private-sector insurance is also available for political risks (*cf.* §11.8.1).

§16.2 EXPORT CREDIT AGENCIES

ECAs are either public-sector institutions in their respective countries, established to provide support for the exports of that country, or private-sector companies that act as a channel for government support for exports from the country concerned.

ECA finance for major projects had traditionally been in the form of buyer credits to public-sector entities, or large utilities in the country concerned, often secured by a Host Government guarantee. This changed after the mid-1990s as major projects (initially mainly in the power sector) were increasingly financed in the private sector rather than by the Host Government—hence the requirement to support project-financing transactions. More recently ECA support has been seen mainly in the natural-resources sector, in oil, gas and pipeline projects.

ECA support is relevant where the Project Company is importing capital equipment—*i.e.* this relates largely to projects being built under an EPC Contract rather than a D&B Contract. This is because the costs in a D&B Contract relate primarily to civil works, where the import of equipment is usually quite limited (*e.g.* only specialized construction equipment) compared to an EPC Contract in which equipment forms a much larger part of the project costs.

---

[2] Information and data on the ECAs, DFIs, and other organizations discussed in this Chapter can generally be found on their websites, links to which are maintained at www.yescombe.com. For summary information on 31 multilateral and bilateral DFIs *cf. International Finance Institutions and Development through the Private Sector* (International Finance Corporation, Washington DC, 2011), Annex.* Another survey can be found in Infrastructure Consortium for Africa, *Donor Debt and Equity Financing for Infrastructure: User Guide Africa* (African Development Bank, Tunis, 2007).* The World Bank maintains a database on PPI (*cf.* §2.5.2) in developing countries at http://ppi.worldbank.org/.

§16.2.1 ECA SUPPORT FOR PROJECTS

ECA support for project financings may be provided in several ways:

Credit Insurance: ECAs may provide lenders with credit support, *i.e.* insurance or guarantees that cover all risks, both political and commercial, thus leaving lenders to provide finance with no risk on the project itself (full cover).

Political-Risk Insurance ('PRI'): ECAs may provide PRI to lenders, so leaving them with only the commercial risks on the project. The use of PRI for lenders is an important product for ECAs, especially in project finance. It is usually dependent on a Sponsor from the ECA's country being involved in the Project Company. Such cover may help to fill gaps in the financing package (*e.g.* caused by export credits only supporting exports of equipment and not civil works). PRI for investors is discussed in §16.3. This type of coverage is not governed by the OECD Consensus (*cf.* §16.2.3).

Financing Support: ECA may also provide projects with financing support, *i.e.*:

- *Direct loans to the Project Company* (which usually means that the ECA is taking the same risk as if it were providing full cover); some countries, such as the United States, Canada, China and Japan, have Export–Import Banks that can lend directly to the Project Company in a similar way to a private-sector commercial bank, but at low fixed interest rates.
- *Interest Rate Equalization.* Other countries, such as France (COFACE) and Italy (SACE), rely on the private-sector commercial-banking market to fund export credits, but provide a subsidy for the difference between the banks' cost of finance and the CIRR (*cf.* §16.2.3). In effect, the ECA enters into an interest-rate swap agreement with the commercial banks (*cf.* §10.3.1), enabling them to provide the Project Company with a subsidized fixed rate of interest. (In some countries the interest rate support is provided by a different body than the provider of the export credit insurance—*cf.* §16.4.)

Some countries, such as the United Kingdom, have advocated abolition of financial support (*i.e.* low-rate loans or subsidized interest rates) for exports, with the aim of restricting ECAs to providing 'pure cover' (*i.e.* credit insurance for exports, but with finance at market interest rates). There are other objections to ECA support programs on the basis that they are just a kind of export subsidy, and exporters should stand on their own feet: but the problem here is that if some ECAs stop offering credit or financing support exporters from other countries that do not stop this will have an unfair advantage.

A decision by an ECA to provide support for exports to a particular country is partly based on the creditworthiness of the country concerned, but also on political factors.

In most cases where ECAs insure or guarantee loans, a payment is triggered only if the covered risks lead to a debt-service default by the Project Company (*i.e.* these are payment guarantees not performance guarantees). Many ECAs do not then repay the lenders immediately, but only according to the original repayment schedule (with interest).

ECAs may also support exports from other countries, depending on arrangements between individual ECAs. In the European Union, for example, ECAs from one E.U. country will cover exports from other E.U. countries up to 30% of the contract value.

Most major ECAs have also now signed cooperation agreements with each other, to deal with the common situation where exports from more than more country, and hence more than one ECA, are involved in a project. A typical structure in this situation is for a 'lead' ECA to be designated, usually the ECA for the lead contractor for the project, and for all the cover or finance to be provided by this ECA. Any other ECA(s) involved then reinsure their share of the risk. Thus the Project Company has only to deal with one set of ECA documentation and payments.[3]

Export credits used in project finance are normally buyer credits (*i.e.* direct loans provided to the importer by the exporter's bank or the ECA itself) rather than supplier credits (*i.e.* loans provided by the exporter to the importer, with finance from the exporter's bank or ECA). Therefore, formally speaking, ECAs deal with the exporter's bank or the Project Company, although Sponsors of major projects usually have their own direct discussions with ECAs.

ECAs have only a small number of staff working on project finance: a number of ECAs therefore use outside financial advisors to help them assess project finance risks.

§16.2.2 BERNE UNION

The International Union of Credit and Investment Insurers, generally known as the 'Berne Union', founded in 1934, promotes international coordination and exchange of information on export credits and (since 1974) investment insurance. It has 78 members, including all major ECAs, and some private-sector insurers (*cf.* §11.8.1).

Business undertaken by members of the Berne Union in recent years is summarized in Table 16.1.

The use of long-term export credits (including cover for project-finance transactions) declined in the 1990s as lenders were increasingly willing to assume risk in

---

[3] Reinsurance between ECAs and private PRI insurers (*cf.* §11.8.1)—both ways—also takes place.

Table 16.1 Project-Finance Business by Berne Union Members

($ millions)	2000	2007	2008	2009	2010	2011
Medium- & long-term business[†]	71,000	142,120	153,591	190,589	173,393	191,175
of which: project finance		2,613	3,419	7,300	13,530	7,658
Year-end exposure[††]	453,000	501,423	523,704	582,792	593,089	647,073
Investment Insurance[†††]	13,000	52,937	58,580	49,337	65,415	77,599
Year-end exposure	57,000	141,868	145,580	145,785	184,398	197,326

[†] Refers to credit insurance, PRI and direct loans; individual sector figures N/A.
[††] Separate figures for project finance N/A.
[†††] PRI for investors in all types of project (*cf.* §16.3); separate project-finance figures N/A.
Source: *Berne Union Yearbooks**.

developing countries without this cover, but this trend reversed after the Asian crisis of 1997, in which significant losses were made by uninsured investors and lenders. The same pattern can be seen in the 2000s: the use of long-term export-credit cover declined somewhat until the financial crisis of 2007–8 and has increased since.

Moreover, direct lending by ECAs, rather than provisions of guarantees, became more important as project-finance banks' ability to provide long-term funding declined (*cf.* §17.2). In the past loans insured or guaranteed by ECAs were generally treated as sovereign risk on the balance sheets of commercial-bank lenders, and hence required no capital to be allocated against them. But the Basel III system (*cf.* §17.3) imposes absolute limits on bank leverage, irrespective of the risk classification of loans, and hence the willingness of banks to fund such loans has declined in line with the general project-finance market.

Having said all this, however, the overall scale of ECA project-finance business is relatively small compared to private-sector financing, but it should be borne in mind that:

- ECA support is often linked to bilateral DFI support for projects, and the two together are significantly more important (*cf.* §16.4).
- ECA support is significant in certain markets, and in developing countries.

§16.2.3 THE OECD CONSENSUS

The detailed terms on which ECAs provide support for export credits (whether direct loans, interest rate subsidies, or credit insurance for lenders) are governed by an international agreement under the ægis of the Organization for Economic Cooperation and Development ('OECD'). *The Arrangement on Guidelines for Officially Supported Export Credits* dates from 1978, and is subscribed to by Australia, Canada, the European Union, Japan, Korea, New Zealand, Norway,

Switzerland, and the United States (*i.e.* most but not all major exporters, China being a conspicuous absentee). This 'OECD Consensus' ensures the operation of an orderly export credit market and seeks to prevent countries from competing to offer the most favorable financing terms for exports. Competition between ECAs is therefore limited to the amount of credit support available (*i.e.* how much credit risk they wish to assume for a particular project in a particular country). The OECD Consensus is not legally binding,[4] although its provisions are given legal effect in some areas (*e.g.* the European Union).

The main provisions of the OECD Consensus (as at 2013—adjustments to the detailed terms of the Consensus are made annually) are:

- 85% of the export contract value including third-country supply can be covered: thus a cash down payment of 15% of the contract value is required.
- 100% of the credit premium charged by the ECA can also be financed.
- Support can also be provided for up to 30% of local costs.
- Countries are classified into two groups:
  - *Category I*: High-Income OECD Countries, as defined by the World Bank based on *per capita* gross national income (GNI);
  - *Category II*: All other countries.
- The maximum repayment term (from final delivery, *i.e.* Project Completion in the case of most project financings) is 5 years for Category I countries and 10 years for Category II (all others). Most project finance with export credits is likely to be to Category II countries; there is a special régime for power plant, which may be financed for up to 12 years.
- Repayments are to be made in equal principal installments at least semiannually, beginning not later than 6 months from completion of performance tests under the Construction Contract. However if project cash flow does not allow for this there is some flexibility on the payment profile.
- Interest (either on direct loans or *via* interest-rate subsidies) is to be charged at minimum fixed rates of 1% over the cost of the equivalent long-term government bonds in the currency concerned. These interest rates, known as 'CIRR' (Commercial Interest Reference Rates) are the same for any one currency irrespective of where the credit is provided (*e.g.* a $ interest rate is the same whether the credit is supported by an ECA in the United States or Europe); the rates are recalculated once a month and are based on market rates for long-term debt.
- The interest rate charged on a particular project can be fixed at contract signing, or based on the CIRR in the month the ECA makes an offer of finance, provided this occurs within 120 days (in the latter case a further 0.2% is to be added to the CIRR).

---

[4] It is a 'gentleman's agreement', and does not have the force of a treaty.

- Minimum Premium Rates ('MPR'), *i.e.* the minimum cost of credit insurance, are to be charged based on a variety of factors including country risk, term of risk, obligor risk, proportion of cover and whether this is full cover or PRI only, and any mitigation of these risks. The MPR is calculated as an up-front payment covering the life of the project. These provisions do not apply to Category I and other low-risk countries.

An arrangement initially agreed to in 1998 (Annex X of the Consensus) allows more flexibility on project finance:

- repayment term of up to 14 years, provided:
  - the first repayment of principal (of not less than 2%) takes place within 24 months;
  - no single principal installment payment shall exceed 25% of the debt; and
  - the weighted average life of the repayment period (*cf.* §12.5.2) does not exceed 7¼ years.
- CIRR rates to apply to loans for up to 12 years, thereafter a margin of 0.2% to be added.
- If the project is in a 'High Income Country' the following also applies to project finance from ECAs:
  - participation in a loan syndicate with private-sector lenders, with the ECA taking a minority share, and total ECA support from Consensus members not exceeding 50%;
  - premium rates not to undercut available private-sector financing costs.

§16.2.4 Assumption of Risks and Scope of Cover

ECAs may not be willing to assume the full risk of a project (*i.e.* by providing full cover or direct loans without any Lender guarantee). Policies between ECAs differ considerably in this respect (these issues do not form part of the OECD consensus), and ECAs also work in other different ways:

Risk Percentage. Some ECAs providing guarantees or insurance have a policy of not covering more than, say, 95% of whatever risk they are assuming, leaving 5% (*pari-passu*) with the lenders (thus they would cover 95% of 85% of the cost of the equipment being exported, after allowing for a 15% down payment), on the grounds that this will help to ensure that the lenders look after the ECAs' interests in the project, rather than relying on the insurance and not pursuing claims with any vigor. Others cover 100% of the relevant risk.

Construction Risk. Some ECAs will not take the construction risk on the project, on the grounds that this risk is mainly within the control of the exporter (*i.e.* the Construction Contractor), and they are not in business to take a risk on the exporter's performance. They thus require commercial banks to take this risk and only guarantee the political risk of the project during the construction phase. In cases where an ECA would normally provide a direct loan, commercial banks may be required to provide the loan for the construction phase (again with political risk cover only during this period), which is then refinanced by the ECA on completion of construction.

Commercial Risk. Some ECAs are not willing to take the continuing commercial risks of the project even when it is operating, and only provide political risk cover throughout the project's life. Others cover the whole of the lenders' risk on the project (*i.e.* provide full cover); others might cover 95% of the political risk and 80% of the commercial risk. There is a general trend towards providing full cover because of the difficulty of distinguishing between political risk and commercial risk (*cf.* §11.5.2). An ECA providing a direct loan obviously takes the full commercial and political risks of the project, although in some cases a completion guarantee from commercial banks is required.

Political Risk. Where only PRI is being provided (with funding by private-sector lenders), ECAs' policies on what is meant by political risk also differ:

- All ECAs provide coverage for the standard investment risks (*cf.* §11.4), *i.e.* currency availability and transfer, expropriation, and political violence, although the precise scope of the cover may vary between ECAs.
- The effects of a change in law (*cf.* §11.3) are normally only covered indirectly (*i.e.* if provisions for compensation for change in law are included in the relevant Project Contract and cause a payment default.
- Some ECAs provide coverage for breach of contract in the narrow sense, if the Host Government has direct contractual liabilities (*e.g.* under a Government Support Agreement) or provides guarantees for liabilities under a Project Contract, provided this involves non-payment which then leads to a default under the loan; this is known as 'enhanced political risk' coverage.
- Some ECAs provide the wider coverage for contract repudiation (*cf.* §11.5.1).
- Whether or not the risk of breach of contract by a sub-sovereign risk (*cf.* §11.6) can be covered is very much a case-by-case question.
- Cover for creeping expropriation (*cf.* §11.5.2) may also be difficult to obtain because of the vague nature of this risk.

Direct Agreements. Some ECAs may require to sign a Direct Agreement with the Host Government under which the latter accepts liability for any payments made to lenders by the ECA in cases where the Offtaker/Contracting Authority is a public-sector body, or gives some weaker assurances to the

ECA in this respect; others do not consider this as appropriate, because project finance is regarded as being in the private sector.

Finance of Premiums. ECA insurance premiums (*i.e.* the payments for an ECA assuming full cover or political risk cover) can be substantial, as they are generally paid at Financial Close, but cover the risk for the whole life of the financing (*i.e.* the premium is the NPV of an annual fee charged for insuring the debt). The level of premium varies according to the risk of the country and the nature of the coverage provided, but on a typical project financing for a developing country may reach or exceed 10% of the amount covered. Some ECAs include their premium within the costs for which they will provide coverage or finance, but others will not.

Interest During Construction. Similarly, some ECAs will cover and finance IDC, but others will not.

Environmental Issues. While not directly a financing issue, there are differences between ECAs on environmental standards; in particular, a minority of ECAs, led by U.S. Exim, require an EIA for projects they finance (*cf.* §9.10.1), while the majority do not unless the Host Country's law requires it.

Eligibility. Similarly, eligibility for ECA coverage differs from country to country, though again this issue is not limited only to project finance. Some ECAs providing guarantees or insurance will only do so for banks incorporated and resident in the ECA's country; others will do so for any bank doing business in the country (*i.e.* including branches of foreign banks); others will do so for any bank wherever located.

Documentation. The nature of the documentation required varies considerably between ECAs, although this has become less of a problem thanks to the cooperation agreements mentioned above.

§16.2.5 CASH COLLATERALIZATION

As mentioned above, some ECAs do not fully cover the amount of risk they are insuring; for example, if 85% of the contract value is being financed by a commercial bank with coverage from an ECA, the insurance may only extend to 95% of this 85%, thus leaving the commercial bank uncovered for 5% of its exposure, or 4.25% of the contract cost. Even this small level of exposure in a difficult country may not be acceptable to the commercial bank.

One approach to this problem is for the Project Company to place cash to this extent in a collateral account, as security for the commercial bank's uncovered exposure. This is likely to be an issue with the ECA concerned; their policy is usually that under their right of subrogation (*cf.* §8.6.5) *i.e.* the right to take over the assets that were insured or guaranteed—the loan in this case—any security must be shared on a 5:95 ratio. The ECA will therefore demand 95% of the proceeds of the cash collateral account on a default, so leaving the commercial bank with the same risk for its 5% exposure as the ECA is for its 95%.

§16.2.6 BENEFIT OF ECA SUPPORT

With the need to keep within the structure of the OECD Consensus rules, the complexity always caused by having another party to the financing, and the relatively high initial premiums charged by ECAs (in lieu of a credit margin), it generally only becomes attractive to use ECA support if private-sector lenders are not willing to provide finance to the country or project concerned without it.

Another key point is that ECAs primarily support exports of equipment, not the whole of the amount payable under an Construction Contract: power or infrastructure projects incur substantial costs under their Construction Contracts for civil engineering work (normally carried out by local subcontractors, with no export element involved), which ECAs can only support under the OECD Consensus to the limited extent of 15% of the total contract value. These costs may be partly covered by the investors' equity contribution, but if a project has a sizable civil engineering component (*e.g.* a road or a hydroelectric power plant), export credits alone will not usually provide enough funding.

The CIRR interest rate charged on export credits is generally attractive if available; moreover, this rate can be fixed when the credit is approved, before the financing is complete, which is very helpful for a project's financial planning, as it eliminates the problem of interest rate movement before Financial Close (*cf.* §10.3.5).

ECA involvement may also provide a degree of intangible political support for the project that could help investors as well as lenders, but this alone is seldom a reason for choosing to use ECA coverage.

§16.3 POLITICAL-RISK INSURANCE FOR INVESTORS

Investors in Project Companies do not necessarily make use of PRI even if their lenders require it on the debt side. The theoretical argument for this is that their investment in the Project Company is well known, and part of their ordinary business, and the risk involved is therefore reflected in their share price. Another similar argument is that if they are not comfortable doing business in the country concerned they should not hide behind insurance, but should not do business there at all. However the high-profile political nature of many project-finance investments may make such insurance prudent (*cf.* §11.2).

There is a potential difficulty with PRI for equity investment in a Project Company. An insurer or guarantor who makes payment under a claim normally has the right of subrogation, although ECAs usually require the commercial bank lenders to continue to attempt to recover the loan on their behalf, as do private insurers. ECAs may thus only pay claims against PRI on equity if the investors' interests in the shares are assigned over to the insurer. This may cause a major problem for investors insuring their equity, as it may indirectly lead to their losing the benefit of the insurance.

Assignment of the investors' shareholding in the Project Company is a standard part of the lenders' security to enable them to control the Project Company more easily after a default (*cf.* §14.7.2). This causes two levels of problem if the investors have insured their equity with PRI, and a political risk-based loss occurs:

- If the loan is not fully repaid after a default, the lenders will be disinclined to release their security over the shares to allow the investors to hand them to their insurer in return for a payment under their PRI; they will argue that lenders should be repaid before investors and therefore the proceeds of the insurance on the equity should be paid to the lenders. But from the point of view of the investors in the Project Company, if the lenders are paid the proceeds of insurance on the equity, this makes the investors' PRI pointless.
- Even if the lenders concede the point, the problem may remain if there are different PRI insurers of equity and debt, since the insurer covering the debt will want to take over the lenders' security, including the pledge of the shares in the Project Company, and recover any value that can be derived from disposal of this equity, which again means that the insurer covering the investors will not be prepared to pay out.

From the point of view of the insurers, the problem is a somewhat theoretical one, since once a Project Company is in default it is unlikely that much value will be recovered on the equity, and the chances of recovering this before the debt has been repaid are very low. Nonetheless it has proved an obstacle to financing on some projects. Even U.S. Exim and OPIC—both owned by the U.S. government—could not agree on this issue until 1999, at which time they signed a joint claims agreement, under which they agreed that they would postpone debate and work together on recoveries and worry about how to divide any proceeds afterwards. This works because both are part of the U.S. Federal budget, so the only issue is which pocket the recoveries go into, but no such agreements are in place between other agencies.

This issue appears to be less of a problem for private-sector insurers, who may be willing to accept a subordinated position to the lenders (*i.e.* they can only recover any payments for the equity if lenders have been repaid).

§16.4 ECAS AND BILATERAL DFIS

ECAs and bilateral DFIs in each country often work together in providing financial support, so it makes sense to look at their activities as a whole.[5] Statistics in

---

[5] It should be noted that if ECAs or DFIs provide direct loans rather than guarantee or insure private-sector lenders these direct loans are not included in the market statistics set out in Chapters 2 and 3.

Table 16.2 Major Export-Credit Insurers, Guarantors and Banks (ECAs), and Bilateral DFIs—Project-Finance Loans & Guarantees

Country	ECA Insurer[†]	ECA Lender	Bilateral DFI	(US$ millions)		
				2010	2011	2012
Japan	Nexi	JBIC	JBIC	4,776	7,691	16,825
Korea	K-sure	KEXIM	KDB	2,578	5,396	8,747
China	SINOSURE	China Exim	CDB	9,578	218	6,013
U.S.A.	US Exim/OPIC	US Exim		1,422	967	3,620
Germany	Hermes	KfW	DEG	5,739	4,260	3,247
Italy	SACE			1,508	3,730	1,286
Denmark	EKF			251	4,054	1,155
France	COFACE		Proparco/AFD	1,013	0	761
Others[††]				2,975	2,146	2,942
Total				**29,840**	**28,462**	**44,596**

There is some double counting against Table 2.1 where ECAs/DFIs provide guarantees for commercial bank loans. Institutions which only provide interest-rate subsidies at the CIRR (*cf.* §16.2.1) are not listed here.
[†]   May also act as a lender.
[††]   9 different entities in 2010, 6 in 2011, 12 in 2012.
Source: as for Table 2.1.

these areas are difficult to find, but *Project Finance International*'s annual survey of project finance markets does collect some numbers, which can be analyzed as in Table 16.2. (Note that this table relates mainly to 'policy-based' project finance provided by these institutions, *i.e.* finance where there is some element of credit support or reduced pricing: as will be seen below a number of the same institutions provide normal commercial project finance, and appear under this guise in Table 4.3.)

Tied Aid. Joint financing between ECAs and their national DFIs is subject to the rules relating to 'Tied Aid' under the OECD Consensus (*cf.* §16.2.3), *i.e.* any bilateral official development assistance ('ODA') grant or loans on a concessional basis to encourage procurement from the donor country:
- Tied Aid is generally governed by the OECD's *DAC*[6] *Guiding Principles for Associated Financing and Tied and Partially Untied Official Development Assistance* (1987)*.
- Tied Aid is not allowed for countries above the World Bank upper limit for lower middle-income countries (GNI per capita of $4,035 as at 2013).

---

[6] Development Action Committee.

- Tied Aid is not to be provided to projects that would be financially viable without it.
- Tied Aid should not be provided with a 'Concessionality Level' of less than 35%, or 50% for a least-developed country. The Concessionality Level is calculated by discounting the Tied Aid payments by the relevant CIRR and comparing this discounted sum to the funds provided.
- The Tied Aid provisions do not apply to export credits or other financing on normal market terms.

§16.4.1–§16.4.7 set out information on the various countries' ECAs and bilateral DFIs shown in Table 16.2, which as indicated on the table have been the largest providers of project finance compared to their peers. Together these examples provide a good cross-§ of the various different approaches used. Despite differences in structure, the combination of market forces and the OECD Consensus ensures that the end results are fairly similar, although as summarized in §16.2.4 there are some differences in risk assumption in the project-finance field.

§16.4.1 JAPAN (NEXI/JBIC)

Finance or guarantees from NEXI or JBIC are heavily concentrated towards projects which are sources of strategic raw materials, *i.e.* the oil, natural gas and mining sectors, as well as major Japanese exports, *e.g.* railway rolling stock.

Nippon Export and Investment Insurance (NEXI). Export-credit insurance was formerly provided by the Export-Import Insurance Division of the Ministry of International Trade and Industry (EID/MITI), established in 1950. In 1993, EID/MITI were one of the first ECAs to provide coverage for project finance transactions, and had a specialized project finance department since 1995. In 2001 the Ministry of Economy, Trade and Industry (METI) replaced MITI, and MITI's export credit and investment insurance responsibilities were transferred to Nippon Export and Investment Insurance (NEXI), an autonomous agency that provides export credit and investment insurance. NEXI's liabilities are reinsured by METI.

NEXI insures up to 100% of lenders' commercial risks (after completion) and up to 100% of political risks. PRI is provided for currency convertibility and transfer, war, revolution, and civil war, and 'any other occurrences arising outside Japan which cannot be imputed to the insured party or the borrower,' which covers matters such as contract repudiation. NEXI also provides investment insurance.

NEXI also makes untied credit insurance available to lenders from Japan, and also has a special program of credit and investment insurance for 'overseas resources development projects' whose purpose is 'securing a stable natural resource supply': for such projects NEXI provides lenders with full cover and investors with cover for war, expropriation, terrorism or *force majeure*, such as a natural disaster.

Japan Bank for International Cooperation ('JBIC'). JBIC was formed in 1999 from a merger of Export-Import Bank of Japan ('JEXIM') and Japan's Overseas Economic Co-operation Fund. In 2008 JBIC became part of the state-owned Japan Finance Corporation ('JFC'), but the name continued to be used for JFC's international operations. It was de-merged again in 2011. JEXIM's first project financing (for an LNG project in Australia) was in 1986, and it set up a specialized project-finance department in 1988.

JBIC's business includes CIRR-based funding for exports (buyer's credits), usually co-financing with commercial banks, and import loans to Japanese companies developing overseas natural resource projects.[7]

JBIC also provides untied funding (ODA) under two main programs: overseas investment loans, which require a Japanese involvement in ownership and management of the Project Company, and untied direct loans as part of Japan's aid program. It also takes equity participations in Japanese investments overseas. Finally it provides guarantees relating to these activities.

§16.4.2 KOREA (K-SURE/KEXIM/KDB)

As compared to Japan, more of Korea's ECA project-finance business relates to Korean exports rather than natural-resource development projects.

Korea Trade Insurance Corporation ('K-sure'). Korean Reinsurance Corporation was established to provide export-credit insurance in 1968; this business was transferred to Kexim (see below) in 1977. In 1992 Korea Export Insurance Corporation (KEIC) was established to provide export-credit guarantees, and changed its name to K-sure in 2010, reflecting a widening of its scope of activities.

K-sure provides buyer's credits with interest-rate subsidies, or direct loans, against CIRR rates, as well as untied loans and guarantees for projects in which a Korean company is an investor. Full cover is also provided to Korean companies for overseas construction projects. K-sure also provides insurance relating to investment and loans for development of natural resources required by Korea.

Export-Import Bank of Korea ('KEXIM'). KEXIM was established in 1976. It provides export credits on a CIRR basis, as well as loans for investments and debt finance for overseas companies in which there is a Korean equity interest, and guarantees to foreign banks making such loans. The Bank also provides financing for imports of essential commodities to Korea, and

---

[7] *Cf. JBIC Project Finance Initiatives: Japanese Enterprise and Global Prosperity* (JBIC, Tokyo, n.d.)*.

manages the Economic Development Cooperation Fund, through which Korea's ODA is channeled.

Korea Development Bank ('KDB'). KDB was founded in 1954. Its policy-based lending (in conjunction with K-sure and KEXIM) is being taken over by the state-owned Korea Finance Corporation ('KoFC'), established in 2009, while KDB itself is being privatized. As to its commercial project-finance lending, and as can be seen in Table 4.3, KDB ranked 5th amongst worldwide project-finance loan arrangers, having provided $5,411 million to 27 loans. Its domestic project-finance business concentrates mainly on infrastructure, and its international business on natural resource projects with a Korean connection.

§16.4.3 CHINA (SINOSURE/CHINA EXIMBANK/CDB

It has been estimated that China Exim and CDB together lent more than $110 billion to developing countries in 2010–11, a figure considerably larger than the World Bank over the same period.[8] However only a limited amount of this was in the form of project finance, primarily in mining and natural-gas projects where the commodity will be exported to China.

China Export & Credit Insurance Corporation ('SINOSURE'). SINOSURE was established in 2001 to provide insurance for China's foreign trade and economic cooperation. As mentioned in §16.2.3 SINOSURE does not adhere to the OECD Consensus. It provides the usual range of ECA products such as insurance for buyer credits and overseas investment. Its involvement in project finance to date seems to have been quite limited.

The Export-Import Bank of China ('China Exim'). China Exim was founded in 1994. It provides *inter alia* buyers' credits, overseas construction loans and loans for overseas investments, and guarantees related to these. Its main mandate is 'to facilitate the export and import of Chinese mechanical and electronic products, complete sets of equipment and new-and high-tech products, assist Chinese companies with comparative advantages in their offshore contract projects and outbound investment, and promote Sino-foreign relationship and international economic and trade cooperation'. Loans are typically made on a LIBOR basis with a margin. Again its project-finance business appears to be limited. (*Cf.* §11.4.1 for its involvement in the 'Angola Model.)

China Development Bank ('CDB'). CDB was founded in 1994. Its main mandate in China is to provide finance for major infrastructure projects. A few of these

---

[8] "China's lending hits new heights", *Financial Times*, London, 17 January 2011.

appear to be on a project-finance basis. (Two domestic projects, for a highway and a coal development, totaling $1045 billion are shown in the *Project Finance International* listings for 2012, making CDB 45th in the *Project Finance International* list of lead arrangers (see Table 4.3)). It also lends to international projects.

§16.4.4 UNITED STATES (U.S. EXIM/OPIC)

Although U.S. Exim and OPIC support for project financing has a long history, the volume of project-finance business undertaken by these agencies is relatively low, and tends to concentrate in the natural resources and power-generation sectors.

The Export–Import Bank of the United States ('U.S. Exim'). U.S. Exim was established in 1934, and set up a project finance division in 1994. U.S. Exim provides long-term loans or guarantees to commercial banks, to the maximum OECD Consensus level. Support is provided on the standard OECD Consensus terms, for the lesser of 85% of the contract price or 100% of the U.S. content. So long as U.S. exports are involved, U.S. Exim will provide support to non-U.S. banks.

Most of the project-finance provided by U.S. Exim relates to power generation, and oil and gas-related projects, and the annual number of project-finance transactions is, as illustrated in Table 16.2, quite small, although the amount of financing for individual projects may be large.

U.S. Exim uses the full flexibility provided by the project-finance provisions of the OECD Consensus, including finance for their risk premium and IDC. After completion, funding is generally provided by U.S. Exim, assuming the full (political and commercial) risks of the project, or full or political risk-only coverage can be given to commercial bank lenders.

Political risks covered are currency convertibility and transfer, expropriation, including creeping expropriation, and political violence (resulting either in physical damage to the project or loss of revenue). Nonpayment because of contract disputes or repudiation is not covered; this is less of a problem than it might seem if U.S. Exim is providing finance post completion: nonpayment by the Host Government before then can only occur if the Project Company terminates its contract and calls on the Host Government guarantee, and the range of defaults that might cause this (before the Project Company is due to begin operations or earn any revenue) is limited.

U.S. Exim may require to sign a bilateral agreement (known as a Project Incentive Agreement) with the Host Government, which gives them recourse to the host government if a default occurs as a result of political risks: this is dealt with on a case-by-case basis.

U.S. Exim provides a useful checklist of its criteria and information required for assessing projects, which may be compared with the information-memorandum requirements set out in §5.2.8 and the risks analyzed in Chapters 9–11: a copy is set out in the Annex to this chapter.

U.S. Exim uses external financial advisors (at the Sponsors' expense) to review the risks in a project financing.

Overseas Private Investment Corporation ('OPIC'). OPIC is a United States government agency, founded in 1971 to take over the political risk insurance responsibilities of the U.S. Agency for International Development ('U.S. AID'), itself the successor in this respect to the post-World War II Marshall Plan, which provided the first insurance for political risks. OPIC (and AID before it) has a good track record of payment of most of the political risk claims submitted. Given this long history, the OPIC approach to political risk insurance has been used as a model by later entrants into the market; the use of OPIC political risk cover, and the direct loans that OPIC can also provide, have become more common in the project finance market.

OPIC can insure up to $250 million per project, covering 90% on equity investments and 100% on loans, for up to 20 years. (There is no requirement to insure both equity and debt, although this can be done.) OPIC can also provide direct loans on similar terms. For equity investments, OPIC typically issues insurance commitments equal to 270% of the initial investment, 90% representing the original investment and 180% to cover loss of future earnings. If a claim arises on a loan insurance, OPIC may choose not to repay the loan immediately, but to make payments on the original debt service schedule.

The eligibility criteria for OPIC support are:

- It is provided to U.S. investors or lenders (*i.e.* U.S. entities owned at least 50% by U.S. citizens, or foreign companies controlled 100% by such entities, or 95% by U.S. citizens).
- The investment or loan relates to project companies overseas where a majority of the equity or the day-to-day management remains in private hands, and 25% of the equity is owned by U.S. investors.
- Total OPIC support cannot exceed 50% of the cost of a new project or 75% on an expansion of an existing project.
- Applicants have to demonstrate that the insurance required cannot be provided by the private sector.

OPIC does not require the investment or loan to be used to cover export of equipment from the United States, although generally equipment imported from industrialized countries would not be covered (since export credit coverage should be available). OPIC is not constrained by the OECD Consensus.

The risks covered are the 'standard' investment risks (currency convertibility and transfer, expropriation, and political violence), as well as creeping expropriation and nonpayment due to breach of contract.

The U.S. and Host Governments sign bilateral agreements covering OPIC programs, and the Host Government has to approve any insurance issued by OPIC.

§16.4.5 GERMANY (HERMES/KFW/DEG)

German concessional project financing is heavily concentrated on supporting exports, especially in the power-generation sector.

Euler Hermes Kreditversicherungs A.G. ('Hermes'). Hermes, majority owned by the insurance company Allianz A.G., administers the German government's export-credit insurance scheme (jointly with PricewaterhouseCoopers' German affiliate). Hermes established a project finance department in 1988. Both commercial and political risks can be covered, on a flexible basis up to 95% of the insured risk. Investment insurance is also provided covering 95% of the risk.

KfW IPEX-Bank ('KfW'). KfW Bankengruppe is a state-owned development bank (80% by the federal government and 20% by the Länder), founded as Kreditanstalt für Wiederaufbau in 1948. Its largest subsidiary, KfW IPEX-Bank, provides direct loans for export credits, co-financing with German commercial banks, and administers the CIRR support on behalf of the German government. KfW also provides untied loans to projects with German investors, or related to the acquisition of raw materials for Germany.

Apart from this policy-related lending KfW also provides project finance on similar terms to commercial banks, and in 2012 ranked just below the top 20 lead arrangers in Table 4.3, at 23rd. In 2008, as a result of European Union concern about IPEX's competition with commercial banks, it became legally and financially independent of KfW Bankengruppe.

Deutsche Investitions- und Entwicklungsgesellschaft ('DEG'). DEG (whose name means 'German Investment and Development Corporation) is also a subsidiary of KfW Bankengruppe. It promotes private-sector investment in developing countries.

§16.4.6 ITALY (SACE/SIMEST)

Italian support for overseas projects is primarily for engineering (EPC) projects.

SACE SpA. Sezione Speciale per l'Assicurazione del Credito all'Esportazione (SACE),[9] was a department of the Italian Treasury, established in 1977.

---

[9] 'Special Section for Export-Credit Insurance'.

Istituto per i Servizi Assicurativi e il Credito all'Esportazione (ISACE)[10] an autonomous state-owned agency, took over responsibility for export credit insurance in 1999. In 2004 it became a limited company, SACE SpA, and is now owned by a state agency Cassa Depositi e Prestiti SpA ('CDP'), which provides long-term infrastructure finance. It provides export-credit insurance on behalf of the Italian government.

SACE's first project-finance cover was provided in 1994. 95% cover can be provided to commercial banks inside or outside Italy for both commercial and political risks: SACE requires that investors take at least 30% of the risk in a project, and at least 35% of the cost is covered by other commercial bank loans (*i.e.* SACE does not cover more than 35% of the total project cost). The cost of SACE's insurance premium cannot be included in its cover or the subsidized financing, and breach of contract is not covered.

Società Italiana per le Imprese all'Estero ('Simest'). Simest, a state-controlled company (CDP now being its majority shareholder), but with other private-sector shareholders, was established in 1991. It provides commercial banks with CIRR support (a rôle that it took over from Mediocredito Centrale in 1999). Simest also provides untied loans to and takes equity interests in projects that are controlled by Italian investors.

§16.4.7 FRANCE (COFACE/DREE/PROPARCO)

Project finance by these French agencies relates mainly to French exports of equipment.

Compagnie Française d'Assurance pour le Commerce Extérieur ('COFACE'). COFACE was established in 1946 as the French ECA. It was privatized in 1994, and 2002 became a subsidiary of Natexis Banques Populaires (now Natixis). It acts on behalf of the French government in providing export-credit insurance. It established a project-finance department in 1995. Coverage is provided to commercial banks in France. Both commercial (post-completion) and political risks (for the standard investment risks) can be covered, up to 95% of the insured risk. The COFACE-covered loan cannot exceed 50% of the total project costs. COFACE also provides investment insurance. Natixis also provides CIRR support on behalf of the state. Export-credit policy is supervised by Direction des Relations Economiques Extérieures ('DREE'), a government agency.

Société de Promotion et de Participation pour la Coopération Economique ('Proparco'). Proparco was set up in 1977 by the predecessor to Agence

---

[10] 'Institute for Export Credit and Insurance Services'.

Française de Développement ('AFD'), the French development agency. AFD holds 57% of its equity, the rest being held by a variety of shareholders from developed and developing countries. Its mission is to be a catalyst for private investment in developing countries.

§16.4.8 DENMARK (EKF)

Eksport Kredit Fonden ('EKF') is one of the world's oldest ECAs, having been established in 1922. EKF's business in 2012 consisted entirely of guarantees for wind-farm projects, in Belgium, Italy Chile and Mexico, reflecting the fact that Denmark is home to a major wind-turbine manufacturer.

In an interesting example of institutional investors becoming involved in what in the past has been primarily commercial-bank business (*cf.* §17.4), in 2011 Pensiondanmark (the state pension fund) signed an agreement with EKF to provide up to $1.8 billion of finance for Danish exports.

§16.5 MULTILATERAL DEVELOPMENT-FINANCE INSTITUTIONS

Table 16.3 sets out information on the scale of project-finance related business undertaken by MDFIs.[11]

The MDFIs discussed below consist of:

- the World Bank (§16.5.1) and its affiliates IFC (§16.5.2), IDA (§16.5.3), and MIGA (§16.5.4);
- the major regional development banks:
  - Asian Development Bank (§16.5.5);
  - African Development Bank (§16.5.6);
  - European Bank for Reconstruction and Development (§16.5.7);
  - European Investment Bank (§16.5.8);
  - Inter-American Development Bank (§16.5.9).

All are owned by governments—the World Bank by governments around the world, and the other MDFIs by governments in their respective regions as well as from other developed countries.

Other smaller MDFIs which have lent in the project-finance market over the last few years have included:

- *Nordic Investment Bank*—the DFI for the Nordic countries in Europe, founded in 1976 and owned by Denmark, Estonia, Finland, Iceland, Latvia,

---

[11] MDFIs are also known as 'IFIs' (international financing institutions), 'MDBs' (multilateral development banks) or 'MLAs' (multilateral lending agencies).

Table 16.3 Multilateral DFIs—Project-Finance Loans & Guarantees

(US$ millions)	2010	2011	2012
World Bank Group	1,070	677	2,721
European Investment Bank ('EIB')	5,735	5,584	2,302
Inter-American Development Bank ('IADB')	131	735	1,094
European Bank for Reconstruction & Development ('EBRD')	1,080	194	788
African Development Bank ('AfDB')	300	57	710
Asian Development Bank ('ADB')		359	586
Others*	1,393	2,234	1,133
Total	9,709	9,940	9,334

*Nine different entities in 2010; five in 2011; six in 2012.
Source: as for Table 2.1.

Lithuania, Norway and Sweden; it provides loans both to its member countries, and to developing countries.

- *Islamic Development Bank* (*cf.* §4.5.4);
- *Eurasian Development Bank*—the MDFI for Russia and CIS countries, founded in 2006;
- *Corporación Andina de Fomento* (CAF)—the MDFI for various Latin American and Caribbean countries, founded in 1968;
- *North American Development Bank*—an MDFI formed by the U.S.A. and Mexico in 1994 to promote development in their border regions;
- *Central American Bank for Economic Integration* (CABEI)—founded in 1960 to promote development in Guatemala, Honduras, El Salvador, Nicaragua and Costa Rica.

'Additionality'. All MDFIs aim to be a catalyst for other sources of finance, and so usually limit the proportion of the debt for a particular project which they are willing to provide (typically 50%). Furthermore, they also have an 'additionality' requirement—*e.g.* they will only lend to a project if finance cannot be raised from other sources (so they are 'lenders of last resort), and therefore do not compete with commercial banks or national development banks.[12]

MDFIs can play an important part, not just as direct lenders to projects, but also in mobilizing additional private-sector funding for projects

---

[12] *Cf.* Stephen Spratt and Lily Ryan Collins, *Development Finance Institutions and Infrastructure: A Systematic Review of Evidence for Development Additionality* (Private Infrastructure Development Group, London, 2012)*.

in developing countries. Private-sector lenders are more comfortable about lending to developing countries under the sponsorship of or in parallel with an MDFI because of the MDFI's general involvement in the economy of the Host Country, the importance of its general lending programs to the economy, and its ability to access the host government at the highest level should the project run into political difficulties (although the degree of their influence in these respects differs widely between different countries). This may give the Project Company the protection of an MDFI 'umbrella,' which can also of course benefit investors.

Preferred Creditor Status. Another important factor in encouraging private-sector lenders to participate in MDFI-arranged financings is the 'Preferred-Creditor' status that arises from the practice of providing a preference to MDFIs when resources for repaying external creditors are limited, and not involving MDFI loans in country debt rescheduling. This status was established to reduce the risk to MDFIs (and their shareholders) due to their special rôle within the international financial community. It is important to note that this status exists by custom and not by law, but it has been honored in practice where countries have run into debt problems. If private-sector lenders participate in 'B' Loans such as those arranged by IFC (*cf.* §16.5.2), they also benefit from this status.[13]

Economic Impact. MDFIs pay more attention than private sector-lenders to examining whether the project to be financed is appropriate in the wider economic context of the Host Country. This can be a double-edged sword, however, as some Host Governments resent attempts by MDFIs to use lending to a particular project as a means of promoting a wider politico-economic agenda. Similarly, if a project gets into trouble, an MDFI may have a more long-term agenda in dealing with the problem that may not be relevant for a lender or investor that is simply trying to get the loan repaid or recover its equity.

Project Preparation. There are a number of MDFI-linked programs which provide funding to support the substantial cost of project preparation by the public sector in the infrastructure and power fields (*cf.* §3.7.3).

§16.5.1 THE WORLD BANK

The International Bank for Reconstruction and Development ('IBRD'), normally known as the World Bank, was founded in 1944, and is an international organization owned by most world governments. Its affiliates IFC, IDA, and MIGA

---

[13] This may raise an intercreditor issue with ECAs—*cf.* §14.14.3.

(discussed below) have been added to the World Bank Group since its original foundation. Its lending mandate is to provide development finance to governments (originally for reconstruction in Europe after the Second World War, and, from the 1960s, for developing countries), and therefore its immediate relevance to project finance, which is always a private-sector activity, might appear limited; however, the increased importance of private-sector funding for infrastructure in developing countries has inevitably led to some change of emphasis in the World Bank's approach.[14] The Bank's funding is provided from the issuance of bonds and other instruments on international capital markets.

Direct Loans. The World Bank first encouraged private-sector bank involvement in its activities through cofinancing operations, also known as B Loans. Under this structure the private-sector bank lends in parallel with the World Bank (which is providing the A loan in this context), and benefits from the Preferred Creditor status of World Bank loans. This is of limited relevance in the project-finance context, because these loans still have to be to the public sector, but as will be seen, the same structure has been used extensively by the World Bank's affiliate IFC and other regional MDFIs.

The only way in which the World Bank itself can provide loans to private-sector projects is by using the Host Government as an intermediary. This can be done by the World Bank's providing finance to the host government, and the latter lending it directly to the Project Company, or, more commonly, *via* a local development bank. Similarly, World Bank finance can also be used by a government to provide Viability Gap Finance to a Project Company (*cf.* §15.11). Alternatively, the World Bank can lend directly to a Project Company under a guarantee of the Host Government.

A Project Company using World Bank finance must follow its procurement rules in purchasing equipment or services to be funded in this way, unless these rules were followed by the Offtaker/Contracting Authority in selecting the Project Company itself (*cf.* §3.7.4). These rules are set out in the World Bank's international competitive bidding ('ICB') procedures.

As with all its lending, the World Bank tries to encourage provision of parallel facilities by other MDFIs, ECAs, and bilateral DFIs. It is also 'lender of last resort' among DFIs, including the other members of the World Bank group, meaning that if finance can be obtained from these other sources, the World Bank will not lend.

Total World Bank loan commitments in 2011/12 were $21 billion, less than half the $44 billion of 2009/10, reflecting the effect of the 2007/8

---

[14] *Cf.* Philippe Benoit: *Project Finance at the World Bank: An Overview of Policies and Instruments* (World Bank, Washington, 1996).

financial crisis (and a major increase on the normal lending commitment levels of previous years of around $12–14 billion).

Partial Risk Guarantee ('PRG'). However, the use of direct loans is no longer the World Bank's preferred approach to supporting private-sector project finance. The instrument now offered is the World Bank Partial Risk Guarantee (previously known as the ECO [expanded cofinancing] Guarantee), which was first used for project finance in 1994.

This is a political-risk guarantee that can be provided to lenders to a Project Company. The PRG is primarily intended to support infrastructure projects. It is not linked to the export of goods from any country, nor does the Project Company have to follow World Bank procurement rules (though procurement should be 'economic and efficient'). It is available in any countries eligible for World Bank loans, which excludes the poorest countries, who obtain funding from IDA (other than the Enclave Guarantee discussed below). Up to 100% of the debt can be covered.

The PRG can cover, *inter alia*, changes in law, failure to meet contractual payment obligations, obstruction of an arbitration process, expropriation and nationalization, foreign currency availability and convertibility, nonpayment of a termination amount or an arbitration award following a covered default, and failure to issue licenses, approvals, and consents in a timely manner. Other political risks not covered directly can be covered indirectly by imposing a contractual obligation in a Government Support Agreement.

As with export credits, this is a guarantee of payment, not a guarantee of performance; therefore, any event giving rise to a claim has to lead to a default on the Project Agreement, and hence the project finance, not just, for example, cause a loss to the Project Company that may affect its investors but does not put its financing in default. The guarantee can cover the Offtaker/Contracting Authority's continuing obligations, or the payment of a Termination Sum (*cf.* §7.10.2).

In all cases the Host Government has to counter indemnify the World Bank for any calls under its guarantee, which means that it cannot be used for sub-sovereign risks; in other words, all the obligations guaranteed have to be direct obligations of the Host Government or obligations of an Offtaker/Contracting Authority guaranteed by the Host Government.

The PRG is intended as a last resort and is thus available only to projects where (a) private-sector financing is not available, and (b) sufficient funding cannot be obtained *via* IFC or with MIGA support (see below). As with direct loans, the World Bank also tries to act as a catalyst to mobilize funding or guarantee support from other multilateral and bilateral development agencies. Unlike other MDFIs, there is no upper limit on the amount of a World Bank PRG, other than general prudence and limits on its overall exposure to the country concerned.

Partial Credit Guarantee ('PCG'). The World Bank can provide a guarantee for part of the loan provided by private-sector lenders; the main use of this has been to cover the later repayments of a loan if the lenders are not willing to lend for the required term. It can also be used to cover a 'balloon' maturity (*i.e.* a large final repayment that the Project Company intends to refinance in due course). Finally it can be used to support bank or other credit in a local currency, to eliminate foreign-exchange risk in projects (*cf.* §10.5.1). Obviously, in such cases this represents a full guarantee rather than political risk cover only. Its use in project finance has so far been limited.

Enclave Guarantee. The World Bank also provides Enclave Guarantees (*i.e.* guarantees for export-based Enclave Projects—*cf.* §11.4.1) in IDA countries. Here there is no Project Agreement involving the Host Government, since the project is based on sale of a commodity internationally. The scope of the guarantee is therefore limited to expropriation, changes in law, war and civil strife, and also excludes currency convertibility and transfer risks, since these should not arise as revenues are earned offshore.

§16.5.2 International Finance Corporation ('IFC')

IFC, established in 1956, is the private-sector financing affiliate of the World Bank, and is therefore the only member of the World Bank group that does not need direct Host Government involvement in projects as a basis for its financing.[15] IFC has been financially autonomous from the World Bank since 1984, and so issues its own bonds on international capital markets.

Loan Program. IFC can invest or lend up to $100 million per project, with a limit of 25% of project cost (50% for expansion of an existing project). Loan maturities can be up to 20 years. IFC loans are based on market pricing (*i.e.* with no element of subsidy), and IFC does not accept direct Host Government guarantees.

B Loans. Apart from its own direct loans (A Loans), IFC has an active 'B Loan' program, under which it brings in parallel private-sector financing for projects.[16] This B Loan program dates back to 1957 and follows similar principles to that of the World Bank: IFC sells participations in B Loans (which carry full market rates of interest reflecting the risk) to commercial banks, but continues to act as the Lender of record, to administer the loans, and to hold security. Thus it is not possible for a borrower to pay IFC but default on the B Loan, since all payments are divided *pro rata* between the A and the B Loan in a transaction, and so a default on a B Loan is a default on IFC's loan.

---

[15] *Cf.* International Finance Corporation: *Project Finance in Developing Countries* (IFC, Washington, 1999).
[16] In other words, IFC syndicates participations in its loans (*cf.* §5.2.8).

Although there is no formal guarantee for political risk, the Preferred-Creditor status accorded to MDFIs applies to IFC B Loans, and most bank supervisory authorities do not require banks to make loan provisions against IFC B Loans merely because the country is in default on its general debt. (Of course the loan can still go into default if the project is not successful.)

It is perhaps worth noting that there is a potential conflict of interest between IFC's rôle as a manager of other banks' B Loans, and as an investor in the same projects, as well as with IFC's rôle as part of the World Bank Group, and therefore concerned with wider development policies that may conflict with the investors of a particular project.

Local-Currency Loans. IFC is able to offer local-currency loans, or long-term currency swaps (*cf.* §10.5.2) in many developing countries. The development of long-term debt markets in developing countries has been quite significant in recent years thanks to the efforts of IFC and other DFIs.

Derivative Products (Hedging). IFC has been offering interest-rate swaps (*cf.* §10.3.1), options (*cf.* §10.3.2), forward exchange-contracts (*i.e.* currency swaps enabling finance in local currencies—see above), and other derivative products to its borrowers to allow them to better manage their financial risks. Project Companies in developing countries cannot easily access directly the markets for such risk-management products. IFC seeks to bridge this gap by providing this market access by intermediating the purchase of hedging instruments, mobilizing the participation of commercial banks in such transactions on a risk-sharing basis, and promoting the development of local capital markets by bringing these techniques to local financial institutions.

Equity Investment. IFC can also take minority equity investments (normally 5–15% and a maximum of 35%) in project companies; IFC does not take an active rôle in company management and is considered a passive investor. To meet national ownership requirements, IFC shareholdings can, in some cases, be treated as domestic capital or 'local' shares. IFC usually maintains equity investments for a period of 8–15 years and is considered a long-term investor. IFC's preferred objective is to sell its shares through the domestic stock market. 'Equity' in this context includes loans convertible into equity, and preferred shares, as well as loans which participate in profits.

IFC's equity investment has been the subject of some controversy, as IFC may insist on purchasing equity at par—*i.e.* neither paying a premium to the Sponsors to cover their initial risks (*cf.* §12.2.5) nor covering any development costs itself.

Equity and Debt Funds. IFC also invests in equity funds managed by private-sector investment banks and is a significant investor in this field of finance for developing countries. It aims to invest about $500 million *per annum* in about 20–25 separate funds. It is now also investing in debt funds (*cf.* §17.4.2).

Guarantees. IFC offers Partial Credit Guarantees similar to those of the World Bank, which cover all credit risks during a specified portion of the loan term and can thus be used to extend the repayment term of loans offered by the private sector.

Advisory Services. Finally IFC is an active advisor on private-sector projects in developing countries, especially IDA countries (see below) and also provides training and other capacity-building.

In the financial year 2011/12, IFC provided debt, equity and other finance totaling $12 billion in 518 projects: obviously only a portion of this related to project finance.

§16.5.3 INTERNATIONAL DEVELOPMENT ASSOCIATION ('IDA')

IDA, established in 1960, is the World Bank affiliate providing development finance on concessionary terms (35–40-year loans, with no interest but a service charge of 0.75% *p.a.*, often combined with grants) for the poorest countries. As of 2012, for a country to be eligible for IDA support, its gross national income (GNI) *per caput* must not exceed $1,175 (in 2010 dollars): 81 countries were eligible for IDA support, of which 39 were in Africa. IDA can provide indirect loans for projects in a similar way to the World Bank, and also has its own guarantee program (for projects where World Bank Enclave Guarantees cannot be used). Total IDA loan and guarantee commitments in 2011/12 amounted to $15 billion.

§16.5.4 MULTILATERAL INVESTMENT GUARANTEE AGENCY ('MIGA')

Another World Bank affiliate, MIGA, was established in 1988 to encourage private-sector investment in developing countries by providing cover to lenders and investors against political risks. It is intended as the primary World Bank group vehicle for political-risk guarantees (and was clearly modeled on OPIC—*cf.* §16.4.4). In 2011/12 $2 billion of political-risk coverage was provided to 50 different projects in 28 countries. MIGA's total guarantee exposure in 2012 was $10 billion, of which $4 billion was reinsured (see below). 58% of this cover related to infrastructure projects, MIGA's largest sector of activity. (Again this coverage was provided to a much wider range of investments than just those in Project Companies.)

The parameters of MIGA coverage are:

- Coverage relates to cross-border investments or loans.
- Both equity (including shareholder loans) and debt can be covered (MIGA previously required equity to be covered if debt was to be covered, but this is no longer required in some circumstances).

- Other forms of investment, such as technical assistance and management contracts, asset securitizations, bond issues, leasing, services, and franchising and licensing agreements, may also be eligible for cover.
- MIGA covers up to 95% of the scheduled payments of loan principal (plus up to 1.5 times the principal to cover loss of interest), or 90% of the equity investment (plus up to 5 times the investment to cover loss of profits).
- Up to $220 million can be insured in any one project for MIGA's own account.
- MIGA can normally provide coverage for 15 years, and for 20 years where justified.
- MIGA operates a Co-operative Underwriting Programme ('CUP') with private-sector insurers, which is based on the principle of the World Bank and IFC's 'B' Loans (*i.e.* MIGA acts as a front for private-sector participation in its risks); using these and other reinsurance arrangements, MIGA can cover significantly more than $220 million in any one project.
- The premiums are in the range 0.50–1.75% *p.a.* on the amounts insured.
- The beneficiary has the option to cancel the coverage after 3 years.

MIGA guarantees cover:

- *Currency convertibility and transfer*: on receipt of the blocked local currency from an investor, MIGA pays compensation in the guaranteed currency; cover includes excessive delays in making transfers.
- *Expropriation (including creeping expropriation)*: *bona fide*, non-discriminatory measures by the Host Government in the exercise of legitimate regulatory authority are not covered. For total expropriation of equity investments, MIGA pays the net book value of the insured investment. For expropriation of funds, MIGA pays the insured portion of the blocked funds. For loans and loan guarantees, MIGA insures the outstanding principal and any accrued and unpaid interest. Payment is made against assignment of the investor's/Lender's interests.
- *War, terrorism and civil disturbance (including revolution, insurrection, coups d'état, and sabotage)*: this covers not only the cost of physical damage to the project, but also extends to events that, for a period of one year, result in an interruption of project operations essential to overall financial viability.
  - For loan guarantees, MIGA pays the insured portion of the principal and interest payments in default as a result of business interruption caused by covered events.
  - For tangible asset losses, MIGA will pay the investor's share of the lesser of the book value of the project assets, their replacement cost, and the cost of repair of the damaged assets.

- Temporary business interruption may also be included and would cover three sources of interruption: damage of assets, forced abandonment, and loss of use. For short-term business interruption, MIGA will pay unavoidable continuing expenses and extraordinary expenses associated with the restart of operations and lost business income or, in the case of loans, missed payments.
- This coverage encompasses not only violence in the country concerned directed against a Host Government, but also against foreign governments or foreign investments, including the investor's government or nationality.
- *Breach of contract by the Host Government (or state-owned enterprises in some cases)*: after a dispute resolution mechanism (court action or arbitration) has led to an award for the Project Company; however, if after a specified period of time, payment has not been received or if the dispute-resolution mechanism fails to function because of actions taken by the Host Government, MIGA will pay compensation. MIGA may make a provisional payment pending the outcome of the dispute-resolution mechanism.

As with the World Bank, MIGA did not cover sub-sovereign risks (unless counter-guaranteed by the Host Government) and only provided coverage under an agreement with the Host Government. However in 2013 MIGA coverage was extended to SOEs (*cf.* §11.6)

In keeping with MIGA's objective of promoting economic growth and development, investment projects must be financially and economically *via*ble, environmentally sound, and consistent with the labor standards and other development objectives of the Host Country. As with the World Bank Partial Risk Guarantees, therefore, the ability to offer coverage may be hampered by policy issues that do not relate to the particular project, but rather the country or sector in general, as well as the requirement for a Host Government counter guarantee.

Note that among the World Bank Group, and the older regional MDFIs (ADB, AfDB, IADB), only MIGA provides political-risk coverage for investments.

§16.5.5 ASIAN DEVELOPMENT BANK

ADB was established in 1966 as a regional MDFI. Total loan commitments in 2011/12 were $23 billion.

ADB began private-sector operations in 1983 and can lend directly to private-sector projects, invest equity (up to 25% of the total equity investment), or provide loan guarantees. Its total exposure to any one project cannot exceed the lower of 25% of the project cost or $50 million (50% or $150 million where guarantees are provided), and it cannot invest more than 25% of the equity. Loans are provided in hard currencies (and in some cases in local currencies where the Host Country's financial markets are sufficiently developed), on market-based terms, for up to 15 years. ADB also has a B Loan program. ADB's main focus in private-sector projects is on capital-market development and infrastructure.

ADB's loan guarantee program is similar to that of the World Bank: two types of guarantee are provided for private-sector projects:

Political-Risk Guarantee. ADB's first political risk guarantees were issued in 2000. Risks covered include transfer restriction, expropriation, political violence, contract disputes, and non-honoring of a sovereign obligation or guarantee, for loan terms of up to 15 years. The guarantee is, however, only issued for projects in which ADB also has a direct loan or equity involvement, and the maximum limit is reduced to the extent of such involvement. A Host Government counter-guarantee may be required.

Partial Credit Guarantee. Similar to the PCG provided by the World Bank, this can cover all events for a specific portion of the debt service, or the principal and/or interest for debt maturities that would be difficult to obtain from commercial lenders. Coverage can be provided to domestic banks in the Host Country's currency, so enabling long-term funding without exchange risks, which might not otherwise be available, to be raised by the Project Company.

§16.5.6 AFRICAN DEVELOPMENT BANK

AfDB was established in 1963. Total financing commitments (loans, equity investments, and grants) in 2011 were UA5.7 billion.[17] As with other DFIs, AfDB's lending increased considerably after the 2007/8 financial crisis but came back to more normal levels in 2011.

Private-sector finance has become increasingly important for AfDB, with the main emphasis on infrastructure, especially energy. Project finance is thus a relatively new product for the Bank. Private-sector project approvals are about $1.5 billion *p.a.*

AfDB can provide direct loans for up to 15 years, with up to 5 years' grace, in hard currencies (including South African rand), or in some cases in local currencies where appropriate hedging arrangements can be put in place. It also has a B Loan program. Partial risk and partial credit guarantees are provided on a similar basis to other MDFIs.

---

[17] The AfDB uses 'units of account' ('UA'), as a basis for its accounting. A UA is equal to 1 special drawing right ('SDR') of the International Monetary Fund, or approximately $1.50.

AfDB also offers risk-management products such as interest-rate swaps, caps and collars (*cf.* §10.3), currency swaps (*cf.* §10.5), and commodity-price hedging (*cf.* §9.6.1).

§16.5.7 EUROPEAN BANK FOR RECONSTRUCTION AND DEVELOPMENT

EBRD was established in 1991. Its initial purpose was to provide support for private-sector investment in Central and Eastern Europe and the CIS. More recently its activities have been extended to Turkey (2009), and various North African countries after the 'Arab Spring' (2012). EBRD promotes private-sector activity, the strengthening of financial institutions and legal systems, and the development of the infrastructure needed to support the private sector. Total financing commitments in 2011 were €9.1 billion. As with other MDFIs its financing activities were increased significantly after the 2007/8 financial crisis. The Bank's funding comes from bond issues.

EBRD's private-sector activities resemble those of IFC; it provides both equity and debt as well as guarantees, encouraging cofinancing (through syndicated loans similar to IFC's B Loan system) and foreign direct investment from the private and public sectors, and helps to mobilize domestic capital. For private-sector projects, the European Bank EBRD is normally prepared to provide, in the form of debt or equity, up to 35% of the long-term capital requirements of a single project or company. Its guarantee program is flexible, with various types available, ranging from all-risk to risk-specific contingent guarantees. In project finance the EBRD has been active, *inter alia*, in the telecommunications, electricity, petrochemicals, and infrastructure fields.

§16.5.8 EUROPEAN INVESTMENT BANK

The most conspicuous case of an MDFI supporting a wide range of project-finance transactions in developed countries is that of EIB.

EIB was created in 1958 under the Treaty of Rome as an autonomous body within the European Union to finance capital investment furthering European integration by promoting E.U. economic policies.[18] Its capital is provided by the member countries of the E.U., but only 5% of this is paid in, the rest being available if required. With this ownership and capital structure EIB benefits from an AAA rating (*cf.* §5.3.1), which enables it to raise its funding at a comparatively low cost on

---

[18] For the legal background to the EIB's activities, *cf.* European Investment Bank, *Statute and other provisions* (Luxemburg, 2009)*.

the capital markets (through bond issues: EIB is the largest non-governmental bond issuer in Europe).

The Bank's primary policy/financing objectives are:

- *cohesion and convergence*: addressing economic and social imbalances in disadvantaged regions.
- *the fight against climate change*: mitigating and adapting to the effects of global warming.
- *environmental protection and sustainable communities*: investing in a cleaner natural and urban environment.
- *sustainable, competitive and secure energy*: producing alternative energy and reducing dependence on imports.
- *the knowledge economy*: promoting an economy that stimulates knowledge and creativity through investment in information and communication technologies, and human and social capital.
- *trans-European networks*: constructing cross-border networks in transport, energy and communications.

These definitions are sufficiently wide to cover a large sector of the European project-finance market, and EIB is a major Lender in this sector. Loans are provided for up to 50% of the project,[19] and can be provided both in € and other major currencies.

Until 2008 the main benefit of EIB financing was its low cost: based on its AAA rating, the Bank raises funds in the bond market at low fixed rates and passes this benefit on to the Project Company. The EIB does not aim at making profits other than to cover its operating costs and risks, which also helps to keep the cost of its financing lower than commercial banks or the bond market. Since this funding was easily available from commercial banks or the bond market, the EIB was ignoring the requirement of Article 16(2) of its Statutes, that EIB should only finance projects where 'to the extent that funds are not available from other sources on reasonable terms', *i.e.* the concept of 'additionality' which normally applies to all DFIs (*cf.* §16.5). However after the 2008 financial crisis EIB financing became essential for many European projects, especially in the infrastructure sector, and hence became truly additional to private-sector financing sources.

Until 2008 EIB's total annual lending amounted to around €45 billion. This increased to over €70 billion in 2009/10 as an extraordinary measure to fill some of the gap created by the decline in commercial bank lending, but had to be reduced back to a normal level in 2012. Following a capital increase in 2013, EIB's

---

[19] As with other DFIs EIB's aim is to act as a catalyst for other financing parties, not just to lend all the required finance.

lending capacity was increased to about €70 billion.[20] (The overall problems in the Eurozone meant that if EIB had continued to lend at the 2011 level without a capital increase, its AAA rating would have been at risk, which would have increased its funding costs significantly.) As can be seen in Table 16.3, its project-finance lending reflected this pattern, reducing from the crisis level of $5.6 billion in 2011 (greater than all other major MDFIs put together) to $2.4 billion in 2012.

EIB behaves in much the same way as a commercial bank when assessing and structuring its project finance, but also needs to be satisfied as to the wider economic benefits of the project. Projects also have to meet EU environmental standards and follow EU procurement rules (*cf.* §3.7). The government of the country in which the project is situated must give the EIB consent to make its loan, but this is normally a formality as EIB agrees in advance with the relevant government how its resources can best be used to support particular projects or sectors.

EIB may not take construction risk on projects (but see the Structured Finance Facility described below), and may only take operating risks on a fairly conservative basis, and not immediately on completion of the project, but based on its initial performance. In such cases the Bank requires commercial-bank guarantees for its loans until it is 'on risk;' the amount of these guarantees covers not only the loan outstanding, but also 6 months' interest and an allowance for the breakage cost (*cf.* §10.3.1) if its loan is repaid early. Guarantees must be issued by 'qualifying banks,' usually based on minimum credit ratings; if a bank's credit rating is lowered, EIB may require the guarantee to be cash collateralized.[21] (The EIB also accepted monoline insurance as an alternative to bank guarantees, but for the reasons set out in §4.3.2 this is no longer a viable structure.)

Structured Finance Facility. In 2001, EIB established a Structured Finance Facility (SFF), under which it takes on a higher level of project risks through providing:
- senior loans and guarantees under which it will assume pre-completion and early operating risks;
- mezzanine finance and guarantees ranking ahead of shareholder equity or subordinated debt;
- project-related derivatives (hedging).

The decision to create this program was probably influenced by the fact that even though EIB financing was cheap, it had become uncompetitive with commercial-bank and bond finance because of the limited risks which the Bank would undertake—again ignoring its additionality required as discussed above.

---

[20] European Investment Bank Group, *Operational Plan 2013–2015* (EIB, Luxemburg, 2012)*, p. 6.

[21] The Portuguese government has counter-guaranteed Portuguese banks which are providing guarantees to EIB, as a way of getting round this problem.

The SFF has been regularly increased and extended since it was first set up; the latest (2008) increase brought the total funds allocated to €3.75 billion.

Europe 2020 Project Bond Initiative. See §15.4.3; §17.5.

Loan Guarantee Instrument for Trans-European Transport Network Projects. See §17.5.3.

Lending Outside E.U. About 10% of EIB's total lending is to countries outside the European Union: these include countries which are candidates or potential candidates for membership of the EU, other adjacent countries (Eastern Europe and Russia; Mediterranean countries), and developing countries elsewhere. This lending is undertaken on the basis of a 'mandate' from the European Commission to provide defined amounts of lending to particular countries and regions, and is in effect a component of EU development assistance. Such loans are managed by the EIB, but the EU provides a guarantee for them.

§16.5.9 INTER-AMERICAN DEVELOPMENT BANK

IADB was established in 1959, and is thus the oldest of the regional MDFIs, covering Latin America and the Caribbean. IADB is the main source of DFI credit in the region, with total new commitments in 2012 of $11 billion. This is roughly double the level of commitments before the 2007/8 financial crisis, following a capital increase in 2010.

IADB's Private Sector Department (now Structured and Corporate Finance Department) was established in 1994. IADB provides direct loans or credit guarantees to private-sector borrowers, mainly in $, and brings in private-sector participation in these loans through a B Loan structure. IADB itself can provide up to $200 million or 25% of total project cost in an A Loan, with typical maturities of 5–15 years.

In 1996, IADB established a program of providing political risk guarantees in favor of commercial bank lenders and bond issues. Coverage is provided for currency convertibility and transfer, expropriation, and breach of contract. In this case, up to the lesser of $200 million or 50% of project cost can be provided.

IADB has an affiliate, Inter-American Investment Corporation, which invests equity in projects.

ANNEX: U.S. EXIM 'PROJECT CRITERIA AND APPLICATION INFORMATION REQUIREMENTS'[22]

(*Cf.* §16.4.4.)

I General Project

- In most cases the project should have long-term contracts from creditworthy entities for the purchase of the project's output and the purchase of the project's major project inputs such as fuel, raw materials, and operations and maintenance. Such contracts should extend beyond the term of the requested Ex-Im Bank financing. In sectors such as telecommunications and petrochemicals if long-term contracts are not available, Ex-Im Bank will evaluate the transactions on a case-by-case basis, looking for economically compelling business rationale.
- The project should contain an appropriate allocation of risk to the parties best suited to manage those risks. Sensitivity analysis should result in a sufficient debt service coverage ratio to ensure uninterrupted debt servicing for the term of the debt.
- Total project cost should be comparable to projects of similar type and size for a particular market.
- Product unit pricing and costs should reflect market based pricing.
- Devaluation risk needs to be substantially mitigated through revenues denominated in hard currencies, revenue adjustment formulas based on changing currency relationships, or other structural mechanisms.

Information Required

1. Summary of all aspects of the project, as contained in an independently prepared feasibility study and/or a detailed information memorandum, prepared by a qualified party. The study or memorandum should include the project description, location, legal status, ownership, and background and status of key elements of the project structure, such as agreements, licenses, local partner participation and financing.
2. Agreements for key elements of the project. Ex-Im Bank considers key agreements to include all contracts necessary for the project to be built and operate. This includes contracts relating to infrastructure as well as supply and offtake agreements. These agreements should be in substantially

---

[22] http://www.exim.gov – Home > Products > Loan Guarantee > Project & Structured Finance > Our Approach to Project Finance.

final form. Ex-Im Bank will not accept summaries or outlines of these agreements.

3. A breakdown of anticipated project costs through commissioning, including interest during construction and working capital requirements, by major cost category and country of origin. This information should also include a breakdown of any 'soft costs' such as development costs, development fees, owner's contingencies and other similar items. A breakdown of the proposed coverage for interest during construction and the method of calculation should also be included.

4. A summary of the anticipated project financing plan and security package, including the proposed source, amount, currency and terms of the debt and equity investments; the sources of finance in the event of project cost over-runs; and description of escrow accounts. Information on the terms, security requirements, and status of financing commitments of other lenders to the project, if applicable, should be provided. All other sources approached for financing (multinational development banks, other export credit agencies, commercial banks, capital markets and private investors) must be disclosed.

5. Projected annual financial statements covering the period from project development through final maturity of the proposed Ex-Im Bank financing, to include balance sheet, profit and loss, source and application of funds statements, and debt service ratios. Projections should include a sensitivity analysis for not only the expected scenario, but pessimistic and optimistic cases as well.

6. This information should also be provided electronically in Lotus 123 or Excel. The structure of the financial model should be in a format that is user friendly. Ex-Im Bank must be able to review and adjust the assumptions in the model.

7. Assumptions for the financial projections, including but not limited to the basis for sales volume and prices; operating and administrative costs; depreciation, amortization and tax rates; and local government policy on price regulation.

8. Market information to include ten years of historical price and volume data; present and projected capacity of industry; product demand forecast with assumptions; description of competition and projected market share of the project as compared to the shares of the competition; identity and location of customers; and marketing and distribution strategy.

9. A description of the principal risks and benefits of the project to the sponsors, lenders, and host government.

10. A description of the types of insurance coverage to be purchased for both the pre- and post-completion phases of the project.

11. Information on infrastructure required for the project to operate, specifically information pertaining to the timing, status and developmental plans.
12. A clear articulation of the need for Ex-Im Bank coverage.

II PARTICIPANTS

- Project sponsors, offtake purchasers, contractors, operators, and suppliers must be able to demonstrate the technical, managerial and financial capabilities to perform their respective obligations within the project.

Information Required

1. Sponsors must provide in English a brief history and description of their operations, a description of their relevant experience in similar projects, and three years of audited financial statements.
2. If the sponsors are part of a joint venture or consortium, information should be provided for all the participants. A shareholders agreement should also be provided. All documents pertaining to this area (joint venture agreement, management and service agreements) should be in substantially final form.
3. Offtake purchasers and suppliers should provide in English a history and description of operations, at least three years of audited financial statements, and a description of how the project fits in their long-term strategic plan. If the project utilizes raw materials (oil, gas, coal, ethane, *etc.*) copies of contracts that have been reviewed by legal counsel for appropriateness and in adherence with local law should be provided.
4. Contractors and operators must provide resumes of experience with similar projects and recent historical financial information.

III TECHNICAL

- Project technology must be proven and reliable, and licensing arrangements must be contractually secured for a period extending beyond the term of the Ex-Im Bank financing.
- A technical feasibility study or sufficient detailed engineering information needs to be provided to demonstrate technical feasibility of the project.

Information Required

1. Technical description and a process flow diagram for each project facility.
2. Detailed estimate of operating costs.
3. Arrangement for supply of raw materials and utilities.

4. Draft turnkey construction contract and description of sources of possible cost increases and delays during construction, including detailed description of liquidated damage provisions and performance bond requirements.
5. Project implementation schedule, showing target dates for achieving essential project milestones.
6. A site-specific environmental assessment, highlighting concerns, requirements and solutions. These documents should demonstrate compliance with Ex-Im Bank's environmental guidelines. All applicants must submit a Preliminary Environmental Assessment report conducted by a third party expert prior to an application for final commitment.

IV Host Country Legal/Regulatory Framework and Government Role

- Host government commitment to proceeding with the project needs to be demonstrated.
- Legal and regulatory analysis needs to demonstrate that the country conditions and the project structure are sufficient to support long-term debt exposure for the project through enforceable contractual relationships.
- Ex-Im Bank's relationships with the host government will be addressed on a case-by-case basis. An Ex-Im Bank Project Incentive Agreement (PIA) with the host government may be required. The PIA addresses certain political risks and Ex-Im Bank's method of resolution of conflict with the host government pertaining to these issues. Only certain markets will require a PIA.

Information Required

1. A description of the host government's role in the project, and progress made toward obtaining essential government commitments, including authorizations from appropriate government entities to proceed with the project. Copies of all permits, licenses, concession agreements and approvals are required in addition to a description of all permits necessary to complete the project and their status. This information is critical for Ex-Im Bank application consideration.
2. A definition of the control, if any, that the government will have in the management and operation of the project, and status of any assurances that the government will not interfere in the project's operation. If the government is also a project sponsor, these issues will be of particular importance.
3. Evidence of the government's current and historical commitment and policies for availability and convertibility of foreign currency.
4. Status and strategy for obtaining government undertakings to support any government parties involved in the project, to the extent that such undertakings are needed to provide adequate credit support for such entities.

Chapter 17

RECENT MARKET DEVELOPMENTS AND PROSPECTS FOR PROJECT FINANCE

§17.1 INTRODUCTION

From the 1980s until 2008, the use of project finance had continued to expand steadily around the world, only marginally affected by previous financial crises such as the Asian crisis of 1997, or the collapse of Enron in 2001. But the direct and indirect effects of the 2008 financial crisis on the project-finance market were much greater in scale. Although by 2009–10 the project-finance market appeared to be recovering, the Eurozone crisis had a further adverse effect, not just on projects in Europe, but also in other parts of the world where the major European project-finance banks were active, especially the Americas.

Although banks' credit losses on project-finance loans were not significant after 2008, liquidity of such loans has been a major issue (§17.2), accentuated by the 'Basel III' requirements (§17.3). The encouragement of non-bank lenders into the project-finance market, especially for infrastructure, has been a priority in the

481

Principles of Project Finance. DOI: http://dx.doi.org/10.1016/B978-0-12-391058-5.00017-5

countries worst affected by declines in bank lending (§17.4), and improving the credit risk of project-finance transactions is seen as a key part of this process (§17.5). New models for project-finance structures may be relevant in a few market sectors (§17.6).

By mid-2013 banks were rapidly coming back into the market and competing strongly with the non-bank lenders, and extraordinary measures to raise private finance for infrastructure project in particular were proving unnecessary. So the major rôle played by commercial banks in the project-finance market may diminish somewhat overall, and decrease considerably in some markets, but is unlikely to disappear (§17.7).

§17.2 THE EFFECT OF THE 2008 FINANCIAL CRISIS

Project-finance loan portfolios survived the economic recession after 2008 very well: the levels of losses incurred by banks and other lenders in project finance were low compared to other areas of lending such as personal loans, home loans or corporate finance. There can be little doubt that the case for project finance as a low credit-risk type of lending—contrary perhaps to first impressions—stood up well under testing conditions. The reasons for the low loss rates clearly relate to the extensive due diligence and careful controls which banks use in project finance.

But project finance did not stand up well in another respect—that of liquidity. There had always been an implicit assumption that project-finance loans were liquid, *i.e.* they could be syndicated (sold off) to other banks (*cf.* §5.2.8) if the original bank wanted to reduce its long-term risk level on a project. The squeeze on lending throughout the banking sector made this impossible in most Western markets, and so sharply reduced banks' risk appetite and hence the funding available for new projects. Lack of liquidity was of course also one major reason for problems in other financial markets at that time.

Another key issue thrown into relief by the liquidity issue is that of banks funding long-term project-finance loans with short-term deposits in the money markets (*cf.* §10.3). Some banks began to face problems in funding their project-finance portfolios from 2008: as banks became very conservative about their counterpart risks, the inter-bank funding markets became more and more illiquid. This again reduced the appetite for new project-finance lending.

So the result was a sharp cut-back of new project-finance lending (as for all other lending). The cut-back was greatest in the regions which suffered most from the recession, as Table 4.1 shows. This was accompanied—not surprisingly—by a sharp increase in interest margins (*cf.* §12.6.1) and a general tightening up of loan terms such as the introduction of soft mini-perms (*cf.* §14.4.4).

Similarly the bond markets suffered severely from the virtual disappearance of the monoline insurers, although business on a somewhat smaller scale continued for non-PPP projects with shorter-term financing requirements (*cf.* §4.3.3).

This reduction in lending led to some governments taking measures to fill the financing gap for PPP projects: *e.g.* the British government set up the Treasury Infrastructure Finance Unit (TIFU) as discussed in §15.7.

These short-term effects were somewhat reduced in 2009/10, and so markets improved, but as the combination of the Eurozone crisis and longer-term issue of bank financing for such long-term debt, following the requirements of the 'Basel process', discussed below, came into focus as a further market contraction took place, especially in Europe.

However by 2013 the bank-loan market was showing signs of revival despite these long-term concerns; in some markets such as North America, ample institutional finance was available for the power and infrastructure sectors, and indeed there was even some competition between institutional lenders and banks returning to the market. A similar position was also developing in Europe. In other markets, such as the Arabian Gulf, local banks picked up the business from the traditional international lenders, and in others, such as India, the government took action to develop the bond market more rapidly.

§17.3 THE 'BASEL PROCESS'

The trend for commercial banks to turn away from project finance, which is not new nor only a result of the 2008 financial crisis (*cf.* §4.2.2), is being accelerated by the 'Basel' process. Basel here refers to the Bank for International Settlements (BIS), based in Basel, Switzerland, which is the central bank for national central banks. It hosts the Basel Committee on Banking Supervision, which sets international capital-adequacy standards for major international banks (to level out the competitive playing field, so avoiding dangerous competition in bank regulation between countries—if this were not done there is a danger that national banking supervisors would reduce capital-adequacy requirements to enable their banks to reduce the costs of their loans; this is especially important where international loans are concerned). These standards have gone though three iterations:

- 'Basel I' (1988), introduced in the G-10 countries in 1992): this proposed a minimum ratio of bank capital to loans; it was applied the same way to all loans other than sovereign loans to governments (hence ignoring credit quality); it also did not take proper account of off-balance sheet liabilities.

- 'Basel II' (2004): this was based on capital relative to measurement of risk, either by external credit rating or the bank's own loss experience.[1] Thus the higher the risk the more the capital required. But banks were required only to hold a small amount of capital—2%—against these risk-weighted assets.
- 'Basel III' (2011, to be introduced from 2013/18) *inter alia* learned the lessons of the 2008 financial crisis, that liquidity is as important for a bank as credit quality. So minimum liquidity requirements are to be introduced for banks, which will discourage too much mismatched funding (borrowing short and lending long). The level of capital required will also be increased to 7% of risk-weighted assets.

For project finance this is likely to mean that a greater emphasis will be based on reducing maturity mismatches by forcing the banks to borrow for longer terms when funding long-term loans. At the very least this will make bank-provided project finance more expensive than it would otherwise be. Some banks may find project finance increasingly especially if loan margins decline to anywhere near the pre-2008 levels, and withdraw from the market entirely, as some major banks had already done even before 2008 (*cf.* §4.2.2). Other banks may remain ostensibly in the market but concentrate on arranging loans which are intended for onward sale to the institutional market: some banks have already set up teams for this work. Alternatively, a bank may continue to be the 'lender of record' to projects (and so can be seen on Table 4.3), but hedge at least some of its credit risks by entering into credit-default swaps with the institutional market.

The problem was most acute for infrastructure finance, where the loan maturities are typically longer (20 years plus) than in other project-finance sectors (less than 20 years). There was also an impact on the cross-border lending market for projects of this nature, with more banks concentrating primarily on their home market. Banks were using 'soft mini-perms' and similar structures to reduce the likely maturity of loans, but by mid-2013 seem to have been spurred on by non-bank competition to return to longer maturities. On the other hand natural-resources projects are often shorter-term, and of strategic interest to the purchasers of these products, and so finance from banks from these countries (such as Japan) is still easily available.

---

[1] Interestingly, when the Basel II scheme was first drawn up, project finance was placed in a relatively high-risk category, along with other structured finance (*cf.* §5.2.2), meaning that banks would have to allocate more capital against such lending, making it less attractive and so diminishing the supply of project-finance credit and increasing its cost to the borrower. Four leading project-finance banks commissioned studies of their historical portfolios by the rating agency Standard & Poor's which showed that in fact the risk of default and consequent loss on project-finance loans was probably lower than on their general corporate-finance business, and as a result the Basel II rules were changed in 2005 to reflect this. *Cf.* Benjamin C. Esty & Aldo M. Sesia, Jr, *Basel II: Assessing the Default and Loss Characteristics of Project Finance Loans* (Harvard Business School, Cambridge MA, 2004). This database continues to be maintained and updated by S&P, and many more banks now provide information to it (*cf.* §9.15).

§17.4 NON-BANK LENDERS

The logical source of debt finance for projects is entities that have a need for a long-term and relatively secure cash flow, *e.g.* life-insurance companies, pension funds, hedge funds, sovereign wealth funds, finance companies, *etc.* (the 'institutional' market). However the limited development of the project-finance bond market (*cf.* §4.3.3),[2] despite many false dawns, shows that there is still a long way to go before such sources could replace bank finance, and the virtual disappearance of the monoline insurers (*cf.* §4.3.2) has obviously not helped.

§17.4.1 INSTITUTIONAL LENDERS

Partly as a result of the sharp contraction in bank project finance after 2008, building on the much longer history of equity-investment funds in the infrastructure market (*cf.* §3.2), and combined with the search for low-risk high-yield assets, the last few years have seen a significant increase in institutional debt finance, *i.e.* non-banks acting as lenders. Another factor which has obviously encouraged this growth is the sharp increase in lending margins which took place after 2008 (*cf.* §17.2). Large life-insurance companies and pension funds are already making direct project-finance loans to projects.

Canada is perhaps the best example of this—the Canadian market had always depended on European and Japanese banks for long-term project finance as the Canadian banks were not allowed to lend at such long maturities. On the other hand there are large and sophisticated life-insurance companies and pension funds in Canada. These parties generally have developed expertise by investing directly in project-finance equity, so providing debt is not an unknown field for them, and they have replaced banks to a considerable extent. The effect of this new source of finance can be seen in that the margin over government-bond rates for such debt had fallen from around 4% in 2008 to around 1.75% by the end of 2012.

Statistics are difficult to obtain, but the rating agency Standard & Poor's (*cf.* §5.3.1) has estimated that project lending from 'alternative sources' in 2012 was comparable in size to the international bond market (*cf.* §4.3.3), at about $20 billion. However growth is constrained by the lack of historical data on portfolio performance, and concerns about construction risk (discussed further in §17.5.1).[3]

---

[2] It is not necessary for non-bank lenders such as life-insurance companies and pension funds to structure their loans as bonds: they can also make direct loans. However bonds have traditionally been the preferred route, as they are structured to enable an easy sale, and hence provide some liquidity for investors, although as discussed below changes are taking place in this respect.

[3] Michael Wilkins, *Out of the Shadows: The Rise of Alternative Financing In Infrastructure* (Standard & Poor's, London, 2013)*.

But there are limits on possible demand from institutional investors: there is no market in which loans to Project Companies can be traded and hence they are illiquid. (And even though bonds are traded in theory, in practice the market for a particular bond issue is not very liquid either.) This means that, as with equity investment, institutional lenders will only want to keep a very limited proportion of their assets (probably less than 5%) in project-finance loans. Institutional lenders also tend to prefer 'plain vanilla' Accommodation Projects rather than more complex and/or risky power-generation or Concession-based projects, so sectors such as these may still have to rely primarily on bank finance. It is also possible that as the general level of interest rates rises, institutional lenders will move away from the complexities of project finance to the relatively simplicity of other debt markets such as corporate bonds.

There are also risks inherent in the fact that information on what is going on in the non-bank market is quite limited, compared to bank loans and bonds, and so, as with the 2008 financial crisis, it is possible that high levels of risk may accumulate without the knowledge of financial-market regulators. It is also not ideal while bank or other regulated lenders have to allocate specific levels of capital and liquidity to support they loans they make, unregulated entities taking the same risks do not have to adhere to such prudential requirements.

§17.4.2 Debt Funds

Another problem for development of institutional debt finance is that only the largest institutions can afford to employ the specialized staff to evaluate and monitor a project-finance loan portfolio. Since project-finance debt will only ever be a small percentage of an institutional portfolio, it is just not worthwhile for smaller institutions to employ the specialized staff required to evaluate and monitor a project-finance loan book. Smaller pension funds, however, may still be interested in allocating a part of their portfolio to the infrastructure sector in particular.

Project-finance debt funds are beginning to address this problem. These provide debt to projects on a similar basis to direct loans, and participations in such funds are primarily taken by parties which already have some involvement in equity investment in this sector, *i.e.* life-insurance companies, pension funds, and—especially in developing countries—DFIs.

There are potential conflict-of-interest issues which may inhibit some of the development in this sector: one model for debt funds is for debt already provided by a bank to be transferred to the fund (with a similar result to a CLO—*cf.* §5.2.10): the risks here are self-evident. The simple solution is to ensure that the bank retains a reasonable part of the loan on its own books, but this is difficult to police as the bank can easily sell a silent participation while remaining the lender of record, or enter into a credit default swap as discussed above.

A further difficulty is that just as non-fund fund managers tend to treat project-finance equity investment as 'high-risk high-return', and charge high fees accordingly (*cf.* §14.17.1), the same philosophy is applied to debt funds, which makes the returns unattractive to many institutional investors.

§17.4.3 PUBLIC-SECTOR PENSION FUNDS

However large public-sector pension funds from developed countries such as Canada and the U.S. are already significant players in project-finance equity and are beginning to get involved in debt. Pension funds of this type usually try to ensure they diversify their portfolio, so they get involved with a variety of types of project on a variety of countries, not just their home market.

So long as public-sector pension funds are able to work on a true arm's-length basis and are not pushed into projects because of political pressure there is no issue here, but this is not always the case. Especially in developing countries (*e.g.* in Nigeria and South Africa), the national public-sector pension fund is often by far the largest potential source of institutional finance (*e.g.* in Nigeria and South Africa), and it is difficult for such funds to resist pressure to invest in projects for the benefit of the national economy. But the main object of a pension fund is to ensure that its members get the pensions they are due, and undue concentration of assets in one sector such as major projects, probably with inadequate due diligence because of political pressures, potentially endangers its primary rôle of projecting pensions.

§17.4.4 SOLVENCY II

A further issue for life-insurance companies in the European Union which may affect their participation in project-finance lending is the 'Solvency II' Directive of 2009,[4] which harmonizes regulation of insurance companies, and could be described as 'Basel III for insurers'. This was supposed to come into effect at the beginning of 2014 but this date was put back by the European parliament and as of mid-2013 no new date had been announced. The main concern relates to the increased level of capital to be held against long-term investments. (No distinction is made in this respect between corporate and project-finance loans.) So Solvency II may make long-term project-finance lending less attractive for the insurance companies which have only just begun to enter the market.

§17.5 IMPROVING PROJECT-FINANCE CREDIT RISK

Improving the credit rating for project-finance projects has been seen as the key to tapping the long-term institutional debt market on a much larger scale. These projects are typically rated at BBB/Baa, *i.e.* the bottom end of investment-grade

---

[4] The 'Solvency I' Directive was issued in 1973.

(*cf.* §5.3.1), which is not attractive to many institutional lenders, who would prefer to see a 'single A' (A/A) rating, although some of the larger institutions are willing to take on BBB/Baa risk in straightforward Accommodation Projects.

Governments have been especially concerned about project finance for the infrastructure sector, including PPPs, which as mentioned above require the longest maturities. The various forms of public-sector support for such projects are discussed in Chapter 15, but there are several possible ways improving project-finance credit risk which can be adopted without necessarily needing public-sector support.

- separate construction risk (§17.5.1);
- mezzanine debt (§17.5.2);
- standby finance (§17.5.3);
- blended tenors (§17.5.4);
- increased equity (§17.5.5).

§17.5.1 SEPARATE CONSTRUCTION RISK

One way of reducing risk and so improving the credit rating for project-finance debt is to remove construction risk. This could be done by commercial banks or other parties giving Project Completion guarantees, or by construction finance being provided separately by banks and then refinanced by institutional lenders once the project is complete (*cf.* §15.6). The logic of involving banks for the construction phase only is obviously that this is the type of short-term finance which is inherently more appropriate as bank business.[5]

But this apparently simple solution raises some issues:

- *Refinancing risk* (*cf.* §10.6). This risk has to be taken by the Contracting Authority unless it can persuade long-term lenders to provide a take-out in advance.[6]
- *Due diligence*: The construction-phase lenders/guarantors have little incentive to carry out due diligence on the post-construction phase risks, so who does this and when?

---

[5] Taking this theme further, the Contracting Authority can provide a full takeout, *i.e.* including equity, at the end of the construction phase, and so benefit from the uplift in the project's value at this stage (*cf.* §14.17.1). The project can then be Franchised out again. But this makes the equity investment quite unattractive to the private-sector investor, as the return on equity will be quite limited, so it is likely that the only party willing to provide some equity would be the construction contractor (perhaps in the form of standby finance rather than equity). In such cases Forfaiting (*cf.* §6.6) is probably the simpler approach.

[6] The interest-rate risk aspect of the refinancing risk could be covered by a long-term interest-rate swap, but there is obviously a question about who would be willing to take on the risk of such a swap, with no corresponding long-term loan in place.

- *Timing of handover*: How would the date on which the construction-phase lenders/guarantors be repaid/released be fixed, and what continuing liability would they have? Even if the project passes any completion tests or meets Output Specifications would it be necessary for the project to operate for some time to ensure no other problems emerge? However, these issues may be more of a problem with projects involving equipment rather than straight-forward Accommodation-based projects.

- *Backstop date*: Typically once the construction of a project is a year behind schedule (other than due to Owner's Risks) both the Construction Contract and the Project Agreement can be terminated for default (*cf.* §7.10.1; §8.2.8). If there are long-term lenders they have the option to Step-in and try to remedy the situation (*cf.* §8.11), and even if this creates losses there is a chance to recover some or all of these losses (at the expense of investors' returns) over the remaining life of the contract. But if there is only a short-term construction loan or guarantee, the construction-phase lenders may crystallize an immediate loss they have no hope of recovering.

Taking these issues into account, construction finance is likely to work best for projects where the construction is relatively low-risk, *e.g.* Accommodation Projects, rather than projects with a high technology risk such as a waste incinerator.

§17.5.2 MEZZANINE DEBT

This logic suggests that provision of mezzanine debt, either by banks or by other parties such as specialized lenders or mezzanine-debt funds, may be a more viable way of dealing with this problem. If a project has 15% equity and 10% mezzanine debt, losses have to be 25% of the total financing before senior lenders have to suffer any loss, as compared to 15% if there is no mezzanine debt. Hence the senior lenders' risk has reduced, which should be reflected in a better credit rating, and a greater willingness to lend on the part of more cautious non-bank lenders.

§15.4 gives examples of using public-sector mezzanine debt (SIBs, TIFIA and the EIB Project Bond Initiative). One key point here is programs of this type offer mezzanine debt at a comparatively low cost, whereas the cost of mezzanine debt from commercial (as opposed to subsidized) sources, such as mezzanine-debt funds, could be almost the same as the required Equity IRR, *i.e.* it comes to almost the same thing as increasing the equity, discussed below. So attempts at creating mezzanine debt funds for projects have not been very successful.

§17.5.3 STANDBY FINANCE

An alternative to the immediate provision of mezzanine debt is an arrangement to provide such finance if it is required. This is most relevant to Concessions, where there may be uncertainty about achieving traffic forecasts, especially during the ramp-up phase (*cf.* §9.6.2). The EIB's LGTT (*cf.* §15.5), for example, provides standby finance to reduce risks for the senior lenders during the ramp-up phase. SIBs, TIFIA and the EIB Project Bond Initiative can also provide standby finance, which unlike the LGTT is available throughout the project life.

As far as equity is concerned, the use of contingent- or standby-equity commitments from the Sponsors to cover unforeseen cash-flow deficits is not new (*cf.* §9.13).

§17.5.4 BLENDED TENORS

Another variant is the use of 'blended tenors', *i.e.* debt finance is provided both by banks and by bonds (or other long-term loans). In this structure these are both lending *pari-passu*, but the bank loan has a shorter term (*e.g.* 7–10 years) and hence is repaid quicker, with the institutional lenders' repayments being 'back-ended' in the cash flow.[7] The overall debt-service profile blends these two repayment schedules together to produce the normal annuity-type repayment. However there are some practical issues when banks are lending alongside bondholders (*cf.* Table 5.2) so this structure works better with institutional lenders or debt funds that are fully involved in the due diligence and control of projects, *i.e.* that behave like banks.

§17.5.5 INCREASED EQUITY

An increase in the proportion of equity in the project financing will have the same result as providing mezzanine debt—*i.e.* risk for senior lenders is reduced, so encouraging institutional lending. The issue here, as discussed in §12.8, is whether the reduced risk for both investors and lenders will result in each of them being willing to take a lower return. If this is not the case the result will of course be a more expensive project.

In its PF2 program, announced in 2012,[8] the British Treasury announced a requirement to increase the usual level of equity in future PFI-Model projects (from roughly 10–15% of project costs to 20–25% in a typical project). This was to be split between the original Sponsors, the public sector[9] and equity to be sold

---

[7] The latter type of loan is known as a 'Term Loan B', as opposed to the bank loan which is the 'A'. Term Loan B is generally used to describe an institutional loan in which the amortization is quite low in the early years, with larger repayments later on, or a balloon repayment.

[8] HM Treasury, *A New Approach to Public Private Partnerships* (London, 2012)*.

[9] The equity will be held by a unit of the British Treasury, not the Contracting Authority, although the latter will benefit from most of the equity return.

in an Equity Funding Competition (*cf.* §12.2.5). Since the non-Sponsor equity was expected to be at a lower Equity IRR, and the debt at a lower cost because of the increased equity, the overall financing costs were not expected to be any greater than under a conventional financing model. This was intended to make project debt more attractive to the institutional market, (and indeed the Treasury said that "*PF2 projects are...expected to source debt finance from sources other than bank debt*") but in 2013 as it became clear that bank financing to PPP projects was becoming more freely available again, the idea of increasing the proportion of equity in PF2 contracts was dropped. [HM Treasury, *op. cit. supra.*, para 8.22][10]

In projects financed with 'soft' mini-perms (§14.4.4; §14.16.4), Sponsors may decide to increase the equity investment when they have to refinance before the mini-perm takes effect, which should be comparatively easy as there will be a stable cash flow. This would then also make debt easier to raise.

§17.6 NEW MODELS

There are some new models, as yet only used to a limited extent, which may be helpful in some sectors, *e.g.*:

- Regulated Asset Base finance (§17.6.1);
- Output-Based Aid (§17.6.2);
- Social Impact Bonds (§17.6.3);
- Tax Increment Finance (§17.6.4).

§17.6.1 REGULATED ASSET BASE FINANCE

Regulation often applies to private-sector utilities which charge end-users. The purpose of this is to ensure that the public is not exploited by monopoly providers of services, while at the same time ensuring that the utility concerned is able to develop the necessary infrastructure and earn a reasonable return on this

---

[10] However the compulsory division of equity between the original bidder, a new investor chosen through an Equity Funding Competition, and the Treasury remains in place. This is intended to deflect criticism of the 'windfalls' made on sale of equity by Sponsors (*cf.* §14.17.1): the windfalls will become smaller and the public sector will have a share in them. It remains to be seen whether Sponsors will be willing to lose control of a project in this way (especially if they become a minority shareholder), and also whether they will consider it worthwhile to bid for projects where their absolute equity return is reduced (because they can't get 100% of the equity).

investment. The roles of the regulator, usually appointed by, but independent of government, are:

- to set service standards, which may result in the utility company having to invest in new projects;
- to agree the cost of new projects, but based on what they should have cost, rather than what was actually spent on them—so leaving construction risk with the utility company's shareholders;
- to agree the utility company's 'asset base', *i.e.* the reasonable cost of its assets, including additions as above, which are required to provide the service, less depreciation;
- to agree the utility company's cost of capital, *i.e.* the reasonable cost of financing its asset base and providing a return to shareholders;
- to agree the utility company's operating costs, including a reasonable profit margin on these costs;

which then results in a calculation of the prices to be charged to end-users, usually fixed for a period of years (say five) until the next regulatory review, with increases over the period linked to CPI.[11]

Given this structure lenders to the utility company know that once the asset base has been agreed it has a secure cash flow, and so the utility company can raise debt at a fairly low cost. Thus there is generally no need for regulated utilities to use project finance rather than corporate finance.

But unlike privatized utilities, PPPs and process-plant projects contracted with a Contracting Authority do not usually operate under the control of a regulator in the sense this is used above. Such projects are based on 'regulation by contract', *i.e.* the Project Agreement sets service standards and the maximum cost which such project can charge an Offtaker/Contracting Authority or an end-user. In fact it would not be that credible for a government-appointed regulator to regulate the price of a contract signed between a private-sector Project Company and a Contracting Authority.[12] But of course this means that if the Contract Payments are perceived as being unreasonably high, a political problem is likely to result (*cf.* §11.2).

In recent years there has been discussion about extending regulation into the PPP sector, so as to make long-term finance easier and cheaper to source, and to counter-act the long-term inflexibility of PPP contracts (*cf.* §7.2.6). This is called

---

[11] This is obviously a highly-complex process, and there is a danger of 'regulatory capture', *i.e.* the regulated entities are better-resourced and informed than the regulator, and so they are likely to be successful in lobbying against regulatory proposals which they regard as detrimental.

[12] *Cf.* Tonci Bakovic, Bernard Tenenbaum & Fiona Woolf, *Regulation by Contract: A New Way to Privatize Electricity Distribution?* (Working Paper No. 14, World Bank, Washington DC, 2003)*.

Regulated Asset Base ('RAB') finance.[13] The idea is that a Project Company will build the project, and raise project finance to cover the construction phase. When the project is complete a regulator will decide whether its cost is reasonable, and if so allow a return on this cost (*i.e.* it becomes the asset base) which will enable the cost of the construction finance to be refinanced by a loan based on the regulated return.

But PPPs and process-plant projects contracted with a Contracting Authority do not usually operate under the control of a regulator in the sense this is used above. Such projects are based on 'regulation by contract', *i.e.* the Project Agreement sets service standards and the maximum cost which such projects can charge an Offtaker/Contracting Authority or an end-user. In fact it would not be that credible for a government-appointed regulator to regulate the price of a contract signed between a private-sector Project Company and a Contracting Authority.[14] But of course this means that if the Contract Payments are perceived as being unreasonably high, a political problem is likely to result (*cf.* §11.2).

So while regulation may be appropriate for privatized infrastructure, it is unlikely to be appropriate for the PPP sector.

§17.6.2 Output-Based Aid

Output-based aid ('OBA') has been defined as:

> "…a results-based mechanism that is increasingly being used to deliver basic infrastructure and social services to the poor… OBA ties the disbursement of public funding in the form of subsidies to the achievement of clearly specified results that directly support improved access to basic services. Basic services include improved water supply and sanitation, access to energy, health care, education, communications services, and transportation."[15]

The concept of OBA was first developed by the World Bank in 2002. It is aimed at the poor who are excluded from basic services because they cannot afford to

---

[13] *Cf.* Dieter Helm, "Infrastructure investment, the cost of capital, and regulation: an assessment", *Oxford Review of Economic Policy*, Volume 25, Number 3 (Oxford University Press, Oxford, 2009)*, and "Infrastructure and infrastructure finance: The role of the government and the private sector in the current world", *EIB Papers*, Vol. 15 No. 2 (EIB, Luxemburg, 2010), p. 34*.

[14] *Cf.* Tonci Bakovic, Bernard Tenenbaum & Fiona Woolf, *Regulation by Contract: A New Way to Privatize Electricity Distribution?* (Working Paper No. 14, World Bank, Washington DC, 2003)*

[15] Yogita Mumssen, Lars Johannes & Geeta Kumar, *Output-Based Aid: Lessons Learned and Best Practices* (Directions in Development 53644, World Bank, Washington DC, 2010), p. 5*. OBA is also known as 'performance-based aid' or 'results-based financing'.

pay the full cost of User Charges such as connection fees. There is now a Global Partnership on Output-Based Aid (GPOBA) which is funded by the World Bank and other bilateral DFIs and provides support for projects using this structure.

There is an obvious link between OBA and output-based PPP Contracts. In particular, this is one way in which the Affordability gap which so often exists in developing countries trying to structure PFI-Model projects in the social sector can be met. OBA could provide long-term funding to cover some or call of the Service Fees on social-infrastructure projects, which would both help to make projects affordable to users, and ensure direct accountability for the way in which aid funding is spent.[16] But one problem may be that aid donors would have to commit to making Contract Payments for the whole life of the PPP Contract, to enable the finance for the project to be raised, whereas most aid is on a shorter-term basis.

§17.6.3 SOCIAL-IMPACT BONDS

Social-impact bonds ('SIBs')[17] have attracted a lot of interest in recent years. They are based on a contract with a Contracting Authority, under which payment is made for improved social outcomes which result in public-sector savings.

The first such bond, issued in Britain in 2010, illustrates how SIBs work. The bond was placed with investors (typically charities and other social investors) and the bond proceeds are being used to pay for a 6-year program of rehabilitation of prisoners after release. If the degree of re-offending is reduced by 7.5%, part of the savings in public-sector costs from this are is paid to the bondholders by the Contracting Authority (the British Ministry of Justice). The further the results are below this threshold the more will be paid to investors, up to a maximum return of 13%. As can be seen from this rate of return, SIBs are high-risk investments, with 'equity-like' risks.[18] The first U.S. SIB was issued in 2012 to finance a program of prisoner rehabilitation in the City of New York ($9.6 million—wholly subscribed by Goldman Sachs). Other countries such as Australia are actively considering using SIBs.

While the example above does not relate to investment in a physical project, there is no inherent reason why SIBs could not also be used to create investment in a project, with its revenue based on social outcomes. However this is obviously rather a niche market.

---

[16] *Cf.* Navin Girishankar, *Innovating Development Finance: From Financing Sources to Financial Solutions* (Policy Research Working Paper 5111, World Bank, Washington DC, 2009)* for a wider discussion on changing the standard models of DFI finance.

[17] To be distinguished from state infrastructure banks ('SIBs') discussed in §15.8; also known as Pay for Success Bond, or Social Benefit Bond.

[18] *Cf.* Social Finance, *A Technical Guide to Commissioning Social Impact Bonds* (London, 2011)*.

§17.6.4 TAX INCREMENT FINANCE

Tax Increment Finance ('TIF')[19] is not a new concept in the U.S., where it has been in existence since the 1950s,[20] and is now used very widely around the country. However it is attracting interest elsewhere in the world as a way for cities to finance urban regeneration and possibly improvement of social infrastructure.

TIF is quite simple in concept: increased property-tax revenue (and sometimes also sales-tax revenue) generated by infrastructure development is used to repay bonds or loans used to finance this new infrastructure. These tax-revenue increases are separately identified, and ring-fenced—project-finance style—to repay the original finance for infrastructure development. Local legislation may be required to ensure the required ring-fencing can be achieved, *e.g.* a special 'TIF district' is established. The infrastructure concerned may be, for example, road or other transport improvements, based on which private investors may construct new housing and commercial development. Other social infrastructure facilities such as police or fire stations, libraries, health clinics, social housing, water-treatment plants, and so on, can also be funded in this way.

The basic requirements in the U.S. for creating a TIF-based project are that the area is 'blighted' by urban decay and needs regeneration, and that regeneration will not happen if TIF is not available (known as the 'but for' test).

The finance can be constructed in different ways:

- *Contracting Authority bonds*: The Contracting Authority can issue bonds (tax-free munis in the U.S.[21]—*cf.* §4.3.1) which are used to fund the infrastructure investment, and repaid by the ring-fenced tax increases.[22]
- *Developer finance*: The Contracting Authority enters into agreement to pay the ring-fenced tax increases to a developer so long as the latter completes the necessary infrastructure investment, and the developer uses this agreement (in effect like a Project Contract) as security to raise finance to undertake the required investments.

---

[19] *Cf.* Council of Development Finance Agencies & International Council of Shopping Centres, *Tax Increment Finance: Best Practices Reference Guide* (CDFA/ICSC, 2007)*.

[20] Ironically California was the first state to use TIFs, but in 2012 effectively abolished them. There were various reasons for this, including a large number of TIF projects resulting in a significant proportion of the state property taxes being 'locked-up' in TIFs at a time when the state was in financial difficulty—and one reason there were a large number of TIFs was that the concept of 'blight' for which regeneration was needed was stretched very widely.

[21] Actually the tax treatment of TIF Revenue Bonds is complex because of their mixed private and public use; appropriate tax advice is needed to ensure that the bonds are tax-exempt if that is the objective.

[22] As with other projects, since the benefits will start to flow only after the construction of the improvements is complete, interest is usually capitalized for up to 3 years. Other typical project-finance characteristics are found in such bonds, *e.g.* a DSRA.

- As a half-way house between these two approaches, the developer may be required to carry out the improvements at its own cost, which is then reimbursed on completion by a TIF bond. This also reduces the risks involved and so can reduce long-term finance costs.

A number of issues have to be considered:

What Kind of Infrastructure? A large sector of the TIF market in the U.S. has been used to develop shopping centers—this is not necessarily the top priority when one considers urban renewal. Misuse of the TIF concept by real-estate developers with good local political connections is clearly a danger.

Social Equity: Some part of the benefit from the increased tax revenues should flow to the Contracting Authority's area as a whole, *i.e.* the benefit should not just be confined to those who are lucky enough to be in a TIF district. This is typically achieved by dedicating no more than, say, 50% of the increased taxes to servicing the TIF debt, so leaving the Contracting Authority free to decide what it wants to do with the other 50%.

Tax-Revenue Risk: Who will take the risk that the increase in tax revenues actually takes place? Depending on the nature of the project, there can obviously be a high risk that not enough new private-sector investment takes place in the TIF district, and hence the debt cannot be repaid. (There is usually a time limit within which the assignment of excess tax revenues applies: this may be 15–20 years in some cases of major investment, or shorter periods in smaller transactions.)

Also the failure of a major developer in the TIF district may affect the recovery on the bonds—*e.g.* if a shopping centre which is the main object of the TIF goes into bankruptcy it will obviously not be paying its property taxes. Concentration of risk (rather than a widely-spread tax base) is thus another key risk issue.

If the Contracting Authority issues Revenue Bonds as in the U.S. muni bond market there is no recourse to its general tax revenues. The same is the case if the obligation to a developer is also limited. It makes little sense for the Contracting Authority to guarantee the tax uplift: if it is going to take this risk it might as well raise the finance on a full-recourse basis (*e.g.* General Obligation bonds), unless there some constraint on its borrowing which does not apply if it gives a guarantee. But on the other hand the risk here is potentially very complex and difficult to assess. In some cases TIF bonds may be secured on the improvements in the district, but this is clearly only helpful if a foreclosure on these could generate any value for the bondholders.

In some states, a state guarantee for the TIF finance can be obtained. Otherwise credit enhancement from monoline insurance, banks or other guarantors may be needed.

Other risk analysis: Some of the risks that would arise on any project financing also apply to a TIF bond, *e.g.* can construction be completed on time and on budget, but of course the key risk of an inadequate tax base is peculiar to TIFs.

Pilot TIF programs are being introduced in local-government finance in Britain, but on a different basis to that used in the U.S.[23] In Britain local government in general does not need to raise its own capital finance by issuing bonds because local governments can borrow from the UK Debt Management Office ('DMO') at attractive rates. So in Britain TIF is just being used as a new basis for local governments to borrow in their own name from DMO, with no private-sector involvement with the TIF risks, which obviously remain with the local governments.

§17.7 THE FUTURE OF PROJECT FINANCE

It would be premature to suggest that the standard bank-financed project-finance debt market is about to disappear. The scale of bank lending in the project-finance sector is still very large, and while some banks have retreated from this market others have joined it. But it is clear that there are long-term trends which may affect the project-finance debt market more and more, especially in particular sectors such as infrastructure, or in particular regions mainly Europe. A significant increase in institutional lending is clearly taking place, but it is too early to say if it is sustainable against stronger bank competition. A European Commission staff working paper concludes that: *"a better channelling of long-term resources via capital markets and reduced dependence on bank funding is required. Nevertheless, such a transformation in funding structure may take some time."*[24] This is a fair summary of the current position, at least in Europe.

Nevertheless, even if traditional bank-provided project finance dried up tomorrow and projects are all financed with institutional debt, this book would not become obsolete—wherever a stand-alone project's financing comes from, the same structuring and risk issues which have been laid out in the previous chapters will continue to apply.

---

[23] Mark Sandford, *Tax Increment Financing* (Standard Note: SN/PC?05797, House of Commons Library, London, 2013)*.

[24] European Commission Staff Working Document, *Long-Term Financing of the European Economy* (SWD(2013) 76 final, Brussels, 2013), p. 18*.

Glossary and Abbreviations

Technical terms used in this book that are mainly peculiar to project finance are capitalized, and briefly explained in this Glossary, with cross-references to the places in the main text where a fuller explanation can be found; other financial terms used in the book are also explained and cross-referenced in the Glossary, as are the various abbreviations used.

Term	Definition	Refer to:
$	U.S. dollars	
3P	*See* public-private partnership	
abandonment	Failure by the Sponsors to continue with the construction or operation of the project	§7.10.1; §8.5.6; §9.5.5; §14.12; §16.5.4
abatement	*See* penalties (for a PFI-Model Contract)	§6.4.3
acceleration	Action by the lenders to make the whole of their debt due and payable following an Event of Default.	§14.12; §14.13
Accommodation Project	Availability-based Contract relating to buildings such as schools, hospitals, prisons, government offices, *etc.*; *cf.* social infrastructure	
accounting officer	The senior civil servant responsible for a PPP procurement	§3.7.1
accreting swap	An interest rate swap drawn in installments to match drawdowns (*q.v.*)	§10.3.1
acknowledgements and consents	*See* Direct Agreement(s)	§8.11
Act of God	*See* Natural *Force Majeure*	
ADB	Asian Development Bank, a regional MDFI	§16.5; §16.5.5
additionality	The requirement for DFIs only to lend if funding cannot be provided by the private-sector markets	§16.5; §16.5.8
ADSCR	*See* Annual Debt Service Cover Ratio	§12.3
advance payment guarantee	Security provided by the EPC Contractor for amounts paid in advance under the EPC Contract by the Project Company	§8.2.9

Term	Definition	Refer to:
AfDB	African Development Bank, a regional MDFI	§16.5; §16.5.6
Affermage	A contract whereby the Project Company takes over an existing public service and is paid a fee by a Contracting Authority or users for service delivery; *cf.* Franchise	§6.6
affirmative covenants	*See* covenants; positive covenants	§14.10.1
Affordability	The ability of the Contracting Authority to make the Contract Payments from its budget, or for users to pay the User Charge	§3.7.3; §7.2.2
agent bank	The bank liaising between the Project Company and its lenders	§5.2.9; §12.6.4; §14.4.1; §14.10.1; §14.13
all risks insurance	Insurance against physical damage to the project during operation	§8.6.2
ALOP insurance	Advance Loss of Profits insurance; *see* DSU insurance	§8.6.1
amortizing swap	An interest rate swap reduced in installments to match reductions in the notional principal amount (*q.v.*)	§10.3.1
Angola Model	Construction of infrastructure projects in return for right to extract natural resources	§11.4.1
Annual Debt Service Cover Ratio	The ratio between operating cash flow and debt service over any one year of the project ('ADSCR')	§12.3
Annuity Contract	*See* Availability-based Contract	§6.4
annuity repayment	A debt repayment schedule that produces level debt-service payments, *i.e.* the sum of principal (*q.v.*) and interest for each period	§12.5.3
Asset Management Plan	Requirements for maintenance and lifecycle renewal of the project assets set out in the Project Agreement	§7.10.7
Asset Register	A register of the Project Company's assets which are to be handed over to the Offtaker/Contracting Authority at the end of the Project Agreement	§7.10.7
assumptions book	The source data for the financial model	§13.3
authorized investments	Low-risk investments by the Project Company of cash in Reserve Accounts	§14.4.1
availability	The project being available as required by the Project Agreement	§6.3.6; §6.4.3; §6.5.5; §9.7.4
Availability Charge	*See* Capacity Charge	§6.3.5

Term	Definition	Refer to:
Availability Period	The period after Financial Close during which the debt is available for drawing	§14.3.1
Availability-based Contract/project	A PFI-Model project under which the Project Company is paid for making the project available for the Contracting Authority's use (N.B. Although there are similarities to process-plant Project Agreements with a Capacity Charge, this type of contract is dealt with separately.)	§2.5.2; §6.4; Chapter 7; §9.6.4; §9.7.4
average life	The average period that the loan principal (*q.v.*) is outstanding	§12.5.2
B Loan	Participation by a private-sector lender in a loan made by an MDFI	§16.5.1; §16.5.2
BAFO	*See* Best and Final Offer	§3.7.4; §3.7.7; §5.6
balloon repayment	A large final repayment of a loan (after a series of smaller repayments); *cf.* annuity repayment; bullet repayment	§10.6; §14.4.4
bankers' clauses	Additional lender requirements on insurances	§8.6.5
Banking Case	The projections of project cash flow at or shortly before Financial Close, agreed between the Project Company and the lenders; *cf.* Base Case	§5.2.8; §7.6.5; §7.10; §13.10
Base Case	The projections of project cash flow at or shortly before Financial Close, agreed between the Project Company and an Offtaker/Contracting Authority; *cf.* Banking Case	§5.2.8; §7.6.5; §7.10; §13.10
Basel process	Internationally agreed capital and liquidity requirements for major international banks	§17.3
basis point	1/100th of a percent	§12.6.1
bbl	Barrel (of oil)	
benchmarking	Adjustment to the Contract Payments based on regular review of the costs of services provided to the Project Company (or additional capital expenditure by the Project Company)	§6.4.5; §7.6.3
Berne Union	International Union of Credit and Investment Insurers	§16.2.2
Best and Final Offer	A second-stage bid in a competitive public procurement ('BAFO')	§3.7.4; §3.7.7; §5.6
BI insurance	*See* Business Interruption insurance	§8.6.2
bid bond	A bond provided by a bidder in a public procurement as security for its signing the Project Agreement if its bid is selected; *cf.* bonding	§3.7.9

Term	Definition	Refer to:
bilateral DFI	A DFI in a particular country, providing loans and equity to projects in developing countries; *cf.* Policy Bank, SFI	§15.8; §16.4
Blended Equity IRR	The IRR received by investors, taking account of all Distributions	§12.2.2
BLOT	Build-Lease-Operate-Transfer; *see* BLT	§6.2
BLT	Build-Lease-Transfer	§6.2
bond	A tradable debt instrument	§4.3; §5.3; §5.4
	A security instrument; *see* bonding	
bondholder	A party which has lent to the Project Company on the basis of a bond	
bonding	Security provided by bidder, or a party to any of the Project Contracts to support its obligations	§3.7.9; §7.5; §8.2.9; §14.8.1
BOO	Build-Own-Operate	§6.2
book runner	The bank in charge of the syndication (*q.v.*) of a loan or a bond placement.	§5.2.8; §5.3.1
BOOT	Build-Own-Operate-Transfer	§6.2
borrowing base	A system of loan drawdown to finance successive tranches of investment, as and when cash flow or other targets have been met	§5.2.2; §14.3.3
BOT	Build-Operate-Transfer	§6.2
breach of contract	*See* contract repudiation	§11.5.1
breach of provision clause	*See* non-vitiation clause	§8.6.5
breach of warranty clause	*See* non-vitiation clause	§8.6.5
breakage cost	The cost of early termination of an interest rate swap, fixed-rate loan or bond, an inflation-indexed loan or an inflation swap	§10.3.1; §10.3.4; §10.4.3; §14.14.1; §14.14.2
BTO	Build-Transfer-Operate	§6.2
Building-Services Contract	A contract to provide 'soft' services such as cleaning, catering and security to the Project Company; *cf.* Hard FM	§2.5.2; §8.4
bullet repayment	Repayment of a loan mainly in one final installment rather than a series of repayments; *cf.* balloon repayment, annuity repayment	§10.3.1; §12.5.2
Business Case	Report prepared by a Contracting Authority as a basis for approval to move to the next stage of project procurement	§3.7.3

Term	Definition	Refer to:
Business Interruption insurance	Insurance against the loss of revenue after damage to the project ('BI insurance')	§8.6.2
buyer credit	An ECA-supported loan to an importer of equipment for a project	§16.2.1
buy-down payment	*See* delay LDs	§8.2.8
	See interest buy-down	§12.8
Capacity Charge	The fixed-charge element of a Tariff payable under a process plant Project Agreement, such as a PPA, payable whether or not the product is required	§6.3.5
Capital Contribution	*See* capital grant	§15.10
capital grant	Payment by a Contracting Authority of part of the capital cost of an Availability-based or other PFI-Model project	§15.10
capitalized interest	IDC which is added to the debt principal (*q.v.*) amount	§10.3; §12.2.3; §13.5.1
CAR insurance	Construction All Risks insurance; *see* Construction & Erection All Risks insurance	§8.6.1
Cascade	The order of priorities under the financing documentation for the application of the Project Company's cash flow	§14.4.2
cash flow	The cash generated (or consumed) by a project	
Cash Sweep	Dedication of surplus cash flow to debt prepayment	§14.4.4; §14.12; §14.16.4; §15.5
Cash Trap	*See* Distribution Stop	§14.4.3
CDB	China Development Bank, a Policy Bank and DFI	§15.8; §16.4.3
CEAR insurance	*See* Construction & Erection All Risks insurance	§8.6.1
Cession de Créance	Concept in French administrative law which enables the Contracting Authority to take over direct responsibility for part of the Project Company's debt; *cf.* Debt Underpinning	§15.17
CfD	*See* Contract for Differences	§6.3.1; §9.6.1
CGF	*See* Credit Guarantee Finance	§15.9
change in law	A change in the law affecting the Project Company or the project, resulting in additional capital expenditure or operating costs; also known as regulatory risk	§7.6.4; §11.3; §14.4.1
change order	*See* Contract Variations	§7.6.3; §8.2.3
China Exim	The Export-Import Bank of China	§11.4.1; §16.4; §16.4.3
CHP	Combined heat and power	

Term	Definition	Refer to:
CIRR	*See* Commercial Interest Reference Rates	§16.2.3; §16.2.6
CIS	Commonwealth of Independent States, the former Soviet Union	
clawback	Requirement for investors to repay Distributions received if the Project Company is later short of cash	§14.4.5
CLO	Collateralized loan obligation	§5.2.10; §14.16.5
COD	*See* Commercial Operation Date	§6.3.3; §6.3.6; §8.5.1
COFACE	*Compagnie Française d'Assurance pour le Commerce Extérieur*, the French ECA	§16.4; §16.4.7
collateral warranties	Agreements under which parties providing services in connection with construction or operation of the project accept liability to the lenders for the performance of the service; *cf.* warranties	§8.11
collateralized loan obligation	A method of refinancing a portfolio of loans though securitization ('CLO')	§5.2.10; §14.16.5
Commercial Acceptance	*See* Project Completion	
commercial banks	Private-sector banks, the main suppliers of debt to the project finance markets	§4.2; §5.2; §5.4; Chapter 17
Commercial Close	Signing the Construction Contract (and/or other major Sub-Contracts) before Financial Close	§8.2.2
Commercial Interest Reference Rates	The interest rates charged on ECA-supported export credits ('CIRR'), based on Interest-Rate Equalization	§16.2.1; §16.2.3; §16.2.6
Commercial Operation Date	The date on which an EPC-contract-based project is complete and the Project Company is ready to begin operations ('COD'). *See* Project Completion	§6.3.3; §6.3.6; §8.5.1
commercial risks	Project finance risks inherent in the project itself or the market for its product or service; *cf.* construction revenue, operating, input supply, and environmental risks	Chapter 9
commitment fee	Percentage fee charged on the available but undrawn portion of a bank loan (*e.g.* during the construction phase of a project)	§12.6.3
Common Terms Agreement	Common lending conditions agreed between different groups of lenders	§14.14
Compensation Event	An event causing a loss or requiring new investment by the Project Company, for which an Offtaker/Contracting Authority is responsible; *cf.* Excusing Cause, Relief Event	§7.6; §8.2.5

Term	Definition	Refer to:
completion risks	*See* construction risks	§7.4.1; §9.5
Concession	A PPP in which the general public pays User Charges in the form of tolls, fares or other charges for using the facility; *cf.* PFI Model	§2.5.2; §6.5
Concession Agreement	A Project Agreement relating to a Concession	§2.5.2; §6.5; Chapter 8
conditions precedent	Conditions to be fulfilled by the Project Company before drawing on the debt ('CPs'); *cf.* conditions subsequent	§14.8
conditions subsequent	Conditions which have to be achieved between the time that loan documentation or Project Contracts are signed and Financial Close	§14.8
consent to assignment	*See* Direct Agreement	§8.11
consortium	The group of Sponsors working together to develop the project	§3.5
Construction & Erection All Risks insurance	Insurance covering physical damage to the project during construction	§8.6.1
construction budget	The cost of construction as agreed with the lenders, deviations from which require lender consent; *cf.* operating budget	§9.5.5; §13.5.1
Construction Contract	An EPC or D&B Sub-Contract	§2.5.2; §8.2
Construction Contractor	The EPC or D&B Sub-Contractor to the Project Company	§2.5.2; §8.2
construction risks	Commercial risks relating to the construction of the project	§7.4.1; §9.5
construction subsidy	*See* capital grant	§15.10
construction-phase insurances	CEAR, Marine Cargo, DSU, Marine DSU and *Force Majeure* insurances	§8.6.1
contingency	Unallocated reserve in the project construction-cost budget, covered by contingency finance	§9.5.6; §9.5.7; §10.3; §12.4.2
Contract for Differences	A Project Agreement under which the Project Company sells its product into the market, but pays to or receives from the Offtaker the difference between the market price and an agreed price level ('CfD')	§6.3.1; §9.6.1
contract mismatch	Incompatible provisions between a Project Agreement and one or more of the Project Contracts	§9.12

Term	Definition	Refer to:
Contract Payments	Payments due to the Project Company under a Project Agreement, *i.e.* the Tariff payable by the Offtaker under a process-plant project, Service-Fee payments by a Contracting Authority under a PFI-Model project, or User Charges payable under a Concession Agreement	§6.3.5; §6.4.1; §6.5.1; §7.3
contract repudiation	Failure by a public-sector body to fulfill its obligations under a Project Contract or by a Host Government to fulfill its obligations to compensate for this under a Government Support Agreement	§11.5.1; §16.2.4
Contract Variations	Changes to a PPP Contract for which the Contracting Authority is responsible	§7.6.3
Contracting Authority	A public-sector entity that is the Project Company's contractual counterpart under an Offtake Contract (other than with a private-sector entity) or a PPP Contract.	§2.4; §2.5.2; §2.6.2; §3.7; Chapter 6; Chapter 7; §9.2; §9.14
Control Accounts	*See* Project Accounts	§14.3.2; §14.4.1
Controlling Creditor	A person making decisions on behalf of bondholders	§5.3.2; §14.13
corporate finance	A loan against a company's balance sheet and existing business, an alternative to project finance	§2.2; §2.6
cost-benefit ratio	The ratio of the NPV of the benefits of a project to the NPV of its costs	§10.2.3
country risk	*See* political risks	§9.1; Chapter 11; Chapter 16
coupon	The interest rate payable on a bond	§12.6.1
coupon swap	*See* interest-rate swap	§10.3.1; §14.14.1
counterparty risk	Technical and financial-capacity risks related to all parties with which the Project Company has Project Contracts	§9.5.4
covenants	Undertakings given by the Project Company to the lenders	§14.10
Cover Ratios	Ratios of the cash flows from the project against debt service, *i.e.*, ADSCR, LLCR, PLCR or Reserve Cover Ratio	§12.3
CPI	Consumer price index, a measurement of inflation	
CPs	*See* conditions precedent	§14.8
credit agreement	*See* loan agreement	Chapter 14
credit-default swap	A risk-hedging contract whereby the credit risk is taken by a different party to the lender	§17.2
Credit Enhancement	Provision of a guarantee, standby loan or other additional financial security for a project financing	§15.3

Term	Definition	Refer to:
Credit Guarantee Finance	The British Treasury's scheme for public-sector financing of PPP Project Companies, with private-sector debt guarantees ('CGF')	§15.9
credit margin	The interest margin over cost of funds charged by a lender to cover its credit risk and provide a return on capital, or the margin over the government bond rate applied to a bond; *cf.* swap credit premium	§12.6.1
credit rating agency	A company providing an independent view on the creditworthiness of the Project Company	§5.3.1; §9.15; §9.16; §17.5
creeping expropriation	A series of actions by the Host Government or another public-sector body that, taken as a whole, have the effect of expropriation	§11.5.2
cross-default	Where there is more than one lender, an Event of Default under one loan agreement is automatically an Event of Default under the others	§14.14
cross-border	Debt or investment made from one country to another	
cross-collateralization	The sharing of security between different groups of lenders	§14.14.3
CUP	MIGA's Co-operative Underwriting Program, based on similar principles to B Loans	§11.8.1; §16.5.4
cure period	A period of time allowed to remedy a default under a contract	§8.11
currency swap	A hedging contract to fix the future exchange rate of one currency against another	§4.2.2; §10.5.2
cushion	An amount of cash flow above that required for making payments to lenders, investors or other parties; *cf.* Cover Ratios	§2.6.1
D&B Contract	*See* Design & Build Contract	§2.5.2; §8.2
Dailly tranche	The portion of a French PFI-Model Contract's Service Fees which are covered by *Cession de Créance* (*q.v.*) arrangements	§15.17
DBFO	Design-Build-Finance-Operate	§6.2
DCF	*See* discounted cash flow	§10.2.1
deal creep	Gradual increases in the originally agreed Contract Payments, or rejection of agreed risk transfers, by the Sponsors during Project Agreement negotiations, usually caused by negotiations after appointment of the Preferred Bidder	§3.7.4; §3.7.7; §14.16.6
debt	Finance provided by the (senior) lenders	§2.4; Chapter 12; Chapter 14

Term	Definition	Refer to:
debt:equity ratio	Ratio of debt to equity; *cf.* leverage	§2.6; §10.5.6; §12.4; §12.8; §14.3.2
Debt Accretion	Increasing the debt amount during the operation phase of a Concession, based on traffic growth above initial projections; *cf.* borrowing base	§14.3.3
Debt Funding Competition	Competitive bidding to provide the debt for a PPP project after a Preferred Bidder has been selected; *cf.* Equity Funding Competition	§5.6.1
debt service	Payments of interest and debt principal (*q.v.*) installments	§12.5
Debt Service Reserve Account	A Reserve Account with a cash balance sufficient to cover the next scheduled debt service payment ('DSRA')	§14.4.1
Debt Tail	Continuing project revenues after repayment of the debt; *cf.* Reserve Tail	§7.2.3; §12.3.4; §12.4; §14.4.4
Debt Underpinning	A second-loss guarantee by the Contracting Authority of part of the debt for a PPP project	§15.17
deductible	Initial loss amount borne before insurance claims are paid	§8.6.3
deductions	Sums deducted from Service-Fee payments of a PFI-Model or from the Tariff of a process-plant project for failure to meet Availability or service requirements; *cf.* abatements, penalties	§6.3.6; §6.4.3; §9.7.4
default interest	An increased credit margin charged after an Event of Default	§14.12
Default Ratio	Minimum Cover Ratio(s) below which an event of default occurs	§14.12
Defaulting bank Lender	A bank which is unable to fund its share of a drawdown	§12.7.3; §14.14.6
defects liability period	The period after Project Completion during which the Construction Contractor is obliged to remedy any defects in the project's construction	§8.2.9
degradation	The decline in operating efficiency of a project caused by usage	§6.3.5; §9.7.3
Delay in Start-Up insurance	Insurance against the loss of revenue or extra costs caused by a delay in Project Completion after damage to the project ('DSU Insurance')	§8.6.1
delay LDs	LDs payable by the Construction Contractor for failure to complete the project by the agreed date; *cf.* performance LDs	§8.2.8
denial of justice	*See* contract repudiation	§11.5.1; §16.2.4

Term	Definition	Refer to:
depreciation	Writing down the capital cost of the project, for tax or accounting purposes	§3.6.1; §4.5.2; §6.3.5; §7.2.8; §12.3.1; §12.5.3; §13.7
derivative	A contract which sets payments and receipts over a period of time, at prices 'derived' from an underlying financial-market movement, *e.g.* an interest-rate swap (*q.v.*); *cf.* hedging	
Design & Build Contract	A turnkey contract to design and build the project ('D&B Contract'); *cf.* Construction Contract, EPC Contract	§2.5.2; §8.2
Design, Procurement and Construction Contract	*See* EPC Contract	§2.5.1
design risk	Risks relating to design of the project by the Construction Contractor, in particular whether the design is complete or especially complex	§9.5.5
developers	*See* Sponsors	Chapter 3; §9.13
Development Agreement	An agreement between Sponsors relating to the development of the project	§3.5
development costs	Costs incurred by the Sponsors before Financial Close	§3.3; §3.5; §9.5.6; §13.3
development fee	A fee payable to the Sponsor(s), usually at Financial Close, to recover their development costs and a profit thereon	§3.7.11; §9.5.6; §12.2.5
DFI	Development finance institution; *see* bilateral DFI, MDFI	§16.4; §16.5
Direct Agreement(s)	Agreement(s) between the lenders and the parties signing Project Contracts with the Project Company, protecting the lenders' interests under these contracts, or similar agreements signed by an Offtaker/Contracting Authority; *cf.* acknowledgements and consents, tripartite deed	§7.4.3; §8.11
Disbursement Account	The Project Company's bank account into which equity and debt advances are paid, and from which payments are made for the project's construction costs; *cf.* Proceeds Account	§14.3.2
discount rate	The rate used to reduce a future cash flow to a current value, and so calculate its NPV	§10.2.1
discounted cash flow	A calculation of the present value of a future stream of funds ('DCF'); *cf.* discount rate	§10.2.1
discounted payback period	A payback period (*q.v.*) calculation which discounts future cash flows to a NPV	§12.2.4

Term	Definition	Refer to:
dispatch	The generation of power by a power project, *e.g.* on instructions from the Offtaker	§6.3.4
dispatch risk	The risk that a power station is required to produce power for a power grid or a power purchaser	§6.3.4
Distribution Stop	Restriction by the lenders preventing payment of Distributions to the investors when Cover Ratio(s) are below a certain level; *cf.* Cash Trap	§14.4.3
Distributions	Net project cash flow paid to the investors as dividends or shareholders' subordinated debt service	§12.2.2; §14.4.2
dividend	The cash amount paid from the Project Company's profits to its shareholder investors; *see* Distributions	
dividend trap	Inability of the Project Company to pay dividends, despite having cash available to do so, because of accounting losses	§13.7.2
Dividend-Stop Ratio(s)	*See* Distribution-Stop Ratio	§14.4.3
domestic	Relating to the country of the project	
DPC Contract	*See* Design, Procurement and Construction Contract, EPC Contract	§2.5.1; §8.2
drawdown	The process by which the Project Company draws monies from the lenders as required during the construction phase of the project	§14.3.2
drawdown request	The formal procedure for request drawdowns	§14.3.2
Drawstop	Suspension of loan drawings from the lenders after an Event of Default	§7.10.1; §14.12
dry closing	Signing of the loan agreement (*q.v.*) and Project Contracts, but subject to conditions subsequent (*q.v.*)	§14.8.1
DSRA	*See* Debt Service Reserve Account	§14.4.1
DSU insurance	*See* Delay in Start-up insurance	§8.6.1
due diligence	Review and evaluation of Project Contracts and commercial, financial and political risks	§2.6; §5.5; §5.6; §9.2; §14.8.1
e.g.	For example	
E.U.	European Union	
easement	A right to use adjacent land, *e.g.* for discharge of water	§8.8.2
EBITDA	Earnings before interest, depreciation, and tax, a financial ratio used in corporate finance	§12.3.1; §12.3.6

Term	Definition	Refer to:
EBRD	European Bank for Reconstruction and Development, an MDFI covering Central and Eastern Europe, CIS and North Africa	§16.5; §16.5.7
ECA	Export credit agency (or export-import bank)	§11.8.1; §16.2; §16.4
economic infrastructure	The infrastructure essential for the functioning of an economy, *e.g.* transportation, communications, energy, water and sewerage; *cf.* social infrastructure	§2.3
Effective Date	*See* Financial Close	§3.1; §3.6.3; §5.2.7; §8.2.2; §13.10; §14.8.1; §14.14
Efficacy insurance	Insurance which covers the Construction Sub-Contractor's liability to pay LDs for delay or poor performance	§8.6.1
EIA	*See* Environmental Impact Assessment	§9.10.1
EIB	*See* European Investment Bank	§15.4.1; §16.5.8; §17.5.2; §17.5.3
EID/MITI	Export-Import Insurance Division of the Ministry of International Trade and Industry of Japan, now superseded by NEXI	§16.4.1
emergency Step-In	The right of a public-sector Offtaker, or a Contracting Authority, to take over the running of the project for reasons of safety or public security	§7.9
Enclave Project	A project whose products are exported, for which payment is received outside the Host Country	§11.4.1; §16.5.1
Energy Charge	The element of a PPA Tariff intended to cover fuel costs; *cf.* Usage Charge, Variable Charge	§6.3.5
Environmental Impact Assessment	A study of the effect of the construction and operation of the project on the natural and human environment ('EIA')	§9.10.1
environmental risks	Risk relating to the environmental effect of the construction or operation of the project	§9.10
EPC Contract	Engineering, Procurement and Construction Contract; *cf.* D&B Contract, Construction Contract	§2.5.1; §8.2
equity	The portion of the project's capital costs contributed by the investors to the Project Company as share capital or subordinated debt	§2.4; §12.2
Equity Bridge Loan	Finance provided by lenders during the construction period for the amount of the equity investment	§12.2.3

Term	Definition	Refer to:
Equity Funding Competition	Competitive bidding to provide part of the equity for a Project Company with a PPP Contract, on or shortly before Financial Close; cf. Debt Funding Competition	§12.2.5; §17.5
Equity IRR	The IRR on the equity paid in by the investors; cf. Blended Equity IRR	§12.2
Equity Subscription Agreement	An agreement between the Sponsors and the Project Company under which they agree to subscribe their equity (and lend subordinated debt) into the Project Company	§3.5; §12.2.3
escrow account	A bank account under the joint control of two parties; cf. Reserve Accounts	§9.6.1; §11.4.1
European Investment Bank	The Policy Bank of the European Union ('EIB'); cf. LGTT, Project Bond Initiative	§15.4.3; §16.5.8; §17.5.2; §17.5.3
Events of Default	Events that give the lenders the right to Drawstop or terminate the financing	§5.4; §14.12
events of default	Events that give parties to Project Contracts the right to terminate them	§7.10.1; §7.10.2; §8.5.6
exchange-rate risks	See foreign-exchange risks	§10.5
Excusing Cause	An event causing a project to be unavailable but for which no penalties are due; cf. Compensation Event, Relief Event	§7.7
export credits	Guarantees or insurance to lenders, or direct loans to the Project Company, linked to export sales, provided by ECAs	Chapter 16
expropriation	Illegal takeover of the project or the Project Company by the Host Government	§11.4.2
facilities agreement	See loan agreement	Chapter 14
facility	The project; or a loan or tranche of a loan	
facility agent	See agent bank	§5.2.9; §12.6.4; §14.4.1; §14.10.1; §14.13
FIM	Final Information Memorandum, the information memorandum on the Project Company used for syndication	§5.2.8
Final Business Case	A review by a Contracting Authority of a PPP procurement before appointment of a Preferred Bidder, to confirm that the procurement has achieved the objectives set out in the Outline Business Case (q.v.)	§3.7.3

Term	Definition	Refer to:
financial advisor	The Sponsors' advisor on arranging finance for the Project Company; or the Contracting Authority's advisor	§3.4.1
Financial Balance	*See* Financial Equilibrium	§7.6.5
Financial Close	The date on which all Project Contracts and financing documentation are signed, and conditions precedent to initial drawing of the debt have been fulfilled	§3.1; §3.6.3; §5.2.7; §8.2.2; §13.10; §14.8.1; §14.14
Financial Equilibrium	Payment for a Compensation Event which is intended to put investors and lenders to a Project Company in the same financial position as they were before the event occurred.	§7.6.5
financial model	The financial model(s) used by Sponsors to structure the project finance, lenders to review and monitor the project, or the Contracting Authority (if any) to review the project	§3.4.1; §3.4.3; §3.7.3; §3.7.6; §5.2.6; §5.5.5 Chapter 13
financial risks	*See* macro-economic risks	Chapter 10
financing agreement	*See* loan agreement	Chapter 14
first loss	A loan or guarantee by a public-sector entity which is subordinated to the senior lenders	§15.3
Fisher formula	A formula for adjusting a real interest rate (*q.v.*) for inflation, to produce the nominal interest rate (*q.v.*)	§13.4.3
Fixed Charge	*See* Capacity Charge	§6.3.5
fixed costs	The element of the Project Company's operating costs which does not vary with output or usage of the project; *see* Capacity Charge; Service Fee	§6.3.5; §6.4.1
floating interest rate	An interest rate revised at regular intervals to the current market rate; *cf.* LIBOR, rate-fixing date	§10.3
FM Contract	Facilities Management Contract; *see* Hard FM Contract, Soft FM Contract, Maintenance Contract, Building-Services Contract	
Force Majeure	An event that affects the ability of one party to fulfill its contract, but that is not the fault of, and could not reasonably have been foreseen by, that party; *cf.* Relief Event	§7.8; §7.10.4; §8.5.2; §8.5.5; §9.9
Force Majeure insurance	Insurance against the loss of revenue or extra costs caused by a delay in completion or interruption in operation due to *force majeure* not covered by DSU or BI insurances	§8.6.1; §8.6.2
forced outage	*See* unplanned maintenance; refers mainly to a process plant	§9.7.5

Term	Definition	Refer to:
foreign-exchange risks	Macro-economic risks resulting from changes in currency exchange rates	§10.5; §13.4.4
Forfaiting	A PPP-like system in which the construction cost of a project is repaid or refinanced in full on completion	§6.6
forward-looking ratios	Projection of future ADSCRs, or the LLCR, once a project has begun operation, for the purposes of a Distribution Stop or Default Ratio calculation	§14.4.3
Franchise	The right to operate existing public infrastructure and receive user payments; differs from a PPP because no substantial new investment is required by the private sector; cf. *Affermage*, Lease	§6.6; §7.2.8; §15.20
fronting bank	A bank acting as a channel for an interest-rate swap	§10.3.1; §14.14.1
Fuel Supply Contract	An Input-Supply Contract to supply the fuel for a project	§8.5
full cover	Guarantees or insurance for both political and commercial risks, provided to a lender by an ECA	§16.2.1; §16.2.4
Gap Financing	Debt provided by a public-sector entity if sufficient finance for a project cannot be raised from the private-sector market; cf. TIFU	§3.7.9; §15.7
gearing	*See* leverage	
GIC	*See* Guaranteed Investment Contract	§5.4; §10.3.4
GOCO	A government-owned, (private-sector) contractor-operated Project Company	§6.6
governing law	The law governing a Project Contract or the financing documentation	§11.5.1; §14.15
government	The central government of the country in which the project is located	
Government Support Agreement	A Project Contract that establishes the legal basis for the project, or under which the Government agrees to provide various kinds of support or guarantees	§11.7
GPA	Agreement on Government Procurement, the framework for public procurement under the World Trade Organization	§3.7.4
GPOBA	Global Partnership on Output-Based Aid; cf. OBA	§17.6.2
grace period	A period of time allowed to remedy a default under a contract	§7.10.1; §14.12
	The period before the first repayments are due on a loan.	§12.5.3

Term	Definition	Refer to:
gross up	Increase a payment to compensate for tax deductions	§7.10.6; §12.7.1
GST	Goods & services tax; *cf.* VAT	§11.3.2; §13.5.1; §13.7.5
Guaranteed Investment Contract	A fixed rate of interest paid by a depository bank on the proceeds of a bond issue until these are required to pay construction costs for a project ('GIC'); *see* negative arbitrage	§10.3.4
handback	The process of handing over the project assets to an Offtaker/Contracting Authority at the end of a Project Agreement	§7.10.7
Hard FM Contract	An FM Contract covering maintenance; *see* Maintenance Contract; the term is used in contrast to Soft FM (*q.v.*)	§2.5.2; §8.3; §9.7.5
Hard Mini-Perm	*See* Mini-Perm; this term is used in contrast to a Soft Mini-Perm (*q.v.*)	§10.6
heat rate	The amount of fuel required to produce a set amount of electrical power	§6.3.6; §9.7.3
hedging	A contract in the derivative (*q.v.*) financial or commodity markets to protect the Project Company against adverse movements in interest rates, price inflation, currency-exchange rates, or commodity prices	§6.3.1; Chapter 10
Hermes	Euler Hermes *Kreditversicherungs* A.G., the German ECA	§16.4.5
Host Country	The country in which the project is located (usually used in connection with a cross-border investment)	§11.4
Host Government	The government of the Host Country	
hurdle rate	The discount rate or minimum IRR used to determine if an investment produces the minimum required return	§10.2; §12.2.1; §12.2.4
IADB	Inter-American Development Bank, an MDFI	§16.5; §16.5.9
IBRD	*See* World Bank	§16.5.1
IDA	International Development Association, a member of the World Bank Group providing development finance to the poorest countries	§16.5; §16.5.3
IDB	Islamic Development Bank, an Islamic financing institution	§4.5.4; §16.5
IDC	Interest during construction	§10.3; §10.5.1; §12.2.3; §13.5.1

Term	Definition	Refer to:
IFC	International Finance Corporation, a member of the World Bank Group which finances private-sector investments	§16.5.2
IFIs	International financing institutions; *see* DFIs	Chapter 16
Implementation Agreement	*See* Government Support Agreement	§11.7
income statement	*See* P&L account	§13.7
incomplete contract	A contract in which the parties cannot provide for all possible outcomes	§9.4
Independent Engineer	An engineering firm not linked to any party to the Project Contracts, who confirms that project construction is being carried out as required by the Project Agreement and EPC Contract	§7.4.1; §7.10.1; §8.2.4
independent power producer	A power-generation project not owned by a regulated electricity utility ('IPP')	§2.3; §6.3
inflation risks	Macro-economic risks (*q.v.*) resulting from changes in the rate of price inflation	§7.3.3; §10.4; §13.4.1
inflation swap	A hedging contract to convert a cash flow subject to inflation adjustment to a fixed cash flow (or *vice-versa*); *cf.* RPI swap	§10.4.3
inflation-indexed bond	A bond whose debt service is indexed against inflation	§10.4.3
Initial Business Case	A PPP pre-feasibility study by a Contracting Authority; *cf.* Outline Business Case; Final Business Case	§3.7.3
Input Supplier	The contractor under an Input-Supply Contract	
Input-Supply Contract	A Project Contract for the supply of fuel or raw materials to the Project Company	§2.5.1; §8.5; §9.8
input-supply risks	Commercial risks relating to the availability and cost of input supplies for the project	§9.8
institutional market/ lenders	The non-bank market for large-scale investment in or loans to projects (mainly life-insurance companies and pension funds); the loans may be made through the bond market, debt funds, or directly.	§3.2.1; §17.4
Institutional PPP	An operating Project Company in which the Contracting Authority sells part of the equity an investor, with the latter actively involved in management of the company.	§6.6

Term	Definition	Refer to:
insurance	Insurance against physical damage to the project, loss of income and for third-party liability; *see* construction phase insurances and operating phase insurances	§7.8; §8.6; §9.9.1
	Insurance may also refer to credit or political-risk insurance of the project debt or equity by monoline insurers, ECAs or DFIs	§4.3.2; §4.3.3; Chapter 16
insurance advisor	The lenders' advisor on insurance aspects of the project (other than credit or political-risk insurance)	§5.5.4
insurance premium	The fee payable to obtain insurance cover	§8.6.8; §9.9.2
intercreditor	Relationship between different groups of lenders	§14.14
intercreditor agent	An agent for the different groups of lenders	§14.14
Intercreditor Agreement	*See* Common Terms Agreement	§14.14
interest buy-down	Reduction in the interest rate in return for providing more equity in the project	§12.8
interest during construction	Interest on loan drawings during construction, which is capitalized (*q.v.*) and forms part of the construction budget ('IDC')	§10.3; §10.5.1; §12.2.3; §13.5.1
interest-rate cap	A hedging contract that sets a maximum interest rate for the Project Company's debt	§10.3.2
interest-rate collar	A hedging contract that sets a floor (minimum) and ceiling (maximum) on the interest rate payable by the Project Company	§10.3.2
Interest-Rate Equalization	The interest subsidy paid by ECAs to banks to cover the difference between the bank's cost of finance and the CIRR (*q.v.*)	§16.2.1; §16.2.3
interest-rate risks	Macro-economic risks (*q.v.*) resulting from increases in interest rates	§10.3; §13.4.3
interest-rate swap	A hedging contract to convert a floating interest rate into a fixed-rate	§10.3.1; §14.14.1
internal rate of return	The rate of return on an investment derived from future cash flows ('IRR'); *see* Blended Equity IRR, Equity IRR, Project IRR	§10.2.2; §10.2.3
investment bank	A bank arranging but not providing a bond issue or other debt	§5.3.1
investment grade	A credit rating of BBB–/Baa3 or above	§5.3.1; §17.5

Term	Definition	Refer to:
investment insurance	PRI provided to investors by ECAs, DFIs, or private-sector insurers	§11.8.1; §16.3
investment risks	Political risks relating to currency convertibility and transfer, expropriation, and political *force majeure*	§11.4; §16.2.4
investors	Sponsors and other parties investing in the equity of the Project Company	§2.4; §2.6.1; §3.2; §12.2
	Investors may also refer to buyers of bonds issued by the Project Company	§4.3; §5.3
IPP	*See* independent power producer	§2.3; §6.3
IRR	*See* internal rate of return	§10.2.2; §10.2.3
IRS	The U.S. Internal Revenue Service	
ISDA	International Swap and Derivatives Association, which produces standard-form documentation for interest-rate swaps and other financial hedging contracts	§10.3.1
Islamic financing	Finance without payment of interest	§4.5.4; §16.5
ITN	Invitation to Negotiate; *see* RfP	
ITT	Invitation to Tender; *see* RfP	
JBIC	Japan Bank for International Co-operation, which provides export credits and untied financing	§16.4; §16.4.1
JEXIM	Export-Import Bank of Japan, now superseded by JBIC	§16.4.1
KDB	Korea Development Bank, a Policy Bank	§15.8; §16.4.2
KEXIM	Export-Import Bank of Korea	§16.4.2
Key Performance Indicators	Measurements of service standards under a PPP Contract ('KPIs'); failure to attain these leads to deductions of Performance Points	§6.4.4; §7.4.2; §8.4
KfW-IPEX Bank	The German import-export bank which provides CIRR funding for German exports, and untied financing	§16.4; §16.4.5
KPIs	*See* Key Performance Indicators,	§6.4.4
K-sure	Korea Trade Insurance Corporation, the Korean ECA	§16.4; §16.4.2
latent defects	Defects in structures on the project site which no-one could reasonably have found and whose effect does not appear until a later date	§9.5.2
LDs	*See* liquidated damages	§6.3.6; Chapter 8; Chapter 9; §13.9; §14.4.1; §14.6.2

Term	Definition	Refer to:
lead arranger(s)	Bank(s) arranging and underwriting project-finance debt, or the investment bank placing a project-finance bond	§5.2.3; §5.2.5; §5.3.1
lease	A form of debt in which the equipment being financed is owned by the lessor; *see* lessor, lessee	§4.5.2; §14.14.4
	A right to use specified land (and buildings) for a certain period of time.	§8.7
	See Franchise	§6.6
lenders	Banks, bondholders or other providers of senior debt to the Project Company	§2.4; Chapter 4; Chapter 5; Chapter 14; §17.4
lenders' advisors	External advisors employed by the lenders	§5.5
Lenders' Engineer	An engineering firm advising the lenders	§5.5.3; §8.2.4; §8.2.7; §9.5.4; §9.5.6; §13.11; §14.3.2; §14.5; §14.8
lessee	The obligor under a lease (*i.e.* the Project Company)	§4.5.2
lessor	The provider of finance under a lease (equivalent to a lender)	§4.5.2; §14.14.4
leverage	The debt:equity ratio	§2.6; §12.4; §12.8; §14.3.2
LGTT	The EIB's Loan Guarantee Instrument for Trans-European Transport Network Projects	§15.5; §17.5.3
LIBOR	London interbank offered rate, one of the leading measures of floating interest rates	§10.3; §12.6.1; §12.7.3
lifecycle	The renewal or replacement of major equipment at the end of its operating life	§7.2.7; §7.10.7; §8.3.2; §9.7.5; §14.4.1; §14.4.4
limited-recourse	Finance with limited guarantees from the Sponsors; *cf.* non-recourse	§9.13
linear project	A project involving construction of a facility over a long stretch of land, *e.g.* a road	§8.6.5; §8.6.9; §9.5.1; §9.5.2
Liquid Market clause	Provision in a PPP Contract that a market sale of the Project Agreement after a default by the Project Company is not required if there are no (or very few) prospective bidders in the market	§7.10.1
liquidated damages	The pre-agreed level of loss when a party does not perform under a contract ('LDs'); *cf.* delay LDs, performance LDs. penalties	§6.3.6; Chapter 8; Chapter 9; §13.9; §14.4.1; §14.6.2

Term	Definition	Refer to:
liquidity support	A standby loan which can be drawn by the Project Company to cover depreciation of the local currency against offshore-currency based debt.	§10.5.4
LLCR	*See* Loan-Life Cover Ratio	§12.3.2; §12.3.6
LMA	Loan Market Association, which produces standard-form documentation for bank loans	§14.2
LNG	Liquefied natural gas	
loan agreement	The agreement between a Project Company and its lenders (*q.v.*); *cf.* credit agreement, facilities agreement	Chapter 14
Loan-Life Cover Ratio	The ratio of the NPV of operating cash flow during the remaining term of the debt and the debt principal (*q.v.*) amount ('LLCR')	§12.3.2; §12.3.6
Lock-Up Ratio(s)	*See* Distribution Stop Ratio(s)	§14.4.3
MAC clause	*See* material adverse change clause(s)	§14.8.3; §14.12
macro-economic risks	Project-finance risks related to inflation, interest rates, or currency exchange rates	Chapter 10; §13.4
maintenance bond	Security to ensure that a PPP or process-plant project is adequately maintained in the later years of the contract before hand-back; *cf.* warranties	§7.5; §7.10.7; §8.2.9
Maintenance Contract	A contract to maintain infrastructure such as a road or a building; *cf.* O&M Contract	§2.5.2; §8.3; §9.7.5
maintenance covenant	A positive covenant (*q.v.*) to maintain a certain level, *e.g.* of Cover Ratio	§14.10.1
Maintenance Reserve Account	A Reserve Account that builds up a cash balance sufficient to cover the major maintenance of the project ('MRA')	§7.10.7; §9.7.5; §14.4.1; §14.4.2; §14.4.4
Maître d'Œuvre	*See* Independent Engineer	§7.4.1
make-whole clause	*See* par floor	§10.3.4
Management Contract	A contract between the Project Company and one or more of its Sponsors under which the latter agrees to provide corporate management services	§3.6.3
	A contract between a public-sector entity and a private-sector company for the management of public infrastructure	§6.6
mandate	Appointment as lead arranger (*q.v.*)	§5.2.3; §5.3.1
mandatory costs	The additional costs of funding a loan which commercial banks charge to a borrower; *cf.* MLA, MLRs	§12.7.2

Term	Definition	Refer to:
margin	*See* credit margin, swap credit premium	
margin ratchet	Increasing the credit margin (*q.v.*) over the term of project loan	§12.6.1
Marine Cargo insurance	Insurance against damage to equipment in transit to the project site during construction	§8.6.1
Marine DSU insurance	Insurance against the loss of revenue or extra costs caused by a delay in completion after damage to the equipment in transit to the project during construction; *cf.* DSU insurance	§8.6.1
market disruption	Inability of banks to renew short-term funding for their loans on the basis set out in the loan agreement	§12.7.3
market flex	The right of lead arrangers to change the proposed lending terms before the loan is signed, to reflect a deterioration in the market	§5.2.7
market stabilization	A hedging exercise in advance of placement of a large bond or swap, to ensure that the placement itself does not move market rates	§10.3.5
mark-to-market	Calculating the current value of a swap, or its breakage cost (*q.v.*)	§10.3.1
material adverse change clause(s)	Clause(s) in the financing documentation that give the lenders discretion to refuse to allow further drawings or to require repayment of the debt following a material adverse change in the project ('MAC clause')	§14.8.3; §14.12
maturity	The scheduled final date of a loan or contract	
MDB	Multilateral development bank; *see* MDFI	
MDFI	Multilateral DFI; a DFI owned by a number of governments	§16.5
Mechanical Completion	Under an EPC Contract, confirmation that the project can meet the required performance and operating criteria	§8.2.7
merchant power plant	An IPP that does not have a PPA, but relies on selling its power into a competitive market	§9.6.2
mezzanine debt	Subordinated debt provided by third parties other than the investors	§4.5.1; §14.14.5; §15.4
MIGA	Multilateral Investment Guarantee Agency, a member of the World Bank Group providing cover to lenders and investors against political risks	§16.5.4
Mini Perm	A loan for the construction period and first few years of operation of a project, to be refinanced in due course by longer term debt; also known as a Hard Mini-Perm, in contrast to a Soft Mini-Perm (*q.v.*)	§10.6

Term	Definition	Refer to:
Minimum Revenue Guarantee	A guarantee by a Contracting Authority of the minimum revenue under a Concession ('MRG')	§15.18
MIRR	*See* modified IRR	§10.2.3; §12.2.3
MLA	Banks' minimum liquid asset requirements; *see* mandatory costs	§12.7.2
	Multilateral Lending Agency; *see* MDFI	§16.5
MLRs	Banks' minimum liquidity ratio requirements; *see* mandatory costs	§12.7.2
mobilization	The transition from the construction phase to the operating phase of the project	§9.5.6
Model Auditor	An independent firm of accountants (or a specialist modeling firm) that reviews and certifies the financial model	§5.5.5; §13.10; §14.8.1
modified IRR	An IRR calculation with a reduced reinvestment rate for cash taken out of the project ('MIRR')	§10.2.3; §12.2.3
monoline insurance	Insurance of an individual financial risk (rather than general casualty insurance)	§4.3.2; §4.3.3; §5.3.2; §15.4.3; §15.9; §16.5.8; §17.2
Monte-Carlo simulation	A method of assessing risk	§9.2; §12.2.4
MRG	Minimum Revenue Guarantee	§15.18
muni bonds	Bonds issued in the U.S. municipal bond market; *cf.* PAB, Revenue Bond, TIF	§4.3.1
Natural *Force majeure*	An unforeseeable natural event affecting the project, *e.g.* fire, explosion, flood, unusual weather conditions; *see* Force Majeure	§7.10.4
negative arbitrage	The loss of interest caused by having to draw the whole of a long-term bond financing and then redeposit the funds in a short-term basis until required; *see* GIC	§5.4; §10.3.4
negative equity	A cumulative accounting loss exceeding the amount of the Project Company's issued share capital	§13.7.3
negative pledge	An agreement by a borrower with its lender not to give security over its assets to any third party	§14.7.1; §14.7.2; §14.10.2
Negotiated Procedure	A public-procurement procedure whereby negotiations take place with bidders to clarify their bids	§3.7.4
net present value	The discounted present value of a stream of future cash flows ('NPV')	§10.2.1; §10.2.3

Term	Definition	Refer to:
network risk	The risks for a Concession resulting from connections outside the project	§9.6.3
NEXI	Nippon Export and Investment Insurance, the Japanese ECA	§16.4; §16.4.1
no-fault termination	Termination of a Project Agreement caused by *Force Majeure (q.v.)*	§7.10.4
nominal interest rate	The interest rate payable including inflation; the actual amount of interest payable; *cf.* real interest rate	§13.4.3
nominal sum	A sum of money in current prices, *i.e.* including inflation; the actual amount of money received or paid; *cf.* real sum	§10.4
non-recourse	Finance relying only on project cash flow, with no guarantee from the Sponsors; *cf.* limited-recourse	§2.2; §2.6.1; §3.2; §9.13; §9.14
Non-Reverting Asset	Assets financed under a PPP Contract which do not revert to Contracting Authority ownership or control at the end of the contract	§6.2; §7.2.5; §7.6.5; §7.10.8; §7.10.9; §9.14
non-vitiation clause	Provision in an insurance policy that the rights of lenders will not be affected by action by the Project Company that invalidates the insurance	§8.6.5
Nordic Investment Bank	The MDFI of the Nordic countries	§16.5
notional principal amount	The amount of debt which is the subject of an interest-rate swap	§10.3.1
NPV	*See* net present value	§10.2.1; §10.2.3
NPV at risk	A method of evaluating risk for the investor in a project	§12.2.4
NPV of Revenues	A system of fixing a flexible term for a Concession, to deal with traffic risk	§9.6.2
NTP	Notice to Proceed, a notice from the Project Company to the Construction Contractor to begin the project works	§8.2.2
O&M	Operation and maintenance	
O&M Contract	Operation & Maintenance Contract, a Project Contract to operate and maintain a process-plant project on behalf of the Project Company	§2.5.1; §8.3; §9.7.2
O&M Contractor	The contractor under the O&M Contract	
OBA	*See* output-based aid	§17.6.2

Term	Definition	Refer to:
obsolescing bargain	The concept that a foreign investor has a strong position *vis-à-vis* the Host Government before making an investment in a project, but the balance of power shifts to the Host Government thereafter.	§11.2
ODA	Official development assistance; *cf.* Tied Aid	§16.4
OECD	Organization for Economic Co-operation and Development	§2.2; §16.2.3
OECD Consensus	An agreement under the ægis of OECD to regulate credit terms offered by ECAs	§16.2.3
Offtake Contract	A Project Agreement under which the Project Company produces a product and sells it to the Offtaker	§2.4; §2.5.1; §6.3; Chapter 7; §9.6.1; §9.14
Offtaker	The purchaser of the Project Company's product, *e.g.* under a PPA	§2.4; §2.5.1; §9.14
operating budget	The budget for operating costs (where these are under the Project Company's control); *cf.* construction budget	§9.7.7
operating cash flow	The Project Company's revenues minus operating costs *i.e.* cash flow before debt service	
operating phase insurances	All Risks, BI, and *Force Majeure* insurances	§8.6.2
operating risks	Commercial risks relating to the operation of the project	§9.7
operational gearing	The ratio in a Service Fee between debt service and equity return, and payments to cover operating costs	§15.10
OPIC	Overseas Private Investment Corporation, a U.S. government agency	§16.4; §16.4.4; §16.5.4
optimism bias	The tendency to under-estimate costs and overestimate the chances of success of a project	§3.7.3
Optional Termination	The Contracting Authority exercises an option to terminate a PPP Contract early; *cf.* Termination for Convenience, Voluntary Termination	§7.10.3
Outline Business Case	A detailed PPP feasibility study by a Contracting Authority, carried out before approaching the market for bids; *cf.* Initial Business Case; Final Business Case	§3.7.3
output-based aid	A system of providing subsidies for projects in developing countries which works in a similar way to PPPs ('OBA')	§17.6.2

Term	Definition	Refer to:
output dedication	The Input Supplier commits to provide all the available inputs from a particular source (but does not commit to a volume or amount of inputs); *cf.* sole supplier	§8.5.1
Output Specifications	Specifications in a PPP Contract of what is required from the project	§6.4.2
over-indexation	Inflation indexation of the Contract Payments by a proportion greater than the Project Company's variable costs	§10.4.2
Owner's Engineer	The engineer supervising the Construction Contractor on behalf of the Project Company	§8.2.4
Owner's Risks	The responsibilities of the Project Company under the Construction Contract	§8.2.3; §8.2.5; §9.5.5
P&L account	The Project Company's accounting-based (instead of cash-based) results; *cf.* income statement	§13.7
p.a.	*per annum*, annually	
PABs	Private Activity Bonds, a method of raising finance for PPP projects in the U.S. municipal bond market	§4.3.1
par floor	Provision in a bond or fixed-rate loan that an adjustment for changes in interest rates at the time of early payment cannot lead to less than a 100% principal (*q.v.*) repayment; *cf.* make-whole clause, Spens clause	§10.3.4
pari-passu	Equal *pro rata* share in security; relates to security shared by different lenders, or payments to other claimants	
Partial Credit Guarantee	A guarantee of part of the credit risk provided by an MDFI ('PCG')	§16.5.1
Partial Risk Guarantee	An MDFI guarantee covering political risk aspects of a project ('PRG'); *cf.* PRI	§16.5.1
payback period	The period of time in which Distributions to investors equal their original investment; *cf.* discounted payment period	§12.2.4
paying agent	A company distributing debt-service payments from the Project Company to bondholders	§5.3.2
Payment Mechanism	The formulæ and other methods for calculating Contract Payments (*q.v.*)	§2.5.1
PBCE	Project-Bond Credit Enhancement: the result of using the EIB Project Bond Initiatives	§15.4

Term	Definition	Refer to:
PCG	Parent-company guarantee (for a Sub-Contractor)	§8.10
	See Partial Credit Guarantee	§16.5.1
penalties	LDs payable by the Project Company for failure to meet service requirements under a Concession; *cf.* abatements, deductions	§6.3.6; §6.4.3; §6.5.5; §9.7.4
performance bond	Security provided by the Construction Contractor (or another Sub-Contractor) for performance under its contract	§8.2.9
	Security provided by the Project Company to guarantee its performance under the Project Agreement	§7.5
performance LDs	LDs payable by the EPC Contractor if the completed project does not meet minimum required performance standards	§8.2.8; §9.5.10; §14.6
Performance Management System	The system for monitoring performance in a PPP Contract ('PMS')	§6.4.4
Performance Points	Penalties for failure to meet KPIs, accumulation of which results in penalties or deductions from the Contract Payments and may eventually lead to termination of the Project Agreement	§6.4.4
performance risks	Completion risks relating to the performance of the project	§9.5.10
performance-based contracting	Contracts which are based on output or performance standards in a similar way to PPPs	§6.6
Permits	The rights or permissions required to construct and operate the project, invest in the Project Company, or for the Project Company to borrow its debt	§8.8; §9.5.3
Persistent Breach	Consistent failure by the Project Company to observe any provisions of the Project Agreement which are not covered by penalties or deductions, or otherwise an Event of Default	§7.10.1
PF2	A revised version of PFI introduced by the British government in 2012; the revisions are quite minor, and the term PFI continues to be used in this book.	§2.5.2; §3.2.2; §17.5.5
PFI	*See* Private Finance Initiative	§2.3; §4.3.3
PFI-Model Contract	A Project Agreement with a Contracting Authority under which the latter pays the Project Company for the right to use the project, also referred to as an Availability Contract (*q.v.*), although a minority of PFI-Model Contracts—*e.g.* Shadow-Toll projects—are not paid for in this way; *cf.* Accommodation Project; Concession	§2.5.2; §6.4; Chapter 7

Term	Definition	Refer to:
PIM	Preliminary Information Memorandum, the information memorandum on the project used as a basis for obtaining financing bids from prospective lead arrangers	§5.2.8
planned maintenance	*See* scheduled maintenance	§9.7.5
planned outage	*See* scheduled maintenance; refers mainly to process plant	§9.7.5
PLCR	*See* Project Life Cover Ratio	§12.3.4
PMS	*See* Performance Management System,	§6.4.4
Policy Banks	State-owned banks providing finance for particular industries or sectors of the economy; *cf.* SFI, bilateral DFI	§15.8
Political *Force Majeure*	Political violence affecting the project, *e.g.* war, terrorism or civil unrest	§7.10.4; §9.9.1; §11.4.3
political risks	Risks related to Political *Force Majeure* and other investment risks (*q.v.*), change in law (*q.v.*), and quasi-political risks (*q.v.*)	Chapter 11
political-risk cover	Political Risk insurance or Partial Risk Guarantee; *cf.* full cover	§11.8; Chapter 16
Political Risk Insurance	Insurance against political risks (*q.v.*) by private-sector insurers, ECA or MDFIs ('PRI')	§11.8; Chapter 16
power purchaser	The Offtaker under a PPA	§6.3; §7.12.1; §9.4
Power-Purchase Agreement	A type of Offtake Contract ('PPA')	§2.5.1; §6.3; Chapter 7
PPA	*See* Power-Purchase Agreement	§2.5.1; §6.3; Chapter 7
PPI	Private participation in infrastructure, *i.e.* privatized and private-sector infrastructure, and PPPs	§2.5.2; §16.1
PPIAF	Public-Private Infrastructure Advisory Facility, a multi-donor trust fund that provides technical assistance to governments in developing countries on PPI programs and projects.	
PPP	*See* public-private partnership	§2.5.2; §2.6.2; §3.7; §6.4; §6.5; §6.6; Chapter 7
PPP Contract	A Concession, or a PFI-Model Contract	§2.5.2; §2.6.2; §6.4; §6.5; §6.6; Chapter 7
PPP Unit	A public-sector centre of expertise to support PPP procurement and contract management	§3.7.1

Term	Definition	Refer to:
PPPI	PPPs for infrastructure (to distinguish from other kinds of PPPs)	§6.6
PQQ	Pre-qualification questionnaire (in a public-procurement)	§3.7.5
præcipium	Net arrangement fee retained by lead arranger(s) after a loan has been syndicated	§5.2.8
Preferred Bidder	The bidder with whom the Contracting Authority intendeds to sign a PPP Contract after going through the procurement process	§3.7.3, §3.7.4; §3.7.7; §3.7.9
premium	*See* insurance premium, swap credit premium	
pre-NTP works	Preliminary works on the project (*e.g.* design) carried out by the EPC Contractor before issuance of the NTP	§8.2.2
prepayment	Early repayment of some or all of the debt	§14.6.2
pre-qualification	The first stage of a procurement process	§3.7.5; §5.6; §9.5.4
PRG	*See* Partial Risk Guarantee	§16.5.1
PRI	*See* Political-Risk Insurance	§11.8; Chapter 16
primary investors	The original investors in the Project Company, including the Sponsors; *cf.* secondary investors	§3.2
principal	The amount (or amount outstanding) of a loan	
Private Finance Initiative	The British PPP program ('PFI'), renamed PF2 in 2012	§2.3; §4.3.3
private placement	Sale of bonds not quoted on a stock exchange	§4.3.3
Proceeds Account	*See* Disbursement Account	§14.3.2
process-plant project	A project in which an input supply (*e.g.* gas) is processed to produce an output (*e.g.* electricity)	§2.5.1; §6.2; §6.3; Chapter 7; §9.6.1
Project Accounts	Operating or Reserve Accounts into which the Project Company's cash flow is paid, with disbursements based on the cash-flow Cascade	§14.3.2; §14.4
Project Agreement	The contract between the Project Company and an Offtaker or Contracting Authority relating to design, construction, finance and operation of a project, and which is the main security for a project financing; *cf.* Offtake Contract, Availability-Based (or PFI-Model) Contract, Concession, PPP Contract	§2.4; §2.5; Chapter 6; Chapter 7
Project Bond Initiative	The EIB's credit enhancement structure for infrastructure-finance bonds	§15.4.3; §17.5.2; §17.5.3
Project Company	The SPV created to construct and operate a project	§2.2; §2.4; §3.6

Term	Definition	Refer to:
Project Company costs	Costs of running the Project Company itself	§9.5.6; §9.7.7
Project Completion	The date on which construction is complete and operations or service provision can begin; *cf.* COD, Commercial Acceptance, Substantial Completion, Service Commencement Date	§3.1; §7.3.1; §8.2.7; §8.5.4
Project Contracts	Contracts signed by the Project Company, which may include a Project Agreement, Construction Contract, Input-Supply Contract, O&M/Maintenance Contract, Building-Services Contract, Government Support Agreement, Direct Agreements and insurance	Chapters 6–8
Project Coordination Agreement	*See* Common Terms Agreement	§14.14
project cost budget	*See* construction budget	§9.5.5; §13.5.1
project finance	A method of raising long-term debt financing for major projects through 'financial engineering', based on lending against the cash flow generated by the project alone; it depends on a detailed evaluation of a project's construction, operating and revenue risks, and their allocation between investors, lenders and other parties through contractual and other arrangements	§2.2
Project IRR	The cash flow of the project before debt service and Distributions, measured as a return on the cash investment required (whether debt or equity)	§7.10.1; §10.2.2; §12.2.4; §13.8
Project Life Cover Ratio	The ratio of the NPV of net operating cash flow during the remaining life of the project and the debt principal (*q.v.*) outstanding ('PLCR')	§12.3.4
Project Preparation Facility	Funding for a Contracting Authority to engage advisors to develop a PPP project	§3.7.2
project risks	*See* commercial risks	Chapter 9
project-finance risks	*See* commercial risks, macroeconomic risks, and regulatory and political risks	Chapter 9–Chapter 11
promoters	*See* Sponsors; may also refer to the Contracting Authority in a PPP	§3.2
protective covenants	*See* negative covenants	§14.10.2
PSC	*See* Public-Sector Comparator	§3.7.3
public liability insurance	Insurance against damage or injury caused by the project to third parties; *cf.* Third-Party Liability insurance	§8.6.1; §8.6.2

Term	Definition	Refer to:
public procurement	Competitive bidding for a Project Agreement, organized by a Contracting Authority	§3.7
public-private partnership	A contract under which the Project Company provides a public service on behalf of a Contracting Authority ('PPP'); *cf.* Concession, Availability-based Contract, PFI-Model Contract	§2.5.2; §6.2; §6.4; §6.5; Chapter 7
Public-Sector Comparator	A calculation of the lifetime cost of a project if built and operated by the public sector, for comparison with the expected cost of a PPP ('PSC')	§3.7.3
pull tolling	A tolling contract with an Offtaker supplying the fuel or raw materials (*cf.* push tolling)	§8.5.1
purchasing-power parity	The assumption that the future exchange rate between two countries' currencies will reflect their inflation-rate differentials	§13.3.4
push tolling	A Tolling Contract with an Input Supplier (*cf.* pull tolling)	§8.5.1
put-or-pay contract	An Input-Supply Contract on a Take-or-Pay basis	§8.5.1
QIB	Qualified Institutional Buyer, an institutional investor to whom Rule 144a bonds can be sold	§4.3.3
quasi-political risks	Project risks on the boundary between commercial and political risks, namely breach of contract (by a Host Government or public-sector body), sub-sovereign risks and creeping expropriation	§11.5.1; §11.6
RAB finance	*See* Regulated Asset Base finance	§17.6.1
ramp-up	The early years after completion of a traffic project, when usage is still building up (*e.g.* for a toll road);	§9.6.2
	The period of time it takes a power station or other process plant to get to its full output	
rate-fixing date	The date on which a floating interest rate is refixed to the current market rate	§10.3
real interest rate	The interest rate excluding the rate of inflation	§13.4.3
real sum	An amount of money adjusted for inflation (*cf.* nominal sum)	§10.4
real tolls	Tolls or fares paid in cash by the users of the project (*cf.* Shadow Tolls)	§6.4.6; §6.5.1; §9.6.2
refinancing	Prepayment of the debt and substitution of new debt on more attractive terms	§5.4; §10.3.1; §10.6; §14.16
refinancing gain	The benefit of a refinancing to the investors in the Project Company	§14.16

Term	Definition	Refer to:
Regulated Asset Base finance	Using a regulated rate of return to raise finance for a project ('RAB finance')	§17.6.1
regulation by contract	Fixing Contract Payments based on the Payment Mechanism in the Project Agreement rather than through an independent regulator	§17.6.1
regulatory capture	The tendency of an independent industry regulator to be over-influenced by the entities it is regulating.	§17.6.1
regulatory risks	Risks of changes in law or regulations (*e.g.* on safety in the workplace) which results in additional capital expenditure or operating costs for the Project Company	§11.3.1
reinsurance	Reinsurance of liability by an insurance company, ECA or DFI	§8.6.6; §16.5.4
Relief Event	Temporary *force majeure* preventing the completion or continuous operation of the project, which the relevant contract party is given time to remedy, without this being a default	§7.8; §8.2.6; §8.5.2; §9.9
representations and warranties	Confirmation by the Project Company of the facts on which the financing is based, and acceptance of liability for any error	§14.9
Request for Proposals	An invitation to bid in a public procurement ('RFP')	§3.7.6
Request for Qualifications	Request for prospective bidders' financial and technical qualifications, at the initial (pre-qualification) PQQ stage of a public-procurement process ('RFQ')	§3.7.5
rescue refinancing	Refinancing of the Project Company's debt caused by problems with the project	§14.16.4
Reserve Accounts	Accounts controlled by the lenders (or their trustee or escrow agent) in which part of the Project Company's cash flow is set aside to provide security for the debt or to cover future costs; *cf.* DSRA, Maintenance Reserve Account	§14.3.2; §14.4.1
Reserve Cover Ratio	The equivalent of LLCR for a natural resources project	§12.3.5
reserve risk	The risk of insufficient extraction of supplies of natural resources required for the project	§9.8.4
Reserve Tail	Proven reserves available after the final maturity of the debt; *cf.* Debt Tail	§9.8.4; §12.3.5; §14.4.4
Residual Cushion	*See* Debt Tail	§7.2.3; §12.3.4; §12.4 §12.4.1; §14.4.4

Term	Definition	Refer to:
residual-value risk	The risk on the value of the project after the maturity of the Project Agreement.	§6.2; §7.2.5; §7.10.7; §7.10.9; §9.11
Restricted Procedure	A public-procurement procedure whereby no negotiation takes places after bids have been made	§3.7.4
retainage	The proportion of each payment under the Construction Contract retained by the Project Company as security until COD	§8.2.9
retained risks	Risks retained by the Contracting Authority, or its obligations, under a PPP or process-plant contract	§7.6; §15.2
retention amount	*See* retainage	§8.2.9
Revenue Bond	A bond in the muni bond market (*q.v.*) repaid only from the revenues of the (public-sector) issuer	§4.3.1; §15.20; §17.6.4
revenue risks	Commercial risks relating to generation of revenue by the Project Company, derived from volume or price of product sales, or level of usage of the project	§9.6
Reverting Asset	A PPP Contract in which the project reverts to the Contracting Authority's ownership or control at the end of the contract; *cf.* Non-Reverting Asset	§6.2; §7.2.5; §7.10.7; §9.14
RFP	*See* Request for Proposals	§3.7.6
RFQ	*See* Request for Qualifications	§3.7.5
right of way	A right of access to adjacent land (*e.g.* for a pipeline bringing fuel to the project)	§8.8.2
risk matrix	Schedule of project risks and mitigations	§9.3
rollover risk	The risk that an interest-rate swap contract may not be amended on acceptable terms if the amount of debt or repayment schedule changes	§10.3.1
RPI swap	*See* inflation swap	§10.4.3
Rule 144a	SEC provisions that allow trading in bond private placements with QIBs	§4.3.3
SACE	SACE SpA, the Italian ECA	§15.16; §16.4.6
SAFETEA-LU	The U.S. Safe, Accountable, Flexible, Efficient Transportation Equity Act: A Legacy for Users of 2005, which raised the limits on PABs for transportation projects, and extended the support offered by TIFIA (*q.v.*) for PPP projects	§4.3.1; §15.4
scheduled maintenance	Time set aside in the Project Agreement for maintenance; *cf.* planned outage; unplanned maintenance	§9.7.5

Term	Definition	Refer to:
SEC	Securities and Exchange Commission (of the United States), that regulates the investment markets	§4.3.3
second loss	A loan or guarantee by a public-sector entity on which a payment or loss only occurs if the loss on the project is greater than the senior loan outstanding; *cf.* first loss, *pari-passu*	§15.3
secondary investors	Investors purchasing some or all of the Sponsors' shareholding in a project after the construction is complete; *cf.* primary investors	§14.17
securitization	The process of packaging bank loans to sell to non-bank investors; *cf.* CLO	§5.2.10
	The process of packaging receivables such as credit-card debt to sell to bond investors	§4.3.1
senior debt	Debt provided by senior lenders (*q.v.*)	
senior lenders	Lenders whose debt service takes priority over debt service over mezzanine or subordinated debt, and Distributions to investors, and who are repaid first in a liquidation of the Project Company; *cf.* mezzanine lenders, subordinated lenders In this book senior lenders are just referred to as lenders, unless the context requires otherwise	§4.5.1; §12.2.2; §14.14.5
sensitivity analysis	Variations on the Banking Case assumptions to review the possible performance of the project in one or more 'downside' scenarios	§13.8
Service Availability Date	*See* Service Commencement Date	§6.4.1
Service Commencement Date	The Project Completion date of a PPP project	§6.4.1
Service Fee	Payments by the Contracting Authority under a PFI-Model Contract; *cf.* Contract Payments, Tariff, User Charge, Payment Mechanism	§6.4.1
SFI	State financial institution; *cf.* Policy Bank, bilateral DFI	§15.8
Shadow Bid Model	A Contracting Authority's estimate, at the feasibility stage, of the costs of procuring a project as a PPP, using project finance	§3.7.3
Shadow Tolls	Tolls based on usage of the project, but payable by the Contracting Authority rather than the general public; *cf.* real tolls	§6.4.6; §9.6.2

Term	Definition	Refer to:
Shareholder Agreement	An agreement between Sponsors relating to their investment in and management of the Project Company; *cf.* Development Agreement	§3.6.2
SIB	U.S. State Infrastructure Banks, which provide mezzanine support for transportation projects using Federal funding	§15.4.1; §17.5.2; §17.5.3
	Social-impact bond (*q.v.*)	§17.6.3
Simest	*Società Italiana per le Imprese all'Estero*, which provides Italian CIRR interest subsidies, and untied financing	§16.4; §16.4.6
SINOSURE	China Export & Credit Insurance Corporation, the Chinese ECA	§16.4; §16.4.3
site risks	Risks related to the acquisition or condition of the project site	§8.2.5; §9.5.1; §9.5.2
site-legacy risk	The risk of pre-existing contamination on the project site	§9.10.3
social-impact bond	A bond in which repayment depends on achieving specific social outcomes	§17.6.3
social infrastructure	Infrastructure to support social services, *e.g.* schools, hospitals, prisons, public housing, other public buildings such as government offices or police stations, *etc*; *cf.* economic infrastructure; Accommodation Project	§2.3; §2.5.2
SOE	state-owned enterprise	§11.6
Soft FM	*See* Building-Services Contract	§2.5.2; §8.4
Soft Mini-Perm	A requirement by the lenders for a Cash Sweep, beginning 2–3 years after Project Completion, to encourage investors to refinance their loan; *see also*: Hard Mini-Perm	§14.4.4; §14.16.4
sole supplier	*See* output dedication	§8.5.1
Solvency II	The E.U.'s 'Solvency II' Directive of 2009, relating to capital ratio requirements for life-insurance companies	§17.4.4
SoPC	H.M. Treasury, *Standardisation of PF2 Contracts* (v. 5, London, 2012), a standard form of PPP Contract which has been adopted (with amendments) by various other countries	§6.1
sovereign risk	A risk carrying the full faith and credit of a country, *i.e.* relating to the Host Government; *cf.* sub-sovereign risks	§11.6

Term	Definition	Refer to:
Spens clause	*Cf.* par floor	§10.3.4
Sponsor(s)	The investor(s) who develop and lead the project through their investment in the Project Company	§3.2
SPV	Special Purpose Vehicle, a separate legal entity with no activity other than those connected with its borrowing; the Project Company is usually an SPV	§3.6.1
standby finance	Finance made available for drawing if the Project Company's cash flow is significantly below projections	§15.5
state aid	E.U. rules which prevent a Contracting Authority from giving support to a project which enables it to compete unfairly with other projects which do not have this support	§3.7.9
Step-In rights	Rights under a Direct Agreement for the lenders to take over management of a Project Contract to protect their security; *cf.* emergency Step-In, substitution	§8.11
structural risk	*See* contract mismatch	§9.12
Sub-Contractor	The obligor under a Sub-Contract	
Sub-Contract(s)	The Project Company's Project Contracts other than the Project Agreement	§2.5; Chapter 8
subordinated debt	Debt whose debt service comes after amounts due to senior lenders, but before Distributions of dividends to investors; *cf.* mezzanine debt	§4.5.1; §12.2.2; §14.14.5
subrogation	Right of an insurer or guarantor to take over an asset on which an insurance claim or guarantee has been paid	§8.6.5; §16.2.5; §16.3
sub-sovereign risk	Risks relating to a public-sector body other than the Host Government	§11.6
Substantial Completion	Confirmation that the project meets the required performance or other specifications	§8.2.7
Substitution	Right under a Direct Agreement for the lenders to substitute a new entity to take over the Project Company's rights and obligations under a Project Contract	§8.11
sukuk bond	A bond based on Islamic principles, with the return based on the underlying business of the borrower rather than interest payment	§4.5.4
Sunset Date	The last possible date for completion of construction of a project before failure becomes an Event of Default	§7.10.1; §8.2.7

Term	Definition	Refer to:
Support Services Agreement	A contract between the Project Company and one or more Sponsors to provide back-up technical support, spare parts, *etc.*	§3.6.3
swap credit premium	The credit-risk margin charged on an interest-rate swap	§10.3.1
swap provider	A bank providing an interest-rate, inflation or currency-swap to the Project Company	§10.3.1; §10.4.3; §10.5.2; §14.14.1
syndication	The process by which the lead arranger(s) reduces its underwriting by placing part of the loan with other lenders	§5.2.8
TA	Technical Advisor; *see* Lenders' Engineer	
take-and-pay contract	A contract under which the purchaser pays an agreed price for the product purchased, but is not obliged to purchase	§6.3.1; §8.5.1
take-or-pay contract	A contract under which the purchaser must buy the product or make a payment in lieu	§6.3.1; §8.5.1
target repayments	A flexible repayment structure to allow for temporary cash flow deficiencies	§12.5.4
Tariff	Contract Payments under a PPA or similar process-plant Project Agreement	§6.3.5
Tax Increment Finance	A method of raising finance for urban redevelopment	§17.6.4
Technical Support Agreement	*See* Support Services Agreement	§3.6.3
technology risk	Risks where the technology for a project is new and untried	§9.7.1
tenor	*See* term; duration of a loan	§12.5.1
term	Duration of a Project Contract	§7.2;
	The period until the final repayment date of the debt	§12.5.1
	One of a number of conditions (*see* term sheet)	
Term Loan B	A long-term loan with low amortization in its earlier years, and/or a balloon repayment (*q.v.*), provided by an institutional lender (*q.v.*)	§17.5.4
term sheet	Heads of terms for the project finance	§5.2.7; §14.2
Termination for Convenience	*See* Optional Termination	§7.10.3
Termination Sum	The compensation payable by the Offtaker or Contracting Authority for the early termination of a Project Agreement	§7.10

Term	Definition	Refer to:
Third-Party Liability insurance	*See* Public Liability insurance	§8.6.1; §8.6.2
third-party revenue	Revenue earned by the Project Company from sources other than Contract Payments	§7.3.4; §7.10.2
third-party risks	Risks that failures by parties not involved with the Project Contracts may affect the completion of the project	§9.5.9
Throughput Contract	A Project Agreement for the use of a pipeline	§6.3.1
Tied Aid	Joint ECA finance and national DFI aid, the latter being linked to the export covered by the former; *cf.* OECD Consensus; *cf.* Untied Financing	§16.4
TIF	Tax Increment Finance	§17.6.4
TIFIA finance	Finance for transport infrastructure projects provided under the U.S. Transportation Infrastructure Finance and Innovation Act ('TIFIA') of 1998, and subsequent legislation	§15.4.2; §17.5.2; §17.5.3
TIFU	The British Treasury Infrastructure Finance Unit, which provided Gap Financing for PPP projects	§15.7
Tolling Contract	An Input-Supply Contract in which the fuel or raw material is supplied free, and the Project Company is paid for processing it	§8.5.1
tranche	Separate portions of a loan or investment, which may be provided by different parties on different terms, or for a specific purpose rather than financing the project as a whole	
Transportation Contract	*See* Throughput Contract	§6.3.1
tripartite deed	*See* Direct Agreement(s)	§8.11
turnkey contract	A Construction Contract covering both design and construction, or engineering, procurement and construction, of a complete project; *see* D&B Contract; EPC Contract	§8.2; §9.5
U.S. Exim	Export-Import Bank of the United States, the U.S. ECA	§16.4.4
Unavailability	A period when the project is not available (*q.v.*)	
undertakings	*See* representations and warranties	§14.9
Unitary Charge	*See* Service Fee	§6.4.1
unplanned maintenance	Maintenance required to deal with an unexpected problem; also known as a forced outage (for process plant); *cf.* scheduled maintenance	§9.7.5

Term	Definition	Refer to:
unsolicited bids	Proposals for a PPP made without any tender request from the Contracting Authority	§3.7.11; §15.18
Untied Financing	Financing or other support by ECAs or other public-sector agencies not linked to exports	§16.4
unwind cost	*See* breakage cost	§10.3.1; §10.3.4; §10.4.3; §14.14.1; §14.14.2
Usage Charge	*See* Energy Charge	§6.3.5
User Charge	Tolls, fares, or other payments by users of a project under a Concession	§2.5.2; §6.5.1; §9.6.3
Value for Money	The basis on which an Offtaker/Contracting Authority decides whether to transfer project risks to a Project Company ('VfM')	§9.2
Variable Charge	*See* Energy Charge	§6.3.5
variation bonds	The right to increase the amount of a bond issue after it has been placed, to cover additional capital expenditure	§5.4; §7.6.3
VAT	Value-added tax; *cf.* GST	§11.3.2; §13.5.1; §13.7.5
vendor finance	Debt provided by a supplier of equipment or services to the Project Company	§4.5.3
VfM	*See* Value for Money	§9.2
VGF	*See* Viability Gap Funding	§15.11
Viability Gap Funding	A construction subsidy (*q.v.*) for a Concession ('VGF')	§15.11
Voluntary Termination	*Cf.* Optional Termination	§7.10.3
WACC	Weighted average cost of capital	§12.8
warranties	Guarantees against poor construction or failure of equipment after Project Completion, provided by the Construction Contractor; *cf.* collateral warranties, representations and warranties	§8.2.9
Waterfall	*See* Cascade	§14.4.2
willingness to pay	The willingness and ability of users of a Concession to pay User Charges in a Concession; *cf.* Affordability	§9.6.2
windfall gains	Politically-sensitive profits made by investors in PPPs resulting from debt refinancing or sale of their investment	§14.16.2; §14.17.1

Term	Definition	Refer to:
winner's curse	The winning bidder taking too optimistic a view of traffic or other usage risks for a Concession	§9.6.2
withholding tax	Host Country tax deducted by the Project Company before paying interest or dividends to an overseas lender or investor	§12.7.1; §13.7.6
without recourse	*See* non-recourse	
working capital	The amount of funding required for inventories and other costs incurred before receipt of sales revenues	§13.5.1
World Bank	International Bank for Reconstruction and Development, an MDFI providing finance to governments	§16.5.1
wrapped bonds	Bonds guaranteed by a monoline insurance company	§4.3.2
yield	The rate of return on an investment or loan	

Index